GODS AND HEROES

GODS AND HEROES

The Story of Greek Mythology

MICHAEL FOSS

NTC *Publishing Group*
Lincolnwood, Illinois USA

Published by NTC Publishing Group
4255 West Touhy Avenue
Lincolnwood (Chicago)
Illinois 60646-1975 U.S.A.

This edition by arrangement with
Michael O'Mara Books Limited, London.

ISBN 0-8442-5600-5
Library of Congress Catalog Card Number: 95-68177

First published in Great Britain by
Michael O'Mara Books Limited
9 Lion Yard, Tremadoc Road
London SW4 7NQ

Cover illustration: *Achilles and Ajax playing a board game* (SCALA)

Map by Stephen Dew
Designed and typeset by Florencetype Ltd, Kewstoke, Avon
Printed and bound by Clays Ltd, St Ives plc

CONTENTS

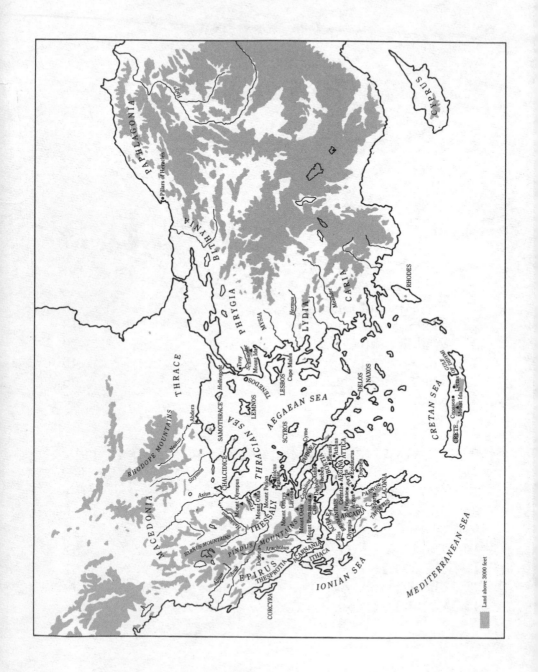

PAPHLAGONIA

Iris

Pillars of Hercules

BITHYNIA

PHRYGIA

MYSIA

LYDIA

Hermus

Mitylene

CARIA

RHODES

CYPRUS

Troy
Scamander
Mount Ida

Cape Malea

TENEDOS

LESBOS

THRACE

RHODOPE MOUNTAINS

Abdera

Nestus

Strymon

CHALCIDICE

SAMOTHRACE

THRACIAN SEA

LEMNOS

SCYROS

AEGEAN SEA

DELOS

NAXOS

CRETAN SEA

CRETE
Cnossos
Mount Ida
GORTYN
GULF OF

Cyme

Axius

MACEDONIA

Mount Olympus

Tempe
Mount Ossa
Mount Pelion
Iolcus

THESSALY

Mount Othrys
Larissa

PINDUS MOUNTAINS

BARNUS MOUNTAINS

Aous

Apsus

Dodona

Arachthus

EPIRUS

THESPROTIA

Mount Oeta
Delphi
Crisa

EUBOEA

Pheneus

Aulis
BOEOTIA
Thebes

Mount Parnassus

ACHAEA

Mount Cyllene
ARCADIA

Mount Maenalus

Elis
Olympia

ATTICA
Athens
AEGINA

Corinth
Mycenae

Epidaurus

PARNON

ARGOLIS

Sparta
LACONIA
TAYGETUS

CORCYRA

ACARNANIA

ITHACA

IONIAN SEA

MEDITERRANEAN SEA

Land above 3000 feet

– Part One –

THE HEAVENLY ONES

Zeus

– 1 –

THE ANCIENT ONES

A s USUAL, the changing seasons caught Mantes in the midst of his travels. Ever since he began to follow his ancient calling – minstrel and storyteller – the road had been his destiny. Now he was coming south from the badlands of Thrace. Early in the year, in the wretched month of Lenaeon, winds that would take the skin off an ox drove him out of the horse-breeding uplands. In those far borderlands, where the wilderness was full of menace from wild men and wilder beasts, who knew when the Fates would flick a life away, like a discarded olive stone?

Once, many years ago, he had not feared those dangerous paths. His stories, and his youth, gave him confidence. He felt he could overcome whatever time and the gods might throw at him. What he had to say – the message that he passed on through the gift of poetry – made him in some sense an accomplice of the Fates. Of course, no man could read their implacable will. They snipped the thread of life whenever they pleased. But it seemed to him that, like certain cunning animals, they only struck when they scented the smell of mortality. He was not contaminated by the stink of death. On the contrary, in his poetry he carried forward the words that gave meaning to life, and his voice was clear and resonant.

But the years on the road had punished him. Mantes was now far from young, and after more than thirty years of travelling he was thin and a little bent, his grizzled hair combed by the wind, his exposed skin as rutted as the path and the colour of faded leather. His step was slow. In the north, the chill morning air made him stiff from an old thigh wound. He faltered more often than he would like to admit, for his eyesight was failing. The voice alone was still strong.

He was glad to be going south. When he sang in the courts of the north, in draughty halls clapped by wind-blown shutters, with his eyes smarting in the smoke – in Thrace, in Chalcidice, even in Thessaly – to whom was he appealing? Tribal ruffians, robber barons, brigands with fresh blood on their hands. They dressed in skins and tore meat apart with brute strength. Gore, revenge, sacrifice, outlandish violence pleased them best. Oh, how they roared and stamped, making the dogs growl beneath the benches. Mantes recalled what the great teacher Homer had said, when he told of the twelve Trojan prisoners killed on the funeral pyre of Patroclus, to assuage the wrath of Achilles – the only example of human sacrifice in all that noble epic. What was Achilles but a Thessalian, as cruel as the whirlwind, a chieftain of barbarous appetites? So Mantes was pleased to have come down the coast road safely, past the craggy massifs of Olympus and Ossa which threw fearful shadows and cramped the narrow trail towards the dark breakers of the Thracian sea. Then the mountains drew back to the west, giving way to rolling uplands studded with pine and pasture. The bleak stretch of the sea, to east and south, began to be colonized by islands. The sky seemed wider, the sun warmer. In this land, the beds were softer, well-fitted doors kept the night air at bay, wine was poured with a free hand. Between household and rich household, the way was easier. Mantes had his dog, his laurel staff – and the road. They had become companions, wound together by the will of the gods.

Though it was early in the year, the midday sun still drew the strength out of an old man. He stopped to rest by a wayside marker which men called a herm, in honour of the god Hermes. A cairn of stones was topped by a stone phallus, reminding travellers that Hermes, messenger and guardian of the road, was also the joker, the jack-in-the-box, the chaser of all females, goddess, nymph or mortal. He was – and had proved himself to be – a god of fertility. The pile of stones on the grass-verge threw a little shade into which Mantes and the dog both sank gratefully. How benevolent the gods were! Mantes reflected, providers of numberless blessings to those who respected them. But a god could be both a friend and a danger. The works of man had become many and complicated. It was necessary for the immortals of Olympus to extend their influence in a way that was wide-ranging, puzzling, and hard for humanity to know.

Reclining in shadow, Mantes let his imagination go over the countryside. Though his sight was now growing dim, many years of wandering these parts had impressed the terrain on his mind's eye. He knew the repose and order of the land under a startling clear light. Even the bad weather was dramatic – a revelation. Field, woodland, meadow, scrub hillside slowly shifted mood and colour from dawn to dusk, changes that were as formal and evocative as a change in music. A white temple on a distant headland in Euboea winked in the sun like a beacon until night put it out. This was the country of Boeotia, a place of good earth. The few small homesteads of the farmers were lapped by tilled and cultivated ground, offering up the seasonal reward for age-old human effort. These farmers told an old tale, as anonymous and almost as long-lived as time itself. It was sufficient for them to follow their fathers' wisdom.

Mantes met them often on the path. Even in good times they seemed to carry a heavy burden. Though the ass carried the load to market, the farmer trudged behind just as wearily, groaning and moaning, weighed down by his destiny. Truly, his life was laborious, in all the senses of that word. Was the sun shining today? Well, that cloud on the distant mountain would dump a plentiful bucket of rain before the milking was done.

'Friend,' Mantes had called out that very morning to a man hoeing around his olive trees, 'how goes it? Earth-shaking Poseidon sleeps, is it not so? and all is well.'

That was altogether too much high spirits. The man reddened and looked aside. He would not answer. He went on plying the hoe, stabbing the ground like a man with a grudge. Mantes imagined the sentence of his ancestor forming in his mind: 'Sparing speech is more than gold; a tongue that seldom moves saves up treasure.' Besides, only the reckless speak lightly of the gods. It's easy to spew out talk, and then the mischief is done. What's left is hard to bear and difficult to get rid of. 'Talk by many people,' said the voice of the ancestors, 'never wholly dies away; even Talk is in some ways divine.'

Mantes smiled. Yes, it was mischievous of him to provoke these countrymen. He knew their set and stubborn ways. Many times he had been in their houses and taken their bread. He knew their solemn, crabbed and cautious rituals. In the dawn, they carefully washed their hands before making a libation to the gods. 'Or else,' they said, 'the holy ones spit back your prayers.' There was always a proper way to do things. Conceive a child in festival-time only – to make love after a funeral was ill-omened. Do not make water facing the sun. A boy who sits on the tombs of the dead is a lout and needs whipping. Marry a virgin five years past puberty and teach her carefully, or your marriage will be a joke with the neighbours. Let the feast-days be simple, with more conversation than food; and remember, when the guests come, not to cut your nails, and never leave the ladle in the wine bowl. Caulk the chinks in the house, or the crow will settle there and croak your fate. A man should not wash in water already used by a woman. In particular, do not make a mock of mysteries, for Heaven also can be angry.

A farmer's business was with land, weather and season. On a winter evening years ago, when the wind made the woods roar and even the shaggy cattle had their tails between their legs, a farmer, surprisingly talkative for a

Boeotian, had given Mantes a lesson in his works and days.

'Pull up to the fire,' he began hospitably. 'Listen, poet, this is how it is with us. Keep the traditional ways and you'll not go far wrong. Follow the lucky days, because sometimes a day is a step-mother and sometimes a mother. The first, fourth and seventh of the month are holy days. On the eighth, geld the boar and the bull. The tenth is a good day for a boy to be born, also for the taming of dogs and the schooling of mules and oxen. Do your shearing on the eleventh and twelfth, but the twelfth is particularly good, for that is the day when the spider spins her web and the ant gets busy about the nest. A woman who sets up her loom on this day finds the work easy. Then in the mid-month, cut the timber for the house beams and for the ribs of ships. The twentieth is favourable, but only in the morning. The twenty-seventh is an excellent day for many things: for opening wine jars, for yoking animals, for hauling boats to the water, though few people seem to know this now, nor do they call this day by its right name.

'Well, that's the good side of the coin. But of course there's a dirty side also. Learn to avoid the ill-omened days. Only a fool plants on the sixth, or begins to sow on the thirteenth. The sixth will make do for fencing but it's tricky for everything else. A boy born that day will be cunning and full of lies. But watch out for the fifth day. Oh, that's terrible. Avoid it like the plague or the north wind. On that day the Furies, daughters of Night, conspire with Strife, making rods for the backs of men. But our fathers have shown us the right and wrong way to go about life, though we know well enough that nothing is certain. The will of Zeus, who holds the aegis, alters from time to time, and it is hard for mortal men to know what he wants.'

Once more, Mantes smiled at this memory. These peasants invoked the name of Zeus but Mantes perceived that the real deities whom they feared and struggled with all their lives were older and more obscure than the Olympian immortals.

In the lee of the stone herm, and fairly comfortable on the grassy wayside – his travels had made the world his living-room and the ground his bed – Mantes pondered the elemental facts: the coming into being, and the stability of the world. He was in no hurry. In an hour or so the worst of the heat would have gone from the sun. His old dog snuffled in the shade. Mantes had some milk curds and a flat loaf in his leather wallet.

In the matter of the oldest gods – the Ancient Ones – it was wise to mark the words of the poets. For what is a poet but the bearer of wisdom? There was a man called Hesiod – peace to his bones! – who lived and sang in this land of Boeotia. He, too, was a farmer. He knew the fields, the hills, the sea, the islands. Winter stung his body, stones made the plough kick in his hands, flood and drought took turns to test him. Disease took the crops or laid low the mules. Yet in the long play of the seasons, unwinding year after year, Hesiod knew that Mother Earth gave forth all good things and sustained the generations of her children.

So Hesiod related the first mystery. There is a distant point where both knowledge and imagination stop. No mind, not even that of the poet, can go beyond. Behind that moment was the realm of Chaos, in which all matter was hidden. Ge, our Mother Earth, was the first and greatest of things to emerge out of Chaos. For without Earth nothing lives, not even the immortal gods who exist on the white peaks of Olympus, high on Earth's wide bosom. And Ge had with her from the beginning the dark pit called Tartarus, a place of troubles, sunk in the bowels of the ground. Then Eros arose, the one who quickens the loins and makes fools of the hearts of gods and men alike. Next, Darkness and Night, whom people call Erebus and Nyx, crept out of Chaos and, seeing there was as yet no light, lay together to bring forth Hemera, the day, and Aether, the luminous air.

By now, Chaos had produced place and time. The moment was ready for the generation of all that lives. What needed to be done? This is no secret to those who deal with crops and animals. Ge – Mother Earth – took it on herself to conceive without help. She strained and brought forth Uranus, the Heavenly Sky, who then covered her entirely and made fertile and productive everything that has a place in the ranks of nature.

That was how the people of Boeotia, that close-mouthed and practical folk, understood the things of the Earth. In the evening, when the household tasks were done, and the cattle chewed quietly in the byre, and the black cat prowled out into the dusk on nameless business, the families offered the day's thanks. A libation, naturally, to Zeus and the deathless gods, for safe-conduct through the dark reaches of the night. But in their hearts they offered a silent and deeper prayer to the Great Mother:

Earth is the mother of all, foundation of everything that is, eldest of beings and support of all nature and all humanity. Hail to the holy and boundless Goddess, Mother of Gods, and bride to the star-studded heavens.

All this Mantes had learnt from Hesiod, his predecessor, and now it was his task to tell this tale of creation in the halls of men. Was it a message that patriarchal man, day by day becoming more distant from the well-springs of Earth, wanted to hear? Legend related that the oracle of Delphi foretold the death of Hesiod, and he was duly murdered at Locris, perhaps for telling too much of the old truth. The nymphs washed his body, the goat-herds sprinkled offerings of milk and honey on his grave. Countryfolk, at least, knew the value of the old man who had tasted at the Muses' pure spring.

By now, the heat had gone out of the day. Mantes roused the dog, clutched his staff and walked firmly but slowly down the path. The road was long and there was no farmhouse in sight to offer him a night's haven. Some gruel or a bite of meat was all he needed, a bowl of wine if he were lucky, and perhaps a straw pallet inside the door.

He walked far into the evening. To the east, the gulf of Euboea darkened like a metal mirror fogged with dew. Behind him, Mantes sensed the rising dusk. The wayside trees thickened with shadows. Rushing down from a hill-side spring, a broad ribbon of water lay across the path, shivering in the half-light like the flank of a black horse. Before he waded the stream, Mantes paused. He spoke a brief prayer to the god of the river and washed his hands in the water as the rites prescribed. He wanted to urinate, but as he began to uncover he remembered that he was entering the realm of Night where none must defile either spring or stream. Quickly, he covered himself again and went on his way unrelieved.

Night, the Dark Nyx, coexisted with Ge before even Zeus was born. One must not offend, Mantes thought. Not Zeus, nor all the gods of Olympus, can withstand the secret power of these Ancient Ones.

And he went steadily on, towards the sound of dogs barking in the darkness.

The Storyteller

– 2 –

THE STRUGGLE

'HOMER,' MANTES was saying, in the confident voice of the professional storyteller, 'greatest of poets, tells us that a rich house is a stately place, and that an assembly of princes is a good sight to see. But better still is a blazing fire on a filthy night when Zeus, son of Cronus, sends the shivering winter weather.'

It is the habit of storytellers to overdo the compliments. This house, where he had landed for the night, was no rich palace, and his host was no prince. He was a retired soldier who now farmed a rambling estate on the plains of Boeotia. The house – if not rich, at least large and comfortable – was set amid lonely fields surrounded by groves and orchards of good earth. Such a place was tempting to bandits and marauders. Men called this wide, productive land 'the dance floor of Ares', because the war-god had trampled here so often with invading or retreating armies. But the owner had remembered his military training and had surrounded his home with a steep bank of earth and a fierce hedge of prickly pears. Strangers were likely to turn aside when the dogs in the gatehouse strained at the leash; and those who ventured beyond the thorns and the barking found a brisk military welcome rather than the luxury of a prince.

But Boreas, the North Wind, was battering the roof and hooting in the chimney. Winter rain scudded across the courtyard and crept under the shutters. The host, who did not believe in small measures, had banked up a fire in the hall capable of putting a regiment of soldiers in a sweat. But Mantes was glad enough to be warm and under cover on such a night. There would be plenty of plain food to go with the roaring fire, and in return for this hospitality only a story was needed.

Listening to the battle of the elements outside, Mantes decided to tell a tale of another, divine strife.

'We poets,' he began, 'sing of the glories of the Immortals and of the deathless sagas of the heroes, but it's hard for ordinary folk to know what we mean. We are a country people in the main, peasants and farmers. For most of us the world ends where the fields stop, or where the river winds into the ravine, or where chestnut and beech straggle out into the sparse scrub and the blue rocks of the hills. What do our peasants care for the great tragedy of the House of Atreus, or for the clash of armies and gods on the plains of Troy? Too often, in the midst of our tales, we are interrupted by creaking voices of country folk: "That Aegisthus sounds like a bad lad. I knew a herdsman with a name something like that, up on the slopes of Mount Oeta. He was a bad one also. They say he cut the balls off a ram from a rival herd." Or "There was a Diomedes down our way, lived on the edge of the swamp. It takes a smart fellow to get out of the swamp and do well. I expect the Diomedes you're talking about was the same family."

'Country people understand best that the sky is their roof and the earth their floor. And between these bounds of nature they feel the tyranny of the land and the pressure of the seasons. Their life is a lottery. What is given with one hand is taken away with the other. The sum of their lives is work, and they do not look far beyond the wisdom of their fathers. They know the old saying: "The idle man who waits on empty hope, ignoring the tasks of the day, reaps a harvest of trouble. Winter will catch him helpless and poor, scratching his swollen foot with a thin hand."

'Mighty Zeus, had he so wished, could have allowed the earth to bring forth in a week enough to keep a prudent family for a year. Nature is kind. Her instructions, which all farmers must learn to follow, are simple. When the Pleiades set, towards the end of the year, harness the team and plough the fields. When they rise again in the spring, weed the crop, sharpen the sickle and make ready for the harvest. Those stars of the Pleiades – daughters of the Titan Atlas – will not let us down. In their constancy, they support the toil of farmers. But the gods are jealous. Too often, they kick the wheel of nature from its regular track, making burdens for the weary shoulders of mankind.'

The old soldier, listening to this beginning, was showing signs of impatience. He was hungry, waiting for the evening meal to be brought in, and in this mood his temper was not reliable. A poet, of course, liked to approach things in a roundabout way, but a soldier plunged straight in. He got up from his couch and prowled before the fire, cracking his knuckles and rubbing his old bones.

'Well, storyteller,' he interrupted, 'you're right about the burdens of mankind. But what's the explanation? I'm only an old campaigner with not much learning, but I know that there were gods before All-Seeing Zeus. Puzzling beings, deities of earth and sky, of space and time. Giants and Titans, unruly broods spawned by Mother Earth, fought in the childhood of time to make the world the dangerous place we know today. Not that we can ever avoid all conflict or opposition. We farmers know that nature must strike a balance. We pay for the good days with miserable ones, such as today. No land has the sole right to warmth and clear skies. At this time of year the chariot of Helius, the Sun-God, has appointments elsewhere. It's over Africa now, turning the people black. But we are satisfied if Helius makes his daily journey across the sky, even though from time to time it pleases Zeus to hide the sun with thunderclouds. It is enough that we can know that Helius is there, and can see the fiery disc and feel the heat. Eos, Goddess of Dawn, gets us farmers out of bed, and we shut our eyes on the pale light of Selene, the Moon. Those gods and goddesses we respect. How else would we divide our seasons and our days?

'But as for the Deathless Ones, the mighty gods of Olympus, country folk don't have much to do with them. We honour them, of course, because it's foolish to risk the anger of immortals. But we remember that everything on earth, including the gods, rests on the bosom of Ge, our universal Mother. Even in the sea there were divine beings before Poseidon, the Earth-Shaker. The old god Pontus ruled the waters at first, as all fishermen know. And he had many strange children whose lives, like our own, grew out of struggle. Some were born to help and some to fear.

'Any sailor can tell you about the terror of the sea. But was the earth any less frightening? Giants and Titans acted like madmen. They even attacked the gods. The ground rumbled and split, islands were tossed around like empty plates, inoffensive little river gods dried up or were torn from their beds. Some of those monsters were so danger-ous they had to have mountains heaped on top of them to keep them quiet. But still they rebelled, fuming and roaring under ground, spewing their anger sky-high in volcanic outbursts. All this I have learnt as I campaigned from one end of Greece to the other.

'So, poet, though we don't know much about the proper history of those Holy Ones on Olympus, I'll tell you how it is with my fellow farmers and country folk. There are spirits of earth and sky and sea, and they lay shadows over our lives. The generations of these beings, like us, tear at each other, for place and favour. We, like them, struggle for light. This begins the day you are born and continues until Charon, the grim ferryman, grabs the obol coin from beneath the tongue of your corpse and begins to cross the black waters to the Underworld.'

The old soldier stopped as the steward and the house-hold slaves bustled forward with the first dishes from the kitchen. Wine was drawn into earthenware pitchers and the wine-cups set out. The fire, stoked by the master's energetic hand, was roaring away with too much enthusiasm and had to be damped to a more comfortable heat. The smell of roast meat drew the men to the table.

'Helius has hurried home with the sun,' Mantes began again, settling into his place with the sigh of the traveller finally at rest, 'and even old warriors may take their ease. After the alarms of the day, neither Hector nor Achilles was ashamed to strip off the sweaty armour and stretch out on the banks of the Scamander. A song or a tale beguiled them while the river ran by. But I see I mustn't beat about the bush with military men. Your life has been struggle. Your reward – as with all mankind – will be the grave. How can it be otherwise, for we follow the path that the gods have trodden before us? Listen, and I'll tell you of fear in heaven and pain on earth.

'At the beginning of things, Ge, our Mother Earth, was lonely in the coldness of the void. So she called to Uranus, the Heavenly Sky, and he covered her and they mated in joy and expectation. Many children were born – the nights of eternity are long. First, the Titans came from the womb of Earth: Oceanus, whose waters encircle the world, and Hyperion, father of Helius and the first to guide the chariot of the sun, and Iapetus, father of Prometheus, that friend to mankind. Then Ge gave birth to a race of goddesses, mysterious, maternal, perhaps beyond knowing, for only with one of them – Mnemosyne – did memory begin. Chief among these immortals were Rhea and Tethys. Then Cronus crept from the Earth's womb, bawling and angry, a powerful deity to pity and fear.

'After the birth of Cronus, it seemed as if Mother Earth began to experiment with the bounds of nature. A floodgate opened and she poured forth monstrous beings. First, the Hundred-Handed Giants emerged, three monsters larger than mountains and each with fifty heads. Then came the Cyclopes, with a round eye in the middle of the forehead – oafish brutes, almost as large as the giants, who later forged lightning and divine thunderbolts for Zeus in their underground smithies. These were the beings of Earth, creatures of riot and destruction, and their father, Uranus, lord of the steel-blue skies who moved serenely among the orderly procession of the stars, hated them all. What had he to do with such ugly, brutal, ungovernable beings? So he took hold of his children one by one and banished them from the light of Heaven, thrusting them deep into the dark body of their mother Earth.

'But Ge groaned and ached to be delivered of her burden. "Dear Mother," her children cried within her, "it's dark and musty down here. Beneath us, Tartarus sends up the stink of Death, and yet we have not lived. Release us into the light and air." And Ge schemed against the injustice done to her and her children by Uranus. In secret she made a flint sickle and gave it an edge keen enough to split one of her hairs. Then she called her children. "Sons," she said, "who is willing to put right this evil done to us all by your father, Uranus? Be bold, and I will show you the way." But all were afraid of their father's heavenly anger. "Well," cried Ge in derision, "such vast and strong and big-hearted children – and so timid!" Then Cronus, the sly one, spoke up. "Mother, I'll do it, whatever it is. Our father, the Heavenly Sky, keeps us from our birthright. He deserves neither respect nor pity."

'Ge gave Cronus the sickle and hid him in ambush. That night, when Uranus, as eager as a stallion, came to cover Earth, Cronus reached out his left hand – that sinister, that unlucky hand! – took his father by the genitals and cut them off with a sweep of the sickle. As he flung the castrated parts towards the sea, drops of blood and semen fell on Mother Earth and fertilized her womb once more. And now, what strange things emerged! Who can fathom the productivity of Earth? She brought forth more giants, and the nymphs of the ash tree, and the three Erinyes, those avenging Furies whom all fear and none can escape. And where the severed member of the god fell, by Cape Drepanum, the sea frothed until the goddess Aphrodite rose from the foam. This is the immortal, the child of lust and violence, the most beautiful, dangerous one, whom men also call Philommedes, the Cock Lover. Aphrodite went to Cyprus, where she was joined by Eros and Desire, and ever since these three mischief-makers have plotted to set the hearts of mankind on fire.

'Once Uranus was castrated he fell away from Ge. No longer did they embrace in the night. Heaven and Earth were now divided and stood apart. The one was the realm of frozen space, and the other the ground for all our pleasure and all our pain.'

They had finished eating. After the earlier tumult of the wind and the rain, the day was dying more peacefully. A smell of damp earth suffused the hall, vying with the lingering aromas of sesame and thyme and rosemary. Stomachs were satisfied. They had eaten barley soup, and a kid roasted with chestnuts, and last year's olives in brine, and handfuls of raisins. There was bread to take the edge off the wine, which was new and a little raw.

The olive logs of the fire were glowing cheerfully and Mantes wrapped himself luxuriously in the woollen cloak laid out for him by the steward. But his host still wore the leather jerkin and the short linen tunic of the old army man. His arms and legs, tanned and time-blotched, and taut with strong sinews, were bare. He had eaten sparingly, and the steward had refilled his wine-cup only once. Something about the tale he had just heard preoccupied him. Leaning back on an elbow, he fixed the poet with a startling, clear eye.

'What you tell me,' he said, 'about the beginning of things is largely news to me. We soldiers have studied fortifications and warfare but we have neglected theology. I listen to you and wonder. The actions of the Immortals are very puzzling. What are blunt fellows such as I to make of it all? As a former commander who has seen many battles, I think it may be better to clear our heads of divine mysteries and stick to learning the heroic virtues. How else can we keep our lands safe from invaders and lawless rogues?'

'Before we ate,' Mantes replied, 'you did not neglect the usual libations and prayers.'

'Respect is easy. It requires neither sweat nor blood. We do what is customary. It is best to sacrifice as our fathers sacrificed.'

'But what do you ask for when you pray to the Deathless Gods?'

'My trade was war, but to the wise man war is only a road to security. Now that I'm a farmer, I ask for peace and good harvests.'

'But for yourself?'

'Health, and to keep the strength of my arm.'

'Strength to do what?'

'To keep family and household safe, and to advance us all in prosperity and happiness.'

'A noble answer, indeed. A soldier's answer. But how does happiness look to you?'

'Alive, to judge the present moment correctly and to march with the demands of the time. To die a death worthy of a soldier. And after death, I see nothing but darkness.'

He frowned. He rubbed his beak of a nose and pushed his couch back a little, as if to put some distance between him and his questioner. A soldier does not like to be confronted by matters of the soul. They upset the simple scheme of war and peace, of survival or death. Is that what poets are for, he wondered, to sow tares and weeds among old certainties?

He rapped sharply on the table, summoning the steward and waving towards the empty wine-cups. A soldier lived in the company of Ares, the war-god, a loudmouth, a slaughterer, whose cruel ways did not encourage any further enquiry into the nature of the gods. No, his life until his retirement to his estate had been that of the campaigner. He had slogged all the roads where Greek fought fellow Greek or invader, from Rhodope in the barbarian north, where the mountains were like broken teeth, to the five gaunt fingers of Taygetus, rising high above the arid plains of the south. In the east, he had seen the ruined and wind-swept gates of Troy. He had tracked across sea-lanes strewn with wrecks and drowned bodies to the bird-spattered cliffs of Corcyra and the little gouged inlets of Ithaca, no bigger than dog-hutches. Reflecting on this long experience, he turned towards his guest.

'The lesson of war, poet, is fear. A soldier clings to fact, not mystery, otherwise he could not endure. Do not worry about the gods. Salute them and let them be, for there's nothing we can do about them. The Fates, or the Furies, have us marked and we'll not escape them. But teach me to live nobly and to do great deeds and you shall eat at my table food fit for the feasts of Olympus every day of your life until Hades greets your shade in the Underworld.'

Mantes poured a little water into his wine. He wanted to get his words straight. He gazed into the fire and hugged the cloak to him, as if he felt the chill of uncertainty. How was he to bring home to this old warrior that conflict was a rank plant that grew out of the nature, the very stuff, of humanity, a poisonous weed sown by the gods them-selves? As soon as Cronus had usurped the place of Uranus, his castrated father, at once ambition, hatred, fear and cruelty were afoot in the universe. Then Cronus reigned, but for how long? He took his sister Rhea as his wife, and his other brothers and sisters joined together, each to each. But in these families there was neither com-fort nor safety. Cronus was afraid.

Mantes put it to the old soldier as he would to a child.

'How did it come about, even among the gods, that those who had risen might also fall? What had been done once could be done again. The door of knowledge, once opened, can never be closed completely. So even Cronus, most powerful of the gods, had reason to be afraid. His parents, Heaven and Earth, from whom all things sprang, foresaw his fate and warned him to beware his destiny. But where would the danger come from? In his panic he suspected everyone. The grim Cyclopes and the Hundred-Handed Giants? They were fearsome enough to do anything. Cronus acted as his father had done and imprisoned them in the bowels of the earth. Or maybe his children? Each one was likely to be his enemy! So Cronus sat by the birth-stool of Rhea, and as each child came from the womb he snatched the baby and devoured it. The goddesses Hestia, Demeter and Hera, the gods Poseidon and Hades– one by one Cronus devoured them.

'Now, imagine the grief of the mother. "Heaven and Earth, dear parents, save me and mine," Rhea called out. They heard her and took pity. When Rhea was big with Zeus, her youngest child, Mother Ge came in darkness and spirited her daughter away to Lyctus, in Crete, where, in a wild and secret place, the babe was safely born and hidden in a cave on Mount Aegaeon. Then Ge took a smooth stone, about the size of a baby, wrapped it in swaddling clothes and gave it to Cronus, who swallowed it down in one lump. Then he was satisfied.'

'Strange satisfaction,' the old soldier snorted.

'Yes, and only temporary at that. What is to come cannot be deflected; even the gods can't do that. Time passed. Though raised in a cave, Zeus knew who he was. Ge and Rhea, the maternal spirits, had brooded over him, guiding each step. And the cunning of Ge – for who, finally, can resist the influence of Mother Earth? – induced her son Cronus to vomit up what he had swallowed. And the first thing he spewed out was the stone he had taken for his youngest son. Zeus honoured this stone, which he set at Pytho, in the vale of Parnassus, so that all mankind might see and remember.'

At this point the host interrupted. 'That much seems clear,' he said. 'Travelling in the place now called Delphi, I saw something like that. There, by the sacred precinct, near the tomb of Neoptolemus, is a stone much rubbed and honoured, though it's nothing much to look at. Every day the people of Delphi anoint it with oil.'

'It is the actions of mankind,' Mantes replied, 'that make

the gods credible. Without worship and sacrifice, who shall know that the gods exist?'

Mantes continued his story. It was easy to see what would happen now. After vomiting up the stone, Cronus spewed up his other children, who could not restrain their enmity against their father. Zeus incited his brothers and sisters against Cronus and they needed few arguments. It was a poor fate for young gods to be imprisoned in the belly of their father! Then Zeus released the Cyclopes and the Hundred-Handed Giants from their dungeon below the earth and in gratitude they rallied to his cause. Preparations began for war. The Cyclopes went to work, beating metal on the anvil, forging for Zeus the lightning and thunderbolts of his wrath. For Poseidon, they made a huge trident, a three-pronged fork with wicked points. And for Hades, later Lord of the Under-world, they fashioned a cap of invisibility. In alarm, Cronus called to his aid the Titans, the first children whom Ge had borne to Uranus. Under their leader, Atlas, strongest of them all, they made ready to defend the rule of Cronus. The gods were at war.

Mantes rose from his couch to stretch his legs. He took a turn or two in front of the fire, pausing to shake the smouldering logs into a sudden flame. Then he went on quietly.

'You know very well what war is. I don't need to remind a soldier what happens when the arm strikes and the blood flows. Yet how much more terrible it is when the gods fall out. What superhuman acts of courage, strength and vio-lence. The madness of battle. The vainglory and boasting. The world of nature torn to shreds. Godlike rage and god-like suffering. For ten years Cronus and the Titans held fast on Mount Othrys. For ten years the army of Zeus could not be shifted from the peaks of Olympus.'

'Stalemate,' the host muttered in sympathy. 'That's how it usually is when equal forces are entrenched in mountain strongholds. Time to try cunning, or treachery, or find new allies.'

'Well said, old warrior, you remember your trade. That's just what Zeus thought. He called for renewed help from the Cyclopes and the Hundred-Handed Giants. The giants, Cottus, Briareus and Gyes, with three hundred hands between them, each as large as a temple courtyard, made the sky black with a hail of boulders. And into this gloom Zeus flashed the lurid shafts of his thunder and lightning, prepared for him by the Cyclopes. Seas boiled. The ground heaved. The sun was draped in dust and rubble. Even the far depths of Tartarus shivered, fearing the collapse of the world above.

'But the bonds of the world held and mighty Zeus, the Thunderer, prevailed. The Titans were overwhelmed. The triumphant gods of Olympus tied them in chains and hurled them below, sinking as far as an anvil would fall in nine days and nights, down to the realm of Tartarus. There, in black mist and bog, they were locked behind triple ramparts of bronze. Poseidon closed the ramparts with a gate of bronze and set the Hundred-Handed Giants, each with fifty heads, eternally on guard. Only Atlas, mightiest of the Titans, was spared this prison. Zeus banished him to the end of the world, to stand upon the last shore by the circling waters of Oceanus, to bear the weight of the sky on his bowed shoulders.'

There was a silence. Then the host banged the table in approval and called for wine.

'A good campaign,' he said with a laugh. 'The enemy beaten, rounded up and well guarded. The leading rogue set apart and made to feel his shame. But tell me: did All-Seeing Zeus now taste the sweet fruits of victory?'

'Not yet. One last opponent arose out of the infinite resources of Earth. Perhaps Ge was offended by the impris- -onment of the Titans, her first-born children. In any case she coupled with Tartarus, the infernal deity of the dark wastes, and gave birth to Typhon, her last and most terrible child. Imagine a being whose head touched the stars. His arms reached from sunrise to sunset. From the waist upward he looked like a man. But what a man! A face huge and voracious. A brow burning like forest fires. Hair and beard like a storm in motion. A hundred snakes lashed around his winged shoulders, each one mouthing weird cries – hissing, squealing, roaring, bellowing, the gasps of the tortured, the laments of the damned. And below his waist, instead of legs, two giant serpents slithered and twinned.

'This was the monster who challenged the victory of Zeus. They began to fight, and once more the world held its breath. Even the Titans groaned in their subterranean prison. Typhon was forced back by lightning and thunderbolts but at Mount Casius, in Syria, he caught Zeus at close quarters. As they grappled Zeus lost his sickle-sword to the monster. With a few rough blows Typhon hacked the sinews from the hands and feet of the god. Then Typhon carried the stricken Zeus to the Cave of the Winds, in Cilicia, and hid the sinews in a bearskin. Delphyne, half hag and half dragon, guarded the mouth of the cave. But the allies of Zeus, aghast at the defeat of their leader, hurried to help him. Pan, who knew best the lie of the country, crept up on Delphyne and roared in her ear, stunning and confusing her. Then Hermes – the slippery one, the god of the light-fingered – stole back the sinews and skilfully sewed them in place.

'Furiously, Zeus mounted a chariot with winged horses, driving Typhon north with tempest and fire, so that he fled towards the lands beyond all knowledge. Prodigious leaps took the monster from mountain top to mountain top, pursued by the vengeful god. Wounded and weak, Typhon made a last stand in Thrace. Tearing a mountain from its roots, he hurled it at Zeus. But the arm was weak and the aim was poor. The mountain dropped harmlessly, stained by the monster's blood. Mount Haemus, it is called – Blood Mountain. Then the game was up for Typhon, for the Fates had called his doom. He dragged his wretched body to Sicily, where Zeus overpowered him and crushed him under Mount Aetna. To this day, a spew of fire and brimstone still bursts out of the mountain from the monster trapped beneath.'

In the hall, the fire had subsided to dying embers. The wine jar was empty. The wick in the lamp was flickering and needed trimming. Tomorrow would be time enough. Outside, beyond the ring of the fence, a late animal called, hunting or hunted. The old soldier yawned and ruffled his white hair, as stiff as snow-strewn stubble. He began to rise, then he paused, listening into the night.

'Fear came into the world,' he said slowly, 'followed by blood. Every soldier finds, in the end, that his path leads to Blood Mountain. And not only soldiers. The gods have imposed upon all mankind a grim pilgrimage up those painful slopes. The good soldier knows that he fights not only the violence of the enemy but also the violence within. Blood is inevitable. It is our duty to temper it with honour.'

'Once more, nobly spoken, old warrior. But do not be too confident of success. We are confused by the evidence of our nature, even though it is revealed to us by the action of the gods. Can we ever conquer Blood Mountain?'

The two elderly men were standing now, ready to bring the day to a close. Two seasoned campaigners, in their different ways, they slowly trod the bars of moonlight that lay across the darkened hall. The experience of their lives had resolved nothing.

'I'll leave you with a fable,' Mantes said, turning towards his bedchamber. 'A hawk was carrying a speckled nightingale high in the clouds. Pierced by the talons, the little songbird cried out piteously. But the hawk silenced her with disdain: "Miserable fool, why do you weep? One far stronger than you now grips you fast. Sing your heart out but I'll do to you what I please. Perhaps I'll eat you, perhaps I'll let you go. My strength, my appetite, my mastery of the air have given me licence to do as I wish. It is your lot to submit and suffer. Be quiet, or I'll kill you now." Reflect on that in the hours of the night.'

Start of a Horse Race from Atlas to Olympia

– 3 –

WALKING THE COUNTRY
OF THE GODS

MEN AND women quarrel, even over the gods. Where do the immortals come from? What lands and which peoples have been blessed by their presence? Mankind acknowledged the greatness of Zeus. After the defeat of Cronus and the Titans, he was unchallenged among the gods, the Lord of the Bright Sky. But on earth, squabbling men, as always ardent for glory, jostled to claim for themselves the holy places of his birth and childhood. The stories told by the poets said one thing, and then another. This place had a claim, and also that one. But the loudest claim came from Crete. Who was right? Since the poets were the historians of the gods, it seemed to Mantes that they, most of all, had a duty to find out. As a Greek and as a poet, Mantes could hardly help himself. He had it in his bones to look into the heart of things: that was the Greek way.

Years ago, when Mantes began to follow his calling, it needed a strong spirit of enquiry, and some courage also, to persuade him to risk the dangers of the voyage to Crete. Poseidon's kingdom, which the sea-god stirred with malicious strokes of his trident from his palace below the waves at Aegae, was often a frightening place, a wind-torn chaos of sea-sickness and terror. Like any landlocked youth, Mantes feared the sea. Besides, Crete was a backwater. King Minos was long dead. His empire was gone, his palace was crumbling into the parched ground. Kites nested in the ruined towers, vermin scuttered in old banqueting halls, now ripped open to the sky. Who, in this wreck of an island, could now afford to support and encourage a storyteller? Men who might once have been princes were now sheep herders and cattle thieves. Their hospitality, always suspicious of strangers, was likely to include a knife in the ribs.

But Crete had its place in the history of the world. If it was the land where gods and mortals played out the divine scheme in the childhood of time, then Mantes had to set aside the fears of a landlubber. Anxiously, he took a trading vessel from Gytheum. He quit the little mainland port, safely backed by the bulwarks of the Taygetus range, and entrusted his life to some scarred and battered planks, heading for the Gulf of Didymi on the north coast of Crete.

To the outsider, there was something shocking about the island. The sun thrust down like a lance, throwing sharp-edged shadows which scythed the ground and seemed to leave behind little but dust. Under the powerful light, the areas of shade looked dangerously obscure, yet beyond their dark borders there was too much clarity. The light overwhelmed, dazzling the head with heat and nausea. Things nearby – trees, rocks, flaking walls, a lone goat moving like a sleepwalker – were sharply chiselled. But distant objects trembled in the heat-haze and the landscape bled out into indistinctness. To focus at that distance made the eyes hurt.

The plain behind the shoreline was large, empty, frightening. In the solitude the hum of the insects was not friendly but too loud and angry. The mountains, with their promise of a greener, cooler world, looked too remote to be of any help. Their pale tops shimmered into the washed-out sky.

'Somewhere over there,' Mantes repeated to himself, to give himself confidence, 'is the birthplace of Zeus.'

There was no road across the plain, only faint animal tracks, which had scuffed through the thin grass to an underlay of dust and grit. A few grazing beasts fidgeted under the attack of the flies. There was no one to show the way. Mantes walked until he saw some smoke lingering under a small grove of pines. Three bearded peasants, as shaggy as the beasts on the plain, had just finished grilling pieces of lamb, and the damped fire was sending coils of greasy smoke into the low branches of the pines. The men hardly glanced at the traveller. They were busy, gobbling the meat, hacking it from the bone with short daggers. Juices seeped into matted beards. Stinking powerfully of dung and sweat, the peasants seemed as much satyr as human, rough beings coated in hair who might drop onto all-fours at any moment and gallop away.

Mantes leant against a pine, wiping sweat from his face. He waited, judging it not quite safe to interrupt their eating. In a while, the smallest peasant, whose face was made particularly villainous by a gummy diseased eye, belched, cleaned his knife in the ground, and grinned at Mantes.

'Hot, eh?' he said cheerfully. 'The god forgets to rain.'

'Which god is that?' Mantes asked, wishing to be polite.

'Zeus, of course, chief of them all.'

Another peasant laughed. 'The Cloud-Gatherer, some people call him. Not round here, he isn't.'

'Zeus,' Mantes repeated. 'I was going to ask you about him.'

'Ask away. If we know, we'll tell you. Yes or no, that's how we deal with questions here.'

'They say this is his land.'

'Yes, that's true. We call it the god-trodden land.'

'Born somewhere over there,' the third peasant put in helpfully, waving his knife in the direction of the mountains.

'So I've heard,' Mantes said. 'But where exactly would that be?'

The answer was vague. None of the three knew anything definite. The Cave of Dicte was said to be the god's birthplace, on the slopes of Mount Aegaeon, somewhere to the west. Or was he born, as other Cretans said, on Mount Ida?

But that miraculous event was untold years ago, before even the fathers of our fathers were in the land. People came and went, and the land devoured them. What remained was grey stone, white dust, a sun like a branding iron, silence. Many dynasties succeeded each other, passing from pomp to disaster. But the god persists. All-Seeing Zeus governs the land, and the land rules all those who live in it. No child of man escapes the rod of Father Zeus.

'No use making a fuss,' the one with the ravaged eye explained. 'A god is a god. Zeus belongs here but we're not what you might call friends. What can we know about him? No more than a sailor on a bad sea can guess about Poseidon, making trouble beneath the waves. If we could see what the gods were up to, we could make our own lives easier. Many people have come here in years gone by – pirates, invaders, merchants, settlers, all kinds of adventurers. Zeus has taken them all in hand and made them Greeks. For this is his territory, such as it is, and no one here can avoid his influence. What more can we say?'

Zeus is *Anax*, the King, and he is also *Hellanios*, great father of all Greeks. But at that moment the starry axe of his thunder was not splitting any rain-clouds, yet peasants still had to scratch a living from the sun-baked plains. Having finished their meal, the three men kicked earth over the dying fire, stuck their knives in their belts, and trudged out from the shade of the pines. Talk of the gods was pointless. There was work to be done.

Mantes continued west, by enquiry narrowing his search towards a high ridge in the broken mountains. He climbed into upland pastures thinly dotted with a summer population of sheep and lonely shepherds. Occasionally he passed a shepherd's temporary camp. Branches were propped in the angle of a rock and covered with skins or cloth. A large, evil dog barked its head off at the approach of a stranger. The rarified air of the hills began to make the lungs of the traveller pant. Above the pasture the way became steep, zig-zagging through fig trees and vallonea and holly-oak

and stunted olives. Wild lupins and thyme grew underfoot. In the evening, when the light changed, crags of limestone put on a sudden golden blush, and the bright scars
left by landslip or winter storm were as vivid as flame.
They looked like tailings and embers pitched out from the
underground forges of the Cyclopes. From the heights, the
traveller saw valleys slowly filling with blue shadow, and
the wide bowl of the Lassiti plains beyond turned a
burnished copper in the sun's declining rays.

As night fell, Mantes forgot the sense of wonder and the
exhilaration of the view. Afraid of darkness and wild
animals, he jammed himself into the small space between a
jumble of rocks and a twisted oak. Curled among the roots
of the oak – the tree sacred to Zeus – he pulled his cloak over
his head and prayed to the Father of the Gods and to Eos,
Goddess of the Dawn, to see him safe through the black
hours. When daylight returned he was refreshed and ready
to approach the birthplace of Zeus in the Cave of Dicte.

'Stop! Wait!' These plaintive commands came from a
small, spry figure puffing up the hillside. When he had
climbed level with the cave, he collapsed on a rock,
fanning himself and getting his breath back. Then he
turned a stern eye on the poet.

'You can't go in there, just like that. Definitely not.
There's a proper way to do things.'

'Who says I can't?' Mantes asked. 'Who are you?'

'I keep an eye on things round here.'

'Are you a priest of this holy place?'

'Not exactly.' The little fellow began to look shifty. 'We
don't run to a priest up here in the wilderness. I'm more of
a caretaker. I take time off from my flocks, guarding the
place and making sure things are done right. Respect and
honour, you know.'

He gazed into the distance with an innocent air, though
he had manoeuvred himself to block the path to the cave.
But a small gift of coins, discreetly slipped into his hand,
changed his humour immediately. At once he was all
business.

'Let's get on with it,' he said briskly. 'I've got to get back to my flock.'

He unfastened from his belt a flask of water and some dried figs tied up in a cloth. Then he poured the water in purification over Mantes's hands and over his own. He laid the figs, as an offering, on a slab of rock that made a natural altar. Then both men prayed, standing with their arms spread wide and their palms upwards. They prayed towards the huge, empty sky in which Helius' chariot was just beginning to drag the heat of the new day up from the eastern rim.

Then the guardian was ready. Solemnly he thrust out his little chest and began to point out the catalogue of holy wonders.

'Those faint dents in the ground were left by the divine hands of Rhea, when she supported herself giving birth to Zeus. The Dactyls, the Finger-folk, sprang from those same marks. They are the brawny smiths who taught us Cretans the use of iron and copper. Those rogues who live around Mount Ida say that all this happened on their mountain, but we know better. And that tree, that poor old oak now gnarled and dying, that's where the golden cradle of baby Zeus was hung. He lay there and his angry father, Cronus, could not find him because he was neither in heaven nor on earth nor in the sea. The golden watch-dog snarled below, pawing the earth just there, scratching up that pile of rubble.

'Come this way now. Here, in the open space before the cave, the youthful Curetes danced and banged their weapons, making a hideous racket that drowned out the squalls of our lusty young god. This is the path where Amaltheia, the goat-nymph, went to and fro with her milk and with honey from our own sweet hillside. She was the divine nurse, and the god rewarded her service. All-Providing Zeus made the Cornucopia out of one of her horns, filling it with a never-ending supply of food and drink. Later, Zeus gave her further honour. When he needed an invincible cloak, he took a goatskin in memory of Amaltheia and made it into his sacred aegis. Such was the respect and affection between the divine babe and his nurse! It teaches us lessons. Look up even today into the night sky and you'll still find Amaltheia, placed by Zeus in the constellation of the Goat.'

By now they had come to the mouth of the cave. They entered with awe. In front of them was a large, dank, cold, slippery, downward-sloping darkness. Some light entered through the low, wide mouth but withered quickly, glancing very faintly off pale, dripping stalactites and then dying, rubbed out by the emptiness. The air was chill and wet. A loose stone clattered down, the cave sounding ever more hollow until the stone was sucked into the deep stillness of an underground pool far below. They stumbled forward for a while, then could see no more. Beyond was mystery, and the heavy oppression of the unknown. Human sight could penetrate only so far into the nursery of Zeus. Overcome by something like fear, they turned back.

Out on the sun-drenched hillside, at once the world looked safer and easier to understand. The Zeus of the cave was a primal god, an infant deity just emerged from the universal womb of Earth, from whom all things descended. He was not yet Lord of the Bright Sky, not until he had defeated his father, Cronus, and the Titans. Only when he had routed them from Mount Othrys did he come into his inheritance, as had been foretold.

Mantes saw that even the gods had a destiny, which they could not avoid. The three Fates, daughters of Darkness and Night, governed the course of all lives, both mortal and immortal. Clotho, the eldest sister, spins the thin thread of destiny. Lachesis, the second, measures the length. Atropos, small and terrible, cuts with her shears each allotted portion. They are beyond appeal, though radiant Apollo once tricked them with drink and extended for a while the life of his friend Admetus. Bad luck to those who try to escape their decision, for it is a delusion to think one may tangle with the Fates. Typhon thought he could unseat Zeus and rule in his place. But when that monster was locked in battle against the King of the Gods, and already growing weak, the Fates cunningly persuaded him to eat human food to regain his strength. But this weakened him still further, for our food is not fit for an immortal, and Zeus struck him down.

With relief, Mantes turned away from the mountains and the Cave of Dicte and set out for the coast. Cretan Zeus, the young god of a bare, denuded land, raked by the sun and worn away by waves of invaders, seemed an unformed deity, like rough clay waiting to be given the shape of a mature god. Crete was the nursery, the initiation of the god into a suffering world. His destiny pointed him elsewhere, towards his allotted place as Lord of Olympus and master of the world.

In his youth, Mantes thought how obscure is the story of the gods! To mankind, they reveal so little. The history of their lives is like a comet glimpsed through clouds, seen and then gone, passing into realms no human eye can reach. The poets, who tell the story to each generation, must laboriously piece together evidence from the brief view through the clouds.

In the years that followed, Mantes grew experienced in his trade. Before a thigh-wound and age took the spring out of his step, he served the Muses well, taking his songs and tales up and down the land, to all who would listen. Gradually, in many wanderings, he saw how the influence of Zeus radiated over the whole country where men and women had become Greek. In many strange places – in a hill shrine still hung with withered garlands, in a grove of oaks, in a rich temple sanctuary, by the altar of an army – suddenly he would sense the overwhelming presence of the King of Gods. It seemed to Mantes that Zeus was educating his servant. 'Look for me in Dodona,' he was saying. 'Search me out in the meadows of Olympia.'

So Mantes went. He travelled to Thesprotia, far to the northwest. This was not fertile country for poets. Few people lived there. The inhabitants were surly and uncommunicative, their language being only a tortured kind of Greek. They had no knowledge of writing. But the Fates led him on. The road was hard among swelling, barren hills. Moisture-laden winds flew off the western seas, settling a melancholy fog in the valleys, or dumping cold rains on the bare peaks. In winter, the mountain lakes froze. In spring, fast-melting waters swept tracks away and carved ever more deeply into ravines where plane trees began to spread leaves as tough as leather. In the warm places, sheltered from the wind, wild ilex grew above bushes of white-flowering myrtle. Neither merchants nor armies came this way. Few sounds broke into the stillness, only wind sighs and the chuckle of tumbling streams and the chink-chink of the stonechat.

'Where are you going?' the lonely bystanders asked, as the traveller went past.

'To Dodona, to the holy precinct where Zeus of the oak tree lives.'

The bystanders gave a smug smile. 'Of course. Why else would anyone come to us? We wish you luck at the oracle of Zeus. Let the god speak to your satisfaction.'

They took pride in the only distinction their land had to offer. All in heartache or doubt turned their prayers towards Zeus at Dodona. When Achilles was in trouble at Troy, lying low and sulking between his burning ships and the walls of the city, he petitioned Zeus of snow-bound Dodona to grant his pretty young friend Patroclus some of his own strength and luck. Shipwrecked Odysseus, blown from his homeward course and cast up on a beach in Thesprotia, climbed wearily to Dodona to ask Zeus the way back to Ithaca. It was well known that Zeus had hidden himself at Dodona. He would speak through his oracle to those who came with humility and gifts.

Mantes was only another in the long chain of enquirers. 'Take this path,' the bystanders said. 'The sanctuary lies at the end of the valley. There's nothing much to see – a big oak on a patch of stony ground, surrounded by a low wall.

Round about are the tripods and cauldrons that the priests use for their prophecies. Approach with reverence. This is sacred ground, which belongs to Zeus and his consort Dione – we call his divine wife by this name, though others call her Hera. Look for the holy priestess of the oracle and her fellow priests. They're easy to find, with their feet unwashed as they have always been, and still sleeping on the bare ground under the oak. If you need them, don't give them coins. They have no use for money. Bring them cattle, oil or wine instead. Ask your question. Zeus will speak through the mouth of the oracle.'

It was a lonely and impressive place. A giant sky peered over the rim of the surrounding hills. Boisterous weather scoured the valley, shaking the limbs of the sacred oak. Wind moaned in the bronze cauldrons of the priests, imitating in chords and whispers the voice of the god. But what did it mean?

'Zeus was, Zeus is, Zeus will be,' the oldest priestess chanted. 'O Great Zeus.'

She shook the grimy locks of her hair. Her eyes speared the questioner through and through.

'Our ancestors,' she told Mantes, 'the people called Pelasgians, prayed at this spot to nameless gods. Then a black dove flew from Thebes in Egypt and settled in this oak. The dove spoke in a human voice and taught us the name of Zeus, the god who dwelt in the roots of this tree. The dove became his oracle. We who are the priestesses are the descendants of that holy dove, and ever since we have served as the mouth of Zeus. In an ecstasy, we voice the divine judgment. But we do not know what the words mean. We wake from a trance and cannot remember what has been said.'

At Dodona, earth-born Zeus, the god of the beginning of the world, was slowly leading his people out of their uncertainty. He was the guide to mankind, the instructor of ways and means, the comfort of the perplexed. When to sow and when to reap? Who to marry? When to make war, and when to sue for peace? Mantes saw that he would not find resplendent Zeus, the Lord of the Bright Sky, among the simple folk of Thesprotia. Their Zeus was still a god of earth, a god among the roots. Mantes knew that he must move on to places where mankind had reached a better prosperity and a fuller understanding. Immortals do not give up their secrets easily. Why reveal mysteries to empty minds?

It was time to abandon the poor and stormy northwest. Mantes went south to Arcadia, where a poet could feed well and be entertained and sleep softly without fear of catastrophe or violence. From a ring of high, protective hills the land fell away westwards towards the plains and the sea. Many streams coursed down the crumbling lime-stone slopes, plunging through dark-wooded valleys but growing broad and lazy on the plain, watering grain-fields and meadows and vineyards. The harsh summer of the Peloponnese was tempered by moist air off the western sea. The country was not tame or easily worked. It needed the care of a vigorous people, but when good soil and good water were put to use, the land became green and produc-tive. Farmers had prospered here for as long as history could recall. Wealth and good harvests had often attracted invaders but the appeal of the country had taken the sting out of military ambition. Soldiers found better things to do. They stayed, built houses, left their weapons to rust in a forgotten chest and stealthily became farmers again. At Olympia, in the flood plain between the reed-fringed rivers Alpheius and Cladeius, they gathered under arbutus and tall cypresses, to trade and talk. They took stock of the world and were at peace. And in return for their good luck they did not forget to honour the gods, in the sanctuary called the Altis at the foot of Kronion Hill.

Long ago the gods had found out this pleasant spot. What appeals to mankind, pleases the gods also. Before even Zeus was born, his parents, Cronus and Rhea, had come to Kronion. The people of Olympia say that when Rhea's time arrived she went in the night to the place where no shadows form, in the mountains of Arcadia, and secretly gave birth to Zeus. She washed the babe in the river and then delivered him to Mother Earth who carried him away to Crete, where he would be safe from the jealousy of Cronus.

Later, Zeus remembered the place so favoured by his parents. When the Titans were defeated, and the long, bitter campaign was over, he recalled the sheltered and abundant land cooled by the western breeze. To the north, a savage wind buffeted the mountains, and parched air dried up the land to the south. But on Kronion the fragrance of asphodel and pine scented the mild evening. Olympia seemed a blessed, if temporary, relief after ten years of warfare on like-named Mount Olympus, the austere citadel of the gods. Zeus journeyed south. Even an immortal may relax.

Feasts, entertainments, conversation, friendship, the company of congenial spirits – that was the rule instituted by Zeus in the lucky country that stretched away from the foot of Kronion Hill. With the Titans overthrown and imprisoned in dark earth, the barbarism of brutality and raw power was at an end. Triumphant Zeus had brought in the age of civilization. In Olympia, at the foot of the hill, mankind followed the lead given by the gods on the heights. Strangers came and settled, safe under the protection of Zeus, God of Guests. To Zeus, God of the Household, each family made an offering. A town grew while Zeus, Lord of the City, looked on. In the streets packhorses clattered, hens flew under the feet, pots banged, merchants and housewives and slaves haggled over the price of lentils or barley. Zeus of the Market Place was fostering trade and commerce. Home, the house well swept, a table laden with fruits of the fecund earth, wine-cups full of the new vintage – these were the gifts of peace and civilization offered by kindly Zeus. But occasionally, when the thunder rolled, echoing between the slopes of the valley, and the downpour threw torrents into the shallow river-beds, Zeus reminded all his subjects that his defeat of Cronus had left him the God of the Sky. He was rightly called the

Thunderer, the stern ruler of both nature and human lives.

Peace called for celebration. The first Heracles, one of the large-muscled Dactyls who had sprung from the finger-prints of Rhea, was summoned from Crete to found a games in honour of Father Zeus. Below the hill, the gods of Olympus sported, glorying in their vitality and good spirits, and in their victory over the Titans. Zeus himself presided. Was it not on Kronion that he had wrestled with Cronus hand to hand, and defeated him? Now the other gods ran and wrestled and boxed. Apollo, God of Light and Grace, won the footrace from the swift but devious Hermes. He then met Ares, the God of Battles, in the box-ing ring and sent the rough bully home with his ears ring-ing. That was the final victory of mind and art over the dark forces of violence.

Respectfully, the people of Olympia continued what Zeus and his divine court had begun. The games were reborn among mankind. The ghostly laughter of divine sport was mirrored in the human cries of the crowd, the victor's shout, the applause as the winner's brow was crowned with a wreath of olive branches. To the name of Dactylic Heracles, founder of the Olympic Games, the people of the land added their own later Heracles, the world-renowned hero, son of Zeus and Alcmene, and grandson of Pelops, father of the whole Peloponnese, of which Arcadia was a part.

In the precinct of the Altis, smoke from burnt offerings rose intermingling to Pelops and Zeus. Nearby, grew the wild olives that Heracles had brought from the headwaters of the Danube, in the savage land of the Hyperboreans. From the young branches of these sacred olives, a youth with a golden sickle cut the wood for the victors' wreaths. Every fourth year the heralds, similarly wreathed, set out from the Altis to the farthest corners of Zeus' dominions. To receive and to accept the invitation to celebrate the games in honour of the Father of the Gods was a privilege for Greeks only. They alone were the people of Zeus.

On the level land between the Alpheius and the

Cladeius, Mantes and the priest of the Altis strolled together. Dusk had brought coolness to the dying day. The wide, shallow streams, much reduced by summer heat, broke over many exposed stones, glittering in the sun's last rays. The sport was over. The winner of the footrace had run the 200-metre length of the *stadion*. He had lit the sacrificial fire to Zeus and now stood apart, naked and muscular, in power and bodily proportion rivalling one of the images of the gods. The crowd dispersed. The purple-clad judges went homeward, down the darkening green lanes of the valley. It was time to give thanks to the Deathless Ones.

In the lee of Kronion Hill, the sanctuary was beginning to sparkle with altar fires. There were no buildings, no temples, no shrines – just low altars of stone or clay dotted among the trees of the Altis. Mankind spoke to the gods simply, without grandeur, heart to heart. Votive gifts hung in the branches of the trees. In the holiest place of the sanctuary was the fire-altar of Father Zeus, only a mound of wood-ash, without structure and unadorned. Within reach were the altars of the Twelve Immortals of Olympus, the companions of the divine struggle who had helped Zeus overthrow Cronus and the Titans. Around and about, some sixty other altars showed that the gratitude of mankind was extended to everything that was holy, to the Nymphs, the Graces, the Muses, and the implacable Fates.

Mantes watched as priests went serenely from altar to altar, touching a torch to the kindling and making fireflies of flame dance in the dusk. He knew that the court of the gods was not here, in Olympia of the barley-fields and vineyards, but far to the north among the jagged peaks of Mount Olympus where cloud and long snowfalls kept the majesty of the gods hidden from human view. The divine presence at Olympia was a happy diversion, a gift to mankind from Zeus, Lord of the Sky. Through this gift the door of knowledge was opened a little, allowing mankind to mirror, through the arts of civilization, the perfect community of the gods.

At peace with himself, refreshed by the breeze and beginning to be lulled by the first stirring of the night insects, Mantes heard with half an ear the invocations of the priest.

'Happy Zeus, ruler of rulers, most blessed of the blessed, most perfect of the perfect,' the priest was crooning softly. 'Zeus is air, Zeus is earth, Zeus is sky.'

Yes, Mantes thought drowsily, after all my travels and toils now at last I understand.

And he gave thanks.

Apollo

– 4 –

THE SUMMIT

THE BOY looked up towards the heavens. To the east, beyond the sea, a vast expanse of sky floated over unknown lands. To the west, at a short distance from the shore, the land started to buckle and rise steeply. The gigantic mass of the mountain was so large that the travellers at the foot could see no beginning and no end. It was a wall that blocked out the imagination. Nor could the eye make out the topmost heights. Dense cloud sat on the heavy shoulders of the mountain, but somewhere beyond that blindfold rose forty-two peaks. The boy became dizzy with looking. He knew this was Mount Olympus, the home of the gods. But was there one peak for Zeus, and forty-one lesser peaks for other gods?

The merchant from Delos was not sure. 'Father Zeus, of course, is there,' he said respectfully, 'and his brother Poseidon. But how many others? They say the Olympian gods and goddesses are twelve in number. But who else? The sky is filled with strange deities. Cat-faced and dog-headed fellows from Egypt. Ruffian-gods from Phrygia, Mysia and Caria, who look to us as if they're up to no good. Odd divinities in Media and beyond, in caftans and fezzes, with hardly enough Greek between them to say "Here's to your health". Are they up there, jostling for our affections? And what of the half-forgotten ones, some still honoured here and there? Are those crags echoing with their lonely sighs?'

The party of travellers was going north, on the narrow road cramped between the mountains and the Thracian sea. The Fates, in whose hands their lives rested, drew them that way, but they went with misgiving. Everyone knew the reputation of the northern lands. Thessaly was dangerous. Chalcidice and Thrace were worse. And somewhere beyond were the Hyperboreans, in the realms of the hardly human.

They had left Mount Ossa behind, like the last lighthouse of civilization. In the vale of Tempe many had paused, to gather courage. And here Mantes had also stopped, hesitating for a moment in the cycle of his wanderings. He saw around him those waiting to go on – merchants, herdsmen, soldiers, wanderers, couriers and servants, a few family groups – and he attached himself to one of these loose bands, seeking safety in numbers. In the dawn, as Eos drew the curtain of the day, they took to the road. Just ahead, Olympus reared up in the path, a place of holiness and dread.

'A salute to Poseidon, at least,' said an old sailor, squinting a practised weather eye at the high, grey turmoil of the clouds. 'When Cronus was defeated, and his three sons drew lots for a share of the world, Zeus took the sky, Hades the Underworld, and Poseidon got the sea. The surface of the earth was common ground, where each had rights, though Zeus, the Thunderer, is mightiest of the three.'

The old sailor was making his way back to his northern island home on Thasos. Damp sea air had crept into his bones. Hobbling with arthritis, he was glad to cadge a ride or a lift in a cart whenever he could. He had had enough of the sea.

'Everyone who's seen the sea in a temper knows the nature of Poseidon. The Earth-Shaker, he's called, for good reason. His mother, Rhea, threw the infant Poseidon into the sea, so that Cronus would not swallow him. And there Poseidon stayed. He had found his element. Capheira, the daughter of Oceanus, was his nurse. The nine Telchines, magicians and cunning craftsmen of the Underworld, were his first companions on the island of Rhodes. Some say that they made him his trident, but in fact the Cyclopes made it, during the War of the Gods.

'We fear the sea. What lies below the shifting waters? A kingdom of mystery and uncertain power. The divine lottery on Olympus gave all this to Poseidon, and the old watery deities – Pontus, Oceanus, Nereus – made way for him. The little gods of rivers and streams were careful to obey him too, lest he shrivel them with heat and drought, or blast them from their beds with storm and flood. Look at his face, huge and surly in a waving forest of sea-green hair, and recognize his power. As the oceans surround the land, so Poseidon is the Girdler of the Earth, and all mankind trembles before him. He is as swift and sudden as the storm, three strides taking him from Samothrace to his golden palace below the waters at Aegae. His horses have bronze hooves and golden manes, shimmering in movement like the evening sun on an in-running tide. Monsters, grotesque beasts, slimy things frisk in the wake of the god. The furious speed of his chariot parts the sea and its axle remains dry.'

'We know all about the Earth-Shaker,' a voice interrupted, 'but tell me this: why is the sea-god's chariot drawn by horses, not by dolphins, or perhaps sea-monsters?'

The new speaker was a horse-breeder from the grasslands of Macedonia. Some months before, he had gone south with a string of ponies to sell in the markets of Attica and Corinth. Trade had been good but towns made him uneasy and he was hurrying back to the unconfined pastures of the River Axius. His large moustache, exuberant and fiercely brushed, spoke of well-being. He wore a thick sheepskin tunic, and the hardy little bay he rode sported a vivid new horse cloth. The horse, used to the free-striding plains, was nervous in the human crowd but riding, to the Macedonian, was as natural as breathing. With a few flicks of his plaited whip he steadied the horse with almost absent-minded skill.

'To us,' he continued, 'Poseidon is Hippios, the Lord of the Horse. Our people say that even before he inherited the oceans he came south with the gift of horses from the limitless plains, where the wild flowers bloom and the grasses ripple like water. We say that when Cronus came to devour Poseidon, Rhea deceived her husband and gave him a young foal instead. Poseidon invented the bridle, not Pallas Athene, as those boastful Athenians claim. Poseidon, the Unharvested, is the god of our plains, and our horses – wild, powerful, noble – share the character of the god. Poseidon is the father of horses. When he felt the sting of lust he coupled with the Gorgon Medusa and she gave birth to Pegasus, the famous winged horse. When Demeter was bothered by the fumbling and the hot breath of the god, as she was searching for her lost daughter, Persephone, she turned herself into a mare. But what was more natural than that he should become a stallion? He mounted her and she brought forth Arion, the horse as swift as the wind.'

'Your horse-god,' the old sailor replied, 'why, that's just Poseidon finding himself space and room. He's the sea-god, but all lands are his to play with, jointly with Zeus and Hades. A god obeys his nature. The violence that Poseidon does at sea, or with horses, was repeated in his violence against countries and cities. Even his fellow gods had to look to their honour. He tried to snatch Naxos from Dionysus, Corinth from Helius, and even Aegina from Zeus. Twice he tangled with Athene. Once he laid claim to her city of Troezen. Then he wanted Athens itself. Frustrated by the judgment of Olympus, he ordered his waters to flood the Attic plain. Then he grabbed Argolis and prepared to defend it against stiff and unforgiving Hera, Queen of the Gods. Zeus tried to steer a course between his wife and his brother. Both were divine trouble-makers. He sent the matter to the arbitration of Inachus, Asterion and Cephissus, three river-gods of the region. They chose Hera, and Poseidon, in a rage, turned against the river-gods – his subordinates! – and shrank their streams so that even to this day their rivers run dry in summer.

'It was, and is, hazardous to cross the Earth-Shaker, in whatever form he might appear. The people of Attica, though protected by the unconquerable arm of holy Athene, still remember his raging flood. Faithfully, they guard his temple at Sounion, on the last headland of their ancestral shores. Below, at the foot of the cliff, as I myself have seen many times, beating up the channels of the Saronic gulf, the waters of the sea-god perpetually heave and growl, lest the people forget.'

By now, a morning breeze was beginning to disperse some of the cloud on Olympus. Rifts of light appeared, revealing long flanks of mountain dusted below with the green of beech and walnut but darkened on the upper slopes by the gloomy bristle of the firs. Then ridges ascended, gaunt with bare rock, and tumbled into the high cols, before soaring onward to the many peaks.

The day was warm and the travellers were making easy progress. The sun was brushing the eastern face of the mountain which seemed, in the friendly light, more a rampart and a comfort against the danger of the wilderness than a place of holy mystery. The boy, sitting on the neck of the ox that pulled the family cart, was still puzzled by the shifting shapes of Olympus. He peered up, seeing peak after peak suddenly unshrouded. How could it be that Hades had a place in such a world of light and space?

'Be quiet, foolish boy,' his nurse chided him. 'It is not wise to mention the name of Hades, the Invisible One, nor to speak about the Kingdom of the Dead. But since you are so ignorant of these matters, you must learn. That grim god has no place on Olympus. The lottery of the gods gave him the Underworld to rule, and he has enough to do in that sad place, overseeing the punishments decreed by the justice of Zeus. We avoid Hades, but we fear him and try to please him with many honourable names. We call him the Hospitable One, or the Good Counsellor. Of course, he is also Pluto, the Wealthy One, for he owns all the gold and silver and jewels that lie beneath the ground.

'Fortunately, being so busy, with so many damned souls to keep his eye on, Hades has little time to visit our lands, to scare us with his chariot of fiery gold and its four black horses. He listens below in darkness, piecing together the news of the world from the oaths and promises that people swear in his name, striking the ground as they do so. Sometimes, lust or curiosity will draw him out from the foul stink of Tartarus. He chased the nymph Minthe and would have raped her had not Persephone, his queen, intervened and changed the timid girl into the sweet-smelling mint. Another nymph, Leuce, was also saved in the nick of time and transformed into a white poplar. When he roams the earth he is dangerous, specially when he sneaks among us wearing the cap of invisibility made for him by the Cyclopes.'

'May kindly Zeus, fount of justice, keep us safe from his dark brother!' exclaimed the boy's mother, looking fearfully around as if the black horses of Hades might erupt from the ground beneath the very feet of her ox.

'And yet,' she continued, 'there is one particular god on Olympus whom we fear almost as much as Hades. I'm talking about Ares, the God of War, that savage god who came to disturb our peace from the barbarian wastes of the north.'

'Now hold on,' the Macedonian horse-breeder cried hotly. 'You people of the south are always trying to blame your troubles on others. Don't tell me that you had no wars before the horsemen – Achaeans and Dorians and others – came galloping out of the lands beyond the North Wind! Whose son is Ares? The son of Zeus and Hera, that's who he is. His birthplace is right here on Olympus, right in the middle of all the Greek lands. This is where he belongs. If he's treacherous and cruel, it's no fault of us northerners. Look in your own souls and you'll find dirty stuff there, too.'

'I'll admit we're not perfect,' the woman rejoined tartly.

'But we need no lessons from your kind. I know the northerners, particularly the Thracians, well enough. They're
filthy, idle, bestial, covered with tattoos. They look like a
freak show. They are ashamed to be seen working. Tilling
the ground is a disgrace to them. All they do is fight and
plunder, and then squabble over the spoils, like mangy
dogs scavenging offal. And their habits! Disgusting. They
keep a string of wives, like horses in heat. They let their
daughters sleep with anyone, and then sell them to slave-
traders.'

'And who buys those girls?' the horse-breeder shouted,
rushing to the defence of all the north. 'You southerners.
You hypocrites.'

'Widow-murderers! Dog-eaters!'

'Effeminate boy-lovers! Pederasts!'

'Ignorant brutes. The gods the Thracians worship are
Bacchus and Artemis – the gods of boozing and hunting.
But their favourite is their own god Ares, the god of
destruction and hate.'

At this, the Macedonian, red with indignation but hating
to lose his temper at a woman, appealed to Mantes.

'You, poet, you're supposed to know these things.
What's the truth about Ares?'

'Many claim that he comes from Thrace,' Mantes replied
soothingly. 'It's true, too, that nobody wants him. Even
Zeus hates his son. It is sometimes said – perhaps Zeus
encouraged this story – that Hera conceived Ares by herself. She ate a magic flower and gave birth, and her son
inherited her ungovernable temper. Zeus and his divine
consort are always quarrelling, and perhaps we should forget these insults. The truth is that the violence of Ares goes
beyond all reason, and that is why both gods and men
avoid him. He has a lust for battle, sniffing after blood like
a pig after truffles. Right and wrong mean nothing to him.
He'll fight at a whim and change sides just as easily.
Where the weapons clang, and the blood flows, and the
most treachery is done – there you'll find Ares, hacking
heads and limbs, with his sons, Phobos and Deimos, by his

side. These are the ones we call Rout and Fear. They are his sons by Aphrodite, children of that infamous piece of adultery when Aphrodite's husband, Hephaestus, caught the heaving and panting lovers in his net.

'The God of War is a huge and powerful figure, and those bulging muscles attracted Aphrodite's ever-lustful eye. Ares knows how to swagger. His roar on the battlefield sounds like ten thousand men, and when he lies down his body measures two hundred paces. But despite his size, and his brutality, he is not always successful. Indomitable Athene, the Goddess of Wisdom, beat him twice on the field of battle. Once, in the Trojan War, she guided the hand of Diomedes, who gave Ares such a wound that he went whining to Zeus. Later, Ares had the temerity to cast his spear at the goddess herself. Contemptuously, she caught the blow on her sacred breastplate, and the spear fell harmlessly. Then she felled him with a boulder. Aphrodite had to take him in her soft arms and help him slink away from the fighting. That was shame enough – to be rescued by the perfumed and wanton Goddess of Love. But even a hero could defeat Ares, and once Heracles gave him a good drubbing. And the two playful giants Otus and Ephialtes, while still in their childhood – though growing at the rate of a yard a year – caught Ares and imprisoned him in a bronze jar. There he stayed for thirteen months, growing weaker and weaker, until Hermes, the Messenger God, heard of his plight and released him.'

Talk of Ares made the travellers thoughtful. The God of War, with his violence and his blood-lust, reminded them of the way ahead, in lands where Greek gave way gradually to barbarian babble. The group drew in a little, forgetting differences in the need for mutual support. Even the Macedonian was quiet, though his face was still brick red and his moustaches quivered like battle pennants in the wind.

'That Ares,' an elderly Athenian burst out, glaring angrily at the heights of Olympus, 'he's a braggart and a bully. He sends many poor folk to the dark halls of Hades.

Yet we speak of him with awe, even with grudging admiration. He's up there now, lolling in the courts of holy Olympus, dining on our respect, with a full share of our prayers and burnt offerings. I'm a man of peace, a craftsman, a maker of useful and beautiful things. I pray to Hephaestus, the Divine Smith, who has taught us the secrets of our art. Yet look how they treat *him* in heaven. He is the butt of divine jokes. Ares yawns at the feast of the gods, while Hephaestus limps around with the wine-cups. They laugh at him because he's lame and clumsy on his feet.'

'Ares is power,' Mantes murmured, 'and we are intimidated by that. The raw facts of life and death are what impress us most.'

But was that the whole story? Was there not a suspicion here also that Greek is good, foreign is bad? There were doubts about both Ares and Hephaestus. Ares, perhaps, was reluctantly allowed to be Greek, for he had, at least, the proportions and the presence, the godlike aspect, which all Greeks admired. But Hephaestus, busy at his forge, was lame and ugly and not at all glorious.

So the birth of Hephaestus was also subject to rumour, to innuendo. He was born prematurely, with his feet turned backwards, during the three hundred years when his parents, Zeus and Hera, kept their marriage secret. His mother, Hera, threw the babe out of heaven, because he looked so peculiar, and Zeus did not lift a finger to save him. They were ashamed of their child. Hephaestus fell in the sea where the gentle sea-nymphs Thetis and Eurynome found him. They took him and looked after him for nine years in an underwater grotto, where he set up his first workshop and began to make many beautiful things. Then Hera, impressed by a jewelled ornament that Hephaestus had made for Thetis, summoned her forgotten son back to Olympus. Again, he felt the wrath of his parents, for he stepped into one of their familiar quarrels, and Zeus hurled him once more from Olympus. He fell a full day and landed with broken legs on the island of Lemnos.

And Lemnos, some say, is his real home, not Olympus. He came to Lemnos from Caria, in Asia Minor, a strange, swarthy god with a hammer in his hand and a bellows under his arm. He is an eastern fire-god, and volcanic Mount Moschylos, on Lemnos, is his workshop. Hephaestus is a wizard, a wonder-worker in metals, a dabbler in laborious rites that the Greeks of old hardly knew. His looks are unworthy of a god. His preoccupation with menial tasks, his busyness, his skill itself, all demean the aloofness of a god.

'As if looks are more important than skill,' the Athenian scoffed. 'We think like fools. There is more to life than noble warfare. What could we do without Hephaestus? We would still be living like animals – or Thracians – if he had not taken us in hand. His invention and his skill put the materials of the world at our command. While his wife Aphrodite is out deceiving him, playing the games of love – their marriage was surely a divine joke, a piece of malice against an outsider – Hephaestus is sweating at the forge, teaching us the dignity and usefulness of work. He has made fire into our servant. When the logs crackle and the sparks jump, we say, "Hephaestus is laughing."

'Even though the other gods on Olympus mock him, look what he has done for them. He made a sickle for Demeter, so the corn may be cut. He fashioned a gold cup for Helius and forged the deadly arrows that Apollo and Artemis use. Heroes and mortals owe him debts as well. For Minos, King of Crete, he made Talos, the bronze giant. He made the gold and silver dogs that guarded the palace of Alcinous, and the bulls with brazen feet that Jason set to the plough. Perseus and Agamemnon thanked the god, the first for his sword and the second for his sceptre. Achilles and Diomedes marched against Troy in the armour made by Hephaestus. All who prefer to live in the ease of a good house rather than in the squalor of byres and stables salute the Divine Smith. Hunched and grimy, with powerful shoulders and lame feet, he drags himself to the forge, always at work, and both heaven and earth are the better for his efforts.'

The merchant from Delos chuckled. 'You Athenians will worship any god, no matter where he comes from, so long as he helps you make things to sell. I'm a trader myself, and I, too, have sent many prayers to that clever Hephaestus for the latest goods and the best merchandise. But we don't need to rely on foreign gods, useful though they are. The greatest and the most truly Greek of the Olympians is radiant Apollo, the god from my own island of Delos. His mother, perhaps, came from Lycia, the wolf-country, but Apollo certainly represents all that we most admire in the character of our people – curiosity, intelligence, grace, and a generous heart.

'You remember the story? Zeus set his heart on the Titaness Leto, and, of course, Hera was jealous once more. Zeus pursued and Leto fled, from the River Xanthos across untold lands to the wastes of the Hyperboreans, where the sun hardly shines. In Lycia, she became a she-wolf, and at Didyma a quail. Zeus caught her there and, turning into a quail also, coupled with her, and she conceived twins. But still she had no rest, for Hera had decreed that no land where the sun shines would receive her. After many wanderings Leto begged the small and rocky island of Delos to let her rest and give birth. At this time, Delos was a mere scrap of land floating in the sea. It was one of the many islands that Poseidon, in a bad temper, had gouged with his trident out of the mainland and scattered into the Cyclades. Now little Delos was afraid. How could one offend Hera? The dragon Python, which she had sent from Pytho to harry Leto, was terrifying enough. How could this barren speck of rock support the dignity of a god? Surely, a divine child would stamp it in contempt to the bottom of the sea, to become a home for black seals, not men. But Leto swore by Styx – the holiest oath an Immortal can make – that her child would honour Delos and build his first temple there. Then Poseidon covered the island with waves, which the sun could not penetrate. Iris, a

messenger of the gods, summoned the divine midwife
Eileithyia. All the other goddesses, except Hera, were in
attendance. No one was in doubt as to the greatness of this
event. For nine days Leto was in labour. Then, clinging to
a palm tree, she gave birth to twins. Holy Artemis leapt
first from the womb and helped her mother deliver her
twin, Apollo.

'No mother's milk was good enough for the new god.
Instead, the goddess Themis fed him nectar and ambrosia
brought from the court of Olympus. At once, Apollo burst
from his swaddling clothes and rose up fully grown. And
our Delos, the fortunate island, was fixed in its place
and touched with gold. The leaves of the olives turned to
gold, and gold swam in the River Inopus. Apollo blessed
the island. He strode to the top of Mount Cynthus and held
out his arms, saying: "The lyre and the bow shall be dear
to me, and I will declare unto mankind the unfailing will
of Zeus."'

This tale pleased the travellers, for everyone knew that
Apollo is the most glorious of the divine sons of Zeus. It
eased the burden of the road to reflect on the grace of
Apollo. He is the beacon of Olympus. As the sun splits
the cloud to reveal the summit, so the radiance of Apollo
illumines the Olympian court of the gods. When he enters
there, all other deities stand. He hands his bow and his
quiver to Leto and takes his place by his father's side. From
there, he spreads his divine influence over the affairs of
mankind. He is the God of the Lyre and the Patron of
Music. To him, doctors owe their medicine. He watches
over navigation, steadies the course by sun and stars, and
guards our people in distant colonies. But most of all, he is
the God of Prophecy.

Within four days of his birth, Apollo set out on his divine
mission. In pursuit of the dragon who had made his
mother's life a misery, he went first to Pytho, to the place
now called Delphi. The Python, earth-coloured with
shining scales, stood at bay, throwing huge coils around a
laurel tree. But Apollo pierced the dragon with a volley of

arrows. And when the wounded beast fled into a cave sacred to Ge, Apollo followed and killed it in the innermost sanctuary. Though the dragon was dead, Apollo had invaded a holy place, and Mother Earth called out to Zeus in protest at this sacrilege. Sentenced to exile and servitude, Apollo walked the road that became known as the Pythian Way, to the vale of Tempe. There, for nine years, he was the slave of King Admetus. Then, purified of guilt and wearing a wreath of laurel, he returned to Delphi with the added title of Phoebus, the Undefiled. One thing more needed to be done. To appease Hera for the death of her dragon, he instituted the Pythian Games. Then Mother Earth relinquished her place and her prophecies to the purified Apollo.

'Such a place deserves such a god,' said a solemn man from Phocis. He was a messenger of the temple at Delphi, and though he travelled all the wild and beautiful lands where Greeks were settled, he could never erase from his mind the sombre chasm of Delphi, caught between the rust-red cliffs of the Phaedriades. From Mount Parnassus, capped with snow, the land fell away in rough slides and rock falls to this point where the Earth-Shaker clove it with a god's axe. The Castalian spring bubbled at the foot of the chasm, and close by that was the fissure in the rock leaking the thin vapours which carried the prophetic voice of Apollo.

'Delphi is the *omphalos*,' said the messenger proudly, 'the navel of the world. At the beginning of time Zeus sent two eagles, one from each end of the cosmos, to determine the centre of things. They met at Delphi. It was natural that Mother Earth should communicate to mankind from this spot. It was natural also that Apollo, when he took on that mantle of prophecy, should make his temple there. But who would build it and keep it? The god is wise, he is also resourceful. Some say the bees made him a shrine out of their wax. But we know that his temple was something grander than that. When this work had to be done, Apollo looked out to sea and saw a Cretan ship heading for Pylus.

He dived into the waves in the form of a giant dolphin and boarded the ship. Huge and cheerful, he commandeered the deck and showed the captain the way to go. Landing at Crisa, the port of Delphi, Apollo transformed himself into a long-haired youth with a lyre, and leading the sailors on with caressing music he took them up the hillside to Delphi and set them to work. When the temple was ready he honoured the Cretans by making them his priests and initiating them into the service of the prophetic Pythia, the priestess who spoke in the voice of the god.

'Then he revealed to them his first prophecy: "From now on, all of mankind will bring you gifts to learn from my wisdom. But if you do not deal justly, or if you become evil or too proud, others will come and force you from your place."'

'A humorous god,' the travellers exclaimed, 'and a just one, too.'

'Glorious Apollo shows in his character everything that is attractive in humans also. But do not be fooled. The gods are jealous of their virtue and will not be mocked. Apollo gave King Midas the ears of an ass, for daring to prefer the music of Pan, the goat-legged God of Shepherds. Midas tried to hide his deformity under a Phrygian cap but could not keep it from his barber, who was sworn to secrecy. Put this talkative fellow could not contain himself, so he whispered the news to a hole in the ground. Some reeds growing nearby heard the secret, and when a breeze shook them they sighed for everyone to hear, "King Midas has the ears of an ass."

'Even worse was the punishment given to Marsyas. This foolish satyr had come across a flute discarded by Athene, though it was still full of godlike music. When Marsyas blew into the flute the listeners exclaimed that Apollo himself could not make better music. Apollo was angry and, to put the satyr in his place, arranged a contest, with the nine Muses as judges. The condition of the contest was this: that the winner should do as he wished with the loser. At first, the Muses could not decide. Athene's flute sounded as beautiful as Apollo's lyre. Then Apollo challenged Marsyas to sing and play at the same time, which no flute-player can do. Apollo played and sang hymns to the glory of the gods on Olympus, and when the Muses gave him the prize he took his revenge on the satyr. Able to do whatever he wished, he had Marsyas flayed alive. Then he nailed the skin to a plane tree by the riverside, as a warning to others who presumed to challenge a god.

'For the rage of a god is a terrible thing, and not even Heracles was safe from the righteous anger of Apollo. When the greatest of heroes defiled holy Delphi with bloodstained hands and stole the tripod that the Pythia used for prophecy, Apollo would have transfixed him with one of his unerring arrows had not Zeus hastily intervened and reconciled his two sons, the one half-human and the other divine.'

'Such cruel punishments, such anger,' a timid voice cut in. 'How do you explain it?'

The temple messenger frowned. He could not admit any criticism of Apollo.

'Far-Shooting Apollo,' he said severely, 'punishes a few so that the many may learn. When we were rough and young, in the days when Ge guarded the sanctity of Delphi, too many of our people were savage, turbulent, without peace or justice. But Apollo taught peace and justice, though it took many a sharp lesson. Now, thanks to the god, things are different, as I know well. It is my task, as a herald from Delphi, to go out every four years to the furthest extent of the Greek lands, to proclaim the sacred armistice that belongs to the Pythian Games. Everywhere I go, I am received with feasts and joy. "Blessed Apollo," the people sing, "he is the one who heals us; he banishes evil government; every house becomes pure by his power." And as for his tolerance, do you not know that gracious Apollo, out of a kind heart, permits his holy place to be shared by Dionysus, the wild one, the orgiastic god? For three winter months every year Apollo leaves Delphi, to live among the Hyperboreans of the north. In those months, no hymns, no paeans are heard. The voice of the Pythia, pronouncing the oracular wisdom of the god, is silent.

'But in the springtime, a chariot drawn by swans brings Apollo back to Delphi. And then, what gladness, what celebrations! The Pythia, the divine priestess, enters once more the *antron*, the sanctum where only she may go. She purifies herself, washing in the Castalian spring. She seats herself on the tripod, poised over the crack in the rock. She inhales the divine vapour. In her trance, she is inspired. She gives voice. Mankind listens, and is all the wiser.

'Outside, in the porch of Apollo's temple, two sentences are carved: "Nothing in excess" and "Know thyself". That is the Greek way, the way to the wisdom of the gods of Olympus. It was not always so, in the days before Apollo. Then blood was paid in blood, and murder was a holy deed. Apollo showed us the better way, that one could atone by catharsis, by penance and purification. "Ah, you new gods of Olympus," cried the Erinyes, those ancient and implacable Furies who made retribution their business, "you have kicked over the old laws, and we can grasp them no more."'

The party of travellers had eaten a midday meal, pausing briefly by the roadside. Afterwards, in the heat and torpor of early afternoon, talk was fitful, the words dying away like a theme forgotten. Feet trudged on mechanically, and the animals swayed forward slowly, with drooping heads. The boy lay full-length in the family cart, staring into the sky through half-closed eyes. High in the heavens, the sun shone directly on the mountain, making the permanent snows of the peaks as bright as mirrors. Idly, the boy began to count.

'One, two, three, four, five,' he said in a dozy voice. 'There are the thrones of five of the Holy Ones. But should there not be one more Olympian god? Where is he?'

'That one is Hermes,' said Mantes, smiling as he walked by the wheel of the cart. 'Phoebus Apollo we all admire and respect. But Hermes is, if anything, even more Greek than Apollo. Listen, and I'll tell you about him.

'Hermes, youngest of the gods of Olympus, is the son of Zeus and Maia, the daughter of Atlas. Zeus came often to Maia, and lay with her secretly, in a cave on Mount Cyllene, while Hera slept. Then the secret was out. On the fourth day of the month Hermes jumped into the world, and soon he had made himself known to all the land of Arcadia. He was born in the early morning; by noon he could play the lyre; in the evening he stole the cattle of Apollo. Nothing could satisfy his curiosity. In a moment, he was out of the cave and roaming around. Soon he found a tortoise plodding through the grass, and he had the spark of an idea. Hermes was never short of ideas, and no mischief was beyond him. He took the poor tortoise and killed it and turned its shell into a musical instrument, stringing it like a lyre. By noon he had already coaxed a tune from it. He thought, "The world is a lively place and worth investigating." So Hermes walked on, to the meadows of Peiria, where fifty cows belonging to Apollo were grazing. Here he had another idea. How amusing to steal the cattle! To disguise the tracks, Hermes drove the cows backwards, following with his own feet bound in twigs, to leave an indistinct trail. In the evening, by the River Alpheius, he slaughtered two cows with the proper ritual, made fire by rubbing two laurel sticks together, cooked meat and filled his belly. He hid the remaining animals in an olive grove and in the night slipped back to the cave, tucking himself into his cradle as if nothing had happened.

'Now, Apollo was both angry and puzzled by the theft. How was it done? An old farmer, who had witnessed the trick, gave him the clue, and soon Apollo was confronting the infant Hermes with a godlike rage. But Hermes, looking all innocence, snuggled into the bedclothes and pulled the covers up to his chin. "I, a mere baby, steal cattle?" he replied impudently. "Why, I'm too young to even know what a cow is."'

'O shame,' the boy's nurse burst out, 'that you should fill the boy's ears with such stuff. Thievery and lies.'

But the boy protested. 'Good nurse, let him go on. I never knew there was such fun among the gods.'

'It's true,' Mantes replied, 'that Hermes is a trickster and a thief. But the divine power of the gods permits them to do everything that we can do, and are there not rogues amongst us? Besides, Apollo was not deceived. Taking a firm grip on the young god, he hauled him off for judgment at the court of Olympus. But Zeus was more amused than outraged. He liked the spirit of enterprise, the refusal to conform, the wild imagination. He told the half-brothers to make their peace, and that is what happened. Hermes gave Apollo his tortoiseshell lyre, in payment for the slaughtered cows, returned the rest of the cattle, and all was well between the two gods. Apollo even began to share a few mysteries with the youngster. He taught Hermes how to prophesy, using stones in water. And Hermes, ever quick to improve on any lesson, devised another method for himself, using knuckle-bones. Apollo, God of Enlightenment, was impressed by such intelligence and zest. He asked Zeus to allow Hermes into heaven. And Zeus, who had need of a brisk, imaginative god to act as intermediary between heaven and earth, graciously gave way. He welcomed Hermes to Olympus and invested him with the marks of his office: the broad hat of the wayfarer, and the *caduceus* of the divine messenger – the herald's staff wound round with two snakes. The silver tongue, the quick eye, and the thieving fingers, Hermes did not have to be given. Those he had already.

'A master of cunning, a robber, a cattle-rustler, a spinner of dreams, a watcher by night, a thief at the gates, a deviser of wonders – that is Hermes. But, on the whole, mankind had won a friend. Was there anything on earth Hermes could not do? He invented, or helped to invent, the musical scales, astronomy, the alphabet, the cultivation of olives, the balance for weighing, the measuring-rod. As the messenger of the gods he is the keeper of the road, and the guardian of all travellers. He sets up the 'herms', the piles of stones that guide men on their way. People should not be lonely or lost; no, they should join together in assemblies and feasts and fairs, looking for entertainment and happiness. At the games, Hermes smiles on the athletes, though he may also, out of devilry, pick the pocket of the crowd. In the gymnasium, he is the patron of the wrestling and the boxing.'

'I like that friendly god,' the boy laughed. 'When I'm a man I'll not forget him in my offerings.'

'But be warned. Enthusiasm is sometimes dangerous. Hermes lacks judgment, and that is why he has the lowest place in the divine court of Olympus. Once, when amorous Zeus sent him to release the water-nymph Io, who was under the watchful guard of hundred-eyed Argus, Hermes lulled Argus to sleep but then cut out his eyes. Such cruelty disgusted the gods. They drove Hermes from their presence with a hail of stones. When a god is rash, who shall put right his errors? Beware lest, in anger or mistake, he sends you to the Underworld, where the dead souls wail. He will lead you by the hand to the banks of the Styx; for that, too, is one of his many duties.'

The boy looked thoughtful, but he was not frightened. He lay at his ease in the cart, rocking with the comfortable slow jog of the ox. The day was beginning to draw in. The ghostly eye of Selene, the moon, was just discernible in the heavens. Soon the travellers would stop for the night. In the firelight under the stars they would eat, then the day would be closed by a long sleep. The wall of Olympus, to the west, was a protection against the night things.

Warm shadows were creeping over the uplands and flooding into the gorges and the hollows of the mountain. But the declining sun, well on its way towards the encircling river of Oceanus, still bathed a brilliant light on the summit of Olympus. The gods held court, sustaining from on high all that is. It is right that Greeks do not talk of the sun setting. They say, instead, that it reigns in splendour.

Armed Aphrodite and Attendant

– 5 –

THE HOUR OF THE WOMEN

TOWARDS EVENING, the travellers heard what they were hoping for: the sound of a strong stream rushing over rocks and gravel. At a bend in the path the little river came in view. The track dipped into a tumultuous swirl of water, which then plunged away down the hill, hurrying to lose itself in Poseidon's realm.

The leading matron of the party stopped at the edge of the stream and scooped up a bowl of water. She sipped, wrinkling her brow in concentration, testing for smell and taste. Then she smiled and pronounced herself satisfied. They had found the most important requirement of all travellers – good water. Now they could camp for the night.

After the men had unloaded the animals, they hobbled them and set them to graze. Then they went in search of a hollow, or a grove of trees, where they could set up shelter for the night. They took with them a lamb, which they would kill and roast for the evening meal. The preparation and cooking of meat was male business and no concern of the women. So the women were left to gather together the produce they had brought with them. They unpacked strings of onions, bags of lentils, chickpeas and beans, straw baskets of figs and raisins and cheese. They took from the panniers goatskins of wine and water, cooking pots, earthenware jars, decorated bowls glazed in sombre colours. Household slaves began to collect firewood. A baby suckled noisily at the nurse's breast. Two or three energetic children played catch and run in the bushes. A younger brother, too tired for games, sucked his thumb under the axle of an up-turned cart. The women set about their oft-repeated task, to impose on the wilderness a moment of comfort and relaxation.

When the bustle died down, and the fire was well lit, and the ingredients of the meal were prepared and mixed, the women and children, with maids and servants, all settled around the fire. This was the hour of the women. When they were gathered the old matron, thin and dignified in her long white tunic, stood and approached the fire. She drew the embroidered edge of her shawl over her head to ward off the humours of the evening air. Taking a cup of pure water, she poured a libation. Then she offered a prayer to Hestia, the Goddess of the Hearth, eldest child of Cronus and Rhea. Hestia, gentlest of the gods of Olympus, is the Virgin One, about whom there is neither scandal nor controversy, though both Poseidon and Apollo vied for her hand in vain. She had sworn an oath on the head of her brother Zeus that she would remain forever a maiden. She is the peacemaker, the friend to women, the keeper of the household flame. Suppliants who reach her fire on the hearth are safe from prosecution, for Zeus honours her greatly. He has granted her the first victim of every sacrifice.

'Praise be to Hestia indeed,' sighed a young wife from Ionia, giving the dough for the bread a last smack. 'Finally, she sends us women a blessed moment of quiet and relief. Just listen to our men out there. They set up camp as if they were fighting lions. Everything they do, even the smallest task, is done with such noise and fuss. How pleasant to be rid of them for a while. I sometimes envy my Carian ancestors. They wouldn't eat with their husbands, nor even call them by name, because they were Greek invaders who had killed our menfolk and forced our poor girls into marriage. Why did we ever forgive them, I wonder, and allow them back to our board and our beds?'

She lay back on the grass, pillowed on clasped hands,

and frowned at the bold, bare hills, looking sternly at them as if they were the bald heads of ancient senators.

A plump, jolly girl laughed. 'Who are we to stand aside from the age-old battles of the sexes, which even the gods cannot avoid? Hestia is too modest. She puts herself beyond the strife by a vow of chastity. That's not to everyone's taste. Certainly not to mine. So why should I fare any better than Hera, Queen of Heaven? Did she not have much to suffer at the hands of Zeus?'

So much rested on the shoulders of All-Seeing Zeus, nothing less than the stability and order of the world. He would marry, but what partner could help him best read the deeply interleaved and barely understandable book of the universe? First, it is said, Father Zeus joined with the goddess Metis, whose name means wisdom. But any son from their loins was destined to topple Zeus, as he himself had thrown down his father Cronus. So Zeus swallowed Metis, to possess her wisdom and to prevent the birth of her child.

But Zeus could not sleep alone. It was his duty to populate the heavens with the many divine beings who give guidance to mankind. He called to his bed many goddesses and nymphs and spirits. He mated with Themis, the Titaness, and their children were Eunomia, Dice and Eirene – Good Government, Justice and Peace. By Eurynome, he fathered the three Graces. He lay with Mnemosyne, Goddess of Memory, and she gave birth to the nine Muses, the spirits who inspire in mortals all the arts of the imagination.

'Duty is good,' protested the Ionian wife, 'but where does duty end and lust begin? What cause was there for Zeus to force himself on his sister Demeter, or on timid Leto who fled from him so fast, or on Maia, daughter of the sky-supporting Atlas?'

'So many assaulted and dismayed,' added a slave-girl, stirring a pot on the fire. 'He covered Danae in a shower of gold. So many other poor women undone.'

From the ring around the fire, other voices chimed in.

'Leda, terrified by his feathered glory when Zeus came to her as a swan.'

'Europa, carried away and forced by Zeus-the-bull.'

'Callisto, changed into a bear and killed by Artemis' arrow.'

'Unsuspecting Niobe, first human ever to lie with a god.'

'Semele, turned to ashes by the blazing splendour of the King of Heaven.'

'Poor deceived Alcmene, tricked by that same King when he took on the form of her husband.'

'Are we nothing more than bodies for bed-work and breeding?' lamented a bitter farmer's wife from Boeotia. 'Men hunger for us, but fear us like the plague. They blame us. They say we flaunt those secret parts that make them go weak at the knees. Hesiod, my own sour old country-man, says that Zeus and Hera argued whether men or women took the most pleasure in sex. They put the question to the prophet Teiresias, one who'd been both man and woman. He said: "A man's joy in sex rates only one in ten. But a woman gets ten full measures." Thus they brand us as nymphomaniacs. The truth is, men are afraid of womanhood and what it represents. Secretly, they want to treat us like oxen. Hesiod – may Hades give him work in the stews of Tartarus! – also said: "Get a house, a field, an ox, a plough, and a slave-girl – not a wife – and all will be well." For men. Do they learn this from the gods?'

The matron, the foremost woman among the travellers, was a little shocked by these outbursts. She came from an aristocratic family and knew her duty to the gods.

'The power of Zeus, the potency of the Father,' she said sharply, 'is a great and necessary power. But it is dangerous if it is not curbed. That was the task of Hera, his co-ruler on Olympus and his divine wife. It was natural that Zeus should be drawn to Hera, so handsome, so stately, the daughter of mighty gods. But cold, it must be admitted. Though mother to four of Zeus' children, she was never hot nor wanton.

'The campaign for Hera's heart was long and stormy. Many are the stories of their troubles. Once, in the woods of Argos, Zeus caused a tempest. Then, turning himself into a cuckoo, he fled from the storm into the shelter of

Hera's robe. She comforted the frightened bird, but Zeus rose in majesty and tried to ravish her. In Euboea, maddened by her "will I, won't I?", Zeus abducted her to Mount Cithaeron. When searchers came to look for her, he claimed that he was busy in the arms of Leto and must be left alone. Then, also on Cithaeron, Zeus tried to force her hand through jealousy. He pretended to marry another. He had a log of wood dressed as a bride, but when a furious Hera broke up the marriage procession the log was undressed to much laughter. Would they ever be reconciled enough to marry? Well, at last they did marry, though the people of Samos claim it was kept secret for three hundred years, to allow an end to hostilities and a godly consummation. Naxos, Euboea and Crete all wanted the honour of the marriage feast. But instead it took place in the palace where the waters of Oceanus touch the farthest western shore. All the gods brought gifts. Mother Earth gave a tree with golden fruit, which Hera planted in the nearby garden of the gods. She appointed the Hesperides, the daughters of Atlas, as the keepers of the garden, and set a dragon at the gate to watch and guard.

'But not even three hundred years of love, on a bed of hyacinths under a golden cloud, could restrain Zeus' monstrous sexual appetite. Hera suffered. Her nature, never warm, froze to ice, and her temper was short. Those who crossed her, she drove to frenzy or madness, as she did the god Dionysus and the hero Heracles. She whipped up storms, she sent pestilent clouds of insects. She struck Teiresias blind and sent the Sphinx to ravage Thebes. Sometimes she went too far. Her son Hephaestus did not forgive her when she threw him out of heaven on account of his ugliness. In revenge, he made her a golden throne which was also a secret trap. When she sat on it, she was held fast, and none of the other gods could release her. She was imprisoned there until Dionysus made Hephaestus drunk and stole the key.'

'Poor lady, to be driven to such distraction,' said a voice from the shadows. 'It was the fault of Zeus.'

'Yes, the Thunderer was the cause of her misery. At last, she was driven to rebel. She plotted with Poseidon and Apollo, who were also angered by Zeus' arrogance and temper. They joined together in revolt. They caught Zeus asleep, with a full belly after dinner, and bound him with a hundred knots. He roared and threatened. But he was entangled in a web of rawhide ropes, and the plotters laughed to see that he could not reach his thunderbolts. Thetis, the Nereid, heard both the rage and the mockery and she went pale. Fearing another War of the Gods, she hurried to fetch hundred-handed Briareus from Tartarus. A hundred knots were no trouble for his hundred hands, and in a moment Zeus was set free. Then he took his revenge. Hera, the ring-leader, was suspended from the sky in manacles, with an anvil fastened to each ankle. She was only released when she swore never again to rebel against her divine husband.'

The women were silent in sympathy. Hera was their goddess, their protector, and every blow against her was a blow against womanhood. They felt her indignity and pain. The cruel pull of the anvils weighed on them too, reminders of their burden, their suffering under custom, insolence and stupidity.

But one of the group was not impressed. A *hetaera*, a courtesan of the temple of Aphrodite at Corinth, was stretched elegantly on a rug of suspicious oriental luxury, a pattern of stylized panthers and lions in an angular green jungle. A small and painted slave-girl had spread the rug on the thickest patch of grass she could find, at some distance from the domestic huddle of wives and families around the fire. Here the courtesan was giving herself careful attention, fastidiously scrubbing her teeth with a willow twig, massaging her arms and legs with aromatic oils, trawling her face for wrinkles in a polished metal mirror.

When she was satisfied with her complexion, she gave herself a little smile and drawled into the silence.

'With the greatest respect to the divine Hera, who is, of course, the Queen of the Gods, I can't help wondering if she is really a victim of her husband's selfish ways. Might we not blame, instead, her own shrewish temper, her spite and her bad grace? The fact is, she's not womanly enough to hold her lord and husband. She lacks the arts of love. It's not that she despises them – just that she's no good at them. She tried, as the poets have often told us. They've left us a pretty picture: Hera, naked, cleansed with ambrosia, then anointed top to toe with perfumed oil strong enough to make heaven and earth swoon. She brushed her hair until it was like spun gold and plaited it into a regal braid, set off with jewels. She slipped into a robe embroidered for her by Athene herself. Around her hips was a girdle with a hundred golden tassels. A triple cluster of pearls hung from each ear. On her feet were sandals as light as air. She was ready to overwhelm the senses of amorous Zeus.

'No, this is not a goddess without conceit. And did she not challenge Athene and Aphrodite for the title of "the fairest"? The apple was the prize, and Paris was the judge. O, Hera certainly had her eye on that delicious youth. But what was the result of all this? Her seduction of Zeus – all that painting and primping – would have come to nothing had she not begged a love-spell from Aphrodite. And the judgment of Paris was no contest. The apple went to Aphrodite, who offered young Paris the most powerful promise of all – the gift of love. Let Hera learn from Aphrodite, my own sweet Lady of the soft arms, that envy and stiff-necked pride are poor substitutes for an understanding of the heart.'

'We thank you for your professional opinion,' the Ionian wife called out insultingly, 'but we need no lessons from the Goddess of the Bed.'

'That's where you're wrong,' the courtesan replied with calm good humour. 'I would lay odds that the beautiful lady whom you scorn has had more influence on the affairs of both gods and men than Pallas Athene, with all her holy wisdom. In fact, to know the nature of Aphrodite is, for mankind, the best wisdom of all.'

'If lechery is wisdom, and adultery is sense!'

'You forget,' the courtesan went on sweetly, 'that Aphrodite is the oldest of the Olympian gods, born of the foam when the severed genitals of Uranus were flung in the sea, long before Zeus was conceived. The gods mock her but neither god nor mortal can avoid her universal influence. She smiles at their mockery and remains untouched. Helius, driving the chariot of the sun through the sky, spied her passionately at play with Ares, in the marriage bed of her husband, Hephaestus. The lame god trapped them there, covering them with an unbreakable net, and invited all Olympus to laugh and stare. What did Aphrodite care? She'd tasted ecstasy and, when at last released, went quietly to Cyprus, to bathe in the waves from which she had been born and so renew her virginity. She knows very well that of all gods and mortals only Hestia, Artemis and Athene can resist her spells and her magic. She bewitched Dionysus, and their son is Priapus, a little imp of a god with a giant phallus. She wrestled in bed with ill-mannered Poseidon. Hermes, in his usual way, won her favours by a trick. For his fraud he fathered Hermaphroditus, a child both male and female.

'Among humans, she strikes impartially, bringing joy or anguish. She was kind to Pygmalion, who made an ivory statue in her image and then fell in love with his own handiwork. She gave the statue life and Pygmalion, most fortunate of men, was able to marry a women formed in the likeness of the goddess. She blessed Anchises with one night of love, coming to him as he tended his flocks on Mount Ida. In the morning she swore him to secrecy and promised him a son, Aeneas, whose name would be famous in the annals of mankind. A human heart can hardly keep from bursting after such possession. When he was drunk, Anchises could not help boasting, and for this indiscretion Zeus struck him down with a thunderbolt.

'Who can deny that love and death are closely intertwined, the one is worth the other? Myrrha, daughter of King Cinyras of Cyprus, thought she was as beautiful as

Aphrodite. So the goddess, to teach her a lesson, filled her heart with incestuous love and she lay with her father. When the King learnt he was deceived he would have killed Myrrha, but she prayed for help and was turned into a balsam, or myrrh, tree. After nine months the bark of the tree split and the handsome boy Adonis stepped out. He was so good-looking that even Aphrodite herself wanted him, and so too did Persephone, Queen of the Underworld. The rival goddesses agreed uneasily to share him. But Aphrodite lured Adonis away with her magic girdle, causing Persephone to appeal to Ares for help. The brutish Ares knew only one way to settle disputes. He turned himself into a wild boar and charged Adonis as he hunted on Mount Lebanon. Severely gored, Adonis bled to death. Red anemones grew out of his bloodstains. And Aphrodite, rushing to his side, was also hurt, cutting her limbs on the thorns of a briar. Roses, which had once been only white, were now tinged with red. From the pain of passion comes beauty. From dying love comes renewed life. When Aphrodite first rose up from the sea and stepped from the scallop-shell that carried her to the shore of her beloved Cyprus, tender blooms and the greenest of grass sprang immediately from beneath her feet. Such, even among plants and dumb things, is the procreative power of love.'

The force of passion – that was something every woman could reflect on. The courtesan, in her shameless way, had put the case for the power of love. But what of the dark side? Neither gods nor goddesses were immune from the failings of the heart, though it was often a tyranny they would thankfully avoid. Even Demeter, daughter of Cronus and Rhea, Goddess of the Corn and the Harvest, was powerless against corrupting passions, which pursued and stung her like summer gadflies.

Demeter, as everyone knows, is mild and kind. She watches tenderly over nature, but even when there is an offence against her bounty she is not vindictive. In Thessaly, she warned Erysichthon not to waste wood from her own sacred grove to make beams for his banqueting hall. But Erysichthon took his axe to the grove, and only then did Demeter afflict him with perpetual hunger, so that he ate his way through his wealth until he was reduced to beggary, rooting for scraps by the highway. Her whole care was given to nature, to everything that grows and fruits. She had no time and little inclination for matters of sex. But perhaps it was her tenderness itself that attracted the attentions she did not want.

In her youth, the Titan Iasius had tumbled her in a thrice-ploughed field, though Zeus struck the Titan dead for daring to touch a goddess of Olympus. She turned herself into a mare to run away from Poseidon, but the God of Horses became a stallion and mounted her. Zeus himself lusted after his gentle sister. How could she resist? He possessed her and she gave birth to Persephone, who is also called Core, a most pretty child but destined to be as sadly used and abused as her mother.

Demeter raised her daughter in all innocence, secluded in Sicily, far from the broad paths trod by gods and men. But Hades, Lord of the Underworld, saw Persephone and desired her. Demeter would not hear of a marriage – to lose her daughter to the Kingdom of the Dead! So Hades planned to abduct her. On a summer's day, when Persephone was gathering flowers in the fields of Enna, she saw a single white narcissus placed by Ge among the violets and irises and hyacinths. As she picked the flower, the earth opened. A golden chariot with four black horses, whipped on by Hades, burst from the split earth. With one arm he scooped the terrified girl from the ground, and then they plunged together into blackness.

Demeter set out to find her daughter. The trail was obscure. No one could tell her what had happened, or where her daughter had gone. Taking two torches from the fires of Aetna to light her way, Demeter wandered from land to land. At the passing of her sad figure, the crops withered and the ground became barren, for in her desperation she forgot to sustain the work of nature. Grim and unrecognizable, she came to Eleusis, where King Celeus and his wife, Metaneira, received her kindly. She said she was an unhappy woman who had lost her child, so Metaneira, who needed a nurse, invited her to look after her own son Demophoon. Demeter was touched, and in gratitude she decided to make the little boy immortal. But as she held Demophoon over the fire, to purge him of mortality, Metaneira entered and screamed in fright. The child fell in the fire and died. Then Demeter rose in god-like splendour and for this unlucky intervention imposed certain rituals on the queen. When these were done Demeter relented and taught the queen and the people of Eleusis her Mysteries, which ever afterwards have been celebrated in the name of the goddess.

Now, Celeus had an older son called Triptolemus, who had been away in the fields, looking after the king's cattle. When he returned to the palace he told a strange tale. One day, he had seen the earth open, and after a rush of fetid wind, stinking of decay, a team of black horses drawing a golden chariot thundered out of the chasm, and a dark charioteer had plucked a girl from the field and then they all disappeared. At once, Demeter knew Persephone's fate, for only Hades drove the golden chariot with the black horses. Demeter cried out for justice and begged Zeus to order the release of her daughter from the Underworld.

Within his own dark realm, Hades took no orders, even from Zeus. But the world was starving while Demeter grieved. Because of this dearth, Hades agreed reluctantly to let Persephone go. She prepared to depart. With a light heart, she plucked a pomegranate to sustain her on the journey to the upper air. But the pomegranate is the fruit of the dead, and those who taste it shall see the world no more. The Fates have decreed it, and not even the gods can alter that decision. At best, the gods could only arrange a compromise, which allowed Persephone to spend a portion of the year away from the hall of Hades.

So in spring and summer Persephone comes into the light of the bright sky and stays in the palace of her mother. Then Demeter smiles, and the crops flourish, and the fruit ripens on the tree. But when winter comes Persephone retreats to the Underworld and sits in gloomy state by her husband, Hades, ruling over the battalions of the dead. Then Demeter's face is clouded and she pulls her mantle over her head. The summer flowers die, and the leaves fall from the trees, and the earth is in mourning, dark and barren.

Now the preparation of the meal was in full swing. Pleasant aromas drifted from boiling pots. Cakes of dough baked on the hot stones, covered with a handful of ashes. Children, hungry and tired of games, snatched titbits from the edge of the fire. From time to time, a small head received a resounding slap. Into the long summer dusk, the fire cast a circle of comfort. It was a haven, administered by women with their many tasks, giving shelter against the doubts of the coming night. The women were busy, but not too busy to release a sigh for Demeter, held on the rack of others' desire.

The Ionian wife was always ready to give voice to the indignation of women.

'One goddess, at least,' she burst out, 'is fierce, and chaste, and unwounded by the darts of love. Artemis, great Apollo's twin, has her bow and her unerring arrows and knows how to shoot straight. She supports us. She is the protector of the child-bed and the Nurse of Youth. Brontes, the Cyclopes, made her a silver bow. Pan sent her from Arcadia ten ferocious hunting dogs, as swift as deer and as strong as lions. Unwise is the person who opposes her. She, of all the Olympians, has the moral courage to stand between male lust and male actions. She shot the giant hunter Orion when he tried to rape the maiden Opis. She turned her favourite follower Callisto into a bear when she forgot her vow of virginity and fell into the arms of Zeus. The giants Otus and Ephialtes, though huge and riotous, and with no respect for the gods, had to face her anger. When they made a lewd attack on herself and on Hera, Artemis caused a deer to start up between the giants. Each of them flung a spear, but in their excitement they missed the deer and killed each other. It is a warning to those with hot breath and groping hands.'

'Nonsense, a lament of the frigid,' interrupted the courtesan. 'Your Artemis is merely the patroness of hunting. She is called the Goddess of the Wild Beasts, and she is as savage as her clients – bloodthirsty and mean. She killed poor Actaeon, because he saw her naked. What prudery! A true woman glories in her body. But Artemis turned Actaeon into a stag and he was torn apart by his own hounds. She filled Admetus' wedding-bed with snakes, because he was busy with guests and forgot to greet her at the wedding. And when Oeneus also neglected her rites at a harvest festival, she sent a wild boar to ravage his land. Such mean-minded spite! And that story about Orion – I can tell you other versions. Some say Artemis was jealous of Orion, who loved Eos and not her. But her real reason for jealousy was Orion's prowess as a hunter. He boasted that he could clear the whole world of wild animals, and this was too much for both Apollo and Artemis. They sent a scorpion to attack Orion. He tried to escape by swimming but Artemis, to show her skill, took long-range aim at his head in the waves and pierced his skull with a single arrow. The gods placed Orion in the constellations of the night sky, but what remedy was that for the poor fellow?

'No, there's not much to admire in your hunting goddess. Hera revealed her true status when she boxed her ears. The gods of Olympus were arguing over the course of the Trojan War. Artemis' speech was biting and without respect, but you know that Hera, for all her faults, is every inch the Queen of Heaven. "O, you're a lioness among women," she scornfully told Artemis, "and you may shoot humans like vermin. But you'll find it better sport to slaughter dumb beasts than to try conclusions with me." Then Hera grabbed the bow and the quiver, and cuffed the goddess once or twice, and sent her snivelling to Zeus, to hide like a pigeon in her father's lap.'

'Peace, friends, peace,' the elderly matron held up her

hands. 'We begin to sound like a council of ministers. Let us not quarrel like menfolk. Remember, we women have one true champion whose power is always equal to the task. Athene, Goddess of Wisdom, is also called Parthenos, the Virgin. It is a title that she bears out of serenity and confidence in her sex. She is not intimidated by the muddle of the heart and the desire of males. On Olympus, in full armour and with spear at the ready, standing with the owl of wisdom on her shoulder and the crested helmet of battle on her head, Athene waits by the throne of Zeus, at one with her father, an intimate sharer in his knowledge and strength. She is his favourite daughter, his "dear grey-eyes", and often she carries his aegis and his thunderbolt.

'Everything about her birth and upbringing is impressive, a hint of future greatness. Zeus swallowed Metis, for fear of a son. But Metis was already pregnant with a girl. When Zeus was walking by Lake Tritonis, in Africa, he was gripped by a raging headache, caused by the infant struggling to be born. So bad was the pain, Zeus begged Hephaestus to strike open his skull. Hephaestus swung his axe, and out leapt Athene, fully armed, shaking her spear and sounding her warcry. It was a moment of terror. Even the Sun hesitated in his track, until the children of the Sun in consternation hurried to Rhodes to honour the new deity. In their rush, they forgot fire for the offering, but Athene, who is as gracious as she is stern, was well pleased. She looked kindly on the island of Rhodes. She granted the people a supreme skill in craftsmanship, so that they made statues that lived, and she permitted them to make sacrifices without fire.

'From the beginning, Athene was a warlike goddess. In her youth she practised arms with a girl companion called Pallas. One day, when tempers were a little heated, Zeus had to thrust his aegis between them. Distracted by this, Pallas did not see Athene's blow, which killed her. In sorrow and repentance Athene took on her dead friend's name and became Pallas Athene. She also made an image of Pallas and covered it in her own aegis. This was the famous Palladion, which fell from heaven upon Troy and on which the luck of the city rested. When Diomedes and Odysseus stole it, at the end of the Trojan War, Troy was doomed. Athene became formidable in arms and no warrior dared to stand against her. Even gods quaked at her name. But, unlike Ares, she always uses the power of her arm on the side of right and justice. For her, war is the grim remedy against tyranny. That is why she twice sent murderous Ares fleeing from the field with her contemptuous blows. And that is why she fought so stead-fastly for us Greeks in the Trojan War. Helen's abduction, by the Trojan prince Paris, cried out for justice. Menelaus and the Greek armies had right on their side.'

'Greeks, yes,' complained a soldier's wife from Tiryns, a tough-looking woman giving the soup ladle a fierce twirl. She resented Athenian pride and superiority. 'That business at Troy was our fight – the people of Argolis under our commanders Agamemnon and Menelaus. Athene stood by us then, I'll admit it. But why does she always show such favour to the Athenians? The rest of us – from Laconia to Achaea, from Elis to Euboea – are we not as Greek as they are?'

An Athenian came quickly to the defence of her city, for it is a place never short of glib tongues.

'Naturally, Pallas Athene prefers our city,' she snapped. 'It bears her own sacred name. She struggled for the city and means to keep it. Poseidon, the surly sea-god, tried to take it from her. He struck the rock of the Acropolis with his trident and gave the people a miracle. A saltwater spring began to flow. We still see it today, under the porch of the Erechtheion. But wise Athene gave us a greater benefit. With a touch of her spear she made an olive tree grow, and soon there were olive groves and prosperous agriculture. No wonder the gods awarded Athens to her, not Poseidon.

'Then Athene became part of our history. She suffered on our land – how can we deny her claim to us? Hephaestus, the lame smith, lusted after her but Athene, who had vowed to remain a virgin, fought him off, even at the gates of the city. In the struggle, he spilt his seed on the ground. Ge, the Earth, was fertilized and she gave birth to Erichthonius. She handed the baby to Athene – for was she not a kind of foster mother? – who hid the infant in a chest which she gave for safe-keeping to the three daughters of Cecrops, King of Athens, half man and half serpent. The contents of the chest were a secret. But Aglauros, his eldest daughter, was too curious. She raised the lid and showed her sisters. What did they see? No one knows. Perhaps a baby in a nest of snakes, perhaps a snake-child. But the sight drove them mad, and they jumped from the Acropolis to their death. A crow brought the news to Athene while she was out collecting a boulder for the fortification of the walls. In her anger she dropped the gigantic stone and cursed the crow. The boulder became the hill of Lycabettus, and the crow turned from white, which all crows used to be, to the accursed colour black.

'But Athene did not remain angry with Athens. When Ares killed Halirrhothius, for raping the daughter of Aglauros, the goddess set up her court in Athens. This was the Areopagus, the court before which even the war-god Ares had to appear, to be judged by Athene and the citizens of Athens. Ares was banished for a period of slavery. And ever after Pallas Athene attended the Areopagus, the highest court of mankind. In judgment, when she threw her pebble to cast her vote, she always threw it on the side of mercy.'

Athene has mixed justice with mercy, and the world thanks her for it. Though she is indomitable in a good cause, when the battle is done she extends the olive branch from her own sacred tree and binds angry opponents to peace and reconciliation. This is reason enough for gratitude, but mankind has other gifts to thank her for. Dance and music come under her care. Both the flute of peace and the trumpet of war belong to her. She is the tamer of horses and showed the hero Bellerophon how to manage Pegasus, the wild winged horse. She encourages all acts of craftsmanship. She helped the Argonauts build their ship and taught Epeius how to make the wooden horse that brought the walls of Troy tumbling down.

But more than anything else Athene is the comforter and the help-mate of women. When Zeus created Pandora, the first woman, Athene gave her a soul. When women needed arts, Athene gave them those, too. She taught them spinning and weaving and pottery. Nor is she ashamed, when she can set aside for a moment her duties as Champion and Counsellor of mankind, to watch over the kitchen as Goddess of the Cooking-pots. The skill of woman's hand is no mean matter, and not to be slighted. Arachne was the greatest weaver in Lydia, but she was too proud of her skill. Athene warned her against presumption. Modesty is a virtue in women. But still Arachne boasted, so Athene in disguise challenged her to a weaving contest. To reinforce her warning, Athene wove a story of punishments given to those who annoyed the gods. But Arachne, foolish woman, wove into her web divine indiscretions, adulteries and scandalous affairs. In a rage, Athene beat her with the shuttle of her loom, so that Arachne at last knew her offence and hanged herself. But Athene, advocate of mercy, saved her life. She turned Arachne into a spider so that she could weave to her heart's content without offence to gods or mortals.

The sun at last had dipped below the horizon and Helius began unshackling his horses in the stables of Oceanus. The snowy frieze of Olympus showed silver in the young moonlight. Out of the growing dark came the crunch of many feet, and the hubbub of male voices suddenly too loud in night stillness.

The wife from Ionia turned her head and listened. An ironic smile slowly formed on her lips. 'Come, children, stop your squalling and misery now. Set out the pots and dishes. At last we can eat. The men are returning, and I smell the roast lamb they bring. And in what triumph! Such enterprise, and skill, and dedication! Now, indeed, the human race is ready to continue– if Hera and Demeter and Pallas Athene will only bless us women with children.'

Triptolemus Receives Corn from Demeter

– 6 –

MYSTERIES

'DIOMEDES, KING of the Bistones,' the merchant said, 'fed human flesh to his horses.'

He had meant to say, 'Now we are among savages,' but he had stopped himself, in case the wilderness had ears.

He looked around fearfully, kneading his hands and cracking the joints of his fingers. They were in strange country, near Meteora. The ground erupted into sugar loafs, humpbacks, needles, spires of rock, some more than a hundred feet in height, rising out of a grassy plain as calm as parkland. Behind the fractured rocks, a range of sullen grey hills shed boulders and scree into the valleys. Beyond, to north and east, were large desolate vistas, rolling landscapes as patched and scabby and scuffed as the disintegrating coat of an old donkey.

Once safely through the dangerous funnel of the pathway between the mountain and the sea, the travellers had split into smaller groups, veering off into the wide regions of the north. The merchant, with his packhorses and his servants, intended to go through Thessaly and Macedonia into Thrace, before hurrying home by the shortest route. He had brought jewels and plate and trinkets, bolts of dyed and embroidered cloth, earthenware pottery, samples of weapons with gilded hilts and decorated blades. Things to please the barbarian eye. He hoped to return with skins, precious metals and uncut stones. But he was apprehensive. He tried to balance profit against danger, and the equation made his head ache. The gods of these parts had a rough sense of humour and a hearty appetite for blood.

'I tremble when I cross the River Peneius,' the merchant confided to Mantes. 'The cornlands give way to pasture. Centaurs prowl, as vicious as men and as powerful as horses. Woods and hills are full of the noisy riot of unpredictable beings – drunken Sileni, insatiable Satyrs, frenzied Maenads. Where the ploughing stops, where corn no longer grows, Demeter protects no further. Then we are at the mercy of Dionysus.'

Whenever he crossed the Peneius, the merchant prayed: 'Holy Demeter, stay with me now.' She was his touchstone. Only Demeter could foster the conditions of civilization, that happy state that lies on the other side of violence, rage and lust. Gentle Demeter had been tempered by sorrow in the long search for her daughter. At the end of that trial lay peace and a state of grace. Demeter smiled once more, and the corn grew and the harvests were gathered in. These are the gifts of civilization. Where Apollo rules there is order. Where Demeter is worshipped, nature releases her bounty to mankind and angry passions subside. Beyond this jurisdiction lie the danger lands.

Demeter blessed the mortals who were kind and gave her help in the search for Persephone. At Eleusis, Celeus and Metaneira had found her in disguise, sad-eyed and travel-stained by the Well of Maidenhead. They gave her a drink of barley water flavoured with mint and took her into their palace and made her the nurse of their child. In gratitude, Demeter made the royal family of Eleusis the first priests of her temple, showing them her Mysteries, and promising certain glories in the afterlife to all who followed this secret way. Triptolemus, son of Celeus and Metaneira, a youth specially favoured by the goddess, received the seed of the corn from her own hand, and she taught him to yoke oxen and sow the seed. He tilled the level plain between Eleusis and Athens, and reaped the harvest and took it to the threshing floor which he had also made according to Demeter's instructions. When that was done, Demeter gave him a chariot drawn by winged dragons and ordered him to carry the seed-corn, and to spread the secret of agriculture, into all lands. In time, Triptolemus became King of Eleusis, the priest of her Mysteries, and the guardian of her cult.

The merchant remembered this old story among the pinnacles and canyons of Meteora, while big slow birds looped ominously overhead. Somewhere there was death in the valley and the scavengers were circling. In these lands, death came suddenly and soon. The merchant was afraid to think of death. He yearned for life and the solemn life-giving order of the Mysteries. The innermost rituals of Demeter were a secret that none would reveal, even on pain of death. But with what fervour, and what love for the goddess, did her initiates dwell on the memory of her public ceremonies and the outward signs of her glory! The Lesser Mysteries were held in Anthesterion, the month of spring flowers. The chief festival, the Greater Mysteries, began before the autumn sowing, in the month of Boedromion.

'This is the time when our hearts swell most with pride and devotion,' the merchant recalled. 'On the fourteenth day of Boedromion, the priests of Demeter carry the sacred objects from the Hall of Initiation, in Eleusis, to the goddess' other sanctuary below the Acropolis in Athens. Next day, the festival begins. The public come to the Painted Stoa in the Agora, and all are welcome, even slaves. Only murderers, and those unlucky people who can't speak our language, are excluded.

'For two days there are public ceremonies, sacrifices, rites of purification. For the initiates, us Mystai, this joyful time passes with impatience. We are waiting for the return. Our spirits surge in anticipation towards Eleusis. On the nineteenth we begin the preparation that will take us into the secret heart of the goddess. At noon, the sacred objects are collected and the procession forms to make the half-day's journey to Eleusis. With torches and singing and dancing we set out. We are setting foot on the Sacred Way of the soul, the straight way to grace and knowledge. At intervals we stop and pray at shrines set up for Iacchus, the cult-god of our Mysteries, who is in some sense Demeter and in some sense Dionysus, though I hardly dare breathe a mention of these hidden matters. It is night when we reach Eleusis. The torches have multiplied and we enter as if under a rain of fire. For two days we look into our souls, meditating alone on the seashore or wandering the wild places, as Demeter had done in her search for Persephone. We come to share her suffering. Then we are ready for the final act. We enter the Hall of Initiation and close the door on profane eyes. There is a sound of music and of a vast sacred drama being enacted – that, at least, one may hear from the outside. No lips may speak of the Mysteries within. But we who have been in the Hall of Initiation emerge rapt and content. Now, however long we may live, we are prepared for death. Through the grace of Demeter, we have become Persephone's servants and we have her promise of certain blessings in the afterlife . . . '

The voice of the merchant trailed away. Had he already said too much, given away divine secrets? He looked around nervously, but he only saw incomprehension or mild derision on rough and homely faces. The merchant's group, sedate and slow-moving, was mixed with local traffic on the road – drovers, horsemen, carters, tribal warriors who might in a sudden excess of spleen turn into bandits or robbers. To all of them, he was the curiosity. Townsman! they thought. And a southerner to boot. A poor fish, lacking in manly courage, muddling life with mystical sentimentality. So neat, with his little curly beard, and his bald patch tucked under a fur cap, and his clean white linen tunic, and smart ox-hide boots halfway up his skinny shanks.

'Well, that's a pretty speech,' said a drover, walloping the rump of a stubborn animal. 'Demeter is a great goddess, and we owe her thanks for the harvest. But it seems to me she might allow a little more fun. The question is not what will happen when Death leads us down to the Court of Persephone. We want to know how to get the best out of this life. You talk of Boedromion. I'm thinking also of that hot lazy month. The artichokes are in flower and the crickets chirp in the trees. Goats are at their plumpest. Young girls are free and easy, giving us the wink, but Sirius has got us parched and we are dying for a flask of a good vintage.'

'A bit of shade and a drink, eh?' cried his fellow herds-man, putting his shoulder to an ox's steaming flank. 'A shady rock and the wine of Biblis, and perhaps a lump of goat's-milk curds and the roasted meat from a young heifer. It's a great thing to sit in the shade and sip the bright wine, while Zephyrus' breeze cools the brow, and the stream gurgles out of the clear spring. Then I'll thank the gods. I'll pour three libations of pure water, and add a fourth of wine for good luck.'

This raised a shout of approval. 'What's the old saying? Where there's no wine, there's no love, and man has no further joy.'

'That's what we believe up here in the north,' a young horseman cavorting on the edge of the group called out cheerfully. 'Dionysus is our god. Born and raised here, or so they say. We lift the wine-cup in his honour. And then we do it again, for the hell of it.'

With unwearied high spirits he pulled on the reins, making his barely tame pony rear and prance.

Dionysus was no god for timid, law-abiding people. He is an outsider, from the ungovernable spaces of Thrace and Phrygia. Always, wild music leads him on and peaceful, rational folk turn their eyes from this carnival. Even his birth was a raw act. Zeus desired the mortal Semele, daughter of Cadmus. It was a familiar case. Zeus strove to possess the girl, and Hera worked to prevent it. The Queen of Heaven came to Semele in disguise, when the girl was already pregnant.

'O most happy girl, to lie with such an exalted lover!'

Then Hera sighed: 'But how can you be sure it's not just a cruel game? He'll have his pleasure and toss you away like the shell of a nut. Test his love. Let him come to you in all his glory, as he would to a lawful wife, for it's a poor thing to be a god's whore.'

So Semele nagged her lover until, in a moment of aggravation, he gave way. But no human body can withstand the divine blaze of Zeus in all his majesty, and Semele was burnt to ashes. Zeus grabbed the baby from her womb, a child already made immortal by contact with the holy fire, and thrust it into a gash in his thigh, to await the full term. When the time came, the infant Dionysus was born from his father's thigh.

Lacking a mother, Dionysus was nursed by Ino, Semele's sister. But Hera was not finished with the family. She sent madness to afflict both Ino and her husband, Athamas, so that he shot his elder son in mistake for a deer. Then pursued by mad Athamas, mad Ino jumped, with her other son in her arms, from the Molurian Rocks into the Saronic Gulf. Dionysus escaped to Mount Nysa where the nymphs of the rain and the mountain cared for him. In this seclusion, except for his tutor Silenus, his companions were women. He even dressed as a woman.

Silenus was cunning and dissolute, pot-bellied, bald-headed, and with horse's ears. He taught Dionysus the elements of self-indulgence and disorder. The wisdom of Silenus was not worth a pin. Once, wishing to test him, King Midas of Phrygia captured Silenus, loosened his tongue with wine and demanded to know the secret of life.

'It is best for man not to be born,' Silenus answered, 'and the next best thing is to die young.'

Was the discovery of wine by Dionysus, in which Silenus undoubtedly had a hand, only an antidote to despair?

'Despair, who talks of despair?' cried the young horseman, side-stepping his mount, wild-eyed and foam-flecked, into the throng of travellers. 'Dionysus is our friend.' His excited face beamed around, challenging opposition. 'He is the great benefactor of mankind. All hail to Dionysus! If you can't handle the divine gift of wine, it's no fault of the god. That's a human failing. There's a story about that. Young Dionysus sat on a stone to rest, on his way to Naxos. It was summer, of course. At his feet he saw a little plant, a vine, which seemed to him so beautiful he wanted to take it with him. To keep it from the heat of the sun he put it in the thigh-bone of a bird. As he went along, the plant grew so quickly that it needed more protection. So he put the bird's bone into a lion's bone, and then that into the bone of an ass. And so he came to Naxos. But when he went to plant the little vine he found bones and roots so entangled that he put the whole lot into the ground. The plant grew, and prospered, and bore good red grapes, which Dionysus made into wine and gave to mankind to drink for the first time. Now this is what happened. When people drank a little, they sang like birds; when they drank more, they were as strong as lions; but when they drank too much, they acted like asses.'

'That's Dionysus for you,' put in a carter who had been testing a new flute with a few dreamy notes. 'Who know's what he'll do next? He's got a surprise for everyone, as those Tyrrhenian pirates found when they captured him on Chios, or perhaps it was in Icaria. They discovered they'd bitten off more than they could chew. He looked so drowsy and befuddled and handsome they thought, "Ah, this fellow will sell well in the slave market". Only the helmsman had a suspicion that they might be dealing with a god. But the rest of the crew wouldn't listen. They forced Dionysus on board and sailed away. But the wind dropped as if by magic. The oars became serpents, a vine wound around the mast, and clusters of grapes hung over the head of the strange youth. Wine seeped up through the deck. Then, suddenly, savage beasts were growling and licking their lips, so that the pirates abandoned ship. As they dived overboard they turned into dolphins. And that's why dolphins are now always kind to sailors. They don't want the god to punish them again.'

Dionysus makes people change. He gets under the skin.

Respectable citizens become wild, irrational, a puzzle even to themselves. For a time, they do not know who they are. His weapons are wine and madness.

Where and how was wine invented? That is the secret of the god. Certain hard-drinking places, like Naxos or Chios, like to claim the distinction of the first vineyard. But Dionysus brought wine with him from Thrace, and crafty old Silenus, his tutor, had something to do with the discovery, on Mount Nysa. All at once the mountain nymphs, who had been so shy that they hid their faces behind winnowing-fans, were transformed into raging Maenads, the female rabble who attended Dionysus wherever he went. They wound snakes around their arms and frightened the country peace with bull-roarers. They brandished the *thyrsus* – a strong staff twined with ivy and topped by a pine cone. With this, they beat all who stood in their way. It was a symbol of office, but also a cruel weapon. These women were possessed, carried away by wine and hypnotized by incessant rhythms of the bacchanal dance.

In truth, they were frenzied, sharing in a madness which Hera imposed on the adult Dionysus, as the last act in her revenge against Semele.

In a whirl of dervishes, Dionysus fled through many lands. Vines grew out of his footsteps as he passed, and the people propagated them and turned the grapes into wine. But no one knew what else Dionysus might leave behind. Sometimes it was wonder and sometimes horror, and sometimes the wonder turned to horror. When King Midas – he to whom Apollo had given asses' ears – helped Dionysus through Phrygia and asked for a golden touch in return, the god granted the request. But then even his clothes, even his last crumb of food, turned to gold, and the King was on the point of starvation. Only the River Pactolus could release him from this fatal gift. The stream washed the golden touch into the riverbed, which gleams to this day with gold sands.

As Dionysus moved on, wild rumours and whispers attended his progress. By the Nile, he founded the oracle of Egyptian Ammon. He defeated Titans in Libya. He fought for, and then against, Amazons. On his way to India he flayed a king in Syria. He crossed one great river on a bridge of vines twisted with ivy, and another on the back of a tiger. He tamed elephants in India and drove them back, or so some say, for their bones to lie in Greek earth.

In time, Dionysus' term of madness was at an end. Rhea, mother of Zeus, purified him, and then showed him the mysteries of the Great Mother. He was ready to return to the lands where the gods make their home.

But those lands, already owing duty and worship to older gods, were reluctant to receive him. He harried the opposition, giving no mercy. In his wake he left riot, disorder, bloodshed.

'That drug he had with him, that wine,' the merchant lamented, 'was too powerful for simple mouths, unused to the divine liquid.'

The marchant eyed his fellow travellers with care. Windswept, sun-baked, dragging an effusion of sweat and animal ordure, they seemed familiar enough with the holy wine.

He continued with less confidence, not quite sure of his effect on this crowd: 'Just look what happened, even in the god's own land of Thrace. King Lycurgus attacked Dionysus and his wild women with an ox-goad, forcing the god to dive in the sea and take shelter with Thetis. So Dionysus made the king mad. He took an axe to his own son, thinking the boy was a vine, and pruned off his limbs. Then a barrenness settled on the earth that could only be relieved by the sacrifice of the king. His own subjects tore him apart with wild horses.'

The young rider on the prancing horse laughed. 'That's right,' he shouted. 'There are no milksops in our part of the world. Rough justice for a rough people. Life for a life.'

'No,' the merchant protested, 'this is a question of danger, not of justice. Justice, whatever it is, is rational. But who can calculate the effects of frenzy? Listen, this is what happened in Thebes, in the city of Semele, Dionysus' own mother. King Pentheus feared the look of the Dionysian rabble at the gates of the city. He had the god thrown into prison and the Maenads driven out to Mount Cithaeron. But the doors of the prison flew open and Dionysus walked free. Then he took Pentheus aside and whispered in his ear, inviting him to witness strange erotic scenes on Cithaeron. What did the king see?

'At dawn, a company of women arose, old, young, matrons, mothers, girls, all jumbled together. Dishevelled hair hung to their shoulders. They wore skins bound with snakes, which licked their cheeks. In their hair were tangles of ivy, oak leaf, briony. Some, with full breasts, suckled fawns or wolf-cubs. One struck a rock with her *thyrsus* and made water spout. Another dug a hollow in which a pool of milk formed. Another jabbed the ground and a fountain of wine gushed out. Honey dripped from the tips of the ivy-clad staffs. From the mountain, they swept down on the cattle pastures. A full-uddered cow was pulled apart and a calf ripped to pieces. Bones and flesh were trampled into the ground, blood-spotted tatters of skin hung on the branches of the pines. Countless female hands dragged a bull to its knees, and before you could blink the flesh was stripped from it.

'Then, like birds of prey, they swooped onto the rich plains of Asopus, where farmers live in peace and contentment. In a moment, the villagers were engulfed by senseless fury. Nothing harmed the wild women, fire did not burn them, nor weapons touch them. But they, thrusting and battering with their *thyrsus* staffs, broke many a head and spilled many a gut, until the villagers were put to flight. Then the Maenads returned to the top of Cithaeron in triumph, their bare shoulders weighted with looted babies. They washed in the springs that Dionysus had caused to flow, and the snakes licked the bloodstains from their faces.

'King Pentheus spied all this and quaked. Some god-demon, he thought, has done this. He has sent these women the mind-corrupting grape, the vine that loosens conscience. Even as he thought this, a gust of wind revealed his hiding place, and the frenzied women were on him in a flash. Like the calf, like the bull, he was ripped asunder with bare hands, and it is said that his own mother, Agave, tore off his head.'

What defence has mankind against the superhuman powers of god-sent dementia? In Attica, Icarius welcomed Dionysus, planted his grapes, fermented wine, and gave it to the people to drink. But becoming drunk, they thought they had been poisoned and killed Icarius. When his daughter, Erigone, having searched everywhere with her faithful dog, found the body, she hanged herself in grief.

Even worse things happened in Orchomenus. The three daughters of King Minyas refused to join in the Dionysian debauchery. They stayed in the palace, quietly weaving, even when Dionysus came in disguise and pressed them to take part. In anger, the god then tormented them with phantasms and weird sounds. Vines grew into the cloth on the loom, and wild animals stalked the room until the girls were driven mad. After casting lots, they tore the son of the eldest, Leucippe, to pieces, as a sacrifice to Dionysus. But he was not appeased. He banished them from mankind, changing them into a bat, an owl and a crow.

No land could hold out against Dionysus. Everywhere he went, fury and ecstasy overwhelmed the people, and they bowed down before the new god. Even the gods acknowledged his divine force. On Olympus, Zeus introduced his wild son into the pantheon of heaven. Then Dionysus plunged through Lake Lerna, to rescue his mother, Semele, from the black wastes of the Underworld. He instated her modestly on the fringes of the divine court, where not even Hera objected to her presence.

Out of the fury of the ritual dance, out of the heavy pulse of the drums and the keening of flutes and shawms, out of waves of nausea and passion, out of the orgy, came inspiration and inner vision. Those are the dangerous gifts, the mysteries, brought by Dionysus from the lands of the north.

Could ecstasy be purged of violence and cruelty, so that the inner voice might be heard without pain, and the doors of perception swing peacefully open? Dionysus and Demeter, it seemed, were far apart. But in the world of visions their paths crossed at least once. This is how it happened. On her way to Eleusis, searching for her daughter, Demeter had met in the road a woman called Baubo. She offered the goddess some barley water but Demeter was preoccupied by grief and did not drink it. Then Baubo lifted her skirts and showed her womb, in which Demeter saw the child Iacchus. The baby was gurgling and smiling and seemed so happy that Demeter laughed too. Then her grief was lifted and she took the drink gratefully. Iacchus was Dionysus in another form, and because he had consoled Demeter he was ever after woven into the secret web of the Eleusinian Mysteries of the goddess.

One miracle was accounted to Iacchus, the hidden Dionysus. When the Persian armies of Xerxes were laying waste the plain before Athens, some Greeks who were with the Persians saw a tower of dust, as much as thirty thousand soldiers would make, rising over Eleusis. The cloud moved over the war-torn land towards Salamis, where the ships of the Greeks waited. Then there came from the dust a swelling sound, the solemn music of the hymn sung to Iacchus in the practice of the Mysteries. The Greeks knew than that the Persians were doomed.

One ecstatic follower of Dionysus pondered the connection with holy and gentle Demeter. He set out to illuminate the visionary world, to divide the Dionysian frenzy from the mystical Dionysus.

To the singer Orpheus, the world was not what it seems. There is another story of primal beings even beyond the Olympian gods. Orpheus sang of these things. First, only Chaos and Darkness existed, out of whom the goddess Night emerged, spreading her wings like a monstrous black bird. The Wind fertilized her and she gave birth to Eros, enclosed in a silver egg. Eros was also called Phanes, the Revealed One, a god who was both sexes, a woman before and a man behind, with four eyes and four horns and golden wings. With his mother, Night, he lived in a deep cave, for none could face his radiance, and for this reason Night called him 'the First-born Shining One'. Then Eros-Phanes made earth and sky and moon, with the sun to watch over them, and he set Rhea, the Great Mother, in front of the cave to beat a bronze drum, as a warning of the divinity within. Eros-Phanes governed the reins of the universe, which he passed on in his own good time to Uranus, and thence to Cronus and Zeus as the poets have related. But Orpheus and his mystical followers believed that the time of Zeus will pass, and then Dionysus will bring in a new age of faith in which all perplexities are resolved.

On the road from Meteora, the caravan of the travellers had settled into the steady rhythm of experienced wanderers. The sun was losing heat, arcing towards the western horizon. The drovers gave an occasional whistle, or a half-hearted crack of the whip, but the animals plodded on as if mesmerized. The carter had his new flute tuned now. Confidently, he began a melody that nearly everyone recognized. Then a singer added the words of the ode, in praise of music.

> 'Golden lyre, gift of Apollo and the bright-haired
>   Muses,
> The dancers hear you and the dance begins.
> First, the prelude, then singers join the trembling
>   strings.
> Music quenches the thunderbolts of ever-flowing fire.
> With folded wings, the eagle sleeps on Zeus' sceptre.
> Enchantment seals its eyelids,
> Its supple back rises and falls,
> To the spell of your sweet sounds.
> The War God drops his spear and his brutal heart is
>   quiet.
> Taught by Leto's son and the rich-breasted Muses,
> The power of music lays even gods to rest.'

Listening to the noble ode, Mantes thought about Orpheus. He was mortal, after all. Apart from being the greatest poet and musician who ever lived, how did Orpheus differ from his countrymen, the untamed and much-feared warriors of Thrace and Phrygia? They, too, were musicians, lovers of songs and dance, followers of Dionysus. Travelling with the men from those lands, Mantes considered his own group on the road. In the day, they endured with stoical strength whatever nature and the gods might throw at them. At night, they took out wine flasks and panpipes and flutes and serenaded the stars until tears of passion or sadness flowed. And then, in contentment, they pulled horse-cloth or sheepskin over their heads and slept.

But Orpheus, like Demeter, went through the refining fire of suffering.

Orpheus was the son of King Oeagrus of Thrace and the Muse Calliope. Taught by his mother and her sister Muses, he understood the arts of poetry and music as no mortal had ever done. Both men and beasts crept close to hear him play, and the trees bent down to him, and the rocks wept, and rivers stopped flowing to hear him. Apollo himself, God of Music, was touched and gave Orpheus one of his own lyres, in recognition of an almost divine skill. Orpheus thanked the god humbly, but in his heart he worshipped Dionysus, the god of his homeland.

Orpheus loved the wood-nymph Eurydice, and she loved him tenderly in return. But Aristaeus, a minor deity who looked after bee-keeping and the olive groves, lusted after Eurydice and tried to rape her in the vale of Tempe. Eurydice fled but in her flight she trod on a snake, which struck out and killed her. Her shade went down to the realm of Hades, leaving Orpheus in despair. He made up his mind to bring her back. With nothing but his lyre and his songs to help him he went to Taenarum in Laconia, where a cleft in the earth leads down to the Underworld.

On the banks of the Styx, Orpheus began to play. Charon, the grim ferryman, heard him, and, forgetting both duty and payment, carried him to the far bank where even Cerberus, the three-headed watch-dog, was lulled by soft sounds to sleep. Orpheus passed the Judges of the Dead, in the Fields of Asphodel, and came to Tartarus, to the court of Hades. When he had listened to the playing of Orpheus, and heard his request, the God of the Underworld made one concession, which was all his icy heart allowed, in recognition of the power of music. Eurydice could return to the land of the living on one condition: Orpheus must not look back at her until they reached the surface of the world.

They set out, through many terraces of pain and darkness. Eurydice followed the sound of the lyre and Orpheus was reassured by the slight rustle of her soft footfall. But as they approached the sunlit world he was no longer sure. Had she lost the way? Where was she? He turned to look back and caught her last agonized glance before Hades plucked her beyond the reach of his arms. The gates of Tartarus closed on her forever.

Bereft of love, Orpheus abandoned hope. His lyre fell from his hands and was taken by the gods into the night sky, as the constellation Lyra. In his despair, he was finished with women. Some say he turned to the love of men, the first among humans to do so; others say he became a celibate priest of Apollo. In any case, he no longer took pleasure in the orgies of Dionysus, and for this the Maenads could not forgive him. Once, when they were mad and heated, they came upon Orpheus in his wanderings. They wanted to correct him, to punish him, to repossess him. Each Maenad grabbed at him with lust and fury until, as had happened to so many others, he was torn apart. When they saw what they had done, the women of Dionysus tossed his head into the River Hebrus. But they could not stop the head from singing. Still singing, it was washed to the sea and came to rest at last on the island of Lesbos.

As the severed head drifted past many lands, nothing could stop it singing. It celebrated a mystery that no Maenad could destroy: it sang of the eternal power of music. As the head floated by, people in many lands heard it, at first with wonder, and then giving thanks from the heart. Out of the divine terror of the Dionysian rout, Orpheus brought them a new solace, the indescribable consolation of music.

Sedately poised above the slow-swaying rump of his horse, the lax reins loose on his knees, the carter still drew from his flute the free-flowing measures of an ancient dance. As he listened, Mantes was at peace, released for a little moment from the tension and struggle of daily living. He looked around. A mellow evening light lay on the empty land, and the uncouth northern faces softened with respect and gratitude.

– Part Two –

HEROES IN THE LANDS OF THE GODS

Boatmen

– 7 –

LIFE AND DEATH

THE WORLD is the gift of Ge, our Mother Earth. She created it, and made all things ready, before the coming of gods and men.

To each, a part was apportioned. High on Olympus, a heavenly place was prepared for the gods. Above mist and cloud, where human eye can penetrate no farther, is a realm of divine peace. No storms shake those sunlit peaks. The Four Winds of the world, feared by the gods for their unpredictable and limitless bluster, are safely caged below, on the floating island of Lipara. Aeolus is their keeper. Seated within the Cave of the Winds, he releases his charges from the hollow island, one by one, through a hole in the cliff. Above, in unblemished days, under golden palace roofs, the gods of Olympus feast and keep council, directing the affairs of man and nature. Their food, unfit for human mouths, is nectar and ambrosia. Instead of blood, the divine ichor runs in their veins. They are immortal.

Then there is the other race called human. In shape, these beings are like the gods. In desire, in intelligence, in feeling, they show their godlike qualities. But they live in a world of many trials, amid drought and cataract, dogged by grief and pain, and Death takes them in the end.

'We are tragic godlings,' Mantes often thought, as he sang the unfolding destinies of gods and heroes. 'We reach for divinity and fail.'

gods and humans are the children of Earth. In the first there was stone, or clay, or water – things of the Earth – and then suddenly there was man. How did it come about? From the time of memory, Ge was accompanied by certain youthful bands – the Cabiri, the Dactyls, the Curetes. Spirits or men, they came from Earth. Blood or semen, spilt on the ground in the course of divine struggle, opened the womb of our Mother. Once, the Sun-god, flying his chariot high above Phrygia, saw the Corybantes growing like trees out of the land beneath. In another place, under the ash trees, the Melioi men dropped to the ground like fruit.

Many lands claimed the honour of Earth's first human progeny. In his travels, Mantes heard many tales. The Boeotians boasted: 'The Titan Prometheus took our clay, which Ge provided, and moulded it to human form. Pallas Athene breathed into the form and it came alive. Look here, at Panopea, here are the clay shards left over from that first man.'

But other Boeotians disagreed: 'Everyone knows that our ancestor Alalcomeneus was the first man. He came out of the water, rising like a seal from Lake Copais.'

In Arcadia, they spoke of Pelasgus, their earth-born man, who taught his descendants to eat acorns, make huts of branches and wear a covering of skins such as simple folk still wear. Arcadia eventually had many people, but the island of Aegina gave birth to Aeacus only. He lived in lonely state until Zeus pitied him and turned the ants of the island into men called Myrmidons. Then Lemnos, or so it is said, brought forth Cabirus; Dysaules grew from the Rharian Fields of Eleusis, and Alcyoneus, first of the giant people, sprang from the ground of Pallene.

'It was not enough for Mother Earth,' an Athenian told Mantes, 'that animals and mere vegetables should possess the world. She made man out of her earthy body so that she could see intelligence at work, and feel the devotion of such beings. Of course, she chose to begin in Attica. Our Attic earth was pure and fertile ground for the generation of such a being, who would surpass all others in reason and give due worship to the gods. Cecrops was the first being of this kind, mortal but not yet wholly human, a man above but a serpent below the waist.'

But that claim got black looks from the people of Argos. Phoroneus was their first man, who had come to land out of the conjunction of the river and the sea. When Prometheus stole fire from the gods, Phoroneus taught the Argives how to use this gift. Armed with holy fire, they claimed to be the first people to emerge from the savage world of beasts.

It amused Mantes to hear all these old tales. Man, whatever he was, certainly had in his nature the wish to be first, and the need to be important.

But in all these histories there was one point of agreement. Prometheus, son of the Titan Iapetus, was the friend and champion of mankind. Prometheus, whose name means Forethought, was no enemy of the Olympian gods. During the War of the Gods, in which his brothers Atlas and Menoetius fought and suffered, Prometheus supported Zeus, because he knew the Thunderer's ultimate victory. The Titan could read the book of the Fates, but that was dangerous knowledge. He knew the secret Zeus most wished to hear: the goddess on whom, if they mated, Zeus would father a son greater than himself. So Zeus feared and distrusted Prometheus, and his suspicion grew to hatred when he saw that Prometheus was the protector of mankind. This new race was growing too proud. Humans began to set themselves against the will of heaven. They even dared to question the division of the sacrificial animals offered on the altars of the gods.

To test the case, gods and men came to Mecone and put the dispute to wise Prometheus to decide. Now Prometheus, who was secretly on the side of man, devised a trick. When he slaughtered the ox, and divided it, he hid the good meat in the bag of the belly but wrapped the skin and bones in a tempting package of fat. Then he offered the portions to Zeus. Either out of greed or in a desire to incriminate Prometheus, Zeus chose the package of fat. The choice was made. Ever after, in the sacrifice, mankind took the meat and the gods took the bones.

It is not wise to mock the gods. As for Prometheus, his punishment could wait. Zeus had plans for his suffering. But in the meantime, there was mankind. In his rage, Zeus withheld fire from the world. Men might have meat but they would eat it raw. But again Prometheus frustrated the will of Zeus. He climbed to Olympus and stole the heavenly fire, though no one saw him do it. Some say he took a live coal from Hephaestus' forge, others that he lit a torch from the flames of the Sun. Then he hid the fire in a fennel-stalk and took it down to man.

The moment of triumph is a moment of danger. Assisted by fire, man began to bind the forces of nature to his command, giving the race of humans a power that was almost divine. But when Zeus looked down and saw the lands below sparkling with useful flames, he felt a renewed fury and determined to send another test, to complete the life of man or to undo him. He would send a partner, an equivocal being in whom the gods placed both comfort and delusion.

Until this time men had existed without women. They came from Earth and lived on her bounty, without work, taking freely the produce of land and sea. Now Zeus ordered Hephaestus, the divine craftsman, to make a clay figure in the form of an Olympian goddess. Athene breathed life into the figure, Aphrodite gave it beauty, Hermes taught it cunning, the Graces and the Hours showed it the pathos and the wiles of womanhood. The figure walked forth, a living being called Pandora, whose name means All Gifts. This was the first woman. Hermes took her by the hand to the world below and presented her to Epimetheus, brother of Prometheus and the most unsuspecting of beings. Prometheus had warned his simple brother to beware gifts from the gods. But Epimetheus thought, 'What harm is there in beauty?' He gladly received Pandora into his household.

The gods had given Pandora beauty and grace. They had also given her a large earthenware jar packed with afflictions as yet unknown in the world. Disease and evil and cruelty and suffering were in the jar, and also old age and toil and hunger and weariness. The jar was sealed, but who can keep a secret from idle curiosity? Pandora was foolish and Epimetheus dull and without guile. Zeus had foreseen the inevitable result. All at once the jar was lying open and mischief was abroad in the world. Only Hope remained in the jar, caught under the rim, the one consolation left to mankind for the loss of innocence.

In his wanderings, many times Mantes had told this solemn history of man, in banqueting halls or sitting among the people in the agora.

'A curse on Prometheus,' a voice would cry. 'It is rash at all times to go against the gods. But to deceive the Thunderer twice! To cheat him of sacrifice, and then to steal fire! Prometheus did it for us, but why should we thank him? It was pride, it was sin. From these benefits come woe.'

All benefits have a double face, Mantes thought. Bad goes with good. Mankind has a choice but chooses blindly. The consequences are hidden. The Fates alone know the future. What can poet or prophet do except unfold for men and women the story of their own mortality?

'Listen,' he would say then, holding up his hand to still the protests. 'We cannot escape our history. We are fallen beings. In the Age of Gold, Cronus, father of Zeus, ruled the universe. Then men lived like gods, free from sorrow and toil, accepting the harvest of nature. After a time, they were gathered into heaven, as if into sleep, and their spirits became the guardians of the next generation. But this age passed and a new Age of Silver began, when Zeus, the son of Cronus, ruled the heavens. Men were not what they were before. In this age, people hardly developed beyond infancy, hiding in their mothers' skirts for a hundred years, then stumbling still immature to death. The altars were empty, the gods waited in vain for offerings. In disgust, Zeus swept this miserable race into the bowels of the Underworld, to become the spirits of the dead.

'Then, in the Age of Bronze, another race of men sprang up from the ash trees. Strong and fierce, they ate meat not bread, and bound themselves to Ares, God of War. In bronze armour, with bronze arms, they fought each other to extinction, and black Death carried them down to the cold hall of Hades. They disappeared and made way for a better race, the men like demi-gods of the Heroic Age. These fought and died by the seven gates of Thebes, in the land of Cadmus, and took ships to Troy and perished nobly in the dust of the plain. To some of these, in recognition of their courage and glory, Zeus gave a life after death, in the Elysium of the Blessed Isles, in a land of peace and plenty still under the kindly rule of Cronus.

'Finally, in the Age of Iron, came the people of the present, a time we know too well, full of wickedness and grief. Nor is the trial of mankind at an end, for things grow worse. Surely we shall see the time when degenerate babes will be born with a foot in the grave, with senile wrinkles and heads of white hair. Then oaths will mean nothing – we move towards it now! – might shall be right, and each man shall raise his hand against his neighbour. Then, when mankind is utterly abandoned, when the last good spirit retreats to heaven, when Reverence is shamed and even Indignation silenced, then Zeus will bring the inglorious human experiment to an end.'

'It is the fault of Prometheus,' the voices cried once more. 'He set us against the gods. He is the false prophet. He gave us meat we could not stomach. Let him suffer.'

Prometheus did not escape the revenge that Zeus had planned for him. Hephaestus summoned the Titans Bia and Cratus, whose names mean Force and Strength, and together they captured Prometheus and bound him fast to a mountain peak in Caucasus, far from the homes of men. Daily, Zeus sent an eagle to tear out his liver, and each night the liver grew again. His suffering was timeless, for Prometheus could not die. One thing sustained him against his tormentor. He alone knew the name of the goddess who was a danger to Zeus. And so for countless years the two opponents remained in tension, the Titan in agony, the Father of the Gods in unforgiving suspense. At last, an exchange was agreed. Heracles, travelling through Caucasus in pursuit of mighty deeds, was permitted to shoot the eagle and set Prometheus free. In return, Zeus was warned not to lie with Thetis, daughter of Nereus, lest he father a son greater than himself.

But the punishment of Prometheus did nothing to exonerate mankind. In all the years of his pain, men did not lose their insolence, and they discovered new ways to offend the gods.

In the Age of Bronze, when the world had fallen into a chaos of war and cruelty, Lycaon of Arcadia sacrificed a boy on the altar of Zeus. And when Zeus himself came in disguise to investigate this impiety, he was given at the sacrificial feast the guts of a youth mixed with the offal of sheep. Zeus was not deceived. He dashed the pot from the table and turned the family of Lycaon into wolves. Then he reflected further. Mankind had become irredeemably evil. Zeus resolved to destroy these loathsome beings in a great flood.

But Prometheus, whose foreknowledge still did not desert him, even with his agony on the Caucasian rock, sent a passing bird to warn his son Deucalion. 'Build an ark,' was the message, 'and go aboard with your wife Pyrrha, daughter of Epimetheus and Pandora, and wait there for the rising of the water.' Then Zeus opened the floodgates of heaven. Notus, the South Wind, roared, the waters piled up, overwhelming the lands and their peoples. Only a few fortunate ones escaped the deluge. Cerambus of Pelion turned into a scarab beetle and flew away. Megarus, founder of Megara, was led to the safe heights of Mount Gerania by the eerie calls of high-flying cranes. Dardanus, later prince of Troy, launched a boat of skins from Samothrace and drifted to the eastern shore as the swelling waters of the flood pushed Europe and Asia apart. These few survived. The little ark of Deucalion floated above the rest, over a waste of water and a drowned people.

After nine days the flood subsided and the ark came to rest on a mountain peak. It was Parnassus, or Aetna, or Othrys, or Athos – no one is sure. With thanks-givings Deucalion and Pyrrha stepped on the ground. But what a world! All around a woebegone land, drenched and seaweed draped, the houses silent, the altars cold. At once, Deucalion and Pyrrha made sacrifice to Zeus, in gratitude for safe delivery. Then they prayed to Themis, at her empty shrine by the River Cephissus, begging her to intercede with Zeus for the renewal of the human race. Zeus was touched. If one man and one woman were capable of such unforced humility and devotion, then there was something in mankind worth saving. Through the mouth of Themis, Zeus gave direction for renewal.

'Cover your heads in penitence,' she ordered Deucalion and his wife, 'and throw over your shoulders the bones of your Mother Earth.'

So they took Earth's bones, which are the rocks and the stones, and threw them over their shoulders. Deucalion's stones became men, and those thrown by Pyrrha grew into women. First of the new race, Deucalion and his wife went to Locris where Pyrrha gave birth to Hellen, a leader of men, destined to be father of all Greeks.

All-Seeing Zeus had ordained a fresh beginning. From the loins of Hellen came a new race of humans. They were people like lions, with spirits forged in iron, standing against the world as tall as trees. They honoured the gods and relit the sacrificial fires.

For a time all was well. The shameful Bronze Age passed, the Age of Heroes had begun. But in this world neither respect nor worship last, for man is always man, his own worst enemy.

But Mantes knew very well that heroes were not gods, however alike in beauty, intelligence and energy. 'We cannot avoid our mortality,' he thought. 'Thanatos, black-clad Death, closes all human eyes. Life twists and turns but leads both Achilles and the beggar to the kingdom of Hades. The shades of the dead let go of the world. Let them be buried well, for without a coat of earth or dust the Lord of the Underworld will not accept them. Pay Charon, the ferryman, with a coin beneath the tongue. Then Hermes will take them from the grave for the last journey. The facts of life are these: birth, and procreation, and death.'

Many hidden and dangerous paths led down to the Underworld – a cleft in a rock, a sombre valley, a ravine from which hot vapours swirl – at Aornum, or Taenarum, or by Lake Lerna. But the ordinary shades depart by one broad road, from the land of the Cimmerians, where the Styx and its four dread tributaries mark out the upper boundary of the Realm of the Dead. Acheron, Phlegethon, Cocytus and Lethe – the Rivers of Grief, of Fire, of Lamentation and of Forgetfulness – run into the Styx, the River of Hate. And here, at this border post of life, stands the Oracle of the Dead.

'It is the duty of the poet,' Mantes reminded himself, 'to find the truth about the gods. We must follow wherever they lead, even to the edge of the afterlife.'

In the spirit of enquiry he journeyed north to consult the priest of the Oracle on the banks of the dark river. Leaving Thesprotia, he entered a land of gloom, for Helius did not come this way but drove the sun's chariot far to the south. Mantes stumbled through a wild country. Zephyrus, the West Wind, came rushing from the nearby stream of Oceanus. The wind battered the hills and tugged at the scant vegetation, shaking rain on the chill ground in which few things grew. The land, raw and bitter, looked spent, like a life near its end. Gaunt bones pushed at the bare and weathered skin.

The people of this land, the Cimmerians, lived with Death as a neighbour. Charon tethered his boat at the foot of the mountain. To these people, Charon and Death were indistinguishable – the servants of Hades. They collected souls. Their shadows, huge and suffocating, hung over all lives. On his journey, in a hut barely lit by a guttering rush-candle, Mantes heard an old woman lay out a corpse. As she rubbed the body with herb-scented oil she harried Charon with a thin protesting wail:

'Why are the mountains dark, and why so sad?
Is it the wind at war, or does the rain-storm scourge them?
It is not the wind at war, it is not the rain that scourges,
It is only Charon passing, passing through with the dead.
He drives the youths before him, and drags the old behind,
And tender babes hang from his saddle-bow in a line.'

Beyond the mountain pass, in the heavy plain, Mantes saw dull waters, grey as lead. Where Acheron and Cocytus flowed into the Styx, he saw Acherusia, the Lake of the Dead. Where did it end? The low, treacherous shore petered out into ghost-haunted marshlands. On the bank, beneath a tall white rock, stood the grove of willow and poplar sacred to Persephone, Queen of the Dead. This was the point of departure. Below in the palace of Erebus, in the palace of black halls, Hades waited.

'He reaps his harvest, which is never short,' sighed the priest of the Oracle, standing with Mantes in Persephone's grove. 'Hades is ever anxious for souls.'

Plucked from the grave by Hermes' guiding hand, shades of the dead began the voyage below. With muffled oar-strokes the ferryman glided slowly from the bank of life to the shore of death where Cerberus, the triple-headed hound, kept guard, to see that none returned. Then the road led down to the Fields of Asphodel, where shades of no distinction dwindled out eternity, existing so close to nothingness that the meanest penury on earth seemed kingly in comparison. Here the dead came to justice and accounted for their lives before the three Judges of the Dead. Aeacus judged Europe, Rhadamanthys judged Asia, and stern Minos was arbiter of doubtful cases. Most shades, too ordinary for special praise or blame, went no farther, destined to rest uneasy in the Fields of Asphodel. A few passed on. For heroes, Zeus had decreed the place called Elysium, or the Isle of the Blessed, a land set apart from Tartarus, bathed by Oceanus. There, under the rule of Cronus, in a perpetual summer, those who had dared and accomplished much contemplated the memory of their great deeds, in an afterlife without toil or pain or worry. But the wicked were condemned to the deep prison of Tartarus, a pit of torment enclosed in metal walls.

'Such punishments,' said the priest in a voice of awe, 'for those who set their hands against the gods! Our own spirits tremble at the thought. Think of Ixion and Tityus, who tried to force themselves on holy goddesses. Remember Tantalus and Sisyphus, whose deceit and trickery enraged the gods.'

Drunken Ixion tried to ravish the Queen of Heaven herself. But Zeus sent a pillar of cloud in the shape of his wife and caught Ixion copulating with air. The Father of the Gods threw him down to Tartarus, to revolve forever on a wheel of fire. Next to him in Tartarus lay Tityus, pegged to the ground. He had tried to force himself on Leto, mother of the holy twins Artemis and Apollo. Two vultures plucked at his liver, rooting in the cavity of his body for all eternity.

Simple justice for simple villains. But Tantalus, once the darling of Olympus, won his terrible fate for betraying the confidence of the gods. He, who had once eaten at the divine banquets, stole the sacred nectar and ambrosia and peddled abroad the divine table-talk. He stole the golden dog that had watched over the infancy of Zeus and hid it on Mount Sipylus. Then, most awful, either in madness or thinking himself divine, Tantalus fed the gods a dish of human flesh made from Pelops, his own butchered son. For this, he went to Tartarus, fixed in an infernal lake. Cool water lapped his chin and the laden boughs of fruit trees grazed his head. Yet he could not rid himself of thirst and hunger. When he dipped his head to drink, the water retreated to a black hole. When he reached for fruit, the wind tore it away.

Who would shed tears for such a wretch? Sisyphus of Corinth deserved some sympathy perhaps. But the gods are implacable. Unlucky Sisyphus fell between Zeus and his love. Amorous Zeus had hidden the nymph Aegina, and her angry father, the river-god Asopus, could not find her. But Sisyphus, who was as clever as he was rash, knew the hiding place. In return for a spring of good water in Corinth, Sisyphus told Asopus where to go. The rough river-god, who was no respecter of the Olympians, set out after the lovers and Zeus had to turn himself into a stone to avoid him.

Then Zeus visited his wrath on Sisyphus. He ordered Hades to seize him and drag him to Tartarus in chains. But wily Sisyphus persuaded Hades to test the chains himself, and when the god did so Sisyphus snapped the locks shut. In consternation, Ares rushed to release Hades, for war is friend to death, and the bodies of the slain were piling up on earth. Once more Hades grabbed Sisyphus but the Corinthian had another trick to try. He whispered to his wife to leave his corpse unburied, for none could go to the Underworld without the rites of burial. But Zeus had spoken. What the Fates had in store for Sisyphus could not be deflected forever. In Tartarus, a huge stone awaited, standing at the foot of a steep hill. With straining muscles and heaving breath, Sisyphus strove to push the boulder to the crest. But every time the stone neared the summit, the hill rolled it back again.

Mantes knew that these warnings from the realm of

Hades had been brought to Odysseus in the Age of Heroes. Odysseus had stood here also, in Persephone's grove, seeking word from the dead. Circe, the witch, had told him what to do. With his sword he dug a pit, a yard in width and length. Then he poured libations of milk, honey and wine, and sacrificed a ram and a black ewe. He bent their heads down towards Erebus and slit their throats and the dark blood flowed into the pit.

'This was the trench, it happened here,' said the priest of the Oracle, pointing out to Mantes the very spot.

'Yes,' the priest continued, 'the road back from the Underworld is not impossible. Orpheus found it and lost it. Even Cerberus can be bribed with honey cake. Ghosts return, released for a time by Hades, from compassion or sardonic humour. They come to drink the blood, the red liquid of life, which has gone from their bodies and for which they crave.

'Here, look at this place. Here is the outline of the pit. When Odysseus' blade struck, the dark blood flowed and the shades of the dead flocked upward from the deep. In disordered haste they came, with their agonies still upon them: maidens and young men cut off from love, the suffering old, girls with broken hearts, troops of warriors bearing wounds like open mouths, slain men encased in bloodstained armour. They howled and cried, but what could they do? The red blood had fled from the pale forms. Sinews no longer held flesh and bones together.

'In the grave, the shade leaves the body as a dream takes wing. The spirits who crowded Odysseus at the trench were as insubstantial as the phantasms of our sleep. They told their news and departed with a sigh. As they left one shade called out – the shade of Lord Achilles himself – "Odysseus, prince of cunning, remember this: I would rather be the least slave to the least of men on earth than lord of all the lifeless throng." Grim Hades chuckled. The race was run. The gods decreed that only Death was the victor in the end.'

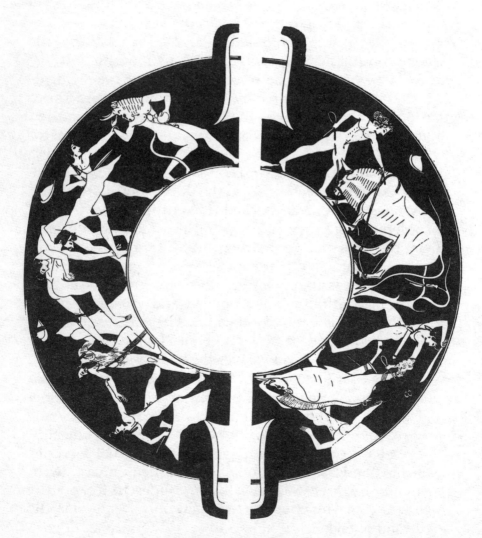

The Contests of Theseus

– 8 –

FOUNDATIONS

THE LISTENERS had become sleepy in the noonday heat. A few, in the shadows, were settling into a quiet doze. All around, eyelids were drooping. Suddenly, at the top of the table, the patriarch stirred and jerked his head upwards.

'No more about the gods,' he yawned. 'We've heard those songs to distraction. The town snoozes, the dog lolls under the step to escape the sun, even the flies have stopped dancing in the sunbeam. But chance has set us in your path. Wake us up. Our hearts are generous and we are not without wit. There, beside you, are the things great Homer himself called for when he sang his songs: the table spread with bread and meat, fruit plucked fresh from the tree, the mixing bowl of wine. The steward will fill your cup again. Come, O teller of tales, give us human stuff. Sing of men not gods. What kind of beings are we, a race so mixed and crossed, dark and fair, soldiers and thinkers, merchants and farmers, seafarers and mountain-men, but all speakers of the same tongue? Where did we come from? Sing of our brotherhood, our history of glory and shame, our rage to become everything that man or woman might be. Tell us, I beseech you, who are we?'

The long afternoon stretched away, waiting to be filled, but Mantes wondered where to begin. The question was not easy. To arrive at man, one must start with gods. The storyteller began, as so often, with Zeus in love.

There was a king called Agenor who went from Egypt to Tyre, in the land of Canaan. The blood of the east ran in his veins. Ancient dynasties had bequeathed him power and wisdom. His people combed the ports of the large, land-locked sea. Agenor prospered in Tyre and part of his prosperity lay in his six children. He had five sons, and a daughter named Europa.

Now, Zeus had little business with these lands at the far edge of his dominion. Other gods reigned in those parts, old inscrutable deities, some with the head of a hawk or a cat, all jealous of their offerings and their worship. But occasionally the all-seeing eyes of Zeus ranged over the far shores. To the south were the burning lands. Helius singed these countries bare, and turned the Ethiopians black in the sun. More distant still, almost unimaginably far, in forests like nightmare, pigmies fought with cranes. But as his eye roved over the land of Tyre, Zeus saw a city rich with trade, good crops in the fields, fat cattle driven out to pasture where the river met the shore and where the women of the palace also came, to bathe in the cool of the day and to play amid the peaceful herds. Europa, flower of all the maidens, went there with her women and Zeus saw her. His eye rested there.

He turned himself into a young bull, white and hand-some and with a fine sweep of horns. He blew down his nose, frisking playfully among the herd.

'Tease me,' the bull called to the girls, 'stroke me, gar-land me. Why bother with lambs and heifers? Am I not beautiful?'

And he kicked his heels, and made a little mock charge, and showed such high spirits that the hearts of the maidens shuddered with apprehension and delight. They collected sprigs of laurel and made garlands of wild flowers and gave them to Europa, to hang about the neck and the horns of the bull.

'Mount me,' the bull whispered as she did so, 'climb on

my back. Do not be afraid. I'll take you on a journey such as you've never seen.'

Europa moved like one in a trance, for was it not the voice of Zeus that spoke through the bull's mouth? She mounted on the broad back and immediately the bull rushed to the sea. Frightened though she was, Europa knew she must cling on. She wound her arms around the muscular neck. The pretty animal was no longer a gentle plaything. The beast had mastered her.

The bull swam west, breasting quiet waves, which did not resist the passage of the god. He swam until he reached the southern shore of Crete. Then he came to land and set the girl down and shook the sea from his coat. The form of the bull had served its purpose and suddenly Europa saw a god standing before her. Zeus led her to a willow grove and possessed her under the trees, where a rill of spring water ran into the bay. In time, she gave birth to three sons: Minos, Rhadamanthys and Sarpedon.

Nothing lasts. Why should a god dally away time with a mere human? It was enough that Zeus had shed greatness on Europa. He had taken her, and blessed her with children, and then he left her. But Europa, though abandoned, had been touched by divinity and her children had some mixture of heaven's blood in their veins. Asterius, the King of Crete, willingly married Europa and adopted her children, who grew up to be proud and powerful lords. As a test of manhood, they entered into the quarrels of the land, which was a wild, rich place, standing in the trade routes of the world. Many people were attracted there, many half-related strangers – Pelasgians, Aeolians, Ionians – turbulent tribesmen, adventurers who might grab a patch of scrub and found a kingdom.

War is the ambition of young princes; it is also their game. The island of Crete was too small for the sons of Europa. Very soon, their differences became irreconcilable when they fell out over the good-looking youth Miletus, with whom all three princes were in love. They came seriously to blows, and in this tumult Miletus fled to Caria, on the Asian coast, where he founded a city which bore his name. Rhadamanthys and Sarpedon soon followed him into exile, defeated and driven out by their brother Minos.

The world was a wide place, full of empty spaces waiting to be colonized by restless men. Sarpedon went to the land ruled by his uncle Cilix from Tyre and lived, by the grace of Zeus, three times longer than man's allotted span. He fought and conquered the Milyans and set his seed in the kingdom later called Lycia. Rhadamanthys, when he left Crete, drifted among the islands of the southern Aegean, where he was well received out of honour for his parentage. He began to govern these islands, and he made such good laws and ruled with such justice that Zeus made him a Judge of the Dead in the Underworld when he died.

When Minos had driven out his brothers, he made himself, by force of arms, the heir to Crete. He married Pasiphae, daughter of Helius, and had many children, among them the girls Phaedra and Ariadne. He was a bold and successful warrior, and when Asterius died Minos did not hesitate to claim the throne. But the people muttered.

'This man is not one of us,' they said. 'He is only an adopted son. Why should we obey him?'

'The gods have marked me,' Minos replied with disdain. 'I bask in their smiles. How can you deny me my destiny?'

And to prove his claim, he boasted that whatever he asked of the gods would be granted. At once, this was put to the test. He made ready an altar on the beach and prayed to Poseidon to send an animal worthy to be sacrificed. When he had finished his prayer a powerful white bull swam out of the sea, which the people took to be a sign from heaven, and they accepted Minos as their king. But Minos deceived Poseidon. The white bull was such a large and splendid animal that Minos could not bear to kill it. He added it to his royal herd and substituted an inferior beast for the sacrifice.

Mantes paused. He reflected how the crooked heart of man leads him into conceit and self-delusion.

'Pride is the father of stupidity,' he said with sudden

venom. 'He who judges himself greater than his fellows must still learn that he is less than the gods. Minos had begged a favour, then he had broken a promise. In truth, Crete had seduced him. He wanted it too much. Was it not the place where Zeus was born? He wanted that kingship. He wanted the gold, the trade, the energy of the people, the fury of the warriors. He wanted the bull that came from the sea. His desire overrode his reverence for the gods, and for this he had to be punished.'

When Minos kept the white bull, and did not repay it in sacrifice, Poseidon sent an appropriate punishment. He inflicted Pasiphae with an unnatural lust so that she longed for the bull and wanted to couple with it. She was sick with desire, but how could she accomplish it? The act was not only inhuman, it was also hardly possible. Driven to distraction by the itch of this unmentionable vice, she went in secret to Daedalus, the greatest craftsman and most ingenious inventor in all mankind.

Many years before, Daedalus had been banished from his native Athens. He had killed his nephew in a fit of jealousy because the boy, Perdix, was beginning to challenge the skill of his uncle. Perdix had at a very early age made a potter's wheel and a set of compasses. He invented the first saw, taking as his model the rows of teeth in a crocodile's jaw. But his precocious talent went no further, for his uncle Daedalus seized him and threw him over a cliff. The gods had mercy on the innocent youth and changed his falling body into the partridge which now bears his name. Daedalus was not saved by this transformation. The Athenians arraigned him for murder and took him before the court of the Areopagus, which condemned him to exile. After many journeys Daedalus wandered to Cnossus, in Crete, where he was welcomed by Asterius. He settled and married and had a son called Icarus, and very soon he began to repay his welcome through the extraordinary skill of his hand. A palace of a thousand rooms rose slowly out of his fertile imagination. He planned fortifications and harbours and roads. He made engines of war and strange inventions that did the work of many men. He built painted birds that whistled and sang, and he contrived toys that danced to please the ladies. Daedalus was as valuable to Minos as he had been to Asterius. The great craftsman had the cunning and the talent to give substance to Minos' dreams for his kingdom.

When Queen Pasiphae came to him, with her tale of illicit passion, Daedalus promised to help. To him, it was only one more technical problem, a test for his ingenuity. He constructed a frame in the form of a cow and covered it with a fresh hide so that it looked and smelt right. He arranged that the queen could fit herself in the rear of the beast and stand with her legs thrust into the hollow legs of the cow. Then moving smoothly by means of levers and wheels, the imitation cow, with Pasiphae concealed inside, was taken to the pasture and set amid the king's herd. In a while, the white bull mounted and Pasiphae had her lust satisfied. Later, when she gave birth to a monster with the body of a man and the head of a bull, Minos went to an oracle for advice. The child-monster, that thing of shame, could not be destroyed, for it was the judgment of Poseidon on the king's impiety. Under the command of the oracle, Minos ordered Daedalus to build a vast, impenetrable maze, or Labyrinth, in which the Minotaur – as the monster was called – could be locked up and hidden from sight.

Minos learnt his lesson. He bowed down before the gods and became a great and just ruler, instituting laws that Zeus himself approved. Crete grew in power and fame. With wise government, strong armies and plentiful trade it began to dominate those lands overlooked by the Holy Ones of Olympus. Every nine years King Minos was called to the summit of Mount Ida, to account to Zeus for the progress of the laws. The Father of the Gods was well satisfied. The country was rich and peaceful. The bronze giant, Talos, constructed for Minos by the divine smith, Hephaestus, guarded the coasts of the island, routing enemy fleets with a barrage of boulders and smothering unlucky invaders in its fiery breast. In old age, Minos could look back on a life lived, for the most part, in accordance with the will of the gods. Heaven forgave him his lapses. And though he died meanly, pursuing an unworthy vengeance against Daedalus, Zeus granted him the recognition of great achievement. In the dark Kingdom of Hades, he joined his brother Rhadamanthys as one of the Judges of the Dead.

But the stain of sin persists. In the heart of Crete, in the mystery of the Labyrinth, lay the secret evidence of shame. The Minotaur grew and lived on, prowling alone in its unfathomable precinct. So long as it lived, it shadowed the mind of the people with guilt and uncertainty. It was a forbidden question. What was the Minotaur? None had seen it. What was the nature of the Labyrinth that contained the monster? Had the cunning of Daedalus put that beyond all conjecture?

Mantes the storyteller stopped speaking and there was silence in the hall as the audience felt a momentary touch of horror.

'I heard a wise man say,' a voice ventured at last, 'that the Labyrinth was nothing more than the double-headed axe that struck down all who dared to enquire too far.'

'Rather, I believe,' said another who was no friend to Crete, 'that it was the palace of a thousand rooms at Cnossus in which King Minos gave birth to his policy of blood and conquest. That was the monster.'

'Perhaps,' Mantes murmured, 'it is only the metaphor for a malign dance, the to and fro of the human heart in which the monster of vanity and presumption lurks perpetually.'

There is no triumph without envy, no conquest without pain, no loss without anger. The power of Crete was hard to withstand and hard to accept. Minos ruled ninety cities. His ships went to the edge of Oceanus, where Atlas held up the sky. The chariot of Helius, flying from sunrise to sunset, barely covered the royal lands. But the success of Minos made others afraid. Daily, in the sharp light of Attica, the people of Athens saw the shadow of the Cretan empire creeping towards them, obliterating the older forms of life and property, obscuring boundaries with bloodstains. What did Crete want? The Athenians looked about them. They saw a modest patrimony: a plain of stones and olive trees and small fields standing amid bold, bare hills; a coast of rugged promontories and wind-blown beaches, turning westward at its southern tip into the sheltered haven of the Saronic Gulf. But the Athenians were not deluded. From the summit of the Acropolis, Pallas Athene had taught her people some of her wisdom. They knew that conquest comes chiefly from the will to power. The spoils of possession are incidental.

The death of a son gave Minos his chance. Androgeus was killed by Athenians, causing Minos to make a punitive expedition against Athens. He subdued the city and imposed a penance on the citizens. Every nine years, seven youths and seven maidens were taken from Athens to Cnossus as an offering to the Minotaur. The Labyrinth swallowed them and none ever returned.

Though Athenians claimed to be as ancient a people as any in the world, springing as they did from the earth-born Cecrops, in this time of Cretan strength Athens had long been weak and troubled. The gods had given with one hand and taken with the other. The kings were not fort-unate. Their families were torn by violence and jealousy. A daughter was snatched away by the North Wind. Other children, defiled by rape and cruelty, were transformed into a hoopoe and a nightingale and a swallow. King Erechtheus, in a moment of victory, was slain by Poseidon. Princes were driven into exile. Plots were afoot continually. Frequent rebellion let no man rest. At this critical time, in answer to the king's prayer, a champion was born.

Aegeus, son of the exiled Pandion, had reclaimed the throne of Athens but he had no children. Unwilling to leave a disputed succession in a turbulent kingdom, he went to Delphi to consult the oracle. The reply, as so often, was mysterious.

'Do not untie your wine skin,' the priestess told him, 'until you reach your home on the Acropolis.'

On his return journey Aegeus puzzled over this message. At Corinth, the sorceress Medea offered to help. Her magic would produce him a son if he would promise her a refuge in Athens, should she ever need it. The King agreed and she cast a spell. But at Troezen, King Pittheus saw the meaning of the oracle: Aegeus must not lie with a woman until he reached home. Now Pittheus saw a chance to influence the affairs of Athens. That night, he made Aegeus drunk and sent him to the bed of his daughter Aethra. In the morning Aegeus feared what might have happened, and he averted his face from the girl.

He mumbled an apology. 'Last night my wits were not with me. How went the night?'

'The night went as it usually goes,' replied Aethra, 'when man and woman lie naked in one bed.'

Then Aegeus swore her to silence and told her what to do if she gave birth to a son. If the boy, when he was old enough, could remove a large rock under which Aegeus would leave his sword and his sandals, then Aethra should send this son to Athens, to claim his inheritance. In nine months a boy was born, as Medea had promised, and he was named Theseus.

Theseus grew up tall and strong, like a tree rooted in rich earth. He was first in the footrace, the most powerful and agile in wrestling and boxing. His arrow split the exact centre of the target, and none could withstand his sword thrust. He feared nothing. Even Heracles, who visited Troezen and scared all the populace with his frown and his battle array, and with the snarling lionskin that hung from his shoulders, did not intimidate young Theseus. The boy, barely seven years old, took an axe from the woodpile and prepared to defend himself. When he reached sixteen he was already a man. He dedicated a lock of hair to Delphic Apollo and easily lifted the rock that revealed his father's gifts. When his mother had explained their significance, Theseus got ready to go to Athens.

He did not go by the short and easy sea route. He went by land, thirsty for experience and adventure. The world was a dangerous place. Cities were at war. The highway was bandit-ridden. Oppression grew fat on victims of turmoil. But Theseus slung his father's sword from his belt, slipped on the sandals and set out cheerfully. He breathed the invigorating air from the Gulf. In the clear light, the distant peaks of Cithaeron and Helicon summoned him onwards. He was eager for challenges. He wished to test himself against the hardship of the world as his great kinsman Heracles had done. He did not have to wait long for his first test.

At Epidaurus, by the sacred grove of the divine healer Asclepius, he was waylaid by Periphetes, the club-man, who robbed travellers with his huge brass-bound club.

'The grove of Asclepius is a place for healing, not for deadly wounds,' said Theseus with contempt. He wrenched the club from its owner and dispatched him with one blow.

Theseus kept the club, which was a murderous weapon very useful against brigands, and went on his way. Soon he was challenged again. Near Corinth, where the isthmus narrowed, he encountered Sinis, the pine-bender, who tore men apart between two springy pine trees. Theseus tied him to his own trees and watched him flung skywards. Next, he turned aside to hunt and kill a savage Grey Sow that was ravaging the land around Crommyon. Refreshed by the chase, Theseus returned to the highway and put an end to Sciron, a rogue who compelled travellers to wash his feet on the cliff top of Megara and then kicked them into the sea. Passing on to Eleusis, Theseus swept the wrestler Cercyon from the path, dashing him to the ground with such force that his skull was broken. Then, at the border of Attica, with Athens in sight, Theseus met Procrustes, the stretcher. This robber lured travellers to his house, overpowered them and bound them to a bed. Those who were too short were stretched, and those who were too long were chopped to fit. Theseus made Procrustes measure up to his own bed, and he did not survive.

At the gates of Athens, Theseus purified himself in the River Cephissus for the blood spilt on the journey. Then he entered his father's city looking so majestic that masons working by the road were amazed, even alarmed, by his presence. Truly, they thought, someone almost godlike has come to Athens.

But only Medea, instructed by her black arts, knew who this stranger was. Years before, while Theseus was growing up in Troezen, Medea had fled from Corinth and taken up the refuge that Aegeus had promised her. She bewitched the King, and married him in his old age, and gave birth to a son, Medus, whose way to the throne would be cut off if Theseus claimed his own birthright. So she prepared a feast for the attractive stranger and poisoned his wine-cup with wolfsbane. As Theseus lifted the cup, the pattern on the hilt of his sword was revealed and Aegeus recognized it at once. The king knocked the cup from Theseus' lips and overwhelmed his son with tears and rejoicing. In the midst of this happy hubbub, Medea wrapped herself in a magic cloud and disappeared.

After the tears and the laughter Aegeus grew suddenly solemn. He addressed Theseus in a serious, worried voice. 'My son,' he said, 'you come just in time. My nephews, the fifty sons of Pallas, are in open revolt. Heracles, that mighty and incalculable man, has inflicted a great trial on us. For reasons we do not know, he has abandoned a gigantic Cretan bull at Marathon and it is now laying waste the country. But worst of all, we approach the moment we most fear, when we must send our seven youths and seven maidens as a cruel tribute to Minos and the Minotaur.'

On the road from Troezen, Theseus had tested and proved his heroism. He had served his apprenticeship. Now he was ready to accept the greater troubles of his father's land. The first two calamities facing Athens were easily put right. Theseus ambushed the sons of Pallas, defeated them and made them beg for peace. Then with bare hands he wrestled the bull of Marathon and dragged it to the Acropolis, as a sacrifice to Athene, holy patroness of the city.

But the tribute of youths and maidens demanded by Minos was a far more difficult problem. Theseus had no definite plan. He decided to go to Crete as one of the condemned youths and then he would see what happened. In any case, he was confident of success.

'We set out with black sails of woe,' he promised Aegeus, 'but we will return under white sails of joy.'

The ship left in gloom, pulled dejectedly towards Crete by the black sails. Even the weather was an enemy, the ship being battered around by the furious breath of Notus, the South Wind. In Crete, Minos stalked the harbour wall, scanning the seas with impatience, and as soon as the ship docked the king went aboard to inspect the victims. His eye was taken by one of the girls and, wishing to enjoy her before she died, he ordered his soldiers to lead her to the palace at Cnossus. In a rage, Theseus intervened. A martyrdom for Athens was at least a brave and dignified death. But to be deflowered first, as a matter of sport, was a cause of shame. He accused Minos of mean-spirited brutality unworthy of a king. The two exchanged angry words, arguing about their rival claims for nobility. Minos called on his father, Zeus, and in reply the Thunderer made the sky roar and the lightning flash. Theseus invoked the name of Poseidon and called on him as a witness.

'If the Earth-Shaker is such a friend,' Minos challenged, tossing a ring into deep water, 'let him help you recover that ring.'

At once, Theseus dived into the sea and plunged down to the palace of Poseidon where he was gracefully received by the sea-goddess Amphitrite. Dolphins were sent to scour the sea bed for the ring, which was soon found and returned. Then Amphitrite gave Theseus the ring and sent him ashore with an added favour from Poseidon: the god granted Theseus three wishes, to be used at any time in the future.

Despite the sign of divine favour, Minos did not intend to spare Theseus. He was paraded with the other Athenians in the streets of Cnossus, for the Cretans to stare at. But among those who stared was Ariadne, the king's daughter, and her heart went out to the bold and handsome youth who strode towards doom as if he had not a care in the world. She fell in love with him at first sight. That night, having bribed the guards, she visited Theseus in prison. On the morrow the Minotaur awaited him in the Labyrinth. But if Theseus would flee with her and marry her, she would show him a way to escape the maze that Daedalus had once taught her. He promised, and then she gave him a large ball of string and directed him how to use it.

Next day, when the sun was hardly up, the fourteen Athenians were driven into the Labyrinth. Acts of tyranny are best done in silence, when the face of the world is turned aside. Theseus tied one end of the string to the gatepost and then set out into the maze. He walked in gloom, for the slanting light was still creeping down the high, narrow walls. All around was stench, decay, whitened bones, the debris of an abandoned world. Theseus did not know where he was going but he carefully unwound the ball of string as he penetrated deep into the maze. In an innermost recess he came upon the Minotaur sleeping on a bed of rotten straw. He took the monster in a brutal wrestler's hold and slowly strangled the life out of the beast. Then he consecrated the dead body as an offering to Poseidon.

Quickly, Theseus retreated through the twists of the Labyrinth, winding in the string as he went. At the gateway, where his fellow prisoners were still cowering in fright, he rallied the Athenians and gave the signal for Ariadne to open the doors. There was no guard. No one had ever escaped from the Labyrinth. In the greatest haste, Ariadne led the Athenians to the harbour where she had prepared a ship for their flight. They tumbled aboard, the rowers strained at the oars, and the ship was away before the alarm could be raised.

The sail was hoisted and the ship fled to Naxos. Theseus judged that they were now safe from pursuit, so all the ship's company went ashore to rest. But when the time came to sail on, unaccountably Ariadne was not on board. Who knew what had happened? Was this the sudden forgetfulness of a man burdened with the larger cares of his people? Some have whispered that there is a fatal carelessness in the nature of heroes, a brutal egotism that makes them discard others like shelled peas. They do not understand the anxieties and fears of ordinary humans. Awe-inspiring Heracles himself was guilty of casual and selfish cruelty. Others exempt Theseus from blame. They say that Dionysus saw Ariadne on Naxos and cast a spell on her, so that he could keep her to himself and bed her at will.

The ship sailed from Naxos to Delos, the birthplace of Apollo, where Theseus stopped to sacrifice and celebrate games in honour of the Divine Twin. Then the Athenians swooped joyously on a good wind towards home.

For a long time, old Aegeus had watched daily from the cliff, anxiously searching for the white sail that would indicate safety and success. But Theseus, in his hurry to reach Athens, forgot his promise. The king saw the ship approach with its black sail still spread. In despair, Aegeus threw himself into the sea, which is now called the Aegean in his memory.

'Consider,' said Mantes after a pause, 'the turning moments in great affairs. Failure and success chase each other, rolling end over end like tumblers at a village fair. Consider Daedalus, Minos, Theseus himself – three mighty men. The Fates bore them up to a dizzy height, then pulled them down with a sudden hand.'

Mantes looked around the dinner guests. The meal had ended and there was an air of content. Idly, some were cracking almonds and walnuts, while others peered with more hope than expectation into the lees of the wine-cup. Mantes saw no reason not to go on.

'When Theseus escaped the Labyrinth, King Minos knew who to blame. Only Daedalus understood the workings of that maze. He had given the secret to Ariadne. So Minos arrested Daedalus and clapped the inventor into his own Labyrinth, and for good measure threw his son Icarus in with him. Daedalus had plenty of time to contemplate his fall: from chief artificer of Crete to prisoner in one step. But Daedalus was not the man to pine. Every physical event had an answer, he felt, somewhere in the ferment of his ingenuity. And lying on his back between the narrow walls of the maze, watching the sky and the shifting clouds and the freedom of the birds, he suddenly saw the answer.

'At once, he set to work, using the left-over pieces and the forgotten material of the Labyrinth. He gathered feathers, cord and wax, and he made two pairs of powerful wings. He strapped one pair to his own arms and the other to the arms of Icarus. Then he gave his son instructions: "Fly not too high, for the fierce flames of Helius will melt the wax; nor too low, for the sea-spray will drench your feathers and bring you down." But who can restrain youth? The freedom of the air was an intoxication that Icarus could not resist. He flew higher and higher, towards the eye of the sun, until the wax melted and he fell like a broken doll into the arms of the sea. Cautiously, Daedalus flew on, leaving Crete far behind, until he came to rest in the Sicilian land of King Cocalus. And there he stayed, in mourning and in retirement.

'But vengeful Minos was not finished with Daedalus. He was determined to pursue him to the edge of the world. He took a ship and roamed the seas, for he did not know where Daedalus' wings had taken him. Wherever he landed he gave the ruler or governor a test which he knew could only be solved with the help of Daedalus. The test was to pass a thread upward through the interior of a spiral seashell. No one could do this until Minos came to

Camicus, in Sicily, where King Cocalus dribbled a thin trail of honey through the shell and then tempted an ant to draw a thread along that path to a hole bored in the tip. Minos guessed at once that Daedalus had devised this method and demanded the surrender of the great inventor. But the daughters of Cocalus, whom Daedalus had amused with many pretty toys and trifles, plotted with their friend against Minos. They ran a pipe into the bath-house, and when Minos was soaking away the cares of his long journey they scalded him to death with boiling water, or, some say, with hot pitch.'

The great king died ignobly, and within a generation his empire was in ruins. The Fates swung the balance. Crete had been too high, too proud. Down it went, and Athens rose into the glare of history.

At first, Theseus could afford to crow over the death of his most powerful opponent. When he returned from Cnossus, and became king, Theseus set out to unify and strengthen his land. When he met opposition, he executed his enemies out of hand. Then he joined the twelve rival clans of Attica into a federation under the leadership of Athens and founded the All-Athenian Games to celebrate the occasion. He made treaties and agreed borders. To settle a long-rankling dispute, he put up a large board at a certain point on the isthmus of Corinth. On one face it said: 'All this way is the Peloponnese.' And on the other face: 'All this way is Ionia.' To the south, pointing towards Crete and the lands of almost forgotten histories, was the old Greece. To the north and east, pointing towards Macedonia and Asia, was the new Greece. In this second direction lay the dangerous future. And Theseus himself had to face this danger. His policies stirred the Amazons into war, and these fierce warrior women swept out of the frozen north to besiege Athens from their camp on the hill of Ares. With difficulty, Theseus defeated them and kept their Queen Antiope as a prize.

After a time, when he had secured his borders, Theseus could turn to the civic affairs of his city. He wrote a constitution for Athens, which set out the duties for the city fathers and the magistrates, for the tradesmen and for the farmers. He minted the first coinage, stamped with the bull of Poseidon. His heralds went throughout Greece, inviting people of talent and energy to go to Athens and become citizens. Even the Delphic oracle acknowledged the success of Athens. The priestess prophesied that Athens would ride the current of history as easily as a pig's bladder rode the sea in a storm.

Theseus had a son called Hippolytus whose mother was the Amazon Antiope. But when Theseus wanted to ally himself to Crete, he set Antiope aside and married the Cretan princess Phaedra, sister of Ariadne and daughter of Minos. It is ever this way with great men, that policy dictates marriage, not love. Hippolytus grew up in Troezen, a severe, silent youth who was devoted to chaste Artemis and lived only for hunting. This coldness towards love was an affront to Aphrodite and she decided to make him suffer. When Hippolytus came to Eleusis to perform certain rites, looking so haughty and unapproachable in his ceremonial robes, Aphrodite made sure that Phaedra saw him. At that moment Eros, God of Desire, released his malicious arrow and Phaedra's heart was lost to Hippolytus.

Phaedra tried to restrain her infatuation. But growing haggard and sleepless she gave way to desire and wrote to Hippolytus, admitting her incestuous passion. Hippolytus rejected her in disgust. Then Phaedra took a despairing revenge. She wrote a note to Theseus, incriminating Hippolytus, and hanged herself from the lintel of the doorway. When Theseus read the letter his mind nearly burst. He called to the gods and cursed his son – he hardly knew what he was doing – but Poseidon heard him and counted the curse as one of the three wishes he had granted to Theseus below the sea. As Hippolytus fled from his father's wrath, whipping his horses into a furious pace along the seashore, Poseidon sent a bull charging out of the waves. The horses bolted in terror, the chariot broke its axle on the root of an old gnarled olive tree, and

Hippolytus was thrown and dragged to death in a tangle of reins and splintered wood.

When the wheel of fortune begins to turn, who can arrest it? After his wife and son were destroyed, Theseus plunged into senseless activity, as if heroic energy alone could save him. He made a wild wager with Peirithous, the madcap and dangerous King of the Lapiths, that each would find a new bride from among the children of the gods. Together, they raided Sparta and abducted Helen, the twelve-year-old daughter of Zeus and Leda, whom Theseus intended to marry when she came of age. But Peirithous, with overweaning vanity, coveted not the child of a god but the goddess Persephone herself, the Queen of the Underworld. Theseus wanted nothing to do with this plan, but he was bound to the Lapith king by oath. The two of them entered Tartarus through the chasm at Taenarum and attempted to lay hands on the dark queen. But Hades easily forestalled them and fixed them to the Seat of Forgetfulness, from which they could not tear themselves. And there they remained for four years, guarded by serpents and lashed by Furies, until Heracles used his superhuman strength to pull Theseus free. Peirithous was left to eternal damnation, for his insolence could not be forgiven by the gods.

And Theseus?' the patriarch interrupted. 'The gods abandoned him also?'

The fringe of the sky was now touched with pink by the declining sun. The dog had shaken off its somnolence and was wrinkling its nose hungrily towards the kitchen door. Inside the house, the hall was brushed with shadows. It was almost time to light the lamps. The patriarch rose briskly. He had neglected the household for long enough, and in any case he thought he knew the end of the story.

'It is truer to say,' Mantes replied, 'that Theseus abandoned the gods. We get no more than we deserve. What king deserves to prosper if he leaves his kingdom adrift for four years? While Theseus was imprisoned in Tartarus, those strong men Castor and Polydeuces – the Dioscuri – invaded Attica and rescued their sister Helen. They left the land in an uproar for which Theseus, rightly, was blamed. When he returned at last, the citizens turned on him angrily and drove him into exile. Menestheus, a grandson of Erechtheus, was installed in his place. Theseus sailed for Crete. But a storm blew his ship to Scyros where King Lycomedes received him with every mark of respect. This king, however, was secretly in league with Menestheus, who feared Theseus and would be glad to see the end of him. As the great hero was taking the air on the cliffs of Scyros, exchanging many gracious words with Lycomedes, the king gave a signal to his servants and they kicked Theseus into the sea.'

The patriarch nodded sadly. 'It is not wise to trifle with the Holy One. There is a limit assigned to humans that none may go beyond, not even a hero, not even Theseus.'

Bellerophon, on Pegasus, Kills the Chimaera

– 9 –

HOMELAND

A SINGLE GREEK,' the dying poet once told his successor Mantes, 'can take any number of barbarians and make Greeks of them. For it is not so much the person, but the land that teaches. The earth, the mountains, the rivers, the valleys, the fields, the very stones are Greek and make Greeks in their turn.'

In his long life, the old poet had searched every corner of the land for its spirit and its story. At last, this illumination had come to him and then he was content, waiting for black-robed Death to call him away. In a hut of mud and rubble, roofed with reeds, he lay patiently, his arms crossed, uneasy breath puckering his toothless mouth. Outside, in the Eurotas valley, harsh light flooded over the laurels and the pebbles of the desert, as it had always done. The Taygetus mountains raised their five powerful fingers into the heavens. In dark fissures, a few silver threads glittered where streams shrank into the ravenous ground.

'Listen,' the old man said urgently, 'the land conquers all and makes us what we are.'

Later, as he buried the poet in the white, sorched soil of the Peloponnese, Mantes pondered on this motherland that nourished her children from such a thin, famished breast.

From the first, it was a land born under disadvantage, under a god's curse. Both Hera and Poseidon claimed it, but when Inachus, the local river-god, awarded possession to Hera, Poseidon afflicted the land with aridity, thirst and perpetual summer drought. Io, daughter of Inachus, was only the first of many who were driven away in suffering but ached to return. Who can forget the realm of the gods?

Io was loved by Zeus, who turned her into a white heifer to deceive Hera. But Hera tethered the heifer in an olive grove at Mycenae and set hundred-eyed Argus Panoptes on guard, until Hermes cut out the eyes of the sleeping Argus and released the heifer. Then angry Hera chased Io through the world in a cloud of gadflies. Maddened by stings the white heifer plunged across the sea – the Ionian – which now bears her name and fled as far as India, where she turned tail and was pursued by the biting flies into the valley of the Nile. At last, she was allowed to rest. Restored to human form, Io looked homeward in vain. She settled by the Nile and had to console herself with the birth of Epaphus, her son by Zeus.

Her children, and the children of her children, ruled in North Africa until, after many years, the brothers Aegyptus and Danaus came to blows. Warned by an oracle to beware of Aegyptus and his fifty sons, Danaus took his fifty daughters and sailed for Argos, the land of his ancestors. The king and the people of Argos laughed at the pretention of this newcomer and his claim to the land. But when a wolf came in the night and killed the Argives' leading bull, the people accepted this sign and made Danaus their king. Soon, the sons of Aegyptus came in arms, besieged the city and demanded the fifty daughters of Danaus in marriage. Danaus pretended to agree. But when the youths came to their brides in the night, the women stabbed their husbands to death, all except for Lynceus who was spared by Hypermnestra because he had not taken her maidenhead.

Danaus died without a son and the kingdom passed to Lynceus. The exiled branches of the family were reconciled and joined. The descendants of Io had come home to their roots which, now as ever, lay deep in the hungry, blood-stained south.

Within two generations the family enmity that had separated brothers on African soil was repeated, in Argos, after the birth of the twins Acrisius and Proetus. These two fought even in the womb. And their later rivalry was so bitter and intense that they decided to share the kingdom.

Acrisius took Argos while Proetus went to Tiryns where seven giant Cyclopes built for him, out of stones too large for even a mule team to shift, massive walls and battlements brooding over sombre gates and arrow-slits and lanes like pools of darkness.

Acrisius, having only a daughter called Danae, went to consult an oracle about his lack of an heir. But the oracle gave him a grim reply: 'You will have no son, yet you will die by your grandson's hand.' In haste, Acrisius locked Danae away in a dungeon, with fierce dogs to guard her. But ever-roaming Zeus, who noted her beauty and her distress, appeared to her as a shower of gold. Penetrated by this radiance, Danae gave birth to a son called Perseus.

Afraid to kill his own daughter, Acrisius locked mother and child in a wooden chest and tossed it into the sea. After drifting with wind and current the chest lodged on the isle of Seriphos where a fisherman walking the shore heard, among the clamour of the sea birds, another despairing wail, which proved to be the bawling of a baby. He broke open the chest and took the sea-bedraggled couple to King Polydectes who, touched by the beauty of Danae and the sorry pathos of her child, took them into his household.

The king's feeling for Danae grew into love, but she rejected all offers of marriage and Polydectes hesitated to push the matter further because Perseus had grown into a formidable youth, quite capable of defending his mother. Anxious to be rid of the threat posed by the young man's strong arm, Polydectes thought of a stratagem.

He announced that he had set his heart on another woman and demanded from each of his nobles the gift of a horse, so that he would not appear at her door as a poor, unworthy suitor. Perseus, ashamed that he had neither horse nor gold to buy one, recklessly promised to bring Polydectes something beyond horses, beyond even gold, 'even, if the king so wished, the head of the Gorgon Medusa'.

Polydectes accepted immediately.

Alone with his task, with nothing but his courage and his foolhardiness to help him, Perseus resigned himself to the will of the gods. Fortunately for him, Athene heard his rash boast and took him in hand. The grey-eyed goddess was an enemy of Medusa. This Gorgon, one of three sisters, was a monster born of the sea, a female with batwings that creaked like leather, claws of brass, the tusks of a boar, and a head that sprouted venomous snakes. One glance into the eyes of Medusa turned animal or human to stone. All this was hateful to Athene, the source of wisdom and reason. To her, the Gorgons were foul emanations from a time of primordial perversity, so she willingly taught Perseus how to go about his dangerous task.

First, she showed Perseus how to tell Medusa apart from her sisters and gave him a polished metal shield, so that he could approach the monster with head averted, homing in on the reflection in the shield. Then Hermes provided an adamantine sickle, able to cut a ship's hawser with one blow. And as further aides in this desperate venture Athene promised Perseus a pair of winged sandals, a magic pouch, and Hades' cap of invisibility. But to fetch them, Perseus would have to seek out the Graeae, for only those strange wizened hags, with but one eye and one tooth between them, knew where to find the nymphs who kept these objects.

The Graeae refused to talk, dribbling age-old malevolence from shrivelled gums. Then Perseus deftly intercepted the eye and the tooth as they passed hand to hand and wrung from the hags the information he needed. Collecting the sandals, the pouch and the dog-skin cap from the nymphs, Perseus was carried aloft by the sandals and flew swiftly to the far northwest land of the Hyperboreans, where rain swept over the cold barrens, scouring into ugly shapes the beasts and humans turned to stone by the eye of Medusa.

The three Gorgons were asleep in a wilderness of mud. Looking steadily into the reflection on the shield, Perseus picked out Medusa and severed her neck with a single stroke, making sure that the head with its corona of writhing snakes dropped into the magic pouch. Immediately, the body of Medusa burst like rotten fruit and from it sprang the winged horse Pegasus and the warrior Chrysaor who clasped a golden sword. These were the children of Poseidon, for the lust of the sea-god was pressed even on monsters. As Pegasus winged towards heaven, Perseus, too, was in flight. Behind, he heard the howling of Stheno and Euryale, the Gorgon sisters, but he was safely hidden from their eyes by the cap of invisibility.

A thing of evil became, through the intervention of holy Athene, a force for good. Medusa's head, with its glance that turned to stone, had spread around it a frozen world of suspended shock and grief. But safely contained in the magic pouch it became, in Perseus' hands, a weapon more powerful than any sword or bow.

Speeding from the land of the Hyperboreans along the north shore of Africa, Perseus paused to show the head to Atlas, turning him into a mountain of stone and thus relieving the weary Titan from the burden of the sky. Aware now of the potency of his prize, Perseus flew high and fast to the east. Over Libya, drops of Gorgon blood dripped from the pouch and became the poisonous snakes of the desert floor. Then, turning homeward, Perseus saw below by the cliffs of Philistia a young woman chained to a rock at which the waves snapped hungrily. On the cliff-top a man and a woman strained their eyes towards the horizon.

When Perseus landed he discovered that King Cepheus and his wife, Cassiopeia, were watching over their daughter Andromeda. Queen Cassiopeia had foolishly boasted that she and her daughter were more beautiful than the Nereid sea-nymphs, and to teach her some modesty Poseidon was sending a sea-monster to devastate the land. Only the sacrifice of Andromeda to the monster would save the kingdom.

Was it the maiden or her danger that struck Perseus' heart? In any case, she was beautiful, and a cause for pity, and Perseus determined to save her and marry her. He mounted once more into the air and flew over the approaching monster, which was distracted by the shadow on the water of this strange winged beast. Suddenly the monster found itself confronted by the Gorgon's head and was turned to stone. When Perseus had released Andromeda – the marks of the chains are still shown on the rock-face at Joppa – he took the girl from the reluctant arms of her parents and carried her back as his wife to the island of Seriphos.

On the island, Perseus found that his mother, Danae, was still in danger from Polydectes who, in final exasperation, had locked her in a temple to choose between marriage and starvation. The king was feasting with his friends when Perseus came to the palace. A ragged, drunken cheer greeted the new arrival.

'Hail to the Gorgon-slayer!' they cried insolently, for they were quite sure that he had failed. 'What's in your pouch, young braggart? Is it as empty as your promises?'

Slowly, with closed eyes, Perseus raised Medusa's head from the pouch, held it high, and then lowered it quietly to its resting place. When he opened his eyes, and looked round, instead of feasting guests he saw only a circle of stones.

Danae was released, the sandals, pouch and cap returned to the guardian nymphs, and the head of Medusa presented to Athene to wear on her aegis. Then Perseus left Seriphos for Argos, the land of his birth. King Acrisius heard of his approach and, remembering the oracle, fled to Larissa in panic, abandoning his kingdom to the grandson he feared but did not know.

It was Perseus' country, but what did he know of it? The ground, when he landed at noon, crinkled with heat and the sun seemed to ooze molten drops from the dusty needles of the pines. The vertical sun gave no shadow, no cloak to hide the extreme nudity of the earth. The lines lay on the land like knife-cuts. A heart-stopping emptiness blazed with light almost too powerful to look on. A shepherd boy, who seemed to be elbowing a thorn tree for its thin cover, threw languid stones at a goat nosing the ground for the last green twig. Something in the absolute clarity, in the shock of an unavoidable, simple choice between surviving and not surviving, welcomed Perseus home.

Now, it happened that some time later Perseus was invited to Larissa to take part in the funeral games of the dead king. In these games, when Perseus came to throw the discus, the wind caught it and carried it far into the crowd where it struck and killed an old man whom Perseus had never seen before. A bystander informed him that the dignified old man was well known in Larissa, a certain Acrisius, once King of Argos.

What the oracle foretold was fulfilled. It is vain to outguess the gods, vain to try to outrun the Fates. To be Greek is to accept no hiding place.

Mantes thought: 'Perseus was born in Argos. In some sense, both the desolation and the stark choices were in his blood. But what drew princes from across the seas? Gold, women, horses? Yes, all of those. Also the sense of a worthy but dangerous trial, the wish to do heroic acts under the very eyes of the gods. Amber, rubbed on a sleeve, will attract the wayward scraps, rich or poor.'

Pelops was the millionaire of Asia Minor, a son of the doomed Tantalus, who had tried to feed human flesh to the gods. But for all his riches he was restless. The mines of Mount Sipylus, in his native Lydia, gave him wealth but he could not settle there. He remembered the blood-guilt of

his father. That was the past. The future was the unimag-
inable weight of Asia that pressed on all sides. Perhaps
also he dreamt of water, and of compact lands with known
boundaries and known gods. He had drifted to
Paphlagonia, to Phrygia, on to the Black Sea and then back
to Lydia. Nothing satisfied him. Then he heard of the fame
of the beautiful Hippodameia, daughter of King
Oenomaus who ruled Elis and Pisa in the territory of
Arcadia. He decided to marry her. He would gladly settle
in a new land, near the playground of the gods at Olympia,
and he would not look back.

Many princes had wooed Hippodameia but her father
was afraid to lose her. Some said he was in love with her
himself, for Oenomaus set each suitor a stern test.

The king was a passionate horseman, with such a high
regard for horses that he forbade his subjects to mate mares
with asses, even though they needed mules to work their
farms. He challenged each suitor to a chariot race and laid
out a long and difficult course between the sacred precinct
at Olympia and the altar of Poseidon on the isthmus of
Corinth. Hippodameia was the prize to be won and
Oenomaus had no doubts about victory, for the horses of
his chariot were a gift from Ares and swifter even than the
North Wind. Losers in the race had their heads chopped off
and their bodies thrown to scavengers. Already, as a warning to others, twelve heads were fixed to poles by the
palace gates.

Blood shed in a great cause, where armies clashed and
noble acts were done – that was something the gods could
accept. But the cruel slaughter of hopeful young men was
offensive to the Holy Ones. They suspected, with disgust,
that Oenomaus intended to build a temple of skulls. So
when Pelops prayed to Poseidon for help in the race, the
Earth-Shaker responded and sent him a golden chariot
pulled by immortal horses. And to make victory doubly
sure Pelops also bribed Myrtilus, the king's charioteer,
offering him the first rites of the wedding night if
Oenomaus were defeated. Myrtilus agreed, for he too

loved Hippodameia. As he prepared the king's chariot, he used wax instead of metal pins to secure the wheels on the axle.

In the fury of the race the wax melted, the wheels fell off, and Oenomaus was flung to his death. Pelops won Hippodameia but he did not keep his promise to Myrtilus. Instead of granting him the first rites of love, Pelops had him hurled into the sea. As he drowned the deceived charioteer laid a bitter curse on Pelops and all his house. For the second time, a curse lay heavy on the southern lands.

But had the gods heard Myrtilus, for he was not without guilt himself? Pelops married Hippodameia and inherited the kingdom. Slowly he extended his power through all the land that spread out below the narrow collar of the Corinthian isthmus until he ruled the whole territory, governing his new domain from the old city of Argos. And having unified the country he renamed it the Peloponnese in his own honour. The years blessed him with fame and even greater riches, and with many children among whom were the sons Atreus and Thyestes.

These two were enemies from birth. They were destined to quarrel, if not for a favourite toy, then over a game of knuckle-bones; if not over a woman, then for a kingdom. When Atreus married the Cretan princess Aerope, Thyestes made it his business to seduce his sister-in-law and together the lovers plotted against Atreus. After the death of Pelops, when the brothers became rivals for the throne of Mycenae, Thyestes saw a way to his ultimate triumph. He would take both wife and kingdom from Atreus.

Atreus had vowed to offer his finest lamb as a sacrifice to Artemis. But when his shepherd brought him a lamb with a golden fleece, he was astonished and could not bear to fulfill the whole sacrifice. So he compromised with the goddess. He slaughtered the lamb at the altar and made Artemis a burnt offering of the meat, but he kept the golden fleece and hid it away in a chest. It seemed to him to be a true emblem of royalty. But Aerope knew what he had done, and she stole the fleece and gave it to her lover, Thyestes.

Soon afterwards the question of the kingship was debated before the people of Mycenae.

'I am the elder,' said Atreus, 'but that is not enough. Kingship is a sacred office. Let it go to him whom the gods favour. I claim that divine favour by right of a golden fleece, which I alone possess.'

Thyestes smiled. 'That indeed is a remarkable sign. I agree that he who has the golden fleece is divinely blessed and he should be king.'

Then Thyestes produced the fleece and his brother, defeated by his own words, gave up the kingdom to him. But Zeus, Provider of Justice, was not satisfied with this trickery. He sent Hermes with a message for Atreus.

'Challenge your brother in this way: "If the sun runs backwards will you give up the kingdom?"'

The proposition was ridiculous and Thyestes accepted with amusement. Then Zeus ordered Helius to turn his horses at midday and drive the chariot of the sun back east, to the stables of the dawn. Thus the anger of Zeus was made known. In shame, Thyestes abandoned the throne and went into exile.

Old wounds fester. When Atreus learnt all the wrongs done to him by his wife and brother, he brooded on their crimes and planned revenge. After a while he pretended to be reconciled to Thyestes and tempted him back to Mycenae with the offer of a half-share of the kingdom. Then he welcomed his brother with a gruesome feast. He forced several of Thyestes' children to leave the refuge of a temple sanctuary, butchered them, and cooked them in a stew which he served to his brother.

Thyestes ate with good appetite.

'You have eaten well, my brother,' said Atreus.

'Truly, it was a tasty dish,' Thyestes replied.

'You are satisfied? Then let me show you the rare ingredients of such a fine stew.'

Then the heads and the hands and the feet of the slaughtered children were brought in on silver platters and set before their father.

Vomiting with horror and grief Thyestes called on the gods for justice and fled once more from Mycenae. He went first to Delphi, to ask the oracle what he should do, and he received a reply that was almost worse than his present torment: 'Your son by your own daughter shall avenge you.'

Desperate for revenge and feeling helpless to avert what the Fates ordained, Thyestes went on to Sicyon where his daughter Pelopia was a priestess of Athene. Disguised in a mask, he waylaid her at night and raped her. She gave birth to a son called Aegisthus.

Now the curses began to bite home in the unlucky land. The great scheme of crime and punishment slowly unfolded. The country withered with disease and famine. Strange omens appeared, beasts with two heads, wells flowing blood, trees bursting with sudden flame. Princes roamed land and sea looking for victims, for scapegoats, to test the edge of their swords. Agamemnon and Menelaus, sons of Atreus, searched for their uncle Thyestes with murder in mind. Aegisthus, when his family history was revealed to him, sent a bloody sword to Atreus, to trick him into believing that Thyestes was dead. In the celebration that followed at Mycenae, when Atreus was off his guard, Aegisthus took the same sword and slit Atreus' throat.

Vengeance began to pall. Men stumbled in the weary round of killing. Atreus had been killed and Thyestes died. Aegisthus was banished. King Agamemnon reigned in Argos. The Furies were satiated and, for the moment, the parched land drank no more blood of family hatred and revenge. But the curse of Myrtilus – the long-echoing and oft-repeated curse that sped to the very summit of Olympus – was not yet expunged.

Not far from Argos, to the north, a young prince set out from Corinth. Going east, on the cliff-top path, he went by ragged fields of barley, stones marooned in a sea of wild flowers, small olive trees as old and seamed as the face of time. His feet, brushing the herbs, raised pungent scents. At his back, bleak mountains stood sharp in the sun, the peaks still capped with snow in the early summer. All around he was aware of land set in an emerald-glitter of water, an untamed land-mass burnished ruddy in the sun, pinched at the isthmus by two seas out of which rose cliffs, bluffs, capes, gulfs, and the confusion of a thousand islands.

Often he looked back, as if to commit home to memory. Nothing escaped the light. Every detail was clear, reinforcing the solemnity of leave-taking. Bees cast their drowsy spell, a few swift birds scouted the inshore waters. A donkey, standing stubborn and still as a grey rock in the midst of restless, grazing wild horses, twitched just the tip of its tail. In a tiny patch of shade a boy held a young goat in his arms, both asleep.

Prince Bellerophon went slowly on, his steps heavy and reluctant. He was going into exile and parting was as painful as a spear-thrust.

Bellerophon had killed a kinsman in a brawl and he was fleeing from Corinth. It was a piece of misfortune, but misfortune dogged his family. His grandfather was Sisyphus, he who had tricked the gods and paid for his temerity in the torments of Tartarus. His father, Glaucus, was torn apart by his own maddened horses in a chariot race at the Isthmian Games. Carrying his burden of ill-luck, Bellerophon fled to the court of King Proetus in Tiryns where he hoped to begin his life again. But misfortune still followed him.

In Tiryns, Queen Stheneboea fell in love with him at first sight, and when Bellerophon rejected her advances she accused him of trying to seduce her. Proetus believed his wife but dared not kill a suppliant, for that would bring down on him the revenge of the Furies. So he sent Bellerophon with a sealed letter on an embassy to King Iobates of Lycia, in Asia Minor. Iobates was the father of Stheneboea, and the letter said: 'Kill the bearer.

He tried to violate she who is your daughter and my wife.'

Iobates had no wish to kill this strange prince, but he had to do something out of respect for his son-in-law. After much puzzlement he thought he saw a way out of his predicament. He would send Bellerophon to destroy the Chimaera, a grim maker of widows and orphans, a fire-breathing monster that was part lion, part goat and part snake. Either Bellerophon would kill the monster, or the monster would kill him. For the king, either course had something to be said for it.

Before he set out Bellerophon consulted a soothsayer who advised him that his task would be easier if he caught and harnessed the winged horse Pegasus. This was no easy matter. What human could hope to bridle a semi-divine beast, born of Poseidon and Medusa? Despondently, Bellerophon looked for Pegasus. The horse was not at its usual home on Mount Helicon where, with a stamp of a hoof, it had brought forth the spring called Hippocrene, the sacred fount of the Muses. Pegasus had flown to the Acrocorinthus where it grazed amid the swift and ferocious wild horses of the isthmus.

Unable to approach the winged horse, Bellerophon gave up for the day and went to rest in the temple of Athene. He prayed in the courtyard, and then he slept. In this sleep Athene appeared to him in a dream and placed in his hands a celestial bridle. When he awoke the bridle lay on the ground beside him. From a short distance, Bellerophon threw the bridle over the neck of the wary horse. With one last thrash of anger Pegasus pawed the ground, causing the Peirene spring to gush, and then he stood quietly, waiting to be handled. Bellerophon mounted and flew to Lycia where the Chimaera withered the country from flame-breathing nostrils. High above, Pegasus swooped from out of the sun while Bellerophon transfixed the monster with deadly arrows.

When Bellerophon returned in triumph to Iobates, the king was still not satisfied. The hero and the winged horse made a powerful instrument of war which Iobates was determined to use. Bellerophon was sent to defeat the Solymians and the Amazons and to repulse an invasion of Carian pirates. His only defeat came from a band of Xanthian women who advanced upon him with skirts raised to their chins, forcing Bellerophon to abandon the field out of modesty.

At last, Iobates was convinced that Bellerophon was innocent of the charge from Tiryns. He produced the letter from Proetus, and when Bellerophon had explained the true circumstances of Stheneboea's jealousy the king asked forgiveness and gave Bellerophon his daughter Philopoe in marriage. Bellerophon became king in time, and he still kept Pegasus in his royal stables.

Although he prospered Bellerophon could not shake off the shadow of his pest. He ruled in Lycia but he was a man of Corinth, city of Sisyphus' sacrilege and Glaucus' pride, bold city of licence where a thousand priestesses ministered to the rites of love in the temple of Aphrodite. In the perfumed, shaded courtyards of the temple lewd and many-breasted Astarte had taken refuge from her eastern home.

Cruel and unlucky acts were woven into the tapestry of Bellerophon's kingship. He killed Stheneboea out of revenge, throwing her from the back of high-flying Pegasus. Deaths came suddenly, his own children being struck down in their prime by war and illness. At last, Bellerophon himself succumbed to pride, his father's sin, the sin of Corinth. He mounted Pegasus and drove the horse towards the summit of Olympus, as if he himself were divine. Zeus, God of Retribution, stung Pegasus with biting insects so that the winged horse bucked high in the heavens and threw Bellerophon from its back. Alone, Pegasus continued to Olympus where Zeus harnessed the magic horse to his thunder-cart. But the flights of mankind, though they might aspire towards the gods, can never mount that high. Disgraced Bellerophon fell into a thorn bush, broken and crippled, and limped away far from the eyes of men.

At first, lands are empty, possessed only by the weather and the beasts, under the eyes of the gods. Then, suddenly, there are humans. Space waits to be filled. An obscure destiny drives the feet of mankind onwards. Who knows where they are going? Each person yearns for some condition, some unknown resolution, that will ease the heart. But the gods dispose.

When Zeus abducted Europa, and Agenor saw his daughter disappear into the sea on the back of a bull, the king could not know where she had gone. He sent his sons to scour the earth for her return. Phoenix searched diligently along the North African shore, then he came back and founded the kingdom of Phoenicia. Cilix travelled to Asia Minor and stayed, giving his name to Cilicia. Thasus, discovering some gold on an island, claimed it and called it Thasos. Cadmus wandered with his mother, Telephassa, first to Rhodes, then through the islands of the Cyclades and Dolopes to Thrace, where Telephassa took ill and died.

Not sure how to go on, Cadmus went to Delphi to question the oracle. The priestess told him to look for Europa no more, for having found the land of All-Seeing Zeus he had, in a sense, also found Europa. Now he was to follow a cow with a moon-mark on its flank and to build a city where the cow lay down to rest. It was an invitation from Apollo to become Greek, and how could Cadmus reject the will of the god? On the road to Phocis, Cadmus found a cow with a moon-mark in the herd of King Pelagon and drove the animal east into Boeotia, a land unknown to him. After they had travelled far without a pause the cow lay down near the River Asopus. It was a pleasant spot for a town, on a hill flank overlooking the green of the river valley.

Once its task was done, the cow's life was forfeit to the gods. But collecting water for the sacrifice, the men with Cadmus were killed by a dragon guarding a spring sacred to Ares. Cadmus was forced to crush the head of the dragon with a large rock. After the sacrifice Athene appeared and ordered Cadmus to gather the dragon's teeth and sow them in the ground. At once, an army of fierce warriors sprang up, clashing their arms and quarreling. These were the Sparti, the 'Sown Men'. Cadmus threw stones among them and they began to brawl, accusing each other of assault, hacking at each other until only five were left alive. Tired of killing, the five survivors acknowledged Cadmus and helped him build a city, at first called Cadmeia but which later became Thebes.

For a while all went well. Cadmus founded a civil society, teaching the rough farmers of Boeotia an alphabet he had brought from the east. By the grace of Zeus, he married Harmonia, becoming the first human to wed a child of the gods. And the Olympians themselves attended the marriage feast in state. Athene wove the wedding robe. Hephaestus made a golden necklace as a gift. Demeter brought seed-corn for the fields, and Hermes gave Cadmus a lyre.

But Ares, the rancorous war-god, had not forgotten the death of his dragon, even though Cadmus had atoned with eight years of servitude. Because of this hatred by Ares, Dionysus, in an inspired fit, foretold a violent and blood-spattered future for Thebes. Cadmus and Harmonia were rescued from calamity, but at the cost of being transformed into spotted serpents. Children of the royal family suffered and died. Foolish Semele looked on Zeus in his glory and perished. Pentheus was torn apart by Maenads. Ino and her husband, Athamas, were driven mad by Hera. Laius, taking refuge at the court of Pelops at Pisa, offended heaven by abducting the son of his host. The crown of Thebes rested on uneasy heads.

Laius, when he became king, married Iocaste, but wished to set her aside after an oracle warned him that his son would kill him. Iocaste, however, made Laius drunk and lay with him and gave birth to a son whom Laius exposed on Mount Cithaeron with a spike through his feet.

But the boy did not die. A shepherd found him and took him to King Polybus of Corinth who, having no child of his own, adopted him and named him Oedipus, or 'Swell-foot', because of his damaged feet.

One day, when Oedipus was grown up, a Corinthian taunted him for being a bastard. In distress, Oedipus went to Delphi to question the oracle, but the priestess drove him away in horror.

'Do not pollute this holy place,' she cried, 'for you are destined to kill your father and marry your mother.'

Knowing no other family and city than those of King Polybus in Corinth, Oedipus got away from there as quickly as possible and fled to Boeotia. At a narrow pass, where the road went through the Divided Ways, Oedipus found the path blocked by King Laius in a chariot, though neither man knew the other.

'Make way, peasant,' the king shouted.

'My birth is as good as yours,' Oedipus answered. 'I stand firm.'

'Then try to withstand this,' cried Laius, whipping the chariot forward so that a wheel ran over Oedipus' wounded foot.

'Violence begets violence,' roared Oedipus in a rage. And he hurled his spear, striking Laius with a lucky hit and killing him.

When Oedipus arrived in Thebes the news of the king's death, by an unknown assassin, had preceded him. The city was in an uproar, for it was already suffering from the ravages caused by the Sphinx. This winged monster, part woman and part lion, devoured all travellers who could not answer its riddle. And now the king was dead. Creon, the regent, harried by two problems, tried to solve them both by offering his widowed sister Queen Iocaste in marriage to anyone who would rid the land of the Sphinx.

Full of the confidence of youth, Oedipus accepted the challenge and confronted the monster.

'What,' said the Sphinx, getting ready to feast on yet

another foolish man, 'goes on four legs in the morning, two in the afternoon, and three in the evening'?

But Oedipus had the answer at once. 'Mankind, which crawls on all-fours as a baby, walks upright in maturity, and leans on a staff in old age.'

Angry and surprised, the Sphinx spread its wings and flew away. Some say that it dashed into the rocks and killed itself out of mortification. But Oedipus was left to claim his reward. In all ignorance, he married his mother, Iocaste, and took the throne of the father he had recently murdered.

Though the sins were unconscious, the gods could pardon neither incest nor patricide. They sent plague and famine on the land and spurned the sacrifices of the people. Then the oracle said: 'Banish from your midst the murderer of Laius.' But who was this person? The old king had been killed long ago, in cloudy circumstances, at a crossroads far from home. The puzzled citizens called on the blind prophet Teiresias, begging him to help them. First, said the prophet, one of the Sown Men who had built the city must die for it. When he heard this, Menoeceus, father of Iocaste, threw himself from the walls.

'Menoeceus has done well,' Teiresias continued, 'but it is not enough. There is another, a descendant of Cadmus, who has sinned deeply. Our king, Oedipus, though he does not know it, has killed his father and married his mother.'

Parts of this dreadful story were confirmed by Queen Merope in Corinth, and another part by the aged shepherd who had found the infant Oedipus on the mountain. When they learnt all this, and saw what they had done, Iocaste hanged herself and Oedipus put out his own eyes. Then in rags and ashes, with only his daughter, Antigone, to guide him, Oedipus was driven from the gates of Thebes.

Banished by Creon, Oedipus cursed his own sons, Eteocles and Polynices, who watched him go without remorse, and wandered blindly away, led by faithful Antigone. Pursued by the avenging Furies who would not let him rest, he made many painful journeys until he came, tired and defeated, to Colonus in Attica. He was finished with life. At the grove of the Eumenides he made a final offering to the Furies and died, still hand in hand with sorrowful Antigone.

After the exile of Oedipus, Eteocles and Polynices agreed to share the throne, ruling alternately, a year at a time. But at the end of the first year Eteocles refused to give way to his brother. Polynices went to Argos in a rebellious frame of mind, married the daughter of King Adrastus, and started to plot against Thebes with the king's help.

Adrastus gathered a powerful war-party to force Eteocles from the throne. This alliance of champions was known as the Seven against Thebes. Only the prophet Amphiaraus stood back from the campaign, foreseeing blood, grief and eventual failure, until Polynices bribed his wife with the golden necklace that Hephaestus had made for Harmonia. Continually nagged by his wife with accusations of cowardice, Amphiaraus set out with reluctance, but first he ordered his sons to kill their mother, if he did not return, and then to take revenge themselves on the city of Thebes.

At the walls of Thebes, Tydeus, one of the Seven and a favourite of Athene, blew the herald's trumpet and issued the challenge to Eteocles. The seven generals took up position before the seven gates and the siege began. Inside the walls there was great fear until the blind prophet Teiresias prophesied a Theban victory if a prince of the royal house would sacrifice himself. Creon's son offered himself up, dying on the walls in full view of the enemy. But the Argives were not impressed. They attacked fiercely. One of the generals, Capaneus, scaled the walls, exulting that not even Zeus could stop him. In a moment, the skies split and Zeus struck him down with a thunderbolt. Tydeus, mortally wounded, begged Athene for help. Since he was her favourite she came quickly with an elixir of life but discovered him, raging like a rabid dog, eating the brains of his enemy Melanippus. The goddess turned on her heel and left him to die.

With the tide of war running against the Seven, and most of them dead, Polyneices offered to settle the matter in single combat against Eteocles. Both were killed in the duel, leaving the Theban defenders triumphant. The army of the Seven scattered and fled. Amphiaraus drove his chariot away from the battlefield, but the earth opened and swallowed him. When King Adrastus saw that he alone had survived of the Seven, he mounted the winged horse Arion and flew in haste to Argos.

Thebes was saved, but at what price? Both princes lay dead and the care of the people was thrust once more into Creon's hands. He surveyed the ruined walls and desolate fields, feeling a burning resentment. Polynices had brought this on. He had brought the enemies of the state to destroy his own home. Neither he nor his confederates from Argos deserved burial. They were carrion fit only for crows and dogs.

But when Antigone heard this sentence she turned pale. Unburied, Polynices was tied to this world forever, condemned to wander as a ghost without hope of the afterlife. So she took a little earth and sprinkled it on the corpse of her brother, lying among the gory mess of the slain, giving him a token burial, even though Polynices had turned his face against both his father and his people. She forgave him, for the needs of his soul were greater than his sins.

Mantes, the storyteller, thought about irreconcilable duties.

'Faithful to the gods? Or faithful to the homeland?' he mused. 'Unhappy Antigone. Even pious acts may have cruel consequences. The full weight of the state bore down on her. Creon condemned her to be entombed alive for disobeying his orders. Teiresias denounced this savagery, and Creon's son, Haemon, who loved Antigone, pleaded for her. Creon relented, but too late. When the rescuers rushed to the tomb, Haemon was dead by the door, and Antigone had hanged herself within.

'Creon had sinned. His zeal for Thebes overrode respect for sacred duty. Some retribution was inevitable for the city already hated by Ares. In Argos, the sons of the prophet Amphiaraus remembered their vow against Thebes. They were the Epigoni, the 'Later-Born', and they succeeded where their father had failed. They stormed the city and sacked it. They pulled down the walls and drove the survivors out into the wilderness. Time to begin again for the people of Thebes, time to send roots once more into the tenacious homeland, time to prove the value of being Greek.

'It is the web, the tangled web of love and duty that catches mankind. And who spins the web? The gods, only the gods.'

Heracles Kills the Lion

– 10 –

THE HERO OF THE GODS

W hen Amphitryon of Troezen returned from the wars he discovered that a god had occupied his marriage bed. It was another step into disaster. His life was unfortunate enough already. How was he to make sense of it?

Amphitryon was betrothed to Alcmene on the understanding that he would first help her father, Electryon, defeat the enemies of Mycenae. He was glad to do this. Beautiful Alcmene was a prize for any man. But before he could join the campaign he was the cause of a serious accident. While he was herding some cattle he threw his club at a stray cow. He missed the cow but hit and killed King Electryon. With family blood on his hands, Amphitryon took Alcmene and fled to Thebes.

Alcmene forgave him the accident and married him, but out of piety to her dead father she insisted that her husband should finish the war before he enjoyed the rites of marriage. After he had been away fighting for some time, one night, in the small secret hours, Alcmene felt a familiar presence by her bed.

'Is it you, my husband?' she murmured, sleepy and content.

'It is I,' answered the voice of Amphitryon, 'come to claim the sweet rewards of the night. The door is closed. It is time to sow for the expected harvest.'

Then Zeus entered her bed in the form of Amphitryon. The King of the Gods had noted her and prepared for this time when she would be alone. He had ordered Helius to unhitch the horses of the sun and arrest the dawn. Darkness reigned and Selene, the moon, slipped slowly across the heavens in an extended night. In one night that was as long as three, Zeus brought comfort and ecstasy to Alcmene. There was great work to be done.

Hardly had Zeus departed, and nature resumed its expected course, when the real Amphitryon returned from the war. He was ready for the wedding bed. His success in the campaign had atoned for the unlucky death of his father-in-law. He was full of anecdotes and energy, and he came to his wife with joyous expectation. But Alcmene was amazed and afraid. This moment had already been consummated. Can the gods duplicate time? Enfolding her husband in her puzzled arms, she did not know what to say. Later, when the prophet Teiresias told him that he had been cuckolded by a god, Amphitryon knew himself to be a victim – or beneficiary – of a divine scheme larger than human lives. Out of respect for Zeus, he no longer slept with his wife. But twice-gratified Alcmene had already conceived twins.

Often, when he related this story, Mantes wondered about the god's intention.

'This was no sudden whim,' he told himself, 'no outburst of passion such as All-Powerful Zeus had given way to on many other occasions. Alcmene was the most perfect and beautiful of womankind. Zeus had marked her as his own. He had a special destiny in store for her. After Alcmene, he lay with no other human. From her loins he intended to bring forth a glorious son, one who was no less than an intermediary between heaven and earth.'

Although Alcmene and Amphitryon submitted humbly to the will of Zeus, Hera, Queen of Heaven, was in no way reconciled to this latest example of her husband's infidelity. She knew that something quite extraordinary was in store, for when the time of delivery was close she heard Zeus make this oath: 'The child of my blood who is born to a mortal woman before this nightfall shall be lord of all the lands of Perseus.'

Now, Hera knew that the wife of Sthenelus of Tiryns – a king descended from Perseus and thus from Zeus and Danae – was also about to give birth. So she sent Eileithyia, Goddess of Childbirth, to sit with crossed legs in front of Alcmene; for no child could be born until the goddess opened her legs, and this she did not do until the infant Eurystheus was safely delivered in Tiryns. Then the restraint on Alcmene's womb was released and she gave birth to twin boys. The younger, by an hour, was named Iphicles and the elder at first was called Alceides, though later he became known as Heracles. This name, which means 'Glory of Hera', was perhaps an attempt to placate Zeus' angry consort. She was the enemy of Heracles and had already stolen part of his birthright and given it to Eurystheus.

At first, Amphitryon was in doubt as to which babe was his, and which the son of a god. When Heracles was eight months old, two large snakes slithered into the nursery. Some say that Hera sent them, and others that Amphitryon himself put them there, to test the children. His doubts were soon resolved, for while Iphicles bawled in terror Heracles calmly took a snake in each hand and strangled both of them.

Knowing now the prodigious and semi-divine nature of Heracles, Amphitryon gave the boy the very best instruction. He himself showed Heracles the art of chariot-driving. Eurytus, a grandson of Apollo, taught him archery. The warrior Polydeuces taught him use of the sword, and Autolycus, master of tricks and sleight-of-hand, initiated him into the finer points of wrestling. Linus tried to teach him music but in this Heracles was a slow learner. When Linus corrected him, Heracles gave him such a blow with the lyre that he killed him. Heracles escaped punishment by pleading self-defence, quoting from a law of Rhadamanthys, but Amphitryon quickly sent him into the country, to work off his dangerous energy as guardian of flocks and herds.

This life suited him well. Alone, under stars by night and the burning sun by day, clothed only in a short tunic and sandals, Heracles perfected his skill with bow and spear. He learnt the ways of animals, and how to tell auguries by the movements of birds. Abstemious by day, drinking water from clear streaming springs, he feasted at evening, eating enough roast meat to satisfy a mountain lion. At night, he slept under the great roof of heaven. He grew to more than four cubits, as large and strong as any human. He was ready to prove himself.

When he was eighteen he went to Mount Cithaeron, to kill a lion that was preying on the countryside. On his way back, he turned aside to the notorious, loose court of King Thespius and in the exuberance of youth serviced the king's fifty daughters, some say in fifty nights, and some say in one.

'Be careful, Heracles,' his friends warned him. 'You over-reach the powers of man.'

'Who cares?' he boasted in reply. 'The gods have made me thus. Whatever I will, I shall do.'

Then, returning to Thebes mightily refreshed, he fell in with the Minyan heralds from Orchomenus, coming to collect a tribute owed to their city by Thebes as the result of a recent war. Angry words were exchanged which put Heracles in such a rage that he cut off the noses and ears of the heralds and strung them around their necks.

'That's the only tribute you'll get from us,' he cried, and beat the Minyans homewards.

King Erginus of Orchomenus immediately declared war, but Heracles raised and trained an army of Theban youths. Then he ambushed and defeated Erginus. After this victory, he forced from the Minyans double the tribute that Thebes had formerly paid to Orchomenus. The Thebans were proud of their new hero. They raised a statue to Heracles, the Docker of Noses, and King Creon gave Heracles his daughter Megara in marriage. Heracles and

Megara had children and for some years lived and prospered in Thebes.

'The early life of Heracles,' Mantes reflected, 'was a glorious chapter, but also a lesson. When a man is a hero, and a favourite of Zeus, who shall govern him? He had molested and painfully wounded the Minyan heralds – those whose persons are supposed to be inviolate – yet he went unpunished. When anger clouded his eyes with blood he smote and killed without compunction. He defeated the Euboeans and tore their king apart between wild horses and dumped the blood-boltered carcass on the river-bank. Hera saw this, and saw the terror of all the lands around, and she remembered her enmity towards Heracles.'

Seeing brutality rampant and justice in despair, Hera afflicted Heracles with a fit of madness. In a homicidal rage he killed Megara and his children and even struck down two children of his brother, Iphicles. Only then did he come to his senses.

When he saw what he had done, Heracles went into a dark place and wept. Sorrowfully, he travelled to King Thespius, to undergo the purification prescribed by the gods for the letting of blood. Then he went to Delphi, to learn his fate from the Pythoness at the shrine of Apollo.

Calling him by the name of Heracles for the first time, the priestess told him: 'You shall go in exile to Tiryns, to the court of Eurystheus, whom you shall serve for twelve years, doing whatever he demands from you. When you have done this, you will become immortal.'

Here was both a penance and a promise. But to serve Eurystheus, that mean-spirited king who had already stolen his birthright! And for twelve years! In dejection, Heracles collected himself for the journey. He wore a bronze breastplate made by Hephaestus and a cloak woven by Athene. He took the sword of Hermes and the bow of Apollo and strode towards Tiryns. On the way, to complete his armoury, he carved a gigantic club from a wild olive tree in Nemea. For Heracles, fancy weapons were hardly necessary. His club was enough.

King Eurystheus greeted the arrival of his new servant with dismay. He did not need this careless and over-powering presence to muddy the quiet waters of his life. The best he could do was to challenge Heracles with dangerous and inhospitable acts, and hope that Heracles might be killed in the process. From all the lands around him, he called to mind the largest variety of impossible tasks, and for his first labour sent Heracles to kill the Nemean lion.

This lion, an offspring of the monster Typhon, had a skin invulnerable to any weapon and an insatiable appetite. Heracles, taking with him his young nephew and friend Iolaus, tracked the lion to its cave high in the hills and attacked it with bow and sword. But arrows bounced from the beast like peas on a stone floor, and his sword grew blunt with the effort. Even blows from Heracles' mighty club only drove the lion into its den. Throwing aside all weapons, Heracles boldly followed, took the lion in a head-lock and strangled it to death.

Since no blade could pierce the pelt, to skin the animal Heracles used the lion's own razor-sharp claws. He dressed the skin and threw it over his shoulders as his own special cloak. The snarling skull fitted his own head like a helmet, and the impenetrable skin kept him safer than armour. In this savage costume, he returned to Eurystheus in triumph.

But the sight of Heracles terrified Eurystheus.

'What is that gruesome figure,' he asked his attendants, 'advancing on us in such a menacing way?'

'Sire, the paths are empty and the children hide because it is Heracles dressed in the skin of the Nemean lion.'

'Let the gates be closed instantly,' cried the king in a panic. 'Life is much safer with Heracles outside the walls. Is it just for the gods to frighten me with this unruly servitor? In future I shall talk to him only from a distance, through a herald.'

And for greater security Eurystheus buried in the ground a large bronze jar into which he could jump whenever he saw Heracles bringing home yet another fearful prize.

But the king felt safest of all when Heracles was far from Tiryns, and so he quickly thought of the second labour, which was to rid the land of the Hydra who lived in the marshes and quicksands of Lerna. This desolate seaside tract, sacred to Demeter and Dionysus, was terrorized by a swamp-creature with the body of a huge dog and nine snake-like heads, of which the middle one was immortal. The monster was venomous, so poisonous that not only its breath but even its body smell could kill.

Again taking Iolaus with him, Heracles chased the beast from the swamp with burning arrows and then, holding his breath, set about the nine heads with his brutal club. But as each head was struck off a new one grew, as angry and venomous as the one before. And while Heracles was tangling with the heads, his enemy Hera sent a giant crab to attack him from the rear. Heracles stamped on the crab, crushing it underfoot. Then he shouted to Iolaus to bring a burning torch, to cauterize the necks of the Hydra and prevent new heads from growing. The last head, the immortal one, he cut off with a golden sickle and buried it deep in the ground. When the Hydra was dead, he opened the body and took the gall from the gall bladder, to use as a deadly poison for the tips of his arrows.

When Heracles returned and the herald shouted through the gates the story of the triumph over the Hydra, Eurystheus was not impressed.

'Iolaus helped you,' he complained from within the bronze jar. 'That was not our agreement. This labour can hardly count. Now, away with you at once, and bring me the Hind of Ceryneia.'

This wild, dappled deer could not be killed, for it was sacred to Artemis, Goddess of Hunting. With bronze hooves and graceful golden horns it lived free on the mountain pastures, so swift that it left the wind behind.

Heracles gave chase, following it doggedly for a year, from the Peloponnese to the land of the Hyperboreans. Easily, the hind outran him but he would not give up. At last, by the River Ladon, he surprised the deer while it slept. He tied the feet fast, threw the animal lightly over his shoulder and set off for home. But Artemis, travelling that way with her twin, Apollo, met him and angrily wanted to know what he was doing with her sacred hind. Adroitly, Heracles laid the blame on Eurystheus and the goddess allowed him to continue, on condition that he let it go when he reached Tiryns.

The pursuit of the Ceryneian Hind had been an invigorating and zestful chase. But the fourth labour, the capture of the Erymanthian Boar, caused Heracles much trouble and regret. On his way to the wooded slopes of Mount Erymanthus, in Arcadia, Heracles stopped to rest at the home of the Centaur Pholus. Pholus entertained his guest well, with roast meat for Heracles and raw meat for himself, but he was reluctant to open a flask of wine because to do so would attract the other Centaurs, who owned the wine communally. And strong drink was known to make Centaurs violent. But Heracles would not be denied. He had travelled far and he was parched. Who could withstand the will of Heracles, specially when the hero was a guest? Pholus opened the wine and the other Centaurs smelt it at once. Already enraged, they attacked Pholus' cave with rocks and flaming brands and uprooted trees.

Indignantly, Heracles struck back with a volley of arrows, sending the horse-like creatures galloping towards the home of Cheiron, their king. Although Heracles had the greatest respect for the learning and wisdom of Cheiron, unfortunately one of his arrows hit the king in the knee. The wound was hardly more than a glance, but the arrow was tipped with the Hydra's gall and Cheiron could not escape the agony of the poison. Though he was immortal, he longed to die and at last chose to do so, voluntarily giving up his immortality. Nor was that the only misfortune. While Pholus was burying the other victims of

Heracles' arrows, he also gashed himself on a poisoned tip and died instantly. Heracles buried his friend with full honours and was glad to leave the unlucky place.

After these difficulties, the capture of the boar was a simple matter. Raising a great din with roars and shouts and the clash of weapons, Heracles frightened the boar from its lair and drove it high into the peaks of Erymanthus until at last it floundered into a snowdrift and was stuck. Heracles jumped on its back and bound it fast. Then he heaved the huge beast on his shoulders and took the homeward road.

But when Eurystheus saw the captive animal, with its coat of bristles like a thorn bush, its tusks as curved and sharp as sickles, and its slobbering angry snout, he took one look and leapt for the safety of his bronze jar.

At Elis in Arcadia, Eurystheus had a neighbour called King Augeias, a son of Helius. Like his father the sun-god, Augeias possessed very many cattle – some say he had the largest herd in the world – and his animals were healthy and fertile and multiplied fruitfully, so that the care of this vast number quite overwhelmed the king and his herdsmen. The stockyards and the stables overflowed with dung. The noisome stench raised a pestilence in the land and the run-off into the fields prevented ploughing and sowing.

The clearing of this foul mess was a particularly unpleasant task which Eurystheus gladly imposed on Heracles as his fifth labour.

Heracles sized up the task and offered to cleanse yards and stables before nightfall, in return for a tenth of the cattle. Augeias laughed at this folly but quickly sealed the offer with an oath. With the help of Iolaus, Heracles made breaches in the walls surrounding the cattle, then he diverted the rivers Alpheius and Peneius into these gaps and watched the rushing waters sweep the yards clean well before nightfall. Suddenly the air was sweet once more, and the night birds called for the first time in as long as people could remember.

Heracles claimed his reward in cattle, but Augeias refused to pay on the grounds that not he but the two river-gods had done the work. He sent Heracles empty-handed back to Tiryns where Eurystheus was waiting with more carping criticism.

'Another mark against you, servant,' the king sneered from behind the gates. 'You tried to work for payment, and once more Iolaus helped you. This labour does not count. Do better now, and rid our lands of the Stymphalian Birds.'

The brackish marsh of Stymphalus, set amid dense woods in Arcadia, was the home of a large flock of man-eating birds. These birds, which migrated from Arabia, were like cranes but had brazen feathers. They attacked in swarms and their beaks were strong enough to pierce a breastplate. Hidden in the thick woods or out of reach on the marsh, they were safe from humans and Heracles was puzzled how to reach them. As he pondered the problem Athene came to him with a large metal rattle and told him to place himself on a mound by the shore and shake the rattle with all his strength. When they heard the noise the birds rose in panic. With his unerring bow, Heracles shot as fast as he could take aim and killed many. The rest flew away to the Black Sea where they settled on an island sacred to Ares.

By now, Heracles had cleared the Peloponnese of its greatest dangers and Eurystheus had to scratch his head to find further test for his heroic servant. He would have to go abroad. For the seventh labour, he sent Heracles to capture the Cretan Bull.

Crete was renowned for its bulls, from that first moment when Zeus, in the form of a bull, had landed on the island with Europa on his back. No one is sure which bull Eurystheus had in mind, but most agree that Heracles captured Poseidon's bull from the sea, the one that serviced Pasiphae and fathered the Minotaur. Heracles grappled with it, and tamed it, and rode it back to Eurystheus. Some say that the King offered the bull to Hera, but the vindictive goddess would have nothing to do with a sacrifice provided by Heracles. Others say that the bull was simply released. This was unfortunate. The bull, which was angry and violent, went rampaging across the land even as far as Marathon, where Theseus was forced to subdue it and drag it as a sacrifice to Athene.

The next task, to tame the horses of Diomedes, took Heracles even further afield, to the far wastes of Thrace.

Diomedes, King of the Bistones, kept his horses tethered with stout chains and fed them human flesh. For this, enemies taken in war were useful, but a guest would do as well. Heracles, expecting a struggle, raised a band of helpers and sailed to Thrace. Then he struck suddenly, raiding the stables at dawn, surprising the grooms, and driving out the vicious horses with swords and spears rather than with whips and bridles. When the king and his soldiers came in pursuit, Heracles left young Abderus to guard the horses and turned to face the enemy. He and his friends routed the pursuers, and having stunned Diomedes with a formidable blow he dragged the king away with him. But when he returned to the horses he found that they had attacked and eaten Abderus. Heracles buried his companion on the spot that later became the city of Abdera. Then he took hold of Diomedes in disgust and threw him to his own horses.

After driving the horses with much difficulty back to the Argolid, Heracles discovered Eurystheus in his usual contrary frame of mind. No, he did not want these horses. They were far too savage and dangerous. So he just let them go, as he had done with the bull from Crete. But the horses, raised on the grasslands of the north and feeding on flesh, could not thrive in the Peloponnese. They wandered into the mountains and soon became prey to wolves and lions.

Now Eurystheus said to Heracles, 'I can see that you're a bold fellow against beasts and monsters, and you hack down men like summer weeds, but let us see how you fare against women. Fetch me the golden girdle of Hippolyte, the Amazon Queen.'

Heracles did not underestimate this labour. The Amazon women, who lived by the stormy banks of the River Thermodon on the shores of the Black Sea, were descended from Ares, a race of warriors who despised peace and lived only for war. They crippled their men and set them to work in the house, while they cut off the right breast – it was this that gave them their name – to give themselves more freedom to draw the bow-string. The female arts, decorous and soft and langorous, were not for them. They wore rough skins, carried a shield like a half-moon, and were expert with a short bow, reinforced with horn and brass. They were fierce and tenacious fighters.

To face them, Heracles had gathered another band of hardy soldiers. After several adventures on the way, the ship sailed into Themiscyra where Heracles was surprised to find Queen Hippolyte waiting for him, not only friendly but positively amorous. Infatuated with the person and reputation of the hero, she was ready for a struggle in arms of another kind and gladly offered her girdle as a token of love. But Hera, always the antagonist of Heracles, frowned at this peaceful intent. She went in disguise among the Amazons spreading the rumour that Heracles was about to abduct their queen. The Amazons rushed to arms and attacked, but Heracles and his allies beat them back. Suspecting that Hippolyte herself had planned this attack, Heracles killed her without compunction, ripped the girdle from her body and sailed hurriedly beyond range of the Amazon missiles.

Held back by the winds in the northern Aegean, Heracles landed for food and water at Troy and found the city in great distress. Some years before, Apollo and Poseidon had built a wall to protect Troy but King Laomedon had foolishly withheld their payment. This rankled with the gods. Apollo afflicted the people with a plague and Poseidon, ever the more brutal, sent a sea-monster to destroy the city. Laomedon soon saw the error of his ways, and at the time when Heracles arrived the king was staking out his daughter Hesione on the shore, as a sacrifice to the monster. In this way, he hoped to placate the angry gods and save the city.

To Heracles, a maiden in jeopardy was an occasion for heroic acts. Why else had All-Seeing Zeus brought him into the world? Immediately, he offered to rescue Hesione if her father would give him in return the wonderful horses that Zeus had once presented to Troy. The king agreed and Heracles killed the monster by jumping down its throat and hacking it with his sword from within the belly. But rash Laomedon, who made a habit of breaking promises, refused to hand over the horses. Heracles was enraged, but with the wind turning he had no time to spare. He was in a rush to complete his service to Eurystheus. So he laid a curse on Laomedon and on Troy and sailed quickly away.

After several years, and nine labours, Heracles had faced unflinchingly the terrors and the hazards of the world. He had been to the limit of the lands of the gods, where the barbarians roam, and he had survived. Now Eurystheus sent him further, to the shadowlands where nature and the supernatural mixed, to places where a human cannot enter without fear and trembling.

On the island of Erytheia, in the western stream of Oceanus, the monster Geryon kept a herd of red cattle. Geryon himself was formidable enough, having three bodies and three heads, but to guard his cattle he was also helped by the watch-dog Orthrus, a two-headed brother of Cerberus, the hell-hound. For his tenth labour, Heracles was ordered to steal the red cattle.

As he journeyed west to the edge of the world, Heracles was hemmed in by the narrow strait that separated Asia from Europe. Wishing to make room for a safer passage he set his shoulders to the continents and thrust them apart, marking the new sea-way with two large rocks that are called the Pillars of Heracles. As he was sweating and straining to push the lands apart he became annoyed that the bright beams of Helius were burning him so fiercely. In a flash of temper he loosed an arrow at the sun, but Helius was so amused at this attempt at the impossible – as if a mere human could stop the sun's chariot with a puny arrow! – that he gave Heracles a golden bowl, in which it was safe to sail on Oceanus to the isle of Erytheia.

When he landed, Heracles felled the dog Orthrus with a mighty blow of his club. But Geryon, a descendant of the Titans, fought strongly and was not defeated until Heracles transfixed his three bodies with a single arrow. Then he herded the cattle into the golden bowl and sailed back to the shores of mankind.

He had stolen the cattle but now he had to drive them home to Eurystheus. The journey was not easy. The red cattle, unused to humans, were almost uncontrollable. Bandits waylaid the herd, waiting for strays. In Liguria, Heracles spent all his arrows beating off the Ligyes and had to pray to Zeus for help. The Thunderer directed him into a plain of stones where he found plenty of ammunition to sling at the raiders. But slowly the herd was diminishing. At Rhegium in Italy, a bull broke away and swam to Sicily, forcing Heracles to swim after it and wrestle the king of the land for its return. From Italy the herd ran north, but before Heracles could turn the cattle towards the Peloponnese, Hera sent a cloud of gadflies that stampeded them into Thrace. Many slipped from mountain paths, or fell into ravines and were killed. Others broke away into the wilderness and were lost. After months of hard travelling Heracles reached the Argolid with only a few lean and foot-sore animals. He had no use for these skeletons and sacrificed them to Hera in a vain attempt to appease his greatest enemy.

By now, Heracles had served Eurystheus for eight years and one month. He had completed ten labours and had reason to hope for his release from bondage. Eurystheus, however, was still quibbling about two of the tasks and was not prepared to remit one moment of the sentence. Far from showing generosity, the king was planning a labour of malicious cunning, which would send Heracles into the territory of the gods. Eurystheus ordered him to go to the Garden of the Hesperides and bring back the golden apples that Ge had given to Hera as a wedding gift.

No human had been to the Garden. It was said to lie far to the west, on the lower slopes of Mount Atlas, near the night-pastures where the sun-god's horses took their rest. Ladon, the hundred-headed dragon, guarded the apples, coiled unsleeping around the apple tree. Heracles set out hopefully, but he did not know the road. He walked at random, questioning all the travellers he met. Some were helpful and some were not. In Macedonia he was drawn into a quarrel with a son of Ares and might have killed him had not Zeus separated them with a thunderbolt. Further on, at a lucky encounter by the River Eridanus, he came across Nereus, the Old Man of the Sea, asleep in the mild sun. He got a grip on the slippery old sea-god and held on grimly while Nereus changed from one bewildering shape to another, until at last he forced the Old Man to reveal the way to the Garden.

Though Heracles now knew his destination, his steps were still wayward, for the geography of the world was a troubling science to mankind, and very few travellers had been far enough even to say what was over the next hill. Heracles veered south and north, though all the time he was trying to bear to the west. He was stopped often by the challenges or the injustice of the world. Passing through Libya, he found Antaeus in his path, a giant who liked to wrestle travellers to the death. Heracles prepared for the contest, rubbing his body with oil. But Antaeus poured hot sand over head and shoulders. When they began to grapple, and the giant was thrown to the ground, he rebounded every time stronger than before, since Earth was his mother and he gained strength from each contact with her. When Heracles realized this, he jerked Antaeus off the ground, held him high and crushed him to death. In Egypt, Heracles barely escaped with his life from King Busiris, who was looking for a stranger to sacrifice to Zeus, in order to end an eight-year famine.

Still Heracles could not find the best route. He went

through Rhodes, where his theft of a cow made later men use a curse when they sacrificed to Heracles himself. Going on through Asia Minor into the Caucasus he stumbled on the tragic figure of Prometheus, still chained to the rock, with the vulture still tearing daily at his liver. After prayers to his father, Zeus, Heracles was permitted to shoot the vulture and cut free the champion of mankind. He had suffered enough for his disrespect of the gods. Then Heracles offered him, again by the grace of Zeus, the immortality which the Centaur Cheiron had renounced.

Wandering on through the icy storms of the Hyperboreans, Heracles at last knew that the end was in sight. He saw the sky-bearing figure of Atlas looming gigantic on the last foothold of the land. Heracles felt now that the apples of the Hesperides were almost in his hand, for he could see them gleaming in the declining light as Helius drove the setting sun into the stream of Oceanus. It was a simple matter to collect his prize, to shoot Ladon with a poisoned arrow, to pick the apples and go on his way. But others say that he could not touch the apples, which were beyond the reach of a mere human, and that he turned to Atlas for help, shouldering the sky while the Titan plucked the fruit for him. But then Atlas was free. He sighed and stretched his arms and smiled once more.

'Now, at last,' he said with overwhelming relief, 'I am free of that burden. Now I permit you to carry the sky!'

'Well and good,' replied cunning Heracles, 'you deserve your rest. But here, the weight frets me a little on the left shoulder. Just take the load for a moment while I settle myself more comfortably.' The unsuspecting Titan agreed. With a laugh and hardly a backward glance Heracles took the apples and went on his way.

But the apples were the property of the gods and Eurystheus could not keep them. Their theft had been permitted, to test the ingenuity and power of Heracles, as a part of his penance, and then Hera demanded their return.

Athene collected them and took them back to their rightful place in the Garden of the Hesperides.

'The time of your release grows near,' said Eurystheus to his heroic servant with grudging respect. 'You have overcome the dangers of the earth and even ventured onto the foothills of divine territory. Now I shall put you to the greatest test of all. For your last labour, you must brave the Underworld and bring me the dog Cerberus from Tartarus.'

Such an undertaking could not be done without the help of the gods. Heracles prayed for assistance from Athene and Hermes. On his way to Taenarum, where a cleft in the rock formed one of the gates to hell, he stopped at Eleusis, to atone for the blood of the Centaurs and to be initiated into the Mysteries of Demeter. Then, with Athene and Hermes to guide him, he entered the realm of Hades.

In the black gloom Heracles – even he! – reached for Athene's hand. He was menaced by shadows. The shade of Medusa ghosted by. The pale form of Meleager raised an arm, but only to warn Heracles of his own approaching death and to offer the hero his sister Deianeira in marriage. Theseus and Peirithous called out from the Seat of Forgetfulness, begging to be released. Heracles strained all his strength to pull Theseus free, but Peirithous, whose sins were great, was left to suffer. And when, in the Fields of Asphodel, the shades clamoured around him with beseeching looks, Heracles slaughtered one of Hades' cattle, so that the shades might drink the blood they craved.

In the deepest hall of Tartarus, Hades waited, grimly amused. He agreed to let Cerberus go, but only if Heracles could capture the dog with his bare hands. With Athene's advice Heracles mastered the dog and dragged it across the Styx and into the light of day by way of the chasm of Troezen. All the way to the Argolid the beast struggled and howled, its three heads scattering saliva from which sprang poisonous aconites.

When Eurystheus saw what kind of a monster Heracles had brought him this time, he went white with terror and sent Cerberus straight back to Tartarus.

What difference did twelve years of servitude make to the greatest of heroes? The character of Heracles had been set from the moment of maturity. He was all of a piece. Out of him poured passion, sentiment, unthinking generosity, egotism, violence, vast acts of the will. It was as hard to stand in his path as to roll back the sea.

'He either saved you or damned you,' Mantes chuckled to himself, 'and the one was just as likely to be painful as the other.'

Even the gods could barely hold him in check, and then only through the corrective of divine punishment.

When Eurystheus released him after his years of labour, Heracles returned to Thebes with undiminished energy, knowing that his only purpose in life was to express fully the extraordinary nature granted him by his father, Zeus. Some say that Megara was waiting for him, having survived his earlier homicidal fit, but that Heracles, unable to face the memory and guilt of his own madness, divorced her and then married her to his faithful nephew Iolaus. In any case, he was soon in the hunt for another wife, going to Oechalia to compete at archery for the hand of Iole, daughter of King Eurytus.

Heracles won the prize but the king, recalling the unhappy story of Megara, refused to honour the agreement. When angry words were exchanged, and then there was a further misunderstanding over some stolen cattle, Heracles took hold of Iole's brother Iphitus and hurled him from the walls of Tiryns. This time, no king would purify his rash and bloody hands. Even the Pythoness at Delphi, horrified by his murderous lack of control, turned him away from the holy oracle. Then Heracles threatened to destroy the shrine, stole the sacred tripod of the priestess and, when Apollo himself intervened, began to wrestle with the god, until Zeus parted them with a thunderbolt. Such a sacrilegious outrage was too much for heaven to overlook. Through the mouth of the priestess, Zeus condemned his favourite son to three more years of slavery.

Since there was now no great competition among the courts of mankind to accept Heracles as a servant, Hermes, God of Trade and Commerce, was told to make the best bargain he could. After some haggling Omphale, the widowed Queen of Lydia, agreed to take Heracles at a price. They were well matched, queen and servant. The witty, easy-going queen understood how best to handle Heracles' overbearing nature. She put his brutal energy to work in the cause of justice, and he found a place for his boisterous humour in the wiles and surprises of her oriental court.

His three years of service in Lydia was a chapter of odd events. Once, he woke to find his goods being rifled by a couple of small, light-fingered rogues called the Cercopes. Heracles seized them and trussed them like fowl for the pot, then he hung them head down from each end of a pole and carried them away. But the little men then had an unusual view of the hero's bottom, which was hardly covered by the lionskin. When Heracles heard the sound of their laughter he stopped to find the cause. The Cercopes explained the joke and then all three of them lay by the road, laughing so hard and long that they could not continue the journey. On other occasions, when Heracles was not taking the field to fight the queen's enemies, he was likely to be indulging her fantasies at home, changing clothes with her, or elbowing her handmaidens in the household chores. And at night, queen and hero joined together to satisfy each other in bed.

When the three years were up, Omphale and Heracles parted with good wishes and with pleasant memories of affection. Heracles left Lydia. He had old scores to settle. Both Laomedon of Troy and Augeias of Elis had broken promises to redeem, and Heracles was not the man to forget. First, he sailed to Troy with a powerful force of eighteen ships. With his Greek army he besieged the city, breached the walls and killed King Laomedon together with all but two of his sons. Podarces, later called Priam, survived and thus had good reason to remember in years to come the fury of Greeks. Next, Heracles turned on Augeias. The king who had refused Heracles the payment of cattle for the cleansing of his stables now paid for that miscalculation with his life. In this warlike mood Heracles swept on across the Peloponnese like an incalculable storm, dealing rough justice with his own well-blooded hands and making kings and princes quake in fear.

This fierce joy in war lasted for some time. Then, tired of slaughter, Heracles turned to softer thoughts and remembered the promise that Meleager had made him in Tartarus. He went to Calydon to seek out Deianeira. He wooed her, fighting off the competition of the river-god Achelous, and won her. Heracles married Deianeira and for a time they lived peacefully and happily, producing a son and a daughter. But then, in a moment of familiar anger, Heracles struck out and killed a young servant who had spilt wine on the table. Once more, he took his family on the doleful road to exile.

As they were travelling towards Trachis, the Centaur Nessus offered to carry Deianeira on his broad horse's back over the rushing spring waters of the River Evenus. Going on ahead, Heracles was just pulling himself up the far bank when he heard the cries of his wife, about to disappear into the trees with the galloping centaur. Heracles drew his bow and felled the centaur with a long shot. As Nessus lay wounded, expecting an inevitable death from the poisoned arrow, he told Deianeira to fill a small flask with his blood, to use on Heracles as a love potion if he ever grew tired of her.

Time passed and Deianeira had cause to wonder. Her husband had set out once more on a trail of vengeance, to punish Eurytus for denying him the hand of his daughter Iole. Deianeira heard that Eurytus was dead and that Heracles was returning with Iole as his concubine. This news she had from Lichas whom Heracles had sent on to fetch a ceremonial robe which Heracles intended to wear when he sacrificed to Zeus in thanks for the victory. When she heard about Iole, Deianeira felt that her husband's heart was stealing away from her and she remembered the words of Nessus. She spread on the robe the blood of Nessus and sent it to Heracles.

But the blood of the dead centaur, which was mixed with the Hydra's gall from the tip of the arrow, was a corrosive poison, not a love potion, and when Heracles put on the robe it burnt him to the bone. In an agony of rage he seized Lichas and hurled the unlucky messenger far out to sea. With his skin on fire he knew that death was close and remembered the old saying of an oracle, that no living person could kill him but that he would die by the hand of the dead. He ordered his friends and his son Hyllus to carry him to Mount Oeta in Thessaly. He was ready for the end. When Deianeira learnt what she had done, she forestalled revenge from husband or son and hanged herself.

Coming painfully to Mount Oeta, Heracles took Hyllus aside and gave his last orders: 'On the summit of this mountain make me a pyre of oak and olive wood. Then, resolutely and without tears, burn me.' When the pyre was built Heracles spread his lionskin over it and lay down with his mighty club as a pillow. But still he could not die, for no one had the courage to light the funeral flames. At last, a passing shepherd offered to do so and received in return for this kindness the bow and the quiver of the hero. As the flames mounted and began to consume the human part of Heracles, the skies opened and his father Zeus threw down a thunderbolt and a shaft of lightning which split the pyre and released Heracles into the immortality of heaven, as the Delphic oracle had long ago foretold.

'It is as well that Heracles went to the realm of the gods,' Mantes used to say with a kind of reverent criticism. 'Superhuman power is not safe unless it is tempered by divinity. Heracles did many good things in our world.

He eradicated monsters, killed tyrants, made roads safe and cities secure. Often, the poor and the weak had reason to bless him. But many innocents were destroyed by the whirlwind of his actions. Mere insects in his path, lesser humans were crushed by his bold, unthinking steps.

'He is better employed in heaven, as the immortal gate-keeper to the court of Olympus and the husband of Hebe the wine-bearer. With what eagerness does he await the daily return of Artemis, the Huntress. How gladly he inspects the results of the chase, anticipating the evening feast. There's good fellowship in the halls of Olympus! And nothing can make Heracles forget his appetite!'

A Goddess with Two Warriors

– 11 –

THE VOYAGERS

THE SAILOR could see that Mantes was nervous. Mantes admitted it. Secretly, he hated the sea. But he could not admit to hatred. He suspected that it was disreputable for a Greek to think in that way. For Greeks, the sea was a familiar companion. Turbulent or serene, it was an inescapable part of their elemental world. One may approach it with a certain caution or nervousness, but hatred was another matter.

The prospect of a sea voyage filled Mantes with ill-disguised apprehension. He feared not just the chance of shipwreck or drowning. No, he also dreaded the giddiness of nausea, the painful retching, the hammer-blows of sick headache, the unbearable loss of equilibrium. Even when the motion was smooth enough to avoid sickness he found much to abominate in the salty confines of shipboard life. Damp sea air sent shooting pains through his lame leg. In the mornings he was so stiff he could barely move, dragging himself by the rigging from bulwark to bulwark. As for the accommodation, prisoners were better lodged. Wind and spray scoured open boats. The cabin – when there was one – was stuffed with musty barrels, sodden cordage, spoilt cargoes, nameless rotting things, all shot through with the smell of unwashed bodies. It was hard to face the cold, dismal food, the spray-blown nights, the growls of the sailors contemptuous of all mere passengers.

But what was he to do? Service of the Muses took him to wherever Greek was spoken. Yearly, he set out for remote lands – Thrace, Phrygia, Mysia, Lydia, Caria, all the kingdoms of the Ionian shore. He had visited Crete and Cyprus and had been battered amid the islands of the Ionian Sea. He had peeped into the Black Sea. He had fumbled down the eastern sea-coast to Egypt and gratefully hurried back again. Once, in a voyage of surprising blissful ease, under the softest of breezes, he had been as far as Sicily.

Today, for the time being all was well. At Chalcis in Euboea, Mantes had boarded a trading vessel bound for the Troad and then on to the southern ports of the Black Sea. His own destination was the shrine of the Great Gods on the island of Samothrace, but he was tied to no itinerary and no timetable. Greek mariners went where the wind blew and hung to the coast like babes at a mother's breast. Mantes was prepared to stop off wherever the whim of the sea might land him. But that decision was far away. They were still in the long sea-channel between Euboea and the mainland, passing so close to the shore that the ship seemed to drift in a sea, not of blue, but of green and grey and brown. The weather was kind.

Perhaps Mantes' gaze was too wistful as he leant on the rail and scanned the solid landscape.

'No cause for worry,' the sailor assured him cheerfully, setting his elbows down next to him. 'This is the best time for a voyage, just after the spring equinox. The leaf on the new shoots of the fig tree is no larger than a crow's foot. That's the moment to take the boat off the blocks and run it down to the sea. With luck we'll be home before the grapes are harvested, when Notus, the South Wind, sends his gales and the Thunderer wrings a downpour out of miserable clouds. Of course, trade means money and money means life to poor mortals, so unwary men will sail at any time, even when Earth-Shaking Poseidon bares his teeth in angry winter. But now Zephyrus is befriending us. There's no danger here.'

'So you know these waters well?' Mantes asked.

'I am a Minyan, from the Gulf of Pagasae. From child-hood, this was my playground. Our people came from the sea, none knows when. We are wedded to water by our history. This is where great voyages begin. From our land, the Golden Fleece was sent to Colchis. From our city of Iolcus, Jason went to bring it back. That much I know, though the details of the story are a muddle to a mere seafarer. But look, poet, we are here entering into your territory. The day is calm, the passage is easy, there's time on our hands. Ease your nerves, settle your stomach, and tell me the true history of those events.'

The woman whose name was Nephele, or 'Cloud', bore King Athamas two children, Phrixus and Helle. But the children grew up under a step-mother, Ino, who hated them and plotted to get rid of them. Ino told the countrywomen to roast the seedcorn before it was sown, so that the next year's crop would fail. When this happened, and Athamas sent to Delphi to learn the meaning of the disaster, Ino bribed the messenger to bring back a false message: 'The land will be barren unless you sacrifice your son, Phrixus.'

Now, the gods noted this abuse of the oracle. They were angry, and Zeus most of all, because he also disapproved of human sacrifice. At the last moment, even as Athamas lifted the sacrificial knife, Zeus sent a golden ram to rescue the children. Phrixus and Helle jumped on the back of the ram and clung to the golden fleece as the ram bounded away to the east. In a few blinks of an eye the ram sped through Macedonia and Thrace, but when it made a great leap over the narrow sea that divides Europe from Asia it caused Helle to lose her grip. She fell and drowned in the strait now called the Hellespont. But the ram ran on, carrying Phrixus along the southern edge of the Black Sea to Colchis, the dawn-land in the east near the stables of the sun. King Aeetes, a son of Helius, recognized the ram as a godsend and received Phrixus with the greatest kindness and solemnity. The ram, its task complete, was sacrificed to

Zeus and its wonderful skin was fixed to an oak in a grove sacred to Ares, where a dragon kept guard. The ram's skin was the Golden Fleece.

Some years later, in the Minyan town of Iolcus in Thessaly, Pelias usurped the throne from his step-brother, Aeson. This usurper, like many of his kind, ruled with cruelty and suspicion. He feared the family of Aeson in particular, since an oracle had warned him to beware of a one-sandalled man of Aeson's blood. When Aeson learnt of the danger to his family, and saw the king's soldiers making enquiries with swords in their hands, he sent his little son Jason to safety on Mount Pelion where the wise old Centaur Cheiron looked after him.

Cheiron taught Jason well. When the youth came to manhood he was eager for his place in the world. He set out for Iolcus in time for a festival in honour of Poseidon. But Pelias, anxious to satisfy Poseidon, had neglected Hera, and she was not pleased. Disguised as an old woman, the goddess waited for Jason by a brawling stream and begged him to carry her across. But in mid-stream she grew so unnaturally heavy that Jason stumbled and lost his left sandal. He was young and fit and bred on the mountain pastures, and this slight nuisance did not delay him. Without a pause he walked on to Iolcus, to confront the king and to claim his rightful inheritance.

When Pelias saw the bold young man with only one sandal and heard his demands, he remembered the oracle and became afraid. The king was old now and his arm had lost its force. Old tyrannies were forgotten. He wanted peace, not insurrection or blood feud. He thought of a way to buy time and to distract this youth with the intoxication of a dangerous adventure.

'This unhappy land,' the old king sighed, 'lies under the curse of Phrixus. His restless spirit lies far from home, banished to the distant place where the Golden Fleece is kept. Bring back the Fleece, appease the shade of Phrixus, and lift the burden of the curse from our shoulders. Then you shall have the kingship.'

The king was sad and old and hardly worth a blow. Moreover, the great adventure was an inescapable challenge. Jason agreed to fetch the Golden Fleece.

What did the task need? First, a ship equal to the demands of strange seas, and then a band of great-hearted companions. Argus, the Thespian, built the ship at Pagasae, using close-grained timber grown high on Mount Pelion. It was a ship of fifty oars, the largest yet made by mankind. Athene fixed in the prow a billet of wood cut from Zeus' sacred oak at Dodona, which could speak with the voice of the oracle. Then the ship was named the *Argo* and hauled to the water.

When the ship was ready, heralds went to every part of the land, inviting young heroes to test themselves against unknown Fate. They came forward readily. Tiphys, the great navigator, was the helmsman and he was aided by eagle-eyed Lynceus in the lookout post. The rest of the crew were all mighty men and it was a puzzle who should lead them. Heracles was the natural choice, but that capricious hero waved the offer aside, conscious of too many other important occasions pressing on his time. So votes were taken and Jason was chosen. As the light faded Jason sacrificed two oxen to Apollo, God of Departures, and then the Argonauts feasted, growing hot and boastful until Orpheus, the great poet and peacemaker of the crew, soothed them to sleep with music.

In the dawn, as the disc of Helius climbed over the Magnesian headland, the Argonauts settled on the benches two by two. They strained into the rhythm of the oars and left Pagasae behind.

Mantes paused and the sailor took up the story.

'Ah, what a moment, that first clean break into the morning light, into the arms of our Aegean! It is the taste of a new world. A new sky, a freshness in the wind, an urgency in the ripple of the water. The huge shapes of the mainland mountains, hugged by mist, fall behind and the sun begins to caress the islands, our multitudinous islands, set like a necklace of flowers dropped in the silver flashes of the sea.

And the birds hover and swoop and squall over the moving ship, waving you away with incoherent cries, both encouraging and fearful. Slowly, the islands of the Dolopes drop astern. Scyros is off the starboard bow. On lonely beaches lean boats lie atilt, nuzzling into the land. Behind, a bridle path mounts through a harsh tangle of rocks into grey hills strewn with a few patches of green. Here and there the small white cube of a house rests amid terraced fields, garlanded with fig trees, or the blooms of the oleander, or a trellised vine. The houses are white, dazzling white in the rising sun. Even the flagstones of the courtyard are edged with whitewash. They are like beacons marking the steps on the roadless seas, through which we Greeks will always move towards discovery and hope.'

While the sailor was talking, suddenly Mantes felt a quiver under his feet. His ship had swung east, passed Larissa, and settled into the swell of the open sea. The wind was picking up, small plumes of spray were whipped from the hurrying wavelets. From the deck, the receding land appeared to roll slightly.

'What is our course now?' Mantes asked with faint beginnings of unease.

'Where the Argonauts led, we follow. Northeast to Lemnos.' And the sailor turned his happy face to the expectant sea.

When, after a fair passage, the Argonauts came to Lemnos, they were surprised to be greeted by the angry scowls of armed women. No men were in sight. Echion, the herald, went first ashore with the staff of peace and discovered that the women were expecting a raid from Thrace. Some time before, the women of Lemnos had been very indolent in matters of love, which offended Aphrodite so much that she afflicted them with a grievous stench. Their husbands, unable to bear the stink, went to Thrace for sweeter-smelling partners, but when the men returned with their concubines the wives waylaid them and killed them all, men and girls. Now they feared Thracian vengeance.

As soon as the Argonauts made clear their peaceful intention, the women became more gracious. The heroes were decidedly handsome and the women were beginning to have second thoughts about celibate life. There was, some recalled, a forgotten pleasure in love, and what if their people should die out? They took the advice of a wise old nurse who urged them to welcome these strangers, and join with them in love, and breed new citizens for Lemnos.

This solution was perfectly agreeable to the Argonauts. Queen Hypsipyle gave herself to Jason, and the other heroes found themselves in such eager and accommodating arms that the departure was put off again and again. Many children were conceived, for the honour of Lemnos. And who knows how long this state of happiness might have continued had not Heracles, always impatient for action, marched through the town with his club, banging on doors, ordering reluctant companions to transfer from the bed to the boat? Colchis was still far away, and there was much to do.

Leaving Lemnos, the *Argo* sailed north to Samothrace where the crew made libations and offerings to Persephone, as was the custom with all seafarers who wished to make a safe passage into the Black Sea. Going on by night, to avoid the truculent men of Troy, the ship slipped through the Hellespont and landed in the country of the Doliones. King Cyzicus greeted the Argonauts well, but in the feast that followed the guests were attacked by certain earth-born giants whom the Argonauts had to beat back with bloodshed. In the morning, with the thanks of Cyzicus and after an exchange of gifts, the Argonauts departed. All day they wrestled with contrary winds and a strong current until, at nightfall, the helmsman put about and headed for safety. As they landed, the Argonauts were ambushed by a band of warriors. In the dark there was a sharp skirmish, but in daylight they saw with dismay that they had killed Cyzicus and several of his soldiers, who had mistaken the *Argo* for a pirate ship.

The dead were given respectful burial and games were held in the king's honour, but day after day the ship was unable to leave in the face of continual storms. At last, the seer Mopsus, who knew the language of birds, heard from a sheltering sea bird that the goddess Rhea held the crew accountable for the death of her earth-born giants. When the Argonauts had made an offering to Rhea, the wind abated and the ship moved on.

As the Argonauts, eager to make up time, sped swiftly through the Propontis, Heracles pulled so strongly on his oar that the blade snapped. Glad for a rest, for Heracles as usual had tested them almost beyond endurance, the crew allowed the ship to drift to land. While fires were lit and a meal prepared, Heracles went in search of timber for a new oar. At the same time, Hylas, his young squire and favourite, went to fetch fresh water. Finding a clear pool, Hylas dipped his pitcher, but the water-nymphs were so taken with his beauty that they pulled him under. When the youth did not return, Heracles went to look for him. Going farther and farther into unknown country, shouting the name of Hylas, Heracles lost touch with the ship. At dawn, with a good breeze blowing and still no sign of Heracles, though many feared Heracles' wrath Jason ordered the crew aboard and sailed away without regret.

'That I can understand,' interrupted the sailor with approval. 'A man like Heracles will lead you onto the rocks. A ship is a delicate thing. It needs a calm and subtle hand to guide it. Bombast and wasteful competition will get you nowhere. I've seen seamen like Heracles and they're nothing but a nuisance.'

The next landfall was Bebrycos in Bithynia. Here, King Amycus, a brutal and vain son of Poseidon, fancied himself as a boxer and refused the Argonauts food and water unless they put up a champion against him. Polydeuces, one of the Dioscuri, was a boxer of repute and gladly put on his thin rawhide gloves. But the king wrapped his meaty fists in metal-studded thongs. Amycus was a powerful, clumsy fighter, given to rushes and wild swings. But Polydeuces boxed skilfully and carefully. For some time, Polydeuces dodged and feinted in the circle of spectators, tiring his opponent with telling jabs and quick counterpunches. Then, when Amycus was panting and sweating heavily, Polydeuces stepped inside his guard and killed the king with a single crushing blow to his temple. At once, the spectators rioted at the death of their king. Standing shoulder to shoulder the Argonauts easily defeated the shaggy and evil-smelling barbarians, put them to flight and swept on to sack and burn the king's palace. After sacrificing twenty bulls to Poseidon, to atone for the death of his son, Jason quickly cast off from Bebrycos.

As he was now approaching the dangerous strait into the Black Sea, Jason headed for Salmydessus, to ask blind King Phineus for advice. Phineus had the gift of prophecy and had displeased the gods by foretelling the future. So Zeus had offered him blindness or death. Phineus chose blindness, but this in its turn had offended Helius, God of Light, who sent two Harpies as a further punishment for the king. These loathsome, birdlike women fouled his every meal so that the king was on the edge of starvation and readily agreed to help the Argonauts if they would rid him of the Harpies. When the filthy hags came to hover over the next meal, Zetes and Calais, two winged sons of the North Wind, flew at them with their swords and chased them beyond the realms of mankind. In thanks, Phineus pointed out the way to Colchis and warned the Argonauts of the many dangers, the first and most perilous of which were the Clashing Rocks of the Symplegades, which guarded the entrance to the Black Sea.

At this dismal narrows, Jason heard the thunder of the impact and saw huge jets of spray spurt into the sky as the rocks clashed together and rebounded, threatening all ships with instant destruction. Phineus had told Jason to release a dove and to follow it closely through the opening gap. The rocks caught the tail feathers of the bird and sprang apart. Then the Argonauts bent into the oars, driven on by the urgent beat of Orpheus' drum, and sped so swiftly through the narrows that only the tip of the stern-post was pinched by the closing jaws.

The broad sea-road of the Black Sea now ran clear towards Colchis in the east. Hugging the southern shore, the *Argo* went steadily on, landing the crew each evening for food and rest. At the River Lycus, Idmon was killed by a boar while hunting for fresh meat. Then Tiphys, the helmsman, grew sick and died. Ancaeus took his place and steered the ship past savage lands barely touched by the benign influence of the Olympian gods. They left behind the land of the Amazon women, and that of the Chalybes who knew no other trade or occupation than the working of iron. Nor did they stay long with the Mossynoechi who lived promiscuously without marriage in sad wooden huts.

The ship was nearing Colchis. By the Isle of Ares, when a storm blew up just after the Argonauts had repulsed an attack from the Stymphalian birds with their spear-like beaks and feathers, the heroes went to the rescue of four castaways clinging to the wreckage of a boat. These four were the sons of Phrixus attempting a return to their father's homeland. Jason was glad to have new hands to make up for the losses in the *Argo*'s crew. But when the sons heard the purpose of the journey they were reluctant to disturb the shade of Phrixus or to desecrate the sacred grove of the Fleece. Since, however, they owed their lives to the Argonauts, they sacrificed to Ares, took their places on the rowing-benches, and guided the ship safely to Colchis.

'The end of the journey!' the sailor's eyes clouded with memory. 'The river mouth lies under the great, hunched shoulders of the mountains. The declining sun lays a russet path before the ship, leading to the tranquil bay. We drop the anchor and make libations of wine and honey. On the whole, the gods have been kind. Thanks be to Poseidon, another passage, another landing.'

In a quiet evening, the *Argo* sheltered at the mouth of the River Phasis, out of sight of the city of Aea and the palace of Aeetes. When they had rested awhile, the Argonauts held a council of war. Some were for guile and some were for force, but Aeetes was no mean opponent and the Golden Fleece was guarded by a dragon as strong and cruel as its master, Ares.

In the morning, still undecided, Jason walked to the city to sound out the king. He offered, in return for the Fleece, to lead his battle-hardened Argonauts against the worst enemies of Colchis. But the king frowned. He was far from being impressed. He did not like men from the west, specially those who burst into the sovereign waters of the Black Sea and dared to claim the holy things that belonged to Colchis. He advised Jason to retreat before he had his tongue torn out. But Jason was not deterred by threats. With the powerful backing of the Argonauts, he argued at such length and so forcefully that at last Aeetes thought he could only get rid of these determined interlopers by setting Jason impossible conditions.

'In the pasture are two of Hephaestus' bulls,' he told Jason. 'You'll know them by their bronze feet and the fire of their breath. Yoke them, plough the Field of Ares, and sow it with some of the dragon's teeth that have come from Cadmus at Thebes. Then you shall have the Golden Fleece.'

When he heard this, the only thing Jason could do was to pray to the gods.

Now, Aeetes had a daughter called Medea who was as lovely as the dawn but was also a witch and a priestess of Hecate. So when Jason asked for divine help, Hera and Athene incited Aphrodite to make Medea fall in love with Jason. Eros struck her heart with his mischievous arrow and Medea, unable to help herself, declared her love to Jason, promising to guide him through the traps set by her father if he would marry her. Jason willingly agreed. Protected by Medea's magic, he yoked the bulls, ploughed the field, sowed the dragon's teeth, and when armed men sprang out of the ground he repeated the trick that Cadmus had used, throwing stones among the warriors so that they quarrelled and fought and killed each other. With the task done, Jason went to claim his reward. But Aeetes suspected some deception and went back on his word. He drove Jason out of the palace and prepared to attack the Argonauts.

With the king's soldiers closing in, Medea quickly led the Argonauts to the grove of Ares. Throwing a potion made from juniper into the eyes of the dragon, she put it to sleep. Then Jason tore the Golden Fleece from the oak tree and the Argonauts turned and ran for their boat, carrying Medea and her little half-brother, Apsyrtus, along with them. Soldiers barred their way. There was a skirmish and some of the heroes were wounded, but all managed to get aboard and their oars, dug deep, made the *Argo* skim from the shore. The king's ships were already on the water, ready to cut off the Argonauts at the point. All seemed lost, with the Argonauts vastly outnumbered, until Medea saved them with a cruel sacrifice. She killed Apsyrtus, cut him in pieces and threw the bits of his body in front of the Colchian ships. As the enemy ships paused to recover the pieces of the little prince, the *Argo* flew between the fleet and the land and made for the freedom of the wide sea.

In the open sea, the ship was lost. Greek mariners were never safe without the comfort of landfalls and islands and a half-familiar coastline. Tiphys, the great pilot, was dead. His successor manned the tiller but Hera chose the course. Following the path of the sun to the west, the ship came to an unknown land. A broad stretch of water led inland. Was it a seaway or a river? The Argonauts dropped the sail and rowed. They struggled against the current, up the Don or the Danube, or some say it was the Eridanus. And when the banks closed in and the ship could no longer make headway against shallows and rapids, they hauled the

Argo on rollers and dragged it to another river, north-flowing, into fir forest and sodden plains and lands of ice. At the cold edge of the world Hera directed them into the stream of Oceanus which swept them south to the Pillars of Heracles and the landlocked sea of their ancestors. With relief, they landed at Elba and lay on the cool pebbles till nightfall, searching for constellations that pointed the way home. When they rose from the beach the pebbles were marked with the pattern of their skin.

Grateful to the friendly stars, the Argonauts eased their way past Sicily into the Ionian Sea. But as they approached Corcyra, on the threshold of home, the oracular voice spoke from the piece of Zeus' sacred oak in the prow of the ship. It warned them that their hands were still stained with the blood of Apsyrtus and that the *Argo* would not reach home until the crew was purified. Across a narrow channel the mountains of Thesprotia enticed them with dreams of the homeland, but the Argonauts had to turn away and sail to the island of Aeaea where Medea's aunt, Circe, an even greater sorceress than her neice, reluctantly purified them.

With the crew freed from the burden of guilt, the *Argo* seemed to have wings. Thetis, the sea-goddess, smoothed a path through the waves and watched over the progress of the ship. At the island of Anthemoessa, where the Sirens drew unwary sailors onto the rocks with the unbearable sweetness of their singing, Orpheus took his lyre and went among the rowing-benches, filling the ears of his companions with an even more ravishing music. Of all the crew, only Butes, the Athenian, jumped overboard and was lost to the Sirens.

Hurrying away from that temptation, the Argonauts came to a danger they could not avoid. Here, the sea ran roaring into a gorge, with the jagged crag of Scylla on one side and the whirlpool of Charybdis on the other. It was enough to strike terror even in heroes. But Thetis saw the peril and put her hand on the helm while her attendants, the Nereids, picked out for the ship the best course through the violent current. Then they came into sunlight and quiet water and sailed calmly on to the island of the Phaeacians.

As the Argonauts landed they saw many sails chasing towards the island. A fleet from Colchis, which had been hunting the *Argo* for many weeks, had picked up the trail and now followed the heels of the enemy into the harbour. King Alcinous found himself with awkward guests. The formidable fleet from Colchis demanded the return of both Medea and the Golden Fleece. Medea was afraid to go back, fearing the just anger of Aeetes, and Alcinous was reluctant to have his peaceful island contaminated by fighting and bloodshed. Offering to mediate between the two sides, he secretly told Jason and Medea to marry that night.

Next day, he delivered his judgment: 'If Medea is still a virgin, she must return to Colchis. If not, she may stay with Jason.'

Displaying the sheets of the marriage bed, Jason proved the coming together of man and wife, and the Colchians, bound by oath to accept the king's judgment, departed with many mutterings.

The seasons were changing. The time of easy sailing, at the spring equinox, was far behind. The *Argo*, after so many delays, left the Phaeacians and was at the mercy of rougher airs, blowing erratically by command of the Four Winds. Boreas, the North Wind, filled his lungs and sent the ship scudding helplessly to the Bay of Syrtes in Africa where it grounded. Unable to relaunch in the teeth of the wind, the Argonauts took heart from instructions given to Jason in a dream. They hauled the ship onto rollers and, shepherded by goat-like deities of the desert, followed a white horse for twelve days to Lake Tritonis in Libya where the god Triton directed them by river back to the sea. Even then troubles were not at an end. After a passage from the African shore in heavy weather, the Argonauts wanted to stop and rest in Crete. But the bronze giant Talos, the sentinel of the island, beat them back with a bombardment of rocks. Medea alone managed to slip ashore and tempted Talos with a narcotic drink. When the potion put the giant to sleep she removed the bronze pin that stopped his veins and watched his lifeblood run into the sands.

After leaving Crete, the *Argo* came within the embrace of the Aegean, moving through well-remembered islands, past Andros, along the double bow of the Euboean coast, and into the welcoming jaws of the Gulf of Pagasae. Weather-worn and weary, the heroes splashed through cool shallows onto land turning sombre and autumnal.

As Mantes related the homecoming, the sailor was suddenly more attentive. His face took on a look of happy solemnity. His gaze across the sea seemed to encompass all its moods, all the possibilities and satisfactions of seafaring.

'Yes,' he affirmed, 'those Argonauts were true Greek mariners: free, equal, bold and enquiring. They had departed with high hearts, set on a noble task. They had battled respectfully with the gods of wind and weather, and they had not been defeated. They were not dismayed in strange places but bent their backs and went on. And heaven, in the main, approved their venture. After many by-ways and surprises, their spirit had been tested and rang true. They came home in triumph to the old world and the new wine, and a girl or a wife on the beach waving a scarf in welcome.'

But on this occasion there were no wives, no women on the beach. Pelias, the old tyrant, still ruled in Iolcus and had taken advantage of Jason's absence to kill the hero's parents. The other Argonauts, too long away, dispersed to their far homes. Jason and Medea faced an uncertain future alone. Jason was unsure how to go on but Medea advised him to hide himself and the *Argo* for the time being and to put his trust in her magic. Then she went to Iolcus disguised as a wise old crone, a votary of Artemis, with an elixir of life to sell. Pelias, who was old and steeped in sin but did not wish to die, heard of the elixir and demanded a demonstration. Sprinkling magic herbs into a boiling cauldron, Medea threw into the broth the dismembered pieces of a tough old ram. After a few minutes a new lamb sprang from the pot. Pelias was convinced. Medea charmed him to sleep and ordered his daughters to cut him in pieces. But this time the herbs in the broth were of a different kind, and no new prince arose out of the cauldron.

The king was dead but his son Acastus, even though he had been an Argonaut, was duty-bound to avenge him. He banished Jason and Medea from Iolcus and they went willingly, for Jason had no further interest in a place where he had never lived and where his parents lay dead. He went first to Minyan Orchomenus and hung the Golden Fleece in the temple of Zeus. Then he sailed the *Argo* to Corinth, dragged it onto blocks and dedicated it as a memorial to Poseidon.

Jason and Medea settled in Corinth where Medea's family had a claim to the throne. For ten years they lived happily enough, then troubles came between them. Jason had seen the ruthless and pitiless nature of her powers, and what was she anyway but a sorceress from the east? There were things about her that no Greek could understand. He grew suspicious of her, and perhaps also afraid. When the chance came he repudiated her and planned a marriage with the Theban princess Glauce. Medea, never more dangerous than in adversity, pretended to submit to his will. Graciously, she sent Glauce a golden crown and a white wedding robe. But the robe was poisoned and burnt Glauce to the bone. Then, in a final act of bitter revenge, Medea put to the sword her own two children by Jason and fled to Athens in a chariot drawn by winged serpents.

With his hopes and his posterity destroyed, Jason left Corinth and wandered homeless from city to city. He was a man apart, marked by his achievement and his tragedy. In his old age, in the course of his travels, he found himself once again on the isthmus of Corinth. A prisoner to old memories, he sat in the shadow of the *Argo* and contemplated the workings of Fate. As he bent his head, overwhelmed by the decisions of the gods, a loose beam fell from the decaying fabric of the famous boat and killed him.

Long after he had finished speaking Mantes remained jammed into a corner by the bulwark, watching the land recede. Underfoot, he began to feel the tricks of the waves, and on his cheek the inconstancy of the wind. The sailor had left him, going about the business of the ship. By mid-afternoon the wind veered and freshened. The mountains to the north and west softened and almost disappeared under a pall of cloud, and a thin rain ruffled the water. The wind was nearly on the beam now, and the ship started to roll in choppy seas. Mantes clung to something solid. He felt wretched.

The sailor came hurrying to his side of the deck and untied a rope. 'Change of course,' he shouted cheerfully through the wind. 'Goodbye to Lemnos. The wind is driving us south and east. We'll run for Cyme. If we miss it on the left, we'll hit Lesbos, and on the right, we'll get to Chios. Good luck to us either way. But you, poet, you'll not see Samothrace for many a day.'

Anywhere will do, Mantes thought in his misery, just so long as it's land. There are times when the destination is not important.

Menelaus and Helen

– 12 –

THE TALE OF TROY

'SHAME,' SAID the old soldier, looking at broken walls. 'All this fuss about a woman! Grown men shouldn't bother with such matters. A man's concern is with great deeds, with courage, fighting, plunder, life at the edge of death. Let us talk of bold voyages, discoveries, dangerous enterprises far from home. Love is a soft blind thing, hardly worth the breath it takes to tell it.'

Mantes smiled at this outburst of male indignation.

'In the consequences that flowed from this one woman,' he replied, 'there are great deeds enough to fill the volumes of the world for a thousand years to come. Besides, this Helen was no ordinary woman. Alcmene, mother of Heracles, was accounted the most beautiful of humans, but she was as nothing compared to Helen. For Helen was the daughter of Zeus, imprinted by the father with a godlike presence. She was semi-divine and her brothers, Castor and Polydeuces, were the Dioscuri, that is to say, the twin boys of Zeus. They lent their strong arms to noble causes, and they were the mariner's guide too, sending the friendly fire that sits on masts and rigging of storm-bound ships. When such a family springs from the fount of divine pleasure, what extraordinary events may be expected? Zeus foresaw it all and let the great tale unfold.'

They had come north, Mantes and the old soldier, thrown together by the chances of travel in a little ship bumping carefully along the coast from Cyme. The ship was an island trader. They had left Lesbos and Tenedos behind. Imbros, Samothrace and Thasos lay ahead, if the gods and the winds were willing. But now the ship was tied up in Sigeum, at the mouth of the Scamander in the Troad, and the two elderly men were making a small inland pilgrimage, to a scene of ancient troubles.

The Asiatic plain was arid, bone dry, dust on top of dust, through which the River Scamander etched a languid, silvery line, as if dragging itself painfully out of a vast, lost interior. A violent, hot wind, a child of the Egyptian khamsin, irritated the gaunt bones of the land. To the south, only the high nude hump of Mysian Mount Ida gave a sense of scale to the low plain. Here, the city of Troy had been built and destroyed and rebuilt again. New walls were slowly rising amid extensive old ruins. Among the rubble of time the old men trod cautiously on shattered skulls, blackened stones, arrowheads, charred fragments of wood. Under their feet lay the ashes and grief of a fallen empire.

Who were these peoples of the plain who incurred the wrath of gods and men? Their lineage was both ancient and obscure. Some say that Scamander, the Cretan, and his son Teucer led some wanderers here in a distant time of famine. Apollo told them to establish themselves wherever beasts of the earth attacked them by night. And when hungry mice came in the dark to eat their bow-strings and their leather tunics, the Cretans made their home in sight of a mountain they called Ida, in memory of their own Cretan peak. Scamander died in battle, drowned in the river which took his name, and Teucer succeeded him.

But others say this Cretan colony was not the beginning of Troy. That event they date from the flight of Dardanus, son of Zeus, from Samothrace, who fled to the Phrygian shore on an inflated oxskin. Teucer received him well, for Dardanus was a powerful warrior and conquered the

explained what had happened. Then they led their brother Paris to Priam who wept and rejoiced at this sudden delivery. He acknowledged his lost son and gave him his proper place in the royal household.

Now, a little before Paris was translated from rustic Mount Ida to the palace of Troy, on Mount Pelion in Thessaly the Olympian gods were preparing for another festive occasion. From the beginning of time, Almighty Zeus had been fretted by a puzzle of the heart. He had long desired the sea-goddess Thetis, daughter of Nereus, but had been warned that her child would become mightier than the father. So he kept his passion in check until at last, to spare himself further temptation, he decided to marry Thetis to the mortal Peleus.

Like many young princes and heroes before him, Peleus was being trained for manhood on Mount Pelion by Cheiron, the King of the Centaurs. Cheiron knew very well that no goddess would be flattered by a mortal husband, and also that Thetis would be no easy catch since, like her father, she could change her shape at will. Cheiron advised Peleus to seize her while she was asleep and not to let go, whatever happened. Stalking her to a quiet cave where she was having an afternoon nap and taking her unawares, Peleus held on grimly while she changed from lion to serpent, from water to fire, from goddess to giant squid hidden behind its veil of ink. But she could not avoid the destiny chosen for her by Zeus and at last grew still in her pursuer's arms.

The gods gathered on Pelion for the wedding, bringing with them many gifts. But Eris, Goddess of Strife, who had not been invited, came out of spite and scattered among the divine assembly her own peculiar gift of dissension. Observing the three queens of heaven - Hera, Athene and Aphrodite – in a rare mood of smiling harmony, Eris threw at their feet a golden apple inscribed: 'To the fairest. '

At once, the good mood vanished and the three great goddesses began to bicker over the prize, growing so heated and angry that Zeus had to step between them. Zeus had noted before, in a dispute concerning Ares, that handsome young Paris, the herdsman of Ida, had pacified the violent war-god with great tact. He now summoned Hermes and told the messenger of the gods to put the dispute for the apple to the judgment of Paris.

Then the court of heaven flew to Mysia, to seek out Paris on Mount Ida. Paris, who thought of himself as a mere herdsman, was abashed and confused by the commission. He was not worthy. He blushed. But his blush was very fetching. The three goddesses took up studied poses.

'Perhaps it would be best to divide the apple?' Paris tentatively suggested to Hermes.

'The prize does not permit it,' Hermes replied sternly. 'All or nothing.'

But who would dare to judge between these three? Hera, the consort of Zeus, a majestic and overwhelming figure, offered Paris the full protection of her position and authority. Serene Athene, who feared neither god nor monster, promised him wisdom and perpetual success in battle. But Aphrodite, beautiful lascivious Aphrodite, took Paris softly by the hand and sighed and looked downcast and breathed in his ear.

'Such a gentle, handsome young man, and I, alas, have so little to offer you. Why, Helen herself, most glorious of all women, would be more than pleased to accept you.'

'Is she not married already?' stammered Paris, with his senses thoroughly confused.

'Yes, that is a little difficulty. But the heart can undo such small impediments. If you were to give me the apple – unworthy though I am – I think I could incline her love towards you. I have, as you no doubt know, some influence in these matters. Yes, her heart shall certainly belong to you.'

And Aphrodite's sweet doleful lips brushed his face with just the ghost of a kiss.

Disengaging his hand from her too tender grip, Paris took the apple and gave it to the Goddess of Love.

Zeus desired Leda, wife of Tyndareus of Sparta. She could not escape him. The Father of the Gods came brutally to her in the form of a swan, great wings beating, and took the nape of her neck in his beak and trod her down and possessed her. As a result of this union she brought forth an egg from which came Helen, the beauty and the wonder of the world.

'That name again,' the old soldier growled. 'We make too much of her. The valley of the Eurotas and the country of Sparta breed fine stock – that much I know from my experience. But was Helen's beauty any more extraordinary than the oleanders and the rhododendrons and the citrus groves in flower? Mankind must keep a sense of proportion about a face and a figure.'

'Some things are judged, not in the sharp light of day, but in the corrupting half-light of the imagination,' Mantes corrected him. 'A king will sometimes throw away his patrimony for a pearl, and a philosopher lose all reason over a barbarian slave-girl.'

'Go on, then,' the soldier said grudgingly. 'Tell me the worst about this woman.'

Helen, indeed, blossomed like the flowers of the Eurotas, and by the time she was fully grown there was none in the world of humans to compare with her. The princes of the Peloponnese, and beyond, were suitors for her hand, all except for Agamemnon, High King of Argos, who was already married to her half-sister Clytemnestra. After much competition, Menelaus of Mycenae, brother of Agamemnon and richest of the princes, won her. But Tyndareus, anxious not to cause friction among great men by this choice, bound all the suitors by oath to abide by his decision and to defend Helen's husband, whomever he might be, against the oppression and spite of jealous men. And to solemnize this oath Tyndareus made offerings to the gods. By an unfortunate oversight, however, he forgot to include Aphrodite.

Tyndareus died. The Dioscuri, Castor and Polydeuces, were taken into heaven by Zeus and set in the stars as the constellation of Gemini. Menelaus became King of Sparta and lived there peacefully with his wife, Helen.

On a certain day in the gocd sailing season, a fleet from the east put into the port that served the inland city of Sparta. Paris of Troy had come to beg King Menelaus to purify him for the accidental killing of a kinsman. Aphrodite had set the events in motion. In Troy, she had drowned out the prophetic laments of Cassandra and Helenus, the far-seeing children of Priam. She had over-ridden the fears of King Priam himself, and she had made Paris deaf to the pathetic pleas of his first love, the nymph Oenone. Aphrodite sent the wind that blew Paris so smoothly west. She put a welcome for the Trojan in Menelaus' stolid and unsuspecting heart. After nine days of feasting, she arranged, providentially, that Menelaus should leave for Crete, to honour the funeral games of his grandfather. In the palace of Sparta, Helen was alone with Paris.

On Mount Ida, the goddess had promised Helen to Paris. When he saw her in the flesh he knew that he wanted her more than anything in the world. Looks passed between them, a light touch of the hand, almost accidental, a sudden flush of heat and embarrassment. Menelaus was her hus-band and they had children. He was noble, dull, worthy and rich. But how could he compete for her heart against a prince invested by the Goddess of Love herself with all the radiance and passionate desire of love-famished youth? That night, they eloped.

Fleeing to the ships, Paris and Helen paused only long enough to dedicate a shrine to Aphrodite on an island by the harbour and there to consummate a new love. Then they sailed on a long journey home, driven about by angry winds which Hera sent against them. They took with them the serving-girls from the palace at Sparta, and some also say the palace treasure. Perhaps that was malicious gossip, an attempt to stain a god-given love with ordinary greed. King Priam and the people of Troy, however, looked for no trea-sure other than Helen herself. Despite omens of doom, despite the certainty of a wrong committed, when the Trojans saw Helen for the first time they forgave her every-thing. The world might be won or lost. Who but the gods could know? But for Helen's sake, the risk was worth taking.

When Menelaus returned from Crete, summoned hastily by a message from Hera, and learnt what had happened to Helen, he began to claim from his fellow princes the duty owed to him by reason of their oath. His heralds went to call men to war, and great warriors came from far and wide, some thirsting for glory and some reluctantly, but bound by their word.

The fleet and the army, as large a force as mankind had seen, began to gather at Aulis. King Agamemnon of Argos, overlord of the Peloponnese and brother of Menelaus, was commander-in-chief. From the ancient cities of giant walls he brought the largest contingent. Menelaus, the wronged husband, supported him with sixty ships, and the brothers had as their chief counsellor the old greybeard Nestor who came from sandy Pylos with no less than ninety ships. From the coastal towns and villages that lay between Epidaurus and Tiryns, Diomedes brought eighty more, while the Athenians sent another fifty under Menestheus. And from farther afield came representatives of all the confederation of Greek peoples – Mycenaeans, Argives, Achaeans, Aetolians, Dorians, Hellenes, Danaans – all sending ships and men from Boeotia, Euboea, Minyan Orchomenus, from the wilder lands of Thessaly, Acarnania and the Epirus, from Crete and Rhodes, and from many, many islands. Even the inland mountain men of Arcadia wished to go, but Agamemnon had to loan them ships, for they knew nothing of seafaring.

But some leaders tried to evade the call to arms. It is said that Idomeneus, the wealthy lord of Crete, offered the grandest fleet of all but only if his ships had the foremost place in the expedition. Cinyras of Cyprus promised fifty ships but sent one real boat and forty-nine small models. Apollo killed him for this deception.

Among the bands of soldiers were many seasoned and formidable fighters. Old Nestor had survived many campaigns. Diomedes, both brave and cunning, had cut his teeth in the battles of the Epigoni against Thebes. The lesser Ajax from Locris, a fearsome man with a spear, paraded his violent, proud, untrustworthy nature. He walked the camp with his nose in the air, followed like a dog by his pet serpent. His namesake, the greater Ajax, son of Telamon, was also a boastful fellow. He was not rich, being somewhat slow-witted, and could raise only twelve ships from Salamis. But he was stronger and braver, a head taller than any Greek, and second only to Achilles in the arts of war. Where the fighting was thickest, there he would be, almost invulnerable, for Heracles had wrapped him in the famous lionskin at birth, making Ajax safe from blows except for a small area around neck and shoulder where the lionskin failed to meet. Besides these heroes, there was also clever Palamedes, Agamemnon's right-hand man, and Philoctetes, who owned the bow and the poisoned arrows of Heracles.

Two men, however, were indispensable for the expedition, and at first Agamemnon waited for them in vain. Odysseus, the fox, was needed for his incomparable understanding of men's motives and the ways of the world. And Achilles, son of Peleus, was needed to be first in battle, the one warrior whom all respected and all feared.

War had no attraction for Odysseus. Wise beyond most, he foresaw the barren waste in lives and treasure. Ithaca, his poor island home in the Ionian Sea, was unable to bear the expense of a long campaign. He was happy in his marriage to Penelope, governing the modest life of a modest land, and an oracle had warned that a voyage to Troy would drag him from home for twenty years. So when Menelaus and Palamedes came to him in Ithaca, to bind him to his oath, Odysseus feigned madness. In rags and a battered felt cap, he yoked an ass and an ox, ploughed, and sowed salt instead of seed. But Palamedes knew the tricks of the man. As Penelope stood by with the infant Telemachus in her arms,

Palamedes grabbed the baby and put him in the path of the plough. To save his son, Odysseus halted the plough and proved his sanity. Reluctantly, he left for the war where his advice fended off disaster and made the best of many a bad day. But he never forgave Palamedes.

With Odysseus within the fold, the Greeks were happier. But the generals could not be completely satisfied until Achilles was persuaded to join them. But where was he?

When the sea-goddess Thetis was forced by the decision of Zeus to marry the mortal Peleus, she still longed for immortal children. As each of her babies was born she held it in the flames, to burn away mortality. But every one of the children died. At the seventh attempt, the desperate father, Peleus, pulled baby Achilles from the fire and substituted a giant's thigh-bone. Since Thetis could not make her son immortal, she tried to make him invulnerable instead by dipping him in the River Styx. Only his heel, by which Thetis held him in the water, remained a place of weakness. Then Thetis, having had enough of humans, returned to the sea, though she still kept a maternal eye on her son, Achilles.

Peleus sent the growing boy to be schooled by Cheiron on Mount Pelion. When Achilles approached manhood, the most accomplished of the Centaur's many warlike pupils, Thetis warned Cheiron to hide him away. He was too young to compete for Helen, or to take the oath of the suitors, but Thetis knew the danger of Aphrodite's scheming. She knew that Achilles' lust for glory would pull him towards Troy, but that he would die if he went there. So Cheiron disguised Achilles as a girl and sent him to the court of King Lycomedes in Scyros. For a time he lived as a woman in the women's quarters, but not so womanly that he forgot his male nature. On Scyros, he fathered Neoptolemus, the flame-haired son who later followed in his dead father's footsteps on the tragic plain of Troy.

With Odysseus to guide them, Nestor and Diomedes traced Achilles to Scyros. Lycomedes calmly denied any knowledge of the youth and allowed the generals to search the palace. As they did so, Odysseus had a suspicion about a certain tall, graceful girl who moved more like a panther than a lowly serving-woman. He planned a little trap. He filled a hall with many gifts, including arms and armour, and invited all the women to choose what they wanted. At that moment, the trumpet sounded the battle-alarm. The women fled, all except for one tall figure who stripped off a woman's clothes, ran for the armour and took up the heaviest sword. With his disguise uncovered, Achilles could not be denied the joy of war. Willingly, he joined the expedition, setting out for Aulis with his bosom friend, Patroclus, and placed himself proudly at the head of his Myrmidon soldiers.

At Aulis, in the sheltered waters between Euboea and Boeotia, the vast fleet jostled for room between shore and shore. The sacrifice to Zeus and Apollo was prepared. The Greeks were ready to leave, to avenge Menelaus against Paris and against Troy.

'**R**espect the gods and give them due worship, by all means,' the soldier was grumbling again. 'But this story you tell me, poet, is barely credible.'

Though old, the soldier was still spritely and his sight was keen. He had made the round of the walls. He had seen the lie of the land and inspected the fallen battlements. In the gaps of the smashed ramparts, in the odd glory of the few remaining towers, in the intermingling of bones and dust, his practised campaigner's eye perceived something of the to and fro of attack and defence. He felt the reality of war.

'Old man, war does not come from poetry,' he went on. 'No, it arises out of commercial jealousy, or loss of trade, or imperial ambition, or deliberate foreign policy, or just the press of people at home clamouring for light and land. I have heard it said that Zeus, Lord of the Thunderbolt, pursued this war because the world was burdened with too many people. He wished to make a void in the race of men.'

'I do not deny,' Mantes replied, 'that rivalries of trade

and the wish for power and the fretful expansion of many peoples helped to bring Greek and Trojan face to face in bitter warfare. Yet the gods look beyond these mundane matters into the hearts of men. Wars are made by man, and man's motives are pride and greed and selfishness. Where there is sin, the gods exact penance. Where there is guilt, there must be punishment and retribution. Learn, O simple-minded soldier, learn before it is too late, that the gods bring down those who climb too high. Thus it was with great Achilles, who choked on pride and anger. And thus it was with Paris, so handsome a youth, and with Troy, so rich and powerful a city in its time.'

Heaven had taken sides. Because of Paris and Helen, Troy was condemned, but the Greeks also were not without fault – what man is? At Aulis, when Agamemnon was making sacrifice for success and safety, a snake with the markings of blood slithered from beneath the altar into a plane tree where it devoured a mother bird and eight young. It was a dire omen, which Calchas, the seer, explained in this way: Troy would not fall until nine years had elapsed. Subdued by the thoughts of time and all its pains, the Greeks departed.

What began with a bad omen continued with ill luck. The fleet was driven off course to Mysia, which the pilot mistook for the Troad. After some purposeless skirmishes the ships were knocked round and about by violent winds until forced to regroup at Aulis. The wind off the sea still blew strongly. Passing the time in hunting, Achilles offended Artemis by boasting of his prowess, and the cold, unforgiving goddess would not let the wind subside until the commander of the army, Agamemnon, had made a sacrifice of his daughter Iphigenia. She, the prettiest of his children, was brought from Mycenae and consented with heroic resolution to die for the Greek cause. Some say that Artemis relented at the last moment, for Zeus hated human sacrifice. As the knife was about to fall, the goddess substituted a hind on the altar and carried Iphigenia to Taurus, to be a priestess of her temple. Then the wind shifted and the fleet sailed again.

This time, fair breezes took the Greeks quickly to Tenedos, where Achilles rashly killed King Tenes, a son of Apollo. Then Philoctetes, the keeper of Heracles' bow and arrows, was bitten by a snake. The bite grew septic and stank, and Philoctetes cried out in such pain that the army could not bear it. A swift boat took him away and abandoned him on a small, bird-stained rock off Lemnos.

Amid these sombre signs, with some gloom in their minds, the Greeks went the last lap to the Asian shore. Protesilaus, who desired the glory, jumped first to the beach and was instantly struck down by Hector. With this warning of the stern contest to come, the rest of the army disembarked more cautiously and camped on the plain. Ahead, the towers and fortifications of Troy looked formidable. The Trojans were prepared and included in their ranks many experienced and skilful fighters. They were no strangers to war. Now the Greeks knew what the omens had already warned, that there is no great achievement without great effort, no conquest without suffering.

For nine years the Greek tide of battle surged and ebbed. Unable to make a dent in the walls that Poseidon and Apollo had built, the Greek army harried the surrounding countryside, stirring up enmity from many barbarian kings in Phrygia and Mysia who had no reason to love the invading Greeks. With the help of these allies, the Trojans easily stood firm. The Trojan generals were not inferior to those of the Greeks. Hector, first among the Trojans and the eldest of Priam's fifty sons, could stand toe to toe against Achilles himself. Paris, the cause of the city's woes, was anxious to redeem himself by the fury of his warlike arm. Even Antenor and Aeneas, two men who spoke for peace and the return of Helen, fought bravely like patriots and won the respect of the Greeks for upright and honourable conduct.

After nine years, soldiers on both sides were weary and despondent. They hated an enemy they could not overcome but also felt despair at their own lack of success. Comrades became quick to quarrel. In the tenth year, after an attack on an outlying town, Achilles returned to camp with two captive girls. One, he took for himself while the other was claimed by his commander, Agamemnon. But this girl, Chryseis, was a priestess of Apollo, who sent a plague on the Greeks until his servant was returned. Annoyed at the loss of a bed-fellow, Agamemnon demanded that Achilles should give way to a superior officer and let him have the other captive instead. Pale with anger, Achilles retired to his tent and vowed that he and his Myrmidons would fight no more until Agamemnon put right this act of injustice. Thetis heard the complaint of her son and made Zeus promise to withhold a Greek victory until the honour of Achilles was satisfied.

It was a moment of Trojan advantage, but the army of King Priam, too, was without heart. Hector, sick of slaughter, tried to resolve the deadly stalemate by a duel between Paris, the adulterer, and his victim Menelaus. Yet when Menelaus had Paris at his mercy, and peace was almost within grasp, Aphrodite wrapped her favourite in a cloud and spirited him away to safety.

For the war, which was a bitter struggle between men, was also being fought in heaven. Aphrodite, the troublemaker, naturally came to the aid of Troy. But the hands of love are soft, unused to weapons, and she was little help on the battlefield. Bold Diomedes spilt her divine blood and sent her whining home to Olympus. Both the twin gods, Apollo and Artemis, also supported Troy. Each had a grievance against Achilles, who had killed Apollo's son on Tenedos and had offended Artemis by his idle boasting at Aulis. Ares, the God of War, sniffed the blood from either side, for nothing pleased him better than death. If he had an inclination, he leant towards Troy, drawn that way by his lover, Aphrodite. But greater deities than he, Athene in particular, set the edge of Greek swords against him and drove him wounded from the battle.

Those gods were powerful allies. But the weight of Olympian support lay with justice and the Greek cause.

Tempestuous Hera and invincible Athene, both spurned by Paris, had good reason to set themselves against the favourite of Aphrodite. Earth-shaking Poseidon and the lame smith, Hephaestus, set sea and fire in opposition to Troy. But Zeus, Father of All, kept heaven in balance. Time and the Fates were not yet satisfied, and so Almighty Zeus withheld the final decision.

While Achilles sulked, and a truce failed, fighting broke out again with renewed fury. In the nick of time, Diomedes and Odysseus stopped Thracian reinforcements from reaching Troy. They killed Rhesus and captured his barbaric white horses, which had been destined, had they got through, to save the city. Then the Trojans, taking advantage of Achilles' absence, counterattacked, stormed the palisade that guarded the Greek fleet and set fire to some of the ships. In this desperate plight, Patroclus put on Achilles' armour and rallied the Greeks. The sight of the golden armour of the hero terrified the Trojans, who turned and ran for home, closely followed by Patroclus. But Apollo had noted the deception. At the gate of the city, the god knocked the weapon from Patroclus' hand, then Hector completed the work of death, hacked him down and stripped Achilles' armour from the body.

The year had turned. Wild flowers dared to show their faces again on the stained and trampled banks of the Scamander. In the absence of Achilles, the armies had fought each other almost to a standstill. Agamemnon, Odysseus and Diomedes were all wounded. Greater Ajax and Hector had fought hand to hand from dawn to nightfall, when they fell apart in exhaustion and mutual respect. That was how things stood when news came to Achilles' tent of the fall of his dear friend, Patroclus. When he heard of this death, Achilles covered his head and rolled in the dirt with grief.

Now nothing could stop Achilles. He cast off lethargy and self-pity and concentrated all his immense powers of destruction into a thirst for revenge. Thetis brought him new armour, forged by Hephaestus, and he drove into the enemy like a wolf among sheep. Hector sheltered behind the Scamander and the river-god lashed his waters in Achilles' face. But Hephaestus sent fire to dry the river-bed and Achilles pursued Hector until the Trojan champion was forced to turn and fight. Who else was capable to taming this murderous Greek? In stunned silence, the armies drew back from the two heroes. Then the spirit of Hector, brave though he was, failed him as he saw in the eyes of his opponent the terrible enormity of his rage. Hector fled, and Achilles chased him three times around the walls before he caught the Trojan and thrust a spear right through his body. There was a shout, of triumph on one side and terror on the other, then a silence in heaven as Achilles hitched the dead man by the heels to his chariot and dragged the body in the dust to the Greek camp.

Long flames consumed Patroclus and his funeral pyre, on which horses, hunting dogs and twelve noble Trojans with their throats cut were also sacrificed. But the battered corpse of Hector was only grudgingly ransomed to Priam for its weight in gold. Now it seemed to Trojan eyes that Death and Achilles stalked hand in hand. The anger of Achilles was without bounds, a tyranny of slaughter that displeased the gods. Though he was half in love with her beauty, he killed Penthesileia when the Amazon queen brought her warriors to help Priam. And it was whispered that he did an unspeakable act with her dead body. Foul-mouthed Thersites, who respected no man, jeered at Achilles for his filthy lust and received in return a single deadly blow which drove his teeth into his skull.

At his wit's end, in the face of this ferocity, King Priam summoned his half-brother, Memnon, to bring an army of black soldiers from the lands of Ethiopia. With fresh arms, and used to heat and hardship, these fighters brought temporary relief. Memnon killed the son of Nestor and for a moment the Greeks were in disarray. Then Achilles called out to Zeus to judge between him and Memnon. Their lives were weighed in the divine scales, and Memnon was found wanting. As the Ethiopian was trading blows with Ajax,

Achilles shouldered his colleague aside and spilled the guts of the black king. In grief, his followers, lost and far from home, turned into birds and circled his grave with forlorn cries.

Here, Mantes paused in the narrative, for the old soldier was growing red again.

'Disgraceful military conduct,' he snapped. 'A soldier without honour is no more than a snarling dog. Achilles should have known what every old campaigner knows, that excessive rage in a general is a kind of disease. It may frighten the enemy, but it clogs the mind with a vision of blood and warps the rational decisions that lead to victory. It is no surprise that the gods eventually look coldly on such a man.'

Achilles' race was run. It was time for the Olympians to rein him in. In the midst of battle Apollo stood by the Scaean Gate, cloaked in mist, waiting for Paris and Achilles to come together. As Paris drew his bow, the Archer God sped the arrow which pierced Achilles through his heel, his only vulnerable part. The blood drained quickly from the wound and Achilles died.

'Achilles was brave beyond compare,' Mantes voiced a mild epitaph, 'and a cause of courage in others. In the web of destiny, he served justice. Though not wholly worthy of praise, he did great deeds, suffered and died. He is remembered. That is enough.'

The body of Achilles was burnt on a funeral pyre, his ashes mixed with those of Patroclus, and his possessions distributed among his companions. Ajax, son of Telamon, fiercest in battle after the dead hero, claimed his arms. But Agamemnon, valuing cunning above strength, awarded the prized weapons to Odysseus, a decision which drove Ajax mad. He attacked a flock of sheep in mistake for Odysseus and his men. When he woke from his fit, and saw what he had done, he killed himself for shame.

Events foretold by the oracle long ago had come to pass. For the Trojans, the killing of Achilles was only a fleeting triumph. With his death the city of Troy began to die also.

But the conditions for a Greek victory were not quite fulfilled, as the Palladium still stood secure in the shrine on the citadel.

Then Calchas, the prophet, spoke once more: 'The stricken tree totters, but before it falls Neoptolemus, son of Achilles, must replace his father. And Philoctetes must bring to Troy the bow and arrows of Heracles.'

When red-headed Neoptolemus was brought from Scyros, Odysseus dressed him in his father's armour, an image that still had power to put terror in the Trojans. With greater difficulty, long-abandoned Philoctetes was rescued from the rock off Lemnos and brought to Troy, either through a trick or with the promise of a cure for his still-festering wound. Machaon, the surgeon, cured him with a poultice of wine and herbs, and soon Philoctetes repaid this care by shooting Paris with one of Heracles' poisoned arrows.

Then Odysseus was free to turn his scheming mind to the capture of the Palladium. He and Diomedes put their clever heads together. Odysseus had himself whipped until he bled. Dressed in rags he went by night as a fugitive to the Trojan gate, howling curses against the Greeks. The gatekeepers admitted him in sympathy and bathed his wounds. But in the dark he sneaked away and killed the sleeping guards of the Palladium. He hefted the large image onto his broad shoulders and carried it to the main town sewer and floated with the foul refuse beneath the walls to the waiting Diomedes outside.

The ripe fruit was almost in hand. All the Greeks had to do now was to reach for it. Athene, the greatest of their protectors, inspired them with the plan. She commanded the craftsman Epeius to take planks of the best fir and build a wooden horse with a hollow interior large enough for fifty picked fighting men. Then, with a great show of despondence, the Greek fleet sailed away, but only as far as Tenedos, leaving Sinon behind, a most plausible fellow and a grandson of the trickster Autolycus. Sinon went to the puzzled Trojans with a tale of woe, crying out against his cold-hearted companions who had run for home and left him at the mercy of the enemy. And when the Trojans enquired about this curious wooden horse, Sinon pointed to the inscription: 'An offering to Holy Athene, in gratitude for our safe departure from this accursed shore.'

Though the horse was too big to fit through the city gates, Sinon promised the Trojans that its presence within the walls would make the city forever safe from further invasion. Cassandra cried out when she heard this, for she feared the Greeks bearing gifts. And the seer Laocoon added his doom-laden voice to hers. But when two sea-serpents crushed Laocoon and his sons to death, the Trojans believed Sinon. They tore down part of their impregnable, god-built walls and pulled the wooden horse into the city.

Listening to the jubilation of the enemy, the Greeks in the belly of the horse waited for night. Some suspicious Trojans tried to thrust spears and swords between the planks, and Helen called to heroes she had once known, imitating the voices of their wives. Homesick warriors jumped up to reply, but Odysseus pulled them down with a hand over their mouths. The Greek fleet had crept back from Tenedos and was hove-to just off shore. In the night, when Troy was dizzy with joy and wine, Sinon lit the beacon to recall the ships. They grounded softly on the beach. Then Epeius opened the trap door in the horse and let down the rope-ladder. Grim men emerged, with faces strained for slaughter.

The horror began. Ten years of rage and frustration were visited on the people of Troy. Few were spared, not children, not mothers with babes at the breast. Men, youths, grand-fathers, honoured matrons were put to the sword, but the best of the young women were taken as concubines. Priam and Hecabe took refuge at an altar of Zeus where the weak arm of the old king made one last feeble thrust at Neoptolemus. Contemptuously, the son of Achilles cut him down. Antenor, the respected advocate of peace, had a better fate. Menelaus hung a panther's skin at his door, as a sign that he should be saved. Deiphobus, the new guardian of Helen after the death of Paris, could expect no such mercy from her husband. Menelaus hunted him to his home and killed him in the heart of his family.

After the slaughter came the division of the spoils. Lesser Ajax captured Cassandra and dragged her from the temple of Athene. But Agamemnon, the commander-in-chief, claimed the prophetess for himself. Neoptolemus, in his father's name, took Hector's widow, Andromache, and Odysseus grubbed up the very roots of that heroic family by throwing her little son, Astyanax, from the walls. Even the dead shared the plunder. Achilles appeared in a dream, demanding the sacrifice of Priam's youngest daughter, Polyxena, and threatening to withhold the homeward winds until this was done. Agamemnon shuddered at this cruelty. But Calchas overruled him. Polyxena was slain on the tomb of Achilles and the good winds began to blow.

When the killing was done, Queen Hecabe stood almost alone in the bloody ruins of city, friends, family and home. In the division of the prizes, she fell to Odysseus. He accepted her, but what use is a grief-stricken old woman? She was more a token and an evil reminder than a prize. The gods had pity on her and turned her into one of the savage black dogs that follow Hecate. In wild Chersonese, far from home, she howled her despair over a cold sea and disappeared under the waves.

The great act was finished. The Fates closed the last chapter in the long history of Troy. The Greeks set fire to the dead city and sailed away on the favourable wind.

At midday, the molten sun poured over the plain. They sat under a ruined tower, grateful for a little, crooked patch of shade. They were silent, overwhelmed by heat and history.

In a while the old soldier said: 'Is this the meaning of that woman? How is it that we Greeks can forgive her still?'

And Mantes, after long thought, answered, 'This also I have wondered, and I reply to you in the words of another poet, a Greek like you and me. "For ten years we staggered on the shore, giving our blood that the image we had of Helen might be clothed once more with warm human flesh. After ten years of pleading and agony, she came. She came! When Menelaus lifted her high in his arms and, striding through the smouldering palace, past the carcass of Priam, the thresholds of Troy and the pebbles of the shore, plunged waist deep into the sea and placed her aboard his ship, all the Greeks turned pale as they saw the beauty of the incomparable woman.

'"Generations passed, but Helen still stirs in song, sits at the law-givers' tables and at the gatherings of the common folk. In the evening she goes to the beds of the newly-weds, like a bride, and all the daughters of Greece bear her resemblance. She is the woman of the Greeks.

'"Blessed be the gods! Before our blood and song gave her birth, Helen was a shadow, trembling like all women, without hope of eternity upon the earth. She walked through the canebrake of the Eurotas, sat at the loom, directed her servants, moved up and down the palace like a shade. She would have died as if she had never lived.

'"But suddenly our poets passed by and caught sight of her, and like the sea, the song rose up and took her, and made her our own, and then gave her to the world forever."'

Dancing Girl

– 13 –

WANDERING MEN

Safe at last on Samothrace, Mantes gave thanks at the shrine of the Great Gods.

For him, this was a refuge and a completion. In his lifetime of service to the Muses and to the Holy Ones, Mantes had never before been to remote Samothrace, the storm-tossed island of the northern seas. Yet this was one of the most venerable of sanctuaries, and also the most hospitable. Greek or barbarian, man or woman, citizen or slave – all were welcomed into the mysteries. Now the home of the Great Gods, Samothrace at first, before even the coming of the Greeks, had been dedicated to the Great Goddess. First, she was primeval Ge, our Mother Earth. Then she was Axierus, goddess of the unknown tribes. She was Phrygian Cybele. She was Greek Demeter. She was Persephone, Guardian of the Dead.

Into these maternal arms mankind came with a simple intent: to seek happiness in the earthly life and peace in the Underworld. And here Mantes joined the initiates in procession by night, advancing by torches along a path on which there was hardly a level footstep. From the crags mountain goats peered down with insatiable curiosity. The ritual was easy, the requirements few. In the sanctuary, the initiates put on white chitons and the priest of the cult showed them certain symbolic objects, which alone must remain secret. That was all.

After the ceremony the initiates wore an iron bracelet, representing the power of the earth, and around their hips they wound a large cloth, which promised protection against the sea. For the Great Gods had the care of navigation in their hands, and lofty, snow-tinged Mount Phengari was a beacon for sailors, and the little coves of the island were a haven to ships when Poseidon raged in this turbulent, wind-swept corner of the Aegean Sea.

'Blessed are the Great Gods,' Mantes sang, celebrating his own release from the sea, 'who safeguard all friends, all strangers on land and sea. Here is the sanctuary we need, for all Greeks are wanderers, in life and in the imagination.'

Wearily, the Greeks of Agamemnon's army abandoned Troy and prayed for peace and rest. But Athene sent a storm that whirled them helplessly onwards. The struggle was not over, for who in a ten-years' war could say he had not sinned? And the gods do not forget.

Ajax, son of Oileus, began this trouble. At the sack of Troy he had pulled down a statue of Athene which Cassandra clung to as he tried to rape her. The statue lay on the ground, outraged eyes pointing skyward. When Ajax went unpunished by the Greeks for this sacrilege, Athene sent the storm that wrecked the returning fleet at Cape Caphereus in Euboea. She herself smashed Ajax' ship with a thunderbolt, but he swam to a rock and boasted of his escape from the will of heaven. When Poseidon heard this ranting, he sent a wave that knocked the wind out of Ajax and drowned him.

After the storm, Demophon, son of Theseus, was driven into Thrace while trying to make his way back to Athens. In the new land he married Phyllis, daughter of the king, and then left for his old home. When he did not return, she hanged herself and was changed into an almond tree, which bore neither leaves nor fruit until her repentant husband came back and put his arms around the trunk and kissed the tree.

Many others were drowned in the storm but Diomedes and Neoptolemus, two favourites of the gods, survived. Athene saved Diomedes but Aphrodite had not forgiven him for wounding her with a spear-thrust before the walls. When he returned to Argos he found his wife thick in adultery and the people of the city turned against him. He took refuge in the temple of Hera, then fled to Italy and lived out unhappy days in exile. Neoptolemus, however, did not sail with the fleet since he had been warned of the danger by the sea-goddess Thetis. Instead, he went by land across Thrace and Macedonia, conquered the Molossians and made a kingdom for himself. But Apollo called him to justice for his cruel slaughter of Priam, which defiled the altar of Zeus. When Neoptolemus seized Hermione, Apollo put hatred in the heart of Orestes, to whom she had been promised, and he killed Neoptolemus at the sacred grove in Delphi.

At the fall of Troy, Menelaus took Helen to his ship and cast off as quickly as possible. His parting with Agamemnon on the beach had been bitter, an argument among drunken soldiers, and the two brothers never met again. In his haste to get away Menelaus neglected to make a sacrifice to Athene, so the goddess marked him down and Apollo shot the pilot of his little fleet. All but five of his ships were lost in the storms of the return. Menelaus was blown to Crete. For eight years he was battered around southern and eastern seas, seeking friendly winds but never finding them, sailing to Cyprus, Phoenicia, Ethiopia, Libya and, finally, Egypt. Proteus, one of the changeable gods of the sea, had charge of these winds and only he could send Menelaus back to Sparta.

After eight years Menelaus caught up with Proteus; hid among the seals of the sea-god's flock when they gathered on Pharos, and then grappled with the slippery god. Subdued at last, Proteus told him that his brother Agamemnon was murdered and that Menelaus must return to Egypt, to appease the gods by sacrifice. Menelaus made offerings on the banks of the Nile and built a memorial to his brother. Then the winds relented and took Menelaus and Helen safely back to their homeland.

How subtly, and with what cruel irony, did the Fates pursue the curse of the House of Atreus against the two brothers. Menelaus did hard penance on alien shores amid other peoples and other gods. At last the gods allowed him home, and he and Helen settled into the exhausted peace of age, their passion spent, their great adventure a story for other generations. But Agamemnon, the elder son of Atreus, came triumphantly home from Troy with hardly a stumble. Hera led him safely through Athene's storm. With all the pomp and dignity of a conqueror, he landed at Nauplia, kissed his native ground, and wept for joy.

But his wife, Clytemnestra, hated him. He had married her by force, killing her first husband, Tantalus, and the child at her breast. He had taken Iphigenia, her prettiest daughter, and had sanctioned her for sacrifice. He had wasted ten years in war, in men's futile business. And now, if the rumour she heard was correct, he was coming home with Cassandra as his Trojan concubine.

Aegisthus, son of Thyestes and the sworn enemy of the sons of Atreus, knew Clytemnestra's turmoil of mind. While Agamemnon was away he took the chance to harm her husband. He flattered Clytemnestra and won the way to her bed and became her lover, despite the warning of Hermes, for they were satisfied both in body and in the spirit of revenge. Then they conspired to murder Agamemnon and his Trojan slut, whomever she might be. For a year, Clytemnestra posted a watchman on the palace roof at Mycenae, to give her notice of her husband's return. When the news came, she and her lover were ready.

Agamemnon and Cassandra climbed from the port on a torrid day, a day over-burdened with sunlight. Behind, the plain of Argos was covered by the mirage of the heat, like a lake on fire. The feet of the travellers dragged, despite Agamemnon's anxiety to be home, and their tongues were parched. But what comfort could Mycenae offer? To Cassandra, it seemed a fearful place. The citadel sat powerfully on its rock, above a gorge, flanked by two grey mountains. The walls built by the Cyclopes were enormous and threatening, too large for humans, as if built to contain some colossal outrage, some deep insult to the gods.

Clytemnestra stood smiling at the gate of the palace. The purple covering of welcome lay over the steps. The bath was ready, the women of the palace were even now adding the last sweet herbs to the water. The feast was prepared. Agamemnon set his foot within the door. But Cassandra, the doom-saying Trojan prophetess whom none believed, could not go on. With the smell of blood in her nostrils, she cried out in despair and stood like stone.

In the bath-house Agamemnon was refreshed. The toil and the bitterness of years flowed away with the water and he was ready now for the feast. As he stepped from the bath Clytemnestra came forward with what seemed to be a towel. But it was a seamless net which she threw over his head, and then Aegisthus struck him two savage blows with a sword. Though Agamemnon was already dying, Clytemnestra made certain with the stroke of an axe which beheaded him. She wiped her axe and her blood-spattered hands on her husband's hair and ran outside to kill Cassandra with the same weapon.

When the deed was done the murderous lovers became king and queen of Mycenae and ruled for eight years. By then, Orestes, son of Agamemnon and Clytemnestra, had come to manhood and the gods reminded him of his duty to his father. The oracle at Delphi demanded the death of Clytemnestra and her lover, though this course was full of danger, for matricide also called for vengeance and the Furies would not let Orestes rest. In disguise, Orestes went to the palace in Mycenae and pretended to his mother that her son was dead. Clytemnestra was relieved. She had been oppressed by bad omens, dreaming that a serpent sucked both milk and blood from her breast. She and

Aegisthus relaxed their vigilance. Then Orestes drew his sword, killed Aegisthus, and turned on his mother. She bared her breast and begged for mercy, but Apollo hardened Orestes' heart and he beheaded her, just as she had done to Agamemnon.

After the fall of Troy, one man, at least, knew that he would see his home again. Odysseus, who had taken the road to Troy so reluctantly, had the promise of the oracle that he would return to his native Ithaca. Son of Laertes, Odysseus was the grandson of Autolycus, famous among all mankind for quick wits and sharp practice. On the plains of Troy, Odysseus had demonstrated his lineage, proving himself to be the most intelligent and cunning of the Greeks. He had endured the war. Now, in time of peace, he would survive whatever happened.

Only one thing clouded the certain knowledge of his return. He knew also that his journey home would take him ten more years.

Odysseus left Troy with a fleet of twelve ships and headed northwest into the Chersonese. Odysseus was a man of the Ionian Sea. The enclosed eastern waters of the Aegean were strange to him. In the manner of Greek sailors he intended to hug the coast, a broad, short man standing astride the tiller, shrewd eyes scanning the shoreline, assessing as always the profit and loss of action or inaction.

At the first landfall, he lost his Trojan captive. Queen Hecabe, Priam's widow and his prize, took the form of a black dog and, too sad to live, vanished into the sea. Landing again further along the coast of Thrace, Odysseus' men made an unprovoked and bloodthirsty attack on a town of the Cicones, sparing only the priest of Apollo, who gave them in gratitude some wineskins full of the strongest wine. While they were sampling the drink and celebrating their easy triumph, the Greeks were surprised by a sudden counterattack which left many dead, forced the remainder to tumble aboard ship and run into a northeast gale that drove the little fleet helplessly south towards the island of Cythera. During a lull in the weather, off Cape Malea, Odysseus tried to round the point and make the short passage up the Ionian Sea to Ithaca. But the wind redoubled in strength and tore him away again to the south, far from his home, to the land of the Lotus-Eaters.

This was a land of dreams. Those who ate the fruit of the lotus forgot the pain and effort of living. The past was closed to them, and the present a mysterious interlude. But for ten years the men of Odysseus had seen blood, horror and the intimacies of death, and why should they not reach now for some blessed state? Some willingly took the fruit and sank to the grass beneath shady trees, listening to the play of the breeze and watching the clouds soar away. But Odysseus roused them with the point of his sword and herded them back to the boats. Man was made for resolution and endurance, not for the sleep of forgetfulness.

The ships sailed on into unknown waters. After a time, needing meat and fresh water, the crews landed on a small, verdant, wooded island, ringing with the plaintive calls of many sheep and goats. No humans were in view. Exploring with one ship on the other side of the island, Odysseus saw a large, airy cave to which he and his men took a goatskin of wine, intending to shelter for the night. Inside, they found meat and milk and cheese, and they were just preparing a meal when a giant with a single eye in the middle of his forehead drove a flock of sheep into the cave and secured the entrance with a massive boulder.

'What?' the giant rumbled in an ugly voice. 'Visitors?'

'We are only poor strangers, driven here by ill winds and the will of the gods,' Odysseus answered humbly. 'In the name of Zeus we ask for your hospitality.'

The giant only laughed. Then he caught two of the men, cracked their heads against the rock and began to eat their flesh.

Fate had brought the unlucky Greeks to the home of Polyphemus, a son of Poseidon, one of the race of Cyclopes who had formerly served the gods as craftsmen and black-smiths. In time, these Cyclopes had degenerated into brutal, ignorant monsters, living lonely lives in island caves and wholly dependent on their flocks for livelihood. In a sleepless night Odysseus wracked his brains. He and his men might kill the giant, but how would they escape from the cave? A team of twenty oxen could hardly move the door-stone.

In the morning, Polyphemus ate two more men and left with his flock, carefully replacing the boulder behind him. During the day Odysseus found in the cave a heavy log of well-seasoned olive wood which he sharpened into a stake, hardening the point in the embers of the fire. Then in the evening, when Polyphemus returned with the flock and satisfied his hunger with two more victims, Odysseus offered him some of the strong wine he had brought from the Cicones. The wine loosened the giant's surly tongue. 'Tell me, little man,' he asked Odysseus, 'what is your name?'

'My name is Nobody,' Odysseus replied solemnly.

Polyphemus giggled. 'Well, Mr Nobody, in return for your gift of wine I'll do you a favour. I'll eat you last.'

At that, the giant rolled onto the ground and began to snore. In the night, Odysseus heated the stake and drove it deep into the round eye of the drunken Cyclopes. Polyphemus woke blinded and roaring with pain, bringing his fellow Cyclopes running from distant caves.

'What is the cause of this fearful noise?' they called out.

'Nobody has blinded me,' Polyphemus answered.

'Is that all? Most likely, you have a fever. Pray to your father Poseidon for relief.' And they went away grumbling.

When morning came, Polyphemus had to let out his flock for water and pasture. He pushed aside the stone and crouched in the entrance, to feel each animal as it passed. But Odysseus had fastened the sheep in threes and tied one of his men beneath each group of three. Then he him-self clutched the thick, long wool under the largest ram. At the entrance of the cave the giant ran his hands over the back of each animal but found no one. The ram was the last to leave.

'You are usually the first to leap from the cave,' Polyphemus said tenderly, groping in the fleece on the ram's back. 'Have you stayed to comfort me in my agony? Go on, old friend, the pasture awaits you.'

With a bound the ram was out of the cave and Odysseus was free. He and his men ran for the ship but when they were safely offshore he could not restrain his triumph.

'Listen, Cyclopes,' he shouted. 'It was not Nobody who blinded you. It was I, Odysseus of Ithaca.'

In rage and pain Polyphemus prayed to Poseidon for revenge and hurled vast lumps of the earth towards the voice that taunted him. Blindly aimed, the volley of rocks fell short, only raising a circle of waves on which the ship rode to safety. But Poseidon heard the petition of his son Polyphemus, and the Earth-Shaker did not forget the name of Odysseus.

Joining the rest of the fleet, Odysseus sailed north to the island of Aeolia, where Aeolus, Lord of the Winds, greeted the wanderers with much kindness. He entertained them for a month and then gave Odysseus a large sack in which the more unruly winds were imprisoned, leaving only Zephyrus, the gentle West Wind, free to blow the fleet swiftly to Ithaca. Under bright skies Odysseus steered the fleet until smoke from the hearths of Ithaca came in sight. Then, overcome by fatigue, he slept. As he rested, his crew untied the sack, hoping to find gold and jewels. In a moment, the angry winds rushed out, caught the sails of the ships in their arms and hurried home. But Aeolus would have nothing more to do with men who misused his gift. Obviously, these sailors were not favoured by the gods. They were not worthy to have the winds as their servants. In future, they had better row.

They rowed laboriously for seven days then came to a land of high, broken mountains under a gloomy sky. Glad for any relief, the other captains took their ships into the narrow jaws of the harbour, which was closed in by steep cliffs. But Odysseus did not like the look of the country and anchored out in the bay. It was as well that he did so, for the Laestrygones, the savages of the land, attacked and destroyed all the ships in the harbour. Then the savages began a leisurely feast on the bodies of the dead. Sick at heart but unable to prevent this massacre, Odysseus cut his anchor-rope and fled with his one remaining ship.

A long voyage east took him to the island of Aeaea, near the realm of Dawn, where the great sorceress Circe lived in the midst of her enchantments. After so long at sea, the island looked peaceful and pleasant under a mild sky, but Odysseus and his men were suspicious. In the toil of their homecoming, they had been hurt by too many alarms and surprises. Cautiously, Eurylochus, the second-in-command, took a party of men to investigate. At a clearing in the woods they came to a fine house in a glade in which many wild animals were prowling. The men drew back, afraid. But these animals seemed to have forgotten their wild habits, and instead of attacking they came forward eagerly to lick the hands of the strangers and to fawn at their feet. From within the house there was the sound of a loom, and of a woman's voice singing the contented songs of the hearth and the home. Eurylochus called, 'Who's there?' Then Circe came to the door with her arms held out in greeting and invited the strangers to enter and eat and rest.

Eurylochus, still full of suspicion, refused to go in. But the rest of the men entered at once. There was something in the quiet glade, in the peaceful house, in the calm figure of the sorceress that reminded them of homes and families so long unseen. Men used to the seafarer's ration of hard-tack and salted meat and water from a mouldy barrel willingly sat at a table laden with barley cakes, cheese, milk, curds, honey and fruit. When they had eaten and were lying back with a cup of wine, Eurylochus, who was spying through the window, saw Circe rise from her place and touch each man with her staff. Instantly, the men were transformed into swine which Circe drove out of doors with kicks and blows. They joined the throng of beasts outside in the glade, those who also had once been humans.

When Odysseus heard what had happened he was furious and reached instinctively for his sword. But an enchantress was no ordinary enemy and Odysseus was not sure what to do until Hermes met him on the path and gave him a magic herb called moly, which would make him safe against the spells of Circe. Now he could fight magic with magic. At the house, Circe charmed him and feasted him, as she had done to the others, but when she struck him with her magic staff Odysseus took her by the hair and held his sword at her throat. Circe begged for her life. She offered him her riches, her bed, all the langorous delights of the enchanted island. She spread ointment on the backs of the swine, bringing his crew back to human form but younger and more handsome than before. Then Odysseus agreed to stay with her and comfort her in her loneliness.

For a year, Odysseus and his men lived at ease in the strange luxury of Aeaea until they grew homesick for their own land. But when, and how, would Odysseus be allowed to see his homeland again? He was beginning to despair, and though Circe was willing to help him, even her witch's eyes could not read the book of his future. She told him that he must seek out the shade of Teiresias in the kingdom of Hades, who would lay before him the will of heaven. So Odysseus' ship ran on the North Wind to the place where Circe had directed him, to the grove of Persephone where sad willows drooped over the Rivers of the Dead. Here, by the entrance to Tartarus, Odysseus dug a pit and filled it with the blood of sacrificial ewes. Ghosts of the dead welled up from the Fields of Asphodel to drink the blood. But Odysseus drew his sword and kept them at bay. He was waiting for Teiresias.

The shade of Elpenor came first, the youngest of the crew who had died in a drunken fall on the island of Circe but a few days before. His body lay unburied and he gazed reproachfully at Odysseus, pleading for remembrance.

Then came many shades, old and young, and among them was Odysseus' own mother, Anticleia, whom Odysseus wept to see. But still Odysseus held them back. Then Teiresias slowly advanced, with blind steps, and drank deeply of the blood.

'Lord Odysseus,' he said in thanks, 'home is sweet and return lightens man's heart. But Poseidon, the Earth-Shaker, has set himself in your path. He hates you because you blinded his giant son Polyphemus. You shall not escape his anger, though you may yet return to your beloved Ithaca.'

After this warning, Teiresias as pointed out to Odysseus the many dangers that lay ahead. He told him to keep a tight hold on his crew, lest suffering make them foolish and rebellious, and in particular to stay well clear of the cattle belonging to the Sun. If Odysseus did return to Ithaca, he would find the island changed, with much trouble in his own house, and a struggle to be taken up against brutal men. And even then his journey was not finished. At last, death would come to him from the sea.

When Odysseus had thanked Teiresias, he put down his sword and let the other ghosts come to the trench to drink. Anticleia had her fill and blessed him. Three times they tried to embrace, but her shade slipped through his arms and departed. Then a throng of the famous dead jostled for the blood. Noble women related to Odysseus their tales of passion and jealousy, and old companions from the fall of Troy mixed memory and regret. Ajax, son of Telamon, stood there, still sulking, and mighty Achilles, unreconciled to death. Odysseus was surprised to see Agamemnon, chief of the Greeks, and learnt from him the horror of his homecoming and death. When the heroes were gone, Odysseus saw others who suffered in Tartarus for their crimes. Even Heracles strode by, scattering the dead like birds from the new corn, and commiserated with Odysseus on the pains of life, and death.

Leaving the borders of Tartarus, Odysseus returned to Aeaea, to give young Elpenor the burial he craved. Next day at dawn, Circe wished him a fond farewell and warned him, adding her voice to that of Teiresias, how to overcome the enmity of Poseidon and the rage of the sea. A good wind carried the ship away, towards the island of the Sirens, whose heart-rending songs drifted out on the dying breeze. As Circe had commanded, Odysseus stopped the ears of his men with wax and ordered them to row swiftly by. But he had himself tied to the mast, for he longed to hear the Sirens' perilous music. And though he stormed and pleaded to be released when the music reached him, so that he might rush to join the Sirens, Eurylochus only tightened the ropes and grimly kept rowing.

Now, the course set by the helmsman took them towards a notorious danger, for the ship could not avoid the narrow strait where Scylla and Charybdis lived and menaced every passing boat. Scylla, with six long necks and six vicious heads, dwelt high in the steep sheer cliff that bordered one side of the narrows. With her weaving necks, she reached down and plucked sailors from the decks of ships which hugged the foot of the cliff. On the other side of the strait, amid the spray and din of rushing water, Charybdis lived under the sea. Deep below a rock with an ancient fig tree, this monster sucked the water into a dizzy whirlpool three times a day, dragging unwary ships into the depths then spewing them up in broken pieces.

Circe had advised Odysseus to chance his luck with Scylla, since Charybdis was too strong even for Poseidon to withstand. At the mouth of the narrows the rowers nearly burst their lungs with effort and the boat went with the speed of fear. But Odysseus steered a little too close to the cliff. The necks stretched out and six jaws snapped on six of the crew. In an instant they were plucked howling into the air, but Odysseus did not dare to pause or turn back. He had nothing but prayers to offer his slaughtered men.

After the terror of the narrows the crew, grief-stricken and exhausted, saw ahead the welcome shelter of the island of Thrinacia, where Helius, the Sun-God, pastured his large herds of placid, well-fed cattle. Odysseus remembered the warnings from Teiresias and Circe and wished to sail on. But his men were on the edge of revolt and demanded a time to rest. Reluctantly, Odysseus landed and made all the crew swear that they would not touch even the least of the Sun's sacred cattle. The island was a pleasant place to sleep and dream of home but the winds remained contrary, blowing hard onto the shore, and the ship could not get away. For a month the men held to their oath. In a while food grew scarce and the men started to eye the cattle. Then, as Odysseus slept, they killed several cows and roasted enough meat for six days of feasting.

A sacrifice was made to Helius, but the Sun-God was not placated. When the wind shifted and the ship, as if in shame, sped from the scene of the sacrilege, Helius called to Zeus for justice. In the storm that followed the Thunderer split the ship with a thunderbolt, sank it and drowned all but Odysseus. He clung to a piece of wreckage, which was carried by wind and tide inexorably back towards Charybdis. Just as the water was sucked into the whirlpool, Odysseus lunged upwards and caught a sturdy branch of the great, overhanging fig tree. Desperately he hung there until Charybdis flung the wreckage out. Then Odysseus regained his raft of broken planks and floated away for nine days until he drifted ashore on the island of Ogygia where Calypso, a daughter of Thetis, entangled him once more in the delights of love.

For seven years Odysseus satisfied the nymph Calypso. She was ardent and loving, and he returned her passion. But the long days drifted by and his heart grew cool. He remembered, more and more, his distant island home, his faithful Penelope, his son, Telemachus. He became distracted, sitting many hours on the shore, gazing at the swell and ebb of the sea. Athene saw his state of mind, and pitied him, and went to Zeus to plead his cause. Zeus was sympathetic. The will of the gods was not that Odysseus should grow thin and sad in the chains of an over-loving bed. Zeus sent Hermes to order his release from Ogygia.

Forlornly, Calypso let him go, for who can resist the decision of Zeus? She told him to build a boat and helped him with wood and tools and cloth for the sail. In four days it was finished. On the fifth, she provisioned it with stores and water and a goatskin of wine. Then she bathed Odysseus, touching so lightly the scars of war on his sturdy body, and dressed him like a bridegroom in the richest clothes. She kissed him, and set him free on a fair wind.

He sailed away most peacefully. For seventeen days, as Calypso had advised him, he kept his eyes on the firmament of heaven. Under the kindly influence of the Pleiades he moved serenely, keeping the Bear always on the left hand. Then Poseidon, returning from a long visit to the far-flung Ethiopians, noticed the lonely boat on the dark sea and burst out in anger.

'Treachery! Behind my back, the gods deceive me. They have sent Odysseus sneaking towards the land of the Phaeacians. But I'm not finished with him yet. He shall have his fill of troubles.'

He massed the clouds and churned the ocean with his trident. Roaring winds came rushing to his call. Lightning lanced through a blue-black sky, the foundations of the earth shook, and a wave as tall as a temple flooded over the boat. Encumbered by his heavy robes, Odysseus was on the point of drowning when Ino-Leucothea, a spirit of the seas, fluttered over him in the form of a seagull. Giving him a veil, which she was carrying in her mouth, she ordered him to throw off his clothes, wind the veil around his waist and plunge boldly into the waves. The celestial veil would take him safely to Scheria, the land at the end of the world where the Phaeacians lived, which already showed dimly in the distance, like a shield looming in the storm of battle.

Poseidon, in his golden chariot, watched the rescue from above. 'This time you go safely,' he grumbled, half-satisfied. 'Though my brother Zeus favours you now, know that your misfortunes are not at an end.' With that, he whipped his horses back to Aegae in a turbulence of tossing manes and flying hooves.

For two more days Odysseus struggled through angry seas towards the shore. He could find no foothold among jagged rocks. But Athene calmed the breaking waves and guided him to a river mouth where Odysseus could drag his bruised and swollen body onto warm sand. He kissed the land, threw the magic veil back to sea as he had promised Leucothea, and collapsed, all naked, into the shelter of some seaside bushes. In a few moments, he was asleep.

While he slept, Nausicaa, daughter of King Alcinous, came with her handmaidens to wash clothes on the banks of the river. When the washing was done, the girls began to play, tossing a ball hand to hand until one missed her catch and the ball fell in the stream. There was a shout of consternation and Odysseus woke with a start in the bushes.

When Odysseus stepped out of the bushes, hiding his nakedness inadequately behind a green branch, he looked like some grizzled sea-thing, with savage eyes and brine-streaked hair. The serving women fled but Nausicaa stood firm. And when silver-tongued Odysseus had explained his sorry state to her, she gladly helped him, giving him clothes and food, and sending him, hidden in Athene's cloud of mist, to plead his cause at the feet of Queen Arete. The queen's heart also softened at the tale told by the master of eloquence. Under gentle pressure from his queen, Alcinous promised to make all things good for this travel-stained stranger, to provide a ship and honourable presents, and a safe passage back to Ithaca. But before the ship sailed, there would be an offering to the gods, and royal games, and a feast worthy of a noble guest, for hospitality is a sacred duty of all mankind.

Next day, in the great hall, when stomachs were satisfied and the wine was flowing, the bard Demodocus took up his lyre and began to sing the well-loved songs, of gods and destiny, of great deeds, of mighty men and lovely women. Blind Demodocus struck the first bold chord and all fell silent. He sang of the trials of war, of wounds and death-agony in the long battle for Troy, of heroic contests on the arid plain. The listeners were sitting in rapt attention. But Odysseus drew his crimson cloak over his head to hide his tears. Then Alcinous stopped the bard and asked his guest the cause of his trouble.

Odysseus answered: 'I am Odysseus, Laertes' son, that same man of whom you sing. All the world knows my subtle ways, and my fame goes up to heaven. In the maze of my wanderings I see no country better than my own dear Ithaca, and yet I cannot reach it.'

Then without pause, in the grief of exile, he recounted to the court the full history of his journeys and his struggle.

At dawn on the next day, Alcinous gave Odysseus many presents and put him aboard one of his swiftest ships, which flew like some great sea bird safely to Ithaca. Worn out by time and travel, Odysseus was asleep when the ship dropped anchor in the little bay of Phorcys. Without waking him, the sailors set him softly on the beach, with his gifts around him, and went quietly on their way.

But Poseidon, no longer able to hurt Odysseus, expended one last burst of fury on the Phaeacians. As their ship reached home, he turned it to stone with a blow of his hand. Let mankind learn, once and for all, not to try the temper of the Earth-Shaker.

A t rest in the sanctuary of Samothrace, at peace with the world, Mantes the storyteller reflected on the homecoming of Odysseus.

'It is a marvellous story, a Greek story, composed of blue sea, storms, shipwreck, danger, and the safety of mysterious islands. Odysseus kept Ithaca always in mind, but the gods did not let him hurry. And they were right. When he left Ithaca, twenty years before, he had been notable for cunning and devious ways, with a head full of stratagems. He returned old in years and wise in experience, his mind stored with riches beyond cunning, a new wealth gained from gods and giants, cannibals and savages, witches and nymphs. Ithaca, when he returned, was the same poor place, a rock with a little earth in the folds, fig trees, olives, lean cattle, leaner children, cracked pots on the doorsteps with bright flowers, and within, pale girls weaving and singing: "Loom of gold, ivory comb . . . "

'He knew now that his journey would never end, but Ithaca had nothing more to teach him. Odysseus had in his hands the reins of his life. The horses of desire and ambition were tamed. They were pulling him towards what he knew to be his destiny. But first, there was work to be done.'

When Odysseus awoke, on a strange beach, his first thought was for his treasure. While he was hiding it, Athene stepped out of the morning mist, told him where he was and explained the state of unhappy Ithaca. One hundred and twenty idle suitors were laying siege to Queen Penelope, convinced that Odysseus was dead, wasting his patrimony and eating her out of house and home. Laertes, his father, had withdrawn from the court in grief and disgust. Telemachus, his son, was searching abroad for news of his father and the suitors planned to murder the young man when he returned. Penelope, his faithful wife, fought off the suitors. She said she could make no decision until she had finished Laertes' shroud. For three years, she wove by day and unpicked the cloth by night. But her trick was now known and the suitors were angry.

When Athene had told Odysseus all these troubles, she disguised him in a beggar's rags and sent him to the hut of Eumaeus, an old swineherd still true to his absent master.

Athene summoned Telemachus from Sparta and father and son were reunited in the swineherd's hut, though neither Eumaeus nor Penelope was yet let into the secret. Cautious Odysseus had a plot to prepare, which was best done with fewest helpers. Taking stock of the enemy at the palace, beggarly Odysseus got only a kick from the goatherd Melantheus, but the old hunting-dog Argus, dying on the dung-heap, recognized his long-lost master and feebly stirred his scabby tail.

Inside the palace, Odysseus found the suitors idling the day away with drink and boastful chatter. He begged for alms in the name of charity but the suitors greeted him with abuse and blows. Antinous, their chief, having thrown a stool at Odysseus, then thought it a pleasant joke to match this new beggar with Irus, a sturdy rogue who hung about the fringes of the table. A prize of blood and bones was offered to the winner. Odysseus tucked up his rags for the contest, surprising all with his powerful muscles. Contemptuously, he felled Irus with one blow.

But Penelope, when she heard of these scenes of riot in her own hall, was ashamed and sent for this unlikely beggar. He had travelled far and might have news of her husband. Still Odysseus did not reveal himself. Instead, he told Penelope a long and pitiful tale which made her weep, and she called for the old nurse Eurycleia to bathe the legs and feet of this long-suffering wanderer. As she did so, the nurse recognized a scar on Odysseus' thigh, the result of a hunting wound from long ago. Before she could cry out, Odysseus gripped her by the throat and hissed, 'Speak at your peril.'

Next day was a feast of Apollo and Odysseus had his plan ready. He told Telemachus to remove all weapons from the hall during the night. Penelope was due to give her decision at the feast. The suitors had lost all patience and had given her an ultimatum. In the hall, when the feasting was done, she announced that she would marry the man who could string Odysseus' great bow and shoot an arrow through twelve axe-rings set in a row.

Still dressed as a beggar Odysseus watched from his lowly position by the door as suitor after suitor failed to bend the bow. Then Odysseus humbly asked if he might try, and Telemachus brought him the bow amid many shouts and insults from the amused suitors. Easily, Odysseus bent the stiff bow, and strung it, and gave the string a sharp twang. Still seated on his stool he pulled the string to its full extent and sent an arrow truly through the rings of the twelve axes. Telemachus ran to his father in the doorway, spear and sword in hand. The suitors sprang for their arms and armour but found them gone and the doors secured. They drew daggers and short swords and faced this presumptuous beggar. On the threshold, with the great door barred behind him, Odysseus threw off his rags and declared himself. He planted his legs apart, steadily took up the bow and with his second arrow pierced the neck of Antinous.

The battle, though fierce, was not in doubt. Athene herself guided the hand of her favourite Odysseus, and sitting among the rafters in the form of a swallow she stiffened his resolve in the bad moments. All the suitors lay dead at last, and of their friends only the bard and the herald were spared, for by sacred custom their persons could not be touched. The serving-girls who had kept warm the suitors' beds were hanged in a row, and the goatherd Melantheus had his extremities chopped off and fed to the dogs.

In the great hall, after the lust of battle, Odysseus stood amid the shambles of the slain, bespattered in gore like a lion who has devoured an ox. Wearily, he summoned Eurycleia.

'Nurse, fetch fire to purify this house, and sulphur to cleanse the pollution. Then seek out Penelope and bring her to me.'

There had been enough killing. Life, not death, was in his mind. It was time to start again.

But words, after so long an absence, were hard to find. Husband and wife, partly strangers now, sat each side of the cleansing fire, gazing in silence into the flames. When they began to talk, pain, resentment, recrimination poisoned their mouths until all hurts were out, and the slate was wiped clean. Then they looked on each other with new eyes, with the eyes of remembered love, and went quietly to their repose.

Strife was almost at an end. The families of the suitors called for revenge but Athene petitioned her father, Zeus, to stop the flow of blood. Zeus, the Reconciler, struck the ground between the enemies with a thunderbolt and all parties laid down their arms, in submission to the will of heaven. Only Poseidon was unsatisfied.

Then Odysseus made the last journey, as Teiresias had instructed him on the banks of the Styx. He took an oar on his shoulder and travelled to the wilds of Thesprotia, walking far into the mountains until he met a people who used no salt and mistook the oar for a winnowing-fan. Here, he planted the oar in the earth and sacrificed a ram and a bull and a boar to Poseidon. At last, the Earth-Shaker was pacified in his surly mind and granted Odysseus the gift of rest. He returned to Ithaca and waited, as it had been foretold, for death to come to him from the sea.

Mantes looked out from the slope of Mount Phengari, high above the breathing plasm of the Aegean, where the evening sun had burnt a violet trail through copper-coloured water and the rising morn was just now breaking over the flank of the hill, pale, but ready to suffuse this hot world with tender, trembling light.

'Odysseus, brother Greek,' Mantes prayed for the wanderer and for all wanderers, 'in my imagination I touch your closed eyes. Life is a flower, a breath, the morning dew, a moment at twilight. On all sides from where I stand, from the depths of the Aegean, from the bowels of this magic earth, there rises into the mind's eye the race of men and women created under the maternal caress of this holy land where the gods live. That is what is substantial, and what endures.

'O gods of Greece, I pray that my eyes too may close in such an hour as this, when only one way remains to express my sense of enchantment, to kneel and kiss my native ground, then to rise up and spread my arms wide in reverence, worshipping the soil and the water and the colour and the sky of Holy Greece.'

INDEX

INDEX

Contents

KEY TO SYMBOLS

✚ Map reference
✉ Address
☎ Telephone number
🕐 Opening times
✋ Admission prices
🚇 Subway station
🚌 Bus number
🚉 Train station
⛴ Ferry/boat
🎫 Tours
📖 Guidebook
🍴 Restaurant
☕ Café
🍸 Bar
🏬 Shop
🚻 Restrooms
🛏 Number of rooms
🅿 Parking
🚭 No smoking
🏊 Swimming pool
🏋 Gymnasium
🍴 Place to eat
🛏 Place to stay

UNDERSTANDING CANADA

Canada is one of the world's most exciting and rewarding countries
to visit. The variety is intense. Stupendous mountain peaks vie with
wide rolling prairies, great lakes, dense forest growth, and
wave-battered ocean shores.
From the midnight sun of the north to the vineyards and fruit orchards
of the south, the landscape unfolds as an unending mosaic.
Sophisticated cities and rural communities house a close-knit
population as diverse as the land.
And over it all, the sky twinkles with stars and glows with the swirling
luminescence of the northern lights.

The distinctive red maple leaf declares in unmistakable terms that, wherever it appears, you are looking at something Canadian—from the national flag to the tourist T-shirt

VAST AND FROZEN GIANT

Say "Canada" and the first three adjectives that pop into most people's minds are "huge," "cold" and "empty." This "big frigid" stereotype makes some Canadians bridle, and it is a bit simplistic, but like all stereotypes it contains a germ of truth. Canada is immense. Almost unimaginably so. Bigger than any country on Earth except Russia, it sprawls more than 6,000km (3,720 miles) from the Atlantic to the Pacific and fills four-and-a-half time zones. An office worker in St. John's, Newfoundland, gets home for supper just about the same time his colleague in Vancouver on the West Coast is getting back to his desk from lunch. From south to north, the country is almost as vast. It stretches from the vineyards of the Niagara Peninsula, where sunset is determined by hour, to the edge of the polar ice cap, where it's determined by month. Even Canada's provinces are huge. It takes 24 solid hours of driving just to get across the province of Ontario, for example, and the entire United Kingdom would fit comfortably into British Columbia three times, with plenty of room left over for Greece.

And let's be honest about this: It can be extremely cold. Stand stationary at the corner of Victoria and Albert streets in Regina,

Saskatchewan, in mid-January for more than five minutes and your cheeks will start to turn white. But go to the same street corner in mid-July and you could fry eggs on the sidewalk. And what about Victoria on the west coast? Every February when Montréalers and Calgarians are still digging themselves out of mountainous snowdrifts, the Victorians go out and count flowers. In 2002 8.5 billion daffodils, lilies, peonies, primroses, violets and snowdrops bloomed. Canada cold? For sure, but not everywhere and not all the time.

URBAN POPULATION

It is only partly true that Canada is empty. Yes, Canada does have just 31 million people (2001 census)—only about half as many as France. And there are indeed great stretches of the country where you can drive for miles and not see another human being. But about 90 percent of Canadians live within 200km (124 miles) of the US border, and the population along some parts of that long narrow strip can be pretty dense. In fact, most Canadians are urbanites, and close to a third of them live in just three cities: Montréal, Toronto and Vancouver, which, incidentally, are among the most vibrant metropolises on the continent. Montréal and the province of Québec are as French as, say, Nice and Normandy. Not

CANADA'S REGIONS

Newfoundland and Labrador One province in spite of the ungainly name. It joined the Canadian federation in 1949, making it the youngest province and very much a place apart, with a fierce sense of identity and its own distinctive accent. Most of its 530,000 people live on Newfoundland, many of them in tiny villages with captivating names like Heart's Delight and Heart's Content (not to mention Dildo) that cling tenaciously to the rocky coast.

Atlantic Provinces Even if all three of the Atlantic provinces—Nova Scotia, New Brunswick and Prince Edward Island—were merged into one, the result would still be by far the smallest province. But what the Maritimes lack in size, they make up for in history. They are among the most settled regions in Canada and the coastline is dotted with historic villages, where French, English and even Gaelic are spoken. The lush farmland of the St. John River Valley, the tides of the Bay of Fundy, the warm-water beaches of Prince Edward Island, and the mountains of Cape Breton are among the region's most famous attractions.

National and provincial flags (left) fly in front of Ottawa's government buildings. Fall colors of the maple (center). Ceremonial uniform of the Royal Canadian Mounted Police (right)

Québec The heartland of French Canada. More than 80 percent of its 7 million residents are French-speaking, which sets it apart from all of North America. Most of its cities, towns and villages are strung along the shores of the St. Lawrence River, but its northernmost point is on the same latitude as Greenland. Its capital, Québec City, is one of the oldest settlements in North America and the only walled city north of Mexico. And while Québec is not a Maritime province or even considered an Atlantic province, it has one of the longest, most varied and most beautiful coastlines in the east.

Ontario Canada's richest and most populous province. Its wealth is centered in the industrial cities of the Great Lakes—Toronto, Windsor, Hamilton, Oshawa and Thunder Bay—and in northern mining towns like Timmins and Sudbury. But it's not all industry and commerce. Toronto is the cultural heart of English Canada and one of the most important theater cities in the world. The Niagara Peninsula is on the same latitude as northern California, and has some of Canada's best farmlands and vineyards. To the north, the wilderness stretches all the way to the shores of James Bay.

Prairies Manitoba, Saskatchewan and Alberta are collectively referred to as the Prairies, and indeed, much of the landscape is flat and filled with wheat farms and cattle ranches, but the landscape is more varied than many people think. Woodlands account for more than half the entire region and Manitoba's Lake Winnipeg is large enough to qualify as an inland sea. The badlands in the southern parts of Alberta are rich in dinosaur fossils and stories of fugitive outlaws. Western Alberta has some of the highest peaks in the Rocky Mountains and two of Canada's most famous national parks—Banff and Jasper.

British Columbia Canada's opening on the Pacific, with a coastline pocked with deep fiords and covered with rain forests. In the interior, the Coastal, Purcell, Kootenay, Selkirk, Monashee, Cariboo, and Columbia mountain ranges ripple across the southern interior like rocky waves. Between them lie deep valleys and long narrow lake systems. Most of the province's 4 million people live in the Lower Mainland area around Vancouver, where the Fraser River empties into the Strait of Georgia. Victoria, the provincial capital, has the mildest climate in the country; it attracts so many retirees that the locals refer to it as God's waiting room.

The Far North That vast stretch of land and ice north of the 60th parallel is really Canada's last frontier. Its three jurisdictions, the Yukon, the Northwest Territories and Nunavut, are quite different. Deciduous forests and high mountains make the Yukon look more like an extension of British Columbia than part of the Arctic. The Kluane National Park, in fact, has Canada's highest mountains and some of its fiercest rivers. Visitors to the Northwest Territories can sail on Great Slave Lake or travel west from Yellowknife to see Virginia Falls in Nahanni National Park. Nunavut is Canada's newest jurisdiction and is administered by the Inuit. It is home to three of the most remote national parks in the world: Auyuittuq, Sirmilik and Quittinirpaaq.

that the country is limited to just two cultures any more. Succeeding waves of immigrants have created a checkerboard of communities across the country: Highland Scots in Nova Scotia, Greeks and Italians in Montréal and Toronto, Icelanders in Manitoba, Ukrainians in Alberta, and Sikhs and Chinese on the west coast.

Trying to stuff all that landscape and all those cultures into a short trip is pretty well impossible. Just driving from Montréal to Toronto, for example—two cities that consider themselves mid-country neighbors—takes at least five hours on a good day, and to get from Toronto to Vancouver takes three days and four nights on Via Rail's

Elizabeth II. Her representative in Ottawa is the governor general, a job once handed out to British peers and minor royalty but now usually held by a prominent Canadian who is appointed to the job for five years or so. It's a purely cere-monial job, but it comes with a fine residence, Rideau Hall in Ottawa, and a regiment of scarlet-coated guards. The governor general must give royal assent to every law passed by parliament.

The 10 provinces are, in theory at least, all equal in autonomy, with their own legislatures and their own health and school systems (and their own lieutenant-governors to handle the ceremonial side of things). But they're wildly

Vast Maligne Lake (left), in Jasper National Park, is fed by glacial meltwaters. Point Armour Lighthouse (center) is a beacon to Newfoundland's fishermen. Calgary's distinctive skyline in winter (right)

transcontinental train. But flying into one of the three big cities will give you quick access to a wide variety of landscapes and people. Toronto is the gateway to Niagara Falls, the Great Lakes and Canada's industrial heart-land; Montréal opens up the way for a thorough exploration of French Canada, from the fishing villages of the Gaspé Peninsula to the ski resorts of the Laurentians; and Vancouver, of course, is the gateway to the Pacific coast and the snow-capped Rocky Mountains of the British Columbia interior. And no matter how cosmopolitan each city might feel, the empty spaces are never far away. The Parc de Mont-Tremblant, for example, a mountainous, lake-spattered wilder-ness more than half the size of Luxembourg, is just a two-hour drive from the cafés and clubs of downtown Montréal.

But don't overlook the smaller cities. The old port of Halifax makes a great base for exploring the Gaelic- and French-speaking villages of the Atlantic provinces, and Calgary and Edmonton are gateways to the Rocky Mountains and the wheat fields and cattle ranches of the Prairies.

POLITICAL DIVISIONS

Canada is the only monarchy on the North American continent, even if royal symbols don't get the respect they once did. Canada's ultimate head of state is still whoever happens to be sit-ting on the British throne—at present, Queen

Canadian population by mother tongue	
English	18 million
French	6.7 million
Chinese	850,000
Italian, German (each)	500,000
Arabic, Portuguese, Polish, Punjabi, and Spanish	200,000
Dutch, Filipino, Greek, Vietnamese (each)	100,000
Other	2 million
Cree	73,000
Inuktitut	29,000
Other First Nations	100,000

unequal in just about everything else. Québec, for example, with more than 1.5 million sq km (half a million sq miles) of terri-tory, is about three times the size of France. Tiny Prince Edward Island, on the other hand, is less than 6,000 sq km (2,375sq miles), which is plenty, consider-ing its population of 133,000 is smaller than that of an average Toronto borough in Canada's most populous province, Ontario. They don't even all speak the same language, either. Québec is officially French-speaking, New Brunswick is officially bilingual (French and English), and the rest are all officially English, although they accord varying degrees of services to their French-speaking citizens.

Three territories, the Yukon, the Northwest Territories and Nunavut, also have their own leg-islatures, but defer to the federal government on many matters. The vast majority of the people in Nunavut, the newest territory, are native Inuit and the discussions in its legislature in Iqaluit are often in Inuktitut rather than French or English.

DEMOGRAPHICS

Canada began as a clash between the French and the English, plus a dash of native North American. But it wasn't long before the Scots and the Irish showed up to add a Gaelic touch to the mix. Succeeding waves of eastern Europeans, Jews (first Sephardic and then Ashkenazi), Italians, Greeks, Germans, Lebanese,

		DK		IS	

Arctic Circle

USA

YUKON

MOUNTAIN
STANDARD
TIME
UTC - 7h

NUNAVUT

NEWFOUNDLAND
STANDARD
TIME
UTC - 3.5h

PACIFIC
STANDARD
TIME
UTC - 8h

NORTH WEST
TERRITORIES

CENTRAL
STANDARD
TIME
UTC - 6h

NEWFOUNDLAND

BRITISH
COLUMBIA

ALBERTA

MANITOBA

EASTERN
STANDARD
TIME
UTC - 5h

SASKATCHEWAN

ONTARIO

QUÉBEC

PRINCE
EDWARD
ISLAND

NEW
BRUNSWICK

NOVA SCOTIA

ATLANTIC
STANDARD
TIME
UTC - 4h

USA

Chinese and Japanese made Canada into one of the most multicultural nations on earth. More recent arrivals include Southeast Asians from Vietnam and Cambodia, Indians and Pakistanis, Iranians and Arabs, and Latin Americans from Nicaragua, Guatemala and Mexico.

CLIMATE

According to an old joke, Canadians split their year into two parts: ten months of winter and two months of bad skiing. A bit of an exaggeration, maybe (southern areas are mostly warm from May to September), but Canadian winters are truly the stuff of legend.

Hikers in Yoho National Park pause to admire the view of Lake O'Hara

January temperatures in Montréal, which shares the same latitude as Venice, often drop to -20°C (-4°F). In cities like Edmonton, Winnipeg and Regina, far from the moderating influences of the sea or the Great Lakes, the mercury regularly drops to -40°C (-80°F) and stays there for a week or two. On the other hand, summers on the Prairies can be blisteringly hot, with temperatures rising to well over 40°C (104°F). The only relief comes in the form of fierce rain storms.

Brutal winters and scorching summers, however, are not universal. In Victoria, British Columbia, for example, the temperature seldom drops below freezing, and the flowers start blooming in early February. Januarys in Vancouver are more likely to be damp than white. Sometimes some of that warm, Pacific weather leaks through the valleys of the Rockies into Calgary in the form of winds called Chinooks, which can make the temperature rise by as much as 20 degrees in a day. Victoria and Vancouver have another distinction: They're the only parts of the country that get a real spring, a season that starts in February on the West Coast and lingers with much blossoming and budding well into May. The post-winter period in the rest of Canada, on the other hand, is nasty, muddy and short, erupting into summer with a speed that's almost rude. But what the east lacks in spring it makes up for with its long, glorious fall. The hills and valleys of Ontario, Québec and the Maritimes, in particular, blaze with glowing foliage. The red maple leaf on the Canadian flag is highly appropriate.

BEST PLACES TO STAY

Murray Premises Hotel, St. John's (see page 308) Luxury hotel located in former warehouse on the harbor.

Auberge St-Antoine, Québec City (see page 315) Hotel of great character in historic Lower Town.

Pillar and Post Inn, Niagara-on-the-Lake (see page 318) Lovely country inn in friendly community.

Hillcrest House, Calgary (see page 326) Warm and welcoming B&B in a fine old house.

Castle Mountain Chalets, Banff (see page 329) Log cabins in wilderness setting, but with all modern conveniences.

Auberge St-Antoine is on place Royale, in Québec City

BEST PLACES TO EAT

Ryan Duffy's, Halifax (see page 307) Famous for its steak and seafood.

L'Express, Montréal (see page 311) Lively bistro on fashionable St-Denis, with great food.

Truffles, Toronto (see page 323) Classy restaurant with the best food in town (some say in Canada).

Tavern in the Park, Winnipeg (see page 328) Glass-roofed atrium, outdoor terrace and the best food in the West.

Blue Water Café, Vancouver (see page 331) Hip restaurant with splendid seafood in trendy area.

Of all the bounty of Canada's waters, the salmon is king

BEST SMALL TOWNS

Lunenburg, Nova Scotia (see page 67) A World Heritage Site and one of Nova Scotia's most historic and attractive towns.

St-Andrews-by-the-Sea, New Brunswick (see page 72) Picturesque town with elegant houses and tree-lined streets.

Niagara-on the-Lake, Ontario (see page 127) One of the most delightful and historic townships in Ontario.

Chemainus, British Columbia (see page 152) Thriving art center with magnificent outdoor murals.

Dawson City, Yukon (see page 178) Living history and one of Canada's most unusual communities.

Historic Lunenburg is full of architectural delights

BEST HISTORIC RECONSTRUCTIONS

Louisbourg, Nova Scotia (see page 66) The great fortress of New France guarding the entrance to the St. Lawrence.

Kings Landing, New Brunswick (see page 61) Splendidly re-created 19th-century Loyalist settlement.

Upper Canada Village, Ontario (see page 129) Imaginative re-creation of early Ontario life.

Heritage Park, Alberta (see page 136) Historic village transporting you back to early 20th-century Calgary.

Fort Langley, British Columbia (see page 152) Carefully re-constructed Hudson Bay Company trading post.

Canada's earliest days live on at Louisbourg

BEST MUSEUMS

Canadian Museum of Civilization, Gatineau (see page 92) Architecturally unique, with displays as diverse as Canada itself.

Royal Ontario Museum, Toronto (see page 114) Bewildering array of choices, but something to interest everyone.

Science North, Sudbury (see page 128) Award-winning science center in two snowflake-shaped buildings.

Manitoba Museum, Winnipeg (see page 142) Spectacular museum with excellent dioramas and historical displays.

Museum of Anthropology, Vancouver (see page 147) Fine museum devoted to the art and lifestyle of the First Nations.

First Nations art, Canadian Museum of Civilization, Gatineau

BEST ROCKY MOUNTAIN SITES

The quintessential image of the Rockies, at Maligne Lake

Moraine Lake (see page 163) Jewel of the Rockies, reflecting the jagged peaks of the Wenkchemna Mountains.

Peyto Lake (see page 158) The almost unbelievable turquoise-blue of the water is created by glacial particles.

Athabasca Glacier (see page 158) Tours on the glacier by giant snowmobile take you onto 300m (1,000ft) or more of ice.

Mount Edith Cavell (see page 161) Serenely beautiful peak in magnificent setting with hanging glacier.

Maligne Lake (see page 161) The largest lake in the Rockies, surrounded by glacial peaks.

BEST NATIONAL PARKS (OUTSIDE THE ROCKIES)

Gros Morne National Park (see page 61) Spectacularly beautiful, with geology of international importance.

Cape Breton Highlands National Park (see page 60) Breathtaking scenery along a wild rocky coastline.

Kluane National Park (see page 179) Majestic mountainscapes in Canada's highest mountains.

Riding Mountain National Park (see page 139) Rising like an island in the farmland, with three distinct landscapes.

Pacific Rim National Park (see page 166) Virgin forests, fantastic beaches and remote offshore islands.

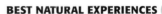

The sun goes down over Riding Mountain National Park

BEST WATERFALLS

Montmorency Falls, Québec (see page 87) Unexpectedly impressive so close to Québec City.

Niagara Falls, Ontario (see page 122) Of course! Is there anyone in the world who has not heard of Niagara?

Kakabeka Falls, Ontario (see page 129) Dramatic falls sometimes called the Niagara of the North.

Athabasca Falls, Alberta (see page 159) Very photogenic as the Athabasca River tumbles over rocky ledges.

Takakkaw Falls, British Columbia (see page 173) Spectacular falls in splendid setting.

Virginia Falls, Northwest Territories (see page 179) Remote, dramatic and twice the height of Niagara.

Niagara's Horseshoe Falls are a compelling sight

BEST NATURAL EXPERIENCES

The tides of the Bay of Fundy (see page 63) One of the world's marine wonders, Fundy tides rise and fall an incredible 16m (52ft).

Whale-watching in Tadoussac (see page 94) A great flotilla of whales summers in the plankton-rich waters of the St. Lawrence.

Polar bears in Churchill (see page 137) A veritable wildlife paradise on the shores of Hudson Bay.

Badlands of Alberta (see page 131) Dramatic with their stark beauty, ocher-colored soil and arid landscapes.

Northern lights in Yellowknife (see page 180) Wildlife and northern lights reflected in Great Slave Lake.

Rolling Breakers on Vancouver Island (see page 171) The rolling swells of the Pacific break directly on Long Beach.

Above: Horseshoe Canyon in Alberta's Badlands
Right: A close-up view of an orca

TOP 20 EXPERIENCES

Hike out to Newfoundland's Signal Hill National Historic Site for a grand view of St. John's and its snug harbor.

Ride the passenger ferry across Halifax Harbor for a view of one of the most fascinating ports in North America.

Go to a church-hall lobster supper in any of a dozen or so Prince Edward Island villages.

Rent a kayak in Tadoussac and paddle up the Saguenay River to look for beluga whales.

Walk the ramparts of Québec City, the only walled city in North America north of Mexico.

Take a romantic evening stroll to the lookout on Mont Royal for a bird's-eye view of Montréal, North America's only French-speaking metropolis.

Go to solemn Mass in Montréal's magnificently ornate Basilique Notre-Dame on Sunday morning.

Pick a bar, any bar, on Montréal's rue St-Denis and sit outside sipping a beer, a glass of wine or a cognac and watch some of the country's most stylish men and women stroll by.

Go to a National Hockey League game in Montréal, Ottawa, Toronto or Vancouver. Failing that, go to any neighborhood rink and watch a Pee Wee tournament.

Skate on the Rideau Canal through the heart of Canada's capital city, Ottawa.

Paddle a canoe through the waterways of Ontario's Algonquin Park, one of the more accessible wilderness areas in Canada.

Go Saturday shopping in Toronto's Kensington Market, where there is a chaotic fusion of cultures, smells, food, secondhand goods and street performers.

Ride the ferry to Toronto's Ward's Island, walk along the outer boardwalk to Centre Island and ride the ferry back.

Ride the Algoma Central Railway train through the blazing fall shades of the Agawa Canyon north of Sault-Ste-Marie, Ontario.

Take the train (or fly, if you're short of time) from Winnipeg to Churchill on the shores of Hudson Bay to see the polar bears.

Spend a night in a tepee at Wanuskewin Heritage Park near Saskatoon. Canadian aboriginals started camping here more than 1,500 years ago.

Cheer the chuck wagon races at the Calgary Stampede. For sheer excitement it's hard to beat.

Rent a horse and a guide, or join a group, in either Jasper or Banff and go riding in the Rockies.

Hike right past the well-walked Lake Louise in Banff National Park and climb to Lake O'Hara, luminescently green and surrounded by snowcapped peaks.

Rent a bicycle and ride around Vancouver's Stanley Park. If you're really energetic, jog or walk.

Pick a clear day or evening and take a 1.6-km (one-mile) ride to the top of Grouse Mountain on the Skyride for a glorious view of Vancouver and the Pacific.

Take a floatplane trip from Vancouver for a remote fishing trip, or just flightseeing.

Take a midnight stroll in daylight along a wooden sidewalks in Yukon's Dawson City.

Taking the ferry across Halifax Harbor (above). Left: The chief ingredient of your lobster supper

Terrasse Dufferin offers a scenic walk on Québec City's ramparts

Saddle up to explore the Rockies on horseback

A Mountie (far left) on guard. Racing (right) at the Calgary Stampede

Skyride to the summit of Vancouver's Grouse Mountain

Fly a floatplane (left) from Vancouver
In summer, the midnight sun shines on Dawson City (right)

Living
Canada

The British influence is still strong in Victoria, BC, not least at this fish-and-chip restaurant (left)

Vancouver's Chinatown (above and below) draws Chinese Canadians. Ukrainian church architecture, Saskatchewan (right)

Canadian SOCIETY

Toronto writer Peter Newman once complained that Canadians are the only people on Earth who aspire to be Clark Kent rather than Superman—an ironic jibe given that one of the two men who created the Man of Steel was Canadian-born Joe Shuster. While the stereotype is probably overstated, Canadians are, by and large, a diffident group of people (except at hockey games, of course). They tend to end every sentence with an interrogative "eh," for example, as if not quite sure of where they stand. They also tend to identify themselves by what they're not—English-speaking Canadians are "not American," for example, and, sadly, a significant number of French-speakers identify themselves as "not-Canadians." Part of the blame probably rests with the country's fractured origins. The founding nationalities—French and English—weren't exactly close to start with and spent the first century or so pretty much keeping out of each other's way. That meant that the succeeding waves of immigrants—Celts, Jews, Ukrainians, Italians, Greeks, Asians, and Latin Americans—did much the same and formed what Canadians prefer to call a cultural mosaic. The end result isn't neat or tidy or homogenous, but it is interesting.

Parades Tell the Story

In the past, nothing reflected Canada's cultural clashes and compromises better than the parades of Montréal. On June 24—Québec's Fête Nationale—thousands of separatists and nationalists took to the streets for a huge parade. This parade has latterly become increasingly representative of Québec's diversity, with ethnic dancers and Scottish pipe bands. A week later, on Canada Day, the Federalists staged a more modest march, and this is now a huge multinational party ending with a big fireworks display. On March 17, Montréalers of every political, linguistc and ethnic stripe turn out to celebrate St. Patrick's Day, which marks the end of winter. They hold fast to the notion that "Everyone is Irish on St. Patrick's Day."

Eating alfresco (above) in Montréal, and the city's Jazz Festival (below). West Edmonton Mall's lagoon (right)

A scene from *My Big Fat Greek Wedding* (above), shot in 2002

Patriotic Suds

One of the few places Canadians display patriotism is in beer commercials. Molson, the brewing company, mounted one of the most aggressive such campaigns in 1998 with a rant by a character named Joe, which was as much anti-American as pro-Canadian. "I speak English and French, not American," he says. "I can proudly sew my country's flag on my backpack. I believe in peacekeeping not policing, diversity not assimilation, and that the beaver is a truly proud and noble animal. Canada is the second largest land mass. The first nation of hockey. And the best part of North America. My name is Joe. And I am Canadian." It was an instant hit, but ironically the actor who played Joe is now working in Los Angeles.

The Great Indoors

Canada is a paradise for outdoor types, but in winter many Canadians tend to prefer the Great Indoors. Albertans, for example, have the West Edmonton Mall (see page 231–232)—48ha (120 acres) of dazzlingly conspicuous consumption with more than 800 stores, 100 places to eat, 20 movie theaters and the world's largest indoor amusement park.

Montréalers can live a full life without ever going outdoors, thanks to their Underground City, which has (at last count) 8 hotels, 3 department stores, 1,000 boutiques, 300 restaurants, 40 bank branches, 90 office buildings, 4 universities, a skating rink (the home of the Montréal Canadiens), a cathedral, the Convention Centre, 2 bus depots, 2 train stations, and nearly 3,000 apartments.

No Hyphens Here

Novelist Neil Bissoondath would appear to be a poster boy for Canada's "cultural mosaic." Of East Indian descent, he was born in Trinidad and came to Canada in the 1960s—the perfect multicultural Canadian. But he has stubbornly refused the hyphenation process that gave us "Greek-Canadians" and "Italian-Canadians", partly because he didn't want to have to describe himself as an East-Indian-Trinidadian-Canadian, but mostly because he thought it was just plain wrong. In his 1994 book, *Selling Illusions*, Bissoondath argued that multiculturalism, with its festivals and celebrations, was paternalistic and condescending, and created a kind of "gentle and insidious cultural apartheid."

"Multiculturalism," he wrote, "has done little more than lead an already divided country down the path to further social divisiveness."

Greek Pride

Winnipeg native Nia Vardalos turned the adventures and misadventures of her huge, eccentric and proudly Greek family into a wildly successful one-woman comedy show. She focused on her family's horrified reaction to her marriage to decidedly non-Greek Ian Gomez—a theme that resonated with thousands of interethnic couples across the country. It also resonated with actress Rita Wilson, who saw the show in Los Angeles and recommended it to her husband, Tom Hanks, who in turn decided to make it into a movie. *My Big Fat Greek Wedding* cost only $5 million to make, but it was a megahit. And while the movie was set in Chicago to please American audiences, the real story happened in Winnipeg.

Bright autumnal hues of *The Pool* (right), by Tom Thomson, in the National Gallery in Ottawa. Street entertainers (right) on Granville Island, Vancouver

Montréal International Jazz Festival (below), and an equally eye-catching performance by Les Grands Ballets Canadien (bottom)

Arts and Media

In recent years Canada has shown a remarkable ability to crank out pop divas. So much so, you could be forgiven for thinking there are no male singers in the country. Sure, homegrown fans swoon over rock bands like the Tragically Hip, and chanteur Roch Boivin sets francophone female hearts aflutter everywhere. But none of these male stars can match the sheer world-busting fame of Céline Dion, Alanis Morrisette, Avril Lavigne, and Shania Twain. Go beyond the boundaries of pop songs, and that list of female superstars could be expanded to include jazz-singer Diana Krall and Cape Breton fiddler Natalie MacMaster. When it comes to the performing arts, Canadian women are top of the bill.

But beyond the musical stage, the genders even out. Filmmakers Denys Arcand and Atom Egoyan, and playwrights Michel Tremblay and Luc Plamondon, for example, have lit world stages and screens with their works. Canadian writers both male and female have made winning the Booker Prize look almost routine. Michael Ondaatje won it in 1992 for *The English Patient*, for example, and Margaret Atwood won it in 2000 for *The Blind Assassin*. When Yann Martel won the Booker for *The Life of Pi* in 2002, contenders included fellow Canadians Rohinto Mistry and Carol Shields.

Reinventing an Old Art

In 1984, Guy Laliberté, a fire-eater and musician, brought together street-performers from around the world to create Cirque du Soleil. They first pitched their blue-and-yellow tent in Baie St-Paul, Québec, and proceeded to revolution-ize the ancient art of the circus. Instead of grumpy tigers and a ran-dom sequence of sepa-rate acts, Cirque du Soleil combined theater, music, lights, dance, acrobatics, and dazzling costumes into a seam-less spectacle that has become a worldwide success.

The troupe now pro-duces five international touring shows in addi-tion to having resident shows in Las Vegas and Walt Disney World, attracting in total about 7 million fans a year.

Montréal is still the Cirque's international headquarters, and the troupe's big tops return to their home city every spring to launch its new productions.

The distinctive Big Top (right) of the renowned Cirque du Soleil, which travels the world but always has a season in its home town of Montréal

Towering billboards in front of the gleaming CBC Building in Toronto

The fantastic acrobatics of the Cirque du Soleil in rehearsal (left)

Avril Lavigne carries on the long line of Canadian singers to reach stardom

Reaching Everyone

Drawing together an officially bilingual, culturally diverse population scattered thinly over a vast landscape has been the daunting mandate of the CBC since the state-owned broadcasting corporation was set up in 1936. Its two national television networks (one French and one English) and four national radio networks (two French and two English) reach every nook and cranny of the country, from downtown Toronto to Inuvik, way up north in the Arctic

The proliferation of private networks and cable channels has diminished the role of the CBC, but it still provides an important platform for Canadian entertainers and journalists. English-language programming has focused primarily on variety and information, while the French television network has produced such classic melodramas as "La Famille Plouffe" and "Il Lance, Il Compte."

Fraud on Stage

In the 1990s, Garth Drabinsky and Myron Gottlieb were the darlings of Canadian theater. Toronto was emerging as a major theatrical hub and Drabinsky and Gottlieb's high-flying company, Livent, was mounting such giant musicals as Showboat and Phantom of the Opera. Then, in 1998, it all came crashing down, just as Livent was taking its latest musical, Ragtime, to New York. Accountants found irregularities in Livent's books and the company went bankrupt. A US court indicted Drabinsky and Gottlieb for fraud, and in Canada the RCMP did the same. Still, despite all the troubles, the last production Livent mounted while Drabinsky was in charge was Fosse, which won three Tony awards in 1999, including best musical. And Toronto is still a major theater city.

Building an Empire

In the 1920s, Roy Thomson was trudging around the mining towns of northern Ontario trying to sell De Forest Crosley radios, but not having a whole lot of luck. He figured he'd sell more if radio reception was better and decided that the only way to achieve that would be to open a radio station. So he did – in North Bay.

This was the start of what was to become one of the biggest media empires in the world. By 1964, the Thomson family controlled hundreds of newspapers and radio and television stations in Canada, the United States and Britain (including the venerable Times of London). Roy, a working-class lad who'd grown up in his mother's Toronto boarding house, became Lord Thomson of Fleet.

Regulated Culture

Defining what is and what is not a "Canadian song" is a serious business for Canadian bureaucrats—and for Canadian singers, musicians and radio stations. Canada has devised a set of radio and television rules to protect its "cultural industries" from the American giant next door. Radio stations, for example, must air a certain percentage of Canadian songs, as defined by bureaucratic guidelines. The results can sometimes be silly: One year, for example, the albums of pop-star Bryan Adams were shut out because he'd co-written the music with an American. But supporters say the rules have helped to create the conditions that produced such homegrown stars as Avril Lavigne and Shania Twain.

First Nations (above) add their own touch to the Calgary Stampede. The retractable roof of Toronto's SkyDome (left) opens to reveal the lofty CN Tower

Snowmobiles (below) are a fun way to enjoy the harsh Canadian winter, and there are plenty of designated trails in the most popular areas

Saskatoon's hockey team (above), and the 2002 Olympic curling gold-medal winners (below)

Top Sports

Polite Rule-followers

For a magic moment during the 1988 Olympics, Canada thought it had the fastest sprinter on Earth when Jamaican immigrant Ben Johnson of Toronto won gold by running the 100m (109yd) in 9.79 seconds. But it turned out Canada just had the fastest cheat on Earth. Johnson tested positive for illegal steroids and was stripped of his medal—a severe blow to the country's self-image as a diffident nation of polite rule-followers.

Canada regained some measure of its lost honor, however, in 1996, when another Jamaican immigrant, Donovan Bailey, won the gold medal in the 100m (109yd) with a time of 9.84 seconds. Slightly slower, maybe, but honest.

The three most important words in Canadian sport are hockey, hockey and hockey—and that means ice hockey, not the game schoolgirls play on grass. The Iroquois game of lacrosse might be Canadians' official national sport, but hockey is their passion. "You don't like hockey," according to writer Stuart McLean, "you believe in it." Which helps explain why there are about as many indoor ice rinks in the country as there are churches. In even the tiniest towns kids can get quality ice time to learn the basic skills of skating and stick handling. Canada's other icy obsession, curling, is even more eccentric. This Scots-bred sport, which involves sliding 18kg (40lb) lumps of granite down long ice sheets, has more than a million aficionados in more than 1,200 clubs across the country. The national television network clears the airwaves to broadcast the national "brier," or championship. Not surprisingly, other winter sports such as skiing and snow-shoeing are also popular, and while soccer's generally a dud as a spectator sport, thousands of kids play it every summer. There are even cricket teams—one of which stunned the world as well as the Canadians by winning a game at the 2003 world championship.

The Calgary Stampede (above) includes exciting rodeo events

Toronto Blue Jays at the practice nets (above). A 1960s snowmobile sales brochure (below left). Lacrosse (below right) at Toronto University

Cross-country skiing (above) in Québec

Curling

Who but Canadians would try to make a hit movie about curling? The result—*Men With Brooms*—wasn't quite the box-office smash its producers hoped for, in spite of the presence of homegrown stars Paul Gross and Leslie Nielsen. Still, the 2002 movie has its hilarious moments as its four unlikely heroes from a northern mining town try to earn the respect of their neighbors by winning the coveted Golden Broom. The final scenes even manage to make so-called "ice-bowling" look exciting. But best of all, the movie is an affectionate portrayal of the important place that curling holds in the hearts of small-town Canadians all across the country.

Women in Hockey

When both the women's and the men's hockey teams won gold for Canada at the 2002 winter Olympics in Salt Lake City, it was a dream come true for millions of fans. It was also eloquent proof that hockey, one of the toughest games in the world, was no longer an exclusive male preserve. Female players aren't allowed to slam each other into the boards the way the men do, but their no-hitting game is fast and exciting. So far, the elite National Hockey League hasn't signed any women, but a couple of minor-league teams have used female goalies, and one of the Salt Lake City veterans, Hayley Wickenheiser, is playing forward with a professional men's team in Finland.

Bombardier's Marvel

In 1958, Québecer Joseph-Armand Bombardier invented an odd contraption that looked a little like a motorcycle but with a tread and skis instead of wheels. This new winter vehicle was an instant success. Inuit hunters, for example, now zip around the Arctic on snow-mobiles rather than on dogsleds. Farther south, a couple of million Canadians ride off into the wilderness on thousands of miles of marked trails, complete with everything from fuel and repair stations to lodgings and restaurants. There's even a snow-mobile Grand Prix at Valcourt in Québec, Bombardier's birthplace and manufacturing plant. The Grand Prix SKI-DOO de Valcourt, the most important event in Canada and one of the most significant in North America, brings together elite racers to compete on an oval track and snowcross events.

A Popular Solution

One of the world's most popular sports owes its birth to the ingenuity of a young Canadian teacher who was looking for a way to keep his bored, trouble-making charges interested in their gym class. It was back in 1891, and James Naismith, an Ontario native and fresh graduate of Montréal's McGill University and Presbyterian Theological College, was trying to teach physical education at the International Young Men's Christian Training College in Springfield, Massachusetts. It was winter, so they couldn't exercise outdoors. Naismith's solution? He nailed a couple of peach baskets to the walls of the gym, and—presto— the game of basketball was born. He even talked the janitor into climbing a ladder to retrieve the ball each time a point was scored—the hole in the bottom was one innovation he didn't think of.

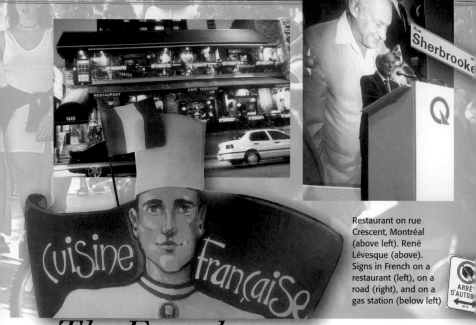

Restaurant on rue Crescent, Montréal (above left). René Lévesque (above). Signs in French on a restaurant (left), on a road (right), and on a gas station (below left)

The French Effect

Depending on how you look at it, Canada has either been blessed with two founding cultures or has been cursed with two warring partners. But even for the pessimists, there is no doubt that *le fait français* (the French fact) lends flash and flair to what could have been a monochromatic culture. There are French-speaking (or francophone) communities across the country, especially in northeastern Ontario and along the Acadian shores of New Brunswick, Nova Scotia and Prince Edward Island, but the province of Québec is French Canada's heartland. More than 80 percent of Québec's 6 million citizens count themselves fran-cophones, and in some parts of the province resident anglophones are as rare as Sherpas. That kind of heft has allowed Québec to develop a rich and unique culture with its own pop stars, soap operas, writers, painters, and musicians. Schools like the Université de Montréal and Québec City's Université Laval are among the world's finest French-language institutions. And there's simply no denying that French Canada, with its sense of fashion and style and its delight in fine dining and night life, has enriched the country.

Parlez-vous Anglais?

Montréal is North America's only French-speaking metropolis and one of the largest French-speaking cities in the world. Its English-speaking population, however, is one of the largest in the country, and while anglophones sometimes grumble about language restrictions imposed by the provincial government in Québec City, they also revel in living in one of the continent's most distinctive and cosmopolitan cities. Their language is peppered with French expressions (like *dépanneur* for convenience store), and conversations in the trendy bars and restaurants of St-Denis and Crescent streets often flit almost effortlessly back and forth between the two languages. Succeeding waves of Italians, Greeks, Portuguese, South and East Asians, Haitians, and Latin Americans have added even more spice to the city's rich cultural stew.

Traffic lights and road signs in Montréal

Québec City's rue St-Louis (left) exudes French charm and architecture. Québec's "fleur de lys flag" and the Acadian tricolor (right) flutter in the breeze

Road signs (below), as well as labeling and other printed matter, are bilingual throughout the country

Into the Mainstream

Until a disgruntled René Lévesque broke with the Québec Liberal Party in the early 1960s, the separatist movement in Québec was pretty much a fringe affair with little mainstream support. Lévesque, however, had a common touch that endeared him to all Québecers. He was also a former television journalist who could explain his ideas in beguilingly reasonable terms. He eschewed the word "separatist" and called himself a sovereignist instead. But just what he meant by sovereignty was a little unclear. He always linked it to a special association with the rest of Canada, an ambivalence that has bedeviled the movement ever since, with the *purs-et-durs* demanding full independence and the softer nationalists hoping for some less final solution.

Loss of Faith

One of the most startling phenomena of the last half-century has been the collapse of Roman Catholic authority in Québec. As recently as the early 1960s, the Church ran the province's schools, hospitals and social services. Large families, and almost universal Mass attendance at church, were the norm. Just about every village and city neighborhood had a cathedral-size stone church. But today, those churches are virtually empty. Québec has one of the lowest church-attendance rates in Canada and one of the lowest birth rates in the world. The turnabout seems a little ungrateful, however. Québec's bishops might sometimes have been a little authoritarian, but no institution did more than the Church to preserve the French fact in Canada.

Québec on Film

Moviemaker Denys Arcand's critically acclaimed *Decline of the American Empire* (1986) offers an incisive if not particularly attractive portrait of Québec's modern and very secular bourgeoisie. Its main characters, four university professors and their various partners, gather for a dinner party and discuss the problems of sexuality, success, fidelity, intimacy, and aging. The movie won an Academy Award nomination and four Canadian Junos. A more recent Arcand movie, *Jésus de Montréal,* takes a gentler look at post Catholic Québec and its loss of faith. It follows the adventures of a group of young actors who make pornographic films by day and re-enact Christ's crucifixion for pilgrims to a Montréal shrine every evening.

Irish Connection

Many French-speaking Québecers have names that are more Gaelic than Gallic. Ryans and O'Neills are particularly common. Most of these French-speaking Gaels can trace their lineage back to the immigrants who arrived in Canada in the 19th century to escape the potato famine in Ireland. Most of them journeyed in deplorable conditions aboard overcrowded ships. Hundreds of new arrivals died of cholera in the fever sheds of the quarantine centers. Encouraged by their bishops and parish priests to help their suffering fellow Catholics, many French Canadian families adopted the orphaned children, but out of respect for their parents and their heritage, allowed them to keep their Irish names.

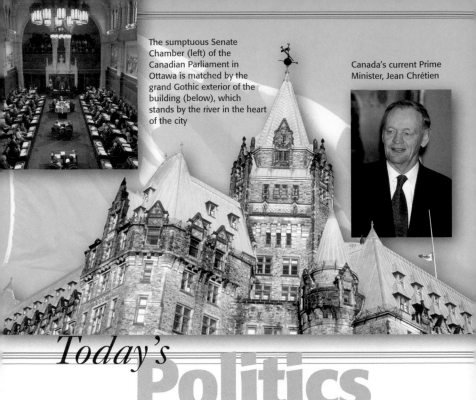

The sumptuous Senate Chamber (left) of the Canadian Parliament in Ottawa is matched by the grand Gothic exterior of the building (below), which stands by the river in the heart of the city

Canada's current Prime Minister, Jean Chrétien

Today's Politics

Canada's Parliament

The Canadian Parliament mimics its British counterpart with a 301-seat House of Commons holding the real power, and a 105-seat Senate filling in for the House of Lords as a "chamber of sober second thought." Canada's senators are appointed for life. Because senate seats come with a handsome salary and plenty of perks, and because they're often handed out to the party faithful, Canada's Upper House is sometimes referred to as the Grateful Dead (the name of a popular rock group in the 1970s). "How does a senator wink?" the old joke goes. "He opens one eye." The jokes are not entirely fair, since the Senate committees do some of the most effective work on Parliament Hill.

Canada's 10 autonomous provinces have exclusive jurisdiction over their own education, culture, health care, and social policy. So provincial politics is as important to most Canadians as national politics. In French-speaking Québec and industry-rich Ontario, who runs the provincial government is often more important than who's in charge in Ottawa. The Liberals have run the federal government for all but 15 of the last 70 or so years. In spite of the fact that Québec's campaign for more autonomy and even independence has dominated the national agenda since the 1960s, the prime minister's job has gone to Québecers for 33 of the last 35 years—a statistic that rankles westerners in Alberta and British Columbia. In fact, western discontent led to the creation of the Canadian Alliance, which merged with the Progressive Conservatives in 2003 to form the New Conservative Party, now the official opposition in Ottawa.

Christian Politicians

Christianity has played a sometimes contradictory role in Canadian politics—especially on the Prairies. Bible Bill Eberhart, for example, founder of his own Protestant sect, turned to the scriptures and the funny-money theories of Major C. H. Douglas to create the populist, right-wing Social Credit Party that held power in Alberta between 1935 and 1971.

Baptist preacher Tommy Douglas, on the other hand, was inspired by the social Gospel and dreams of the New Jerusalem to found the Co-operative Commonwealth Federation, forerunner of the socialist New Democratic Party. In 1961, while he was premier of Saskatchewan, Douglas introduced Canada's first universal Medicare plan, overruling the angry protests of the province's doctors. The rest of the country followed suit some five years later.

The Story of Canada

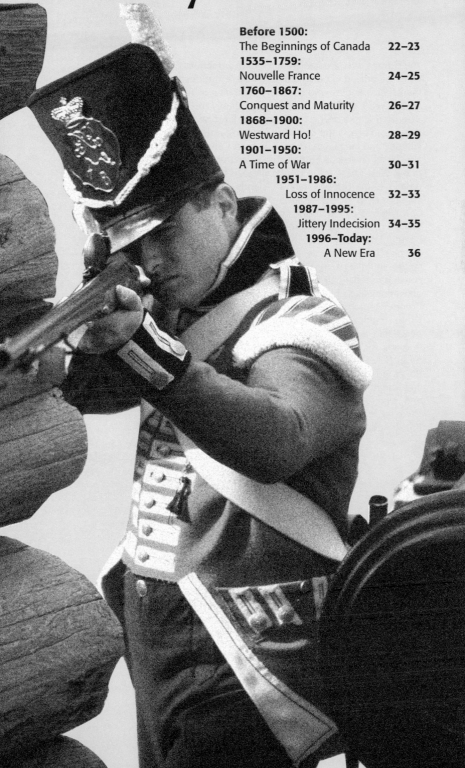

The Beginnings of Canada

The Hurons who greeted French explorer Jacques Cartier when he arrived in Canada in 1534 were the descendants of the Asiatic peoples who had started arriving in the Americas 13,000 years earlier. Most of them probably trekked from Siberia to Alaska over a now vanished land bridge and spread out across the continent, creating a rich tapestry of cultures and languages. Pre-Columbian Canada was, in fact, at least as diverse as Europe. The salmon-rich rivers and seas of the West Coast, for example, allowed the seafaring Haida people, of the Queen Charlotte Islands, to develop a complex culture rich in art and sculpture. In the Arctic, the Inuit not only survived by harvesting seals and whales in one of the world's most hostile climates, they flourished, developing beautiful decorative arts. The seminomadic nations of the Iroquois Confederacy developed a sophisticated political system in the eastern woodlands, with a constitution that laid out rights and obligations and enfranchised women. Contrary to popular myth, however, North America was not an entirely peaceable land. The Huron and the Iroquois, for example, had clearly never heard of Jean-Jacques Rousseau's "noble savage," and fought over territory and resources with the same vigor as, say, the British and the French.

Canoe

It's no wonder the semi-nomadic hunters and farmers of what's now eastern Canada never developed the wheel; in a land of trees and hills, it would not have been much use. Instead, some unknown wilderness genius invented the birch-bark canoe, a fast, maneuverable craft superbly adapted to a land of lakes and rivers. It was strong and flexible, yet light enough to be carried around rapids. If a rock did puncture its tough skin, the canoe could be quickly patched with a piece of bark and some tar (pitch). A scarcity of craftsmen and suitable trees has made bark canoes rare, but the design lives on, using materials as varied as cedar strips, aluminum, fiberglass, and Kevlar.

Paul Kane's *Mah-Min* (an Assiniboine chief) hangs in Montréal's Musée des Beaux-Arts

Before 1500

War canoe (above) on show in Georgia Park, Nanaimo

Wall painting (right) at Saskatoon's heritage park. Haida carvings (inset right and above right) at Vancouver's Museum of Anthropology

Totem Pole

Most West Coast totem poles are made of cedar, which carves easily and has a natural resistance to rot. But there the similarities end. Each nation or tribe has an individual style. The Haida, for example, barely sculpt their poles, carving instead low-relief figures that look as if they have simply been wrapped around one half of the trunk. Their Tsimshian neighbors on the mainland carve away much more vigorously, creating birds with projecting beaks and men with projecting arms. For both Haida and Tsimshian totem poles are not simply a random assortment of carved figures, but a banner to proclaim their identity. The animal and human figures on each pole represent a collage of personified family, tribal myths and history.

Gaudy totems, at Vancouver's Stanley Park (below), in Québec (below left) and in Victoria (right)

Igloo

Life in an igloo is not as chilly or precarious as it might appear. To begin with, two blubber lamps and body heat will keep the temperature hovering around 57°F (14°C) —not exactly toasty, but not like living in a refrigerator, either. It's sturdy, too, even when made from blocks of snow carved from fresh drifts. Dome-shaped buildings stand up well, anyway, as Inuit hunters discovered long ago, but the harsh arctic climate gives the igloo added strength. Fresh snow melts when it lands on an igloo then refreezes, a constant process that hardens the igloo into a solid lump that could support a full-size polar bear, should one happen along.

First Encounter

Some time in the summer of 1007, a Norse woman named Gudrid, wife of Thorfinn, gave birth to a son named Snorri—an event that would hardly be worth a mention if it weren't for the fact that it happened at l'Anse aux Meadows in what is now Newfoundland. That made Snorri the first European child born in North America. He didn't stay long. His parents abandoned their settlement on the rugged coast after one too many run-ins with the local natives, but this was 500 years before Christopher Columbus set sail for the West Indies. Norse explorations of Canada's east coast began in 1001, but attempts at settlement were short-lived. Stories of their adventures, however, became part of European lore.

Maple Syrup

Legend has it that an Iroquois chief and his wife were responsible for the discovery of one of Canada's sweetest treats. In a fit of pique, apparently, the chief hurled his ax at a tree. His intrigued and perhaps fearful wife collected the faintly sweet sap that dripped from the resulting hole in the bark, and boiled the next day's hunt in it—thereby inventing both maple syrup and sugar-cured venison. Canadian maple farmers still boil sap to produce 80 percent of the world's supply of maple syrup, although these days they use plastic tubes to collect the stuff and industrial-size boilers to reduce it—a process that requires 20L (5 gallons) of sap to produce just a liter (2 pints) of syrup.

Explorer John Cabot (left) "discovered" Canada in 1497 while in search of a westerly route to the Orient

Viking encampment at L'Anse aux Meadows (above) recalls the earliest visitors

Huron Ouendat Indian village (right) at Georgian Bay, Ontario

Nouvelle France

French navigator Jacques Cartier was looking for gold, diamonds and a route to China when he explored the St. Lawrence River in the mid-1500s. He failed on all three counts, but his voyages brought him as far inland as what is now Montréal, opening the way for later adventurers to prosper on more prosaic products. Salt cod, for example, a Lenten staple in Catholic France, brought in enough money to build the magnificent walled city of Louisbourg on Cape Breton Island, while merchants in Québec City grew rich buying beaver pelts from native tribes with axes, guns and, less creditably, booze. Catholic missionaries followed traders into the wilderness, braving hardship and martyrdom to convert the Huron and Iroquois tribes. All this commerce and conversion, along with a few well-armed troops, made the colony's fertile lowlands safe enough for farmers and tradesmen. Slowly, Nouvelle France evolved into a mirror of the mother country, with walled cities full of stone homes and grand churches, and a countryside peopled with tenant farmers and aristocratic seigneurs. But the colony was never well defended, and the Seven Years War effectively ended the French Regime, with British troops capturing Québec City in 1759 and Montréal a year later.

1535

Canada's First Social Club

Samuel de Champlain, explorer of note, was also Canada's first bon vivant. During the grim winter of 1606, he founded the *Ordre du bon temps* (Order of Good Cheer), to buck up the spirits at the tiny French outpost of Port-Royal in what is now Nova Scotia. Colonial officers prepared feasts for themselves and local native leaders, using the region's ample fish and game, and organized music, jokes and skits to keep everyone merry. These soirees began with a ceremonial procession led by the host for the evening, proudly wearing the order's chain around his neck.

Francophone areas have a strong tradition of Celtic-style music

Map (right) depicting the siege of Québec. Bust of Jacques Cartier (inset above right)

Painting of the death of General Wolfe (below) in the National Gallery, Ottawa

Fashion Statement

It was male vanity that made many of Canada's early merchants wealthy. What they had that European haberdashers needed were beaver pelts—not for fur coats, but to make the tall, stylish felt hats that were all the rage among European men from about 1550 to 1850. At first, traders preferred old pelts that native trappers had used as coats for a couple of years. That sort of wear and tear got rid of the coarse guard hairs and made it easier for hatmakers to get at the dense underfur they used to make sturdy, water-resistant felt. However, Russian techniques for removing guard hairs cheaply eventually made new furs more desirable than "coat grade" pelts.

Displays about fur trapping (below and bottom left) at Calgary's Glenbow Museum

Female Power

Montréal owes much of its early success to the religious fervor of two formidable French women. The first was Jeanne Mance, who abandoned the comforts of her well-to-do home in France in 1635 to help Paul Chomedy de Maisonneuve establish what they hoped would be a model Christian community in the middle of the wilderness. She was Canada's first lay nurse and built Canada's first hospital. The second was Marguerite Bourgeoys, who was the city's first schoolteacher and founder of a religious order that still runs schools in Canada. Marguerite Bourgeoys's nuns also taught homemaking skills to the "Filles du Roy," young, orphan girls who came to Canada at royal expense to find husbands among the largely male settlers.

The Scots Connection

Scotsman James Johnstone seems to have had a habit of picking losing causes. First, he joined Bonnie Prince Charlie's failed Highland rebellion in 1745 and only barely survived the disastrous Battle of Culloden. Fourteen years later, he was in a French uniform fighting yet another losing battle against the British, this time to defend Québec City against the army of General James Wolfe, who'd served as a major on the winning side at Culloden. When the brief battle ended, both Wolfe and French General Louis-Joseph de Montcalm were dead, leaving Johnstone, Montcalm's aide-de-camp, to parlay a battlefield ceasefire with fellow Highlander General James Murray, Wolfe's second in command. Legend has it the pair negotiated in Gaelic.

Oriental Obsessions

Robert Cavalier Sieur de La Salle was so obsessed with finding a route through North America to China that many of his contemporaries doubted his sanity. And the man did travel a lot—to Lake Michigan in 1679 and to the mouth of the Mississippi in 1682, for example. He was murdered in Texas by mutineers while trying to invade Spanish territory in 1687. Back home on the island of Montréal, where he held land near the rapids that blocked the way west, his neighbors were unimpressed. They derisively referred to his estate as *la Chine* (China), a name that is still attached to the city borough of Lachine and the nearby rapids.

Victor of Québec, James Wolfe (below left), and determined explorer Robert Cavalier (below)

Marguerite de Youville (above left), founder of the Sisters of Charity (Grey Nuns), was canonized in 1990

German-Swiss settlers founded Lunenburg (right) in 1753

The star from the Acadian flag adorns a house in Cheticamp (below), known for its strong French heritage

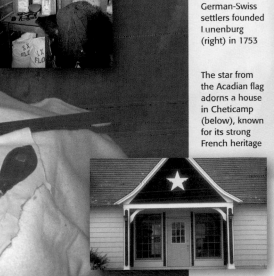

1759

Conquest and Maturity

When the British took possession of Canada in 1763, they allowed their new subjects to keep their language and their religion, an act of imperial tolerance that helped guarantee *Canadien* loyalty during the American Revolution. A few years later, the *Canadiens* had their turn to be tolerant when thousands of British Loyalists fled the new American republic to settle in the Maritimes, southern Québec and what is now Ontario, changing Canada's linguistic and cultural makeup forever (and hopelessly complicating Canadian politics). The Loyalists also formed a solid bulwark against Yankee expansionism, which came in handy when the Americans marched north again during the War of 1812.

But devotion to king and country had its limits. Living under the crown was fine, but as the country matured and cities like Halifax, Montréal, Kingston, and Toronto grew and prospered, both Loyalists and *Canadiens* began agitating for self-government.

Their struggle led to protests, riots and even armed rebellion. By the 1860s, it was clear that Canada and Britain needed a new arrangement, and on July 1, 1867, Canada became the first British possession to achieve independence by peaceful means.

Hudson's Bay Company

While settlers cleared farmland in the east, the NorthWest Trading Company and the Hudson's Bay Company fought a no-holds-barred battle for control of the still lucrative fur trade in the west. The Nor'Westers had youth, vigor and a willingness to do just about anything to win. Their traders pushed the boundaries of exploration to the Rockies, the Arctic and eventually the Pacific. But the Hudson's Bay Company had one huge advantage—control of the ports on Hudson's Bay and hence a much shorter route to Europe. In 1821, the two companies merged as the Hudson's Bay Company, ending one of the most ruthless trade wars in Canadian history.

The traditional dress (left) of the Crow tribe. Burial place (below) of Chief One Arrow, in Winnipeg

CHIEF ONE ARROW
Signatory to treaty #6
KA-PAYAK-WASKUNAM
1810 – 1886

CHIEF ONE ARROW, chief of a Willow Cree Tribe along the Saskatchewan River, was incarcerated at Stony Mountain for his participation in the North – West Rebellion of 1885. He was released and died shortly thereafter in Arch - Bishop Taché's residence, St. Boniface, Manitoba, Apr. 25, 1886.

His last words to the Government of Canada were:
"Do not mistreat my people."

1760

Historical reenactments at Fort York (top) and Île-Ste-Hélène, Montréal (right). First Nations culture (above) can be seen in traditional ceremonies across Canada

Crossing the Continent

When Alexander Mackenzie found himself on the shores of the Arctic Ocean in 1789, he was so dejected he called the long and beautiful waterway that had brought him there River Disappointment. It was the Pacific Ocean the Scots-born explorer had been aiming for, not the Arctic. Mackenzie, a partner in the NorthWest Trading Company, thought it worth another try. In May 1792, after a trip to England to learn new navigation skills, he set out in an 8m (26ft) canoe with six paddlers, two native guides and his dog. In July, he and his team reached the Pacific and became the first Europeans to cross the continent. River Disappointment is now called the Mackenzie River.

License to Rob

Of the hundreds of privateers who got rich raiding American merchant ships during the War of 1812 between Britain and the United States, none was more famous than Captain Joseph Barss, Jr., of Liverpool, Nova Scotia. As soon as hostilities started, Barss obtained a letter of marque, essentially a license to rob enemy merchantmen, from the Royal Navy and set out to make a fortune. Within a year his armed schooner, the *Liverpool Packet*, had captured 33 ships and brought them back to Nova Scotia. His luck didn't hold, though. In 1813, a bigger and better armed American ship captured his vessel and took Barss and his crew to Portsmouth, New Hampshire, as prisoners of war.

A New Nation

Sir George Étienne Cartier, who persuaded French Canada to join the new Canadian Confederation in 1867, was a former revolutionary who had participated in an armed rebellion against the British crown. Cartier had joined the brief Patriote rebellion of 1837 and had fought British troops at the Battle of St-Denis. But after a few years of exile in the United States, he came home to Montréal to become a lawyer and railroad promoter. Later he helped Sir John A. MacDonald persuade Queen Victoria and her government of the benefits of a new North American nation. Cartier was convinced that the federal system would give French Canada the tools it needed to defend its language, culture and religion.

Rebel Raid

During the US Civil War, Confederate forces used Montréal as a base for launching their only attack on the northern states of New England. On October 19, 1864, Lieutenant Bennett Young and 20 cavalrymen rode south to St. Albans, Vermont. With gun drawn, Young mounted the steps of a hotel and shouted, "This city is now in the possession of the Confederate States of America." His troopers herded the townsfolk to the village green and emptied three local banks. They dropped most of their loot and failed to burn down the town, but they still had about $200,000 when they got back to Montréal. Many Canadians had Southern sympathies—mostly because they feared a victorious North would turn its attention to Canada.

Explorer Alexander Mackenzie (below)

Sir John A. MacDonald (below center) was Canada's first prime minister

Sir George Étienne Cartier (left) was one of the founding fathers of Canada's Confederation

1867

The American frigate *Constitution* ("Old Ironsides"), sinking the British warship HMS *Guerriere* off the coast of Newfoundland, 1812

Costumed interpreters at King's Landing, New Brunswick (left). The tools of the trade (right) for First Nations hunters

Westward Ho!

Canada owes its early expansion to a combination of red-coats, railroadmen and daring. The redcoats were the North West Mounted Police, a tiny force of 300 lightly armed men who rode west to patrol a wilderness the size of European Russia. They used courage, discipline and not a little bluff to drive American whiskey traders from the Prairies, to pacify the native tribes and to make the land safe for settlement. This also made way for an audacious gamble—building the Canadian Pacific Railway across 4,000km (2,500 miles) of muskeg and mountains to link Montréal to the British colonies on the West Coast. The project nearly bankrupted the tiny dominion, but its completion in 1885 assured Canada's nationhood. British Columbia entered the Confederation and new settlers poured into the west, trans-forming the Prairies into a breadbasket, and tapping into the mineral and lumber wealth of the Rockies and the West Coast. But opening the west didn't happen without blood-shed; two uprisings led by the mixed-race, French-speaking Métis of Manitoba and Saskatchewan gave Canada its first and last taste of warfare with native tribes and created a bitter-ness that endured for decades.

Freedom Fighter or Traitor?

The strongest resistance to western expansion came from the Métis, a mixed-race nation of devoutly Catholic, French-speaking buffalo hunters and farmers who feared that new settlers would drive them from their lands and destroy their way of life. Largely because the government did little to reassure them, they rebelled twice. In 1870, their magnetic leader Louis Riel declared a provis-ional government and executed a white settler who defied his authority. Canadian troops crushed the second rebellion of 1885 and Riel surren-dered. His subsequent trial and execution split Canada along linguistic lines: The French hailed him as a visionary free-dom fighter; the English condemned him as a half-mad traitor and mur-derer. The tragic truth was probably some-where in the middle.

Winnipeg (left), as it looked in 1875. Gold nuggets (below) sparked the Yukon Gold Rush

1868

The Château Frontenac hotel (below), built in 1892 for the Canadian Pacific Railway. The completion (right and inset opposite) in 1885 of the trans-Canadian railroad

Red River Carts

While American settlers moved their goods west in huge covered wagons, early Canadian homesteaders favored the much humbler Red River cart, a two-wheeled vehicle designed by the Métis to haul their goods around on hunting trips. The carts were hardly pretty, but they were easy to build, easier to repair, and were superbly adapted for wilderness travel. Their outward angled wheels allowed them to carry loads of more than 360kg (800lb) without sinking into the soft prairie dirt, and their watertight construction meant the boxes could double as rafts once the wheels were removed. The carts did have one irritating characteristic, however—their greaseless axles emitted a high-pitched squeal that could be heard for miles.

Mounted Police and Sitting Bull

When Superintendent James Morrow Walsh of the North West Mounted Police heard that Sitting Bull and 5,000 followers had crossed the border from the US into Canada in 1877, he figured he had better go and lay down the law for the Sioux leader, whose tribesmen had just wiped out the US Seventh Cavalry.

To accomplish this daunting task, he took with him exactly three men. But all went well. Morrow, a bit of a dandy in his buckskin coat, got along famously with Sitting Bull. The pair spent the best part of a day together, and Sitting Bull agreed to respect the laws of the Great White Mother (Queen Victoria)—which is just as well, since Walsh had only 90 men under his command to enforce those laws.

Gassy Jack

When John (Gassy Jack) Deighton arrived by rowboat on the south shore of Burrard Inlet in 1867, he had "little more than $6 in his pocket, a few sticks of furniture, a yellow dog, and a bottle of whiskey." But within 24 hours he'd opened the first bar in what would one day become Vancouver. The Globe Saloon was not much more than a shack, but it served as a blessed oasis for the workers from a nearby sawmill, who had nowhere else to go.

Life wasn't easy, though. "Surrounded by Indians, I dare not look outdoors after dark," Jack wrote his brother Tom back home in Yorkshire. "There was a friend of mine, about a mile distant, found with his head cut in two."

Taciturn Wisdom

The North West Mounted Police owed much of their early success in the west to the skills of a short, bow-legged, hard-drinking man named Jerry Potts. The son of a Scottish trader and a Blackfoot woman, Potts seldom spoke more than two words at a time. "What's over that hill, Jerry?" the disoriented Mounties would often ask. "Nother hill," was Potts's invariable reply. But the stubbly little Potts was a superb guide, tracker and hunter. His 22-year career with the police began in Fort Benton in 1874, when he led Commissioner George French's lost column to water and pasture, and found suitable campgrounds for them. He also taught the Mounties how to do business with the First Nations peoples according to their own traditions.

Prolific inventor Alexander Graham Bell made his home at Baddeck, on Cape Breton Island

YOU ARE INVITED TO HELP "MAINTAIN THE RIGHT"

Join the RCMP

Royal Canadian Mounted Police

An early recruitment poster for the Mounties

HERE WAS DRIVEN THE LAST SPIKE COMPLETING CANADIAN PACIFIC RAILWAY FROM OCEAN TO OCEAN NOVEMBER 7, 1885

1900

Toronto's neo-Gothic Parliament Buildings were constructed in 1885–92

Defiant to the last, Louis Riel's statue takes a stance outside Winnipeg's Legislature

A Time of War

The two world wars of the 20th century had oddly contradictory effects on Canada. On the one hand, they helped the country mature and take its place on the world stage. On the other, they threatened to tear it apart. The valor of Canada's troops at the Battle of Vimy Ridge during World War I was unexcelled, and the country's contribution to World War II, especially the war at sea, was prodigious for a nation of fewer than 15 million people.

But at home the bitter conscription battles of both wars split the country along linguistic lines, leading to riots, internment and tottering governments. French Canadians argued fiercely against being forced to fight wars they viewed as both foreign and imperial. Yet, despite their opposition to the draft, French Canadians volunteered for service in numbers roughly proportionate to their share of the population.

Meanwhile, the population was changing. Canadians were abandoning the land and moving into the towns and cities, and by the midpoint of the century, Canada had become an urban country. It was also less English and less French, in spite of its often unwelcoming policies controlling new immigration.

Radio pioneer Marconi sent the first transatlantic signal from Newfoundland

1901

British ex-servicemen arrive with their families (top) in 1927 to start a new life. Reminders of World War II: HMS *Sackville* (above), in Halifax, and men of the Royal Canadian Airforce in 1940 (right)

Nobel Prize

After reading an article about the pancreas in the fall of 1920, Dr. Frederick Banting jotted down an idea that led, after two years of twists and turns, to the discovery of insulin as a treatment for diabetes. It also led, unfortunately, to an unseemly battle over who should get the credit. Banting claimed that he and graduate student Charles Best had done all the important work and deserved all the glory. He deliberately set out to discredit his overseer at the University of Toronto, J.R.R. Macleod, and his protegé, James Collip. When the Nobel Committee shared the 1923 prize for medicine between Banting and Macleod, an angry Banting split his share with Best and Macleod split his with Collip.

Valiant Canadian airman leaves for war

Gangsters in Moose Jaw

Moose Jaw, Saskatchewan, was a pretty lively place during the 1920s, thanks to Prohibition in the United States. Some of the continent's biggest gangsters used it as a hideout and a depot for smuggling booze into the States. River Street (aka Little Chicago) became the hub for gambling, prostitution and bootlegging. Particularly appealing to mobsters was a network of tunnels under the town that had been built to hide illegal Chinese immigrants. One frequent visitor was Al Capone, who used to stay in a River Street hotel whenever Chicago got too hot for him. Legend has it that an ill Capone had a doctor brought to his room to remove an infected tonsil—without anesthetic.

The Duke of Windsor—later Edward VI—in a feathered headdress (right) at a First Nations display in Banff during 1919

Canada's Most Interesting Man

When King George VI paid a visit to Montréal in 1939, his host was Camillien Houde, the city's irrepressible mayor. As the two drove past cheering crowds, the enormously popular Houde told the King with a grin, "Some of this is for you, your majesty."

Later at dinner, Houde made the King hoot with laughter when he breezily showed him a list of topics his worried advisors had forbidden him to raise. One of them, no doubt, was the impending war with Germany. While it was raging, Houde was interned for opposing the draft.

In spite of Houde's politics, however, the Queen reportedly told friends in England that the mayor was the most interesting man she'd met in Canada.

Victory at Sea

Angus Walters doesn't look like the finest seaman that Canada ever produced. Pictures show a small, almost wizened, man wearing a cloth cap and an enigmatic smile. But Walters was the skipper of the legendary *Bluenose*, a sleek Nova Scotia schooner that fished the Grand Banks of Newfoundland in the 1920s and 1930s. In 1921, Walters and the *Bluenose* wrested the Fishermen's Cup from the Americans and held it for the next 17 years, in spite of the best efforts of designers in American ports such as Gloucester, Massachusetts, and Portsmouth, Maine, to come up with something fast enough to beat them. "The wood of the vessel that will beat the *Bluenose*," Walters once boasted, "is still growing."

Evocative shipping line poster (above left). The Alaska Highway (above), which was built during World War II to supply northwestern defense posts. The Memorial et Parc Canadien (left) remembers Canadian soldiers who died at Vimy Ridge in 1917

A TIME OF WAR 31

Loss of Innocence

Canada celebrated its 100th birthday in 1967 with a giddy year of parties, fireworks and royal visits. There was a centennial song, a centennial flag and hundreds of centennial projects, including a World's Fair in Montréal and a UFO landing pad in St. Paul, Alberta. But just three years after all this merriment, armed soldiers were patrolling the streets of Montréal in the wake of a series of terrorist kidnappings, and just six years after that, French-speaking Québec elected its first separatist government.

The roots of the unrest could be traced to the 1950s, when French Canada began to lose its Catholic fervor and assert itself as a political power to be reckoned with. At the time, the huge baby-boom generation, galvanized by the civil-rights struggle and antiwar movement in the United States, started to look around for causes of its own. But it wasn't all power and protest. The same forces also generated a torrent of literature, music and art. Somewhat later, in 1982, Canada also got a new constitution of its own, along with a Charter of Rights and Freedoms. Canada began carving out a role for itself on the world stage as a peacekeeper and a mediator between the rich and the poor.

In 1955 hockey goalies wore no face guards

Strained Relations

Prime ministers often had a strained relationship with American presidents. Prime Minister John Diefenbaker, for example, claimed that President Jack Kennedy had referred to him as an s.o.b. in a briefing paper. Kennedy denied the charge, saying "I couldn't have called him an s.o.b., I didn't know he was one—at that time." Diefenbaker's successor, Lester Pearson, had an even more abrupt encounter with President Lyndon Johnson in 1964 after making a speech at Temple University in Philadelphia criticizing American policy in Vietnam and calling for a pause in the bombing of Hanoi. Later, at a meeting in Washington, an angry Johnson thumped Pearson on the chest and snapped, "You don't come down here and piss on my rug."

1951

Québécois inventor and entrepreneur Joseph-Armand Bombardier alongside his B1 snowmobile in 1942 (right)

The St. Lawrence Seaway (left) opened in 1959. The Dionne quints meet the Queen (above) in 1951

Relief on Ice

It was supposed to be a cakewalk. There was no way, Canadians firmly believed, that Soviet amateurs could beat Canada's seasoned professionals at hockey. To predict anything but a rout was heresy. "We'll need calculators to keep score," confident pundits predicted. Instead, the eight-game series in 1972 opened with a seven-to-three Soviet victory that rocked the country. From then on it was a heart-stopping roller-coaster ride that had thousands of Canadians ducking work and skipping school to watch the games. Only when Paul Henderson scored the winning goal in the dying seconds of the last game to give Canada a razor-thin victory with four wins and a tie, did the nation heave a sigh of relief and get back to work.

J.A. Bombardier, 1907–1964

Running for Hope

After jogging 5,390km (3,369 miles) from St. John's, Newfoundland, to the western shore of Lake Superior, Terry Fox stopped outside the city of Thunder Bay. He was tired and his chest ached. A medical exam confirmed his worst fears: The cancer that had taken his right leg three years earlier had spread to his lungs. His dream of running across Canada was over.

Less than a year later, on June 28, 1981, Fox died at home in British Columbia. But the image of Terry Fox, his curly head bobbing as he half-jogged, half-hopped the long lonely miles, captured Canada's imagination. Now, every year, thousands of runners keep his Marathon of Hope alive by jogging to raise money for cancer research.

Yvette aux Barricades!

A character in a children's textbook helped save Canada from disintegration in 1980. As Québec prepared for its first referendum on independence, separatist forces under the charismatic René Lévesque were well supported by men but not so much by women. Lise Payette, a TV talk-show host turned separatist politician, suggested it was meekness not conviction that kept women in the pro-Canada camp. She compared them to the fictional Yvette, the mild-mannered mother of a traditional family in a textbook that had been used to teach Québec children to read. Outraged pro-Canada women organized Yvette clubs and a massive rally, which helped turn the tide and win the day for national unity.

René Lévesque, 1980

Sexy Secrets

Steamy security scandals aren't Canada's strong suit. But there was the case of East German agent Gerda Munsinger, who seems to have slept with several cabinet ministers in the late 1950s, most notably Defense Minister Pierre Sevigny. It was never clear that she ever found out anything useful. Then there was Defense Minister Robert Coates, who resigned in 1985 after newspapers revealed he'd visited a strip club during a tour of Canadian bases in Germany. It was rumored he had a briefcase full of top-secret NATO documents with him, but no one ever suggested that anyone saw them. As one wag remarked: "A typical Canadian sex-and-security scandal: no secrets got passed and no one went to bed."

Pierre Trudeau, 1969

1986

Expo 67, the World Fair held in Montréal, was a futuristic affair (left). Even more futuristic—Toronto's CN Tower (above), built in 1976

Monument to the courageous Terry Fox (above left) in Thunder Bay. The curved twin buildings of Toronto's attractive City Hall (below)

LOSS OF INNOCENCE 33

Jittery Indecision

It couldn't have been much closer. On October 30,1995, Québecers voted to stay in Canada—just barely. The difference wouldn't have filled a good-size bar. The final score: 49.4 percent for independence, 50.6 against. The cliffhanger ended a decade of constitutional to-ing and fro-ing that obsessed Canada's political and chattering classes. Meanwhile, for millions of others the whole French-English argument seemed sterile and irrelevant. As accords and crises followed each other with dizzying frequency, Canadians with names like Nguyen, Guiterrez and Singh increasingly tuned out. Even some Québec heroes were losing interest. When Formula 1 driver Jacques Villeneuve opened a restaurant on Montréal's trendy Crescent Street, he called it Newtown—the English translation of his family name. And there seemed to be so many more important issues. Canada sent soldiers and sailors to the first Gulf War, and more soldiers to keep the peace amid the ruins of what had been Yugoslavia.

Meanwhile, writers such as Michael Ondaatje (*The English Patient*) and Margaret Atwood (*Cat's Eye*), pop stars like Céline Dion, Alanis Morissette, and Bryan Adams, extravaganzas like Montréal's Cirque du Soleil and world-beater companies such as Bombardier were giving Canada a new presence on the world stage.

1987

Bouchard
When Lucien Bouchard stepped forward to lead Québec's independence forces in 1995, nationalists were delirious. A wily politician given to changing parties, Bouchard began with the populist Creditistes, moved to the separatist Parti Québécois, switched to the Conservatives and then founded the Bloc Québécois. Along the way, he served in the cabinet and as ambassador to France—an ironic posting for a man who would subsequently describe Canada as "not a real country."

Lucien Bouchard (below). Female Mounties (left)

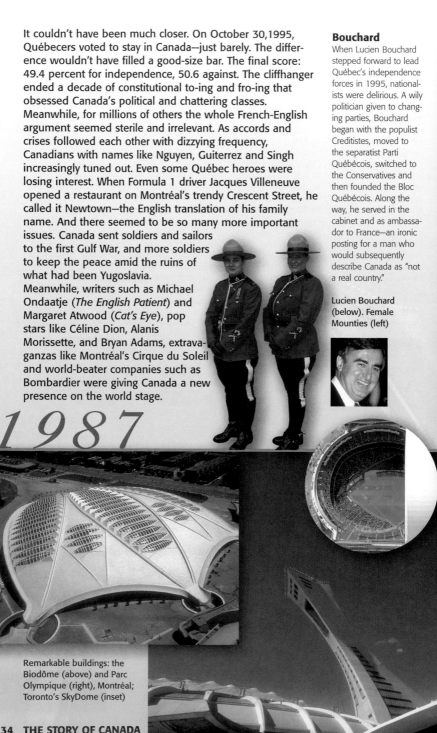

Remarkable buildings: the Biodôme (above) and Parc Olympique (right), Montréal; Toronto's SkyDome (inset)

Indestructible Tilleys

Alex Tilley claims he makes the best darned yachting hat in the world, an uncharacteristically forceful claim for a Canadian entrepreneur. But the stylishly brimmed canvas hat is good enough to have impressed Canada's armed forces, which ordered 6,000 of the things to protect its sailors from the broiling heat during the first Gulf War in 1991. "Tilleys" quickly became a hot barter item among the forces of other nations as well. But the military endorsement wasn't Tilley's best marketing coup. About 10 years earlier, an Ontario zookeeper had reported his Tilley had made a trip through an elephant's digestive system and emerged at the other end soiled but unscathed. The story, Tilley says, "turned out to be a fantastic selling point."

The Great Turbot War

The Great Turbot War of 1995 pitted Canada's tiny navy—seven ships and a submarine—against a fleet of Spanish trawlers fishing off the Grand Banks of Newfoundland. Given that the trawlers were armed with nothing more deadly than nets and hooks, the match was hardly fair, but the conflict made Canada's diminutive fisheries minister, Brian Tobin, something of a hero. Even British fishermen—no fans of Spanish fishing practices—hoisted Canadian flags in his honor. Canadians accused the Spanish of overfishing, cut their nets and confiscated one of the trawlers, escorting it into St. John's Harbour in triumph. The Spanish protested that all this happened in international waters and the Canadians were little better than pirates.

Canadian Peacekeepers

Canadians have become so used to thinking of their soldiers as peacekeepers, they actually seem embarrassed when they show they can fight, too. This might explain why the government kept so quiet about the 1991 Battle of the Medak Pocket. Nearly 900 members of Princess Patricia's Canadian Light Infantry took part in that desperate two-day firefight to prevent Croatian regulars from murdering Serb villagers. The Canadians, about half of them weekend reservists, drove a wedge between the two sides and stopped the killing. But they didn't come home to a hero's welcome. In fact, they had to wait nine years before their government finally honored them with a unit commendation.

Mohawks Don't Play a Round

A dispute over a golf course led to the most serious Native North American uprising in modern Canada. In 1990, the town of Oka, Québec, near Montréal, tried to level a small pine forest to add a few holes to its municipal course. Mohawks from the nearby community of Kanehsatake, however, considered the threatened forest sacred ground and took up arms to defend it. The town sent in the Québec police, the Indians opened fire, and a policeman was killed. What followed was a tense 78-day stand-off between the army and armed Mohawks, who occupied a local social club and blockaded one of the four major bridges leading to Montréal Island. The Mohawks finally surrendered, but the golf course was never built.

Writer Margaret Atwood (right) is one of Canada's foremost authors. Québec singer Céline Dion (left)

1995

The Turbot War of 1995 brought hostility to the high seas off the Canadian coast

A New Era

Northern Dream

A long-held dream came true in 1999 for the Inuit people of the north when Canada sliced off the eastern half of the Northwest Territories to create Nunavut, a vast piece of land four times the size of Spain.

The Inuit—called Eskimos in a less enlightened era—constitute about 85 percent of the region's 29,000 people, and Inuktitut is the official language of courts and legislature. Nunavut doesn't have the same autonomy as a Canadian province, but its existence gives the Inuit an unprecedented level of self-government. Its 19-member legislature tries to blend British parliamentary rules with native traditions of consensus government. There are no political parties, for example, and the legislature selects the premier from among its members.

The second millennium closed with some humbling reminders to Canadians that for all their technology and sophistication, they were still at the mercy of Mother Nature. But for all the unruly weather, the country entered a period of relative calm. The death of Pierre Trudeau in 2000 seemed to mark the end of a tumultuous era. As prime minister from 1968 to 1984, Trudeau brought home Canada's constitution from London, made French and English equal as official languages, and sparred ceaselessly with separatists. His disputes with the much-loved René Lévesque often chafed the sensibilities of his fellow French-speaking Québecers.

Fool's Gold

Shares in Bre-X Minerals skyrocketed to $280 in 1997 when the Calgary firm claimed it had struck it rich in the Indonesian gold fields. Thousands bought in and became millionaires on paper overnight. Then Bre-X's chief geologist committed suicide and independent experts found the company had salted its assay samples in Canada's biggest stock-promotion scam ever.

Sparkling Disaster

For five days in January 1998, a freakish, super-cooled rain fell on much of eastern Canada, coating every surface it touched with layers of ice. The effect was beautiful but crippling. Trees buckled, roofs caved in and dozens of electrical pylons crumbled under the weight. Much of Montréal, the nation's second-largest city, was without power for considerably more than a week. People huddled around fireplaces and cooked their food on barbecues. Thousands found shelter in schools and hotels. In the countryside, livestock froze to death in unheated barns. But the hardship had its good side, as well. People came together to share and keep each other's spirits up, and many look back on the "Great Ice Storm" with nostalgia.

1996–today

An Inuit citizen of Nunavut (top right). Tall Ships Race 2000 (right), Halifax. Every year an ice bridge links Hudson and Oka, Québec (far right). Canada Day, Prince Edward Island (below). The 1998 blizzard (right)

On the Move

ARRIVING

By Air

The major international airports in Canada are in Toronto, Montréal and Vancouver. International flights are also handled at the Ottawa and Québec City airports, and in other major cities such as Halifax, Edmonton, Calgary and Winnipeg, which are all connected to each other as well as to nearby cities in the US. All have efficient websites (see panel opposite) with information that includes airport and/or terminal plans, details of terminal facilities, transportation options and flight schedules.

Departures at Montréal-Pierre Elliott Trudeau International Airport

AIRPORT	DISTANCE TO CITY	TAXI	CAR	TRAIN/ SUBWAY
TRANSFERS TO MAJOR CITY DOWNTOWNS				
Vancouver International	15km (9 miles)	**Price:** Allow about $30. **Journey time:** About 30 mins.	South of city via Highway 99, the Arthur Laing Bridge and Grant McConachie Way.	n/a
Toronto Lester B. Pearson International Airport	27km (17 miles)	**Price:** In region of $40–45. **Journey time:** 45 mins (longer during rush hour).	Northwest of downtown by the Queensway and Highway 427 north.	n/a (but see bus/coach details).
Montréal-Pierre Elliott Trudeau International Airport	15km (9 miles)	**Fixed-rate fare:** $30 (drivers accept credit cards). **Journey time:** 30 mins (depends on traffic).	West of city via Autoroute Ville-Marie (Highway 720) and Autoroute 20 west.	n/a (but see bus/coach details)
Ottawa Airport	11km (7 miles)	**Price:** About $25. **Journey time:** Around 20 mins.	South of downtown via Bronson Avenue south and Airport Parkway.	n/a
Québec City Jean Lesage Airport	20km (12 miles)	**Fixed-rate fare:** $24.50. **Journey time:** Allow 20 mins.	West of downtown via Blvd. Charest, Route 40 north, Blvd. Wilfrid-Hamel and Route de l'Aéroport.	n/a

MAJOR AIRPORT WEBSITES

Vancouver International Airport
www.yvr.ca

Toronto Lester B. Pearson International Airport
www.lbpia.toronto.on.ca

Montréal-Pierre Elliott Trudeau International Airport
www.admtl.com

Ottawa Airport
www.ottawa-airport.ca

Québec City Jean Lesage Airport
www.aeroportdequebec.com

INTERNATIONAL AIRPORTS

Vancouver International Airport (YVR)

Located 15km (9 miles) south of downtown, Vancouver International Airport (tel: 604/276-6101) has the full range of facilities, including duty-free stores, cafeterias, restaurants, money exchange services, tourist information, and car rental desks.

An Airport Improvement Fee is imposed on all departing passengers, who have to pay $5 for flights within British Columbia, $10 for other destinations in North America, and $15 for travel to other parts of the world. However, this is not applied to passengers in transit. This fee will be added to the cost of your ticket.

Toronto Lester B. Pearson International Airport

Lester B. Pearson Airport (tel: 416/247-7678) is 27km (17 miles) northwest of downtown. Already Canada's biggest and busiest airport, it is undergoing further expansion. A fourth terminal— the Infield Terminal— was completed in 2003 and a greatly enlarged and improved new Terminal 1 is due to open during 2004. This will combine the current Terminals 1 and 2. Terminal 3 remains unchanged. There are duty-free stores, car rentals, restaurants, currency exchange and tourist information

All departing passengers have to pay the Airport Improvement Fee of $12, and people in transit have to pay $8. Payment will be added to the cost of your ticket.

BUS/COACH

Airporter bus (tel: 604/946-8866) offers regular shuttle service to the downtown hotels and bus terminal.
Frequency: Regular half-hourly schedule in summer, a bit less frequently the rest of the year.
Price: $12 one way (single), $18 round trip (return).
Ticketing: Must be purchased on the spot.
Journey time: 45 mins.

Airport Express Bus to and from downtown hotels and the bus station (tel: 905/564-3232 or 800/387-6787; www.torontoairportexpress.com).
Frequency: Runs on a half-hourly schedule.
Price: $14.25 one way (single), $24.50 round trip (return).
Ticketing: Reservations can be made online.
Journey time: About 45 mins depending on traffic.

Regular transit bus is the cheapest option (tel: 416/393-4636; www.ttc.ca), providing a number of options, all of which pick up at Terminals 2 and 3 (a shuttle connects Terminal 1 to the others).

• 192 "Airport Rocket" provides an all-day service to the Kipling subway station at the west end of the Bloor-Danforth line (journey time: 20 mins).
• 58A offers an all-day service to the Lawrence West Station on the Spadina subway line (journey time: 45 mins).
• 307 provides a service at night (1.30am–5am), seven nights a week, to the Eglinton West station when the other two buses stop running (journey time: 45 mins).
Price: Regular transit fare of $2.25 for all options, which includes transfer to the subway.

L'Aérobus shuttle service (tel: 514/931-9002 or 800/465-1213) runs between airport and downtown "L'Aérogare" bus station at 777 de la Gauchetière West, which is connected to the VIA Rail train station. Shuttle buses also continue to the Central bus station located at the corner of de Maisonneuve and Berri streets (metro Berri-UQAM).
Frequency: Buses depart every half-hour during the day.
Price: One-way (single) trips $12, round trip (return) $21.75. (From the L'Aérogare, there is a free shuttle service to more than 40 hotels in downtown Montréal.)
Ticketing: Tickets can only be purchased on the spot.

Shuttle bus service to major hotels downtown (tel: 613/260-2359).
Frequency: Regular service every half-hour all day.
Price: $12 one way (single), $20 round trip (return).

n/a (no shuttle bus service downtown)

Montréal-Pierre Elliott Trudeau International Airport

Montréal's international airport (tel: 514/394-7377) is 15km (9 miles) west of downtown. It has many food outlets and stores (at even more extortionate prices than most airports). All major car rental services have desks on the main floor and there's a tourist information booth.

Departing passengers (but not those in transit) have to pay the Airport Improvement Fee of $15; credit cards are accepted.

Ottawa Airport

About 11km (7 miles) south of downtown, Ottawa Airport (tel: 613/248-2000) is small compared with the three airports above, but nevertheless has all

Preparations for departure

the regular facilities. It also levies an Airport Improvement Fee of $15 on all departing passengers.

Québec City Jean Lesage Airport

Québec City's Jean Lesage Airport (tel: 418/640-2700) is located 20km (12 miles) west of downtown. It has food facilities but not much else.

No separate Airport Improvement Fee is levied but you will find that one has been included in the price of your ticket.

GETTING AROUND
Air Transportation

Since Canada is such a huge country, the second biggest in the world, air travel is generally the fastest and most practical means of getting from region to region. In some instances in the north, it is the only way of getting to some communities.

ON THE MOVE

AIRLINES

Air Canada
Air Canada (tel: 888/247-2262) is the country's largest carrier and, in many instances, it has a monopoly. It serves more than 100 destinations, many of them in the US. In addition to its regularly scheduled services, its subsidiaries, **Air Canada Tango** (tel: 800/315-1390) and **Air Canada Jazz** (tel: 888/247-2262), offer budget services. Their low fares are available only by advance reservation and payment, and changes to bookings are either not allowed or incur substantial charges.

AIR CANADA'S FUTURE

In May 2003, Air Canada, which has been a private company since the 1980s, filed for bankruptcy protection. As of December 2003, they are still flying, but the future of the national carrier is uncertain. The Federal Government might step in .

Other Canadian Airlines
● WestJet, founded in 1996 to provide a budget air service in western Canada, has recently begun offering services into Ontario and the Atlantic provinces. It is Canada's second-

Symbol of the national carrier

largest carrier, after Air Canada. The head office is in Calgary. For reservations, call 403/250-5839, 888/937-8538, or 800/538-5696.
● Based in Montréal, **Air Transat** is best known for its charter flights to Europe during summer and services to vacation destinations in Florida and the Caribbean in the winter months. In addition, the airline is beginning to provide links between the major Canadian cities. For general information, tel: 877/872-6728; for reservations tel: 866/847-1112.

● Northern Canada (Yukon, the Northwest Territories and Nunavut) is served by **Air Canada**. Other carriers include **Canadian North** (tel: 800/661-1505), **First Air** (tel: 800/267-1247) and **Air Inuit** (tel: 800/361-2965). Be warned that flights are very expensive. In addition, there are many charter companies providing air services to remote areas; the tourist offices are the best places to obtain further information about these (see page 317).

US Airlines
The major US airlines offer regular flights between the US and Canada. **American Airlines** (tel: 800/433-7300), **Delta** (tel: 800/221-1212), **Northwest** (tel: 800/447 4747), **United** (tel: 800/241-6522), and **US Airways** (tel: 800/428-4322) all service Canada's major airports. Visitors from outside North America may find it worthwhile investigating prices for international connections on the busy US–Canada routes. There are many special offers, but these require you to fly at specified times or dates.

Other International Airlines
International airlines with nonstop services between

AIRLINE WEBSITES		
CANADIAN AIRLINES	**US AIRLINES**	**OTHER INTERNATIONAL AIRLINES**
Air Canada www.aircanada.ca	**American Airlines** www.aa.com	**Air France** www.airfrance.com
Air Canada Tango www.flytango.com	**Delta** www.delta.com	**British Airways** www.british-airways.com
Air Canada Jazz www.flyjazz.ca	**Northwest** www.nwa.com	**KLM** www.klm.com
WestJet www.westjet.com	**United** www.united.com	**Lufthansa** www.lufthansa.com
Air Transat www.airtransat.com	**US Airways** www.usairways.com	**Qantas** www.qantas.com
Canadian North www.canadiannorth.com		
First Air www.firstair.ca		
Air Inuit www.airinuit.com		

Europe and one of Canada's major cities (Toronto, Montréal and Vancouver) include **Air France** (tel: 800/237-2747), **British Airways** (tel: 800/247-9297), **KLM,** operated by Northwest (tel: 800/447-4747), and **Lufthansa** (tel: 800/563-5954). **Qantas** offers flights from Australia (800/227-4500).

SECURITY CONCERNS

You must carry government-issued photo identification if you take a flight within Canada. You will be asked to produce this when you check in. For foreign visitors, a passport is the best way of proving identity. Canadians can use a driving license or medical card provided it contains a recent photograph.

Before boarding, all passengers and their carry-on baggage must pass through x-ray machines, possibly on two occasions. You should be prepared to open all bags and have all your personal effects checked before boarding the plane.

CHECK-IN TIME

As a rule of thumb, passengers on international flights to the US or other overseas destinations should check in two hours or

Checking in at Montréal airport

more before take-off. For flights within Canada, this time can be cut slightly depending on the airport. For example, at St. John's, Newfoundland, you can check in an hour before departure because it is a small airport. At Lester B. Pearson in Toronto, Canada's biggest and busiest facility, it is advisable to check in at least two hours before take-off because there can be long lines waiting to pass through security; you could miss your flight if you arrive later. All that being said, it is always important to contact your airline just prior to flying and ask what time they recommend you check in.

DOMESTIC AIRPORTS

● **Winnipeg International Airport** (tel: 204/987-9402; www.ywg.com) is about a 20-minute drive northwest of the city (allow longer in heavy traffic). A cab will set you back $15 or more, but a city bus costs just $2 (tel: 204/986-5700; www.winnipegtransit.com).
● **Calgary International Airport** (tel: 403/735-1200; www.calgaryairport.com) is 16km (10 miles) north of the city. The trip downtown will take you about 30 minutes and a cab will set you back about $30. Calgary Airport is serviced by several of the major US carriers. The Airporter bus provides a service to and from downtown Calgary

MAJOR AIRPORTS OF EACH PROVINCE AND TERRITORY

St. John's, Newfoundland
Charlottetown, Prince Edward Island
Halifax, Nova Scotia
Saint John, New Brunswick
Québec City and Montréal , Québec
Ottawa and Toronto, Ontario
Winnipeg, Manitoba
Regina and Saskatoon, Saskatchewan
Calgary and Edmonton, Alberta
Victoria and Vancouver, British Columbia
Yellowknife, Northwest Territories
Whitehorse, Yukon
Iqaluit, Nunavut

Edmonton
AIRPORTS

for $10 each way (tel: 403/531-3909).
● **Edmonton International Airport** (tel: 800/268-7134; www.edmontonairports.com) is nearly 30km (19 miles) south of the city (halfway to Calgary if you believe the locals). A cab will set you back at least $35 and take a good half-hour; the Airporter bus costs $12 each way and takes more or less the same time.
● Saskatchewan's capital, **Regina**, has a small airport (tel: 306/761-7555; www.yqr.ca) that is only a 15-minute drive west of the city. It will take five minutes to check in and another five minutes for security, so arriving an hour in advance of your take-off time would be more than adequate.
● **Halifax International Airport** (tel: 902/873-4422; www.hiaa.ca) is 35km (22 miles) north of downtown, sited inland in an attempt to avoid the fogs common on the Atlantic coast. But fog does sometimes reach the airport so it is advisable to call ahead to make sure your flight is on time. There is a shuttle service to downtown hotels (tel: 902/873-2091), which costs $12 one way (single) and $20 for a round trip (return); allow at least 45 minutes for the journey.
● The capital of Newfoundland, **St. John's** has a small airport (tel: 709/758-8500; www.stjohns-airport.nf.ca), 4.5km (3 miles) from downtown. A taxi will cost about $20 and take 15 minutes. There is no shuttle bus.

Details of other airports in Canada can be obtained from the appropriate provincial or territorial tourist office.

City Transportation: Toronto

In general, Canada's cities have invested in extensive public transportation systems, which makes travel around them relatively easy for visitors. The major cities, Toronto, Montréal and Vancouver, have excellent and reliable public transportation. Both Toronto and Montréal operate subway systems as well as buses and streetcars. In Vancouver, there are buses, trolleys, the SeaBus catamaran ferries and the above-ground Skytrain rail service.

ON THE MOVE

GETTING AROUND TORONTO

Toronto Transit Commission (TTC)

The TTC (tel: 416/393-4636; www.ttc.ca) operates buses, streetcars, the subway, and a light rapid transit system (LTR). One-way (single) fares, which can include transfers from one mode to another, are $2.25 for adults, $1.50 for students and seniors, and 50¢ for children under 12. Tickets (small metal

TTC TIPS

● You need a ticket or exact change on buses and streetcars; drivers do not give change but they do give out free transfers if you intend continuing your journey on the subway.
● In subway stations, look for the push-button transfer machine by the entrance.
● Visitors can purchase a special day pass for $7.75, good for unlimited travel after 9.30am on weekdays, Sundays and holidays. No pass is available on Saturdays.

tokens) can be purchased at all subway stations and at other authorized places displaying the TTC sign.

Toronto Subway

The Toronto Subway has two lines: the Bloor-Danforth line, which crosses the metropolitan area from east to west, and the Yonge-University-Spadina line, which forms a great north–south loop. There are 63 stations, from which buses and streetcars leave to service the rest of the city. The popular harborfront area is accessible via a Light Rapid

Streetcars form part of Toronto's efficient transportation network

SUBWAY TIPS

● The Toronto subway opens at 6am every day except Sunday, when it opens at 9am; the system operates until 1.30am daily
● "Ride Guides" with maps of the subway system, are available at all subway stations, tourist offices and other public places.

Transit system, which runs from Union Station all along the waterfront to Spadina subway station. (See map on page 44.)

Taxis

The most expensive mode of transportation is the taxi–fares soon mount, especially at rush hour. Taxi stands can be found outside the major hotels. Cabs can also be hailed on the street, or contacted by telephone. You should tip the driver 10–15 percent of the fare.

Toronto taxi cabs are easy to find and usually efficient

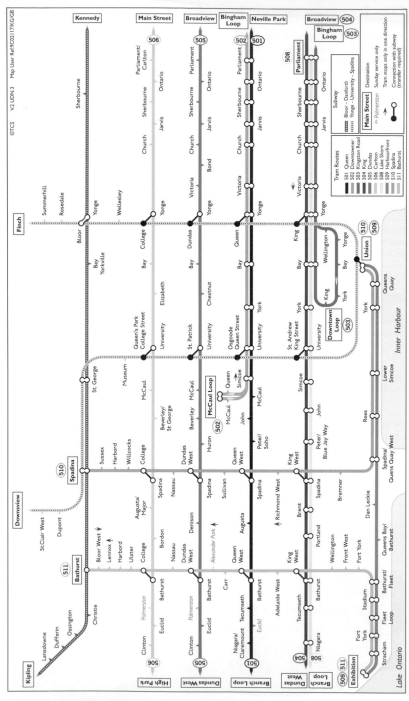

ON THE MOVE

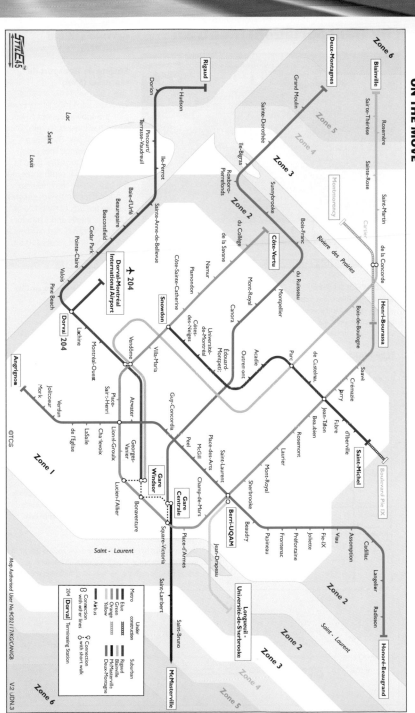

City Transportation: Montréal

Montréal's Lionel-Groulx métro station on the green and orange lines

GETTING AROUND MONTRÉAL

Société de Transport de Montréal (STM)

The STM (tel: 514/288-6287; www.stm.info) runs all city buses plus the subway system (métro), which has four color-coded lines and 65 stations. The métro's green and orange lines cross downtown, the yellow goes to the islands and south shore, and the blue serves the university.

A ticket for a one-way (single) ride on the bus or métro costs $2.50 for adults and $1.25 for seniors, students and children. A strip of six tickets costs $10 for

UNDERSTANDING THE MONTRÉAL MÉTRO (SEE MAP ON PAGE 45)

COLOR-CODED LINES

There are four color-coded métro lines—green, orange, yellow, and blue—and also four above-ground suburban commuter train lines. Métro lines are referred to by their color, suburban trains by their suburban destination (or start point).

TERMINATING STATIONS

When journeying by métro, look for the name of the station at the terminus of the line to ascertain the direction of travel. For

example, the terminating stations on the orange line are Côte Vertu and Henri Bourassa.

NAVIGATION

Follow the color-coded sign with the name of the terminus in the direction you wish to travel. For example, if you are at Berri-UQAM and you wish to go to Atwater, you would take the green line in the direction of the Angrignon terminus.

INTERCHANGING LINES

Some métro stations are served by more than one line. These are indicated by white circles on the map. It is easy to change from line to line—all you have to do is follow the color-coded sign in the direction of the terminus you want.

INTERCONNECTIONS WITH SUBURBAN TRAINS

From several métro stations, covered walkways (indicated by dots on the map) link to the two downtown suburban train stations—Central and Windsor. The suburban train to Blainville links to Vendôme métro station. Connections between métro and suburban trains are indicated by a double white circle.

FARES

There is one flat fare for travel on the métro and bus system on the Island of Montréal. Suburban trains have fare zones as indicated on the map, the fare increasing the farther you travel.

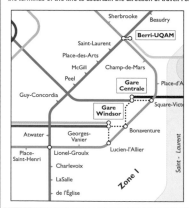

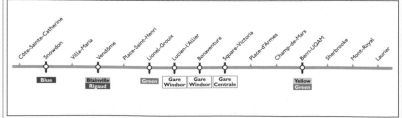

adults and $5 for seniors, students and children.

Taxis

Taxis are the most expensive means of transportation, but are convenient and plentiful in Montréal. Taxi stands are at many strategic points downtown and taxis can be hailed on the street or contacted by telephone. You should tip the driver 10–15 percent of the fare.

MONTRÉAL MÉTRO TIPS

● One-day passes allowing unlimited travel cost $7; three-day passes are $14. In summer, these passes are on sale at all the downtown métro stations; off season you must go to the central Berri-UQAM station.
● In every métro station, a transfer can be obtained from the push-button machine signed "Correspondance," enabling you to transfer to any bus.
● Free maps of the métro system are available in all stations and include a map of Montréal's extensive Underground City (see pages 84–85), together with a list of what is available at each station.
● The métro is open daily 5.30am–1am.
● If you start your journey on a bus, you will need a ticket or exact change.

Vancouver's Skytrain offers a fast, elevated ride between major downtown and suburban destinations

City Transportation: Vancouver

Vancouver taxi cabs can usually be found at stations and main hotels

GETTING AROUND VANCOUVER

Translink

The Vancouver transit system, Translink (tel: 604/521-0400; www.translink.bc.ca), includes buses, trolleys, SeaBus ferries and the above-ground Skytrain. Services run from 6.30am until about 1am (earlier on Sundays). The fare system is rather complex, with three zones operating during weekday business hours. The fare is the same for all: $2 one way (single) for adults, $1.50 for seniors and children. If you cross a zone, you pay more during weekday business hours. Transfers are available between modes, and day passes cost $8 for adults and $6 for seniors and children.

Skytrain has 20 stations along a 28-km (17-mile) track that runs between downtown Vancouver, Burnaby, New Westminster and Surrey.

The **SeaBus** catamarans cross Burrard Inlet to the north shore from the Waterfront station. The 15-minute trip is popular with visitors.

Taxis

Taxi stands are located in front of all the major hotels and transit stations, or taxis can be contacted by telephone. Hailing cabs on the street is less common than in other major cities. Tip the driver 10–15 percent of the fare.

TRANSLINK TIPS

● Be sure to have a ticket or exact change for rides on the buses and trolleys; drivers do not give change, but they do give out transfers.
● Tickets can be purchased at a number of convenience stores and drugstores; look for the "FareDealer" sign.
● The free booklet "Discover Vancouver on Transit," gives the bus numbers and other details for getting to and from the city's top tourist attractions.

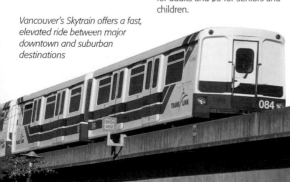

Transportation Outside Cities

On both the East and West coasts of Canada, ferries form an important part of the highway system as well as offering major means of access from the US.

FERRY SERVICES

Nova Scotia

Two ferry services link Yarmouth, Nova Scotia, with the state of Maine in the US.
- **Prince of Fundy Cruises** (tel: 800-341-7540; www.princeoffundy.com) operates between Portland and Yarmouth. The journey takes 11 hours and reservations are essential for any type of vehicle.
- **Bay Ferries** (tel: 888/249-7245; www.nfl-bay.com) operates a fast service by catamaran between Bar Harbor and Yarmouth. The trip takes only three hours and reservations for all vehicles are essential in the summer.

Bay Ferries also operates a ferry between Digby, Nova Scotia, and Saint John, New Brunswick. This three-hour crossing of the Bay of Fundy is spectacular and therefore popular, so book well in advance.

Prince Edward Island (PEI)

The province of Prince Edward Island is accessible by the Confederation Bridge (see page 68), but there is still one ferry in operation.
- **Northumberland Ferries** (tel: 888/249-7245; www.nfl-bay.com) runs a service from May to mid-December between Pictou, Nova Scotia, and Wood Islands, PEI; the trip takes 75 minutes. Like the bridge, tolls are paid only on leaving the island. The service runs back and forth constantly in the high season; no reservations are accepted, so expect lines at peak periods.

Newfoundland

- Two different ferries operated by **Marine Atlantic** make the crossing to Newfoundland from Nova Scotia (tel: 800/341-7981;

BC ferry leaving Swartz Bay

www.marine-atlantic.ca). One operates year-round from North Sydney, Nova Scotia, to Port-aux-Basques, Newfoundland; the trip takes about five hours. The other is a seasonal service three days a week (Monday, Wednesday and Friday) between North Sydney and Argentia, Newfoundland; a 14- to 15- hour trip. Many visitors to Newfoundland cross by one and return by the other; booking is essential in summer.

Victoria, British Columbia

Three different ferries operate between the US state of Washington and Victoria, the capital of British Columbia.
- **Black Ball Transport**

(tel: 250/386-2202; www.northolympic.com/coho) runs a one-hour service between Port Angeles and Victoria, and carries both cars and passengers.
- **Clipper Navigation** (tel: 800/888-2535 or 250/382-8100; www.victoriaclipper.com) runs a three-hour catamaran service for passengers only between Seattle and Victoria, with some stops in the San Juan Islands.
- From June to October, **San Juan Cruises** operates a three-hour service between Bellingham and Victoria, and includes a free salmon dinner on the return run.

MAJOR FERRY SERVICES		
	from	**to**
East Coast	Portland, Maine	Yarmouth, Nova Scotia
	Bar Harbor, Maine	Yarmouth, Nova Scotia
	Digby, Nova Scotia	Saint John, New Brunswick
	Pictou, Nova Scotia	Wood Islands, Prince Edward Island
	North Sydney, Nova Scotia	Port-aux-Basques, Newfoundland
	North Sydney, Nova Scotia	Argentia, Newfoundland
	St. Barbe, Newfoundland	Blanc Sablon, Québec
West Coast	Port Angeles, Washington	Victoria, British Columbia
	Seattle, Washington	Victoria, British Columbia
	Bellingham, Washington	Victoria, British Columbia
	Horseshoe Bay (Vancouver)	Nanaimo, British Columbia
	Tsawwassen (Vancouver)	Swartz Bay, British Columbia
	Port Hardy (Vancouver Island)	Prince Rupert, British Columbia
	Prince Rupert, British Columbia	the Queen Charlotte Islands

British Columbia Coast
● **BC Ferries** (tel: 888/223-3779; www.bcferries.bc.ca) operates a number of routes with more than 40 ports of call. Their key services operate between the British Columbia mainland and Vancouver Island, notably the one-hour crossing from Horseshoe Bay (in North Vancouver) to Nanaimo, and the two-hour service between Tsawwassen (19km/12 miles) south of Vancouver) and Swartz Bay, just north of Victoria.

BC Ferries' famous Inside Passage service, which runs between Port Hardy on Vancouver Island and Prince Rupert, takes 15 hours (reservations are mandatory). An assured service between Prince Rupert and the Queen Charlotte Islands is also available.

Icefields Parkway (above and below). A Toronto ferry (left)

LONG-DISTANCE BUSES

Travel by long-distance bus is relatively cheap and it gives access to most of the country. The major company is **Greyhound Canada** (tel: 800/661-8747; www.greyhound.ca), but there is a host of smaller ones. Greyhound covers most of western Canada, the Yukon and Ontario, with frequent cross-border links to US cities; it also has links with **Voyageur** (tel: 514/842-2281; www.voyageur.com), which serves Québec and the Maritimes.

WINTER TRAVEL

Canada functions relatively normally throughout its long cold winter. If you are nervous about driving in snow, take the train or long-distance bus. Both services run year-round and there are surprisingly few delays due to bad weather. The same is true for flights. Canadian airports are well equipped to de-ice aircraft and clear runways of snow.

You should be equipped with warm mittens, a hat, scarf, a warm coat and boots; long underwear is also advisable.

DRIVER PRECAUTIONS IN WINTER

Make sure your car is fitted with snow tires or chains.

On long trips make certain you carry the following in case you break down or get stuck in a snow drift:
● spare food
● flashlight (torch)
● blanket
● candle (this keeps the temperature in the car above freezing, but you must keep a window open a crack)
● cell phone with fully charged battery.
Remember, help is never very far away.

Train Transportation

Canadian trains are clean, fast and efficient, and are a pleasant way of seeing this scenic country. Most of the passenger service is provided by **VIA Rail** (tel: 888/VIA-RAIL; www.viarail.ca). In Europe, you can contact **Leisurail** in the UK (tel: 0870 750 0222); in Australia, contact **Asia Pacific** (tel: 02 9319 6624).

VIA RAIL SERVICES

The Canadian
Canada's most famous train crosses the country between Toronto and Vancouver three times a week in each direction, and the schedule allows passengers to see the Rockies in daylight. The trip takes three days and three nights. You can travel in Economy or in the famous Silver and Blue Class which offers private rooms, showers, and

Via Rail's Bras d'Or train runs from Halifax to Sydney, NS

- —— VIA
- —— VIA local
- —— GCRT
- —— Ontario Northland
- —— Algoma Central

Arctic Circle

Churchill

Prince Rupert
Jasper
Edmonton
SASKATOON
VANCOUVER
The Pas
Sioux Lookout
WINNIPEG
Moosonee
Oba
Cochrane
QUÉBEC
Sault Ste Marie
MONTRÉAL
HALIFAX
OTTAWA
TORONTO
Windsor
Niagara Falls

VIA RAIL FARE CONCESSIONS

CANRAILPASS

- Offers 12 days of travel in Economy class over a 30-day period.
- High-season (June to mid-October) rates are $678 for adults, $610 for seniors, students and children.
- Low-season rates are $436 for adults, $392 for seniors, students and children.
- Seats are limited, so reserve as early as possible.

CORRIDORPASS

- Offers 10 days of unlimited travel in the Windsor–Québec City corridor.
- The pass is available in both VIA 1 ($613 for adults, $552 for seniors, students and children) and Economy class ($235 for adults, $212 for seniors, students and children).
- The price is the same year round, and must be purchased at least five days before the first date of travel.

NORTH AMERICA RAIL PASS

- With Amtrak, VIA Rail offers a North America Rail Pass valid for 30 days in Economy class and giving access to over 900 cities.
- High-season rates (June to mid-October) are $1,060 for adults, $954 for seniors, students and children.
- Low-season rates are $747 for adults, $672 for seniors, students and children.
- Seats are limited, so reserve as early as possible.

---

access to a two-story observation car, which has a dome lounge with wraparound windows on the higher level and a restaurant below. All meals are included. This is an extremely popular trip, so reservations should be made well in advance.

The Hudson Bay
Leaving Winnipeg, this train travels 1,700km (1,054 miles) through the untamed beauty of northern Canada to Churchill on the shores of Hudson Bay. It runs three times a week in each direction and the trip takes one

day and two nights. Two classes are offered: Sleeper and Coach (economy).

The Corridor
VIA Rail offers a regular service in what it calls "The Corridor" between Windsor and Québec

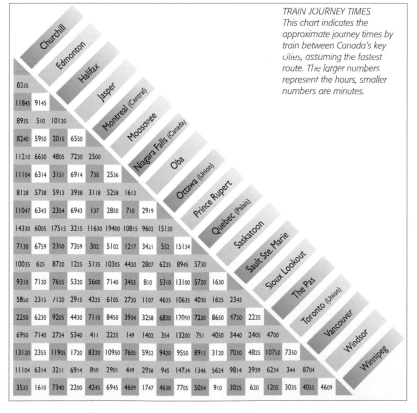

TRAIN JOURNEY TIMES
This chart indicates the approximate journey times by train between Canada's key cities, assuming the fastest route. The larger numbers represent the hours, smaller numbers are minutes.

ON THE MOVE

VIA RAIL CONTACTS IN CANADA

From all over Canada and the USA
tel: 888/VIA-RAIL; www.viarail.ca

For Newfoundland, Prince Edward Island, Nova Scotia, and New Brunswick
tel: 800/561-3952

For Québec
tel: 800/361-5390

For Ontario
tel: 800/361-1235
(except in the 807 area code:
tel: 800/561-8630)

For Manitoba, Saskatchewan, Alberta, British Columbia, Yukon, Northwest Territories, and Nunavut
tel: 800/561-8630

City. VIA's new Renaissance cars between Montréal and Toronto and between Montréal and Québec City run a particularly good and efficient service.

Other VIA Rail Trains

The **Malahat** runs between Victoria and Courtenay on Vancouver Island; the **Skeena** runs from Prince Rupert through the mountains to Jasper; the **Chaleur** is a splendid trip from Montréal to Gaspé along the shores of the Baie des Chaleurs; the **Ocean** links

Montréal to Halifax on the Atlantic coast; and the **Bras d'Or** runs from Halifax to Sydney, Nova Scotia, along the shores of Bras d'Or Lake.

AMTRAK

From the US, Amtrak (tel: 800/872-7245; www.amtrak.com) has a regular train service to Montréal from New York and Washington; to Toronto from Chicago and New York; and to Vancouver from Seattle.

OTHER TRAIN SERVICES— TOURS AND DAY TRIPS

Rocky Mountaineer Railtours
Rocky Mountaineer runs a two-day trip between Vancouver and either Banff or Jasper through the Rockies. Both routes overnight in Kamloops, so the whole trip is in daylight, a spectacular experience. For information, contact Rocky Mountaineer Railtours in Vancouver (tel: 604/606-7245 or 800/665-7245; www.rkymtnrail.com).

ROCKY MOUNTAINEER RAILTOURS®

Viewing from an observation car on Via Rail's Bras d'Or train

Day Trips
● From Skagway, Alaska, the **White Pass and Yukon Narrow-Gauge Railway** runs trips to the top of the White Pass and back daily from mid-May to mid-September, (tel: 800/343-7373 or 907/983-2217; www.wpyr.com). See page 182.
● From Sault Ste Marie, the **Algoma Central Railway** offers a splendid trip north through the wilderness of the Canadian Shield to Agawa Canyon from early June to mid-October (tel: 800/242-9287 or 705/946-7300; www.agawacanyontourtrain.com). (See page 128.)

Observation cars (below) offer wonderful views

Driving

Canadian highways are generally well maintained and present few problems in the inhabited south and between main towns and cities. However, once you venture off the beaten path, you may encounter unsurfaced sections that can make for difficult driving in wet weather. The harsh winters also have an effect—edges often crumble and pot-holes appear.

DRIVING YOUR OWN CAR

From the US, crossing the Canadian border presents few problems. You must have proof of citizenship, vehicle registration papers and proof of insurance coverage with you, and be prepared for the vehicle to be searched for illegal substances.

Fall colors and quiet roads (right).
*This chart details distances in kilometers (green) and journey times (blue) for routes within Canada. An * indicates a quicker route via the USA*

Distance chart (cities listed along the diagonal): Calgary, Charlottetown, Dawson, Edmonton, Fredericton, Halifax, Montreal, Ottawa, Prince George, Quebec, Regina, Saskatoon, Thompson, Thunder Bay, Toronto, Vancouver, Victoria, Whitehorse, Winnipeg, Yellowknife

Upper-triangle values (journey data):

8132	6232	335	7453	8222	*6150	5903	1442	6515	1142	1302	3301	3320	*5648	1407	1741	5053	2111	4045
14347	8311	700	415	1950	2221	9545	1630	7004	7427	7914	4811	2719	9631	9829	13157	6033	11934	
6049	13708	14437	12405	12123	4803	12731	7304	6929	8928	9536	11904	6342	6540	1218	8377	5767		
7632	8402	*6330	*6048	1248	6655	1228	853	2857	3500	*5820	1631	2005	4859	2251	3637			
750	1311	1542	8906	951	6325	6748	7235	4132	2040	8952	9150	12518	5354	11255				
2040	2311	9635	1720	7054	7517	8005	4901	2809	9721	9919	13247	6123	12024					
203	7604	742	5022	5143	5933	2830	539	*7650	*7848	11215	4051	9952						
7322	431	4740	5203	5651	2548	437	*7408	*5018	10933	3809	9711							
7929	2502	2127	4126	4734	7102	1552	1750	3624	3525	3832								
5348	5811	6258	3155	806	*8015	*8213	11541	4417	10318									
344	2245	2153	4521	2641	2839	6114	944	4851										
2024	2616	4944	2716	2914	5738	1407	4516											
3103	5431	4715	4914	7738	1854	6515												
2328	4820	5018	8345	1221	7123													
*7148	*7346	10714	3550	9451														
344	5203	3611	5013															
5401	3809	5211																
7137	4714																	
5914																		

Lower-triangle values (kilometers):

4675																		
2795	7104																	
294	4645	2468																
4315	375	6743	4285															
4744	231	7173	4715	444														
*3530	1155	5958	*3500	795	1224													
*3360	1328	5788	*3330	967	1397	199												
756	5381	2049	745	5021	5451	4236	4066											
*3767	924	6196	*3737	564	993	252	445	4473										
751	3940	3235	776	3580	4010	2795	2625	1512	3032									
816	4125	2984	526	3765	4194	2980	2810	1262	3217	256								
1588	4125	3759	1298	3765	4195	2980	2810	2034	3217	937	821							
1987	2688	4416	1957	2327	2757	1543	1373	2693	1780	1252	1437	1438						
*3277	1673	5705	*3247	1313	1743	542	450	3983	795	2542	2727	2727	1290					
972	5575	2777	1160	5215	5645	*4430	*4260	737	*4667	1651	1636	2408	2887	*4177				
1054	5660	2862	1242	5299	5729	*4515	*4345	822	*4752	1736	1721	2493	2972	*4262	109			
2327	6953	495	2318	6590	7022	5807	5637	1580	6044	3084	2833	3606	4265	5554	2308	2393		
1315	3348	3714	1285	2988	3411	2203	2033	2022	2440	580	765	766	660	1950	2216	2300	3593	
1783	6129	2332	1494	5769	6199	4984	4814	1550	5221	2260	2010	2782	3442	4731	2324	2408	1901	2770

ON THE MOVE

REGULATIONS
- In Canada, you drive on the right and pass on the left.
- Right turns are allowed at red lights, after coming to a full stop, unless otherwise indicated—but not in Montréal, where it's illegal.
- All persons in a vehicle must wear seat belts.
- Speed limits are given in kilometers per hour (see conversion chart on page 131) and vary slightly between provinces. Generally, expect speed limits of 100kph (62mph) on expressways, between 70 and 90 kph (43 and 56mph) on other major roads, and 50kph (31mph) or less in urban areas.

FILLING STATIONS
These are common along major routes and on the approaches to cities. In the north, you should fill your tank regularly as gas stations are sometimes far apart. Usually there will be signs giving the distance to the next station. Fuel is sold by the liter, and costs about 70 cents per liter, though the price varies from province to province. This converts to a very inexpensive 30 pence per liter for UK visitors, but visitors from America will find it expensive at about US$2.50 per US gallon.

RENTING A CAR
To rent a car, you must be over 21, and have ID and a valid driving license, which you need to have held for at least a year. Drivers over 80 may need to provide a medical certificate as

Bilingual road sign on the TCH

guarantee of competence. Reservations can usually only be made using a credit card as a guarantee, and at the moment of rental, the company will take an imprint of your card for the full expected amount. If you have no credit card, you will have to leave a hefty deposit. Check whether there are any restrictions on

ROAD SIGNS

Distances are given in kilometers

Route numbers are clearly indicated

Turn left for Alaska, ahead for the Yukon

Train crossings don't have road barriers

Promoting road safety on a Toronto street

Lights and signposting in Montréal

Moose and caribou are a hazard on roads

MAJOR CAR RENTAL COMPANIES			
NAME	**TELEPHONE**		**WEBSITE**
	Canada	**USA**	
Avis	800/331-1084	800/331-1212	www.avis.com
Budget	800/268-8900	800/527-0700	www.rent.drivebudget.com
Dollar	800/800-4000	800/800-4000	www.dollar.com
Hertz	800/263-0600	800/654-3131	www.hertz.com
National	800/387-4747	800/CAR-RENTAL	www.nationalcar.com
Thrifty	800/THRIFTY	800/THRIFTY	www.thrifty.com

taking the vehicle out of the province in which you organize the rental.

It is easy to rent a car in Canada, but rental vehicles are at a premium in the tourist season (mid-May to mid-October), so make an early reservation.

Rates and Companies

Car rental rates vary widely across Canada, depending on location, availability and how long you want a vehicle for. Starting rates can be as low as $20 a day or as high as $35. It's worth checking on fly-drive deals.

RECREATIONAL VEHICLES

Trailers (caravans) and other types of recreational vehicle are subject to the same entry requirements and driving regulations as cars. Renting RVs (motor caravans) is possible from any of the companies listed above, but reservations should be made well in advance because the rental offices may

RENTAL TIPS

● Don't forget that Canadian taxes (GST plus provincial tax—see pages 342–343) will be added to quoted rental rates
● If you want to drop off the car in a different place from where it was rented, there's likely to be a huge surcharge to cover the cost of getting it back.
● Unless you have collision insurance (Loss Damage Waiver) provided by your credit card, you will have to pay extra for insurance against accident or damage. This can add several dollars to the daily rate.
● Be careful to check whether your daily rental charge covers unlimited mileage, or whether an additional charge cuts in after a set daily limit.

not always keep them on site, and numbers are limited.

In addition, a wide range of recreational vehicles for long- and short-term rentals is

available from **Owasco Recreational Vehicles**, 2000 Champlain Avenue, Whitby, Ontario, tel: 905/579-7573 or 800/263-2676; www.owasco.com

Many campgrounds handle RVs, since a lot of Canadians have them. Each provincial government tourist office can supply a list of campgrounds detailing their facilities and costs (see page 317).

DRIVING IN REMOTE AREAS OR IN WINTER

See Winter Travel, page 49.

BREAKDOWN OR ACCIDENT

If you are going to drive long distances in Canada, especially in remote areas, it might be a good idea to take out membership of the Canadian Automobile Association (tel: 800/222-4357; www.caa.ca). They or their local affiliate can help you in case of breakdown.

Members of the American Automobile Association are entitled to full service with the CAA, but must have their membership card with them.

In case of an emergency or accident, call 911 (see page 314) where possible, and be sure to report any accident to the police. This is usually a condition of your insurance coverage.

Stunning Icefields Parkway drive

TRAVELING WITH A DISABILITY

In recent years, the travel industry in Canada has become increasingly aware of the needs of visitors with disabilities. Unfortunately, the process is a slow one and there is still much room for improvement. There is all too often a difference between what ought to be there and what is actually in place. This makes getting around with a disability frustrating at times, although there has definitely been progress toward making amenities and tourist sites accessible to all.

ON THE MOVE

GENERAL ADVICE

● If you are disabled, plan your trip carefully and check facilities in advance.

● Where possible, travel with able-bodied friends or consider touring with a travel agent who specializes in travel for people with disabilities as this will make arrangements easier.

● Contact both your departure and arrival airports in advance to let them know what assistance you will require. Airports and airlines are exemplary in helping travelers with disabilities–as long as they have advance warning.

● Make hotel reservations well in advance and again be specific about your requirements.

● Before any trip, do some research and find out what your rights actually are. Never hesitate to let it be known if you encounter unhelpful or obstructive behavior. There is often a legal requirement for your needs to be met.

WHAT TO EXPECT ONCE YOU ARE IN THE COUNTRY

● By law, all public buildings must have wheelchair access and provide special toilets.

● By municipal ordinance, kerbs in the major urban centers are dropped at cross streets to meet the needs of wheelchair users. This is not, however, always the case outside the major cities.

Public Transportation

● Buses in the major cities are increasingly being adapted to accommodate wheelchairs. This is less frequently the case in rural areas. Once again, careful checking in advance will make you aware of major problems.

● All VIA Rail trains can accommodate wheelchairs as long as 48 hours' notice is given.

Hotels

● Some of the major hotels provide wheelchair access and some offer special suites for guests with disabilities. Careful checking in advance will avoid problems.

● Be aware that strict codes are in effect for new properties but older accommodations and restaurants may still have barriers.

● Details of hotels accessible to visitors with disabilities can usually be obtained from local tourist offices.

OFFICIAL POLICY

The Canada Transportation Act lays out the government of Canada's commitment to equitable access to transportation services for all. Under the Act, the Canadian Transportation Agency (an arm of the federal government) has the power to remove "undue obstacles" from Canada's transportation network, and this applies to planes and airports, trains and stations, and ferry services and their terminals.

For more information, contact the Accessible Transportation Directorate, Canadian Transport-ation Agency, Ottawa, Ontario, K1A ON9, tel: 819/997-6828 or 800/883-1813; www.cta-otc.gc.ca/index_e.html.

You should indicate your language preference (English or French) and the alternative format you require. This agency produces a number of publications, including:

● *Fly Smart*, a brochure with general information about flying to, from and within Canada.

● *A Guide for Persons with Disabilities—Taking Charge of the Air Travel Experience,* a booklet addressing issues such as seat selection, getting to the terminal, checking in, boarding and leaving the aircraft.

USEFUL ORGANIZATIONS

● **Canadian Association of the Deaf** (www.cad.ca), protects and promotes the rights, needs and concerns of deaf Canadians.

● **Canadian National Institute for the Blind** (www.cnib.ca), provides services to individuals with loss of vision.

● **Canadian Paraplegic Association** (www.canparaplegic.org), assists those with spinal cord injuries and other disabilities.

● **National Federation of the Blind** (www.nfbae.ca), increases awareness of rights and responsibilities for blind, deaf-blind and partially sighted individuals; also produces the *Blind Monitor* magazine available in Braille, large print, diskette, audiocassette, and email formats.

OTHER SOURCES OF TRAVEL INFORMATION
Society for Accessible Travel and Hospitality
www.sath.org
Touring Friends Assisted Travel Association
www.mgl.ca/~touring/
Disability Travel and Recreation Resources (International)
www.makoa.org/travel.htm
Accessible Travel Source
www.access-able.com
Travel Insurance for Pre-existing Health Conditions
www.travelability.com
Scoot Around America (delivers scooters to hotels in major cities throughout North America)
www.scootaround.com

This chapter is divided into six regions, with places of interest arranged alphabetically—though major cities feature prominently at the start of the relevant sections. There's a list of the key sites on each section opening page. For the full list of the sites, turn to the Atlas on pages 365–385.

The Sights

ATLANTIC PROVINCES

On the east coast, the beautiful Atlantic Provinces—New Brunswick, Newfoundland and Labrador, Nova Scotia and Prince Edward Island—are steeped in tradition and the spray of the ocean. They reflect Acadian French roots and the Celtic cultures of Highland Scots and Irish settlers, and boast some lovely old Loyalist settlements.

MAJOR SIGHTS

The waterfront boardwalk at
Annapolis Royal

Spirit of Harbour Grace at the
Conception Bay Museum

Canadian Navy and Coastguard
vessels docked at Baddeck

ANNAPOLIS ROYAL

⊞ 367 W16
www.parkscanada.gc.ca

On the wide basin of the
Annapolis River, where it meets
the Bay of Fundy, tiny Annapolis
Royal is a place of immense historic charm, and its main street is
lined by elegant homes, craft
shops, art galleries, and restaurants. Twice a day, the huge
Fundy tides (see pages 62–63)
rush in, reversing the flow of the
river with a mighty thrust that
generates the town's electricity.

Annapolis Royal was the first
French colony in North America,
settled 15 years before the
Pilgrim Fathers landed in the USA.
It was also the most fought over
place in Canada during the hostilities between the English and
French. Port Royal National
Historic Site (daily, mid-May to
mid-Oct), about 10.5km
(6.5 miles) from town across the
causeway, recalls those days. It
was built in 1605 and survived
only until 1613, but the compound, reminiscent of an old
Normandy farm, has been meticulously reconstructed.

Canada's oldest national historic
park, Fort Anne (daily, mid-May to
mid-Oct), off Upper St. George
Street, was built by the French
in 1702–1708, with later additions
by the British. It houses historical
displays, plus the huge Heritage
Tapestry, a masterpiece of needle-
craft that illustrates four centuries
of Annapolis Royal history.
Don't miss The Port Royal
National Historic Site offers a
splendid insight into the lives of
early settlers.

AVALON PENINSULA

⊞ 367 Z13 🛈 City Hall 2nd Floor
Annex, 35 New Gower Street, St. John's,
Newfoundland and Labrador, A1C 5M2,
tel 709/576-8106

Sometimes called "Canada's Far
East," this is the most easterly
part of the entire North American
continent, suspended from the
rest of Newfoundland by a narrow isthmus. It's wild and beautiful, with the vital city of St. John's
(see pages 70–71) on its eastern coast, a distinctive lifestyle
and sense of history. European
settlement started early here,
and British fishermen first visited
the harbors around the 1520s.

The rugged beauty of the coastline is matched by the wonders
of nature: whales at St. Vincent's
and at the ecological reserve of
Witless Bay (where thousands of
humpbacks and minkes come to
feed); and seabird colonies on
the islands of Witless Bay and at
Cape St. Mary's in the southwest,
home to northern gannets, razor-
bills and murres. And most years
there is the spectacle of 10,000-
year-old icebergs drifting past.

The most easterly point is
Cape Spear. From this headland
there are wonderful views along
the rocky coast and over the
entrance to St. John's harbor,
and it's a prime whale-watching
spot. Now a national historic
park, the cape has a visitor
center (daily, mid-May to mid-
Oct) and two lighthouses. It's
supremely peaceful, but nature
has its hazards too, so heed the
safety notices.

Northwest of St. John's, at
Harbour Grace, the Conception
Bay Museum (daily, summer
only) recalls the town's role in
transatlantic aviation—a number
of pioneering flights set out from
here. Farther north still, Trinity
Bay has a trio of communities
with names that beckon: Heart's
Delight, Heart's Desire and
Heart's Content. At the latter, in
1866, the first successful attempt
to lay a transatlantic communications cable ended. The old cable
station is now a museum (daily,

mid-Jun to mid-Oct), looking
back to the days when cables
cost $5 a word and this station
handled 3,000 messages a day.

On the west coast lies
Placentia, its name derived from
the French plaisance, given to it
in 1662 when it became capital
of the French colony. Located on
a narrow strip of land between
the natural harbor and two deep
inlets, the town is overlooked by
the remains of the 17th-century
French fortress atop Castle Hill
(visitor center: daily, mid-May to
mid-Oct; grounds: year round),
with spectacular views.
Don't miss Cape Spear is great
for whale-watching.

BADDECK

⊞ 367 X15

Baddeck lies at the heart of Cape
Breton island on the shore of St.
Patrick's Channel, part of the
enormous Bras d'Or Lake, and
because of this scenic location
the 1,000-strong community
swells in summer with visitors.
The town has a long history of
attracting emigrating Scots, one
them was Alexander Graham Bell
(1847–1922), inventor,
researcher and all-round genius,
who in 1885 built a summer
home here—Beinn Bhreagh,
Gaelic for "beautiful mountain."

Bell's many achievements are
recalled at the Alexander Graham
Bell National Historic Site (daily)
at the east end of the village on
Chebucto Street (Route 205). It
was, of course, the telephone
that made the inventor rich and
famous, but his experiments
delved into many other areas. In
1907, Bell's Silver Dart flew
across Baddeck Bay in the first
manned flight in Canada. Later,
one of his hydrofoils, the HD-4,
set a world record with a speed
of 114kph (almost 71mph) on
Bras d'Or Lake.

THE SIGHTS

The lights of Cape Bonavista's lighthouse

The Cabot Trail, one of the most scenic drives in the world, winds around the hills, forests and coastline of northern Cape Breton

BONAVISTA PENINSULA

🚩 367 Y12

It is thought that John Cabot's first North American landfall in 1497 might have been on this scenic spot on Newfoundland's east coast. "*O buona vista,*" the Italian-born explorer is said to have declared, and few would hesitate to echo his sentiment. Today, a statue of the explorer stands above Cape Bonavista and its pounding waves. The red and white lighthouse here *(daily, mid-Jun to early Oct)* dates from 1843, and costumed guides re-create life in the 1870s.

About 5km (3 miles) from the cape is the tranquil community of Bonavista, a thriving center for international trade only a generation ago, when its little harbor was filled with schooners and its docksides were alive with scurrying workers. The Ryan Premises *(daily, mid-Jun to mid-Oct)*, on the waterfront, are the former headquarters of James Ryan Ltd., which created an economic empire here based on the Labrador and Newfoundland inshore fisheries. The company closed in 1978, but the buildings have been restored to tell the story. Also on the harborfront is a locally built replica of John Cabot's ship, the *Matthew (daily, mid-Jun to Sep)*, in which he crossed the Atlantic from Bristol, England.

Another explorer, Portuguese Gaspar Corte Real, arrived on Trinity Sunday 1501, and thus the tiny coastal village of Trinity was named. It has colorful "box" houses on its hilly peninsula, looking out across the small harbor to the open seas. Trinity's main claim to fame today is the New Founde Land pageant *(Wed, Sat and Sun 2pm, Jul 1– Labor Day weekend)*, a musical parade through the town with vignettes of characters from Trinity's history. Hiscock House *(daily, Jun–Oct)* is a typical early 20th-century merchant's home, where guides in period costume show you around.

Don't miss You can board the replica of John Cabot's ship.

CAMPOBELLO ISLAND

🚩 367 W16 🚢 From Eastport, Maine, or via Deer Island (Jul–mid-Sep only)
www.campobello.com

At the point where the Atlantic Ocean roars up into the Bay of Fundy lies Campobello, one of the Fundy Islands (see pages 62–63) and long famous for its invigorating climate. In the late 19th century the island attracted wealthy US industrialists keen to escape the polluted air of their cities. Among those who had vacation houses here were James and Sara Delano Roosevelt, whose son Franklin later became US president (1933–45). Young Franklin spent his summers on Campobello, which he called his "beloved island," and later he and his wife Eleanor bought their own summer home here. In 1921, FDR contracted polio while cooling off in the icy Fundy waters after fighting a forest fire for hours. He did not return to Campobello for 12 years, by which time he was president. The 34-room Dutch-gabled Roosevelt Cottage *(daily, mid-May to mid-Oct)* is now the focal point of the 1,133ha (2,800-acre) Roosevelt-Campobello International Park *(daily)*, impeccably maintained by the governments of both Canada and the United States as an international peace park. Simply furnished, the house is a poignant return in time, full of reminders of its former owners. The neighboring visitor center *(open as Roosevelt Cottage)* offers excellent interpretive displays on Roosevelt's life.

Walk down to the wharf for the splendid view of the coast and Eastport, Maine—if the famous fog hasn't set in—or explore the hiking trails and drives that wind through the forest to headlands and rocky shores.

Don't miss Take a guided tour of Roosevelt Cottage.

CAPE BRETON HIGH-LANDS NATIONAL PARK

🚩 367 X15 ℹ️ Ingonish and Chéticamp information offices, daily, mid-May to mid-Oct 🅿️ Permit: adult $5, child (6–16) $2.50, children under 6 free. Fees apply mid-May to mid-Oct only.

Cape Breton is one of the most beautiful places in eastern Canada, and its scenery is nowhere more breathtaking than in the northern part of the island, where the Cabot Trail (see tour and walk on pages 260–263) winds through dense forests and skirts sections of wild, rocky coastline. Much of this road falls within the Cape Breton Highlands National Park, which was created in 1936 and encompasses 950sq km (366sq miles). You need a permit to enter the park, even if you are just driving through, and you can pick this up, along with a free map, from the information building just north of Chéticamp.

The national park has 26 hiking and walking trails, ranging from short family walks to challenging overnight adventures. Some lead to viewpoints offering panoramas of the spectacular coastline; others explore forests and secluded lakes. Here, moose, black bear, bobcats, and coyotes roam, while bald eagles circle overhead. Off the coast, whales and dolphins break the surface, watched by a multitude of sea birds—there is no shortage of whale-watching

Fredericton's Reaverbrook Art Gallery also offers art classes

Bonne Bay, in Gros Morne, is actually two connected fiords

Below, left: Sentries at Fredericton's Military Compound

trips between June and September, notably from Chéticamp and Pleasant Bay (see page 260), but you can often see the marine mammals from the coastal viewpoints.

FREDERICTON

367 W16 · 11 Carleton Street, Fredericton, New Brunswick, E3B 4Y7, tel 506/460-2041
www.city.fredericton.nb.ca

Set on a wide bend of the Saint John River, New Brunswick's capital is a quiet, attractive city of elm-lined streets and elegant houses, and you can easily explore it on foot. The city began life as a Loyalist settlement and was named after the second son of George II, Prince Frederick. Opposite the Legislative Building is the modern Beaverbrook Art Gallery (daily; closed Mon off season), the finest art gallery in Atlantic Canada. Pride of place goes to Salvador Dali's huge Santiago el Grande, high above the entrance lobby, and there are good collections of Canadian and British paintings.

From Fredericton, drive east for 34km (21 miles) on the Trans-Canada Highway 2 to reach King's Landing (daily, end May to mid-Oct), a splendidly re-created 19th-century Loyalist settlement amid woodland, pasture and riverbank. Staffed by costumed interpreters, it's one of the largest cultural sites of its kind in

Canada and includes homes, farms and workshops, plus a fascinating water-driven sawmill. **Don't miss** Enjoy traditional cuisine and a unique beer at the King's Head pub, King's Landing.

FUNDY NATIONAL PARK AND ISLANDS

See page 62–63.

GROS MORNE NATIONAL PARK

367 X13 · Gros Morne National Park Headquarters, Rocky Harbour, Newfoundland and Labrador, A0K 4N0
709/458-2066 · Daily · Adult $7.50, child (6–16) $3.75, family $15 (includes Discovery Centre) · Deer Lake Airport (32km/20 miles from park entrance) · Connections to Rocky Harbour from airport and ferries
www.parkscanada.gc.ca/grosmorne

This wild area of fiords, sea coast, forest, and mountains on Newfoundland's west coast, was designated a World Heritage Site by UNESCO in 1987, not only for its spectacular scenic beauty but also for the global importance of its geology. The flat-topped and almost barren ocher-hued Tablelands (4km/3 miles from the Discovery Centre on Route 431) are peridotite from the Earth's mantle. Formed far below the ocean floor, they were transported hundreds of kilometers to their present position some 450 million years ago.

The formation at Green Point, 12km (7.5 miles) north of Rocky Harbour, a tilted, slanted chunk of rock that rises abruptly from the ocean, is considered one of the best examples of exposed sedimentary rock in the world; there are guided walks with naturalists in summer. The park has a number of other trails, including the arduous 16km (10-mile) hike up flat-topped Gros Morne, 806m (2,644ft) high.

The best introduction to Gros Morne is at the Discovery Centre (daily, May–Oct), in Woody Point on Route 431. It has a wonderful location, and its displays explain the geological phenomena that attract international interest. The Park Visitor Centre (daily, May–mid-Oct; Mon–Fri, mid-Oct to mid-Nov), on Route 430 near Rocky Harbour, also has background information (see tour and walk on page 255–259).

About 27km (17 miles) north of Rocky Harbour is Western Brook Pond. Newfoundlanders are noted for understatement, and to describe this remarkable body of water as a "pond" is one example of this. It's 16km (10 miles) long, bordered by cliffs up to 700m (2,300ft) high, and is 160m (525ft) deep and up to 3km (2 miles) wide. An oligotrophic lake, it contains almost no nutrients and therefore supports little plant life—this water is some of the purest in the world.

There is a dramatic view of the remarkable Western Brook Pond from Route 430, but the only way to appreciate this scenic fiord-lake fully is to walk to its edge (6km/4miles return) and take the boat trip (daily, late June–early Sept). Face to face with nature at her wildest, it's truly awe-inspiring.

About 6km (4 miles) south of the pond is Broom Point (daily, mid-May to mid-Oct), which offers an insight into the lives of a mid-20th-century fishing family.

Head north from Gros Morne to the northern tip of Newfoundland and you'll find a place of enormous historic significance to the whole of North America. L'Anse au Meadows (daily, Jun–Aug) is an excavation and partial reconstruction of the only Viking settlement found on the Continent. It provides a fascinating insight into the lives of those early explorers.

Fundy National Park and Islands

Southern New Brunswick's last true wilderness, on a coast with the highest tides in the world.

One of the famous New Brunswick covered bridges

SEEING FUNDY NATIONAL PARK AND ISLANDS

Situated on the Bay of Fundy, this 206sq-km (80 sq-mile) park is a wonderful combination of coastal highlands and shoreline. The bay, with its vast tidal range and cold waters, influences the entire park. You can experience the tidal fluctuation on its shores by watching fishing boats come and go or by strolling on the beach. You can also walk on more than 100km (60 miles) of inland trails or explore its islands.

HIGHLIGHTS

NATIONAL PARK COASTLINE

At the park's eastern entrance is Alma Beach, where many visitors time their arrival with low tide so that they can walk across the kilometer-wide (0.6-mile) tidal flats. A pole in the sand indicates how deep the water is at high tide. Be sure to walk back well before high tide, as it takes less than and hour for the water to go from nothing to waist deep.

In the 19th-century, a thriving sawmill stood at the mouth of the Point Wolfe River, 10km (6 miles) southwest of Alma. By the 1920s, however, all the easy accessible trees had been cut and the mill closed. You can follow a path overlooking a small gorge and dam and view a cove that was once filled with schooners used to transport the wood; explanatory panels bring the place to life. Look out also for the old wooden covered bridge here. At low tide you can walk down the long beach with its wide gravel bar, though be sure to check the tide tables before wandering too far (people have been known to become stranded in coves as the tide rises).

At Herring Cove, 4km (2.5 miles) southwest of Alma, you can explore the tidal pools, seaweed-draped rocks and mud flats at low tide, and then return at high tide to find them all gone.

CALEDONIA HIGHLANDS

Stretching back from the coast are forested highlands, a wilderness area with dense forest, rivers with waterfalls, and plentiful wildlife. Fundy is on the Atlantic bird migration route, and more than 260 species have been identified within the park; 95 of these have nested in the park and the peregrine falcon has been reintroduced. The park has excellent visitor facilities, including campgrounds and a nine-hole golf course *(mid-May to early Oct)* at its eastern entrance.

CAMPOBELLO ISLAND

See page 60.

DEER ISLAND

✚ 367 W16 ℹ Lord's Cove, Deer Island, New Brunswick, E5V 1W2 ⛴ Free ferry from L'Etete, New Brunswick

Deer and the other two islands—Campobello (see page 60) and Grand Manan (see opposite)—lie in the mouth of Passamaquoddy Bay. They are evergreen-cloaked, often windswept and fog-bound, but are popular because they are so peaceful and have abundant wildlife—particularly birds and whales. Island life is dominated by the

sea, and the high tides, whirlpools and swirling currents of the bay act as giant pumps, bringing up the nutrients that feed tiny marine organisms. These, in turn, are food for all kinds of hungry sea creatures, and the 900 people who reside on Deer Island, which lies on the 45th Parallel midway between the Equator and the North Pole, live largely by harvesting lobsters and clams and by salmon farming. Off Deer's southern tip is the Old Sow Whirlpool, the largest tidal whirlpool in the western hemisphere. It is best viewed from Deer Island Point, three hours before high tide at new and full moon. There's a campground, picnic tables and a pebble beach, but swimming is not recommended!

GRAND MANAN ISLAND

➕ 367 W16 🏠 130 Route 776, Grand Manan, New Brunswick, E5G 4K9, tel 506/662-3442, 888/525-1655 🚢 From Black Harbour, New Brunswick
Grand Manan is the largest of the Fundy Islands, and has towering cliffs, rugged scenery and a population of about 1,000. This is the North American capital for dulse, an edible seaweed used as a seasoning, or eaten raw as a snack (an acquired taste). The island is also a bird sanctuary, where a total of 230 species have been sighted, and Machias Seal Island offshore has a puffin colony. Interestingly, Machias Seal is the subject of a boundary dispute between Canada and the US, an unresolved leftover from the War of 1812.

BACKGROUND

One of the world's marine wonders, the Bay of Fundy experiences the highest tides anywhere on the planet. At the head of the bay, the gravitational pull of the sun and moon causes tides that rise and fall up to an incredible 16m (52ft) twice a day—every day! This huge rise is caused by a combination of factors: Like water in a bathtub, the water in the bay has a natural rocking motion, called a seiche, that takes about 12 hours to rock from the mouth of the bay to its head and back again. This coincides with the frequency of the pulse from the Atlantic tides that flood into the bay. Accentuating the rise even further is the shape of the bay; because it becomes narrower and shallower towards its head, the water is forced higher up the shores.
Other places in the world have large tides, but their tidal ranges measure only about 10m (30ft) and they don't move as much water; in the Bay of Fundy, the tidal contribution is equal to the total daily discharge of all the world's rivers.

Point Wolfe is a great place for birding and beachcombing

TIPS
● If you walk out on beaches at low tide, be aware of the times when the tide changes. The water rushes in—from nothing to waist-deep in less than an hour—and it's not always easy to scramble up the cliffs.

Point Wolfe River Gorge, once busy with loggers and ships

Halifax

●

International gateway to the Atlantic provinces, with the second-largest natural harbor in the world.

SEEING HALIFAX

Halifax can be wet and foggy, and it can be very windy, but on a fine summer's day or during its comparatively mild winter it is an exciting and interesting place to visit. Many attractions are along the waterfront, but the best place to start is up on Citadel Hill—for its fortress and panoramic overview of the city, and also because everything else is downhill from here. Ferries cross the harbor to the twin city of Dartmouth.

HIGHLIGHTS

CITADEL NATIONAL HISTORIC SITE

✉ Halifax, Nova Scotia, B3K 5M7 ☎ 902/426-9080 ◷ Daily (animation Jun 1–Sep 15) 🎫 Adult $8, child (6–16) $4; free mid-Sep–May 🔲 🏛 🔲
Halifax is crowned by Citadel Hill, where the massive star-shaped fortress still dominates the city despite modern high-rise construction. There are views in every direction: of the city (including the famous Town Clock), the harbor, Dartmouth, across The Narrows, and the bridges that connect it to Halifax. Fortified since 1749, the present Citadel was completed in 1865. Inside, you are back in the year 1869 when the 78th Highland Regiment was stationed here, now represented by costumed guides dressed in MacKenzie tartan kilts, feathered bonnets and bright red doublets—an impressive sight. You can visit the barracks, guardroom, garrison cell and powder magazine, and see the "Tides of History," a spectacular audiovisual presentation.

THE WATERFRONT

Halifax's magnificent natural harbor extends nearly 16km (10 miles) inland—only Sydney Harbour in Australia is larger. It remains ice-free all winter and is almost divided into two by a stretch called The Narrows, which separates the outer harbor from the Bedford Basin. The city's lively waterfront area is colorful and fun, with a walkway stretching for 4km (2.5 miles), waterfront restaurants, fine museums, and the ever-present salty smell of the ocean. Besides all the activity on the water, there's much to see and do on land.

A group of old warehouses on Upper Water Street were innovatively renovated in the 1970s and are now collectively known as the Historic Properties. An early but still very successful urban regeneration scheme, they house restaurants, craft stores and offices. There's a particularly good food market area offering fresh fish and seafood to eat in or take out, breads, coffee and more. From here, you can walk along to the casino in one direction and to Pier 21 (see opposite) in the other. Along the way you'll pass the Maritime Museum (see opposite), *Bluenose II* if she is visiting (see Lunenburg, page 67), tugboats, the Dartmouth ferry, and the Court House. Don't miss HMCS *Sackville* (*daily, Jun–Sep; can be visited at HMC Dockyard, Oct–May*), a World War II corvette floating at Sackville Landing. More than 100 corvettes were built in Canada to escort convoys, and she's the sole survivor, restored as a museum commemorating all who served in the Canadian Navy.

Halifax's Citadel (top) and one of its costumed sentries

RATINGS

Good for kids	● ● ● ○
Historic interest	● ● ● ●
Photo stops	● ● ● ○
Shopping	● ● ● ○

BASICS

✚ 367 X16
ℹ Nova Scotia International Visitors Centre, 1595 Barrington Street, Halifax, Nova Scotia, tel 902/490-5946
ℹ Waterfront Visitor Info Centre, Sackville Landing, Halifax, Nova Scotia, tel 902/424-4248
www.halifaxinfo.com • A clear and informative website with details of attractions and facilities in and around the city

MAKE A DAY OF IT

Annapolis Royal (see page 59)
Lunenburg (see page 67)

Halifax's huge natural harbor has hosted the Tall Ships Race (above). The city's fine historic buildings include the Old Red Store (inset)

MARITIME MUSEUM OF THE ATLANTIC

✉ 1675 Lower Water Street, Halifax, Nova Scotia, B3J 1S3 ☎ 902/424-7490 ⏰ Daily, May–Oct; Tue–Sun, rest of year 💰 Adult $5 🏛 ♿

The city's distinguished seafaring history is reflected in this excellent museum on the waterfront, partly located in a 1879 ship's chandlery. It houses a collection of full-size and model ships, some of them floating, tells the stories of the *Titanic* (150 of the drowned were buried in Halifax, many unidentified) and the Cunard Steamship Line (Samuel Cunard was from Halifax), and has an excellent film about the Halifax Explosion (see Background). Other displays include shipwrecks, hidden treasures and a reconstruction of the ship's chandlery of 100 years ago.

PIER 21

✉ 1055 Marginal Road, Halifax, Nova Scotia, B3H 4P6 ☎ 902/425-7770 ⏰ Daily, May–Oct; Wed–Sun, rest of year 💰 Adult $12 🏛 ♿ ▢

Pier 21, at the end of the waterfront walkway, was Canada's "front door" from 1928 to 1971. More than a million immigrants entered the country here (not to mention wartime evacuees, refugees, and war brides). Today, it's an interactive visitor center where Canadians can record their memories. The dramatic multimedia presentation is a fascinating and emotional experience for immigrants and their descendants. It also includes the World War II balcony overlooking the harbor where half a million troops boarded ships to serve in Europe.

BACKGROUND

Halifax was founded in July 1749 on land the native peoples called Chebucto (Big Harbor), and from the start it was a military stronghold. The city's history was frequently eventful, but one episode left a terrible mark. In December 1917, during World War I, the *Mont Blanc*, a French munitions ship carrying picric acid, guncotton, TNT, and benzol, had a fatal collision with the *Imo*, a Belgian relief ship, in The Narrows of the harbor. There followed the greatest man-made explosion the world saw prior to the bombing of Hiroshima in 1945. A huge area of the city was completely flattened, more than 2,000 people died and 9,000 were injured, many blinded for life.

IF YOU'VE TIME

ART GALLERY OF NOVA SCOTIA

✉ 1723 Hollis Street, Halifax, Nova Scotia, B3J 3C8 ☎ 902/424-7542 ⏰ Tue–Sun, year round 💰 $5 (more for temporary exhibitions) 🏛 ♿ ▢

The gallery's star attractions are the works of Naive artist Maud Lewis, including parts of her house moved from Digby after her death, and the extraordinary collection of folk art.

MUSEUM OF NATURAL HISTORY

✉ 1747 Summer Street, Halifax, Nova Scotia, B3H 3A6 ☎ 902/424-7353 ⏰ Daily, May–Oct; Tue–Sun, Nov–Apr 💰 $3 ♿

This is a small but interesting museum that houses a comprehensive survey of the province's wildlife, plantlife, minerals, and archeology. The displays on the Acadians and Mi'kmaq are interesting, but pride of place goes to the whale display.

A number of those who perished in the Titanic tragedy were buried in Halifax. This memorial is among those at the Fairview Cemetery

Hopewell Rocks, supporting tiny islets, are exposed at low tide

The northern lights—nature's spectacular light show

Military life is re-created in realistic style at Louisbourg

THE SIGHTS

HOPEWELL ROCKS

367 W16 • 131 Discovery Road, Hopewell Cape, New Brunswick, E4H 4Z5 ☎ 506/734-3534, 877/734-3429 (within Canada) Daily, mid-May to mid-Oct Adult $5, child (5–18) $3, family $12
www.thehopewellrocks.ca

It is a strange experience to be walking on the sea-bed, knowing that within a few hours the water will be 10m (30ft) deep on that very spot. To get the best of this unique place on Shepody Bay, visit first at high tide, when the bay is dotted with tiny tree-covered islands, then return at low tide to walk among them. The "islands" are actually narrow red sandstone columns up to 15m (50ft) high and wider at the top, and you wonder how they can remain upright—in fact, some have fallen, since the fierce Fundy tides batter the supporting columns mercilessly twice a day.

Hopewell Rocks are 40km (25 miles) south of Moncton on Route 114, going toward Fundy National Park. At the top of the cliff is an interpretive center *(daily, mid-May to mid-Oct)* with displays explaining the Fundy phenomenon. Make sure you consult the tide tables to time your visit so that you don't get cut off by waters that rise at up to 2.4m (8ft) per hour. At low tide you can descend from here to the rocky beach via wooden staircases.

LABRADOR

366 V12 Government of Newfoundland and Labrador, tel 800/563-NFLD
www.gov.nf.ca/tourism

This is one of the last great wilderness areas on the face of the Earth, where glacial action, erosion and internal upheaval have carved a land of unsurpassed beauty. There are towering mountains,

massive rock faces, huge lakes and fast-flowing rivers. The air is clean, the water is pure and there is an amazing diversity of wildlife.

Labrador stretches 1,000km (600 miles) south to north, from the Strait of Belle Isle to the shores of Ungava Bay, and covers a staggering 1,560,000sq km (more than 600,000sq miles). The people have to be self-reliant: Innu and Inuit cultures are rooted in a deep, spiritual relationship with the environment, and settlers from Europe have learned to survive in this sometimes hostile land.

Much of Labrador is inaccessible, but the road from Blanc Sablon, Québec, is gradually being extended and now reaches Cartwright; an unsurfaced road cuts across country from Labrador City to Lake Melville. Communities farther north can be reached only by coastal ferries that ply what is locally known as "Iceberg Alley." Much of Labrador is easier to reach in winter, as long as you have a snowmobile or dogsled!

In the 16th century, the old Basque community of Red Bay, 78km (48 miles) from Blanc Sablon, was the whaling capital of the world; the interpretation center here *(daily, mid-Jun to mid-Oct)* has items retrieved from shipwrecks.

The paved section of Route 510 ends at Red Bay, but a gravel road continues another 65km (40 miles) north to Mary's Harbour, from where you can cross (make arrangements with the Riverview Hotel) to Battle Harbour *(daily, Jun–Sep)*. Here, mercantile saltfish premises established in the 1770s developed into a thriving community recognized as the "Capital of Labrador" for 200 years or so. Since the decline of the cod fishery in recent decades, Battle

Harbour has been deserted, but its former state can still be appreciated in restored historic structures, walkways and work areas, and in a collection of fishery-related items.
Don't miss Look out for caribou, moose and eagles.

LOUISBOURG

367 Y15 • 259 Park Service Road, Louisbourg, Nova Scotia, B1C 2L2 ☎ 902/733-2280 Daily; full animation and services Jun–Sep, limited late May and early Oct Adult $12, child (6–16) $6, family $30
www.parkscanada.gc.ca

Louisbourg glowers into the mists, fogs and storms of the North Atlantic, a mighty symbol of the fierce struggle between France and Britain. This was the great fortress of New France guarding the entrance to the St. Lawrence River and the approach to Québec. Not only did it have the largest garrison in North America, but it was also a commercial hub with a fishing harbor, a governor's palace, a hospital, homes, arsenals, and warehouses.

Construction of the star-shaped fortified town began in 1719. The cost was enormous—the equivalent of about $200 million today—but Louisbourg was not impregnable and was subsequently largely destroyed. The Canadian government has now faithfully re-created about a quarter of the original site to reflect a town of the 1740s.

Louisbourg covers 4.8ha (12 acres), with more than 50 buildings and extensive stone fortifications. From the visitor center, you can walk or take a shuttle bus to the fortress where each summer costumed interpreters reenact every level of society.
Don't miss Be sure to visit the King's Bastion.

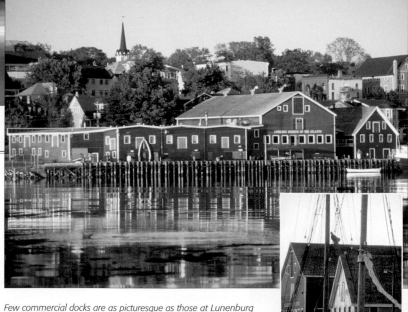

Few commercial docks are as picturesque as those at Lunenburg

LUNENBURG

A beautiful colonial heritage town with a maritime history.

One of Nova Scotia's most historic and attractive towns, Lunenburg has narrow streets lined with colorful buildings that reflect its seafaring heritage. In 1995, UNESCO, when adding Lunenburg to its list of World Heritage Sites, declared it to be an "outstanding example" of British colonial settlement in North America. Set on a neck of land 92km (57 miles) east of Halifax, the town maintains its original rectangular grid pattern and the wonderful variety of brightly painted wood-framed buildings—in Classical, Second Empire, Cape Cod style—that the early settlers constructed here.

ON THE WATERFRONT

The attractive waterfront remains active with the fishing and shipbuilding activities that have been the backbone of the town's prosperity for 250 years. Here, the Fisheries Museum of the Atlantic (*daily, May–Oct, Mon–Fri, rest of year*), in a group of red-painted buildings, includes floating vessels at the wharfside, and you can board the banks schooner *Theresa E. Connor*, or the *Cape Sable*, an early steel-hulled side trawler.

The museum also has an exhibit dedicated to the famous *Bluenose*, which was built in Lunenburg. She was the undefeated champion of the North Atlantic fishing fleet from 1921 to 1942, and graces the back of the Canadian dime. In 1963, an exact replica 43.6m (143ft) long, was constructed, and in the summer months the *Bluenose II* travels up and down the coast between Halifax and Lunenburg offering tours and cruises. You can't miss her if she's in port, and a schedule of her visits is available from the tourist information center.

Don't miss Stop by the antiques and craft shops along Lincoln and Pelham streets, and be sure to take a cruise on the *Bluenose II*.

MARITIME HERITAGE

Established in 1753, Lunenburg was the next British colonial settlement in Nova Scotia after Halifax and soon became the focus of a bustling economy based on fishing, shipbuilding and maritime commerce. By the 19th century, the town was a hive of activity, its harbor filled with masts and sails, and today it's also home to one of the largest fish and seafood processing plants in the world. Where once the cod ruled, now the scallop is king, the most important catch of Lunenburg-based vessels.

The Fisheries Museum of the Atlantic includes floating exhibits

RATINGS	
Historic interest	● ● ● ● ●
Photo stops	● ● ● ●
Specialist shopping	● ● ● ●

BASICS

✠ 367 X16

🛈 Tourist information center, Blockhouse Road, Lunenburg, Nova Scotia, tel 902/634-8100; Seasonal opening times

www.explorelunenburg.ca • Classy website that's easy to use, with solid information and some good photographs

MAKE A DAY OF IT

Halifax (see pages 64–65)

Many of the historic buildings are now put to other uses

Prince Edward Island

Home of the much-loved fiction character, Anne of Green Gables. A tranquil island with fine beaches and a gracious capital.

Green Gables House recalls the story of Anne, set on PEI (above). Cycling is a great way to soak up the charm of PEI (above right)

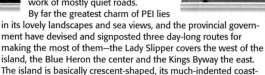

RATINGS	
Good for kids	●●●●
Historic interest	●●●
Photo stops	●●●●
Specialist shopping	●●●

IF YOU'VE TIME

GREEN PARK PROVINCIAL PARK
✚ 367 W15 • Port Hill, near Tyne Valley, Prince Edward Island ☎ 902/831-7947 ◉ Daily, mid-May to mid-Oct 🎫 $4 ⊞ ⛊
In the west of the island at Port Hill is the former home of James Yeo, the richest and most influential man in the colony during the 19th century. His wealth came from the shipyard on PEI, and a museum here documents the island's shipbuilding industry.

ORWELL CORNER HISTORIC VILLAGE
✚ 367 X15 • Orwell Corner, Prince Edward Island ☎ 902/651-8510 ◉ Daily, mid-May to mid-Oct 🎫 $4
About 28km (17 miles) east of Charlottetown, is this re-creation of the life of a rural crossroads community in the 1890s. It really gives a taste of the times, with a farm, animal barns, forge, general store, and school.

SEEING PRINCE EDWARD ISLAND
Getting to the island has been easy since the Confederation Bridge—at 13km (8 miles) the longest bridge in the world over ice-covered waters—opened in 1997. You cross for free, but pay a toll ($38.50 for cars) on the way back. The island is also connected by ferry to Pictou, Nova Scotia. There's a good network of mostly quiet roads.

By far the greatest charm of PEI lies in its lovely landscapes and sea views, and the provincial government have devised and signposted three day-long routes for making the most of them—the Lady Slipper covers the west of the island, the Blue Heron the center and the Kings Byway the east. The island is basically crescent-shaped, its much-indented coastline dotted with distinctive lighthouses, and there is no shortage of superb sandy beaches (some are tinged red by the same oxide that colors the soil). Inland—which is never farther than 16km (10 miles) from the coast—the altitude rarely exceeds 90m (300ft).

HIGHLIGHTS

CHARLOTTETOWN
✚ 367 X15 ℹ Box 940, Charlottetown, Prince Edward Island, C1A 7M5, tel 902/368-7795
Charlottetown, the provincial capital, has a great deal of charm, with a laid-back atmosphere in the commercial areas, leafy residential streets and some fine buildings. The latter include Province House, where, in September 1864, the Fathers of Confederation met for the first time, giving rise to the nation and to Charlottetown's claim to be the birthplace of Canada. Founders Hall *(daily, mid-may to mid-Oct)* includes a "Time Travel Tunnel," which explores the pageant of Canadian history. The city has a pleasant waterfront area.

PRINCE EDWARD ISLAND NATIONAL PARK
✚ 367 W15 • 2 Palmers Lane, Charlottetown, Prince Edward Island, C1A 5V6 ☎ 902/672-6350 ◉ Daily (animation Jun 1–Sep 15) 🎫 Adult $4, children (6–16) $2; free mid-Sep–May ⊞ ⛊ ▢
The national park stretches for 40km (25 miles) along the shores of the Gulf of St. Lawrence from Cavendish (see below) to Dalvay, and encompasses some large and highly mobile sand dunes that are a rare phenomenon in North America. Walking trails thread through a varied landscape of dunes, red sandstone cliffs and some of the finest saltwater beaches in Canada, and the Interpretation Centre at Greenwich has displays on the ecology of the area, plus a 3-D model of the entire Greenwich Peninsula.

CAVENDISH
✚ 367 W15
Up on the north coast, Cavendish has become a major tourist center for one reason only—it was the home of author Lucy Maud

Green Gables House, in the PEI National Park near Cavendish

Founders Hall, Charlottetown, where Canada was born

Montgomery, who has made PEI famous worldwide. She wrote a total of 20 novels, 19 of them set on the island, as well as short stories and poems, and they have been translated into many languages. Montgomery's vivid descriptions of the island have drawn thousands of visitors from as far away as Japan to see the locations firsthand, but the book she is most remembered for is her children's classic, *Anne of Green Gables,* which Mark Twain described as being "the sweetest creation of child life ever written". Green Gables House *(daily)*, a small green and white house organized to reflect the story of *Anne of Green Gables,* is one of the most visited homes in Canada. *Anne of Green Gables, The Musical* is a popular feature of the Charlottetown Festival each summer. There's every chance that you will have had your fill of Anne before you leave the island—there are at least eight houses claiming some relationship, and her name is bandied about wherever a dollar or two can be made out of it.

BASIN HEAD FISHERIES MUSEUM

✚ 367 X15• Basin Head, near Souris, Prince Edward Island ☎ 902/357-7233
◐ Daily, mid-May to mid-Oct 🖫 Adult $4 🎫 🚻 ▣
PEI maintains a strong fishing heritage ($65-million-worth of lobsters were landed in 1995), and over in the east off Route 16 near the little town of Souris (French for mouse; the town was named after a one-time infestation), this museum gives a feel for the life of the inshore fishermen. Displays include fishing shacks and a cannery to visit.

BACKGROUND

Canada's smallest province, 230km (140 miles) from tip to tip, is affectionately known as "Spud Island" for the principal crop that comes out of its bright red soil (look for the brick-red souvenir "PEI Dirt Shirt," dyed with earth!).The island is an extremely popular holiday destination for residents of the other Atlantic provinces, and is fast gaining ground with vacationers from farther afield, who enjoy its peaceful, gently rolling countryside, its fine beaches and its unhurried pace of life. There's a tradition of fiddle music here to rival that of Cape Breton, plus an island-wide culinary love affair with seafood—in addition to the excellent restaurants, you'll see signs inviting you to "Lobster Suppers" in the most unlikely places.

✚ 367 X15
🛈 Tourist information center, Box 940, Charlottetown, Prince Edward Island, C1A 7M5, tel 902/ 368-7795
www.peiplay.com • Masses of island information updated daily

● Before crossing to PEI, stop at the visitor center on the New Brunswick side for splendid views of the bridge.
● Don't leave without sampling the delicious local Cow's Ice Cream.

Lighthouses such as this dot the coastline around PEI

PRINCE EDWARD ISLAND 69

Newfoundland's lively capital retains a strong seafaring heritage around its beautiful harbor

St. John's

A city of enormous character, its steep streets lined with brightly painted clapboard houses.

BASICS

➕ 367 Z13

ℹ Tourist information center, City Hall 2nd Floor Annex, 35 New Gower Street, St. John's, Newfoundland and Labrador, A1C 5M2, tel 709/576-8106
www.stjohns.nf.ca

SEEING ST JOHN'S

The capital of Newfoundland faces the Atlantic Ocean on the Avalon Peninsula, and its location is nothing short of spectacular, on hills that rise behind a superb natural harbor whose narrow entrance is appropriately called The Narrows. The city's major attractions are clustered on, and below, the great rock of Signal Hill. Before you drive up here, be warned that the hill is prone to strong winds, with considerably greater velocity than down in the town—which is why there are no trees. There are some wonderful trails starting up here from Cabot Tower: to the Queen's Battery, with its views of the city, and the Ladies Lookout, the highest point on Signal Hill at 160m (525ft); you can even descend the North Head to The Narrows by a really steep path on the ocean side (not advisable if it is very windy!). Other trails lead to Gibbet Hill, the fishing village of Quidi Vidi and Cuckolds Cove.

HIGHLIGHTS

SIGNAL HILL NATIONAL HISTORIC PARK

✉ Signal Hill Road, St. John's, Newfoundland and Labrador, A1C 5M9 ☎ 709/772-5367 🕐 Daily. Visitor center: daily, summer; occasionally, winter 🎫 Adult $3, child (6–16) $2 🏛 🚹

St. John's was captured by the French three times in the 18th century, which led the British to fortify Signal Hill in order to guard the harbor entrance. Today, it would be unthinkable to visit St. John's without driving up here for the panoramic view across the city, harbor and coastline—Cape Spear, North America's most easterly point, is visible to the southeast. The hill, now a national historic park, is topped by the squat stone Cabot Tower, the city's best-known landmark, built in 1897 to commemorate the 400th anniversary of John Cabot's arrival. Today, it houses displays on communications to commemorate a

A simple monument on Signal Hill commemorates Marconi's historic achievement

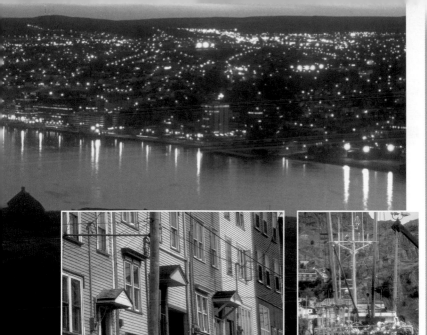

particular function of the hill. As early as 1704, signal flags were flown from the summit to inform merchants of the arrival of their vessels, but in 1901 communications history was made here when Guglielmo Marconi received the first transatlantic wireless signal—the letter "s"' in Morse code, beamed from Poldhu in Cornwall, England, more than 2,700km (1,700 miles) away.

In July and August, a military tattoo takes place on Signal Hill, performed by students in the uniform of the Royal Newfoundland Companies that were stationed in St. John's in the 19th century.

JOHNSON GEO CENTRE

✉ 175 Signal Hill Road, St John's, Newfoundland and Labrador, A1A 1B2
☎ 709/737-7880 🕓 Daily, summer; Tue–Sun, winter 💷 Adult $5 🏛 👫
This is a sensational showcase explaining why the province of Newfoundland and Labrador is so spectacular in geological terms. In Labrador, rocks date back almost to the birth of our planet 4.5 billion years ago, and on the island of Newfoundland, younger rocks provide evidence of plate tectonics, attracting scientists from all over the world. Don't be misled into thinking this is all very dull—you start with a thrilling introductory audiovisual presentation in which you experience earthquakes and volcanoes, and by the time you leave, geology will be so fascinating you'll be analyzing every rock you see.

BACKGROUND

St. John's looks out across the waters that brought the earliest explorers to the North American continent. Some sceptics dispute a number of St. John's two major claims to fame: that John Cabot entered the harbor in 1497 to "discover" the New World; and that on August 5, 1583, Sir Humphrey Gilbert chose this spot to proclaim Queen Elizabeth I's sovereignty over Newfoundland, the first act in the creation of the vast British Empire. But it doesn't really matter. There is no doubt in anyone's mind that this is a city with a very long history. A community first sprang up here because of the rich fishery, the city grew commercially in the 19th century, and the harbor was an important gathering place for convoys during World War II. In recent years, the fishery has declined, but prosperity has come from the exploitation of offshore oil reserves. St. John's has a character all of its own, and its citizens, mainly of Irish descent, have a distinctive accent and a wry wit—and they adore their rocky, treeless, wind-blown city.

Fishermen still land sizable catches (inset, opposite).
Fine old townhouses line Gower Street (inset, above left).
Fishing remains an important industry in Newfoundland (inset, above right).

MAKE A DAY OF IT

Bonavista Peninsula (see page 60)
Terra Nova National Park (see page 72)

TIPS

● Take a boat tour from St. John's to view whales among 10,000 year-old icebergs.
● When the sun goes down and the attractions close, seek out a pub with live traditional Newfoundland music.

The Blockhouse at St. Andrews, recalls more troubled times

One of the spectacles of the Terra Nova National Park is the icebergs that float by; some of them are 10,000 years old

THE SIGHTS

ST-ANDREWS-BY-THE-SEA

➕ 367 W16 ℹ️ St. Andrews Chamber of Commerce, 46 Reed Avenue, St. Andrews, New Brunswick, E5B 1A1, tel 506/529-3555
www.standrewsnb.ca

St. Andrews sits at the end of a peninsula jutting into Passamaquoddy Bay, part of the Bay of Fundy, and is a captivating, neat and orderly community, with elegant houses along wide, tree-lined streets. Kept free of fast-food outlets and chain stores, the main street is an attractive mix of restaurants and small stores selling crafts, antiques and general supplies. There's also a harbor, from where you can go on whale-watching trips.

The first people to settle St. Andrews were Loyalists from the United States. They had moved to Castine (now in Maine) after the American Revolution, only to discover, when the border was surveyed, that they were on the "wrong" side of it. In 1783 they moved, lock, stock and barrel, across the St. Croix River into Canada to create the orderly and disciplined community we see today. Some houses are open to the public, as is the lovely 11ha (27-acre) Kingsbrae Garden *(daily, mid-May to mid-Oct)*.
Don't miss Browse the spruce little shops on Water Street.

Standing guard over the harbor, a cannon at the restored blockhouse at St. Andrews

SAINT JOHN

➕ 367 W16 ℹ️ Market Square, Saint John, New Brunswick, tel 506/658-6000

Saint John—spelt out in full with no apostrophe "s" (St. John's is in Newfoundland)—is the largest city in New Brunswick and is commonly called "Fog City" because of the dense mists that roll in off the Bay of Fundy. Home to the wealthy and powerful Irving family, Saint John is also an important port, with the biggest oil refinery in Canada and a mighty pulp mill.

A trip to see Reversing Falls Rapids is almost obligatory. At low tide, the Saint John River empties into the Bay of Fundy through a narrow rocky gorge where there is a series of rapids and whirlpools. At high tide, the force of the Fundy tides (see pages 62–63) carries water upstream, rising as much as 4.4m (14.5ft) in the gorge. This reversal of the water flow and rising of the level means that, for a very short time, boats can actually navigate over the rapids. To view the phenomenon, go to Fallsview Park (west side of Route 100 as it crosses the Saint John River). The Falls Restaurant in the park offers a film presentation of the phenomenon in the rooftop theater *(small charge)*. You really need to visit the spot twice—near low tide and near high tide—but be warned, the smell of the pulp mill upstream can be rather strong!

Apart from the falls, don't miss the old City Market, downtown on Charlotte Street *(Mon–Sat, year-round)*, which sells lobsters, cheese, the edible seaweed dulse, and other fresh produce.
Don't miss The Reversing Falls are a remarkable natural display.

ST. JOHN'S (NEWFOUNDLAND)
See pages 70–71.

TERRA NOVA NATIONAL PARK

➕ 367 Y13 ☎ 709/533-2801 ◎ Daily 🏃 Mid-May to mid-Oct: Adult $4, child (6–16) $2, family $8; Rest of year, free www.parkscanada.gc.ca/terranova

On Newfoundland's east coast, along the shores of Bonavista Bay, the Terra Nova National Park protects 400sq km (154sq miles) of boreal forest and coastline. It's easy to get here, since the Trans-Canada Highway between St. John's (240km/150 miles) and Gander (80km/50 miles) bisects the park.

Most of the facilities are on Newman Sound, including the Marine Interpretation Centre *(daily, Jun–Oct)* at Saltons. From here, you can take interpretive boat tours *(mid-May–Oct)* to view bald eagles, whales and other aspects of life in the sound.

VILLAGE HISTORIQUE ACADIEN

➕ 367 W15 • P.O. Box 5626, Caraquet, New Brunswick, E1W 1B7 ☎ 506/726-2600, 877/721-2200 ◎ Daily, Jun–early Sep; limited opening, early Sep–mid-Oct 🏃 Adult $12, child (6–16) $7, family $30 🍴 🚻 www.villagehistoriqueacadien.com

In northern New Brunswick, on what is known as the Acadian Peninsula, this attraction provides a remarkably authentic representation of the life of the Acadians—settlers of French descent—between about 1770 and 1939. Acadian pride in their heritage shines through at the village, 50km (30 miles) east of Bathurst. More than 40 buildings are staffed by interpreters in period costume, and visitors who really wish to be immersed in the atmosphere can stay overnight within the village at the Château Albert.
Don't miss Sample Acadian cuisine at La Table des Ancêtres.

QUÉBEC

The heart of French Canada and resolutely distinct in its culture and lifestyle, the province of Québec is a land of contrasts, including the cosmopolitan, sophisticated atmosphere of Montréal, the spectacular scenery of the Gaspé Peninsula and the Saguenay Fjord, and the old-world charm of Québec City.

THE SIGHTS

MAJOR SIGHTS

Montréal's Biodôme is an inspired re-creation of four separate ecosystems, supporting examples of relevant flora and fauna

The Biosphère was constructed for the World's Fair of 1967

MONTRÉAL

Montréal sits majestically on an island in the St. Lawrence River. It is the heartbeat of Québécois culture, and the second-largest French-speaking city in the world, yet a third of its residents are non-French and it is increasingly cosmopolitan. This city of great cultural vitality has a *joie de vivre* otherwise unknown in North America. Though it's a long way from the open ocean, the city is also a major port, lying at the head of a great inland waterway. It has a modern and vibrant business district innovatively linked by the vast and attractive underground city, yet there are such areas as Old Montréal, where the clock seems to have stood still. See plan on pages 358–359 and walk on pages 270–271.

BASILIQUE NOTRE-DAME DE MONTRÉAL
See pages 76–77

Mother and Child in Chapelle-Notre-Dame-de-Bonsecours

BIODÔME DE MONTRÉAL

✚ Off map, 358 A1 • 4777 avenue Pierre-de-Coubertin, Montréal, Québec, H1V 1B3 ☎ 514/868-3000 🕐 Daily 9–6, end Jun–early Sep; 9–4, rest of year 💷 Adult $10.50, child (5–17) $5.25 🚇 Viau 🚌 La Brise, Le Nordet Bistro 🛍 Gift store
www.ville.montreal.qu.ca/biodome

In 1992, the Olympic velodrome underwent a spectacular refit and reopened as an indoor zoological park. Under the 190m (625ft) span of its vast scalloped roof, four ecosystems representing the Americas have been re-created.

The Tropical Forest—a lush and humid South American rainforest—is home to animals such as capybaras, golden lion tamarin monkeys, anacondas, parrots, piranhas, and poison arrow frogs. Hardwoods and conifers flourish in the Laurentian Forest, where beavers, porcupines, otters, and lynx prowl around.

In the replica St. Lawrence ecosystem, cold salty waters are home to hundreds of fish, other marine life and sea birds. Polar World includes a rocky stretch of Labrador coastline populated by Atlantic puffins, common murres and black guillemots.

Don't miss The penguins in the Antarctic area are the stars of the Biodôme.

BIOSPHÈRE

✚ 359 D4 • 160 chemin Tour-de-l'Isle, Île-Ste-Hélène, Montréal, Québec, H3C 4G8 ☎ 514/283-5000 🕐 Daily 10–6, mid-Jun–Sep; Wed–Mon 12–5, Sat–Sun and holidays 10–5, rest of year 💷 Adult $8.50, child (7–17) $6.50, family $19 🚇 Jean Drapeau 🚌 167 Casino, 169 Île Ronde (in season) 🍴 Snack bar 🛍 Gift shop
www.biosphere.ec.gc.ca

The Biosphère occupies the geodesic dome created by visionary

American architect Richard Buckminster Fuller (1895–1983) as the US Pavilion for the 1967 World's Fair, which became the symbol of Expo 67. This is the largest building of its kind in the world, and important in the history of contemporary architecture.

Principally dedicated to the St. Lawrence River and the Great Lakes, the Biosphère is North America's only museum devoted to water, and each of its four exhibition halls showcases a specific aspect, with interactive displays and multimedia presentations. The Biosphère is Canada's first Ecowatch Centre.
Don't miss There's a magnificent view from the open terrace on the fourth floor.

CARRÉ DORCHESTER (DORCHESTER SQUARE)

✚ 358 A4 🛈 Centre Infotouriste, Ground Floor, 1001 Carré Dorchester, Montréal, Québec (postal address: Tourisme Québec, C.P. 979, Montréal, Québec, H3C 2W3), tel 514/873-2015, 877/266-5687; daily 🚇 Peel
www.tourism-montreal.org

Dorchester Square and its southern continuation, place du Canada, is an area of interesting buildings centered on a pleasant green space. It was the city burial ground, but when the cemetery was moved to Mont-Royal in 1855, Bishop Ignace Bourget decided to build his cathedral here. Originally called Dominion Square, it was renamed in 1988 to honor Lord Dorchester, governor of British North America in 1768–78 and 1786–95.

The Centre Infotouriste is in the Dominion Square Building, an attractive 1927 Florentine stone structure. Counterclockwise is Le Windsor, a former hotel and slim 45-story tower housing the Canadian Imperial Bank of Commerce headquarters, built in

Statues atop the Cathédrale Marie-Reine-du-Monde

The Chapelle Notre-Dame-de-Bonsecours is Montréal's loveliest little church, sumptuously decorated and with fine views from the tower

1962. The Laurentienne Building, set at an angle to the street, is clad in copper and glass, and behind it looms the 50-floor IBM Marathon Building. St. George's Anglican Church, hidden away in the corner, was built in 1870 in Gothic Revival style, and has a lovely wooden interior. The former Windsor train station, with its towers, turrets and round arches, dates mainly from 1889. Hôtel Marriott Château Champlain, with distinctive half-moon windows, is known as the "cheese-grater" by Montréalers. The tallest building in the city is 1000 de la Gauchetière, its copper rotundas reflecting the domes of Cathédrale Marie-Reine-du-Monde across the street (see right). The silver-granite Sun Life Building, 1918–31, occupies the whole east side of the square.

CATHÉDRALE ÉPISCOPALE DE CHRIST-CHURCH (CHRIST CHURCH CATHEDRAL)

🕂 358 B3 • 635 rue Ste-Catherine Ouest, Montréal, Québec, H3A 2B8 ☎ 514/843-6577 🕙 Daily (tel for info on services and noontime concerts) 💵 Free 🚇 McGill www.montreal.anglican.org/cathedral

The Anglican cathedral, on busy rue Ste-Catherine, is a fine example of neo-Gothic architecture, with its flamboyant triple portico. Built in 1856–59 by Frank Wills and Thomas Scott, Christ Church had problems with its foundations from the start, and by 1927 the stone spire was leaning precariously and had to be removed; the aluminum substitute was added in 1940. In the 1980s, developers built the huge postmodern tower behind the church and the shopping mall below it, and finally the cathedral stood on firm foundations—financially and architecturally.

The nave, with its Gothic arches, leads to the chancel, with a carved stone reredos and a copy by Poade Drake of Leonardo da Vinci's *Last Supper*. The stained glass is from the studio of William Morris, and the organ was built by Karl Wilhelm of Mont-St-Hilaire in 1980. The cross above the pulpit is made of nails collected from the ruins of England's Coventry Cathedral after it was bombed in 1940. **Don't miss** The icon of the Holy Trinity, by Montréal artist Viorel Badoiu, in the Lady Chapel is a superb work of art.

CATHÉDRALE MARIE-REINE-DU-MONDE (MARY, QUEEN OF THE WORLD CATHEDRAL)

🕂 358 B4 • 1085 rue de la Cathédrale, Montréal, Québec, H2B 2V3 (main entrance at boulevard René Lévesque and rue Mansfield) ☎ 514/866-1661 🕙 Daily; guided tours in summer (tel for info, and for times of Masses) 💵 Free 🚇 Bonaventure www.cathedralecatholiquedemontreal. org

A reproduction on a smaller scale of St. Peter's in Rome, Montréal's Catholic cathedral was built 1870–1994 in the heart of what was then the city's Anglo-Protestant business sector, a strong statement of Montréal's Catholic heritage and position as the "Rome of the North American continent." The plans for the cathedral were drawn up by architect Victor Bourgeau, and its fine-cut stone façade is topped by the patron saints of Montréal's parishes of 1890.
Inside, the nave is dominated by a fine replica of Gian Lorenzo Bernini's baroque baldachin, the canopy over the altar. It was handmade, in red copper decorated with gold leaf, in Rome in 1900 by Victor Vincent. Large

dramatic paintings by Georges Delfosse represent episodes in the history of the Canadian Church. Look for the portrayal of the martyrdom of Jesuit priests Jean de Brébeuf and Gabriel Lalement, and also the one showing the drowning in the rapids near Montréal of Nicolas Viel, the first Canadian martyr, and his companion Ahuntsic.

CHAPELLE NOTRE-DAME-DE-BONSECOURS AND MUSÉE MARGUERITE-BOURGEOYS

🕂 359 F1 • 400 rue St-Paul Est, Montréal, Québec, H2Y 1H4 ☎ 514/282-8670 🕙 Daily 10–5, May–Oct; 11–3.30, Nov–mid-Jan and Mar–Apr (tel for hours of summer presentations about Marguerite Bourgeoys, and for Masses) 💷 Museum: adult $6, child (6–12) $3, family $12 🚇 Champ de Mars www.marguerite-bourgeoys.com

With its copper steeple and large statue of the Virgin with arms outstretched toward the river, this little chapel has long been a city landmark. Before the expansion of the port, the statue was visible from way downstream and sailors would come to give thanks for their safe arrival.
Marguerite Bourgeoys arrived in Montréal in 1653, founded the city's first school and an order of teaching nuns, looked after girls sent from France to marry settlers, and built the original chapel on this site in 1678. Destroyed by fire in 1754, it was rebuilt in 1771–73. It is decorated with frescoes (1886) of scenes in the life of the Virgin by François-Édouard Meloche. The chapel left of the altar is devoted to Marguerite Bourgeoys, who was canonized in 1982. The adjoining museum displays objects and art related to the chapel and its foundress.

Basilique Notre-Dame de Montréal (Notre Dame Basilica)

Montréal's most famous church, with a stunning, unforgettable interior. Far and away the city's most visited tourist attraction.

RATINGS	
Historic interest	● ● ● ●
Specialist shopping	● ●
Value for money	● ● ● ●

TIPS

● Try to visit the basilica at lunchtime, when there are fewer tour groups.

● Alternatively, attend Mass, which is the only time you can see the interior with all the lights on.

● You are not allowed to walk around the basilica during Mass.

SEEING THE BASILIQUE NOTRE DAME DE MONTRÉAL

Luciano Pavarotti sang here, Céline Dion was married here and absolutely everyone who visits Montréal comes here—tour buses line up around the block. The twin towers of Montréal's most famous church rise over 69m (226ft) on the south side of place d'Armes in the heart of Old Montréal. Once they dominated the whole city, but now they are dwarfed by high-rise office blocks.

HIGHLIGHTS

THE INTERIOR

The magnificent interior of the basilica never ceases to amaze, with its handcarved wood—mainly red pine—painted and decorated with 22-carat gold. It's an experience just to walk down the nave—68m (223ft) long, 21m (69ft) wide and 25m (82ft) high—toward the altar and be bathed in the light of the three rose windows Check out the stained-glass windows, depicting scenes from Montréal's history—they were designed by J.-B. Lagacé and produced in Limoges in 1930–31.

The altar and impressive reredos were designed by Victor Bourgeau and carved by Henri Bouriché, with central statues of white pine representing scenes of sacrifice from the Bible. To the left is the huge pulpit, also designed by Bourgeau and carved by Louis-Philippe Hébert; note the statues of Ezekiel and Jeremiah at its base.

The magnificent interior is a stunning sight

A distinctive Montréal landmark

Notre Dame's massive organ, one of the biggest in the world, was made by Casavant and has nearly 7,000 pipes, 84 stops, four manual keyboards, and a pedal-board. Because of its excellent acoustics, the basilica is frequently used for concerts. There is also a sound and light show, celebrating the founding of the city and the basilica.

CHAPELLE DU SACRE COEUR

The original Sacred Heart Chapel was added to the church in 1888–91 for intimate services, principally weddings. In 1978, it was completely destroyed in an arson attack but, rebuilt and reconsecrated in 1982, it is now a masterpiece in its own right, combining the architecture of the former chapel with contemporary elements. The galleries and side altars were reconstructed as before; the vault, however, is of steel covered with linden wood, with big skylights bringing in daylight.

Dominating the chapel is an impressive bronze reredos, the work of Charles Daudelin. Cast in 32 panels by the Morris Singer Foundry in Basingstoke, England, it is 17m (56ft) high and represents humanity making its way along the difficult paths of life toward heaven. On sunny afternoons, the head of Christ at the top is bathed in sunlight entering through the skylights, a spectacular and inspiring effect.

BACKGROUND

The church, built on classical principles but with striking neo-Gothic ornamentation, was designed by James O'Donnell, an Irish architect living in New York, who supervised its construction from 1824 to his death in 1829. John Ostell completed the towers according to the original design in 1843, and Victor Bourgeau was responsible for the interior, finished about 1880. On the façade, note the statues of the Virgin Mary (Notre Dame), St. Joseph and John the Baptist. The east tower contains a 10-bell carillon, including the 12-tonne "Gros Bourdon" which is rung only on special occasions. When consecrated in 1829, Notre Dame was the biggest church in North America.

BASICS

✚ 359 E3 • 110 rue Notre-Dame Ouest, Montréal, Québec, H2Y 1T2

☎ 514/842-2925, 866/842-2925

🕐 Daily, except during Mass (tel for times); sound and light shows: Tue–Sun eve at varying times in year (tel for exact times)

💲 Adult $3, child $1. Sound and light shows: $10

🎧 20-minute guided tours in French and English (free with admission)

🚇 Place d'Armes

🎁 Religious gifts

www.basilicanddm.org • A fairly basic website in French and English, offering a simple history of the basilica and information on Masses, guided tours, the sound and light show, and so on

The Jardin Botanique includes this wonderful representation of a tranquil Chinese garden, complete with pagodas

One of the exhibits at the Musée McCord d'Histoire Canadienne

JARDIN BOTANIQUE DE MONTRÉAL (MONTRÉAL BOTANICAL GARDENS)

✚ Off map, 358 A1 • 4101 rue Sherbrooke Est, Montréal, Québec, H1X 2B2 ☎ 514/872-1400 ⏰ Daily (times vary through year, tel for info) 💵 May–Oct: adult $10.50, child $5.25. Rest of year: adult $7.75, child $4 (entrance includes conservatories and Insectarium) 🚇 Pie 1X or Viau 🚻 ♿ www.ville.montreal.qc.ca/jardin

These glorious gardens extend to more than 73ha (180 acres), and display more than 22,000 species of plants, including 3,000 trees and 1,500 types of orchid. Created in 1931 by Brother Marie-Victorin, the gardens have 10 exhibition greenhouses and some 30 thematic gardens.

The Japanese Garden aims to create a feeling of serenity by balancing the elements, while the tranquil Chinese Dream Lake Garden was inspired by gardens from the Ming Dynasty (1368–1644). These two gardens are beautiful in spring, summer and fall. The First Nations Garden represents the natural environment, and is at its best in midsummer, as are the Annuals and Perennials gardens—look out for Lea Vivot's controversial bronze sculpture *Lover's Bench*.

Two conservatories cover the tropical regions, while another is devoted to ferns. Flowering orchids are displayed in a conservatory resembling an ancient ruined fortress. In the Garden of Weedlessness are *penjings*—miniature trees that embody the Chinese art of living sculpture.

The Insectarium, in the shape of a giant bug, is great fun. Most of the specimens on display are dead, but there are a few live ones. The Insectarium is famous for insect tastings, including "leg of cockroach."

Don't miss The Roseraie, with more than 10,000 rose bushes— it's at its best in August.

MONT-ROYAL
See pages 80–81.

MUSÉE D'ARCHÉOLOGIE ET D'HISTOIRE DE MONTRÉAL
See page 82.

MUSÉE D'ART CONTEMPORAIN (MUSEUM OF CONTEMPORARY ART)

✚ 358 B2 • 185 rue Ste-Catherine Ouest, Montréal, Québec, H2X 3X5 ☎ 514/847-6226 ⏰ Tue–Sun 11–6 (also Wed 6–9pm) 💵 Adult $6, child (over 12, with I.D.) $3, family $12 🚇 Place des Arts 🍴 La Rotonde 🏛 Olivieri art bookstore, The Boutique gift store www.macm.org

The contemporary art museum, with its copper roofs, is part of Montréal's great cultural complex, place des Arts. It moved to this spot in 1992 after years of being "exiled" in an out-of-the-way place on Cité du Havre. Now in the heart of the city, this innovative museum is the only one in Canada devoted solely to contemporary art.

The permanent collection comprises some 6,000 works, produced by 1,500 artists, of whom 1,200 (80 percent) are living. It includes the largest collection of art by Paul-Émile Borduas in existence. The works are shown in ever-changing thematic exhibitions, and the museum is constantly making acquisitions that it considers significant of the latest trends, in traditional media as well as the most innovative means of expression.

Place des Arts is Canada's only cultural complex devoted to both the performing and the visual arts. The Musée d'Art

Contemporain presents educational activities that aim to familiarize the general public with contemporary art. It also stages multimedia events, including performances, new dance, experimental theater, contemporary music, video and film.
Don't miss Geneviève Cadieux's giant lips, called *La Voie Lactée*, crown the building.

MUSÉE DES BEAUX-ARTS DE MONTRÉAL (MONTRÉAL MUSEUM OF FINE ARTS)

✚ Off map, 358 A3 • 1379–1380 rue Sherbrooke Ouest, Montréal, Québec, H3G 1J5 ☎ 514/285-1600, 800/899-6873 ⏰ Tue–Sun and holiday Mons 11–5 💵 Free for permanent collection, but donation appreciated; fees for temporary exhibitions 🚇 Guy-Concordia 🍴 Le Café des Beaux-Arts 🍽 Cafétéria 🏛 Museum boutique and bookstore www.mmfa.qc.ca

The venerable Museum of Fine Arts, founded in 1860, is one of Canada's oldest museums. It is located in buildings on both sides of Sherbrooke Street, with underground links for ease of access. The permanent collection represents all types of art dating from antiquity to contemporary times, and the museum is also well known for its blockbuster temporary exhibitions.

On the north side of Sherbrooke Street is Edward and William Maxwell's imposing 1912 neoclassical building. It houses the Canadian Collection and the Decorative Arts Galleries. On the south side, the main building, designed by Moshe Safdie and opened in 1991, houses the galleries of European and Contemporary Arts. The beautifully decorated European Masters Galleries contain an impressive array of works by Memling, Mantegna, Poussin,

The Musée d'Art Contemporain provides a fabulous showcase for modern works of art, and is the only one of its kind in Canada

Painting of Mah-Min, Assiniboine chief, Musée des Beaux-Arts

Rembrandt, Largillière, Renoir, Gainsborough, Canaletto, Tiepolo, Tissot, Pissarro, Picasso, Matisse, Dalí and Otto Dix.

Under Sherbrooke Street, large vault-like galleries display African, Oceanic, Oriental, Middle Eastern, pre-Columbian, Roman, Greek, and Egyptian art. On the north side, the former Erskine and American United Church is to be incorporated into the museum to display religious art. **Don't miss** The Inuit Galleries display sculpture portraying the traditional lifestyles and legends of the people of the Far North. Tapestries, furniture, porcelain and silver are a highlight of the Decorative Arts Galleries.

MUSÉE MCCORD D'HIS-TOIRE CANADIENNE (MCCORD MUSEUM OF CANADIAN HISTORY)

✚ 358 A3 • 690 rue Sherbrooke Ouest, Montréal, Québec, H3A 1E9 ☎ 514/398-7100 🕐 Tue–Fri 10–6, Sat–Sun 10–5; open Mon holiday weekends and in summer 10–5 💺 Adult $9.50, child (7–12) $3 or (over 12) $5, family $19 🚇 McGill 🛍 The McCord Café 🏛 The Boutique www.mccord-museum.qc.ca

In 1965, the McGill Union Building was converted into a museum to house the vast collections of David Ross McCord (1844–1930), whose abiding ambition was to shed light on the history and cultures of Canada. This has been admirably achieved, and today, the museum is considered one of North America's most significant historical institutions.

The collection numbers over a million objects, including beaded Indian headdresses, hand-forged tools, fine porcelain, glass negatives, and historical letters and documents. The renowned costume and textile collection has a

plethora of women's dresses, and accessories such as parasols, hats, fans and footwear, all made and worn in Canada. An impressive collection of paintings evokes visual memories of the 18th and 19th centuries, including winter scenes, traditional Indian lifestyles and portraits.

However, the McCord is probably most famous for the Notman Archives. Montréal photographer William Notman (1826–91) recorded people, places and events in Montréal and Canada over his long career, and his work was continued by his sons, providing an unequalled archive—nearly half a million photographs—of 19th- and early 20th-century life. **Don't miss** There's a huge totem pole in the stairwell, with the stairs built around it. Simply Montréal magically conjures up both the joys and tribulations of living in a city that receives 3m (10ft) of snow every winter.

PARC DES ÎLES

✚ Off map, 359 F1 🚇 Jean-Drapeau (Île-Ste-Hélène) 🚢 From Vieux-Port in summer months

Parc des Îles, made up of two islands in the St. Lawrence River, is one of Montréal's most precious resources. Île Ste-Hélène was named in 1611 by Samuel de Champlain after his wife, Hélène Boulé. In 1760, the Chevalier de Lévis burnt his regimental colors here before surrendering to the British army. After the conquest, the island was fortified by the British and then

handed over to Canadian troops after confederation in 1867. It became a city park early in the 20th century. Linked to Montréal by the Jacques Cartier Bridge since 1930, it was dramatically increased in size in the 1960s to host the World's Fair, Expo 67. Today, Île Ste-Hélène is best known for its huge amusement park,

Thrilling La Ronde amusement park in the Parc des Îles

La Ronde, but is also home to the Biosphère (see page 74) and the Stewart Museum *(daily 10–6 mid-May to mid–Oct; closed Tue, rest of year))*, housed in the Old Fort and devoted to European settlement in Québec.

Île Notre Dame, a totally artificial construction, was originally created in 1959 using material that had been excavated to form the St. Lawrence Seaway. Later, it was extended with landfill excavated during the extension of the métro in preparation for Expo 67. It's home to the Montréal Casino, the Gilles Villeneuve motor racing circuit, and a lovely floral park. **Don't miss** The model of Montréal in 1760 is worth seeking out in the Stewart Museum.

Mont-Royal

**Montréal's biggest and best park; in the middle of the bustling metropolis.
Traditionally, the origin of the name "Montréal."**

BASICS
➕ Off map, 358 A1
☎ 514/872-6559
🔍 Mont-Royal, then bus 11
🅿 Extensive parking; charges apply 24 hours a day, year round

Montréalers keep fit and active in lovely Mont-Royal park

SEEING MONT-ROYAL

In Montréal, "*la Montagne*" (the Mountain) is not only at the heart of the city, but also part of its soul. The bulky lump of Mont-Royal rises 228m (748ft), graced on its main summit by a lovely park that's perennially popular with residents and is precious to them. For the visitor, it provides some spectacular views of the entire island and the St. Lawrence River. The artificially created Lac aux Castors (Beaver Lake) has year-round appeal—in the winter months, the snow is cleared from the surface and it makes a splendid skating rink; in summer, paddle boats can be rented. To climb the mountain on foot from downtown, walk to the top of rue Peel and follow the path with short staircases to a steep flight of 200 steps (allow 20 minutes).

HIGHLIGHTS

MONT-ROYAL'S VIEWPOINTS

A five-minute walk from the parking area is the Chalet Viewpoint. From the large stone "chalet," built in 1931–32, the view is spectacular: The silver ribbon of the St. Lawrence winds its way around the city, the downtown highrises are prominent, and immediately below you lies the campus of McGill University, with its distinctive gray buildings topped with copper roofs. Farther afield, several of the Monteregian Hills can be identified, notably the imposing lump of Mont St-Hilaire. At night, the view of the illuminated city is equally wonderful, and in winter, the cold gives it an additional clarity. While taking in the view, spare a moment to look for the carved squirrels on the chalet's roof.

From the Camilien Houde Viewpoint, the northern and eastern parts of the city are visible, dominated by the huge form of the Olympic Stadium. The St. Lawrence can be seen flowing toward Québec City. To the south, some of the Monteregians are visible, while to the north are the Laurentian Mountains (see page 98).

The view over Montréal from atop Mont-Royal is spectacular

L'ORATOIRE ST-JOSEPH (ST. JOSEPH'S ORATORY)

✉ 3800 chemin Queen-Mary, Montréal, Québec, H3V 1H6 ☎ 514/733-8211
🕐 Daily (tel for hours of Masses) 🚇 Côte-des-Neiges 🍴 Cafeteria 🎁 Religious gifts

Set on the north slope of Mont-Royal, this famous Roman Catholic shrine is visited by millions of pilgrims every year. Its huge dome, one of the biggest in the world, is visible from all over the northern part of the city. Founded in 1904 by Brother André, the basilica was inaugurated in 1955. The interior has an austerity that is in itself impressive.

OTHER FEATURES

Mont-Royal has three cemeteries on its northern slopes, along with the Université de Montréal, the city's largest institution of higher learning, its campus dominated by a distinctive art-deco tower. The city's most prestigious residential areas, Westmount and Outremont, are also located on its slopes. The 83m (272ft) metal cross *(La Croix)* on the summit commemorates the placing of a wooden cross on the mountain in January 1643 by the city's founder, Maisonneuve, after the new settlement was saved from a flood. A hundred lightbulbs illuminate the cross at night, so that it can be seen from all over the city. More visible by day is the enormous transmission tower.

BACKGROUND

This 200ha (494-acre) park, the jewel in the city's crown, was created in 1876 by the great landscape architect Frederick Law Olmstead, of Central Park, New York, fame. It required a great deal of foresight on the part of the municipal government of the time, since an investment of $1 million was required to expropriate the land. Mont-Royal is one of a series of eight peaks in the St. Lawrence Valley that were created during tectonic activity some 60 million years ago. Rising dramatically from the otherwise flat landscape, these are the Collines Montérégiennes (Monteregian Hills), from the Latin name for Mont-Royal—*mons regius*. According to most historians, Mont-Royal gave the city its name when, in 1535, Jacques Cartier scrambled to the top and exclaimed "It's a royal mountain!" when he saw the view. There are other versions of how Montréal was named, but this is the one that's most popularly accepted.

RATINGS	
Good for kids	●●●●●
Historic interest	●●●●
Photo stops	●●●●●
Walkability	●●●●●

TIP

● Montréalers do not appreciate remarks about the height of their mountain—if you're used to higher peaks, try to refrain from calling Mont-Royal a pimple!

There's a challenging climb up to the Oratoire St-Joseph (below). Much less taxing is a pedalo ride (inset, top) in Mont-Royal park

The Where Montréal was Born exhibit shows a time line of the city

An eye-catching modern building is home to historic collections

RATINGS

Good for kids	●●●●
Historic interest	●●●●●
Value for money	●●●●

BASICS

✠ 359 E3 • 350 Place Royale, Montréal, Québec, H2Y 3Y5
☎ 514/872-9150
🕐 Mon–Fri 10–6, Sat–Sun 11–6, late Jun–early Sep; Tue–Fri 10–5, Sat–Sun 11–5, rest of year
💰 Adult $10, child (6–12) $3.50 or (over 12) $6
🚇 Place d'Armes
🍴 L'Arrivage—fresh, creative menu, plus city's best view of Vieux-Port
🏛 Boutique
www.pacmuseum.qc.ca • Site in French and English, with information on exhibitions and activities, a virtual tour of the museum and interactive games

An informative walk through the history of Montréal

MUSÉE D'ARCHÉOLOGIE ET D'HISTOIRE DE MONTRÉAL (POINTE-À-CALLIÈRE MUSEUM OF ARCHEOLOGY AND HISTORY)

Fascinating exhibits provide an interpretation of old Montréal with the help of a few former residents.

Located on the spot where Montréal began in 1642, this fascinating and innovative museum is devoted to what is often a very dry topic—archeology. Opened in 1992, on the 350th anniversary of the foundation of Montréal, it occupies a striking modern building designed by Dan Hanganu. The structure is dominated by a tower, which is strange since most of what you see inside is underground. The "point" of Pointe-à-Callière no longer exists. Originally it lay between the St. Pierre River, which used to run along place d'Youville to join the St. Lawrence at this point, but the St. Pierre was covered over in the 19th century. The name Callière refers to the second governor of Montréal, Hector de Callière, who built his house near here.

INSIDE THE OLD CITY

It's a good idea to start your visit with the multimedia presentation, which lasts about 15 minutes. This is a very high-tech but clear introduction to the city. Afterward, you can descend into the basement to see the remains of buildings that have stood on this spot since the 17th century. Next, walk through the huge brick conduit into which the St. Pierre River was channeled in 1832 to find yourself in a large archeological crypt, with remains of the foundations of the city walls, old streets and buildings.

You even meet a few of the former residents en route, by means of laser holograms. They answer your questions in both French and English, and really bring the place to life. From the crypt, take the elevator up into the old Customs House, built in 1836–38, where there are more displays on the history of this location.

Don't miss An elevator ride to an outdoor observatory at the top of the tower for a great view of the port, river and part of Old Montréal; more great views and good food at the museum's restaurant, L'Arrivage—in summer, doors open onto an outdoor terrace.

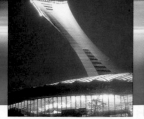
The Olympic Stadium is a first-class sports facility

Place Jacques Cartier is the vibrant hub of the old city

The Vieux-Port is the focus of many festivals and events

PARC OLYMPIQUE (OLYMPIC PARK)

✚ Off map, 358 A1 • 4141 avenue Pierre-de-Coubertin, Montréal, Québec, H1V 3N7 ☎ 514/252-8687 Ⓓ Unless attending an event, accessible only by 30-min guided tour, available all year (tel for hours and cost). Ascent of tower: daily Ⓖ Ascent of tower: adult $10, child (5–17) $5 Ⓠ Pie IX or Viau www.rio.gouv.qc.ca

In 1976, the XXI Olympiad was celebrated in Montréal, leaving the city a legacy of debt (which is still not paid off) and a very fine collection of sports facilities, mainly within the 204ha (504-acre) area still known as the Olympic Park. Resembling a giant mollusk because of its elliptical shape, the Olympic Stadium is dominated by its tower, which rises 175m (574ft) at a 45-degree angle, and by its strange roof, which looks like a plate of meringues. Originally the brain-child of French architect Roger Taillebert, the stadium was completed with the expertise of local engineers. Constructed of concrete with 30 massive can-tilevered ribs, the "Big O," as it is called by Montréalers, has no interior columns to block the view. Controversial, hugely expensive and for many years incomplete, the stadium is nevertheless an amazing architectural achievement.

The spine of the tower can be mounted by a funicular elevator, which climbs at a 27- to 57-degree angle. Three huge sky-light windows give spectacular views, and on a clear day you can see for 80km (50 miles). In the tripod base of the tower, several of the Olympic swimming pools are open to the public. The former velodrome has been transformed into the Biodôme, an indoor zoological park (see page 74).

VIEUX MONTRÉAL (OLD MONTRÉAL)

✚ 359 E3 ⓘ 174 rue Notre-Dame Est, on corner of place Jacques Cartier, Montréal, Québec, tel 514/873-2015 Ⓠ Champ-de-Mars, place d'Armes, or Square Victoria

Old Montréal comprises the narrow streets, old houses, and cobblestones of the original French city. The little mission, founded in 1642, was encircled with great stone walls as defense against First Nation and English attack. The walls have long gone, but today the area they once enclosed is attractive and vibrant, popular with residents and visitors alike.

The impressive former market building, Marché Bonsecours *(350 rue St-Paul Est, tel 514/872-7730)*, has been converted into a showcase for local designers and craftspeople. Place Jacques Cartier has outdoor cafés, street performers, musicians, and flower vendors, and is lively all summer. At one end stands City Hall, close to a 15m (48ft) column topped by a statue of Admiral Lord Horatio Nelson. Nearby, tiny rue St-Amable is lined with artists who sell their wares.

On rue Notre-Dame Est, Château Ramezay, built in 1705 for Claude de Ramezay, Governor of Montréal, is today a museum *(daily, Jun–Sep; Tue–Sun, rest of year)* devoted to local history. The attractive Governor's Garden can be visited free of charge. Other highlights are the Basilique Notre-Dame (see pages 76–77), the Chapelle Notre-Dame-de Bon-Secours (see page 75), and the Musée d'Archéologie et d'Histoire (see opposite).
Don't miss A ride in a horse-drawn calèche, from the place d'Armes area or rue de la Commune, is a novel way to tour the old streets.

VIEUX-PORT (OLD PORT)

✚ 359 F2 ⓘ Old Port of Montréal Inc, 333 rue de la Commune Ouest, Montréal, Québec, H2Y 2E2, tel 514/496-PORT, 800/971-PORT Ⓠ Champ de Mars, place d'Armes or Square Victoria www.oldportofmontreal.com

For many years, the Old Port—the area south of rue de la Commune between rue Berri and rue McGill—was an active commercial port. By the end of the 19th century, concrete piers, steel sheds, docks, and jetties had been constructed, and in the early 20th century huge grain elevators blocked the river off from the city. By 1922, Montréal was the continent's biggest grain port, and was second only to New York in the volume of traffic.

With the opening of the St. Lawrence Seaway in 1959, and the introduction of containerization, the port changed. New container facilities were constructed farther east, and the old part of the port was unused.

This shift in commercial use was, however, turned to advantage, and today the old port forms an attractive linear waterfront park, a people place that is popular year round. Activities range from cycling and walking along the paths to boat trips, and there's a skating rink in winter. Numerous exhibitions and festivals are held here throughout the year, and the city's Science Centre *(daily, summer; Tue–Sun, rest of year)* is located here, along with an IMAX theater *(tel 514/496-4724)*.
Don't miss Mosaïcultures *(daily, late Jun–early Oct)* is a fine display of floral sculptures in Parc des Écluses. Climb up the 192 open metalwork steps of the Tour de l'Horloge (Clock Tower) on quai d'Horloge to enjoy the wonderful views.

THE SIGHTS

MONTRÉAL

Ville Souterraine (Underground City)

Beat the weather and explore Montréal via 30km (19 miles) of subterranean passageways.
Emerge to admire the city's architectural highlights.

RATINGS

Historic interest	● ● ●
Shopping	● ● ● ● ●
Specialist shopping	● ● ● ● ●
Walkability	● ● ●

BASICS

🛈 Centre Infotouriste
✉ 1001 Carré Dorchester, Montréal, Québec
☎ 514/873-2015; daily
Ⓜ Peel
www.tourism-montreal.org

The bright and lofty entrance to the Underground City

SEEING VILLE SOUTERRAINE

Temperatures in Montréal change dramatically from season to season. Nearly 3m (10ft) of snow falls every winter and temperatures can dip to -35°C (-31°F). In July, the mercury soars to a hot and sticky 35°C (95°F). Living with such a climate has many problems, some of which have been solved by the development of a weatherproof, covered-in system in the downtown business district, which gives priority to pedestrians. The connections are not always underground—there are also light, airy atriums full of stores and restaurants. The walkways connect more than 60 buildings, 7 hotels, about 1,700 stores, 200 or so restaurants and bars, 1,600 apartments, about 34 movie theaters, 2 train stations, 2 bus termini, 8 métro stations, some 10,000 indoor parking places, about 45 bank branches, 2 universities, the place des Arts cultural center, the Palais des Congrès, and nearly 2.3 million sq m (25 million sq ft) of office space. To appreciate the importance and extent of the Underground City, take a walk through some of it. The following highlights have linking instructions, as well as details of how to reach each one separately.

HIGHLIGHTS

PLACE VILLE-MARIE TO PROMENADES CATHÉDRALE
Ⓜ Bonaventure or McGill
This was where the Underground City began. A huge cruciform tower and three smaller buildings, developed in 1959–62, sit on a shopping plaza and parking garage, covering the railroad tracks as they enter Central Station. Conceived by I. M. Pei, place Ville-Marie was the largest mixed office and commercial complex in the world when it opened. The cruciform shape reflects the city's origin as a Catholic mission, and its title comes from the city's first name, Ville Marie (City of Mary). Stand in the outdoor plaza here and look north—there is a superb view up McGill College Avenue of McGill University and Mont-Royal. From place Ville-Marie, take the underground passageway to the Centre Eaton and then continue into Les Ailes de la Mode *(métro: McGill)*. When Eaton's department store closed, the massive building was redeveloped to house this fashion store, with its spectacular skylight. Attached to Les Ailes to the east is the Promenade Cathédrale. The construction of this architecturally impressive complex successfully underpinned the rapidly sinking Cathédrale Épiscopale de Christ-Church (see page 75). Walk back through Les Ailes to the Centre Eaton, then continue through Place Montréal Trust and Carrefour Industrielle Alliance to:

LES COURS MONT-ROYAL TO 1000 DE LA GAUCHETIÈRE
Ⓜ Peel or Bonaventure
This elegant complex, with its enclosed interior courtyards, originally housed the Mount Royal Hotel; it was redeveloped in 1988. Note the huge bird figures hanging from the roof. The work of Inuit sculptor David Piqtoukun, they represent Tingmiluks, shaman who are able to

transform themselves into birds. Return to place Ville-Marie, and walk in the other direction through Central Station to 1000 de la Gauchetière, at 205m (672ft) the tallest building in the city, with a huge and spectacular indoor skating rink *(tel 514/395-0555; adult $5.50, child $3.50, family $16. Skate rental: $4.50; www.le1000.com)* on the main floor. It is possible to continue via the Underground City, but construction for the Cité Internationale may complicate matters. Follow the walkway to Place Bonaventure and then follow signs to place de la Cité internationale; after that, continue toward Square Victoria métro station, turning right just before the station and following signs along a long passageway to:

The Atrium of 1000 de la Gauchetière makes a great indoor skating rink

CENTRE DE COMMERCE MONDIAL DE MONTRÉAL

Square Victoria

Quite the most spectacular part of the Underground City, the Montréal World Trade Centre comprises an entire city block enclosed as an atrium. High, light and luminous, the complex surrounds a fascinating fountain and a piece of the Berlin Wall given to Montréal on the city's 350th anniversary in 1992 as a monument to peace.

BACKGROUND

The idea of an underground city dates back to Leonardo da Vinci, but Montréal's began in the 1960s with the construction of the place Ville-Marie complex over the railroad tracks. At the same time, the métro was built, with stations connected by a network of covered passageways to many downtown facilities.

TIPS

● Signing in the Underground City is not as good as it could be. Arm yourself with a map and ask for directions from locals, but note: Montréalers seem to enjoy pretending that they find the Underground City confusing, while managing to stride effortlessly through it!
● Montréalers proudly call their métro system (see page 45) "the largest underground art gallery in the world." Each station, designed by a different architect to link into the area in which they are located, has relevant artworks.

The sumptuous interior of the Cathédrale Notre-Dame-de-Québec filters natural sunlight through delicate French stained-glass windows

Distinguished Château Frontenac is the place to stay in Montréal

QUEBÉC CITY

With its magnificent, lofty site and its sweeping views of the St. Lawrence River, Canada's oldest city has captivated visitors for centuries. A walled city with massive citadel, gates and cannon, it has narrow, cobblestoned streets, splendid mansions and venerable churches to explore. Québec City is first and foremost the birthplace of French culture on the North American continent. Its distinct European feel is enhanced by fine restaurants, lively outdoor cafés and plenty of nightlife. This combination of fortified site and French culture has given it a place on UNESCO's World Heritage List, one of only two Canadian cities to have received this accolade. See plan on page 356 and walk on pages 268–269.

CATHÉDRALE ÉPISCOPALE DE LA SAINTE-TRINITÉ (HOLY TRINITY ANGLICAN CATHEDRAL)

🖽 356 B2 • 31 rue des Jardins, Québec City, Québec, G1R 4L6 ☎ 418/692-2193 🕐 Daily 🎟 Free 🗂 Guided tours in summer
www.ogs.net/cathedral

Standing behind a screen of trees, this wood-frame church, with its 47m-high (154ft) spire, was the first Anglican cathedral to be built outside the British Isles. Consecrated in 1804, it was modeled after the famous church of St. Martin-in-the-Fields in London's Trafalgar Square.

Holy Trinity is utterly Georgian in feeling and atmosphere, hardly surprising since its construction was paid for by King George III. The interior is unexpectedly spacious. Its furnishings include the royal pew, surrounded by a brass balustrade and decorated in royal blue—reserved for British sovereigns or their representatives. This, and the bishop's chair and the box pews, were made of oak from Windsor royal forest. King George also provided a folio Bible, large prayer books, and a magnificent set of communion silverware, the most prestigious gift the colony ever received.
Don't miss The triptych window in the chancel has particularly fine stained glass.

CATHÉDRALE NOTRE-DAME-DE-QUÉBEC (NOTRE-DAME CATHEDRAL)

🖽 356 B2 • 29 rue de Buade, Québec City, Québec, G1R 4A1 (main entrance on rue Ste-Famille) ☎ 418/694-0665 🕐 Daily 7.30–4.30; 30-minute sound and light shows in French and English May–mid-Oct (call for hours) 🎟 Free. Sound and light shows: adult $7.50, child $5 🗂 Guided tours May–Oct (call for hours)
www.patrimoine-religieux.com

Québec's Roman Catholic cathedral stands in the heart of the Upper Town, facing the Hôtel de Ville. Distinguished by its neoclassical façade and two dissimilar towers, the cathedral has an opulent interior. On entering, your eyes are immediately drawn toward the sweeping wooden canopy high over the altar. Made by André Vermare and finished in gold, it glows in splendor.

During the 1759 siege, the cathedral was destroyed by British bombardments. Rebuilt soon afterward, it was destroyed again by fire in 1922, but was again rebuilt, to the original plans.

In 1993, a funeral chapel was dedicated to the first bishop of Québec, Monsignor de Laval. At its heart is a bronze statue of the bishop in a prone position, eyes toward the heavens. A map of his immense diocese is etched in the black granite floor. The crypt houses the remains of the bishops of Québec and four governors of New France.
Don't miss A good sound and light show is held in the cathedral in the summer months.

CHÂTEAU FRONTENAC

🖽 356 C2 • 1 rue de Carrières, Québec City, Québec, G1R 4P5 ☎ 418/691-2166 🕐 Tours daily in summer, weekends only in winter 🎟 $6.50
www.fairmont.com

This massive structure of green-roofed turrets and towers is Québec City's most stylish hotel (see page 315), and is inextricably linked with the city's image. Named for one of the greatest and most flamboyant French governors, Louis de Buade, Comte de Frontenac, the original hotel was built by Bruce Price in 1893 for the Canadian Pacific Railway, in the style of a Loire Valley château. The distinctive central tower was added in 1920–24.

Famous people who have stayed at the château have included King George VI and Queen Elizabeth, Princess Grace of Monaco, Chiang Kai-shek, Charles de Gaulle, Ronald Reagan, François Mitterrand, Prince Andrew, the Duchess of York, Charles Lindberg, Alfred Hitchcock and Montgomery Clift. In 1943 and 1944, the Château Frontenac hosted the Québec Conferences of World War II, when US President Franklin D. Roosevelt and British Prime Minister Winston Churchill planned the Normandy landings.

Even if you are not staying there, you can step inside to have a look. Better still, take a tour, given by guides in 19th-century costume (maid, railroad porter) to hear about various famous—and infamous—guests.

The Anglican Cathedral is a set-piece of Georgian architecture

Historic place Royale, lined by stately old buildings, is the site of the original town, which was established as a fort in 1642

CHUTE MONTMORENCY (MONTMORENCY FALLS)

✉ Parc de la Chute Montmorency, 2490 avenue Royal, Beauport, Québec, G1C 1S1 ☎ 418/663-3330 🕓 Daily; Lower Park and cable car closed off season 🚋 Cable car: adult $4.50 one way, $7.50 round trip 🅿 $7.50 Apr–Oct, otherwise free 🚌 10km (6 miles) east off Highway 440 www.chutemontmorency.qc.ca

No visit to Québec City would be complete without taking a trip to see this waterfall, higher than Niagara. Here, the Montmorency River cascades 83m (272ft) from the clifftop to a deep, bowl-shaped basin at an average rate of 35,000 liters (9,247 US gallons) per second—more during the spring melt.

CITADELLE AND FORTIFICATIONS

See pages 88–89.

MUSÉE DE LA CIVILISATION (MUSEUM OF CIVILIZATION)

➕ 356 C2 • 85 rue Dalhousie, C.P. 155, Succursale B, Québec City, Québec, G1K 7A6 ☎ 418/643-2158 🕓 Daily 10–5, late Jun–early Sep; Tue–Sun 10–5 rest of year 🚋 Adult $7, child (12–16) $2; free Tue except in summer 🍴 The Museum Café 🏛 The Museum Boutique in Maison Estèbe www.mcq.org

Located in the Lower Town close to the river, this museum occupies a modern building that is beautifully integrated into the architecture of the old city. Its copper roof is pierced by stylized dormer windows, and it has a glass campanile and monumental staircase. The Maison Estèbe, a four-story French Regime stone house of 1751, is incorporated into the museum. Excavations carried out during construction unearthed many treasures,

including the remains of a boat dating from the mid-18th century, showing that the house was once on the waterfront.

Designed by architect Moshe Safdie, the Musée de la Civilisation was opened in 1988. Exhibitions are thematic, devoted to civilization in the broadest sense. There's a wonderful collection of Québécois furniture, sculpture and crafts, as well as important Amerindian objects and permanent exhibitions. Mémoires recalls aspects of life past and present in Québec, and Nous, Les Premières Nations (We, the First Nations) displays the lifestyle of the 70,000 Amerindians who live in Québec today. Other shows reflect the whole human adventure.

MUSÉE DU QUÉBEC (QUÉBEC MUSEUM)

🔼 Off map, 356 A4 • Parc des Champs-de-Bataille, Québec City, Québec, G1R 5H3 ☎ 418/643-2150 🕓 Daily 10–6 (also Wed 6–9pm), Jun–Labor Day; Tue–Sun 10–5 (also Wed 5–9pm), rest of year 🚋 Permanent collection free. Temporary exhibits: adult $10, child (12–16) $2 🅿 Charge 🚌 11 🍴 Le Café 🏛 La Boutique du Musée www.mnba.qc.ca

Québec's art museum occupies two buildings on the Plains of Abraham. The original, constructed in 1933, was joined to a former prison in 1991 by a modern wing. The prison building, which retains the original cells, is, surprisingly, more interesting architecturally than the rest.

The permanent collection is primarily devoted to Québec art. Displayed with aplomb, the early works are dominated by religious subjects and sculptures made for churches, and reflect the importance the Roman Catholic Church held in Québec society.

Among the non-religious works, essential viewing includes the paintings by Jean-Paul Lemieux and Horatio Walker. The museum also organizes major retrospectives and hosts important visiting exhibits.
Don't miss The Wolfe monument outside the museum marks the spot where British General James Wolfe died in the famous battle of 1759.

PLACE ROYALE

➕ 356 C2 🚋 Lower Town Funicular between Terrasse Dufferin and Lower Town, $1.50 one way

Place Royale is a delightful cobblestone square in the heart of the Lower Town (but visit after 11am to avoid the delivery trucks). It is lined with tall stone houses of French Regime style, rebuilt to give the square its original appearance (before it was blasted to bits by the British). At its heart is a bust of Louis XIV, a copy of the 1686 original that gave the square its name. On the ground, an outline denotes the exact position of Champlain's original "habitation" of 1608.

The lovely little church of Notre-Dame-des-Victoires commemorates two victories over the British in the 17th and early 18th centuries. It was destroyed during the siege of 1759, rebuilt in 1763–66 and has been much restored since.

The attractive adjoining streets reward exploration. There is a huge mural on rue Notre-Dame, and on place de Paris is Dialogue avec l'Histoire, a contemporary work donated by the city of Paris. Maison Chevalier, on rue de Marché Champlain, offers a free exhibition, Ambiances d'Autrefois (Feeling of Days Gone By), featuring French and English 18th- and 19th-century interior designs.

THE SIGHTS

QUÉBEC CITY

Citadelle and Fortifications

The most important fortification built in Canada under British rule. Headquarters of the famous Royal 22nd Regiment.

THE SIGHTS

QUÉBEC CITY

Colorful military pomp is still a feature of this active garrison

RATINGS	
Historic interest	●●●●●
Photo stops	●●●●○
Walkability	●●●●○

TIPS
- Don't arrive late for the Changing of the Guard—not even a minute—they won't let you in.
- Ceremonies can be cancelled because of bad weather or operational considerations.
- Don't laugh when you see Batisse, the regimental goat.

Military hardware on display at the Citadelle

SEEING THE CITADELLE

This vast defensive earthwork, covering 15ha (37 acres) is still an active military garrison, and if you wish to see the inside you must join one of the guided tours (led by soldiers) and stay with the group—whatever you do, don't wander off on your own. Once you have penetrated the vast array of moats and bastions and joined a tour, you will be taken onto a huge parade ground surrounded by buildings bearing the names of the various campaigns of the regiment, including Vimy, the Somme, Normandy and Korea. It's well worth walking around the *enceinte* (ramparts), either completely or in part (see walking tour on pages 268–269).

HIGHLIGHTS

MUSÉE DU ROYAL 22e RÉGIMENT

This small museum, which is visited on the tour, is located in a 1750 French powder magazine and an 1842 British military prison. It preserves historical documents, a collection of guns and small arms, insignias, medals, uniforms, and other exhibits covering the history of the Royal 22nd. Don't miss the diorama illustrating the principal battles fought around Québec under the French regime.

In summer, traditional military ceremonies such as the Changing of the Guard take place *(daily 10am, Jun 24–early Sep)*, and it's something to see. Soldiers in scarlet jackets and bearskin hats are accompanied by the regimental band and by Batisse, the regimental goat.

FORTIFICATIONS AND GATES

An entire network of walls and gates, erected under both the French and English regimes, encircles the old part of the city of Québec, stretching over a total 4.6km (2.9 miles), making this the only historic district in North America to have preserved its ramparts.

Québec City was a site of great strategic and tactical importance to both the French and the British—the key to communication with the mother country, and the place where fresh supplies were stored and relief was housed. Its defense system therefore reflects the evolution of European fortification techniques from the 17th to 19th centuries, when the era of fortified cities came to an end. After the British garrison departed in 1871, there were plans to demolish what remained, but in 1874 Lord Dufferin (Governor General of Canada 1872–78) began a movement to preserve them. As a result, the Terrasse Dufferin was built over the cliffs (see page 90), and the original narrow gates were replaced to provide easier movement between the old and new parts of town. The current St. Louis and Kent gates were built between 1878 and 1881, and the St-Jean Gate between 1938 and 1939. In 1983, Parks Canada rebuilt the Prescott Gate over Côte de la Montagne in order to complete the walkway.

Near the St-Louis Gate is the Fortifications of Québec Initiation Centre and Esplanade Powder Magazine *(daily,*

Historic cannon sited atop the Citadelle give a good idea of what potential attackers would have faced

Seen from above, the might of the fortifications is apparent

May–mid-Oct), beneath the city's ramparts. Exhibitions concentrate on the history of Québec's defensive system. There's an interesting model illustrating the various fortification projects drawn up for the city. The powder magazine, built in 1815, is the only one to have been restored out of many gunpowder stores located here.

ARTILLERY PARK NATIONAL HISTORIC SITE

☎ 418/648-4205 ⏰ Artillery Grounds: all year. Arsenal Foundry, Dauphine Redoubt, Officers' Quarters: daily 10–5, mid May–Oct 💲 Artillery Grounds: free. Arsenal Foundry, Dauphine Redoubt, Officers' Quarters: adult $4, child (6–16) $2.75 or (17 and over, with I.D.) $3.50, family $10

Artillery Park, in the heart of Old Québec, has a remarkable history. First used by French soldiers, it was occupied by the British garrison in 1763–1871, and its name comes from the Royal Artillery Regiment quartered here for most of that time. It later became an industrial complex comprising a munitions factory, workshops and foundries— the Québec Arsenal, the first of its kind in Canada. When it finally closed in 1964, the site was taken over by Parks Canada.

The Arsenal Foundry now serves as an interpretation and reception center, and contains a wonderful scale model of Québec City, made in 1808 in the tradition of military engineers. The Dauphine Redoubt, a remarkable fortified building, was originally equipped with a battery of cannon. Built by the French in 1712, it served as barracks before becoming home to the Arsenal superintendents. Inside, you can visit the 19th-century kitchen, the luxurious English officers' mess and the Arsenal superintendents' lounge. The officers' quarters have been restored with period furnishings.

BACKGROUND

The Citadelle was designed according to a defense system developed by the famous French military engineer Vauban, and is a four-pointed polygon, each point forming a bastion. Started in 1820, it took 30 years to complete and encloses two buildings constructed by the French, plus later additions. It is still a military base, home of the elite Royal 22e Régiment—the "Van Doos" (from Vingt Deux)—the Canadian army's only completely French regiment. It's also the summer home of the governor general.

BASICS

➕ 356 B4 • Citadelle mailing address: C.P. 6020, Succursale Haute-Ville, Québec City, Québec, G1R 4V7, access is via Côte de la Citadelle

☎ 418/694-2815

⏰ Admission by guided tour only (lasts 1 hour), daily, Apr–Oct (tel for hours)

💲 Adult $6, child (8–17) $3, family $14 www.lacitadelle.qc.ca • Easy to use, with information on the history of the Citadelle and the museum's collection (English and French)

The Terrasse Dufferin (top) has superb views over the river

Promenade des Gouverneurs (above) encircles the old walls

RATING	
Historic interest	● ● ●
Photo stops	● ● ● ● ●

TIP

● The town of Lévis, seen across the river, is pronounced "lay-vee"—there's no more obvious way of declaring yourself a tourist than to pronounce it like the jeans.

BASICS

🟦 356 C3 • Dufferin Terrace: adjoining place d'Armes in front of the Château Frontenac hotel. Governors' Walk: access from the west end of the Dufferin Terrace or from avenue du Cap-Diamant in National Battlefields Park

🕐 Closed in snow and ice of winter, Nov–Apr

🎟 Free

PROMENADE DES GOUVERNEURS (GOVERNORS' WALK) AND TERRASSE DUFFERIN (DUFFERIN TERRACE)

Cliff-face boardwalk with magnificent views.

Built in the late 1950s, the Promenade des Gouverneurs was opened in 1960 by Canadian Prime Minister, John Diefenbaker. This spectacular boardwalk, clinging to the cliff face about 90m (300ft) above the river, goes round the outer walls of the Citadelle. It offers magnificent views of the St. Lawrence, the Lower Town, Lévis, Île d'Orléans, and as far as Mont-Ste-Anne on a clear day. It provides an excellent—if vertiginous—means of getting to the Plains of Abraham from Terrasse Dufferin, as long as you don't mind climbing the 310 steps. It's also a splendid way of arriving in Québec if you descend it from the Plains of Abraham. It takes about 20 minutes (maybe more going up).

TERRASSE DUFFERIN

Suspended high above the river, the Dufferin Terrace is one of the glories of a visit to Québec, a wide wooden boardwalk with magnificent views. A mighty 670m (2,200ft) long, it is popular day and night, year round. On fine summer evenings, lovers entwine to the sound of performing musicians; in midwinter, there is an impressive toboggan slide and tourists slither about, trying to take photographs.

The history of this terrace is almost as interesting as the view. In 1630, Samuel de Champlain (whose statue stands here) moved up from the bottom of the cliff and built the first Château St. Louis here as a defense against the Iroquois and the English. This château served as the residence of the French and British governors until it was destroyed by fire in 1834. Lord Durham, the British governor at the time, built a platform over the ruins that was accessible to the public. It became such a popular visit that it was increased in size in 1854.

In 1878–79, Governor General Lord Dufferin worked with architect Charles Baillairgé to extend the boardwalk once more as part of his vast beautification project for Québec (see page 88). It was opened on June 9, 1879, and has remained a cherished part of the city ever since. The six covered pavilions, or kiosks—named Frontenac, Princess Louise, Lord Lorne, Victoria, Dufferin, and Plessis—offer a shady place to sit and admire the view on hot summer days. The Frontenac Kiosk houses the top of the funicular, which runs down to the Lower Town (see Place Royal, page 87).

Granby Zoo (above and below right), in the Cantons-de-l'Est

Magog, in the Eastern Townships, sits at the north end of lovely Lake Memphrémagog; scenic boat tours are a popular diversion

CANADIAN MUSEUM OF CIVILIZATION
See page 92

CANTONS-DE-L'EST (EASTERN TOWNSHIPS)
✚ 366 U17 🛈 Tourisme Cantons-de-l'Est, 20 rue Don-Bosco Sud, Sherbrooke, Québec, J1L 1W4, tel 819/820-2020, 800/355-5755 www.easterntownships.cc

Land of mountains, lakes and delightful villages, the Eastern Townships are a unique mixture of Anglo-Saxon charm and Québécois joie de vivre. Despite their name, they are actually in the southwest of the province of Québec, and are only east of Montréal. After the American Revolution, the uninhabited land along the border east of that city was surveyed and granted to Loyalists, mainly from New England, who preferred to live on British soil rather than in the new United States. The towns and villages reflect this heritage. From 1850 on, however, more and more French-speaking people moved into the region, and today the population is more than 50 percent Francophone.

The mountains here are part of the Appalachian Chain, which stretches north from Alabama to Gaspésie (see pages 96–97) and Newfoundland. Nearly 1,000m (3,000ft) high, they are rolling and tree-covered, with lakes filling the valleys. Montréalers escape to the ski slopes in winter and the lakes in summer. For visitors, there is a string of delightful villages and a stunningly located abbey.

Knowlton is an attractive Victorian village with a variety of craft stores, art galleries, restaurants, and boutiques on England Hill, which descends to the mill stream. It is now part of the municipality of Lac-Brome, and the buildings are an eclectic mix of styles—including some costly homes on the shores of the lake. Ducks reared here are a delicacy in many of the local restaurants.

Magog has a wonderful site on the north end of beautiful Lake Memphrémagog. Summer boat trips (daily, mid-May–Sep) give constantly changing views of islands and the surrounding Appalachian peaks, notably Mt. Orford. A monastery, on the shores of the lake, has a fairy-tale quality, with striking white-granite and multicolored-brick buildings. The splendid modern church is open to the public. The monks are famous for Gregorian chant (Eucharist 11am, Vespers 5pm). They also raise Charolais cows and produce cheese, notably L'Ermite and St. Benoit.

The forested Mt. Orford Park covers 57sq km (22sq miles) of the Appalachians and is dominated by its namesake mountain, which rises 876m (2,873ft). It's a popular ski resort, and in summer it is sometimes possible to take the chairlift up Mt. Orford for a magnificent view of Lake Memphrémagog and the surrounding mountains.
Don't miss Granby Zoo (see page 212), with 1,000 animals, is a major attraction.

CHARLEVOIX COAST
See pages 94–95.

GASPÉSIE
See pages 96–97.

ÎLE D'ANTICOSTI
✚ 367 W14 🛈 Sépaq, Box 179, Port-Menier, Québec, G0G 2Y0, tel 418/535-0156 (800/665-6527) www.sepaq.com; 🛈 Municipalité de l'Île d'Anticosti, Box 119, Port-Menier, Québec, G0G 2Y0, tel: 418/535-0250, www.anticosti-ile.com

Nature lovers in search of tranquility will adore Anticosti. Just over 300 people live on this huge island (nearly 8,000sq km/ 3,120sq miles), which resembles a giant cork in the mouth of the St. Lawrence Estuary. It is a paradise for birdwatchers (up to 220 species, including bald eagles, have been spotted here). Impressive rock formations, —caverns and waterfalls have been carved out of its fossil-rich limestone, and about 200 shipwrecks lie off the island's rocky shores.

If you can, plan a two-day visit; the Anticosti Reserve (daily, Jun–Sep), run by Sépaq (a government agency), offers vacation packages that include rental of a four-wheel-drive vehicle, essential for getting around.

Anticosti was once part of the seigniory of Louis Jolliet, who explored the Mississippi. In 1895, it was purchased for $125,000 by wealthy French chocolate-maker Henri Menier as a private hunting and fishing reserve. Menier introduced, among other things, 220 white-tailed deer; today, the herd numbers, conservatively, 120,000, the greatest concentration of these deer in North America. Menier is commemorated in the name of the island's only community, Port-Menier.
Don't miss The spectacular 76-m (249-ft) Vauréal Falls, plunge into a steep-walled canyon, and the limestone cliffs that rise dramatically from Baie de la Tour, 24km (15 miles) east of Vauréal Falls.

History comes to life with reenactments at this vibrant museum

CANADIAN MUSEUM OF CIVILIZATION

One of Canada's top museums, in a spectacular building. Fabulous displays on traditional culture in the Grand Hall.

RATINGS	
Good for kids	● ● ● ○
Historic interest	● ● ● ●
Specialist shopping	● ● ●
Activities	● ● ●

BASICS

✚ 380 T18 • 100 Laurier Street, P.O.Box 3100, Station B, Gatineau, Québec, J8X 4H2

☎ 819/776-7000, 800/555-5621

🕐 Daily 9–6, May–mid-Oct (also Thu–Fri 6–9pm, Jul–Aug); Fri–Wed 9–5, Thu 9–9, rest of year

💲 Adult $10, child (3–12) $4 or (over 12) $6, family $22; free Thu 4–9, half price Sun; guided tours $2.50 ($4 for two exhibitions)

🎫 45-minute tours of permanent galleries and selected temporary exhibitions (register at information desk, where schedules are available)

🍴 Café du Musée: elegant restaurant, outdoor terrace in summer

☕ Cafeteria; Café Express

🛍 Canadian crafts and souvenirs

www.civilization.ca • Excellent and user-friendly site with fairly detailed information on the collections and images of selected exhibits. The self-guided tour can be downloaded from the site

Where architecture in Canada is concerned, this superb museum has no equal. Designed by Edmonton architect Douglas Cardinal, it has roughly 25,000sq m (270,000sq ft) of display space. The curved lines of the building—there are no straight lines—reflect First Nations traditional imagery and evoke the North American continent, sculpted and eroded by wind, water and ice. The Manitoba limestone used as cladding is millions of years old, and contains fossils from the earliest epochs. The museum faces Ottawa, Ontario, across the Ottawa River and has the best view of the Parliament Buildings there.

THE GRAND HALL

The architectural centerpiece of the museum is the majestic Grand Hall, overlooked from the floors above, with floor-to-ceiling windows 112m (365ft) high that frame a view of Parliament Hill. It houses six Pacific coast Indian houses with a splendid collection of totem poles, connected by a shoreline and boardwalk with a forest backdrop. Displays focus on traditional culture but also examine contemporary issues, animated with storytellers, demonstrations and dramatic performances. At the far end is the original plaster of Bill Reid's *Spirit of Haida Gwaii*, a large and complex sculpture representing a Haida canoe crammed with paddlers and passengers, which was used to cast the famous bronze at the Canadian Embassy in Washington, D.C.

THE CANADA HALL

Under a domed ceiling 17m (56ft) high, a panorama of Canadian history unfolds. Life-size buildings and complete environments are furnished with appropriate objects re-creating the country's history, sometimes animated by actors. Highlights include the re-creation of a Basque whaling station, place de la Nouvelle-France, Métis bison hunters, a shipyard from the Maritimes, and an Orthodox church from the Prairies where weddings are still celebrated. This area is still under development, with new sections being added every year.

The complex also contains a Children's Museum, with interactive learning displays, the Canadian Postal Museum with interesting philately exhibits, and an IMAX movie theater.

The Île d'Orléans is a rural area dotted with historic settlements

A miraculous event in 1878 led to the building of this shrine at Cap-de-la-Madeleine, and pilgrims still flock here to worship

ÎLE D'ORLÉANS

✚ 366 U16 ℹ Chambre de Commerce de l'Île d'Orléans, 490 Côte du Pont, St-Pierre, Québec, G0A 4E0, tel 418/828-9411
www.idedorleans.qc.ca

Beautiful and fertile, the almond-shaped Île d'Orléans is about 40km (25 miles) long and sits wedged in the St. Lawrence River as it widens after passing Québec City. Settled by the French in the early 17th century, it has Norman-style stone farmhouses, ancestral country homes and several fine old churches. Église St-Pierre (daily, May–Oct), built in 1717–19 and now classified as an historic monument, is Québec's oldest country church.

The island is noted for the fresh produce it supplies to Québec City, and, in summer, Île d'Orléans becomes a vast open-air market, with vegetables and fruit—especially strawberries—on sale at roadside stands. At Domaine Steinbach (year round, but call first, tel 418/878-0000), the Steinbach family harvests organic apples and makes apple cider, mustard (including a maple syrup version) and preserves, and raises ducks and geese.

The jewel of the island is the meticulously restored Manoir Mauvide-Genest (daily, summer; Mon–Fri, winter) in St-Jean, a French manor house built in 1734. Costumed guides explain the seigniorial system and re-create the life of a wealthy seigneur during the French regime.

LAC ST-JEAN

✚ 366 U16 ℹ Fédération Touristique Régionale du Saguenay-Lac-St-Jean, 455 rue Racine Est, Bureau 101, Chicoutimi, Québec, G7H 1T5, tel 418/543-9778, 800/463-9651
www.tourismesaguenaylacsaintjean.qc.ca

Named for Father Jean Dequen, who visited its shores in 1647, Lac St-Jean was originally called Piékouagami (Flat Lake) by the Montagnais. Large (1,350sq km/526sq miles) and saucer-shaped, it is the source of the mighty Saguenay River. The land is flat and fertile, and the water supports a highly prized species of trout known as ouananiche.

In 1912, French author Louis Hémon stayed in the village of Péribonka and was inspired to write his beautiful love story Maria Chapdelaine, which is celebrated at the Louis Hémon Museum (daily, summer; Mon–Fri, winter). The author's life is traced from his birth in Brittany to his tragic death under a train in Chapleau, Ontario.

On a magnificent site beside falls on the Ouiatchouan River is the fascinating deserted village of Val-Jalbert (daily, mid-May to mid Oct), conjuring up dreams of another age when it was a flourishing mill town. After the mill closed in 1927, the population drifted away and the village fell into ruins., but it has been re-created for visitors.

Don't miss The 400-step climb (or cable-car) to the top of the 72m (236ft) Ouiatchouan Falls is rewarded with fine views.

LES LAURENTIDES
See page 98.

SAGUENAY FJORD
See pages 99–100.

TROIS-RIVIÈRES

✚ 366 U17 ℹ 1457 rue Notre-Dame, Trois-Rivières, Québec, G9A 4X4, tel 819/375-1122, 800/313-1123
www.v3r.net

An important industrial hub and the province's third city, Trois-Rivières stands on the St. Lawrence River where it is joined by the St. Maurice River. At its mouth, this mighty tributary branches around two islands—hence the name Trois-Rivières (Three Rivers). In 1634, Samuel de Champlain sent the Sieur de Laviolette to establish a fur trading post here, making Trois-Rivières the second-oldest settlement in New France. Today, it is a pulp and paper town—not pretty, and it can be extremely smelly, but there are a few pleasant older streets to explore.

Some of the oldest buildings stand on rue des Ursulines. The most striking is the Ursuline Convent, with its silver dome and large wall sundial, built soon after the Ursulines arrived in 1697. The nearby Terrasse Turcotte has a waterfront promenade with views of the port and the Pont Laviolette.

In Cap-de-la-Madeleine, a twin community, the river mysteriously froze over in the mild winter of 1878–79 just long enough for the inhabitants to cross it carrying stone to build a new church. In gratitude, the parish priest created a shrine devoted to the Virgin in the old chapel, and, ever since, pilgrims have flocked to the site. In 1964, the gorgeous octagonal Rosary Basilica (daily) was built to accommodate them. It has a magnificent interior with seating for 6,000 and no columns to block the view.

Les Forges du St-Maurice (daily, mid-May to mid-Oct), the old ironworks on the banks of the St. Maurice River, was Canada's first industrial community, and iron was smelted here between 1730 and 1883. You can visit the blast furnace and forges, and wander down to the river, where there is a fireplace from which natural gas escapes; known as the Devil's Fountain, it can be ignited with a match.

Charlevoix Coast

A UNESCO World Biosphere Reserve, with captivating mountain, river and village scenes.
Feeding ground for several species of whale.

Low tide grounds boats in the harbor of Baie-St-Paul (above)

Le Manoir Richlieu (right) is one of the area's finest resort hotels

Guilded angels (below) outside the village of Baie-St-Paul

BASICS

➕ 366 U16

ℹ Association Touristique Régionale de Charlevoix

✉ 630 boulevard de Comporté, C.P. 275, La Malbaie, Québec, G5A 1T8

☎ 418/665-4454, 800/667-2276

www.tourisme-charlevoix.com

ℹ Société des traversiers du Québec

✉ St-Joseph-de-la-Rive to Île aux Coudres ☎ 418/438-2743 St-Siméon to Rimouski ☎ 418/862-9545; Baie-Ste-Catherine to Tadoussac, ☎ 418/235-4395

www.traversiers.gouv.qc.ca

THE CRATER

Charlevoix owes its mountainous profile to a 15-billion-tonne meteorite that hit the earth 350 million years ago. The crater of this meteorite extends from Baie-St-Paul as far as La Malbaie, a distance of about 56km (35 miles), the biggest such crater in the world.

SEEING CHARLEVOIX COAST

The Charlevoix Coast, on the north shore of the St. Lawrence River, officially starts in Beaupré, northeast of Québec City, and finishes at Tadoussac on the Saguenay River. It is one of Québec's most varied and beautiful regions, a combination of mountains sweeping down to the water's edge, attractive villages nestling in the valleys, and the mighty St. Lawrence. It is rural and wild, with ever-changing views of the river and the opposite shore, and on a bright summer day it is stunning. Whale-watching tours leave from Tadoussac, and Baie-Ste-Catherine has a viewpoint high above the river on Pointe-Noire on Route 138, just before the descent to the Saguenay—as well as the views, there are displays and films on the marine mammals.

HIGHLIGHTS

WHALES

Every June, a flotilla of whales swims from the Atlantic up the St. Lawrence to the deep waters off Tadoussac at the mouth of the Saguenay River, waters that are rich in all kinds of flora and fauna. The tidal St. Lawrence sweeps into its tributary every day and in turn is invaded by the fresh waters of the Saguenay, creating an ecosystem where plankton flourishes. This attracts small fish and shellfish such as krill, shrimp and capelin, on which the whales feed. It is a wonderful experience to see these huge creatures. The most common species are fin and minke, and there is a resident population of white whales (belugas). Occasionally, humpback whales are sighted, and if you are very lucky you may glimpse the great blue whale, the biggest mammal on earth, which can be as much as 30m (98ft) long.
All through the summer there are whale-watching cruises from the wharf at Tadoussac (see panel on page 100). The St. Lawrence River is more than 10km (6 miles) wide at this point, and it is in the middle that the whales rise to the surface. Great jets of water issue from their blowholes just before they surface, so it isn't too difficult to locate them. There are wonderful views of Tadoussac, the mouth of the Saguenay and the 15m-high (50ft) lighthouse that marks the junction of the two rivers.

CHARLEVOIX COMMUNITIES

A row of attractive communities lies strung out along the Charlevoix Coast. Baie-St-Paul has a beautiful site among rolling hills on the bay formed by the Gouffre River as it joins the St. Lawrence. It has inspired many artists and today there are a dozen or more art galleries in the town, giving Baie-St-Paul an enviable reputation as a cultural center. High in the hills on the west side, the Maison de Tourisme de Baie-St-Paul has displays on the Charlevoix crater (see panel left) and fine views.

Les Éboulements sits more than 300m (1,000ft) above the river, with splendid views. In 1710, Pierre Tremblay settled here and had a large family. He is the ancestor of all the Tremblays living in Québec today—the Montréal telephone directory lists nearly 6,000.

St-Joseph-de-la-Rive, an old ship-building community squeezed between the St. Lawrence and the mountains, has lovely views of Les Éboulements, the river and the enchanting Isle-aux-Coudres, which can be reached by ferry from St-Joseph. This island, 11km (7 miles) long and up to 5km (3 miles) wide, is a haven of rural peace and charm. In 1535, Jacques Cartier named it for the hazelnut trees (*coudriers*) that once grew here in abundance. From Pointe de l'Islet at the southern end there are exceptional views of Baie-St-Paul, while from Pointe-du-Bout-d'en-Bas at the northern end, Les Éboulements can be seen high on its cliff. Ste-Irénée is best known for the prestigious international music festival held in July and August at Domaine Forget.

Three communities hug the shores of La Malbaie—Pointe-au-Pic, Cap-à-Aigle and La Malbaie itself. Legend has it that the bay was given its name, *malle baye* (bad bay), by Champlain in 1608. He anchored his ships offshore, but the next day discovered that they had run aground. Since the 19th century La Malbaie has been a popular resort, its most famous hotel being the Manoir Richelieu in Pointe-au-Pic, a vast château and casino overlooking the St. Lawrence.

The pretty cove of Port-au-Persil on the St. Lawrence has long been a favorite with artists, and has a tiny church and a small waterfall.

BACKGROUND

The name Charlevoix comes from the Jesuit father, François-Xavier de Charlevoix (1682–1761), the first historian of New France. As early as the 1760s, people visited the Charlevoix for its beauty. Later, lavish summer homes were built in places like La Malbaie, and cruise ships brought wealthy tourists to its shores. In 1899, Canada Steamship Lines built the enormous Manoir Richelieu as a luxury hotel.

Baie-St-Paul has many delightful art and craft galleries

Lofty arches in the Church of Ste-Anne de Beaupré (inset)

RATINGS				
Good for kids	●	●	●	
Historic interest	●	●	●	
Photo stops	●	●	●	●
Activities	●	●	●	

Water tumbles through Canyon Ste-Anne, near Beaupré

Gaspésie

**Rugged mountainous landscapes and a glorious scenic coast.
Extraordinary fossil beds of worldwide renown.
Beautiful and unexpected European-style gardens.**

Properties in Gaspé are built to take advantage of the views

The rocky coastline (above right) of the Parc National de Forillon

RATINGS	
Good for kids	●●●●
Historic interest	●●●●●
Photo stops	●●●

BASICS

➕ 366 V14
ℹ️ Association Touristique Régionale de la Gaspésie
✉️ 357 rue de la Mer, Ste-Flavie, Québec, G0J 2L0
☎️ 800/463-0323
www.tourisme-gaspesie.com

IF YOU'VE TIME

BONAVENTURE

Bonaventure was founded in 1760 by Acadians fleeing deportation by the British. Today, 80 percent of the inhabitants of the island still claim Acadian descent. The Musée Acadien du Québec *(daily 9–5 or 6, late Jun–mid-Oct; Mon–Fri 9–noon, 1–4.30, rest of year)* traces their history and forms a cultural center for the community.

CARLETON

This community is dominated by Mont-St-Joseph (555m/1,820ft), which is topped by a shrine. Drive up to the Oratoire Notre-Dame-de-Mont-St-Joseph for a magnificent panorama of Chaleur Bay.

SEEING GASPÉSIE

Also known as the Gaspé Peninsula, this rugged, remote area of eastern Québec juts into the Gulf of St. Lawrence between Chaleur Bay and the mouth of the river. It is about 240km (150 miles) long and 115–135km (70–85 miles) wide, with a mountainous, forested interior divided by rivers and lakes. Its highest

peak is Mont-Jacques Cartier (1,268m/4,160ft) in the Chic-Choc Mountains. See also tour and walk on pages 264–267.

HIGHLIGHTS

FORILLON NATIONAL PARK

➕ 367 W14 ℹ️ 122 boulevard de Gaspé, Gaspé, Québec, G4X 1A9, tel 418/368-5505; daily, May–Oct 💵 Adult $4, child (6–16) $2.25, family $9.25
This wonderful park is like a massive tilted block arising from the sea. Shaped by erosion, it has a rugged coastline of sheer limestone cliffs, notably Cap Bon Ami and Cap Gaspé on the north side. The interpretive center in Cap-des-Rosiers has large aquariums, displays and films. Plaques along a short discovery trail explain the geographical features of the park and describe its wildlife. Cruises *(late Jun–early Sep)* leave the nearby wharf to view the cliffs up close.

GASPÉ

➕ 366 W14 ℹ️ 27 boulevard York, Gaspé, Québec, G4X 2K9, tel 418/368-8525
The administrative and commercial center of the peninsula, Gaspé has a fine hillside site, dominated by a former religious building on the hilltop, which today houses the hospital. The Cathédrale de Christ-Roi is an all-wood structure built in 1969, its somewhat strange exterior contrasting with the spacious and impressively simple interior. The back wall is dominated by a luminous abstract glass window by Claude Théberge and Pierre Osterrath. The Musée de la Gaspésie includes an excellent exhibit on Jacques Cartier *(Tue–Sun)*.

PARC DE LA GASPÉSIE

➕ 366 V15 • 900 route du Parc, Ste-Anne-des-Monts, Québec, G4V 2E3
☎️ 418/763-5435 🕐 Daily 💵 Adult $3.50, child $2
Encompassing the highest peaks of the Chic-Choc Mountains, including Mont-Jacques Cartier, Mont-Albert, Mont-Richardson, and Mont Ste-Anne (see pages 266–267), the park covers 802sq km (310sq miles). It offers a variety of trails in its deep valleys and forested slopes; information is available at the interpretive center.

PERCÉ

Percé is the scenic culmination of the Gaspé Peninsula. Here, the rock has been squeezed, folded and pushed into an incredible variety of cliffs, bays and hills. Most famous of all is the great pierced rock, Rocher Percé, a limestone block 438m (1,437ft) long and 88m

The massive Rocher Percé is most impressive seen from the water

(289ft) high, formed by layers of sediment deposited on the seabed about 375 million years ago. It had two arches until 1848, when one collapsed, leaving just one hole and a separate block known as the Obelisk. A boat trip to Bonaventure Island *(daily, mid-May to mid-Oct)* passes close to the rock and then makes a circular tour of the island, which is famous for its seabirds, especially the huge gannet colony (an estimated 50,000 birds) on the cliffs on the far side.

BATTLE OF THE RESTIGOUCHE NATIONAL HISTORIC SITE
366 V15 • Route 132, Pointe-à-la-Croix, Québec, G0C 1L0 ☎ 418/788-5676
Daily, Jun–mid-Oct Adult $4
The final naval battle between France and Britain for possession of North America took place at the mouth of the Restigouche River. The French were defeated on July 8, 1760, sealing the fate of New France for ever. On display at this historic site are vestiges from the wreck of the French frigate *Machault*, part of a relief expedition dispatched to retake Québec, which had fallen to the British the previous fall. A dramatic interpretation re-creates the battle.

PARC DE MIGUASHA
366 V15• 231 Route Miguasha, Nouvelle, Québec, G0C 2E0 ☎ 418/794-2475
Daily, Jun–mid-Oct Adult $3.50, child (6–17) $1.50, family $5
The remarkably rich fossil beds exposed in a cliff on the shores of Chaleur Bay are protected in the Parc du Miguasha and are included on the UNESCO World Heritage List. The diverse collection of fossils includes some that help us to understand how fish evolved into land animals. The museum contains some impressive examples.

BACKGROUND

From the Mi'kmaq to the arrival of Jacques Cartier, the Acadians, the Loyalists, and the settlers from the British Isles, people came here to exploit the rich fisheries. It was in 1534 that the French explorer Jacques Cartier planted a cross at Gaspé, claiming the land in the name of the king of France. There's a running dispute about where exactly he put this cross—a stone cross in front of the cathedral commemorates the event in 1934, and there's a bronze monument on the cliff top in front of the Musée de la Gaspésie. Both spots have their champions.

NEW RICHMOND
Dominated by its huge pulp mill, New Richmond was founded by Loyalists after the American Revolution, and has a strong British tradition. This is celebrated at the Gaspésian British Heritage Village *(daily, Jun–mid-Oct),* focusing on British architecture, traditions, culture, and folklore.

PASPÉBIAC
The name of this small community comes from a Mi'kmaq word meaning "broken foreshore," describing the shape of the harbor. For a century or more, Paspébiac was an important base for two fishing companies. A number of wooden buildings remain from this era where the traditional life of fishermen on this coast is featured and reenacted.

REFORD GARDENS
366 V15 • 200 Route 132, Grand-Métis, Québec, G0J 1Z0 ☎ 418/775-2222 Daily 8.30–6.30, Jun and Sep–mid-Oct; 8.30–8, Jul–Aug
Gardens only: adult $8, child (6–13) $3, family $20 Visitor Pavilion self-service restaurant Garden Café
Created by Elsie Reford between 1926 and 1959 on her family's estate overlooking the river, the designs here were inspired by the great gardens of Europe. With the region's harsh winter climate, it is a small miracle to see lilies, rhododendrons, azaleas, gentians, Tibetan blue poppies, primroses, and crabapples growing. Because of the late arrival of spring on this northern coast, the plants all bloom at the same time.

The Village Pietonnier is at the heart of the Tremblant resort

Ste-Adèle is located on the lovely Lac Rond

RATINGS

Good for kids	●●●
Historic interest	●●●
Photo stops	●●●●●
Activities	●●●●●

BASICS

⊞ 380 U17

ℹ Association Touristique des Laurentides

✉ 14142 rue de la Chapelle, Mirabel, Québec, J7J 2C8

☎ 450/436-8532, 800/561-6673

www.laurentides.com • A really useful site to help you plan an action-packed visit

TREMBLANT

⊞ 380 717

ℹ Station Mont-Tremblant

✉ 1000 chemin des Voyageurs, Mont-Tremblant, Québec, J8E 1T1

☎ 800/461-8711

www.tremblant.ca • A comprehensive site giving details of lodging, snow conditions and other activities

Floatplane on Lac Mercier

LES LAURENTIDES (THE LAURENTIANS)

**The oldest mountains in the world.
A four-season vacationland.**

The Québec Laurentians stretch right across the province north of the St. Lawrence River. They were formed in Precambrian times, more than 500 million years ago, and are part of the Canadian or Laurentian Shield, a vast horseshoe of land that nearly encircles Hudson Bay.

Few people lived here before the arrival in the mid-19th century of a Roman Catholic priest, Antoine Labelle, who devoted his life to persuading his fellow French Canadians to settle in the Laurentians rather than seeking work in the "Protestant" United States. Labelle founded more than 20 parishes north of Montréal; today, most of these are still named after their parish saint, such as St-Jérôme, St-Sauveur, Ste-Adèle, Ste-Agathe and Ste-Marguerite.

The 1930s saw the beginning of the ski industry, and the parishes turned into retreats for wealthy Montréalers. Boating, swimming, fishing, hiking, horseback riding, and golf are popular pastimes in the summer, while in the fall the tree-clad mountains become a riot of color and attract many visitors. St-Sauveur-des-Monts, the oldest resort, is surrounded by mountains. Often called "La petite Suisse des Laurentides," the village abounds in restaurants. The main street, rue Principale, has little boutiques and handicraft stores, while the nearby parish church sports a distinctive silver roof and steeple.

The lively resort of Ste-Agathe is located around the lovely Lac-des-Sables (Sandy Lake). There is a famous summer theater here called Le Patriote. A boat cruise on the lake *(daily, mid-May–Oct)* enables you to see the palatial residences where many famous visitors have stayed, including Jacqueline Kennedy, Queen Elizabeth II and Baron Von Ribbentrop.

The resort of Tremblant, surrounded by wilderness, is an amazing place. The striking buildings here house every type of restaurant, bar, boutique, and accommodations imaginable. The resort takes its name from the Laurentians' highest peak, Mont-Tremblant (960m/3,150ft), which dominates the site—the streams tumbling off this great ridge create the sensation of trembling.

Saguenay Fjord

The most southerly fiord in the northern hemisphere, with a stark and dramatic natural beauty.

SEEING SAGUENAY FJORD

The Saguenay is not a long river by any means, but it is incredibly dramatic. It flows out of Lac-St-Jean (see page 93), drops about 90m (300ft) through a wild and rocky upper section, then, for its final 60km (37 miles), it is transformed into a deep and majestic fiord. In places it can be as wide as 1,500m (5,000ft), and it has an average depth of 240m (787ft). Few highways touch its edges, and by far the best way to appreciate it is from the water. Cruises on the fiord are among the most impressive and popular activities in Québec, and are available from both Tadoussac and Chicoutimi.

HIGHLIGHTS

CAP TRINITÉ

The highlight of any cruise on the fiord is the arrival at dramatic Cap Trinité, which rises 500m (1,600ft) out of the dark waters. The name comes from the three ledges that punctuate the face of the cape; on the first of these, about 180m (600ft) above the water, there is a statue of the Virgin, carved in 1881 by Louis Jobin. He undertook the work at the request of Charles-Napoléon Robitaille, whose life was saved twice after an appeal to the Virgin. The statue, which stands 9m (30ft) high, had to be transported here by boat, then painstakingly raised into position in three separate sections. Energetic visitors can walk the steep path in the Parc du Saguenay (see page 100) to the top of Cap Trinité and then descend to the statue, from where there is a superb view.

RATINGS	
Good for kids	● ●
Historic interest	● ● ●
Photo stops	● ● ● ● ●

TIP

● The trail in the Parc du Saguenay that leads to the statue of the Virgin is plagued by mosquitoes in midsummer, so apply plenty of repellent.

BASICS

🗺 366 U16

ℹ Fédération Touristique Régionale du Saguenay-Lac-St-Jean

✉ 455 rue Racine Est, Bureau 101, Chicoutimi, Québec, G7H 1T5,

☎ 418/543-9778, 800/463-9651

www.tourismesaguenaylacsaintjean.qc.ca

Saguenay Fiord, as seen from above St-Rose-du-Nord

Whale-watching trips are well organized and extremely popular

One of the leviathans of the deep that frequent the fiord

VIEWPOINTS

It is quite possible to enjoy the fiord from the land—viewpoints are accessible from Route 172 on the north side, and also from Route 170 on the south side. The pretty village of Ste-Rose-du-Nord has an exceptional site with excellent vistas, especially from the wharf. From St-Fulgence there are views of the final stretches of the fiord. In the city of Chicoutimi there's a marvelous panorama from Croix de Ste-Anne (St. Anne's Cross) on the north side of the Saguenay. Late-afternoon light is best for photography here. From the wharf in the community of L'Anse-St-Jean on the St. Jean River, there are more great views and a covered bridge, built over the river in 1929.

CRUISES

Croisières La Marjolaine
✉ Boulevard Saguenay Est, C.P. 203, Port de Chicoutimi, Québec, G7H 5B7 ☎ 418/543-7360, 800/363-7248 ⚫ 2-hour cruises daily, Jun–Sep (reservations essential) 🎫 Adult $25, child (under 15) $12.50
www.quebecweb.com/marjo

Croisières AML
✉ 124 rue St-Pierre, Québec City, Québec, G1K 4A7 ☎ 418/692-1159, 800/563-4643 ⚫ Daily, Jul–early Sep (from Tadoussac and Baie-Ste-Catherine) 🎫 Adult $50, child (under 15) $20
www.croisieresaml.com

Famille Dufour Croisières
✉ 22 quai St-André, Québec City, Québec, G1K 7B9 ☎ 418/692-0222, 800/463-5250 ⚫ Daily, Jun–Sep (from Tadoussac) 🎫 Adult $65, child (6–15) $36
www.groupedufour.com

PARC DU SAGUENAY (SAGUENAY PARK)

Saguenay-St. Lawrence Marine Park Headquarters ✉ 91 Notre-Dame, Rivière-Éternité, Québec, G0V 1P0 ☎ 418/272-1509 ⚫ Baie-Éternité: daily; trails closed mid-Nov to mid-Dec and Apr 🎫 Adult $3.50, child (6–17) $1.50, family $7

This park was created in 1983 to protect the edges of the fiord, and covers about 300sq m (3,228sq ft) between La Baie and Tadoussac. The most popular and accessible section is on the edge of Baie-Éternité, where the Éternité River joins the main stream. This is one of the most attractive coves on the Saguenay, dominated by twin capes, Trinité and Éternité, which can be seen from a path beside the bay. An interpretive center has displays on the origins of the fiord.

BACKGROUND

The deep channel through which the Saguenay flows beyond Chicoutimi was gouged by glaciers 60 million years ago. When the ice receded, the sea invaded, and today tidewaters still reach Chicoutimi. The upper section of the river has been extensively harnessed for industry—La Baie, on a magnificent site on an inlet of the fiord, is dominated by port installations, and bulk carriers transport more than 3 million tonnes of bauxite each year from the Caribbean and South America to feed the aluminum smelters here and in Jonquière. The bay is actually called Baie des Ha! Ha!—according to local legend, early explorers, who mistook it for the main stream, gave it this name—ha ha meaning dead end. In contrast, industry is unknown in the lower section and man's influence is barely visible.

ONTARIO

Taking its name from the great lake whose name means "shining waters," Ontario has a profusion of lovely lakes and waterways. Ottawa, the handsome federal capital of Canada is here, along with the provincial capital, Toronto—the country's largest city—a vibrant cultural, commercial and financial hub, with a particularly interesting ethnic diversity.

Hudson Bay

Chisasibi

WINNIPEG

Thunder Bay
Lake Superior

Timmins

Sault Ste Marie

Lake Huron

MONTRÉAL

OTTAWA

TORONTO

Lake Ontario

Niagara Falls Parkway Ontario

Windsor

Lake Erie

MAJOR SIGHTS

One of the best museums of its kind in the world, the Canada Aviation Museum contains an impressive collection of airplanes

A 1942 locomotive at the Science and Technology Museum

OTTAWA

Ottawa defies the image most people have of a capital city, for it's an attractive and low-key place full of parks and pleasant boulevards. Certainly it has its imposing architecture, and there are some notably splendid museums here, but it is not too overpowering, and this is perhaps its ultimate charm. While the Canadian capital is the hub of high-tech industry and home to the federal government, it comes across as a fresh and clean place. Images of the city show civil servants skating to work along the frozen Rideau Canal, the millions of tulips that decorate the parks and roadsides in spring, the joggers and cyclists of the summer months, and the bright produce stands of Byward Market. See plan on page 357.

CANADA AVIATION MUSEUM

⊞ Off map, 357 B1 • 11 Aviation Parkway, Ottawa, Ontario, K1K 4R3 ☎ 613/993-2010, 800/463-2038 🕓 Daily 9–5, May–Aug; Wed–Sun 10–5, rest of year 🎟 Adult $6, student $5, child (6–15) $3, family $13 🚌 129 🍴 ♿
www.aviation.nmstc.ca

Housed in a huge hangar, this museum—part of the Canada Science and Technology Corporation—tells the story of aeronautical history from the first attempts at flight to the jet age. It is also home to one of the most impressive collections of vintage aircraft in the world.

Airplanes have been essential in opening up Canada's vast and rugged landscape, and today Canadian planes and designs are used in similar terrains all over the world. Although the emphasis here is on Canadian aircraft, there are planes, both military and civil, from many nations, and the collection is still growing.

The Walkway of Time takes you on a journey through the eras of aviation development, while Pushing the Envelope showcases the achievements of Canada's aviation industry since 1945. You can relive the adventures of Canada's bush pilots and see examples of two of Canada's most important contributions to international aviation: the Beaver and the Twin Otter. Other highlights include a replica of the *AEA Silver Dart*, built by Alexander Graham Bell's Aerial Experiment Association in 1901, plus a World War I Sopwith Snipe and a De Havilland Fox Moth.
Don't miss Take a turn on the virtual-reality hang glider.

CANADA IN THE WORLD PAVILION

⊞ Off map, 357 B1 • 50 Sussex Drive, near Rideau Falls Park, Ottawa, Ontario, K1M 2K1 ☎ 613/239-5000, 800/456-1867 🕓 Daily 10–6, late Jun–Sep 1; Wed and Fri–Mon 10–5, Thu 10–8, early May–late Jun and Sep 2–mid-Oct 🎟 Free 🚌 3
www. canadascapital.gc.ca

Canadians are quite reticent about their achievements, and consequently many of them go unnoticed in the outside world. However, this award-winning exhibition, which opened in a bright new building in 2001, sets the record straight and takes a fascinating look at Canada's interaction with the rest of the world and at Canadians who have made significant contributions—from discovering insulin to inventing the IMAX.

There are galleries dedicated to scientific and technological innovations, international trade, humanitarian and peacebuilding issues, and to achievements in the worlds of sport, entertainment and the arts. Some take the form of interactive displays, and there's a collection of items that includes the costumes worn by the Cirque du Soleil's acrobats, Céline Dion's first Grammy, Olympic medals, and the Oscar awarded to the Canadian National Film Board.

There's a schedule of special activities, including concerts, along with the chance to meet remarkable Canadians and experience the work of Canadian peacekeepers.

CANADA SCIENCE AND TECHNOLOGY MUSEUM

⊞ Off map, C3 • 1867 St. Laurent Boulevard, Ottawa, Ontario, K1G 5A3 ☎ 613/991-3044 🕓 Daily 9–5, May–early Sep, Tue–Sun 9–5, rest of year 🎟 Adult $6, child (6–14) $3, family $14; additional $5 for the Simex Virtual Voyages™ Simulator 🚌 85, 86 🍴 Cafeteria for light refreshments; picnic area ♿ Scientique
www.sciencetech.technomuses.ca

The Canada Science and Technology Museum is the largest of its kind in the country. Devoted to the ingenuity of Canadian inventions, it is immediately recognizable by the huge lighthouse outside. Every aspect of the scientific spectrum is covered, from the snowmobile to the Canadarm (part of the space shuttle). The key words are "hands on." You can push buttons, turn dials and pull levers to experience science and technology first hand. Exhibits cover transportation, astronomy, communications, space travel and computers.

The Locomotive Hall offers an incredible display of huge and powerful locomotives, including the Canadian Pacific No. 926 used across Canada right up until the end of the steam era in the early 1960s.

Ottawa's Rideau Canal is a year-round focus of outdoor city life, with walking, cycling and rollerblading in summer and skating in winter

The Supreme Court is at the heart of Canada's legal system

CANADIAN MUSEUM OF CIVILIZATION
See page 92.

CANADIAN WAR MUSEUM

➕ 357 B1 • General Motors Court, 330 Sussex Drive, Ottawa, Ontario, K1A 0M8 (moving to LeBreton Flats, about 2km/1.2 miles west of Parliament Hill, in 2005) ☎ 819/776-8600, 800/555-5621 🕐 Fri–Wed 9.30–5, Thu 9.30–8; closed Sat, mid-Oct–May (will be closed Sep 2004–May 2005 during move to new location) 🎟 Adult $4, child (2–12) $2 or (13–17) $3, family $9; free Thu 4–8, half price Sun 🚌 85, 86 ☕ Cafeteria; picnic area 🍴 Scientique
www.warmuseum.ca

This is a lively and interesting museum devoted to a topic not often associated with Canadians. In fact, Canada has a rich military history, and this museum has one of the finest collections of its kind in the world, all splendidly envisaged in life-size dioramas and other displays. In 2005, the 60th anniversary of the end of World War II, the museum will reopen in a new site beside the Ottawa River, almost doubling the exhibition space.

In its current location, trench signs tell of Canada's contribution to World War I. Out of a population of just over 8 million, more than 650,000 Canadians signed up to fight in Europe. At the Battle of Vimy Ridge in 1917, Canadians really earned their spurs. A diorama illustrates Canada's part in the D-Day landings in 1944, and other displays tell of Canadians in South Africa during the Boer War and in Korea in the 1950s, and of the Iltis jeep used by Canadian peacekeepers in Bosnia.

NATIONAL GALLERY OF CANADA
See pages 104–105.

PARLIAMENT HILL
See page 106.

RIDEAU CANAL AND LOCKS

➕ 357 C2 • Rideau Canal Historic Site, 34A Beckworth Street South, Smiths Falls, Ontario, K7A 2A8 ☎ 613/283-5170, 800/230-0016
www.parkscanada.gc.ca
ℹ National Capital Commission Infocentre, 90 Wellington Street (opposite Parliament Buildings), tel 613/239-5000, 0800/465-1867; daily
www.canadascapital.gc.ca

Cutting right through the heart of the capital, the Rideau Canal forms an attractive linear park. On Sundays the driveways on either side are closed to traffic, and you can walk, cycle or rollerblade in peace. In winter, the canal becomes a 7.8km-long (4.8-mile) skating rink.

The canal leaves the Ottawa River by a flight of eight locks, located between the Parliament buildings and the Château Laurier hotel. From there it stretches some 202km (126 miles), with a total of 47 locks. The canal was built by the British government in 1826–32 to provide a safe route between Montréal and the naval base on Lake Ontario, avoiding the stretch of the St. Lawrence River that forms the border with the US (during the 1812 war, British boats on the river frequently came under fire). The construction was entrusted to Colonel John By of the Royal Engineers, and although it ranks among the greatest early civil engineering works of North America, By got no credit for it—in fact, it cost so much money that he was recalled to Britain in disgrace.

There's a permanent exhibition on the canal in the Bytown Museum (daily, May–Oct; Mon–Fri, Apr and Nov), housed in Ottawa's oldest stone building beside the entrance to the Rideau Canal locks.
Don't miss Watch the boats going through the locks in summer or, in winter, skate on the frozen canal, and stop for hot chocolate at a booth along the way.

SUPREME COURT OF CANADA

➕ 357 B3 • 301 Wellington Street, Ottawa, Ontario, K1A 0J1 ☎ 613/995-4330, 613/995-5361 for information about guided tours 🕐 Daily 9–5, May–Aug; Mon–Fri 9–5, rest of year 🎟 Free
www.scc-csc.gc.ca

Canada's Supreme Court Building, designed by Montréal architect Ernest Cormier, stands high above the Ottawa River, just west of Parliament Hill (see page 106). Set back from busy Wellington Street, the building provides a dignified setting for the country's highest tribunal.

In front of the building is a statue of former Prime Minister Louis S. St-Laurent (1949–57), by Vancouver sculptor Erek Imredy. Two tall statues by Toronto artist Walter S. Allward, entitled Truth and Justice, stand on the steps of the building.

Inside is the impressive marble Grand Entrance Hall, and busts of former chief justices are displayed in the adjoining gallery. On the first floor, the Main Courtroom has black walnut walls and vast windows opening onto interior courtyards.

Visitors can learn about the Canadian judicial system by taking one of the 30-minute guided tours, which are conducted by law students. These take place daily from May to August, and by pre-arrangement the rest of the year. When the court is in session, it is also possible to sit in on the hearing of an appeal.

THE SIGHTS

OTTAWA

National Gallery of Canada

**Over 1,500 Canadian works of art displayed in a stunning building.
The result of 200 years of erudite collecting.**

*Statuary in the cool Water Court
of the National Gallery*

RATINGS	
Historic interest	● ● ● ● ●
Specialist shopping	● ● ●
Value for money	● ● ●

BASICS
✚ 357 B2 • 380 Sussex Drive, Box 427, Station A, Ottawa, Ontario, K1N 9N4
☎ 613/990-1985, 800/319-2787
🕐 Fri–Wed 10–5, Thu 10–8, May–mid-Oct; Wed and Fri–Sun 10–5, Thu 10–8, rest of year
💵 Permanent collection free; admission fee for special exhibitions
🚶 Guided tours daily at 11 and 2 in English and French
🍴 Cafétéria des Beaux-Art, Café l'Entrée
📖 The Bookstore: books, posters and gifts
🅿 On-site pay parking
www.national.gallery.ca • Easily accessible general information (in English and French) on each of the permanent collections, details of current and forthcoming special exhibitions, calendar of events

SEEING THE NATIONAL GALLERY

The National Gallery of Canada occupies a wonderful site in the heart of the capital, with great views of Parliament Hill, and the glittering prisms of its tower echo the Gothic turrets of the Parliamentary Library across the Rideau Canal. The Great Hall in particular has splendid vistas, and the elegant galleries, courtyards and skylights diffuse natural light throughout the building.

HIGHLIGHTS

CANADIAN COLLECTION

Not too surprisingly, the National Gallery of Canada is home to the world's largest collection of Canadian art, on view in the permanent collection galleries. The tone is set as soon as you enter these galleries. New France springs to life with painted and gilded altarpieces, sculptures of saints and religious paintings. Gradually, there is a transition to splendid landscapes, such as Lucius O'Brien's *Sunrise on the Saguenay*, followed by some of the famous names of Canadian art. The genre scenes of Cornelius Kreighoff and Paul Kane record the long-lost lifestyle of native Canadians. Pride of place is given to the magnificently evocative works of Tom Thomson and the Group of Seven. Thomson's *The Jack Pine*, A. Y. Jackson's *The Red Maple* and Lawren Harris' *North Shore Lake Superior* capture the glorious wildness and stunning beauty of the country. More contemporary artists are not ignored, with fine offerings by Jean-Paul Riopelle and Paul-Émile Borduas.

OTHER COLLECTIONS

The gallery owns some outstanding examples of art from other cultures. Over 400 works of art are on display in the spacious European, American and contemporary galleries, reflecting the core and substance of artistic tradition and innovation in Western culture. The collection is arranged chronologically from the Middle Ages through the 1960s to today. Don't miss Lucas Cranach's *Venus* (c1518), Gian Lorenzo Bernini's marble bust of Pope Urban VIII (c1623), John Constable's *Salisbury Cathedral from the Bishop's Grounds* (1820), and the original of the much-reproduced work by Benjamin West, *The Death of General Wolfe*. In the contemporary art galleries, Barnett Newman's enormous abstract work *Voice of Fire* (1967) features three huge stripes. The American artist's work cost the Canadian tax-

payer $11 million. Controversy still surrounds this purchase, so you may well find a group of out-of-towners here to see what their money was spent on.

Hidden away on the lowest level, but accessible from the Great Hall, you'll find a suite of five octagonal rooms devoted to the art of the North. Full of wonderful prints and sculptures in soapstone and whalebone, they provide a great overview of Inuit art. One section is reserved for mini-exhibitions that focus on individual artists.

Important special exhibitions are presented here throughout the year, and there is a schedule of talks, art-related performances, tours and movies.

RIDEAU STREET CHAPEL

At the heart of the Canadian Galleries, you will suddenly come upon this dramatic presentation of the rich artistic traditions of French Canada. Previously a part of the Convent of Our Lady of the Sacred Heart in Ottawa, this splendid chapel was saved from threatened destruction, dismantled and moved into the National Gallery, which was at that time under construction. Designed in 1887, with a neo-Gothic fan vaulted ceiling, cast-iron columns, three altars, and splendid windows, it is the only known chapel of its kind in North America.

BACKGROUND

The National Gallery was originally launched in 1880, and in 1988 moved to these splendid new premises. The new venue was designed by Moshe Safdie, and its architecture is as elegant and remarkable as the art it contains.

The gallery building resembles a huge, glittering prism

GALLERY GUIDE

Ground Level
Main entrance
Information desk
Cloakroom
Bookstore
Auditorium
Colonnade to Level One

Level One
Great Hall
Cafeteria and restaurant
Canadian Art
Contemporary Art I
Rideau Chapel
Temporary exhibition galleries
Inuit Art

Level Two
Contemporary Art II
Asian Art
Prints and drawings
Library and archives

Three splendid Gothic-style buildings house the national government

Flags of the individual provinces flutter in the breeze

RATINGS	
Historic interest	●●●●●
Photo stops	●●●●●
Walkability	●●●●

TIPS

● If you go inside, you will be given a very thorough body search and x-ray check—allow at least 15 minutes for this. Any potential "weapon" will be confiscated during your visit.
● The guided tours are very popular in midsummer—arrive early and reserve your time in advance at the Info-tent.
● Pick up a self-guiding booklet to the grounds at the Info-tent.

BASICS

✚ 357 B2 • National Capital Commission Infocentre, 90 Wellington Street (opposite Parliament Buildings); Info-Tent on Parliament Hill, mid-May–early Sep
☎ 613/239-5000, 800/465-1867
🕒 Daily
💻 In Info-tent mid May–early Sep
www.canadascapital.gc.ca • catering to Canadians and visitors, this is a comprehensive and user-friendly website
www.parl.gc.ca • Practical information relating to Parliament.
www.parliamenthill.gc.ca • Information on the Parliament Buildings

PARLIAMENT HILL

**The home of the Canadian government.
A glorious fantasy of High Victorian Gothic architecture.**

With their turrets and towers, carved stones and copper roofs, the Canadian Parliament Buildings—commonly referred to as Parliament Hill—stand high on a bluff above the river. The best view of them is from the rear, from the Ottawa River or Gatineau on the other (Québec) side; approaching them on Wellington Street, all you see is a large, flat, open park surrounded by three distinctive stone buildings.

The site was purchased from the British military in 1859. Three buildings were constructed in the 1860s—the middle one for the Houses of Parliament and the Parliamentary Library, the east and west blocks for offices. In 1916, the Centre Block was largely destroyed by fire. It was rebuilt in 1920 in a more sober rendering of the Gothic style. The Peace Tower, added in 1927 as a monument to Canadians killed during World War I, contains a carillon of 53 bells.

Free tours are offered of the Centre Block (unless Parliament is in session). For Canadians, the tour is a sort of necessary pilgrimage, but non-Canadians may prefer simply to walk around the exterior for wonderful views of the city and river.

THE GROUNDS

In front of the buildings is the Centennial Flame, a fountain with a natural gas flame burning at its heart. Lit in 1967 (centenary year), it symbolizes the first 100 years of Canadian Confederation and portrays the shields and emblems of all the provinces and territories, and the date each joined Canada. From here, head left around the Centre Block to the Summer Pavilion, for gorgeous views of the Québec shore and the Canadian Museum of Civilization (see page 92). At the back of the Centre Block is the extraordinary 16-sided Gothic Parliamentary Library, which survived the 1916 fire. The statues you pass are mostly of former Canadian prime ministers or fathers of Canadian Confederation. Two commemorate British monarchs—Queen Victoria, during whose reign Canada came into existence, and Queen Elizabeth II, depicted on her horse, Centennial.

From late June to late August, the 30-minute Changing of the Guard ceremony takes place on the main lawn (get there by 9.45am); a 45-minute sound and light show, twice a night alternately in French and English (times vary), uses the Centre Block as a screen.

An outstanding collection of sculptures by Henry Moore take pride of place at the Art Gallery of Ontario

Casa Loma is a testament to the excesses of Sir Henry Pellatt

TORONTO

Innovative, energetic and stimulating, Toronto is the lifeblood of Canada and its largest city. Set on the north shore of Lake Ontario, it is the heart of the "Golden Horseshoe," the area at the west end of the lake where most of Canada's manufacturing industry is located. Toronto is also Canada's financial hub, where the country's great fiscal institutions have vied to build bigger and more impressively than each other, resulting in some spectacular modern architecture. It is a city of great variety and diversity, too: The 2001 Canadian census showed that Toronto has become one of the world's most culturally and racially mixed cities. See plan on pages 360–361 and walk on pages 272–273.

ART GALLERY OF ONTARIO

➕ 360 B3 • 317 Dundas Street West, Toronto, Ontario, M5T 1G4 ☎ 416/979-6648 ◷ Tue and Thu–Fri 11–6, Wed 11–8.30, Sat–Sun 10–5.30 ⬚ Adult $12, child (6 and over) $6, family $25; free Wed 6–8.30pm ◉ St. Patrick ⬚ 505 ⬚ Agora Restaurant ⬚ Cultures ⬚ ⬚
www.ago.net

This is one of Canada's principal art galleries, and among the most highly regarded in North America. Its good Canadian collection includes works by Tom Thomson and the Group of Seven, plus the Salon Gallery, recalling late 19th- to early 20th-century exhibitions of the Royal Canadian Academy.

There are superb Impressionist works such as Claude Monet's *Vétheuil in Summer*, Pierre-Auguste Renoir's *The Seine at Chatou* and Alfred Sisley's *View of Saint-Cloud, Sunlight*.

One of the gallery's best-known features is the Henry Moore Sculpture Centre, with a total of 900 pieces. Many were donated by the artist, who had a soft spot for Toronto ever since the city purchased one of his works in the late 1950s,.

In 2002 the entire Thomson Collection of nearly 2,000 works, the greatest private art collection in Canada, was donated to the gallery. In addition, Lord Thomson provided funding, enabling the gallery to undertake a major expansion. Frank Gehry is designing the project, which is due to complete in 2007. The Thomson Collection will then go on show.
Don't miss The Henry Moore Sculpture Centre was designed by the sculptor himself.

BLACK CREEK PIONEER VILLAGE

➕ Off map, 360 C1 • 1000 Murray Ross Parkway, Toronto, Ontario, M3J 2P3 ☎ 416/736-1733 ◷ Daily May–Dec; closed Christmas Day ⬚ Adult $10, child (4 and over) $6 ◉ Finch ⬚ 60 ⬚ ⬚
www.blackcreek.ca

A complete small rural community, of the type you would have found in southern Ontario in the early Victorian era, is a delightfully unexpected find in the northern part of the city. More than 35 homes, workshops, stores, and other buildings have been constructed and laid out as a town, with tree-lined dirt roads, boardwalks, and split-log fencing around old-fashioned gardens. The friendly, knowledgeable staff create a welcoming down-home atmosphere, and it's on the site of a real pioneer farm.

Most of the buildings are occupied by costumed interpreters, who bring the whole experience to life—craftsmen are actually working, farmers are tending

animals, housewives are sewing or spinning in their parlors, and all are ready to chat to you about what life was like in pioneer days.

This is a lovely place to spend a summer's day, and in winter roaring fires will warm you.
Don't miss Have a chat to the craftspeople about their work.

CASA LOMA

➕ Off map, 360 B1 • 1 Austin Terrace, Toronto, Ontario, M5R 1X8 ☎ 416/923-1171 ◷ Daily 9.30–5 (last admission 4; closes 1pm Dec 24); closed Dec 25, Jan 1 ⬚ Adult $10, child $6 ◉ Dupont ⬚ 127 ⬚ $2.30 per hour ⬚
www.casaloma.org

Casa Loma, with its turrets and towers, chimneys and machicolations, has been described as a mixture of 17th-century Scottish baronial architecture and 20th-Century Fox. It's a rich man's fantasy on a grand scale.

The rich man was stockbroker Sir Henry Pellatt, and his architect was Edward Lennox. Construction began in 1911, and they gave it 15 bathrooms, 5,000 electric lights, an elevator, a private telephone, and every other luxury money could buy—by the time the house was finished, three years later, it had swallowed up $3.5 million of Pellatt's fortune. It needed 40 servants to maintain it, and the cost of its upkeep skyrocketed just as his fortunes took a downturn. Ten years later he had to sell his dream home and auction off his belongings, and in 1939 he died almost penniless.

For years Casa Loma sat unoccupied while the city debated tearing it down, but in 1937 the Kiwanis Club suggested making it into a tourist attraction; they still run it on behalf of the city today.
Don't miss A 244m (266yd) tunnel leads to the stables, which have mahogany stalls and Spanish tiles.

THE SIGHTS

TORONTO

CN Tower

The world's tallest free-standing tower, with 160km (100-mile) views.
The ultimate symbol of Toronto.

Top of mast

Steel antenna mast

SkyPod

Elevator machinery

Technology Radio/TV

360 Restaurant

Look Out and glass floor viewing platforrms

Parabolic antennae

Glass-fronted elevator

Shaft of tower

Entrance area

From the SkyPod city skyscrapers are dwarfed below

SEEING THE CN TOWER

The view from the top of the 553.33m (1,815ft 5in) CN Tower in downtown Toronto is spectacular—on a clear day you can trace Yonge Street as it disappears in a straight line over the far horizon and see small planes pass beneath you, and it's great to stay up there long enough to watch the sun go down and the city light up far below. For a really special treat, you can dine in the revolving 360 Restaurant (see page 322) while the cityscape and lake drift slowly past the window. To get up the tower, you take a stomach-churning ride in an external glass elevator at a speed of 6m (20ft) per second.

HIGHLIGHTS

THE LOOK OUT

The big bulge two-thirds of the way up, at a height of 346m (1,136ft), is the Look Out, reached via the glass elevator. Here, you can spend some time inside, identifying the city landmarks, before descending one floor to an observatory. If you have a good head for heights, you can even stand on a (strong) glass panel and look straight down at the ground far below.

If you don't want to ride the elevator you can't get up the tower—unless, that is, you join in one of the organized Stair Climbs in which thousands of people climb the 1,776 stairs to raise money for charity. Both the United Way and the World Wildlife Fund hold annual climbs that raise more than $300,000 each. In 1989, Brendan Keenoy set a world record for the fastest climb, accomplishing it in just 7 minutes and 52 seconds! And in 2002, paraplegic athlete Jeff Adams went up the stairs in a wheelchair to support a campaign highlighting accessibility issues. The stairs are not otherwise accessible to the public.

SKYPOD

From the Look Out level, there's an internal elevator up to the SkyPod, another 447m (1,465ft) above the ground. You emerge onto the highest man-made observatory in the world, where the thick enclosing glass curves beneath you to maximize the wonderful views. Visibility can be over 160km (100 miles), and if humidity is low and clouds are few, you might just make out the spray of Niagara Falls and the city of Rochester, New York state, on the far side of the lake.

The observation platform also includes a glass floor (inset), looking straight down the tower's side

The elegant minaret-like tower is an unmistakable icon of Toronto

BASICS

✚ 360 B4

✉ 301 Front Street West, Toronto, Ontario, M5V 2T6

☎ 416/868-6937

🕐 Daily (times vary seasonally); closed Dec 25

💵 Adult $23.99, child $18.99; Look Out and Glass Floor only, adult $18.99, child $15.99. Taxes not included. Free if you have a restaurant reservation

🍴 360 The Restaurant at the CN Tower (see page 322)

Ⓤ Union Station

🚋 Streetcar 510

🚈 GO-Train to Union Station

🍽 Horizons Café and Marketplace Café www.cntower.ca • Information on all the attractions, plus fascinating facts, online ticketing and restaurant reservations

RATINGS

Good for kids	●●●●●
Photo stops	●●●●○
Value for money	●●●○○

TIPS

● Arrive early in the day, as the lines to ascend the tower can be long at peak times.

● Unless you've teenagers in your party, you'll probably want to hurry past the tacky attractions—video-game arcades, motion simulators, etc.—at the bottom of the tower. However, the 15-minute "To The Top" movie about the construction of the tower is interesting.

● Check the weather before you plan your trip—it's a lot of money to pay just to have your head in the clouds.

● Be aware that on windy days you can feel the tower swaying (up to 1.8m/6ft from the vertical). Staff will tell you that it's quite normal, but it can still be very unnerving.

● The best way to get here is to take the subway to Union Station and follow the Skywalk.

● If you make a reservation to dine in the 360 Restaurant (see page 322), you'll avoid any wait to get to the top on busy days. Afterward you can walk down to the Look Out and glass-floor level.

BACKGROUND

The CN Tower was not intended to be a tourist attraction, but was constructed to solve a communications problem. In the 1960s, Toronto's low-rise skyline was transformed with a cluster of downtown skyscrapers that got in the way of the airwaves, so in 1976 Canadian National Railways (CN) built the tower to hold microwave receptors and an antenna, giving Torontonians some of the clearest TV and radio reception in North America. CN had the foresight to provide viewing platforms, too, and it soon became not only a city icon, but also a place visitors just have to go. Since the railroad company sold the tower, the CN in the name has been adapted to stand for "Canada's National."

Historical reenactments are a popular feature of Fort York, but the fighting that took place here was bitter and brutal

Mesoamerican ceramic figure at the Gardiner Museum

FORT YORK

🏛 360 A4 • 100 Garrison Road, Toronto, Ontario, M5V 3K9 ☎ 416/392-6907 🕐 Daily 10–4 or 5; closed Dec 15–Jan 1 🎫 Adult $5, child (12 and under) $3 or (over 12) $3.25 🚇 Bathurst 🚋 Streetcar 511 P 🏛 🛍 www.city.toronto.on.ca/culture/fort_york

In 1793, Toronto, then called York, was founded at this very spot, and became the capital of Upper Canada. Today, the Gardiner Expressway and railroad tracks have replaced the fort's defenses and the waters of Lake Ontario no longer lap against its walls, but it still gives a vivid insight into Toronto's history.

It may be hard to visualize this peaceful spot as the scene of bitter military action, but an American army invaded this growing community on April 27, 1813, and attacked Fort York. Vastly outnumbered, the fort's defenders retreated, but not before they had blown up the city's gunpowder supply, destroying the fort and killing hundreds of the attackers. The city fell to the Americans, who subsequently set fire to the Parliament Buildings and Government House. There's an interesting sideline to the story: When the British occupied Washington, D.C., in 1814, they set fire to government buildings in retribution for the destruction of Toronto. The Americans quickly painted the blackened walls of the presidential residence white to cover the damage—which is how the White House got its name.

Fort York was rebuilt immediately after the War of 1812, and a number of the structures we see today date from that time. The officers' quarters and soldiers' barracks reflect life in a military base in the 1830s. Other buildings house exhibits on the history of the fort and Canadian military history since the War of 1812. There are seasonal tours given by guides in period costume, as well as summer events such as military drills and musket firing, and fife and drum music. There's a pedestrian walkway leading up from the streetcar stop on Fleet Street, but be aware that it's very steep and not recommended for small children, the elderly or people with mobility difficulties.
Don't miss Demonstrations of military drill and drumming are staged by costumed interpreters.

GARDINER MUSEUM OF CERAMIC ART

🏛 360 C1 • 111 Queen's Park, Toronto, Ontario, M5S 2C7 ☎ 416/586-8080 🕐 Mon, Wed and Fri 10–6, Tue and Thu 10–8, Sat– Sun 10–5 🎫 Adult $10, child (5 and over) $6, family $24; free first Tue of every month 🏛 Museum www.gardinermuseum.on.ca

This little gem of a museum, surrounded by buildings of the University of Toronto and overshadowed by the high-profile Royal Ontario Museum across the street, is easy to miss, but it is well worth visiting. The Gardiner is devoted to ceramic art, and was founded in 1984 by local philanthropists George and Helen Gardiner to house the comprehensive collection they had amassed from Europe, Asia and the Americas. The pieces are arranged chronologically, starting with a fine display of pre-Columbian objects, predominantly unglazed earthenware, figures, vessels and ritual items.

There is a splendid collection of 15th- and 16th-century Italian majolica, tin-glazed earthenware from Faenza, Florence, Urbino and Venice, and some 17th- and 18th-century delftware from England, named because of its similarity to the products of the Dutch town of Delft. Note in particular the chargers—large plates with portraits of English monarchs. Meissen, Du Paquier, Sèvres, and the great English companies of Worcester, Chelsea and Derby represent 18th-century European porcelain. The exquisite scent bottles come from different parts of Europe, but particularly notable are the elaborate rococo models made in England. The 19th-century Minton china is excellent, and a small but interesting display of the work of contemporary ceramicists brings the collection up to date.

In 2002, the government announced that it was giving a grant to the Gardiner, and as a result the museum is to be expanded.
Don't miss The *Commedia Dell'Arte* figurines by Johann Joachim Kändler are a standout.

THE GRANGE

🏛 360 B3 • 317 Dundas Street West, Toronto, Ontario, M5T 1G4 ☎ 416/979-6648, ext. 237 🕐 Tue and Thu–Fri 11–4, Wed 11–8.30, Sat–Sun 10–4 🎫 Adult $12, child (6 and over) $6, family $25; free Wed 6–8.30pm 🚇 St. Patrick 🚌 505 www.ago.net/information/grange/index.html

The oldest remaining brick building in Toronto was also the first home of the Art Gallery of Ontario (see page 107), and remains an annex of that gallery. An elegant Georgian house of 1817, it has been meticulously restored to reflect the 1830s period, when it was the home of D'Arcy Boulton Jr. Of Loyalist descent, Boulton was a member of what was known as the Family Compact, a small group of wealthy people with strong British ties, who controlled every

Basketball fan shooting some hoops at Ontario Place

The Purple Pipe is one of many exciting features of Ontario Place's Soak City, a superb facility in the heart of the city's lakeshore

aspect of the government of the colony, and who only appointed from within their own ranks. He played a major part in putting down the Revolt of 1837 led by William Lyon Mackenzie. The house epitomizes the privileged lifestyle of Toronto's ruling elite, with its beautiful curved cantilever staircase and sumptuous decoration, and historical exhibits provide information about other members of the Family Compact. The grounds of the house, which once stretched all the way from Bloor to Queen Street, are a peaceful haven.

Don't miss In the kitchens, volunteers are hard at work preparing 19th-century treats for visitors.

HARBOURFRONT CENTRE

See pages 112–113.

HOCKEY HALL OF FAME

➕ 361 D4 • 30 Front Street, Toronto, Ontario, M5E 1X8 ☎ 416/360-7765 ◷ Mon–Fri 10–5, Sat 9.30–6, Sun 10.30–5 🚇 Union Station 💲 Adult $12, child (4 and over) $8 www.hhof.com

This shrine to Canada's sporting obsession has a comprehensive collection of hockey memorabilia and features hockey greats such as Maurice "The Rocket" Richard, Bobby Orr and Wayne Gretzky. At the interactive consoles you can experience the challenges that have made these sporting heroes great, and you can see the original Stanley Cup, North America's oldest sports trophy, donated by Governer General Lord Stanley in 1893.

KENSINGTON MARKET

➕ 360 B3 🚇 St. Patrick 🚋 Dundas streetcar

Canada's 2001 census revealed that Toronto had become one of the world's multicultural places, and one of the best areas to appreciate this diversity is at Kensington Market. Portuguese spice merchants, Chilean butchers, Italian fishmongers, Laotian restaurants, Jamaican fast food—you name it, you can probably find it. With its cacophony of sounds, Kensington is chaotic, eclectic and constantly evolving.

Based on Kensington and Augusta avenues and Baldwin Street, the market is an amazing potpourri of businesses and street vendors amid a warren of narrow streets. Houses have been converted into individualistic stores and informal restaurants that spill out onto the street, and people fill just about all of the available space between them.

You can buy all kinds of food here—fresh fish, vegetables, unusual cheeses, fruit, bread, nuts, exotic spices—and there are stores selling carpets and furniture. This is also a great place to seek out secondhand or vintage clothing.

The area now occupied by the market was originally settled by British immigrants, but in around 1900 they moved north, to be replaced by Jewish refugees fleeing persecution in Europe. Finding that they weren't particularly welcome in Toronto's business community, the refugees opened stands outside their homes to sell produce and other merchandise, and that's how the market began. There's not much sign of the Jewish community here today, but the tradition is in the capable hands of more recent incomers.

If you want the full market experience, go on a Saturday, when it's at its busiest, but if you want to do some serious shopping, choose any other day.

ONTARIO PLACE

➕ Off map, 360 A5 • 955 Lakeshore Boulevard West, Toronto, Ontario, M6K 3B9 ☎ 416/314-9900; 866/663-4386 ◷ Daily from 10am, Jun–Aug; some weekends May and Oct; closing time varies 💲 "Play-all-day": adult $28, child (4 and over) $14. Grounds only: $10. Also "pay-as-you-play" packages 🚇 Union Station, then free shuttle bus 🅿 $10 in summer, $5 off season 🍴 Zoots Bar and Grill in Atlantis Pavilions; also a variety of restaurants and fast-food outlets www.ontarioplace.com

In 1971, Ontario Place was constructed as a futuristic showcase for the province of Ontario, brightening up what was then an underdeveloped waterfront area and including the construction of three manmade islands and lagoons. Today, it has developed into a popular amusement park, with more than 30 exciting rides, lots of things for children to do and top-quality entertainment.

Soak City and Adventure Island are a huge hit with children— bigger kids love the giant waterslides and the heart-stopping Hydrofuge, and there are gentler areas where the little ones can splash around. The Wilderness Adventure is an animated flume ride through a scenic simulation of the forests and steep canyons of northern Ontario. There are also high-tech diversions and simulator rides.

Outdoor attractions are open only in summer, but entertainments continue year-round in the IMAX movie theater, the Atlantic Pavilions—with nightclub, rooftop terrace and 450-seat theater—and the 16,000-capacity Molson Amphitheatre, hosting concerts starring big-name international performers.

Don't miss The Festival of Fire fireworks displays take place on three nights in June and/or July.

THE SIGHTS

TORONTO

Harbourfront Centre

●

A former dockland area that is now a shining beacon of cultural, commercial and leisure activities.

York Quay Centre (above) is a place to shop for art and crafts

Queen's Quay Terminal (above) is a conversion of an old warehouse into a smart shopping mall

RATINGS	
Good for kids	● ● ● ○
Photo stops	● ● ● ○
Specialist shopping	● ● ● ○
Value for money	● ● ● ● ○

BASICS

✚ 360 B5 • 235 Queens Quay West, Toronto, Ontario, M5J 2G8

☎ 419/973-4600 (admin), 416/973-3000 (info hotline), 416/973-4000 (box office)

🕐 General area always accessible; call for event information

💷 Free access; charges vary for individual events

🚇 Union Station

🚋 Harbourfront streetcar from Union Station

🏬 Large variety of stores and craft shops

🍴 Lakeside Terrace and Café, World Café, Spinnakers Seafood Bistro (Queen's Quay Terminal)

www.harbourfront.on.ca • Easy-to-use website, giving plenty of information about the center and what's on, plus online ticketing facility

SEEING THE HARBOURFRONT CENTRE

Between downtown and the lakeshore, there might seem at first glance to be little more than a tangle of railroad tracks heading for Union Station and traffic thundering by on the wide Gardiner Expressway. Look closer, however, and you will see that these are just barriers separating the bustle of the city streets from a different world of waterfront shopping and entertainment. On the section between York and Spadina is a superb 4ha (10-acre) leisure complex that has transformed the old docklands.

HIGHLIGHTS

PERFORMANCES AND FESTIVALS

The Harbourfront Centre has a full and exciting schedule of music, dance, drama and other events, both inside and in the open air, by international performers. It's also the venue for various festivals, including the World Stage Festival each April, hosting theater companies from all over the world, and the Milk International Children's Festival of the Arts, which takes place over eight days in May. This popular event includes theater, comedy, dance, music, workshops and crafts for children, with plenty of audience participation. The Harbourfront Reading Series, approaching its 30th year, is one of the most admired public reading events in the world, and has hosted more than 2,500 distinguished authors, including a dozen Nobel laureates. The International Festival of Authors, 25 years old in 2004, is another popular event where you can rub shoulders with literary icons. On summer Sunday afternoons, various outdoor "cushion concerts" take place, including storytelling for children and live music.

GARDENS AND GALLERIES

The enchanting Music Garden, outside Queen's Quay Terminal (see opposite), was designed jointly by renowned cellist Yo Yo Ma and landscape artist Julie Moir Messervy to reflect Bach's First Suite for Unaccompanied Cello. Another horticultural attraction is the Artists' Gardens, where plants are used to create living installations.

York Quay Centre hosts exhibitions in a broad range of media, including photography and multicultural themes. Meanwhile, the Power Plant specializes in contemporary art, including paintings,

sculpture and installation work, and, though it exhibits work from the rest of Canada and other countries, it maintains a strong commitment to Toronto artists. The Canada Quay Building also stages temporary exhibitions; features include computer-based displays.

Canada Day is celebrated in fine style at the Harbourfront Centre

SHOPPING

The York Quay Centre, at 235 Queen's Quay West, includes the Bounty Contemporary Canadian Crafts store (see page 216), where you can buy quality Canadian crafts made by some of the country's brightest and most innovative artists. You can also see some of these crafts in the making, in the studios of the artists-in-residence. On summer weekends, the open-air International Market at the water's edge has vendors selling arts and crafts from across the globe, including native works, Oriental textiles and South American jewelry.

Queen's Quay Terminal, at 207 Queen's Quay West, is a glittering and imaginative conversion of a 1920s warehouse that contains more than 30 chic stores, galleries and restaurants, the former selling crafts, fine arts and designer clothing. Luxury condominiums and offices are on the upper floors, with some of the best lake views in the city.

The Harbourfront Antiques Market moved out in 2003 and, at the time of going to print, its replacement is unknown.

There's plenty of waterborne activity on the lakeshore here

ACTIVITIES

There is always plenty to see and do on the water. Nearby, ferries leave for the Toronto Islands and cruise ships disgorge their passengers. The Nautical Centre offers all kinds of water-based activities, including sailing, kayaking, sightseeing cruises, and environmental awareness events. In winter, you can bring your ice-skates down (or rent them) and skate to music at Toronto's biggest open-air ice rink, with changing facilities and hot food and drinks to warm you up.

BACKGROUND

In 1974, the center, then known simply as Harbourfront, was set up as a nonprofit organization (so events are reasonably priced or free) to bring a wide variety of artists and art forms to the people of Toronto, to introduce ideas that would not normally be showcased at commercial venues, and to push the boundaries of creative expression. At just about any time of the year, you can drop by the Harbourfront Centre and find something going on, even if it's just Torontonians taking the air beside the water.

Royal Ontario Museum

Canada's largest museum, with 40 galleries and 6 million objects.
One of the best collections of Chinese art in the world.

Detail of a Chinese relief carving in the Bishop White Gallery

The Chinese Collections (right) are in an appropriate setting

BASICS

✚ 360 C1 • 100 Queen's Park, Toronto, Ontario, M5S 2C6
☎ 416/586-5549, 416/586-8000 (recorded information)
🕐 Mon–Thu and Sat 10–6, Fri 10–9.30, Sun 11–6 (closes at 4pm Dec 24 and 31); closed Dec 25 and Jan 1
💵 Adult $16.50, child $10; free Fri 4.30–9.30 (except special ticketed exhibitions)
🚇 Museum
🚌 5
🚻 Free guided tours daily
🅿 No parking, but museum issues discount vouchers for nearby parking lots
🍴 Closed while construction of museum extension is underway
☕ Little Café and cafeteria
🏬 ROM Reproductions store
www.rom.on.ca • Very clear and user-friendly website that is regularly updated

TIPS

● Try to avoid weekday mornings during the school term, when the ROM tends to be invaded by school groups.
● Excess baggage (umbrellas, knapsacks, etc.) must be checked. Photography is not allowed inside the museum.

SEEING THE MUSEUM

Popularly known as the ROM (to rhyme with Tom), this superb museum covers just about everything, from dinosaurs to gemstones, from Buddhist temple art to bat caves, and from Egyptian scarabs to English military helmets. It truly has something to interest everyone, but it is huge and has a bewildering array of choices. Rather than wander aimlessly around, stop by the area called Mankind Discovering, close to the entrance, which gives an overview of all the collections. Then arm yourself with a map and plan which exhibits you especially want to see.

HIGHLIGHTS

BISHOP WHITE GALLERY AND MING TOMB

The stunning Bishop White Gallery is part of the ROM's world-class collection of Chinese art. It contains one of the most important collections of Chinese temple art in the world, and features three wall paintings and 14 monumental Buddhist sculptures dating from the 12th to 16th centuries AD. The gallery beautifully evokes the atmosphere of a Chinese temple, with long roof beams, subdued lighting and a high coffered ceiling. Priceless Ming and Qing porcelains, embroidered silk robes and objects made of jade and ivory are also on show. In addition, the ROM has the only complete Ming tomb in the Western world, with a processional way passing archways and monumental figures of animals and people to the burial mound.

DINOSAUR GALLERY AND BAT CAVE

If you are traveling with children, and they groan at the suggestion of a museum, bring them straight up to the famous Dinosaur Gallery. Set in vivid walk-through dioramas, there are 13 real fossil dinosaur skeletons, including the savage, carnivorous *Albertosaurus* and a rare duckbilled dinosaur called *Parasaurolophus*. These dioramas have video stations that explain details of each dinosaur, its habitat and way of life, and there's a theater where you can learn all about fossil-hunting in the Badlands of Alberta (see pages 131–133), one of the richest dinosaur-collecting areas in the world.

Children may also find the Bat Cave fascinating, though it has nothing to do with the superhero—it's a walk-through diorama that replicates in miniature the St. Clair bat cave in Jamaica. Once you cross the threshold into the darkness of the cave, more than 3,000 lifelike bats become visible, amid other realistic creatures such as tailless scorpions and cave crickets. The bats roost in the cave's high domes and fly in between the stalactites. Deep in the rocky recesses, you'll see the nursery where thousands of bats roost with their young.

EUROPEAN GALLERIES

These galleries illustrate European lifestyles from the Middle Ages to the 20th century through excellent period room displays. Each one is

complete with furnishings, domestic articles, sculpture, and arms and armour, and the social life of each era is explained to a background of period music. Special exhibits explore such diverse topics as costume and textiles, domestic sanitation and the history of warfare.

Earlier epochs are covered in the Ancient Egypt, Roman and Greek galleries, containing everything from mummies to coins and jewelry.

CANADIANA

More period room settings are to be found in the Sigmund Samuel Canadiana Galleries down in the basement, which have been designed to show the museum's splendid collection of Canadian decorative arts and historical paintings.

Also in the basement is the fascinating Gallery of Indigenous Peoples, which hosts changing exhibitions that explore the culture and lifestyle of Canada's First Nations. There are also displays relating to the contribution to Canada's development made by the French and English settlers.

EARTH SCIENCE AND BIODIVERSITY

On the main floor, the state-of-the-art Gallery of Earth Sciences portrays the powerful forces that affect the earth. As well as the interactive displays, there is a splendid collection of gold samples and gemstones. Upstairs, you'll find the Biodiversity Gallery, which explains the complex relationships between living things. Facilitators engage visitors in educational activities here, and living displays include a beehive and a Great Lakes stream.

BACKGROUND

The ROM has been an independent institution since 1968, but it first opened to the public in 1914 when it was part of the University of Toronto. Rapid expansion over the years has provided 40 galleries, and it is set to get even bigger. The Renaissance ROM project, announced in 2002, is a scheme to restore the current heritage buildings and to add spectacular new galleries so that even more of the museum's collection of 6 million objects can be put on view.

Chinese warrior statue in the Bishop White Gallery

Walk-through dioramas bring the dinosaur era to life (almost)

TORONTO

GALLERY GUIDE

First Level
Entrance lobby
Mankind Discovering
Bishop White Gallery
Ming Tomb
East Asian Galleries
Gallery of Earth Sciences

Second Level
Dinosaur Gallery
Bat Cave
Biodiversity Gallery

Third Level
European Galleries
Ancient Egypt Gallery
Roman Gallery
Greek Gallery

Basement Level
Sigmund Samuel Canadiana Galleries
Gallery of Indiginous Peoples

NB Some galleries may move when the Renaissance ROM project is completed

The Ontario Science Centre was one of the first to make science fun with hands-on exhibits—and it is still one of the best

The magnificent SkyDome hosts sport and entertainment events

ONTARIO SCIENCE CENTRE

361 D1 • 770 Don Mills Road, Toronto, Ontario, M3C 1T3 ☎ 416/696-3127. OMNIMAX: 416/696-1000
Daily 10–5; closed Dec 25
Eglinton, then take bus 34
Adult $13, child $7. Combined ticket with OMNIMAX: adult $18, child $10; OMNIMAX also available separately
$8 Galileo's Bistro Valley Marketplace Mastermind gift store
www.ontariosciencecentre.ca

This is the science center to beat them all—you don't just stand and look here, but can really get involved with the exciting and entertaining exhibits. There are 13 multi-themed exhibition halls with more than 800 high-tech, interactive displays, plus live hands-on demonstrations and an OMNIMAX theater with a giant 24m-wide (80ft) domed screen.

The building, designed by Raymond Moriyama and opened in 1969, cascades down the Don Valley ravine, with different levels connected by enclosed escalators. In the Space Hall you can use a rocket chair to navigate on the Moon; in the Sports Hall you can test yourself by climbing a rock wall or racing an Olympic bobsled; in the Food Hall you can choose your favorite meal and check its nutritional value. You can find out how weather systems form in the Earth Hall and perform chemical experiments in the Matter, Energy and Change display.

Popular sections include the Science Arcade, with its demonstrations about generating your own electricity, and the Human Body exhibit, where you can learn how to catch a criminal with DNA fingerprinting. And when you have had enough with doing all that, you can sink back into a tilted seat at the OMNIMAX theater and enjoy a spe-

cially filmed large-format movie on its huge wrap-around screen, with 13,000W of digital sound.
Don't miss There are daily science demonstrations—check on arrival to see what's on.

ROYAL ONTARIO MUSEUM

See pages 114–115.

SKYDOME

360 B4 • 1 Blue Jays Way, Toronto, Ontario, M5V 1J3 ☎ 416/341-2770 (tours) Guided tours daily, when there are no events scheduled Tour $12.50 Union Station
www.skydome.com

In the shadow of the CN Tower (see pages 108–109) is SkyDome, a superb multipurpose megastadium that was a world leader when it opened in 1989, and its massive retractable roof makes it a year-round, all-weather facility. SkyDome is huge, covering 186,000sq m (2 million sq ft), which makes it large enough for eight Boeing 747s to fit inside, and at 95m (310ft) high it could accommodate a 31-story building even with the roof closed. It also has a luxury hotel built into one side, with many rooms overlooking the field (see page 324).

The SkyDome is first and foremost a sports venue, being home to the Toronto Blue Jays baseball team (see page 225) and the Toronto Argonauts (see page 225), who play in the Canadian football league. It also hosts other sporting events, pop and rock concerts, trade shows, and festivals (see page 230). Seating capacity is just over 50,000 for sporting events and 67,000 for concerts. If the roof needs to close over any of these events, it takes 20 minutes for the 11,175-tonne structure to slide across the 3.2ha (7.9-acre) opening.

If you are unable to attend one of the sporting fixtures or other events here, you can still see the interior by taking a guided tour. This includes a 15-minute film about the construction and a 45-minute behind-the-scenes walking tour.

Before you go in, have a look at the entertaining sculptures squashed into the structure on the Front Street side. The work of Michael Snow, they are called *The Audience* and feature figures hooting, hollering, thumbing their noses and making other rude signs. This is indeed a city with a sense of humor.

See also Walk Nine, "The Heart of Toronto," on page 272.

ST. LAWRENCE MARKET

361 D4 • 92 Front Street East, Toronto, Ontario, M5E 1C4 ☎ 416/392-7219 Tue–Sat Union Station
Paddington Pump pub

This historic market building contains a wonderful assortment of stands on its main floor, selling a huge variety of foods. It is particularly well known for fresh fruit and vegetables (locally grown in season), but is also home to dozens of meat and deli vendors and fishmongers. In season, you can buy fresh cut flowers, and there are carts piled high with an array of crafts and specialty items.

Cheese and dairy foods, dry goods and organic health foods are available on both levels, and there's prepared food to eat on the spot. Try the peameal bacon on a bun. Peameal bacon is salt- and sugar-cured extra-lean ham, rolled in cornmeal. It's a trademark Toronto delicacy (though it is available throughout Canada) and Torontonians eat it for breakfast.

There has been a market in this area since at least 1803, but

Toronto's waterfront playground features an excellent marina and the lovely Toronto Islands; Hanlan's Point is shown here

Cool and classy Yorkville is great for people-watching

not in the present building. This was originally built in 1844 to serve as Toronto's first city hall, and only became a market in 1899 when the city administration moved into what is now "Old" City Hall on the corner of Bay and Queen streets. The old council chamber still exists on the second floor and now houses the Market Gallery, with exhibitions of photographs, paintings and other documents relating to Toronto.

The market is lively and fun at any time, but more so on Saturdays, the busiest day. This is also the day when a smaller farmers' market is open in the north market building directly across Front Street from St. Lawrence Market's main doors.

TORONTO ISLANDS

✚ Off map, 361 D5 ☎ 416/392-8186 (Toronto Parks and Recreation), 416/392-8193 (ferry info) 🚢 From Mainland Ferry Docks at foot of Bay Street to Hanlan's Point, Centre Island and Ward Island, 10-minute trip, daily, every 20 minutes, but first and last ferry times vary seasonally (no winter service to Centre Island) 🎫 Ferry round trip: Adult $6, child (2 and over) $2.50 🍴 Iroquois and Paradise restaurants ☕ Rectory Café, and various fast-food outlets 🚻
www.city.toronto.on.ca/parks

The Toronto Islands are just a short distance from the shore, but the ferry ride to get there makes it feel like a real excursion, and the relaxing parkland and beaches are a world away from the heat and noise of the city. Almost completely traffic-free, the islands offer pleasant walks and bicycle trails, marinas and public moorings, various sporting facilities, an amusement park for children, and fantastic views back across the water to the city.

Centre Island is the principal

destination for most visitors to the islands, and has a superb beach (including a nudist section on the north side of the island), Centreville amusement park (see page 228) and an animal park Other facilities include barbecues and picnic tables, tennis courts, bicycle rental, playgrounds, wading pools and fast-food outlets.

To the west is Hanlan's Point, named after the Hanlan family, who were among the first year-round inhabitants of the Toronto Islands. They built a hotel, and during the second half of the 19th century this was a popular resort with an amusement park. In 1909, a 10,000-seat baseball stadium was built (and rebuilt a year later after a fire), and it was here that baseball legend Babe Ruth scored his first professional home run. The stadium and amusement park closed in the 1930s to make way for Toronto Islands Airport, where you can get helicopter sightseeing trips (see page 227).

From the ferry dock, you can walk to the 1806 Gibraltar Point Lighthouse, Toronto's oldest surviving structure, which has a wonderful site on the lakeshore. It is also home to the Gibraltar Point Centre for the Arts, promoting artistic achievement and development.

Ward's Island, at the east end, is a more peaceful spot than Centre Island, and it has a nice beach (with restrooms) and a children's playground.

Ferries go to different points on the islands, so make sure you get on the right one for the area you want to visit, though you can rent bicycles and buggies to get around once you are there.
Don't miss There are great views of the city back across the water.

TORONTO ZOO
See page 118.

YORKVILLE

✚ 360 B1 🚇 Bay

This is Toronto's ritziest neighborhood, where Bugattis vie with Porsches for parking space, and where the beautiful people, hiding behind sunglasses, sip their lattes after spending a fortune on some bauble in the Gucci, Hèrmes or Louis Vuitton stores.

Yorkville is synonymous with haute couture boutiques (check out Hazelton Lanes), exclusive art galleries, designer stores, and expensive restaurants. In addition, the annual glamfest of the Toronto International Film Festival is based here, attracting Hollywood's biggest names.

Back in the 1960s, this was an altogether different place—the hub of the city's counterculture, hang-out of the flower children, and proving ground for Canadian musicians such as Neil Young, Joni Mitchell and Gordon Lightfoot, who went on to find lasting international renown. The rents here were low, the drug culture prevailed, and it was definitely not an area where Toronto's glitterati would ever have been seen.

Today, the Victorian townhouses—some of the most expensive real estate in Canada—have been restored. Many of them contain antiques shops, art galleries and designer boutiques; some are chic cafés with outside tables shaded by trees. There's a pleasant village atmosphere and an almost tangible aroma of privilege and wealth.

Amid all this, the Village of Yorkville Park is an award-winning transformation of a parking area into parkland gardens with wildflowers, pines and rock outcrops.
Don't miss Indulge in some people-watching from one of the sidewalk cafés.

Canada's wildlife can be viewed in comfort, in near-natural habitats

Animals from all the world's major regions can be seen here

RATINGS	
Good for kids	●●●●●
Photo stops	●●●●
Value for money	●●●●

BASICS

🚩 Off map, 361 D1 • Meadowvale Road, Scarborough, Ontario, M1B 5K7
☎ 416/392-5900
🕐 Daily 9–6, early Mar–mid-May and Sep 2–mid-Oct; 9–7.30, mid-May to Sep 1; 9.30–4.30, mid-Oct–early Mar (last admission 1hr before closing)
💲 Adult $17, child (3 and over) $9
🚇 Kennedy or Sheppard, then bus
🚌 85, 85B, 86A 🚉 GO Train to Rouge Hill, then bus
🅿 $6 per car (Mar–Oct only)
🍴 Various kinds of fast food
📅
www.torontozoo.com • Excellent web-site giving an overview of each area and animal video clips

TIPS

● Arrive early and even then don't try to see everything—it's just too big. But don't miss the gorillas.
● Wear comfortable shoes—even if you take the Zoo-mobile ($5 per day), there's plenty of walking to do.
● Pick up a schedule for the daily "Meet the Keeper" events and feeding times.

TORONTO ZOO

Animals from every continent enjoy spacious enclosures that closely resemble their natural habitats.

Covering 287ha (710 acres) in the valley of the Rouge River at Scarborough 37km (23 miles) northeast of Toronto, this enormous zoo, with 10km (6 miles) of walking trails, opened in 1974. It is more a celebration of wildlife than a zoo in the traditional sense, and its concept has always been to allow visitors to see the animals in as natural a setting as possible. More than 5,000 animals, representing more than 450 species, come from all six of the world's major zoo-geographic regions. In addition to the outdoor paddocks, there are four giant indoor pavilions and several smaller indoor viewing areas. Huge in size, the zoo is also hugely popular, with more than 1.2 million visitors annually. It's a nonprofit organization, and in addition to the public access, it maintains a serious commitment to scientific research and conservation. The annual running costs are around $24 million, and those who balk at paying for parking *(Mar–Oct only)* in addition to admission should know that this alone pays the animals' food bill.

THE CONTINENTAL AREAS

Not surprisingly, the African area is one of the most popular, since that continent is blessed with some of the most spectacular wildlife in the world—elephants, giraffes, rhinos, antelopes, crocodiles—even a termite mound. And, most popular of all, in a huge pavilion covering almost a hectare (2 acres), a troop of western lowland gorillas.

The Australasian continent has a large number of species that are not found anywhere else in the world, such as the Komodo dragon, and there are also plenty of kangaroos and wallabies, emu, possums, wombats, and the Tasmanian devil. In addition, the Edge of Night exhibit switches night and day so that the nocturnal marsupials are active when visitors are present. There's also an Indomalayan pavilion, with a tropical rain forest and waterfall, clouded leopards, exotic birds, and a Sumatran orangutan family; the Eurasia area, with camels, Siberian tigers and Barbary apes; the Americas, featuring animals as diverse as polar bears and Brazilian cockroaches, and including alligators, sloths, bird-eating spiders and llamas.

The rugged Canadian Domain features elk and moose, bison and musk oxen, grizzly bears, cougars, Arctic wolves, and bald eagles, and there's a spectacular variety of waterfowl on Weston Pond.

The tranquil waters of Smoke Lake, in the Algonquin Provincial Park, provide a classic Canadian scene

A superb log building houses the McMichael Canadian art gallery

ONTARIO PROVINCE

ALGONQUIN PROVINCIAL PARK

➕ 380 S18 • Box 219, Whitney, Ontario, K0J 2M0 ☎ 705/633–5572
🕐 Daily 🎫 Adult $2, child $1; additional fees for facilities such as camping (see page 317)
www.OntarioParks.com

The call of a loon echoes from a rocky lakeshore, the sunset silhouettes a solitary pine tree, a moose raises its massive head to stare at a beaver forging a ripple across a glassy pond; Algonquin Park is the essence of the wilderness. Established in 1893 and covering 7,725sq km (2,983sq miles) of maple-clad hills, lakes, rivers, and bogs, this is Ontario's best-known provincial park. The only way to explore the interior is by canoe or on foot, but Highway 60 crosses the park for a 56km (35-mile) stretch, offering easy access to part of it. Trails leave the highway for the interior, and the Visitor Centre (daily, summer; Sat–Sun only off season), the Logging Museum (daily, late Jun–Oct), and the Algonquin Gallery (daily, late Jun–Oct) are on the highway.
Don't Miss The park's famous Wolf Howls are held in August.

HAMILTON

➕ 378 S9 ℹ️ City of Hamilton Tourism Development Department, Hamilton City Hall, 71 Main Street West, Hamilton, Ontario, L8P 4Y5, tel 905/546-4222, 800/263-8590
www.city.hamilton.on.ca

At the western end of Lake Ontario, Hamilton has a natural harbor and is known for its steel industry. It's not a natural tourist center, but two sights close by are of major interest.

The Royal Botanical Gardens (daily), occupying 1,000ha (2,470 acres) on the western side of the lake, offer splendid displays in five different dispersed areas (a shuttle-bus service runs between them).

Overlooking Hamilton's harbor is the neoclassical, porticoed mansion of Dundurn Castle (daily, late May–early Sep; Tue–Sun, rest of year). A showpiece of 19th-century privilege, it was home to Sir Allan Napier MacNab, Canada's prime minister from 1854 to 1856, and contains a fine collection of 19th-century furnishings.
Don't miss The Rose Garden in the Botanical Gardens is at its best in early summer.

GEORGIAN BAY
See page 120.

KINGSTON AND THE THOUSAND ISLANDS
See page 121.

McMICHAEL CANADIAN ART COLLECTION

➕ 378 S9 • 10365 Islington Avenue, Kleinburg, Ontario, L0J 1C0
☎ 905/893-1121, 888/213-1121
🕐 Daily 10–5, May–Oct; 10–4, rest of year; closed Dec 25 🎫 Adult $15, child (5 and over) $12, family $30 🅿 $5 🍴
📷
www.mcmichael.com

"We fell under the spell of works by a few passionate artists who had captured not only the form and color of the wilderness that we loved, but its very soul"—the words of Robert McMichael, explaining why he and his wife decided to collect the works of the Group of Seven. They gave their splendid collection (and their home) to the province of Ontario, and the paintings are exhibited in a stunning setting within a series of sprawling log

buildings. Also on display are contemporary First Nations art and Inuit sculpture. The original Group of Seven—Franklin Carmichael, Lawren Harris, A.Y. Jackson, Frank Johnston, Arthur Lismer, J.E.H. MacDonald and Frederick Varley—sought a Canadian way of representing their country, believing that Canadian art must be truly inspired by Canada itself.
Don't miss The dramatic works by Norval Morrisseau in the Native Galleries are a must-see.

MIDLAND

➕ 378 S8 ℹ️ 575 Dominion Avenue, Midland, Ontario, L4R 1R2 ☎ 705/526-4275
www.town.midland.on.ca

Midland, on Severn Sound, has a picturesque harbor and waterfront, and is a tourist base for nearby Ste-Marie-Among-the-Hurons and the Martyrs' Shrine.

Jesuit missionaries, keen to spread the faith to the Huron, or Wendat, built a mission close to present-day Midland and called it Ste-Marie-Among-the-Hurons. But when two French Jesuit missionaries were massacred by the fierce Iroquois tribes (old enemies of the Wendat), the site was abandoned. A reconstruction of the mission (daily, mid-May to mid-Oct) stands as a poignant memorial, and its 22 buildings are peopled by costumed interpreters representing the Jesuit fathers and their Huron converts.

Martyrs' Shrine (daily, mid-May to mid-Oct) is a twin-steepled church 3km (2 miles) east of Midland on Route 12, built in 1926 to commemorate eight Jesuit martyrs. The striking interior features wood paneling and a cottonwood roof shaped like a ship's hull.
Don't miss Bronze Stations of the Cross stand in Martyr's Shrine.

A fun mural gives this Midland house a whole new perspective

Beautiful Georgian Bay has rocky shores, sand beaches, and islands

RATINGS	
Good for kids	● ● ●
Historic interest	● ● ●
Photo stops	● ● ● ●
Activities	● ● ● ●

BASICS

✚ 378 S8

ℹ Bruce Peninsula National Park and Fathom Five National Marine Park, P.O. Box 189, Tobermory, Ontario N0H 2R0, tel 519/596-2233, visitor center open daily, late Jun–early Sep
www.parkscanada.gc.ca

Tobermory
✚ 378 R8 ℹ Tobermory Chamber of Commerce, P.O. Box 250, Tobermory, Ontario, N0H 2R0, tel 519/596-2452 www.tobermory.org • This comprehensive and enticing site includes the lovely Legend of the Flowerpots

Ontario Northland Ferry
(Tobermory to Manitoulin Island)
M.S. Chi-Cheemaun
✚ 378 R8 ☎ 519/596-2510, 800/265-3163 for info on times and schedules
🗓 May–Oct

GEORGIAN BAY

Canada's "Sixth Great Lake."
Setting of a UNESCO World Biosphere Reserve.

The large expanse of Georgian Bay is part of Lake Huron, but because the Bruce Peninsula and Manitoulin Island nearly cut it off, it is almost a lake in its own right, sometimes referred to as the "Sixth Great Lake." The southern part of the bay has sandy beaches and resorts; the northern and eastern shorelines are indented; and there are thousands of small granite islands with windswept trees and ospreys winging overhead. It's a wild area with a raw beauty.

The Bruce Peninsula, part of the Niagara Escarpment, tilts toward the west, with a gentle side facing Lake Huron, and huge rock walls and rugged capes on the Georgian Bay side. It was declared a World Biosphere Reserve by UNESCO in 1990, and is also a Canadian national park. Manitoulin Island is the largest freshwater island in the world, covering 2,590sq km (more than 1,000sq miles). Named after Manitou, the Great Spirit, it was set aside as an Amerindian reserve in 1837.

COMMUNITIES OF THE BAY

Penetanguishene, commonly called Penetang, is set at the head of a deep inlet. A British naval base was located here in the 19th century, and the site is known today as Discovery Harbour *(Mon–Fri 10–5 mid-May–late Jun; daily 10–5, late Jun–early Sep)*. In the original officers' quarters of 1845 you'll see period furniture and, if you're lucky, a "period" officer. H.M.S. *Tecumseth* and H.M.S. *Bee* are full-scale active replicas of the original Royal Navy vessels.

Tobermory, at the tip of the Bruce Peninsula., is very much a sailors' town, with twin harbors full of yachts and pleasure craft in the summer. It is the headquarters of two national parks: Bruce Peninsula, which protects the land, and Fathom Five National Marine Park, an underwater park preserving the many shipwrecks in the depths—a mecca for scuba divers. Less ambitious visitors can see the wrecks in glass-bottom tour boats.

Another boat trip from Tobermory will take you to Flowerpot Island *(daily, late Jun–early Sep)*, one of Ontario's most recognized natural attractions after Niagara Falls. It is renowned for its picturesque rock pillars, and visitors can take a cruise around the island, with an option to land and hike to the two sea stacks along the walking trails.

Cottages on the lakeshore reflect the popularity of this destination

Old locomotive on display on Kingston's waterfront

KINGSTON AND THE THOUSAND ISLANDS

A pleasant city of limestone buildings, tree-lined streets and lake views.
Sparkling waters dotted with 1,000 islands—more or less.

Located on Lake Ontario just before the St. Lawrence River leaves the lake, Kingston started life as a French fur-trading settlement but was subsequently settled by Loyalists, who gave it the name. In the early 19th century, the British built a naval base and dockyard here, followed by the Rideau Canal (see page 103) and, finally, Fort Henry. By the 1840s, Kingston was so important that it was briefly the capital of the province of Canada—its grand City Hall was built as a possible Parliament building, but it lost the honor after confederation. Today, it retains its military role as home to the Royal Military College, and is a gracious place to visit. It is also on the doorstep of one of southern Ontario's loveliest regions, the Thousand Islands.

Set on Point Henry, high above the St. Lawrence River, the massive Fort Henry (daily, mid-May–early Oct) was constructed in 1832–36 to protect the town, the naval dockyard at Point Frederick and the entrance to the Rideau Canal. It never saw military action, and began to decay in the early 20th century. Restored to its full splendor, it provides a vision of mid-19th century military life, with barracks, officers' quarters, kitchens, guard room and powder magazine. There are costumed interpreters and military performances in summer.

THE THOUSAND ISLANDS

Called the Garden of the Great Spirit by native peoples and the Mille Îles by the early French explorers, these islands set in sparkling waters became one of the most popular vacation areas of northeastern North America in the 19th century. As it leaves Lake Ontario, the St. Lawrence is littered with islands for about 120km (75 miles). They vary in size—some are large and forested, others simply boulders of granite supporting a few jagged pine trees. No one agrees about their number—estimates vary between 990 and 1,800. In places, the rock has a pinkish hue, beautifully set off by the crystal waters and the surrounding greenery. It is possible to appreciate the region's beauty from the Thousand Island Parkway, but by far the best way is on one of the many boat tours.

RATINGS				
Good for kids	●	●	●	○
Historic interest	●	●	●	●
Photo stops	●	●	●	●

BASICS

✚ 379 T8

ℹ Kingston Tourist Information Office,

✉ 209 Ontario Street, Kingston, Ontario K7L 2Z1

☎ 613/548-4415, 888/855-4555

🕐 Daily

www.kingstoncanada.com/www.city.kingston.on.ca

ℹ Thousand Islands Gananoque Chamber of Commerce

✉ 2 King Street East, Gananoque, Ontario, K7G 1E6,

☎ 613/382-3250

🕐 Daily

www.1000islandsgananoque.com

Boat tour companies

Gananoque Boat Line/Ivy Lea/Island Memories, 6 Water Street, Gananoque, Ontario, K7G 2B7 ☎ 613/382-2144, 613/382-2146 (information line) www.ganboatline.com

Rockport Boat Line Ltd, 23 Front Street, Rockport, Ontario, K0E 1V0 ☎ 613/659-3402, 800/563-8687 www.rockportcruises.com

Kingston 1000 Island Cruises, 263 Ontario Street, Kingston, Ontario, K7K 2X5 ☎ 613/549-5544 www.1000islandscruises.on.ca

Niagara Falls

**One of the most spectacular natural sights in the world.
A breathtaking experience that no amount of commercialization can mar.**

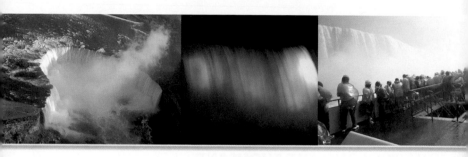

The spray above the falls can be seen long before you get there

Colorful floodlighting extends the viewing day at the falls

The Maid of the Mist *takes you as close as it's safe to get*

BASICS

✚ 379 S9 • Niagara Parks Commission, 7400 Portage Road South, P.O. Box 150, Oak Hall Administrative Building, Niagara Falls, Ontario, L2E 6T2
☎ 905/371-0254, 877/642-7275
🚍 People Mover runs along the Niagara Parkway; every 20 minutes in summer, reduced service off season, no service Jan–Feb; adult $5.50, child $2.75
🅿 Rapids View Parking Lot: $9 per car per day. Falls Parking Lot: $10 per car per day. Queenston Heights Park: free
www.niagaraparks.com

TIPS

● Arrive early or late for the *Maid of the Mist* on hot summer days, as this is the most popular thing to do at the Falls.
● The falls are impressive in winter when partially frozen, but the spray freezes in midair and lands on you as ice pellets.
● Avoid the hucksters on Clifton Hill unless you really want your photograph taken in a barrel "going over the falls."

The sight of deep water disappearing over the edge (opposite) is compelling

SEEING NIAGARA FALLS

The Niagara River divides when it reaches tiny Goat Island. About 10 percent of the water heads for the American Falls (on the US side of the river), which are more than 300m (nearly 1,000ft) wide, and 54m (177ft) high. The other 90 percent of the water heads for the Canadian, or Horseshoe Falls, so named for their shape. They are nearly 800m (2,600ft) wide and about 51m (167ft) high. The Canadian side of the falls has the best views, and attractive parks with beautiful flower displays line the river. Avoid the town—it's tacky and touristy—and its US twin, Niagara Falls, New York, an industrial city full of chemical plants and factories exploiting the power of the falls. However, a trip to the US side can lead you to Goat Island, which separates the Canadian and American falls. There are various ways to enjoy the falls, most of which involve some degree of getting wet, but waterproofs are provided on the *Maid of the Mist* boat trip and for the walk behind the falls. If you want to stay dry, you can take a helicopter ride. Don't ever expect solitude—around 14 million people visit every year. See walk on pages 276–277.

HIGHLIGHTS

TABLE ROCK

While they have their place in the Niagara experience, the boats, helicopters and cable cars should take second place. By far the best way to appreciate the power of the falls is to stand here at the very top, at the point where a dark green mass of water, about 2m (6ft) deep at the edge, silently slithers into the abyss. It is totally mesmerizing. It is also rather wet, especially on windy days. When you can tear yourself away, descend by elevator to the two outdoor observation decks *(daily)*, directly behind the falls.

MAID OF THE MIST

✉ 5920 River Road ☎ 905/358-5781 🕐 30-minute trips daily, late Apr–late Oct
🎫 Adult $12.25, child $7.75
A trip on one of these little boats is quite an experience. You board in calm waters (and don the waterproofs provided), then voyage right

The Maid of the Mist *(above) is dwarfed by the mighty Horseshoe Falls*

The Skylon Tower (opposite and inset) gives an excellent view

Goat Island separates the Horseshoe and American falls (opposite, bottom of page)

The geological profile and composition of the rocks behind the falls (below)

Disposable waterproofs are provided for the boat trip (above)

into the horseshoe and the turmoil of water at the foot of the falls, venturing just a little bit farther than might seem sensible. Soaked by the incredible spray, you can look up at the huge wall of water plummeting down on three sides—Niagara means "thundering water."

BACKGROUND

The falls came into existence about 12,000 years ago, when the retreating glaciers created the Niagara Escarpment (see page 126) and diverted the waters of Lake Erie into Lake Ontario. The top layer of rock is a hard dolomite limestone, with softer layers of sandstone and shale beneath. The force of the water tumbling over the falls cuts away at this underlying layer, causing the top layer to erode and break off. This erosion used to be about 1m (3ft) every year. In fact, 12,000 years ago the falls were 11km (7 miles) downstream. Since the 1950s, water diversion to power plants has spread the flow of water more evenly and thus reduced the rate of erosion, now estimated to be 36cm (1ft) every 10 years. Eventually, in a few hundred thousand years, the falls will erode their way back to Lake Erie. In 1678, a Récollet priest, Louis Hennepin, became the first European to see the cataract. In his journal, he described it as "a vast and prodigious cadence of water which falls down after a surprising and astonishing manner, insomuch that the universe does not afford its parallel." Few have

Rock formations

Height meters		
10		Lockport (dolomite)
20		Decew
30		Rochester (slate)
40		Irondequoit / Reynales
50		Neahga
60		Thorold
70		Grimsby (sandstone)
80		Power Glen
90		Whirlpool
		Queenston (slate)

disagreed with him since. He continued: "The waters which fall from this vast height do foam and boil after the most hideous manner imaginable, making an outrageous noise, more terrible than that of thunder; for when the wind blows from off the south, their dismal roaring may be heard above fifteen leagues off." Little has changed—except you cannot hear the falls from Lake Ontario today; traffic noise and the diversion of much of the water to power plants have seen to that. Since that sighting in 1678, the falls on the Niagara River have enticed people from all over the world. By the 19th century, Niagara had become a hucksters' paradise, with every conceivable device being employed to separate visitors from their money. In 1885, the Ontario government stepped in and created Queen Victoria Park to protect the natural environment around the falls from unbridled commercial development. This was the beginning of today's Niagara Parks Commission, which regulates development in a total of 1,700ha (4,200 acres) of land along the river's edge In the early 20th century, Niagara attracted stuntsmen of all types. Some went over the falls in a barrel, others walked over them on a tightrope. This type of stunt was banned in 1912. Nonetheless, a total of 15 daredevils have tried to go over the falls in one way or another since then. Five of them drowned, included someone on a jetski as recently as 1991.

Niagara Parkway

A 53km (33-mile) drive taking in Niagara Falls,
tranquil river scenes, beautiful gardens,
and fascinating historic sites and communities.

Laura Secord's House, home of a Canadian heroine

Historic Fort Erie (above right), and a costumed interpreter (right)

The orca show at Marineland (above, center)

RATINGS

Good for kids	●●
Historic interest	●●●●
Photo stops	●●●●●
Activities	●●●●●

BASICS

✛ 379 S9 • ℹ The Niagara Parks Commission (and Niagara Historic Sites)

✉ 7400 Portage Road South, P.O. Box 150, Oak Hall Administrative Bldg. Niagara Falls, Ontario, L2E 6T2

☎ 905/356-2241

www.niagaraparks.com • Comprehensive site about the park and falls, including information on special events and on-line shopping (gifts, maps and tickets)

TIPS

● A number of Niagara wineries are open to the public and offer tastings and tours.
● In summer, look for roadside stands selling juicy fresh peaches and other fruits direct from the farm.

SEEING THE NIAGARA PARKWAY

The Niagara Parkway follows the Niagara River between lakes Erie and Ontario. It is a wonderful drive, encompassing Niagara Falls (see pages 122–125) as well as tranquil river scenes, beautiful gardens and the lovely community of Niagara-on-the-Lake. The Niagara River is 56km (35 miles) long; the upper part is a wide, steadily flowing stream with islands both large and small in its channel, and it is only after Chippawa that it begins to pick up speed as it approaches the falls. The parkway is slightly shorter than the river (53km/33 miles), running from Old Fort Erie to Niagara-on-the-Lake. The best way to see it is to follow the drive on page 274.

HIGHLIGHTS

NIAGARA ESCARPMENT

The Niagara Escarpment is sometimes known as Ontario's Great Wall. Essentially, it is a massive ridge of fossil-rich sedimentary rock, which began to form 450 million years ago. Several hundred meters (over 1,000ft) high in places, it stretches 725km (450 miles) from Queenston on the Niagara River to Tobermory at the tip of the Bruce Peninsula (see page 120). In 1990, the escarpment was declared a World Biosphere Reserve by UNESCO, and in the Niagara peninsula, it provides good soil for the rich farmlands, orchards and vineyards.

FORT ERIE

This town stands at the place where Lake Erie empties into the Niagara River. It is a major crossing point into the United States, with the 1927 Peace Bridge—opened by the then Prince of Wales—connecting it to Buffalo. An interesting place to visit is Old Fort Erie *(daily, May–Oct)*, a reconstruction of a British fort that stood here during the War of 1812 and was destroyed by the Americans in 1814. It has a scenic location, and costumed guides really bring the place to life.

IF YOU'VE TIME

WHIRLPOOL AERO CAR
✚ 379 S9 • 3850 Niagara Parkway, Niagara Falls, Ontario ☎ 905/356-2241
🕐 Mon–Fri 10–5, Sat–Sun 10–6
💵 Adult $6, child (6–12) $3
About 4.5km (3 miles) downstream from the falls, the river changes direction abruptly, and the strong currents create a massive whirlpool. You can see it from above on the cable car that has operated here since 1916.

The historic Whirlpool Aero Car crosses above the vortex

Blooms at the Niagara Botanical Gardens

QUEENSTON

Queenston Heights, 106m (348ft) above the river on the edge of the Niagara Escarpment, was the original location of Niagara Falls before erosion forced them upstream. This was also the site of a battle during the War of 1812, when British commander Isaac Brock was killed; a 50m (64ft) monument stands here in his honor. A bridge crosses the river at this point to Lewiston, New York. At the bottom of the escarpment is Queenston, once home to the Canadian heroine Laura Secord, who, in 1813, set out on a 32km (20-mile) journey to warn the British that the Americans had crossed the river and were preparing to attack. The Laura Secord homestead *(daily 11–3, end May–Sep)* is immaculately maintained. Beyond Queenston, the parkway is lined with gracious homes, orchards and vineyards in the heart of the most important fruit- and wine-producing area in Canada.

NIAGARA-ON-THE-LAKE

✚ 379 S9 ℹ Chamber of Commerce, 26 Queen Street, P.O. Box 1043, Niagara-on-the-Lake, Ontario, L0S 1J0, tel 905/468-1950
This community on Lake Ontario at the mouth of the Niagara River is one of the most captivating in Ontario, well known for its annual Shaw Festival (see page 230). Settled by Loyalists after the American Revolution, it was the first capital of Upper Canada. The Americans burned it to the ground during the War of 1812, but it was rebuilt soon afterward. Since then, time seems to have stood still here, and gracious 19th-century houses stand on tree-lined streets. Nearby Fort George *(daily 10–5, Apr–Oct)* was built in the 1790s and is today a national historic park. It played an important role in the War of 1812 and has been restored to its original condition, with a wooden stockade, officers' quarters, guard house, powder magazine, and barracks.

BACKGROUND

The Niagara Parkway was created in 1923 by the Niagara Parks Commission (see page 125), which still regulates development in a total of 1,700ha (4,200 acres) of land along the river's edge.

Carving of a First Nations man by an Iroquois artist

WHITE WATER WALK

✚ 379 S9 • 4330 Niagara Parkway, Niagara Falls, Ontario ☎ 905/356-2241
🕐 Daily 10–5 💵 Adult $5.75, child (6–12) $2.90
Close to the Whirlpool (see above), an elevator takes you 46m (150ft) down into the rocky gorge to a boardwalk alongside the rushing torrent, which safely leads you close to one of the wildest stretches of water in the world.

Boardwalks across the marshes in Point Pelee National Park provide access for visitors while preserving the delicate ecology of the area

Thunder Bay monument to Terry Fox, a courageous fundraiser

THE SIGHTS

POINT PELEE NATIONAL PARK

✚ 378 S10 • 407 Robson Street, R.R.1, Leamington, Ontario, N8H 3V4, ☎ 519/322-2365, 519/322-2371 (info line) 🕒 Daily 📅 Apr–Oct: adult $3.25, child (6–16) $1.60, family $8.55. Nov–Mar: adult $2.25, child $1.10, family $5.35 ☕ Cattail Café 📖 Bookstore www.parkscanada.gc.ca

This tiny oasis of green, protruding into Lake Erie and the most southerly point of the Canadian mainland, was formed when tons of sand were deposited here by the retreating glaciers of the last Ice Age and a lush woodland of deciduous trees took root. Point Pelee is on the same latitude (40°N) as Rome, Sapporo in Japan, and northern California, and has a plant and animal life unique in Canada. For this reason, its 20sq km (8sq miles) have been preserved as a national park since 1918. It is also famous for its spring and fall bird migrations, when more than 350 species pass through. For a few days each fall, it hosts thousands of migrating monarch butterflies, on their way south to the mountains of central Mexico 3,000km (1,860 miles) away. They come to find their only food—milkweed—which grows in abundance here.
Don't miss Visit the Tip, focus of birding activity, and take a walk along the marsh boardwalk, where a sea of cat-tails stretches to the horizon—you may see turtles, muskrats and snakes.

SAULT STE. MARIE

✚ 368 Q18 ℹ The Corporation of the City of Sault Ste. Marie, 99 Foster Drive, Sault Ste. Marie, Ontario, P6A 5X6, tel 705/759-2500 www.city.sault-ste-marie.on.ca

Sault Ste. Marie, commonly called "The Soo," is an industrial city on the north side of the St. Mary River. This 96km (60-mile) stretch of water, obstructed by rapids, connects lakes Superior and Huron and forms the international border between Ontario and the state of Michigan. In a single turbulent mile, the river drops more than 6m (20ft) in a series of rapids *(saults)*.

Mighty locks enable large ships to travel the St. Lawrence Seaway, a major shipping route for iron and copper ore, steel and lumber, between the two lakes, and the four side-by-side Sault Ste. Marie locks—an engineering marvel—are the final step in the 16 locks between the Atlantic and Lake Superior. Two of these locks are 24m (80ft) wide and a massive 411m (1,350ft) long, among the longest in the world. A lock-boat cruise *(daily, mid-May to mid-Oct)* enables you to view the lake freighters and seagoing vessels up close on one of the world's busiest canal systems.

North of town is the wilderness of the Canadian Shield. A day trip by train *(daily 8am, early Jun–mid-Oct)* runs 184km (114 miles) through this rugged landscape, with a two-hour stop at the spectacular Agawa Canyon.

The Big Nickel is a huge icon for Sudbury's nickel mines

SUDBURY AND SCIENCE NORTH

✚ 369 R15 • 100 Ramsey Lake Road, Sudbury, Ontario, P3E 5S9 ☎ 705/522-3701 (info line 705/522-3700) 🕒 Daily (times vary, tel for info) 📅 Adult $16, child (12 and under) $13 🍴 Landings restaurant 📖 Whizards gift store www.sciencenorth.on.ca

Sudbury sits in a huge oval-shaped crater, about 100km (62 miles) wide and 15km (9 miles) deep, in the rocky Canadian Shield in northern Ontario's vastly rich mineral belt. Nickel and copper were discovered here in 1883 during construction of the Canadian Pacific Railway, and today Sudbury is one of Canada's largest mining towns.

Science North, Sudbury's superb science museum, is housed in two glittering snowflake-shaped buildings, representing the glaciation that sculpted the landscape. The smaller building, the reception area is linked to the one with the exhibits by a rock tunnel, ending in a cavern where a spectacular 3-D movie is shown. From here, a glass-enclosed ramp reveals part of the underlying bedrock, excavated at this point for its geological interest.

Science North has a hands-on approach—you can get close to a beaver, watch a flying squirrel in action, lie on a bed of nails, or operate a Canadarm. There are laser shows, an IMAX theater, a tropical greenhouse and the Virtual Voyages Adventure Ride, plus science camps and workshops.

THUNDER BAY

✚ 368 P18 ℹ 550 Donald Street East, Thunder Bay, Ontario, P7E 5VE, tel: 807/625-2270, 800/667-8386 www.city.thunder-bay.on.ca

Located on the northwest shore of Lake Superior, Thunder Bay is

Old Fort William at Thunder Bay is an authentic re-creation

Bringing in the pumpkin harvest the old way

Canada's lakehead—the head of navigation between the Atlantic and the Great Lakes—and a major port for various goods.

From about 1798 to 1821, Thunder Bay (then called Fort William) was an important rendezvouz for the Northwest Fur Trading Company of Montréal. Every spring, brigades of canoes carried fur traders from northwestern Canada to the lakehead to meet their Montréal counterparts, but these meetings ended in 1821 when the Northwest Company merged with the Hudson's Bay Company.

Old Fort William *(daily, mid-May to mid-Oct)*, an authentic reconstruction commemorating the fur trade, looks just as it did in 1815. The fort is huge, with a whole cast of characters. There's an Ojibwa encampment, carefree *voyageurs* in bright clothing, and Scottish fur traders in top hats, long coats and cravats, as well as working artisans.

The Kakabeka Falls, sometimes called the Niagara of the North, are dramatic. The Kaministikwia River plunges 39m (128ft) over sheer cliffs around a pinnacle of rock, then cuts a narrow gorge where platforms and a trail offer great views. Fossils found in the rock here are on display at a visitor center *(daily, May–Oct)*, which also tells stories of the *voyageurs*, for whom the falls posed quite an obstacle.

The spectacular steep-sided Ouimet Canyon, about 1.6km (1 mile) long and up to 100m (320ft) deep, is the result of a fault in the bedrock. Rare vegetation grows on the canyon floor—Arctic-alpine plants such as fir-club moss, lichen, saxifrage and shield fern are a remnant of the colder conditions of the last Ice Age. A trail *(daily, May–Oct)* follows the top of the canyon for about 1km (0.6 mile).

UPPER CANADA VILLAGE

An imaginative re-creation of Ontario life in the mid-19th century.
Over 30 carefully preserved heritage buildings.

✚ 380 T18 • RR1, Morrisburg, Ontario, K0C 1X0 (mailing address)
☎ 613/543-3704, 800/437-2233
🕐 Daily 9.30–5, mid-May–early Oct
💷 Adult $16.95, child (5–12) $7.50, family 10 percent discount

RATINGS	
Good for kids	● ● ● ●
Historic interest	● ● ● ●
Photo stops	● ● ● ●
Specialist shopping	● ● ● ●

🍴 Willard's Hotel: period-style food. Harvest Barn Restaurant: deli, salad bar, luncheon specials
☕ Village Café: light lunches
🏪 The Village Store: 1860s reproduction products, Canadian crafts, gifts and souvenirs
www.uppercanadavillage.com • Comprehensive site including information on activities and events, a virtual tour of the village, and aspects of 1860s life

Upper Canada Village, located beside the St. Lawrence River in a rural setting, was created during the construction of the St. Lawrence Seaway in the 1950s. In order to build the new power dams and shipping channels, engineers dammed the historic Long Sault rapids to form Lake St. Lawrence, drowning 200 farms, eight villages and thousands of homes. Just over 30 heritage buildings were carefully moved here to preserve them, and today the fairly tough early existence of the Loyalists who settled in this area at the end of the 18th century is brought back to life.

VISITING THE VILLAGE
The village transports you into an era when life was simpler, and costumed staff tend livestock in barns and farmyards, spin wool and quilt, make cheese and bread, grind wheat into flour in a steam-powered mill, and travel about in every type of 19th-century conveyance imaginable—visitors can ride some of them too. Tradesmen forge iron, sharpen and solder tinware, make furniture, shoe horses, and print a newspaper. There's a woolen mill, sawmill, school, church, tavern, and a doctor's surgery.

The buildings show the progress of the early settlers from pioneer shanties to substantial homes of brick and stone. The Ross farm, one of the oldest buildings, is a single-roomed log home of a type built by the early Loyalists. In contrast, the much larger 1860s Loucks farm has an air of affluence. Crysler Hall is a magnificent mansion, which would once have been luxuriously furnished. Today, it houses the village's Orientation Centre.

THE SIGHTS

THE PRAIRIES

The three Prairie provinces—Alberta, Manitoba and Saskatchewan—offer awe-inspiring landscapes and an ever-changing rainbow of colors. With a total population of just 4 million, the extent of cultivation is impressive, and there are interesting cities, splendid national parks and the amazing dinosaur graveyard of the Badlands.

MAJOR SIGHTS

The Badlands

●

**A unique region of dramatic arid landscapes bisected by
the 48km (30-mile) Dinosaur Trail.
The site of more dinosaur fossil finds than anywhere else in the world.**

SEEING THE BADLANDS

The Badlands stretch roughly north to south
through Alberta in the region of the Red Deer
River Valley. They have a stark beauty, with ocher-
hued soil that reflects the light and changes
aspect constantly, glowing as the sun strikes it.
The soil is dusty dry in summer and thick mud
when it rains, and little grows here—hence it is
bad for agriculture, it was bad for the early pioneers to travel through, and it can be bad underfoot for tourists in wet weather. Drumheller—the
"dinosaur capital of the world"—makes an excel-
lent base. As well as the Dinosaur Trail (see page 133), there's a
driving loop and numerous self-guiding walks in the Dinosaur
Provincial Park. Best of all, though, are the excellent ranger-led
hikes and the park-bus tour, with a fascinating commentary.

*You can climb the World's
Largest Dinosaur for great views*

HIGHLIGHTS

THE ROYAL TYRRELL MUSEUM

✉ Highway 838, Midland Provincial Park, Drumheller, Alberta, T0J 0Y0
☎ 403/823-7707, 888/440 4240 🕐 Daily 9–9, mid-May to early Sep; daily 10–5,
early Sep–mid-Oct; Tue–Sun and holiday Mon 10–5, mid-Oct to mid-May
💵 Adult $10, child (7–17) $6, family $30 🎧 65-minute audio guides in various lan-
guages: $4 ($7 for two) 🍴 Cafeteria: meals, grills, snacks and refreshments

*Real and replica dinosaur
skeletons at the Royal Tyrrell*

Conservators (inset) at work in Dinosaur Provincial Park

The rugged landscape of the Dinosaur Provincial Park has given up more dinosaur bones than anywhere else in the world

BASICS

⊕ 373 G16

ℹ Drumheller Tourism, P.O. Box 999, 60 – 1st Avenue West, Drumheller, Alberta, T0J 0Y0, tel 403/823-8100 www.canadianbadlands.com • A practical site with a little history, useful visitor information, and some links to other sites.

www.dinosaurvalley.com • A site about Drumheller.

🛍 Dinosaur-related souvenirs, including genuine fossil bones and teeth www.tyrrellmuseum.com

This is one of the finest museums of its kind in the world, named after Joseph Burr Tyrrell, who made the first dinosaur fossil discoveries here in 1884. It houses a paleontology collection covering a staggering 3.9 billion years, whose most dramatic specimens date from the Mesozoic Era, and there is a fantastic range of huge fossil skeletons (some real, some replicas) displayed in replicated natural surroundings. You can see scientists working on recent finds, coaxing the fossilized bones out of their rocky jackets, and view others at work at the Field Centre in the Dinosaur Provincial Park (see below).

Albertosaurus was one of the many dinosaurs discovered here, hence its name. A giant predator, it was up to 10.5m (35ft) long and weighed 2.5 tons. Not quite as big as *Tyrannosaurus rex*, but still a tremendous sight.

This statue outside the Royal Tyrrell Museum hints at what is inside

DINOSAUR PROVINCIAL PARK

⊕ 373 G16 • ✉ P.O. Box 60, Patricia, Alberta, T0J 2K0 ☎ 403/378-4342 ⏰ Daily 💵 Free, but fees for bus tours and hikes

The remarkable Dinosaur Provincial Park, around 110km (68 miles) southeast of Drumheller, is a UNESCO World Heritage Site. Within its 73sq km (28sq miles) paleontologists have unearthed in excess of 300 dinosaur skeletons—more than anywhere else in the world. There are five interpretive hiking tours and a driving loop past some of the more interesting areas. Otherwise, you can go on a guided hike or a bus tour *(late May–Sep)*. The Royal Tyrell Museum (see above) has a field station in the park where scientists are working on new discoveries. Four display areas show nearly complete skeletons in situ, protected under glass.

BACKGROUND

Centuries of rain and river erosion in the Badlands have created some fascinating landscape features, including "rills"—narrow crevices incized down a hillside by rivers of rain—and the extraordinary "hoodoos", towers of soil topped by a harder stone. The latter are formed when rain washes away the surrounding softer soil but the soil beneath the harder capstone is protected. The area has a rich seam of coal, and over 120 mines were active at the peak of the industry, between the two world wars. This has declined in the last 30 years, resulting in the abandonment of several once-thriving settlements.

Dinosaur skeleton (inset above) at the Royal Tyrrell Museum

THE DINOSAUR TRAIL

This 51km (31-mile) trail passes through some of the Badlands' most dramatic landscapes along the Red Deer River Valley and around the little town of Drumheller. There are several spots with excellent views across the region's eroded valleys. The major attractions are Horsethief and Horseshoe canyons; here, the multihued layers of the Badlands' soil has eroded into vertical walls to create something of the look of a Tuscan cathedral.

TIP

● There are some superb viewpoints you really shouldn't miss—from the top of the Horsethief and Horseshoe Canyons, and from the top of the World's Largest Dinosaur in Drumheller.

Erosion of the surrounding soft rock has formed these columns, giving the Badlands an otherworldly appearance

Calgary

Where the Prairies meet the Rockies.
Home of the "Greatest Show on Earth"—the annual Calgary Stampede.

SADDLEDOME

City lights pierce the darkness of a Calgary night

Calgary Tower still offers the best all-round view of the city

Display in the First Nations Gallery of the Glenbow Museum

RATINGS	
Good for kids	● ● ●
Historic interest	● ● ● ●
Photo stops	● ● ●
Activities	● ● ● ●

BASICS

✚ 373 F16
🏠 200, 238.– 11 Avenue S.E., Calgary, Alberta, T0G 0X8, tel 403/263-8510, 800/661-1678
www.tourismcalgary.com

Old-style Mountie at Fort Calgary Historic Park

SEEING CALGARY

Calgary sits on prairie grassland on the banks of the Bow River, and takes its influence from the cowboy culture to the east, where today thousands of miles of flat wheatland stretch away. To the west, the jagged peaks of the Rockies rise out of the horizon, their snowy caps glinting on sunny days. Calgary's compact downtown core is a concentration of highrise towers, reflecting the city's thriving economy, with an efficient light rail transit system running through its heart. The main pedestrian focus is Stephen Street Mall, which links several modern shopping malls with older streetside emporia, cafés and restaurants. To combat the sometimes severe winter weather, shopping malls are linked to office blocks by indoor walkways, either above street level or underground; the downside of this is that the outside streets can seem a little empty and lacking in atmosphere.

HIGHLIGHTS

CALGARY TOWER

✉ 101 9th Avenue S.W., Calgary, Alberta, T2P 1J8 ☎ 403/266-7171 🕐 Daily
Dominating downtown Calgary is the Calgary Tower, built in 1968 and recently refurbished. It offers one of the best panoramic views in Canada, extending from the snow-capped Rockies to the vast expanse of prairie—you can see it while enjoying a meal in the revolving Panorama Dining Room, which takes an hour to make a full circuit. The tower was constructed using the innovative "slip-forming" method, where concrete is poured continuously (in this case, for 24 days) until the required height is reached. It is 190m (623ft) high and the top of the observation tower (reached by a 62-second elevator ride) stands 1,228m (4,028ft) above sea-level.

FORT CALGARY HISTORIC PARK

✉ 750 9th Avenue S.E., Calgary, Alberta, T2G 5E1 ☎ 403/290-1875 🕐 Daily, May–mid-Oct 💲 Adult $8
The original Fort Calgary, established in 1875, served as a barracks for the North West Mounted Police, who brought law and order to this region of Canada and were sent to Calgary specifically to put a stop to whiskey trading. The fort was demolished in 1914 and the one on

The Saddledome is a prominent feature of downtown Calgary

site today is a reconstruction, built using period tools and techniques. Fort Calgary Historic Park brings history to life through interactive interpretation, dynamic exhibits, short dramatic performances and hands-on activities. There is an interpretive center with exhibits about Calgary from 1875 to the 1940s, plus the 1875 Fort site, the Deane House Historic Site and 16ha (40 acres) of riverside park and pathways.

GLENBOW MUSEUM

✉ 130 9th Avenue S.E., Calgary, Alberta, T2Q 0P3 ☎ 403/268-4100 🕔 Daily 🎟 Adult $12 weekdays, $14 weekends

This is western Canada's largest museum, designed originally around the collections of local entrepreneur Eric Harvie, who bequeathed them to the city in 1966. The museum is famed for its treatment of First Nations exhibits. The layout of the newest gallery, The Blackfoot Gallery—Nitsitapiisinni: Our Way of Life, symbolically traces the history and culture of the people who lived in the area for generations before the arrival of Europeans. Harrowing tales of suffering, both physical and emotional, culminate in the hope and cooperation of the present day. Other galleries include the Cultural History Collection, the European Collection, Many Faces, Many Paths: Art in Asia, the Military History Gallery, and an impressive library and archive.

OLYMPIC STADIUM

✉ 88 Canada Olympic Road S.W., Calgary, Alberta, T3B 5R5 ☎ 403/247-5452 🕔 Opening hours vary; call for info 🎫 2-hour guided tours: $15 per person, $40 per family. Self-guided tour booklets: $4.50

www.coda.ab.ca

In 1988, Calgary hosted the XV Winter Olympics, and this stadium was built to the west of the city. Today, it houses the Olympic Hall of Fame, with film footage, displays and exhibits, and serves as a sports center, with facilities for bobsledding, mountain biking and skiing.

PRINCE'S ISLAND PARK

Set on an artificial island in the Bow River, just off Eau Claire Market, Prince's Island is Calgary's urban park, a traffic-free oasis for visitors and citizens alike. There are formal gardens (best seen in the spring and summer) and lawns, hiking, cycling and in-line skating trails, and canoe rental for trips on the river in the summer. Sections of deciduous woodland are home to coyotes, raccoons and other wild urban dwellers.

Costumed interpreters help visitors to get the most out of the Fort Calgary Historic Park

The Glenbow Museum has displays relating to the early pioneers who conquered the West

THE CALGARY STAMPEDE

Once a year the city turns cowboy town for the spectacular, world-renowned Calgary Stampede (see page 238), held in the second week in July. The highlights of this "Wild West" extravaganza are the bull riding, steer roping and bareback riding, but there are also street fairs and entertainments, a native American village, a frontier town, a gambling hall and a range of other activities that turn the city into one big party.

The Calgary Stampede is one of Canada's most exciting annual events, recalling pioneer days

ZOO, BOTANICAL GARDEN AND PREHISTORIC PARK

✉ 1300 Zoo Road NE, Calgary, Alberta, T2E 7V6 ☎ 403/232-9300 🕐 Daily 9–5 💵 Adult $15, child (3–12) $6.50 🚊 LRT: Zoo 🍴 Kitamba Café: fast food, salads, pasta 🎁 Animal-related souvenirs
www.calgaryzoo.ab.ca

This complex occupies 32ha (79 acres) on the banks of the Bow River east of the city and plays an important role in wildlife conservation. As well as animals from around the world, it has a collection of species found in the wilds of Canada. There is a primates exhibit; a Eurasia exhibit, including tigers and snow leopards; the Prehistoric Park, with lifesize models of dinosaurs and a model volcano; and a tropical garden with butterflies and birds. Destination Africa includes a rain forest and Africa savannah, with appropriate wildlife.

HERITAGE PARK HISTORIC VILLAGE

✉ 1900 Heritage Drive S.W., Calgary, Alberta, T2V 2X3 ☎ 403/268-8500 🕐 Daily 9–5, mid-May to early Sep; Sat–Sun 9–5, early Sep–Oct 💵 Adult $13 ($22 including rides), child (3–17) $8 ($17 including rides), family $45 ($79 including rides) 🚊 LRT: Heritage, then shuttle bus 🍴 Wainwright Hotel 🎁 Gift shop
www.heritagepark.ab.ca

At nearly 27ha (67 acres), this is Canada's largest living historic village, transporting you back to the Calgary of the early 20th century. The park has over 150 old buildings with a feel of the old West, and is populated by costumed "citizens." Main Street is lined with saloons, stores and tack merchants from *c*1910, and there's an antique midway (funfair) and a working forge. You can travel back to the halcyon days of the Canadian Pacific Railway on a locomotive, or take a carriage ride through town. And between 9 and 10am you can get a free Stampede Breakfast of cowboy-style barbeque and beans.

BACKGROUND

Calgary was established very rapidly, initially around the site of Fort Calgary, built in 1875 just to the east of today's downtown, then later around the train station, which allowed trade to flourish and the population to grow. Beef was the major commodity, with large ranches dominating the surrounding areas; this gave way to wheat, and then to oil. Since the 1970s, the city, thanks to its oil and natural gas revenues, has grown to become the major commercial hub of Alberta.

Simple graves at the Métis Cemetery at Batoche

Cardston's Remington-Alberta Carriage Centre has more than 250 historic horse-drawn vehicles in its collection

BATOCHE NATIONAL HISTORIC SITE

➕ 370 J16 • Rosthern, Saskatchewan, S0K 3R0 ☎ 306/423-6227 🕐 Daily 9–5, early May–Sep 🎟 Adult $5.75, child (6 and over) $3, family $14.50 💻 📖 www.parkscanada.gc.ca

Batoche, high on a bluff above the South Saskatchewan River, was the stronghold of the Métis people (a mixed French and First Nations population) and the place where they made their final stand. Their leader, Louis Riel, chose it as his headquarters when he declared a provisional regional government during the rebellion over land titles in 1885. Government forces were sent to quell the uprising, and in the ensuing battle the insurgents were quashed; many Métis died.

Little remains of the village, today, save for a few original buildings and a modern interpretive center, where staff in period costumes act out the role of the Métis, but it holds a special interest in the history of the nation. **Don't miss** There are simple Métis graves in the churchyard, the highest point of the site.

CALGARY
See pages 134–136.

CARDSTON

➕ 373 F17 ℹ On Highway 2, south of Fort MacLeod, Alberta, T0K 0K0 ☎ 403/653-2499

This tiny town in southern Alberta has one major claim to fame—a monumental Mormon tabernacle *(only grounds open to non Mormons)*, the largest outside the USA, dedicated in 1923. A group of Mormons left the enclave in Utah in 1887 and founded a settlement here, and today the town has a population of 3,500, the single-story homes overshadowed by the temple.

The Remington-Alberta Carriage Centre *(daily)* has one of the largest collections of horse-drawn vehicles in North America. Sit by a campfire surrounded by pioneer wagons or admire the elegance of the landau, and see the horses that pull them.

The town's most famous daughter was actress Fay Wray, who shot to fame in the movie *King Kong* (1933) as the girl carried by the gorilla to the top of the Empire State Building.

CHURCHILL

➕ 371 M13 ℹ Parks Canada Visitor Reception Centre, Bayport Plaza, Churchill, Manitoba, R0B 0E0 ☎ 204/675-8863 www.parkscanada.gc.ca

Self-styled "Polar Bear Capital of the World," Churchill sits on the shores of Hudson Bay at the mouth of the Churchill River. The town was established in 1929, though the first European, Danish explorer Jens Munck, arrived in 1619. The Hudson's Bay Company built a post here in 1717 to trade and store furs for shipment to England.

However, it's not just the polar bears that are the drawcard here: Churchill is a veritable wildlife paradise, with beluga whales arriving during the summer, seals resident year-round, caribou migrating through the region twice a year, and over 250 species of birds nesting in the summer months. And, in winter, the spectacular aurora borealis lights up the town's night sky.

Just a short boat trip across the river from the town is Fort Prince of Wales *(daily, Jun–mid Nov)*, constructed by the Hudson's Bay Company (1731–71) as its trading post and protection against rival French colonial interests. The Eskimo Museum *(Mon pm, Tue–Sat all day, summer;*

Mon–Sat pm, winter) in town, is devoted to Inuit history and lifestyle.
Don't miss The polar bears are a highlight of any trip to Churchill.

CYPRESS HILLS INTER-PROVINCIAL PARK

➕ 373 G17 • 27km (17 miles) south of Maple Creek, Saskatchewan, S0N 1N0 🎟 Day pass $7 ℹ Loch Leven, tel 306/662-5411, Mon–Fri 8.15–4.30 year round. Elkwater, tel 403/893-3777, daily 9–5 mid-May to early Sep www.cypresshills.com

Rising 600m (1,968ft) from the surrounding prairie, Cypress Hills are the highest land between the Rockies and Labrador. The 18,400ha (45,448-acre) lush forested environment is an oasis amid millions of hectares of grassland. It supports rare wildflowers (best in spring) and more than 200 species of birds, and at its heart is Fort Walsh National Historic Site (see page 139), birthplace of the Mounties.

Shared between Alberta and Saskatchewan, this was Canada's first interprovincial park, but back in the 1860s and '70s it was a hub of the notorious whiskey smuggling trade from the US.

In Saskatchewan, the 22km (13.6-mile) unmade single-track Gap Road is similar to that used by the first Mounties, while Loch Leven is home to the park administration. In the Alberta sector the major settlement is Elkwater, a pretty town on the banks of Elkwater Lake. From here it's 5km (3 miles) or so to Horseshoe Canyon for panoramic views of the prairies to the north, while Head of the Mountain offers views south over the border into Montana.
Don't miss The Gap Road, leading through the heart of the park, gives an idea of the terrain the early settlers had to cross.

The vast World Waterpark is just one of many attractions at West Edmonton Mall. Detail from totem pole (inset) at the Legislature

EDMONTON

Canada's "Gateway to the North."

Edmonton, the most northerly of Canada's major cities, originally grew around a Hudson's Bay Company post called Edmonton House, founded in 1795 to trade in furs with the local Cree and Blackfoot tribes. At the end of the 19th century, the population doubled with the Klondike Gold Rush. In 1905, Alberta entered Canadian Confederation and Edmonton was chosen as the provincial capital, and in 1912 it amalgamated with the nearby town of Strathcona—today an area of early 20th-century architecture with one-of-a-kind boutiques, cafés, restaurants, antiques markets and theaters.

In downtown Edmonton, City Hall is an interesting modern glass structure built for the city's centennial in 1992. Other buildings flanking Sir Winston Churchill Square (the city's arts district) include the Art Gallery, the Citadel Theatre and the Francis Winspear Centre for Music, home to the Edmonton Symphony Orchestra. A short walk south is the Provincial Museum of Alberta *(daily 9–5),* which has a range of galleries explaining the natural and social history of the province, with particular emphasis on First Nations' culture.

South of the river, just across from downtown on A Street, is the Muttart Conservatory *(Mon–Fri 9–6, Sat–Sun 11–6),* where tropical and exotic gardens are housed in a surreal collection of glass pyramids that were designed by Peter Hemingway in the early 1970s.

ALBERTA LEGISLATIVE ASSEMBLY

☎ 780/427-2826 🚋 LRT Grandlin 🎫 Daily tours from visitor center on 107th Street: hourly 9–noon, half-hourly 12.30–4, May–mid-Oct; Mon–Fri hourly 9–3, Sat–Sun and holidays hourly noon–4, rest of year

West of downtown is the Alberta Legislative Assembly, an imposing construction of 1913 with a dome and portico.

FORT EDMONTON PARK

✉ Fox Drive and Whitemud Drive, Edmonton, Alberta ☎ 780/496-8787 🕐 Mon–Fri, mid-May to mid-Jun; daily, mid-Jun–early Sep 🎫 Adult $8.25, child $4.50, family $26

Fort Edmonton was the earliest settlement here, and this re-creation takes you back to the founding of the community. It also has representations of the main street as it was in 1885, 1905 and 1920, and costumed staff and a historic streetcar add to the atmosphere.

RATINGS

Good for kids	●●
Historic interest	●●●
Specialist shopping	●●●
Activities	●●●

BASICS

➕ 373 F15

ℹ️ Edmonton Tourism, 9797 Jasper Avenue, Edmonton, Alberta, T5J 0Y9, tel 780/426-4715

www.tourism.ede.org

IF YOU'VE TIME

HISTORIC STREETCAR

✉ Edmonton Radial Railway Society, P.O. Box 45040, Landsdowne P.O., Edmonton, Alberta, T6H 5Y1

☎ 780/496-1464 🕐 Daily 11–4, mid-May to early Sep (10am–11pm during Edmonton Fringe Festival); Fri–Sun and hols 10–4, early Sep–Oct 🎫 Adult $3, child under 6 free, family $10

www.edmonton-radial-railway.ab.ca

For a fun trip, take the Historic Streetcar from the Legislative Assembly to the Old Strathcona district

WEST EDMONTON MALL

✉ 170 Street, tel 780/444-5200

This is the largest shopping mall in the world, with 800 stores, a waterpark, a fairground, the Deep Sea Adventure ride, a skating rink, and the Dolphin Show. (See also pages 231–232 and 237.)

Inside the stockade at the Fort Battleford National Historic Site

A realistic depiction of ingenious First Nations hunting methods at the Head-Smashed-In Buffalo Jump interpretive center

FORT BATTLEFORD NATIONAL HISTORIC SITE

⊞ 370 H16 • PO Box 70, Battleford, Saskatchewan, S0M 0E0 ☎ 306/937-2621 🕐 Daily 9–5, mid-May to early Sep 🎟 Adult $5.75, child (6–16) $3, family $14.50 🖵 🏛
www.parkscanada.gc.ca

Headquarters of the North West Mounted Police from 1876 until 1924, when it was abandoned, Fort Battleford has been restored to offer an insight into the role of the 19th-century Mountie in a troubled and developing land. In 1885, during the Métis uprising, when First Nations warriors converged on Battleford, the stockade provided refuge to over 500 settlers. Standing firm against its attackers, it was in part instrumental in the uprising's failure.

Today, several of the original buildings have been restored and equipped in the style of the times. The barracks now house an interpretive center, with photographs, documents and other objects that bring the history to life, while costumed staff act as Mounties going about their daily duties. The nearby Fred Light Museum *(daily, mid-May–early Sep)* has military uniforms from the 1880s and the world wars. **Don't miss** The fort's original buildings contain genuine period furniture.

FORT WALSH NATIONAL HISTORIC SITE

⊞ 373 G17 • P.O. Box 278, Maple Creek, Saskatchewan, S0N 1N0 ☎ 306/662-2645 (May–Oct), 306/662-2645 (off season) 🕐 Daily, mid-May–early Sep 🎟 Adult $7, child (6–16) $3.75, family $15 🖵
www.parkscanada.pch.gc.ca

Set in the lee of rolling hills and woodland on the banks of Battle Creek, Fort Walsh was an important center of law and order, and

of Canadian justice. From 1878 to 1883 it was the North West Mounted Police headquarters, and a base for their efforts to control the illicit whiskey trade from the US. And, when Chief Sitting Bull and a band of Sioux warriors escaped here across the US border after the Battle of Little Big Horn in 1876, the Mounties under James Walsh (after whom the fort is named) controlled the situation. Eventually, Walsh persuaded Sitting Bull to head back over the border to life on a reservation. Between 1942 and 1968, Fort Walsh was used by the Royal Canadian Mounted Police as a ranch for breeding police horses.

Today, visitors can take a tour of the buildings, the townsite, two cemeteries, and the Farwell Trading Post—a reconstructed 1872 whiskey-trading post. Costumed staff re-create the pioneering atmosphere of the time. **Don't miss** The whiskey den re-creates a 19th-century illegal liquor stockpile and trading post.

HEAD-SMASHED-IN BUFFALO JUMP

⊞ 373 F17 • Highway 785 off Highway 2, north of Fort Macleod, Alberta, T0L 0Z0 ☎ 403/553-2731 🕐 Daily 9–6, mid-May to mid-Sep; 10–5, rest of year 🎟 Adult $8.50, child (7–17) $4, family $19, mid-May to mid-Sep; adult $6.50, child $3, family $15 rest of year
www.head-smashed-in.com

Where the foothills of the Rockies meet the Great Plains, the bluntly named Head-Smashed-In safeguards one of the oldest, largest and best-preserved buffalo jumps in existence, listed by UNESCO as a World Heritage Site in 1981. For over 5,500 years buffalo were driven to their deaths over this precipice, a traditional part of Native Plains culture. And, despite the popular image of

hundreds of dead buffalo, mass killings were not the norm—tribes are believed to have killed only as many animals as they needed.

An interpretive center, built into the sandstone cliff, explains the phenomenon in an entertaining way via a series of dioramas that draw visitors toward the climax—several fearful, lifesize buffalo standing at the edge of a cliff. **Don't miss** View the actual jump site—from both top and bottom.

REGINA

See page 140.

RIDING MOUNTAIN NATIONAL PARK

⊞ 371 K17 🚹 Wasagaming, Manitoba, R0J 2H0 ☎ 204/848-7275, 888/707-8480 🕐 Visitor center: daily 9–5.30, mid-May to late Jun and Sep–mid-Oct; daily 9–8, late Jun–Aug; closed mid-Oct to mid-May (administration office deals with winter inquiries) 🎟 Day passes: adult $5, child (6–16) $2.50, family $9 🚌 Grey Goose Bus Lines (summer only) to Wasagaming
www.parkscanada.gc.ca

At the meeting place of three distinct landscapes—deciduous forest, boreal forest and aspen parkland—that meld over part of the Manitoba Escarpment, Riding Mountain is home to a wide variety of wildlife and plants. Wasagaming, the park's low-key main townsite, sits on the southern shore of Clear Lake, the largest stretch of water here and the focus of summer watersports and fishing. Over 400km (248 miles) of hiking trails make this one of the most accessible parks in western Canada, and back-country trails are open to mountain bikers. Anishinabe Village at Shawenequanape Kipichewin on Lake Katherine *(mid-May to mid-Sep)* offers the opportunity to experience First Nations culture. **Don't miss** Sleep out in a tepee.

A Royal Saskatchewan Museum exhibit (above) and Regina's Legislative Building (inset)

REGINA

Home of the famous Royal Canadian Mounted Police.

The capital of Saskatchewan, Regina—named in honor of Queen Victoria—rises up out of a vast area of wheat-producing prairie as if out of nowhere. The city was founded in 1882 as the new provincial capital, replacing the original capital, Battleford, farther north. Located where the new Canadian Pacific Railway crossed the Wascana Creek, Regina was seen as a gesture of validation for the railroad and a nod toward the importance of communications, but the decision caused a great deal of controversy at the time. The new capital was incorporated as a city in 1903 and Saskatchewan became a province in 1905. In 1912 a tornado destroyed it, and what is seen today—a small downtown core of high-rise office blocks, surrounded by pleasant low-rise residential areas—is the redevelopment that followed the disaster

RATINGS

Good for kids	● ● ●
Historic interest	● ● ● ●
Photo stops	● ● ●
Activities	● ● ●

BASICS

✚ 370 J17

ℹ Tourism Regina, P.O. Box 3335, Regina, Saskatchewan, S4P 3H1, tel 306/789-5099, 800-661-5099
www.tourismregina.com • Very useful site with everything you need to know about visiting Regina

THE ROYAL CANADIAN MOUNTED POLICE

The RCMP moved to Regina in 1882, some 10 years after the force was established at Fort Walsh (see page 139). Although the headquarters moved to Ottawa in 1920, the Training Academy, or Depot Division as it's officially known, remained here. There's a good museum *(daily 8–6.45, mid-May to early Sep; 10–4.45, rest of year)* within the academy, telling the story of what must be the world's most famous police force. The Sunset Retreat features a colorful drill display.

WASCANA CENTER

South of the largely unremarkable downtown area is the real heart of Regina, the Wascana Center, one of Canada's largest urban parks, covering 121ha (299 acres) around the undulating line of the Wascana Creek. It's a focus for all sorts of outdoor activities, from birding to picnics, but several museums and galleries are also located here. The Royal Saskatchewan Museum *(daily)* has three main galleries—Earth Sciences (geology), Life Sciences (ecology) and an interesting First Nations Gallery. The collection in the MacKenzie Art Gallery *(daily, year-round)* includes regional, national and international works, including famous names such as Henry Moore and Andy Warhol, plus more than 650 contributions by Saskatchewan artists. The Saskatchewan Science Centre *(daily, year-round)* is great fun for children, staging demonstrations with irresistible themes: Cotton Candy Show, Mud Madness, Bat Show, and Blood and Guts Show.

The Delta Bessborough Hotel blends harmoniously with the city architecture that stretches back from the river

SASKATOON

A friendly city with a lively arts scene.

Saskatoon was founded on the banks of the South Saskatchewan River in 1883 by John Neilson Lake, a representive of the Temperance Colonization Society, who had secured a government grant of land. Unfortunately, Lake's efforts to establish an abstemious settlement were not altogether successful, and in the census of 1901, the population of Saskatoon was registered as a mere 113. With the opening of the Canadian Pacific Railway, however, people gradually began to look upon it as a decent place to live. Farming remains the primary industry hereabouts, and the city has become a major hub for agricultural distribution.

CITY MUSEUMS

The history of Saskatoon c1910 can be relived at the Saskatchewan Western Development Museum *(daily)*, on Lorne Avenue South, which features the longest indoor museum street in Canada. A series of dioramas and interpretive displays focuses on agricultural development in the last 150 years. The city's railroad heritage is celebrated in the Saskatchewan Railway Museum *(daily, May–Sep)*, where visitors can take rides on working stock. The Mendel Museum *(daily; free)* on Spadina Crescent East, is the city's premier art gallery, with a revolving exhibit of contemporary and historical works by local, national and international artists.

On Highway 11, the Wanuskewin Heritage Park *(daily)* is Saskatoon's First Nations interpretive center, depicting the lifestyle of the Northern Plains tribes. There are tepees, dioramas explaining the techniques hunters would use to catch and kill buffalo, and a café offering a taste of First Nations cuisine.

OTHER ATTRACTIONS

Saskatoon's most famous son was John G. Diefenbaker, who became Canada's 13th prime minister, and he is remembered at the Diefenbaker Canada Centre *(daily)* on Diefenbaker Place, where his office and cabinet room are displayed with a large archive relating to Canadian history and politics.

Saskatoon has five theaters and during the summer months there are various open-air concerts. You can also take a river cruise from Mendel Gallery Wharf.

Exhibit at the Wanuskewin Heritage Park, Saskatoon

RATINGS	
Good for kids	●●●
Historic interest	●●●
Activities	●●●●

BASICS
✠ 370 H16
🛈 Tourism Saskatoon, 6–350 Idylwyld Drive North, Saskatoon, Saskatchewan, S7L 0Z1, tel 306/242-1206, 800/567-2444
www.tourismsaskatoon.com • Saskatoon Shines! Lots of information, including a photo/video gallery.

Bronze bison at the Wanuskewin Heritage Park

Winnipeg

The geographic heart of Canada and the edge of the prairies.

THE SIGHTS

SEEING WINNIPEG

Winnipeg is the capital of Manitoba province. Downtown covers several city blocks around the Portage and Main crossroads, and is an eclectic mix of modern glass-sided skyscrapers and early 20th-century brick and stone edifices. An underground shopping mall comes into its own in the harsh Winnipeg winters.

Lower Fort Garry National Historic Site, north of Winnipeg. Winnipeg's Legislative Building (inset right) is splendidly imposing

RATINGS	
Good for kids	●●●●
Historic interest	●●●●●
Photo stops	●●●
Shopping	●●●

HIGHLIGHTS

THE EXCHANGE DISTRICT
🚩 314–363 Albert Street, Winnipeg, Manitoba, R3B 1G4, tel 204/942-6716
The Exchange District is a National Historic Site, and its most interesting buildings include Confederation Life, a 1912 skyscraper; the 1903 British Bank of North America, the oldest bank building on "bankers' row"; the 1913 Pantages Theatre, with its lavish interior; and the 1903 Criterion Hotel. Observe trading in action from the viewing gallery of the Winnipeg Commodity Exchange *(Mon–Fri)*, Canada's only agricultural futures and options exchange. This regenerated district also has a lively collection of arts companies, galleries, boutiques, restaurants, and nightclubs. The Centennial Centre (see page 234) is home to the Winnipeg Royal Ballet, Opera Company and Symphony Orchestra. Oseredok *(daily)*, the Ukrainian cultural and educational center, commemorates the Ukrainians who settled in Manitoba through folk art and musical instruments, tools and an art gallery.

Old-style street lamps in The Forks National Historic Site

MANITOBA MUSEUM
✉ 190 Rupert Avenue, Winnipeg, Manitoba, R3B 0N2 ☎ 204/943-2835 🕐 Daily, mid-May to early Sep; Tue–Sun, rest of year 🎫 Adult $6.50, child $5, family $20
This spectacular museum presents a history of the province, from its fossil records (dating from 80 million years ago) to the industries that drive it today. The main theme is man and the environment, and an excellent range of dioramas depicts Manitoba's various ecosystems, with beautifully preserved specimens of animals and birds.
One gallery charts the Hudson's Bay Company's development, with a re-created company store and a York boat used to ply the river systems on trading missions. A highlight exhibit is the replica of the two-masted ketch *Nonsuch*, which sailed from England into Hudson Bay in 1668 to found trade with Canada.
The Grasslands Gallery examines European settlers and their effects on the prairie grasslands. The rise of Winnipeg city is illustrated in the Urban Gallery, with its re-created 1920s street.

THE FORKS NATIONAL HISTORIC SITE
✉ Main Street and Waterfront Drive, Winnipeg, Manitoba, R3C 1N7
☎ 204/983-7752 🕐 Daily 🎫 Free 🚌 38
www.theforks.com
On a bend in the river, this refurbished district is Winnipeg's favorite place to gather, for visitors and locals alike. The Forks

combines leafy parks, river walkways, the national historic site, an excellent marketplace, eating, shopping, and a host of arts organizations in regenerated Canadian Pacific Railway yard buildings.

York boat diorama in the Manitoba Museum

ST. BONIFACE CATHEDRAL

✉ 190 Avenue de la Cathédrale, St. Boniface, Manitoba, R2H 0H7 ☎ 204/238-7304 🕒 Daily 🚻 Free

Across the river from The Forks, and built in 1968, St. Boniface Cathedral incorporates the haunting remains of the original 1908 Gothic Revival church, which was destroyed by fire. The cathedral cemetery is the final resting place of many important French and Métis citizens, including Louis Riel (see page 28), seen by Manitobans as the founder of the province, and two of the earliest bishops—Provencher and Tache. The cathedral museum has displays relating to the rise of the Métis.

DALNAVERT NATIONAL HISTORIC SITE

✉ 61 Carlton Street, Winnipeg, Manitoba, R3C 1N7 ☎ 204/943-2835 🕒 Tue–Thu and Sat–Sun, Mar–Dec; Sat–Sun, rest of year 🚻 Adult $4, child $2, family $8

This is a typical well-to-do family home of the late Victorian era. Built in Queen Anne Revival style, it rejoices in luxuries of the day, including indoor plumbing, central heating and electric lighting, and is furnished and decorated in keeping with its period. The neoclassical Legislative Building, in a pleasant park nearby, overlooks the Assiniboine River.

WINNIPEG ART GALLERY

✉ 300 Memorial Boulevard, Winnipeg, Manitoba, R3C 1V1 ☎ 204/786-6641 🕒 Tue and Thu–Sun 11–5, Wed 11–9; closed Mon 🚻 Adult $6, child (6–12) $3, family $15

Just north of the Legislative Building, this lively gallery, founded in 1912, is designed by local architect Gustavo da Roza to look like a ship rising out of the water. The specialist collection comprises over 22,500 works, from a fifth-century AD Roman bust to 20th-century videos. The emphasis is on Manitoba artists, but international names are also represented. The museum has the world's largest collection of contemporary Inuit art. Other exhibits include Gothic and Renaissance altar paintings and tapestries, mid-18th-century decorative pottery, and around 200 photographs by André Kertész, one of the founding fathers of modern photography.

BASICS

🗺 371 L17

ℹ 279 Portage Ave., Winnipeg, Manitoba, R3B 2B4, tel 204/943-1970; Mon–Fri 8.30–4.30

www.tourism.winnipeg.mb.ca

TIP

● Free concerts and street entertainment are staged in summer in the Old Market Square.

The Golden Boy tops the dome of the Legislative Building

IF YOU'VE TIME

MANITOBA CHILDREN'S MUSEUM

✉ 45 Forks Market Road, Winnipeg, Manitoba, R3C 4T8 ☎ 204/924-4000 🕐 Daily 💰 Adult $5.50, child $6, family $25

Right by the river, this is a wonderland for play and exploration. The Wonderworks Gallery encourages children to get to grips with building cities using child-size equipment. In the Tree and Me Gallery, children can experience the rainforest environment and dress as their favorite animal. The Livewire Gallery enables children to film themselves and then edit the film. All Aboard has a 1954 diesel engine pulling early 20th-century carriages. In the TV studio, children can present their own shows or operate the cameras. (See also page 238.)

Nonsuch *ketch diorama in the Manitoba Museum*

THE FRENCH QUARTER

On the St. Boniface (eastern) banks of the Red River, the French Quarter reflects the city's diverse population and gives a real taste of the city's history. From the early 18th century this area was a main settlement of the French and Métis population, and now offers some interesting attractions, including the Grey Nuns Museum, in an 1846 convent, the Precious Blood Church and St. Boniface Cathedral (see page 143).

The Exchange District is an area of restored, converted warehouses

LOWER FORT GARRY

✉ 5981 Highway 9, St. Andrews, Manitoba, R1A 4A8 ☎ 877/534-3678 🕐 Daily 9–5, mid-May–early Sep 💰 Adult $5.75, child (6–16) $3, family $16.50 🚌 Beaver Lines bus from Winnipeg 🍴 Snacks and full meals 🎁 Lower Fort Garry mementoes

Lower Fort Garry, founded in 1881 and the oldest stone trading post still intact in western Canada, lies 32km (20 miles) north of Winnipeg and was a key component in the Hudson's Bay Company network. The bulk of trade here was in farm produce, which the company bought to feed its workers farther north on Hudson Bay itself. From the 1840s, the company expanded the fort to include a brewery, distillery, sawmill and lime kilns. The original stone enclosure is still intact, and costumed staff describe life in the mid-1800s.

MENNONITE HERITAGE VILLAGE

✉ P.O. Box 1136, Steinbach, Manitoba, R0A 2A0 ☎ 204/326-9661 🕐 Mon–Sat 10–5, Sun noon–5, May–Jun and Sep; Mon–Sat 10–6, Sun noon–6, Jul–Aug 💰 Adult $8, child (6–12) $2 or (13 and over) $4, family $20 🍴 Livery Barn Restaurant: traditional Mennonite dishes 🎁 General store with Mennonite crafts, seeds, books and souvenirs

Set in a 16ha (40-acre) park, 61km (38 miles) south of Winnipeg, the Heritage Village authentically re-creates the traditional lifestyle of Mennonites, a Protestant German-speaking sect, from the 17th century to the present day. There are more than 30 buildings and monuments here, including a windmill, a schoolhouse c1919, a machine shed with old tools and equipment, a barn and animal pens, an 1881 church, and various dwellings.

BACKGROUND

Winnipeg was founded as a Hudson's Bay Company outpost for trading with local First Nations tribes who hunted the prairies. The rival North West Company set up here in 1738. In 1821 the Earl of Selkirk purchased land locally, and the area was settled by Scots fleeing from the Highland Clearances. Winnipeg was declared a city in 1873 and, with the arrival of the Trans-Canada Railway, became the Gateway to the West. Now the capital of Manitoba, the city's heyday was c1900–1930, and the Legislature Building, topped by the shimmering statue *Golden Boy*, was completed during this period.

BRITISH COLUMBIA AND THE ROCKIES

Canada's most westerly province, British Columbia is a land of spectacular coastal scenery, with deep fiords and high peaks surrounding the cities of Vancouver and Victoria. Inland, the Rocky Mountains, shared with Alberta, offer some of the world's most magnificent scenery, with great glaciers and glittering lakes.

MAJOR SIGHTS

Cruise ships dock beside the imitation sails at Canada Place

Chinese characters and motifs announce you're in Chinatown

Granville Island is a lively and entertaining part of the city

VANCOUVER

Set on the deep Burrard Inlet of the Strait of Georgia, and protected from the Pacific Ocean by the island of the same name, BC's largest city has one of the finest sites of any in the world. To the north, the snow-capped Coast Mountains rise abruptly above the city, to the south, the peaks of the Cascades are visible, and to the west lie the mountains of Vancouver Island. This gives Vancouverites an enviable lifestyle with opportunities for skiing, golf, sailing, and hiking available close at hand. And despite the dense forest of downtown buildings, there's breathing space in enormous Stanley Park, one of the world's loveliest urban parks. See plan on pages 362–363.

CANADA PLACE

✚ 363 E2 • 100–999 Canada Place Way, Vancouver, British Columbia, V6C 3E1 ☎ 604/775-8687 ◷ Daily 🎫 Free 🚌 1 on Burrard; 3, 4, 6, 7, 8 on Granville 🚇 Skytrain: Waterfront 🔲 🏛

Stroll the boardwalks at this stunning waterfront building for an overall impression of Vancouver's beautiful setting. The majestic white building, with five vast fiberglass sails, the centerpiece, was designed by architect Eberhard Zeidler and constructed as the Canada Pavilion for World's Fair, Expo '86. In the following year it became home to the Vancouver Trade and Convention Center. Today, Canada Place is also home to an IMAX movie theater and chic hotels, restaurants and stores. Vancouver's cruise ship terminal is here—a huge cruise liner alongside Canada Place is one of the signature images of the city.

CHINATOWN

✚ 363 F3 • Between East Pender, Abbot, Gore and Keefer streets, Vancouver, British Columbia 🚌 19, 22 east of the city on Pender Street 🚇 🔲 🍴 🏛

From Vancouver public library, a pedestrian walkway called the Silk Route (signed by banners on streetlights) leads through the impressive Millennium Chinese Gate into Vancouver's Chinatown, with its lively milieu of authentic restaurants, supermarkets, apothecaries, and stores. East Pender Street and the parallel Keefer house the bulk of the eateries, where you can find delicious dim sum, and on summer weekend evenings, *(Fri–Sun 6pm–11pm, Jun–Sep)* there's a night market, with everything from CDs and clothing to food specialties.
Don't miss Both Chinese New Year (Jan/Feb) and the Spring Festival are marked by lively events in Chinatown.

GRANVILLE ISLAND

✚ 362 B5 • Across False Creek, south of downtown 🛈 1398 Cartwright Street, Vancouver, British Columbia, V6H 3R8, tel: 604/666-5784 ◷ Information Center: daily 9–6. Public market: daily 9–6, Feb–Dec; Tue–Sun 9–6, Jan 🎫 Granville Island: free. One admission for all museums: adult $6.50, youth (13–18) $5.50, child (4–12) $3.50 🚤 Aquabus 🚌 Bus 50 links to the aquabus station 🔲 🍴 🏛 www.granvilleisland.com

A mélange of art schools, studios and workshop theaters makes Granville Island one of the most vibrant cultural areas in Vancouver. Add the wonderful bustling food market, one of the best in North America, the inviting eateries, stores and the weekend street entertainers, and you have a mix that attracts visitors and locals alike throughout the year.
   Three minor museums are housed under one roof: the Sport Fishing Museum, Model Train Museum and Model Ship Museum *(all open daily 10–5.30)*, and don't miss the Net Loft *(daily 10–6)* and its surrounding galleries, with a comprehensive range of quality arts and crafts. Originally swampland, the area was reclaimed after World War I for shipbuilding and ironworks. When the industry declined, the site became derelict, but an ambitious regeneration scheme in the early 1970s transformed the area into the attractive waterside area it is today.

MARITIME MUSEUM

✚ 362 A4 • 1095 Ogden Avenue, Vancouver, British Columbia, V6J 1A3 ☎ 604/257-8300 ◷ Daily, mid-May–early Sep; Tue–Sun, rest of year 🎫 Adult $8, child (6–18) $5.50, family $18 🚌 2, 22 🚤 Water taxi from Granville Island 🏛 www.vmm.bc.ca

The prize exhibit of Vancouver's Maritime Museum is the Royal Canadian Mounted Police ship *St. Roch*, restored to her 1944 appearance and housed in an impressive glass display building since 1966. The first ship to navigate the Northwest Passage between Baffin Island and the Beaufort Sea, the *St. Roch* plied the route as a supply ship for RCMP depots in the Arctic between 1928 and 1948.
   The museum tells stories of pirates, shipwrecks, cruising and the shipping trade, and illustrates Vancouver's strong ties with the sea with models, photographs and memorabilia. Marine enthusiasts can browse in the museum's library of research material and books relating to maritime history and technology.

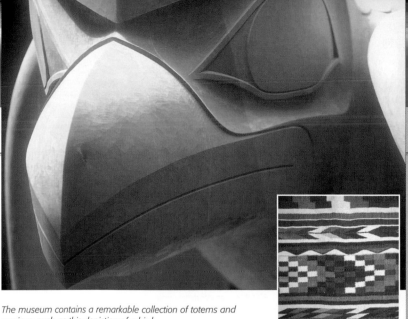

The museum contains a remarkable collection of totems and carvings, such as this depiction of a bird

The collection includes some fine textile exhibits

MUSEUM OF ANTHROPOLOGY

A vast store of ethnographic and archeological objects.

This museum displays objects and art of the local Haida, Salish, Tsimshian, and Kwaiuti First Nations people, and is custodian of a vast archive relating to Haida traditional practices and social history. It was created at a time when the voices of First Nations were being heard, perhaps for the first time, in government circles—their demands for rights over tribal lands was a major political issue during the latter decades of the 20th century, with many tribes receiving land and millions of dollars in settlement of claims. The intense focus on First Nations' rights prompted an interest in their traditions, in contrast to efforts throughout the 19th and early 20th centuries to crush native ways.

THE COLLECTION

Although the collection covers all the tribes in British Columbia, precedence is given to the Haida, the most artistically creative of all North America's native peoples. It was they who fashioned totems as historical records (the forest of poles in the totem gallery is one of the highlights), carved exquisite jewelry and decorated household items.

Haida artist Bill Reid (1920–98) attracted world renown. A sculptor, carver, canoe-builder, poet, and illustrator, Reid was at the forefront of the rebirth of First Nations' artistic endeavor, working tirelessly to keep all aspects of the culture alive. The collection of his work here includes the powerful *The Raven and the First*, depicting the legend of the first Haida men, and the gallery also has fine examples of his jewelry, masks and sculpture, all in traditional materials.

THE BUILDING

The museum building was designed by Arthur Erikson in 1976. The huge expanse of the Great Hall, created to reflect traditional longhouses, is a perfect setting for the fantastic totem collection, and is linked to the outside by more totems set in the gardens.

Two traditional Haida longhouses sit at Point Grey, overlooking the ocean. The Masterpiece Gallery houses jewelry and ceremonial masks, along with much of Bill Reid's work. In the Visible Storage Galleries, 15,000 objects are stored in glass display cabinets and pull-out drawers.

RATINGS				
Good for kids	●	●		
Historic interest	●	●	●	●
Value for money	●	●	●	
Specialist shopping	●	●	●	

MAKE A DAY OF IT

● Combine your trip to the museum with a visit to the University of British Columbia Botanical Garden close by.

BASICS

✚ 381 C17 • 6393 Northwest Marine Drive, Vancouver, British Columbia, V6T 1Z2

☎ 604/822-5087

🕐 Wed–Mon 10–5, Tue 10–9, mid-May–Aug; Tue 11–9, Wed–Sun 11–5, rest of year 💷 Adult $9, child (6–17) $7, free entry Tue 5–9 🚌 4, 9, 10, 25, 99 to UBC 🎫 Free self-guided tours available in English, French, Italian, German, Spanish, Korean, Chinese and Japanese; free gallery walks (twice daily) 📖 Multilingual mini-guides: free 🍴 Café with a range of snacks 🛍 Gifts, books and souvenirs with a northwest coast theme www.moa.ubc.ca • An easy-to-use, informative site with information on the collections and special exhibits

Capilano Gorge has the world's longest suspension footbridge

Lonsdale Quay blends modern stores and an old-style market

The geodesic dome of Science World is a distinctive landmark

THE SIGHTS

VANCOUVER

NORTH SHORE

✚ Off map, 363 F1 🛈 North Shore Tourism, 102–124 West 1st Street, North Vancouver, British Columbia, V7M 3N3, tel 604/987-4488 🚌 247 (Capilano/Grouse Mountain); 255, 257, 258 (Wyn Valley); 246 (Park Royal) www.nvchamber.bc.ca

The North Shore has a different flavor from the rest of the city, and its own special attractions. There is a lively arts scene here, and the North Vancouver Museum and Archives *(Tue–Sun pm)* is the best of a clutch of museums charting the region's development. Shoppers can enjoy the Park Royal mall and the market at Lonsdale Quay.

North Shore is also a gateway to some of Vancouver's best outdoor attractions. Hills rise steeply behind this part of the city, offering expansive views. Just 3km (2 miles) north of Lion's Gate Bridge, the Capilano River Regional Park protects temperate rainforest and huge Douglas firs, and a fish ladder takes salmon around the Cleveland Dam to their traditional spawning beds. About 3km (2 miles) farther north, Grouse Mountain has a cable car to whisk visitors to a base station for panoramic views over the city. Lighthouse Park, about 8km (5 miles) west of Lion's Gate Bridge, is 75ha (185 acres) of coastal virgin forest containing some of the largest Douglas firs in Greater Vancouver, with trails leading through the forest and down to the lighthouse. **Don't miss** Lighthouse Park has some great views.

SCIENCE WORLD

✚ 363 F4 • 1455 Quebec Street, Vancouver, British Columbia, V6A 3Z7 ☎ 604/443-7440, 604/443-7443 (recorded information) 🕐 Mon–Fri 10–5, Sat–Sun and public holidays 10–6;

closed Christmas 💲 Adult $12.75, child (4–18) $8.50. Omnimax theater: single film (daytime), adult $11.25, child $9; double film (evening), adult $13.30, child $10.50; combination ticket, adult $17.75, child $13.50; family $42.50 🚌 3, 8, 19, 22 🚇 Skytrain: Science World 🛒 ♿ www.scienceworld.bc.ca

Built as part of the 1986 World's Fair, the large geodesic dome of Science World appears like a lunar module on the southern shore of False Creek and is home to a series of hands-on science exhibits. Daily scientific demonstrations are given on the stage at the heart of the ground level. On the middle level, main galleries explore the natural environment, and special areas are given over to children: Eureka! suggests experiments with air- and water-powered machines, and explores the workings of gears, electric circuits and wheels; Kidspace has children building dams and flying saucers, and finding out about what happens in a tornado. The upper floor houses Omnimax, a curved screen showing the latest blockbuster movies.

STANLEY PARK
Sees page 150–151.

VANCOUVER ART GALLERY

✚ 363 D3 • 750 Hornby Street, Vancouver, British Columbia, V6Z 2H7 ☎ 604/662-4719 🕐 Fri–Wed 10–5.30, Thu 10–10; closed Mon in winter. Temporary exhibitions: Sun 10–5.30 💲 Adult $12.50, child (over 12) $8, family $30 🚌 1, 5, 15, and tourist trolley 🛒 ♿ www.vanartgallery.bc.ca

Housed in the 1910 former Vancouver courthouse, this gallery concentrates on historical and contemporary art and artists that represent the development of art in British Columbia.

A highlight is the permanent collection of the works of Emily Carr, perhaps the best-known British Columbian artist. A tour de force during the 1930s, her paintings of the deep BC forests display a unique energy and intensity, and her influence is still strong today. The gallery also hosts prestigious international temporary exhibitions.

Vancouver's first law courts occupied this building, and murder victim William Hopkinson reputedly walks the corridors and haunts the catacombs below it with his ghost friend "Charlie." The gallery shop has an excellent range of unique handcrafted items by both established and up-and-coming artists. **Don't miss** Emily Carr's monumental pictures of totems are one of the highlights.

VANCOUVER MUSEUM

✚ 362 A4 • 1100 Chestnut Street, Vanier Park, Vancouver, British Columbia, V6J 3J9 ☎ 604/736-4431 🕐 Fri–Wed 10–5, Thu 10–9; closed Christmas 💲 Adult $10, child (5–18) $6 🚌 2, 22 and trolley bus 🚤 Water taxi from Granville Island to Heritage Harbor ♿ www.vanmuseum.bc.ca

Set in a futuristic building designed by local architect Gerald Hamilton, the museum traces the history of Vancouver from its roots as a First Nations settlement to the development of the modern city. The fine First Nations Gallery depicts the area before Europeans arrived. The Pacific Rim Collection, with displays from China, Japan and Oceania, promotes cross-cultural pan-Pacific relations, while the World Heritage Collection contains objects from around the world. **Don't miss** The re-creations of the Vancouver of colonial times include an outpost of the Hudson's Bay Company.

The aquarium's Beluga Encounter Program is enormously popular with visitors—and the whales seem to like it too

VANCOUVER AQUARIUM

A state-of-the-art aquarium.
Marine life of all types and sizes, from great beluga whales to humble crustaceans.

Located on the eastern edge of Stanley Park, this superb facility is one of the city's main draws with more than a million visitors annually, and is Canada's second most popular attraction—only Toronto's CN Tower (see pages 108–109) gets more visitors. It's the third-largest aquarium in North America, and contains more than 8,000 creatures representing 600 different species.

To get the most out of your visit, stop off first at the information board in the Upper Pacific Canada Pavilion to check out the list of shows and activities that are happening each day. A range of behind-the-scenes tours allows you to get closer to the animals with the Trainer Team, and learn about the aquarium's research, conservation and animal care projects. Children (accompanied by a parent) can join a sleepover beside the giant tanks (see page 248).

NORTHWEST AND ARCTIC EXHIBITS

Outdoor attractions include the BC Forest Headwaters exhibit, where you can see a salmon hatchery, and the Wild Coast pools, with above- and below-water viewing of sea lions, dolphins and seals. There's a separate pool for viewing the entertaining and enchanting sea otters, and the impressive Arctic Canada habitat contains graceful beluga whales, seals and walruses. There's controversy about keeping these creatures in captivity, but they are nonetheless a wonderful sight and a major attraction of the aquarium. Indoor exhibits include the Pacific Canada Pavilion, displaying marine life of the Strait of Georgia, just offshore from the city, and beavers that inhabit the freshwaters inland. Treasures of the BC Coast introduces creatures from deeper waters along the coast, including a huge octopus.

TROPICAL ECOSYSTEMS

The Tropical Gallery features life on a reproduction Indonesian coral reef, including sharks, stingrays and turtles, and there's a steamy Amazon Jungle area, which takes you away from the sea and into the rain forest—an ecosystem of bright tropical birds and fish, crocodiles, eels, snakes, and somnolent giant sloths.

You can watch from below as divers swim with beluga whales

RATINGS	
Good for kids	● ● ● ● ●
Photo stops	● ● ●
Specialist shopping	● ● ●
Activities	● ● ●

BASICS

➕ Off map, 362 B1 • 845 Avison Way, Stanley Park, Vancouver, British Columbia, V6B 3X8
☎ 604/659-3552 🕐 Daily 10–5.30, Sep–Jun; 9.30–7, rest of year 💵 Adult $15.95, child (4–12) $8.95 or (13 and over) $11.95 🚌 35, 135 ☛ Various behind-the-scenes tours must be booked in advance; adult $20, child $15 ☕ Upstream Café 🏪 The Clamshell, with everything from educational to fun items to pure kitsch
www.vanaqua.org • A well-organized and comprehensive site giving full details of the aquarium's attractions, events, attractions for kids and other amenities

Stanley Park

**One of the largest urban parks in North America.
A fantastic mix of forest, beaches, open parkland and formal gardens.**

RATINGS	
Good for kids	● ● ● ○
Historic interest	● ● ● ○
Specialist shopping	● ● ○ ○
Walkability	● ● ● ● ●

BASICS

✚ Off map, 362 A1 • Western tip of downtown Vancouver
☎ 604/257-8400
🕐 Daily
💵 Free (fee for some attractions and facilities)

The Girl in a Wetsuit *statue looks out toward BC's world-class diving waters*

SEEING STANLEY PARK

Often described as the "lungs" of Vancouver, Stanley Park is the largest urban park in North America, providing a place where city-dwellers can escape from the traffic and bustle to relax, breathe fresh air, have fun, and keep fit in environments ranging from temperate forest to formal gardens and beaches. The park sits west of the downtown Vancouver skyscrapers and occupies the northwestern tip of land sheltering Burrard Inlet to the east. It has water on three sides, with road and footpath access on its southern side. It is estimated that 8 million people visit the park each year, which makes it all the more remarkable that it is still possible to feel alone here. The wilder forest side (over two-thirds of the total area) has trails for running, cycling and hiking, while the eastern side—where most visitors tend to stay—has been transformed into a combination of open parkland and formal gardens. The park protects towering cedars, hemlock and fir trees, and the freshwater Lost Lagoon—named after poet Pauline Johnson's *Ode to the Lost Lagoon*—is a haven for birds and waterfowl. The Lost Lagoon Nature House has information on the park's flora and fauna. See also walk on pages 286–287.

HIGHLIGHTS

THE SEAWALL

Surrounding the outer edge of the park is an 11km (7-mile) seawall, which was originally conceived in the early 1920s to prevent erosion, and took nearly 60 years to complete. Today, it is Vancouver's most popular recreational facility, with a walkway and a cycle/Rollerblade track (counterclockwise direction only). There are wonderful views across to the North Shore and out into the Pacific Ocean beyond English Bay—the sandy beaches on this side come as a real surprise, being so close to the heart of this huge metropolis.

This green oasis in the heart of the city is where Vancouverites come to exercise and enjoy the wonderful views. The Seawall (inset, opposite) and trolley-bus tour (inset, above) are two ways to enjoy it

HORSE-DRAWN BUS TOURS

P.O. Box 1134, Station A, Vancouver, British Columbia, V6C 2T1 604/681-5115 Daily, departs every 20–30 minutes mid-Mar–Oct Adult $20.55, child (3–12) $13.05 or (13 and over) $18.65

Traveling around on a horse-drawn bus is a highly enjoyable way to tour the park and get an overview of what is on offer before you set out to explore on foot.

ACTIVITIES AND ENTERTAINMENT

There are plenty of activities in the park to amuse visitors of all ages. The best-known is Vancouver Aquarium (see page 149), but there is also the Children's Farmyard and Miniature Railway, the Totem Pole garden at Hallelujah Point, the attractive Brockton Point Visitor Centre, the Nature Park, the Kid's Waterpark, the Theatre Under the Stars, a heated ocean-side swimming pool, tennis courts, a pitch and putt golf course, and wonderful flower gardens, including the spring-blooming Rhododendron Garden and Rose Garden, with 5,000 roses. In summer, a trip on the free Stanley Park Shuttle ensures that you take in all the most popular attractions as well as the natural highlights.

BACKGROUND

This area of first-growth forest was partly logged in the 1860s to accommodate the growing city, and was also used as an army camp. However, in an early act of environmental protection the newly formed city council designated the area as permanent public parkland in 1886, naming it after Lord Stanley, Canada's Governor General when the park was officially opened in 1888. An elected committee—the Vancouver Board of Parks and Recreation, unique in Canada—was appointed to oversee the management and running of this new resource. The board still exists, and now manages over 190 parks in the Greater Vancouver area.

The figurehead of the SS Empress of Japan can be seen in the park

BASICS

35, 135. Shuttle bus operates within the park; free if you also buy a ticket to Aquarium at the horse-drawn carriage ticket office at the entrance

Restaurants at Prospect Point, Ferguson Point and Stanley Pavilion

Cafés at the Totem Poles, Lumberman's Arch, Third Beach, Lost Lagoon and swimming pool

Shop at the Brockton Park Visitor Centre (Totem Poles) sells a small range of First Nations crafts and Stanley Park souvenirs

www.city.vancouver.bc.ca/parks/parks&gardens/stanley.htm • A comprehensive summary of the background and attractions of the park, with tantalizing color photos

Vancouver Board of Parks and Recreation, 2099 Beach Avenue, Vancouver, British Columbia, V6G 1Z4, tel 604/257-8400
www.city.vancouver.bc.ca

Giant Douglas firs in Cathedral Grove are hundreds of years old

One of the 34 murals on Chemainus buildings

Totem at the Cowichan Valley Museum in Duncan

BRITISH COLUMBIA & THE ROCKIES REGION

BANFF AND THE NATIONAL PARK
See page 154–156.

BUTCHART GARDENS
See page 157.

CATHEDRAL GROVE

⊞ 381 C16 • 114km (70 miles) north of Victoria, on Vancouver Island–take Route 1 followed by a left at Route 4 ◎ Daily, dawn–dusk ▣ Free ₱ $3 www.britishcolumbia.com/parksandtrails

Officially MacMillan Provincial Park, after the company that gave the land to the province, this 136ha (336-acre) park is known to all as Cathedral Grove. It preserves giant Douglas fir trees, some of which are up to 800 years old—the largest is 76m (250ft) high, 3m (9ft) in diameter and 9m (30ft) in circumference.

Walking between the huge trunks below the high forest canopy gives you an impression of being in a vast natural cathedral. A 500m (550yd) interpretative walk south of the highway takes you past some of the oldest trees, with explanatory panels on the temperate ecosystem along the way. A trail to the north of the highway leads through groves of Western Red Cedar to Lake Cameron, where you can swim or picnic along the shore.

CHEMAINUS

⊞ 381 C17 🖈 Chemainus Visitor InfoCentre, 9796 Willow Street, Chemainus, British Columbia, V0R 1K0, tel 250/246-3944 www.chemainus.bc.ca www.muraltown.com

Street art has earned this long-established port in the southeast

of Vancouver Island the title of Canada's largest outdoor art gallery. The town has risen phoenix-like from the ashes of its declining forestry industry to become a thriving artistic and commercial hub. In 1983, following the closure of the town's large sawmill, a mainstay of the local economy for 120 years, enterprising residents set up the Festival of Murals. Building on the success of the first five murals commissioned in 1982, 34 now grace the walls of downtown buildings, depicting the town's history and cultural life: loggers felling trees, a locomotive steaming across a bridge, the interior of the company store c1917, and portraits of First Nations chiefs. Apart from the murals, the town is attractive, its painted clapboard cottages turned into boutiques selling antiques and collectibles, clothing, or arts and crafts. The Chemainus Theatre has a professional cast that performs throughout the year, and the town is well supplied with art galleries and eateries.

DUNCAN

⊞ 381 C17 🖈 Duncan Visitor Information Centre, 381 Trans-Canada Highway 1, Duncan, British Columbia, V9L 3R5, tel 250/746-4636 www.duncancc.bc.ca

Duncan calls itself the "city of totems," and displays over 80 of these unique carved symbols along the Trans-Canada Highway and in the town. The Cowichan people are highly regarded for their totem-carving skills, and each totem tells a story, perhaps a legend or a real family history. Pick up a self-guiding tour map from the visitor information center, or take a free guided tour (May–Sep) starting from the historic train station, now the Cowichan Valley Museum (daily,

Jul–Aug), on Canada Avenue. At the Quw'utsun Cultural and Conference Centre (daily) on Cowichan Way, you can watch totems and other items being crafted, experience a multimedia presentation on First Nations lifestyle and social history, and try your hand at native crafts or buy the real thing.
Don't miss Watch totems being crafted at Quw'utsun Cultural and Conference Centre.

FORT LANGLEY

⊞ 381 C17 • 50km (30 miles) east of Vancouver, signposted off Route 1 ☎ 604/513-4777 ◎ Daily, Mar–Oct; Mon–Fri, rest of year ▣ Adult $5.75, child $3, family $14.50 www.parkscanada.gc.ca/langley

This carefully reconstructed fort gives you a good idea of how the pioneers lived and traded in the early 1800s, with costumed staff setting the scene. The Hudson's Bay Company established a trading post here in 1827, at the southern narrows of the Fraser River, to trade pelts for food and other supplies with the local First Nations tribes.

The trading post was fortified in 1839 and, as the fur trade declined, Fort Langley pioneered farming and fish processing for export to San Francisco, Hawaii and Australia. During the Cariboo gold rush, when thousands made their way north from the US along the Fraser River, the governor of Vancouver Island, fearful of an American takeover, declared British Columbia a crown colony here at the fort in 1858. Within the wooden stockade are barracks, the Big House (the chief trader's home), a forge and a storehouse, the latter being the only original building. Inside here you can see furs and some of the goods for which they were traded.

THE SIGHTS

Locomotive in the West Coast Railway Heritage Park, Squamish

The MV Le Conte *sailing the Inside Passage, part of the Alaska Marine Highway System*

FRASER CANYON/ HELL'S GATE

➕ 381 D16 • 43111 Trans-Canada Highway, Boston Bar, British Columbia, V0X 1L0. On Highway 1, 200km (125 miles) northeast of Vancouver
☎ 604/867-9277
www.hellsgateairtram.com

The main section of Fraser Canyon extends from Yale to Boston Bar, and Hell's Gate is its most spectacular attraction. Here, the river crashes through a narrow 35m-wide (110ft) opening between the 180m-high (600ft) canyon walls. The river is named for Simon Fraser, an American-born fur trader and explorer who navigated its length in a canoe in 1808. Today's visitors no longer need be so intrepid. Airtram *(daily, mid-Apr to mid-Oct)* carries you on a scenic journey from the east side across the seething waters to a plateau on the west bank, a descent of 142m (500ft). Once across you'll find observation points and a display on the life cycle of the salmon that return here to spawn each fall. There's also a restaurant, gift shop and fudge factory.
Don't miss The Airtram journey is well worth the ticket price.

GLACIER NATIONAL PARK

➕ 373 E16 ☎ 250/837-7500 🎫 Adult $5, child $2.50, family $12.50
www.parkscanada.gc.ca/glacier

Aptly named, the Glacier National Park is more than 12 percent solid ice; the rest is made up of the stunning mountain scenery of the Selkirk range of the Rockies. It is one of the least accessible national parks in the Rockies, with few trails that anyone but the most experienced hikers/mountaineers could tackle.
Many visitors simply sail through the park on the Trans-

Canada Highway, enjoying the spectacular views from their car and halting only at the Rogers Pass Visitor Centre *(daily; closed Tue–Wed in Nov)*. Rogers Pass is a national historic site at the place where railroad engineer A. B. Rogers overcame immense technical difficulties to find a way through the mountains for the Canadian Pacific Railway's transcontinental line in 1882. But the line was never stable and closed in 1916 when the Cannaught rail tunnel opened. Now a self-guiding trail reveals old stone bridges, trestle supports, equipment and other railroad structures.
The park was established in 1886, shortly after the line was completed, when railroad executives saw the potential for tourism. The main attraction was, and still is, the Illecillewaet Neve Glacier, located south of the visitor center. Trails leading to stunning viewpoints were laid out by Swiss guides about a century ago, and rangers lead guided walks to see the glaciers.

HOWE SOUND

➕ 381 C16 ℹ️ Squamish Visitor Information Service, 37950 Cleveland Avenue, Squamish, British Columbia, V0N 3G0, tel 604/892-9244; daily www.squamishchamber.bc.ca

The fiord-like landscape of Howe Sound is beautifully unspoiled, a stunning scene created by a mixture of receding iceflows, volcanic action and water erosion. It is an easy drive to the sound from Vancouver on the Sea to Sky Highway, or you can take a leisurely boat trip. Sadly, the Royal Hudson Steam Train is no longer operating, but you can take at look at it at the West Coast Railway Heritage Park *(daily 10–5, closed Dec 25 and Jan)* in Squamish, at the head of

Howe Sound. The town is not particularly picturesque, but is a good place for activities, notably mountaineering and watersports. This ancestral home of the Skomish peoples didn't prosper until the railroad and highway arrived in the late 1950s.
A big attraction in the area is the British Columbia Museum of Mining *(daily, early May–mid-Oct)* at Britannia Beach, on the site of a copper mine that employed 60,000 workers during its 70 years of operation. The mine closed in 1974, and a year later the museum opened, incorporating mine tours and mining exhibits. You may recognize the setting from one of a long list of movies and TV shows that have been shot on location here.

ICEFIELDS PARKWAY

See pages 158–159.

INSIDE PASSAGE

➕ 372 B15

For dramatic scenery and sightings of whales, porpoises, seals, and bald eagles, the 15-hour day trip along the Inside Passage is unbeatable. During the early days of exploration, vessels sailing the western seaboard were at the mercy of the unpredictable Pacific Ocean. The Inside Passage provided a safe route through the offshore islands.
Today, ferries, freight carriers and private yachts ply up and down between the islands and the thickly forested, fiord-incised mainland. The ferry carries supplies and passengers to places accessible only by boat or seaplane. Toward the northern end of the route, you pass through the Grenville Channel, only 500m (1,600ft) wide at its narrowest point. You catch the ferry from either Port Hardy northbound or Prince Rupert going south.

The park is full of wonderful vistas, such as this view of Vermillion Lake, with spectacular mountains in the background. Inset: Banff town as the sun goes down

Banff and the National Park

The grandfather of all Canadian national parks encircles the sophisticated town of Banff with spectacular scenery.

RATINGS	
Photo stops	● ● ● ●
Good for kids	● ● ●
Shopping	● ● ●
Walkability	● ● ●

There is always a sight to see in this superb national park, so bringing binoculars is a good idea

SEEING BANFF AND THE NATIONAL PARK

Surrounded by sublime mountain landscapes, Banff township sits in a natural bowl on the banks of the Bow River and makes an excellent base for touring the area. You'll need a car to do proper justice to the park—start by taking the Bow Valley Parkway (see page 156). Summer and winter, think of any activity associated with mountains, lakes and rivers, and the great outdoors in general, and there'll be the opportunity to pursue it here. Summertime offers guided hikes, river rafting, family kayaking, horseback riding, caving, fishing, golf and helicopter sightseeing. In winter, there's downhill and Nordic skiing, ice-fishing, dogsled tours, sleigh rides, snowmobiling, tobogganning, skating and guided snowshoe walks.

HIGHLIGHTS

BANFF

With stupendous mountain views all around, it's hard to resist the lure of the wild, but Banff has some interesting attractions to make it worth lingering a while. These include Canada's oldest natural history museum at Banff Park Museum Heritage Site *(daily)*, with Victorian glass-case displays of animals. The Whyte Museum of the Canadian Rockies *(daily)* has a more contemporary feel, with art galleries full of

THE SIGHTS

The Sulphur Mountain Gondola
(inset, above) at Banff. Left:
Atop Sulphur Mountain there are
far-reaching views

mountainscapes and a fascinating photographic archive; it also owns
six heritage homes in the city. Buffalo Nations Luxton Museum *(daily)*
showcases the heritage of local First Nations tribes, with reenactments
of their traditional lifestyles.

Banff may be rather tourist oriented in summer and full of skiers in
winter, and prices may be a bit higher here, but standards are high
too—with lots of expensive designer stores, art galleries and craft
shops—and Banff is an attractive and lively place to visit.

HOT SPRINGS

The Cave and Basin National Historic Site *(daily, mid-May–Sep),*
southwest of downtown Banff, was central to Canada's first national
park and attracted early tourists. There are historical displays in the
interpretive center here. However, bathing is no longer allowed

BASICS

✚ 373 F16

ℹ Banff and Lake Louise Tourism
Bureau, P.O. Box 1298, Banff, Alberta,
T1L 1B3, tel: 403/762-8421
www.banfflakelouise.com • Attractive,
comprehensive site including up-to-
date weather reports, trail conditions
and daily accommodations vacancies

ℹ Visitor Centre and National Park
Office, 224 Banff Avenue, Banff, Alberta,
T1L 1K2, tel: 403/762-1550; daily 8–6,
mid-May to mid-Jun and mid Sep–late
Sep; 8–8, mid-Jun to mid-Sep; 9–6, rest
of year
www.parkscanada.gc.ca/banff • Easy to
use website with full information about
all of Canada's national parks

This sign welcomes visitors to the town of Banff

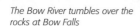

The Bow River tumbles over the rocks at Bow Falls

Cascade Mountain rises high above Banff's Main Street

because the site is sacred to the local Stoney First Nations people. If you want to take a dip, head for the Upper Hot Springs *(daily)* on Mountain Avenue, south of downtown, a modern lido complex belching sulfurous water at a temperature of 42°C (108°F). It shares a parking lot with the Sulphur Mountain Gondola *(daily, mid-May to mid-Oct)*, which rises to 2,281m (7,686ft) and offers fantastic views.

BOW VALLEY PARKWAY

This is a wonderfully scenic drive, passing through some pretty aspen woodland and evergreen forest where you may see elk, moose and even an occasional bear. After 25km (16 miles), you'll come to Johnston Canyon, where you can walk along the canyon side to two pretty waterfalls (1km/0.5 mile to the first and 2.7km/1.7miles to the second).

Johnston Canyon Old Gas Station, on the Bow Valley Parkway

LAKES IN THE NATIONAL PARK

The park's lakes are justly famous. Lake Louise (see page 162) and Moraine Lake (see page 163) are the best known, but don't miss the lovely Lake Minnewanka, north of Banff, where you can take a boat trip *(mid-May to mid-Oct)*, and Vermillion Lakes, to the west, which offers fantastic photo opportunities, particularly at sunset.

BACKGROUND

The whole Rockies tourist phenomenon started when the Canadian Pacific Railway built the Banff Springs Hotel in 1888. It was modeled on a Scottish castle and named after the town of Banff in Scotland. Today, it is one of the world's great hotels, and even if you don't want to stay here, at least call in for a British-style afternoon tea or the legendary Sunday brunch, and wallow in luxury, surrounded by breathtaking mountain scenery.

The Banff National Park, Canada's first, was created in 1885 to protect the hot springs discovered during construction of the Canadian Pacific Railway.

The gardens are a riot of color in spring and summer

There is a large number of exotic plants here

BUTCHART GARDENS

Spectacular formal gardens in an old limestone quarry, planted with rare and exotic species.

Celebrating its centenary in 2004, this remarkable garden was created by Jenny Butchart in and around a worked-out limestone quarry of her husband Robert's Portland cement works. Her lifelong interest in plants inspired the idea, and the garden's inception coincided with a time when exotic plants were the very latest thing in garden fashion. Jenny imported hundreds of species from around the world, and over the decades, the garden has been developed and expanded to cover some 55ha (136 acres). It is still owned and run by the same family, currently by Robert and Jenny's grandson.

GARDEN TOUR

On arrival, visitors get a route map of the meandering pathways. It begins with the Sunken Gardens, 25m (82ft) down on the floor of the original quarry, with classical statuary among the plants. The Ross Fountain here was installed in 1964 to commemorate the 60th anniversary of the gardens. Next comes the Rose Garden, best in July and August, planted with hybrid tea roses around an Italian wishing well. From here you move on to the Japanese Garden, which dates to 1906 and was laid out with the help of a Japanese landscape artist—look for the rare Himalayan blue poppy. Last comes the Italian Garden, the most formal of all the garden areas, planted in 1926 on what used to be the Butchart's tennis court.

SEASONAL ATTRACTIONS AND EVENTS

There is color and interest at any time of the year here. Even in the first quarter of the year, when everywhere else around is still in the grip of winter, the indoor garden, in a stone-flagged conservatory, is an inspiration to gardeners anticipating the spring, with its beds of daffodils and tulips, and flowering shrubs. Outside, stunning displays continue throughout the seasons, including fall foliage and winter berries.

Dazzling by day, the gardens sparkle when illuminated on summer evenings with thousands of lights connected to North America's largest underground wiring system. From mid-June to mid-September there's daily afternoon and evening entertainment, except on Saturdays when spectacular fireworks displays take place, followed by music from a historic pipe organ.

RATINGS	
Good for children	●●
Photo stops	●●●●●
Specialist shopping	●●●
Value for money	●●●

BASICS

⊞ 381 C17 • 800 Benvenuto Avenue, Brentwood Bay, Vancouver Island, British Columbia, V8X 3X4 ☎ 866/652-4422, 250/652-5256 (recorded info) ⊘ Daily 9am–10.30pm, midsummer; 9am–sunset, rest of year 🎫 Adult $16–21 depending on season, child (5–12) $1.50–2 or (13–17) $8–10.50 🚌 Gray Line Shuttle from Victoria (May–Oct); fare includes admission 🅿 🍽 Dining Room Restaurant; Blue Poppy Restaurant ☕ Coffee Shop, Soda Fountain, The Gazebo 🏪 Seeds, gardening accessories, souvenirs and First Nations crafts 📖 Flower identification guide

www.butchartgardens.com • Beautiful photographs, plus details of events and entertainments

TIP

● If you want time to stop and smell the roses, avoid the busiest times of year, when the unbroken conga line of visitors has its own momentum.

Icefields Parkway

One of the world's most spectacular drives, where majestic mountain scenery has been sculpted by massive ice flows.

Snocoach tours of the Athabasca Glacier (above, left) are popular. Big-horned sheep (above, center) live alongside the Icefields Parkway. Peyto Lake (above, right) offers one of the best views of the parkway

BASICS

✚ 373 E15
ℹ Columbia Icefields Centre, Icefields Parkway, Jasper, Alberta, tel 877/423-7433; daily 9–5 or 6, May–mid-Oct
🅒 Icefields Parkway open all year, unless there's heavy snow
🚌 Brewster Grey Line bus from Banff to Jasper uses Icefields Parkway
🚐 Snocoach from Columbia Icefields Centre (daily, May–mid-Oct)
🅿 Free parking at regular intervals
🍴 Columbia Icefields Centre, North Saskatchewan River Crossing, Sunwapta Falls
🏨 Columbia Icefields Centre, North Saskatchewan River Crossing, Sunwapta Falls
www.brewster.ca

SEEING THE ICEFIELDS PARKWAY

Officially Route 93, the Icefields Parkway (see also tour and walk on pages 282–285) reveals a never-ending series of stunning vistas as you drive the 230km (143 miles) from Lake Louise to Jasper. And, best of all, the attractions along the route are easily accessible—at the roadside or within a short walk. There's free parking at all the viewpoints and trailheads—but definitely no parking along the roadside or on the verges. At km127 (mile 79) from Lake Louise is the Columbia Icefields Centre, a comprehensive information center with interactive displays; it also has a restaurant and snocoach tours out onto the ice.

HIGHLIGHTS

THE ICEFIELDS

The route is so named because it leads past the major icefields (glaciers) of the Canadian Rockies. After 40km (25 miles) of lovely alpine meadows dotted with lakes, you reach the first of them, the Crowfoot Glacier, whose three ice flows resemble the claws of a bird. After Saskatchewan Crossing you enter the most spectacular section. From the parking area for Parker Ridge, the 2.4km (1.5-mile) trail to the ridge is a steep climb, but well worth it for the fantastic views to the north. Farther north is the Columbia Glacier and Icefields, made up of several glaciers (notably the Athabasca), where you can take a snocoach ride or a guided walk out onto the ice. Do not venture out here without a guide as the hazards are many.

THE LAKES

The sapphire lakes here are a compelling attraction: tiny Herbert Lake, with a backdrop of Mt. Temple, larger Hector Lake and lovely Bow Lake, where there is a 3.4km (2-mile) lakeshore walk. Some 40km (25 miles) into the route you'll reach the turnoff for the Peyto Lake view, which has one of the best panoramas of the entire highway, extending down over pine forests to the mountain-encircled lake. The unusual blue of the lake's waters is the result of the fine rock particles that wash off the Peyto Glacier, away to the left.

Heed these warning signs in the park and drive carefully

Bow Lake makes a perfect mirror for the mountains above

VALLEYS AND WATERFALLS

Four rivers have carved their way through the mountains, sometimes tumbling as waterfalls. First is the Bow River, which flows south toward Banff, and, after crossing the North Saskatchewan River, there are terrific views of Cirrus Mountain and the Bridal Falls. Farther north are the wider, rock-strewn valleys of the Sunwapta and Athabasca rivers, with the splendid Sunwapta Falls and Athabasca Falls. The latter is the most photogenic waterfall of the route, but the Weeping Wall (105km/65 miles from Lake Louise) is perhaps the most astounding: a giant rock face with water constantly seeping down it. At km72 (mile 45) from Lake Louise, a short trail leads to Mistaya Canyon.

The Athabasca Falls rush down a rocky gorge

Snocoaches are built to drive safely on ice and snow

WILDLIFE

At various points you may catch sight of black bears and moose, and you might even see a gray wolf. More common are the shaggy, white mountain goats that frequent the area, making light work of the landscape with their suction-cupped feet. In the most northerly section, you might also encounter bighorn sheep. If you want to see the rare mountain caribou, head for the Sunwapta gravel flats/Beauty Creek area around May, when they come to feed here. Grizzlies and elk also inhabit this area.

BACKGROUND

The Icefields Parkway was built to provide jobs during the Depression and was intended as a scenic route, so viewpoints and stopping places were an integral part of the plan. It follows the route of the early fur-trappers, and several features are named after pioneers, including Hector Lake, named after geologist James Hector, who was the first white man to travel the area in 1858.

Jasper Town and National Park

A spectacular park with towering peaks and lakes of unbelievable hues.

RATINGS	
Historic interest	● ● ●
Photo stops	● ● ● ● ●
Value for money	● ● ● ● ●
Walkability	● ●

BASICS

✚ 373 E15
ℹ Jasper Tourism and Commerce, T.P.O. Box 98, Jasper, Alberta, T0E 1E0, tel 780/852-3858
www.jaspercanadianrockies.com
ℹ Jasper National Park and Tourism Information Centre, 500 Connaught Drive, Jasper, Alberta, T0E 1E0, tel 780/852-6176; daily 9–5, Apr–mid-Jun; 8–7, mid-Jun–Labor Day; 9–6, Labor Day–end Sep; 9–5, Oct; 9–4.30, Nov–Mar
www.parkscanada.gc.ca/jasper
www.skijaspercanada.com
🚂 Rocky Mountaineer Scenic Railway, ViaRail Station, 607 Connaught Drive, Jasper, Alberta, T0E 1E0, tel 1-800 665-7245
www.rockymountaineer.com

SEEING JASPER TOWN AND NATIONAL PARK

Jasper National Park spans an area of 10,878sq km (4,200sq miles). An excellent introduction to it is a visit to the information office, almost opposite the train station in Jasper town, where you can discover why the park has a reputation for great whitewater rafting in summer, and snowboarding and skiing in winter. Jasper is a stop on the Rocky Mountaineer scenic railroad that runs from Vancouver to Edmonton, and the ViaRail train *Skeena,* linking Edmonton with Prince Rupert on a scenic journey, also stops here. The park has more than 1,200km (660 miles) of hiking routes, mostly long range or difficult, but the main attractions and some of the best scenery are easily accessible by car or via the Jasper Tramway (see opposite).

HIGHLIGHTS

JASPER TOWN

Jasper is not be as pretty or as sophisticated as Banff (see pages 154–155), and those who come do so mostly for the outdoor attractions and activities of the park, giving the place the atmosphere of a real mountain town. You'll certainly want to visit the park information office *(see side panel),* built in 1914 to house the park superintendent and the administrative offices, and now a national historic site in an attractive setting of flower gardens.

To learn about Jasper's history, visit the Yellowhead Museum *(daily, mid-May to mid-Oct; Thu–Sun, rest of year),* which focuses on the town's role in the fur trade and also has exhibits relating to the surrounding landscapes, plus a small art gallery.

THE WHISTLERS AND MT. EDITH CAVELL

You can ride the Jasper Tramway *(daily, mid-Apr to mid-Oct)* 1,200m (3,936ft) up The Whistlers for panoramic views of the surrounding area; a steep climb, around 1.5km (just under a mile) long, takes you to the true summit and the scenic Treelin restaurant *(tel 870/852-5352)*. The name of The Whistlers comes from the high-pitched whistle made by a hoary marmot when it senses danger; you may be lucky enough to see one of these engaging animals near the summit. Another panoramic viewpoint is of the serenely beautiful Mt. Edith Cavell, reached via a 4.5km (2.8-mile) twisting road.

LAKES AND HOT SPRINGS

The nearest lakes to the town (Edith and Annette) are just 5km (3 miles) to the northeast, but more dramatic are Patricia and Pyramid lakes, just over 7km (4 miles) northwest of Jasper. All four lakes have sandy beaches, boat rental and trails to enjoy. One of the highlights of the park is Maligne Lake and the 48km (30-mile) route to reach it, passing Medicine Lake on the way. Maligne Lake Road is a good place for wildlife spotting, especially early or late in the day— look out for elk, deer, bighorn sheep, coyote and black bear. You can also hike Maligne Canyon on a 3.7km (2.3-mile) route.

Miette Hot Springs *(daily, early May–mid-Oct)*, towards the eastern border of the park and reached via a drive up the wild Fiddle Valley, has the hottest naturally occuring water in the Rockies, flowing from the mountains at a temperature of 54°C (129°F).

BACKGROUND

Jasper was one of the first areas of the Rockies to be reached by Europeans when, in 1811, members of David Thompson's expedition to find a northern route over the mountains arrived here. One of Thompson's companions established a depot called Henry House for the North West Company (a rival of the Hudson's Bay Company, but later amalgamated with it). This was renamed Jasper House after a man called Jasper Hawse, and the name stuck when the town grew. Activity declined through the 19th century, but the arrival of the railroad in 1908 saved the settlement. The park was created three years later.

Maligne Lake is the largest in the Rockies. The best way to explore the area is on horseback (inset, opposite) or on one of the hiking trails (inset, above)

TIPS

● The top of The Whistlers is extremely exposed to the elements, so bring warm clothing, even in summer.
● The Columbia Icefields Center, Athabasca Glacier, Sunwapta Falls and Athabasca Falls are also within Jasper National Park (see Icefields Parkway, pages 158–159).

Self-contained vacationers travel the scenic highways by RV

Radium Hot Springs at Kootenay are wonderfully relaxing

KOOTENAY NATIONAL PARK

🔲 373 E16 ℹ National Park Visitor Center, P.O. Box 220, Radium Hot Springs, British Columbia, V0A 1M0, tel 250/347-9505; daily
www.parkscanada.gc.ca/kootenay

THE SIGHTS

Together with Banff, Jasper and Yoho, Kootenay National Park forms part of a UNESCO World Heritage Site and protects an area of 1,406sq km (550sq miles) on the western slopes of the Rocky Mountains. The least busy of the major parks in the Rockies—though it gets 3 million visitors per year—Kootenay is an easy day's excursion from Banff or Lake Louise. In a three-hour drive you can take in all kinds of terrain, from the glacier fields in the north, through mountains, meadows and grasslands to the arid land farther south.

Kootenay owes its existence to the road that cuts through it from north to south. Construction began before World War I with private and provincial money, but that soon ran out, and the highway was completed with federal government funds on condition that a strip of land 8km (5 miles) each side of the road was given over to a national park.

Trails lead from the Kootenay Parkway to most of the main attractions. The best of the short trails are to Marble Canyon and Paint Pots, each about a 15-minute walk from their parking areas. At Marble Canyon the dolomite and limestone walls of the 36m-deep (120ft) gorge have been polished marble-smooth by the waters that carved it. The trail crisscrosses the rushing creek several times before reaching a waterfall. The Paint Pots are pools with a build up of minerals around their rims. Nearby, the Ochre Beds are also the result of seeping minerals.

LAKE LOUISE

One of the most beautiful views in the Rockies.

🔲 373 F16 ℹ Banff and Lake Louise Tourism Bureau, P.O. Box 1298, Banff, Alberta, T1L 1B3, tel 403/762-8421
www.banfflakelouise.com
ℹ National Park Visitor Centre and Park Office, 224 Banff Avenue, Banff, Alberta, T1L 1K2, tel 403/762-1550; Lake Louise Visitor Centre, Samson Mall, summer months only
www.parkscanada.gc.ca

RATINGS	
Historic interest	●●●
Photo stops	●●●●●
Walkability	●●●

TIP
● The view can be spoiled by the crowds, so arrive early if you want to get the place almost to yourself.

Ravishing Lake Louise sits in a bowl carved by glacial ice, framed by dark green forest and with a backdrop of snow-capped mountains. The beautiful iridescent blue of the water is created by microscopic particles that are trapped in the spring meltwaters—these absorb the light of all the colors in the rainbow except blue and green, which are reflected back in the most astonishing way, and appear even more intense viewed from above lake level.

It was called Lake of the Little Fishes by the native Stoney Indians, but when Tom Wilson, a European outfitter working for the Canadian Pacific Railway, saw the lake in 1882, he immediately christened it Emerald Lake for its brilliant color. In 1884 it was renamed Lake Louise in honor of Queen Victoria's daughter, married to the then Governor General of Canada, Lord Lorne.

HIKING TRAILS

Though it is not possible to follow a complete circuit around the lake, there are some wonderful walks, the most popular of which are to the Plain of Six Glaciers and the climb up to Lake Agnes (see page 284). A great way to enjoy the scene without the effort of hiking is from the Lake Louise Gondola *(daily, May–Aug; skiers only in winter)*, which opens up panoramic views.

FAIRMONT CHÂTEAU LAKE LOUISE HOTEL

In 1890, the Canadian Pacific Railway built a wooden chalet for visitors, but work soon started on the Château Lake Louise Hotel (see page 285), which sits on glacial moraine left behind as the ice retreated and now dominates the lakeside. There's a viewing area in front of the hotel, with a splendid outlook toward the surrounding mountains.

Lake Louise is one of the most visited places in the Rockies

Monashee Mountains, as seen from the Mt. Revelstoke Parkway

MORAINE LAKE

The beautiful lake that decorated the old $20 bill.

🞣 373 F16 ℹ Banff and Lake Louise Tourism Bureau, P.O.Box 1298, Banff, Alberta, T1L 1B3, tel 403/762-8421
www.banfflakelouise.com
ℹ National Park Visitor Centre and Park Office, 224 Banff Avenue, Banff, Alberta, T1L 1K2, tel 403/762-1550; Lake Louise Visitor Centre, Samson Mall, summer months only
www.parkscanada.gc.ca

RATINGS	
Historic interest	●●
Photo stops	●●●●●
Specialist shopping	●●●●

TIP

● Visit early or late in the day to enjoy the beauty of the lake without the crowds.

MT. REVELSTOKE NATIONAL PARK

🞣 373 E16 • Box 350, Revelstoke, British Columbia, V0E 2S0 ☎ 250/837-7500 🕐 Open during the snow-free season 💲 Adult $5, child (6–16) $2.50, family $12.50
www.parkscanada.gc.ca/revelstoke

Mt. Revelstoke National Park was created in 1914 after Revelstoke townspeople lobbied for action to preserve the beauty of the alpine meadows below the mountain summit, where wildflowers create a swathe of brilliant color in high summer.

Covering only 260sq km (101sq miles), Mt. Revelstoke is one of Canada's smallest parks. It offers walking on trails such as the Giant Cedars Trail, through a stand of ancient Western Red Cedars, and the Skunk Cabbage Trail, through jungle-like wetland, excellent for birdwatching. The park protects a small herd of the threatened mountain caribou, and provides habitats for grizzly bear and mountain goat.

The 26km (16-mile) Meadows in the Sky Parkway *(closed when snow arrives—usually mid-Oct–early Jul)*, winds uphill through the dense old-growth rain forest of giant cedar and pine, then subalpine forest, and finally crosses alpine meadows and tundra to the Balsam Lake parking area. From here, the mountain summit can be reached either on foot or, in summer, by shuttle bus, a distance of 2km (1.25 miles). A gentle hike on the Meadows in the Sky Trail takes in the best of the woodland landscape. Revelstoke itself is a quiet town of pretty clapboard houses nestling in the valley below the mountain.
Don't miss The view from the lookout near the start of the parkway is awesome.

Discovered in 1899 by Walter Wilcox, who described it poetically as a place of "inspiring solitude and rugged grandeur," Moraine Lake—the Jewel of the Rockies—sits at an elevation of 574m (1,884ft) and, like the nearby Lake Louise, was created by glacial action. Though it is smaller than Lake Louise, it's no less picturesque. In fact, its location at the foot of a range of the jagged peaks of the Wenkchemna Mountains, which are much closer to the water than those surrounding Lake Louise, exaggerates the bowl-like effect and creates a much more intimate atmosphere.

A tea lodge erected in 1912, when such lodges were fashionable, was replaced several times during the 20th century. The most recent (1991) lodge, designed by Arthur Erickson, is a beautiful yet suitably rustic place to lunch or spend the night.

VIEWPOINTS AND TRAILS

At the outlet of the lake, a small hill, created by a landslip, makes a perfect viewing point—this is the view that appeared on old $20 bills. There are a number of trails, all starting from the lodge, whether you just want a gentle walk around the lake or a longer hike. The route to Consolation Lake (3.2km/2 miles) passes a stand of rock called the Tower of Babel; a steeper climb leads through Larch Valley (3.6km/2.2 miles) and, for an even more demanding hike continues to Sentinal Pass; while the trail to Eiffel Lake (5.6km/3.5 miles), involving an ascent of almost 1,200m/3,936ft, is the least walked trail in spite of the grandiose scenery that awaits at its end.

Lovely at any time of the year, the area around the lake becomes unspeakably beautiful during the fall foliage season.

The Wenkchemna Mountains rise above Moraine Lake

THE SIGHTS

The Bastion in Nanaimo dates from the mid-19th century

The little settlement of Oak Bay, just along the coast from Victoria, has many large homes with lovely gardens, plus a yacht club

THE SIGHTS

NANAIMO

🚹 381 C15 ℹ️ Tourism Nanaimo, Beban House, 2290 Bowen Road, British Columbia, V9T 3K7, tel 250/756-0106 🚌 Island Coach runs daily services linking communities on Vancouver Island 🚆 ViaRail E & N/Dayliner along east coast of Vancouver Island from Victoria to Courtenay 🚢 BC Ferries from Horseshoe Bay northwest of Vancouver and from Tsawwassen south of Vancouver ✈️ Regular scheduled flights from Vancouver www.tourismnanaimo.com

The town of Nanaimo revolves around its harbor. A working fishing fleet still operates here, and there seem to be more pleasure boats, kayaks and sailboards on the water than there are cars in garages. On the last weekend in July the town holds the Great International World Bathtub Race, in which tubbers race their craft around offshore islands before returning to Nanaimo. There's a lovely seafront walk that takes you around the harbor from the apartment village in the south, around Georgia Park with its First Nations kayak and totems, and on to the Millstone River inlet where salmon come in the fall to spawn.

The local Snuneymuxw people fished here, and later the Hudson's Bay Company opened a trading post. The Bastion, built in 1853 and overlooking the harbor, was the company's only attempt at fortification. It now houses the Nanaimo District Museum (daily, mid-May–early Sep; Tue–Sat, rest of year), where you'll find First Nations items, a reconstructed street from the old town, and an exhibit on coal mining—once a major industry in the area.

As you travel northward, Nanaimo is the last settlement of any size on Vancouver Island. Beyond here the island is sparsely populated.

OAK BAY

🚹 381 C17 ℹ️ Tourism Victoria, Greater Victoria Visitor and Convention Bureau, 4th Floor, 31 Bastion Square, Victoria, British Columbia, V8W 2B3, tel 250/414-6999 🚌 2 from downtown Victoria www.tourismvictoria.com

This leafy suburb on the coast around 5km (3 miles) east of downtown Victoria is the nearest thing to a piece of Great Britain in Canada. Large family homes are surrounded by gardens planted with roses and hollyhocks. Most date from the early to mid-20th century, when wealthier residents of Victoria moved out of town. In keeping with the area's

British character, many hotels and cafés here serve afternoon tea, often in locations that overlook the sea.

You can drive through Oak Bay on the scenic Marine Drive out of Victoria. Along the road there are good views of the architecture of the place, and glimpses of the rocky coves and sandy bays along the shoreline, and of the spectacular Cascade Mountains of Washington state (USA), across the Strait of Georgia, dominated by Mt. Baker.

OKANAGAN

🚹 381 D17 ℹ️ Thompson Okanagan Tourism Association, 1332 Water Street, Kelowna, British Columbia, V1Y 9P4, tel 250/860-5999, 800/567-2275 ℹ️ Penticton Visitor Information Centre, 888 Westminster Avenue West, Penticton, British Columbia, V2A 8R2, tel 250/493-4055, 800/663-5052 🚆 ViaRail services to Kamloops, 2 hours' drive to the north www.thompsonokanagan.com

The valley of the Okanagan River, with its lakes and rolling hills, is an area of fruit growing and wine production, and is a popular recreation spot, especially in summer. Many of the wineries welcome visitors to taste and buy their products, and the British Columbia Wine Centre, in the same building as the Penticton Visitor Centre, will help you join a tour or plan your own itinerary. The signposted Okanagan Wine Route takes in 25 of the wineries. Four wine festivals take place annually, one for each season. From south to north, the three main towns are Penticton, Kelowna and Vernon, all good bases from which to explore the

A First Nations war canoe, on display at Georgia Park, Nanaimo

Summerhill Estate Vineyard is one of many in the Okanagan area, and has some of the best visitor amenities

The Skeena River cuts through spectacular scenery

region. The Historic O'Keefe Ranch *(daily 9–5, May–mid-Oct)*, 11km (7 miles) north of Vernon, dates back to the 1860s and was a family ranch for 100 years before opening to the public. You can tour its preserved and reconstructed buildings, which have some original furnishings. As elsewhere in British Columbia, there are plenty of opportunities for outdoor pursuits, from watersports on the lakes to mountain biking, hiking, fishing, horseback riding, golf, and skiing in winter. **Don't miss** The Historic O'Keefe Ranch has a fascinating collection of old buildings.

PACIFIC RIM NATIONAL PARK

See pages 166–167.

PRINCE RUPERT/ SKEENA VALLEY

➕ 372 B14/C14 ℹ️ Prince Rupert Visitor Centre, Suite 100, 215 Cow Bay Road, Prince Rupert, British Columbia, V8J 3S1, tel 250/624-5637 🚢 BC Ferries from Port Hardy on Vancouver Island ✈️ Scheduled flights from Vancouver www.tourismprincerupert.com

If you take the ferry north from Port Hardy on Vancouver Island along the Inside Passage, Prince Rupert is the last ferry stop before Alaska. A former Hudson's Bay Company post and natural deepwater port, it was chosen as the western terminus for the Grand Trunk Pacific Railway, begun in 1906 and completed in 1914. But two years earlier the railroad's chairman, Charles Hayes, died on the *Titanic*, and the town never achieved his dream of rivaling Vancouver in importance.

Cow Bay, a renovated area of stores, galleries and restaurants along the waterfront, has original 1905 clapboard buildings painted black and white like a

Holstein cow. Totem poles carved by the Tsimshian and Haida peoples are dotted throughout the town, and the crafts and everyday items of these First Nations are on display in the Museum of Northern British Columbia *(daily, Jun–Aug; Mon–Sat, rest of year)*. Along the Skeena Valley you'll see waterfalls, tiny islands and densely forested slopes backed by snow-capped peaks.

Near the small settlement of New Hazelton, where the road and the river part company, a traditional Gitksan village, called Ksan, has been reconstructed. An open-air museum *(daily)* preserving a vanishing culture, it features tribal longhouses, a carving school, and arts and crafts. **Don't miss** Look for the totem poles in the Skeena Valley.

QUEEN CHARLOTTE ISLANDS/HAIDA GWAII

➕ 372 B14 ℹ️ Queen Charlotte Visitor Centre, 3220 Wharf Street, Queen Charlotte City, British Columbia, V0T 1S0, tel 250/559-8316 🚢 BC Ferries from Prince Rupert to Skidegate ✈️ Daily flights from Vancouver and Prince Rupert www.qcislands.net/tourism

The remoteness of this archipelago of two larger and 150 smaller islands, lying around 130km (80 miles) from Prince Rupert across the Hecate Strait, is perhaps part of its attraction. Visitors come here for the spectacular, often mist-shrouded landscape, wildlife, hiking, boating and fishing, and to experience the culture of the Haida.

This First Nations tribe is

believed to have been here for thousands of years before the islands were claimed for the British Crown in 1787 and named after the wife of King George III. Haida Gwaii means "islands of the Haida people," and the Haida are still thriving here, managing the islands and its tourism industry. The Haida Gwaii Museum in Skidegate on Graham Island is a good introduction to their history and culture, and you can see how Haida craftsmen produce jewelry and sculpture from argillite in the Arts Cooperative in Skidegate.

The Gwaii Haanas National Park Reserve *(May–Oct)* covers the southern tip of the archipelago, and protects the dense rainforest and accompanying wildlife, which would otherwise be threatened by logging interests. There is no vehicular access to the park, and independent visitors must make a reservation and attend an orientation session before being allowed to visit. Taking a trip with a local charter company approved by Parks Canada is your best option. **Don't miss** Gwaii Haanas National Park Reserve, occupying most of Moresby Island, is home to several ancient Haida villages.

The Okanagan area is famous for its first-class wines

Pacific Rim National Park

Strung out along the wild Pacific coast, this huge park has three very different ecosystems.

Clayoquot Sound (above, left) can be explored on a boat trip. A magnificent bald eagle (above, center) perches above Tofino Hot Springs. Sea lions (above, right) often bask on the rocks of Clayoquot Sound

RATINGS	
Good for kids	● ● ●
Photo stops	● ● ● ● ●
Walkability	● ● ● ●

It's easy to explore the national park on one of these boardwalks

SEEING THE PACIFIC RIM NATIONAL PARK

As its name suggests, this national park, covering 49,962ha (123,406 acres), sits on the very western edge of Canada on the Pacific side of Vancouver Island. Many visitors come to see the whales that migrate through the coastal waters, but the land and marinescapes demand equal attention, with virgin temperate rain forest, fantastic beaches and remote offshore islands. Summer sunsets are magnificent, and in winter pounding waves and sea-spray encourage storm-watching. The park, running along the coastal strip, is divided into three main sections: Long Beach, the Broken Islands and the West Coast Trail. There are regular boat trips to the islands. To walk the West Coast Trail you must obtain a permit and attend an orientation session. Port Alberni, though inland from the park, offers access along Barklay Sound by boat and day trips on ferries, and is home to the Pacific Rim Tourism office. Two small settlements—Ucluelet and Tofino—sit like book-ends at either side of Long Beach, and both offer a range of day trips, boat charters and seaplane charters. Ucluelet, to the south, is the perfect departure point for trips to the Broken Islands.

HIGHLIGHTS

LONG BEACH

This is the most accessible area of the park—a broad coastal plain between Barkley Sound and Clayoquot Sound protecting 13,715ha (33,876 acres), of which 7,690ha (18,994 acres) are on land. A walk along the beach here (see pages 290–291) is a wonderful experi-ence, whatever the weather. Long sandy stretches of beach are bro-ken by rocky outcrops and backed by temperate forest. The rolling swells of the mighty Pacific break onto the beach, making it a great place for surfing. The Wikannish Interpretive Centre *(mid-Mar to mid-Oct)* offers tours along the beach, information and a theater program.

THE BROKEN ISLANDS

Scattered across Barkley Sound in the coastal waters south of Long Beach are the Broken Islands, an archipelago of over 100 islets and rocks that protect populations of bald eagles, sea lions and seals. The islands are accessible only by boat, but you can take a daily charter

Whale-watchers can get closer to the whales in inflatable craft. Inset: Relaxing in Tofino Hot Springs

from Ucluelet, or a full day trip *(three times a week, year-round)* from Port Alberni on the MV *Lady Rose* or MV *Frances Barkley*.

THE WEST COAST TRAIL
Even more remote than the Broken Islands is the totally unspoiled strip of land south of Barkley Sound between the tiny settlements of Bamfield and Port Renfrew. The West Coast Trail, originally designed as an escape route for sailors stranded by shipwreck in the 1880s and running for 75km (47 miles) along this strip, is not for novices; it takes around five days to complete.

MEARES ISLAND AND HOT SPRINGS COVE
These two attractions are both reached via Tofino. Meares Island consists of 8,800ha (21,736 acres) of pristine temperate forest said to be 1,500 years old. At Hot Springs Cove, reached along a half-hour boardwalk through forest, pungent sulfurous water at a temperature of 50°C (122°F) flows from natural fissures.

BACKGROUND
The first European to explore this coast was Captain Cook in 1778, followed by Captain Charles William Barkley, after whom Barkley Sound is named. The area was populated by the Nuu-chah-nulth people, but settlers were not drawn to the remote location, with an annual rainfall of 300cm (117in) and treacherous waters known as "the Graveyard of the Pacific." As first-growth forest along the coast began to fall to the lumberman's ax, it was its remoteness that saved the forest. The national park now has some of the finest examples of first-growth temperate rain forest in the world. Though the First Nations population declined steeply in the 19th century, they still have a presence here, and the park protects 290 native archeological sites.

BASICS
✚ 381 C17
ℹ Pacific Rim National Park Office, 2185 Ocean Terrace Road, Ucluelet, British Columbia, V0R 3A0, tel 250/726 7721
ℹ Pacific Rim Tourism, 3100 Kingsway, "The Station," Port Alberni, British Columbia, V9Y 3B1, tel 250/723-7529
🚶 2-hour guided walks on Long Beach in summer
www.pacificrimtourism.ca

TIP
• Sightings are not guaranteed on whale-watching trips, but chances are very good during the migration season.

The western end of the Trans-Canada Highway

PACIFIC TERMINUS
TRANS·CANADA HIGHWAY
TOFINO B.C.

Victoria

**The prettiest city in western Canada.
Regularly voted among the top ten cities in the world by *Traveler* magazine.**

The start of the Trans-Canada Highway in Victoria (above, left). Woolly mammoth (above, center) in the Royal British Columbia Museum. Harbor tour boats in Victoria (above, right) allow maximum vision

SEEING VICTORIA

Victoria sits on the southern tip of Vancouver Island on a fine natural harbor, with magnificent views of the US state of Washington's Olympic Mountains to the south and Cascade Mountains to the east. It was among the leading settlements in colonial Canada and still has a very traditional English feel, with its historic buildings and red buses, and its post boxes, window boxes and hanging gardens. The city is eminently walkable, with old-fashioned shopping streets devoted to craft and souvenir stores, and the main attractions located conveniently close together. The historic Inner Harbour is still at the heart of the city and, with its waterside promenade, is a wonderful place to stroll around. The yachts moored here during the summer add to the atmosphere, and the 1908 Empress Hotel and 1898 Legislature (known as the Parliament Buildings) are architectural treasures.

HIGHLIGHTS

THE INNER HARBOUR

Heart of the city, the Inner Harbour is surrounded by many of the most interesting places in Victoria, including the superb Royal British Columbia Museum (see page 170). The Parliament Buildings *(daily 8.30–4.30, summer; Mon–Fri 8.30–4.30, rest of year)* are worth inspecting for their flamboyant architecture, a meld of Victorian Gothic, Italianate and American Romanesque styles. The buildings were designed in 1893 by the eminent architect Francis Rattenbury and opened in 1898, replacing the original small and rather insignificant Legislature Building. Hundreds of lights over the exterior come on at dusk every evening, making a very pretty sight at sunset.

Other attractions nearby include the Pacific Undersea Gardens *(daily)*, featuring more than 5,000 creatures native to the British Columbian coast. Miniature World *(daily)* includes a fully functioning miniature saw mill and a scale model of the Canadian Pacific Railway. Helmcken House *(daily, Feb–Dec)*, the 1852 residence of doctor and politician John Helmcken and the oldest house in British Columbia, has a wonderful medical collection. The Royal London Wax Museum *(daily)*, housed in a neoclassical building, exhibits wax figures in galleries with themes such as Royalty Row and Chamber of Horrors. The

RATINGS	
Good for kids	●●●
Photo stops	●●●●●
Specialist shopping	●●●●●
Walkability	●●●●●

BASICS

✚ 381 C17 ℹ️ Victoria Visitor Information Centre, 812 Wharf Street, Victoria, British Columbia, V8W 1T3, tel 250/953-2033; daily www.tourismvictoria.com • Easy-to-use and very comprehensive and informative site, with links to attractions.

TIPS

● There's no better way to soak up the "English" atmosphere of Victoria than to take afternoon tea here, either in the Empress Hotel, or at the Blethering Place (see page 333).
● The ferry companies down at the Inner Harbour also do some good sightseeing tours. The shorter trips provide superb views of the city and mountains, or you can take full days of whale-watching or exploring the Gulf of Juan de Fuca and the San Juan Islands.
● See also tour on pages 288–289.

Totem pole (opposite) in Victoria's Beacon Hill Park

Crystal Garden *(daily)* occupies a huge glass-roofed conservatory originally designed as a swimming pool for the Empress Hotel in the style of London's Crystal Palace. Today, it houses over 50 endangered species of birds, small mammals, reptiles and butterflies in a tropical environment.

Slightly farther afield, Craigdarroch Castle *(daily)* is a 39-room Victorian Gothic mansion built in the 1880s for coal magnet Robert Dunsmuir, with some of the finest stained and leaded glass in western Canada, exceptional wood paneling, and period furnishings. The Victoria Bug Zoo (see page 248) features a variety of creepy-crawlies from around the world, while Beacon Hill Park, a five-minute walk south of the Inner Harbor, covers 75ha (185 acres) and is a great place to stroll in the gardens or grassland, visit the petting zoo, or admire the world's largest freestanding totem pole, a dramatic sight.

The outline of the Parliament Building (above, left) is picked out in lights when the sun goes down. Afternoon tea, English style (above, right), is an institution at Victoria's Empress Hotel

ROYAL BRITISH COLUMBIA MUSEUM

✉ 675 Belleville Street, Victoria, British Columbia, V8W 9W2 ☎ 250/356-7226, 888/447-7877 🕐 Daily 9–5 💵 Adult $11, child $7.50, family $28
www.rbcm.gov.bc.ca

Covering the natural, social and cultural history of British Columbia, this fine museum is regarded as one of the best in North America for its excellent displays—there are some superb dioramas. The Natural History Galleries, divided into Living Land, Living Sea and Open Ocean, display appropriate plant and animal species, with full explanations of how they interact. The First Nations Gallery exhibits are divided into two sections, covering the periods before and after the arrival of European settlers in a groundbreaking approach to First Nations history. The Modern History Gallery concentrates on European influence in British Columbia: industry, agriculture, transportation and the development of cities.

Ceramics and glass on display in one of Victoria's craft shops

DOWNTOWN VICTORIA

Situated north of the Inner Harbour, downtown Victoria is a mixture of historic buildings and one-of-a-kind stores in a neat collection of narrow streets, and is a great place for browsing. Bastion Square, close to the site of Fort Camosack's north bastion, contains the Martime Museum (see below), while Market Square, built in 1858, is flanked by some fine period houses, now excellent stores, and has plenty of atmosphere. Little Fan Tan Alley in Chinatown (the third largest in Canada) is full of tiny shops, while the Sticky Wicket Pub in the Strathcona Hotel on Douglas Street is a Victoria institution.

MARITIME MUSEUM

✉ 28 Bastion Square, Victoria, British Columbia, V8W 1H9 ☎ 250/385-4222
🕐 Daily 9.30–4.30 💵 Adult $8, child $3, family $20

Housed in the former 1889 provincial courthouse in Bastion Square, the Maritime Museum reflects the importance of the sea to the development of Vancouver Island, British Columbia and, indeed, the whole of Canada. The Exploration Gallery focuses on navigation, concentrating on world exploration and the development of trade routes. "Commerce" examines the Hudson's Bay Company and its role in trade, and the role of Victoria's docks in the local economy. "Adventure" highlights the

The Empress is the most distinguished hotel in this stately city

achievements of single-handed yachtsmen, while "Passenger" looks to the time when Canada's immigrants arrived by sea, enduring terrible conditions on the journey across the Atlantic. "Government Fleets" looks at the development of the Royal Canadian Navy and its role in conflicts during the 20th century, and "BC Ferries" charts the history of this locally important company, whose headquarters are in Victoria.

BACKGROUND

In 1790 Vancouver Island was claimed for Spain by a ship-wrecked Spanish sailor found by the native people. However, it was the Hudson's Bay Company who brought European settle-ment in the form of a depot. A fort was built in the Inner Harbour in 1843 on a site now occupied by Bastion Square. In 1846 the new US border was created along the 49th parallel, dipping south at the Georgia Strait to leave Victoria and southern Vancouver Island as non-US territory.

The British government granted the island to the Hudson's Bay Company in 1849, with the proviso that settlements be created and a new crown colony of Vancouver Island be declared, with Victoria as capital. In 1852 Fort Victoria became the city of Victoria and the townsite was developed. Later in the decade, the Cariboo gold rush saw a great influx of people to Victoria, and the economic boom was further extended when the Royal Navy chose Esquimalt (just west of today's downtown) as a base. British Columbia became a crown colony in 1858, and Victoria was declared its capital when the mainland and island were amalgamated in 1868.

There's a very strong British heritage in Victoria

These buffalo don't roam too far—they are contained in a paddock within the Waterton Lakes National Park

Blackcomb Mountain is one of the premier winter sports resorts

THE SIGHTS

WATERTON LAKES NATIONAL PARK

🔲 373 F17 • Box 50, Waterton Park, Alberta, T0K 2M0 ☎ 403/859-2224
🔘 Daily, Information center: May–Sep
💲 Adult $5, child (6–16) $2.50, family $10
www.parkscanada.gc.ca/waterton, www.watertonchamber.com

Waterton Lakes is a tiny national park (525sq km/203sq miles), yet the four ecosystems that meet here—mountains, lakes, prairie, and alpine meadows—support a fantastic variety of wildlife. The rugged peaks rise steeply out of the surrounding flat lands with very little in the way of foothills, and the views as you approach are dramatic. The mountains were formed by the Lewis Thrust, their sedimentary rocks pushed up over the younger rocks of the prairies. Erosion has carved deep valleys, often filled by lakes, and sharply sculpted peaks. Grizzly and black bears—best viewed through binoculars—are attracted to the scree slope vegetation. Upper Waterton Lake is the deepest in the Canadian Rockies, and the unusually cold water in the park's chain of lakes supports unusual fish species. Waterton town site is the social heart of the park, and very popular in high season as it's a good place from which to take boat trips and road excursions. In 1932, Waterton Lakes was

Snowboarding is popular with winter thrill-seekers in the Rockies

linked with Montana's Glacier National Park south of the US border to form the Waterton-Glacier International Peace Park *(daily, Jun–early Oct; adult US$4, child US$2)*—the first peace park in the world. There are good long-distance hikes between the parks (non-Canadian visitors must enter Glacier at an official crossing and show passport and visa).
Don't miss Check out the view across the steep-walled Cameron Lake cirque, a glacial hollow.

WELLS GRAY PROVINCIAL PARK

🔲 372 D15 🅸 Clearwater Visitor Centre, 425 East Yellowhead Highway, Clearwater, British Columbia, V0E 1N0, tel 250/674-2646
www.wellsgray.ca

The best of British Columbia's provincial parks, Wells Gray has scenery to rival many national parks. It's a little off the tourist track, but you can take the scenic mountain route along Highway 5 from Jasper and Mt. Robson in the northeast, or make faster progress along the gentler road from Kamloops and the Okanagan in the south.
The access road from Clearwater leads to most of the park's attractions, including several hiking trails. Spahats Falls, around 8km (5 miles) from Clearwater and technically in Spahats Creek Provincial Park, are a taster of what's to come. From the observation platform above the falls you get a good view of the Clearwater River below, framed by the pinky-gray volcanic rock that is found throughout the park. Green Mountain Lookout, just inside Wells Gray, gives an even better view, revealing a breathtaking panorama of the whole park. Dawson Falls are another cataract to look out for, while Helmcken

Falls are definitely on the "must see" list. More than twice the height of Niagara, the waters here plunge 137m (450ft) into a deep bowl surrounded by dense forest, sending up plumes of spray. The road ends at Clearwater Lake, where there's a campsite and plenty of walking trails.
Don't miss Helmcken Falls are higher than Niagara.

WHISTLER

🔲 381 C16 🅸 Tourism Whistler, 4010 Whistler Way, British Columbia, V0N 1B4, tel 604/664-5625 🚍 Several departures daily from Vancouver and Vancouver Airport ✈ Small charter airplanes from Vancouver
www.mywhistler.com

Set to host the winter Olympic Games in 2010, Whistler is a year-round playground for Vancouverites, who live just two hours down the valley to the south. Most drive here via the scenic Sea to Sky Highway, taking in panoramas of Howe Sound (see page 153), although the center of the resort is traffic-free. Nestling between the twin peaks of Whistler and Blackcomb, the village was developed only in 1977 and now has around 2 million visitors every year. The skiing is first class: plenty of snow, a long season, excellent visitor facilities, high-speed lifts, and a good range of slopes for all abilities, including one that runs for almost a vertical mile (1.6km).
In summer, Whistler is still a magnet for visitors, close to Garibaldi Provincial Park for hikers and mountain bikers, and with outdoor activities of all kinds, from river rafting, windsurfing and paragliding to horseback riding, fishing and golf. All of this is backed up by a range of accommodations, from campgrounds to luxury hotels, plus excellent restaurants and great shopping.

Aptly named Emerald Lake reflects the surrounding lush forests

YOHO NATIONAL PARK

A stunning park that does justice to its name—a Cree First Nations word meaning "awesome."

Yoho National Park, 1,310sq km (511sq miles) in size, was established in 1886. The park's history is inextricably linked with the Canadian Pacific Railway and the huge climb required to reach Kicking Horse Pass. The natural features, pretty lakes and spectacular waterfalls are surrounded by towering peaks, many over 3,000m (9,840ft) in height, and sit alongside man-made spiral tunnels built deep into the mountainside.

KICKING HORSE PASS
When this stretch of the railway was being built, the route—which climbs rapidly out of the valley floor—posed problems for the engineers. Runaway trains that headed down the pass and boilers that exploded under the strain of the uphill climb were not unkown. The solution was to create spiral tunnels under the hillsides, allowing the trains to climb and descend at a more sedate pace along a series of overlapping switchbacks. Kicking Horse Pass was named when Sir James Hector came to explore the site for the best rail and road route—he was kicked by a horse and taken for dead.

LAKES, FALLS AND FOSSILS
The park offers 400km (248 miles) of hiking, though many of the trails are long-distance ones. The most spectacular of these is to Lake O'Hara, a 26km (16-mile) return trip to a jewel of a lake surrounded by alpine meadows, while a guided hike is the only way you can get to see the Burgess Shale, an important geological feature containing some of the oldest fossils ever found, dating from more than 500 million years.

However, most of Yoho's highlights are accessible by car. Takakkaw Falls (from the Cree word meaning "magnificent") are reached via the twisting Yoho Valley Road. The falls, with a drop of 385m (1,263ft), are one of the highest in Canada, and the surrounding ice-capped peaks add to the splendor. Emerald Lake is another major attraction, and one of the prettiest vistas in the Rockies. The natural setting is enhanced by a couple of diminutive log cabins, the hand of man on this wild land.

Emerald Lake Lodge sits right on the lakeshore

RATINGS	
Good for kids	● ● ●
Historic interest	● ● ● ●
Photo stops	● ● ● ● ●
Walkability	● ● ●

BASICS

✚ 373 e16 ℹ Yoho Visitor Center, Box 99, Field, British Columbia, V0A 1G0, tel 250/343-6783

💷 Adult $7, child $3.50, family $14
www.parkscanada.gc.ca/yoho

TIPS

● A bus shuttle runs to Lake O'Hara from mid-June to early October; numbers are limited, but you can book a seat up to three months in advance (tel 250/343-6433).
● Contact the Yoho Burgess Shale Foundation (Box 148, Field British Columbia, V0A 1G0, tel 250/343-6006) to arrange a guided hike to the fossil site.

THE NORTH

Comprising one third of the country's total area, the Canadian North is divided into three territories—Yukon, Nunavut and the Northwest Territories. Their varying landscapes offer some remarkable experiences, including the long summer days of the midnight sun and the glory of the northern lights.

Ellesmere Island

Beaufort Sea

Parry Islands

Baffin Bay

Davis Strait

Victoria Island

Baffin Island

Arctic Circle

Dawson City

Alaska Highway

Whitehorse & White Pass

Yellowknife

Southampton Island

Fort Smith

Hudson Bay

Hazelton

Peace River

Churchill

Prince Rupert

Lynn Lake

Banff

EDMONTON

CALGARY

Saskatoon

WINNIPEG

Regina

MAJOR SIGHTS

This is an original Hudson's Bay Company building on Baffin Island, a far cry from The Bay stores in every self-respecting modern mall

Inuvik's Igloo Church is in fitting style for the Far North

ALASKA HIGHWAY
See pages 176–177.

BAFFIN ISLAND

➕ 377 Q7 ℹ️ Nunavut Tourism, Box 1450, Iqaluit, Nunavut, X0A 0H0, tel 867/979-6551 ✈️ Flights to Iqaluit from Edmonton, Québec City and Montréal
www.nunavuttourism.com
www.arctic-travel.com
www.baffinisland.ca

Baffin Island forms the major part of Canada's newest territory, Nunavut, created on April 1, 1999, from the eastern part of the Northwest Territories. Nunavut means "our land" in the language of the Inuit, who have lived here for 5,000 years. No longer nomads, they live mostly in conventional Western-style homes, and many work in office jobs, but they preserve elements of their former lifestyle—in spring, groups may go off on hunting and fishing expeditions.

Three-quarters of the land mass of Baffin Island lies north of the Arctic Circle, and the landscape is primeval and glaciated, with rugged peaks and vast areas of tundra. Ecotourism offers the chance to enjoy hiking, kayaking and canoeing, dogsledding, and snowmobiling. You can spot wildlife (polar bears, whales, narwhals, seals, and walruses) on a boat trip or a floe-edge expedition, which could include staying in an igloo. Birdwatching is best in spring and summer, when migrant species return to nest.

DAWSON CITY
See page 178.

DEMPSTER HIGHWAY

➕ 374 C8 ℹ️ Dempster/Delta Visitor Information Centre, daily mid-May to mid-Sep ℹ️ Klondike Visitors' Association, Dawson City, Yukon or Northwest Territories Tourism, Inuvik, Northwest Territories, tel 867/993-5573

✈️ Flights to Dawson City from Whitehorse. Flights from Inuvik serve the northern end of the highway
www.town.inuvik.nt.ca
www.dawsoncity.org
Completed in 1979, this 736km (457-mile) highway runs from 40km (25 miles) east of Dawson City in the Yukon to Inuvik in the Northwest Territories, and is the only Canadian highway to cross the Arctic Circle, which it does 450km (251 miles) from Dawson. It links remote settlements and crosses vast expanses of wilderness. Dawson City's Arctic Circle Gateway Interpretive Display has information.

There are two river crossings—the first over the Peel at 539km (334 miles) and the second over the Mackenzie at 608km (377 miles). In summer, ferries carry vehicles across, and in winter there are ice bridges. In the intermediate seasons, when bridges form and melt, the road is impassable. The surface is mostly gravel, and there are few facilities—mainly small motels and campgrounds—so driving the route in an RV (motorhome) is popular.
Don't miss The Tsiigehtchic traditional Gwich'in community, at 608km (377 miles) on the Mackenzie River is a thriving First Nations village. At 692km (429 miles) is the Gwich'in Territorial Park, protecting an area of natural beauty.

INUVIK

➕ 374 D7 ℹ️ Western Arctic Visitor Centre, Mackenzie Road, Inuvik, Northwest Territories, tel 867/777-8618
🚌 Twice-weekly connection between Dawson City and Inuvik (12- to 14-hour trip with lunch stop) ✈️ Six flights a week from Yellowknife
www.town.inuvik.nt.ca
www.nwttravel.nt.ca

With a population of around 3,400, Inuvik is the largest

Canadian settlement north of the Arctic Circle and makes a good base for exploring the western Arctic. First Nations Inuvailut and Gwich'in make up most of the population here, and live by hunting, sport hunting and ecotourism activities. Multicolored housing units are raised above the ground, clear of the permafrost, and water, sewage and heating run in conduits above the ground to prevent freezing. The Igloo Church of Our Lady of Victory on Mackenzie Road, built in 1958, is the town's major landmark. Circular and white-walled, with lines to simulate blocks of ice, it does indeed resemble an igloo. Inside, the *Stations of the Cross* were painted by a local Inuit artist, Mona Thresher.

The town lies in the delta of the Mackenzie River, surrounded by hundreds of tributaries that are separated by islands blanketed in baby pine forest. The mass of islets and channels of the delta, one of the world's most important wildlife corridors, are a haven for migratory wildfowl and large fish populations. Herds of caribou migrate here to calve, and the vast tundra is the ideal environment for polar bears.

Several national parks can be reached by small charter plane, and activities include whitewater rafting, kayaking and hiking. Guided wildlife viewing is also popular. The aurora borealis is a big draw in winter, when you can explore by snowmobile, dogsled or snowshoe. Just east of Tuktoyaktuk, 164km (102 miles) north of Inuvik, is the world's largest area of pingos—odd, cone-shaped mounds formed when pockets of water freeze, and are forced upward by pressure from the permafrost below.
Don't miss The Igloo Church of Our Lady of Victory has a style of its own.

Alaska Highway

**An epic journey, recalling the days of the intrepid explorers.
Wild landscapes of incredible beauty.**

Magnificent mountain scenery (above, left) around Haines Junction. Turn left (above center) for the United States, straight on for the Yukon. The sun sets quickly on the Chilkot River (above right)

RATINGS	
Good for kids	●●
Historic interest	●●●●●
Photo stops	●●●●

BASICS

✚ 374 D12 ⬛ Northern Rockies
Alaska Highway Tourism Association,
Box 6850, 9923 96 Avenue, Fort St.
John, British Columbia, V1J 4J3,
tel: 250/785-2544
www.northeasternbc.com
⬛ Tourism & Culture, Government of
Yukon, Box 2703, Whitehorse, Yukon,
Y1A 2C6, tel: 867/667-5340
www.touryukon.com

Don't leave picnic food in the open where you see this sign

SEEING THE ALASKA HIGHWAY

The Alaska Highway stretches for 2,400km (1,488 miles) between Dawson Creek, BC, and Delta Junction, Alaska (USA), and is an adventurous trip across the northern frontier of old. You'll need at least two days to drive the Canadian section of the highway, three if you want to continue to the end at Delta Junction, Alaska, and longer if you're going to do real justice to the experience. If you're planning to drive the entire route, remember that this involves crossing into the US, so make sure you have the necessary documentation and currency or credit cards. The Canadian customs point is at km1,937 (mile 1,201) and the official border with the US is at km1,967 (mile 1,220), from where it's another 321km (199 miles) to the end of the highway.

HIGHLIGHTS

DAWSON CREEK

The symbolic start to the trip is the Mile Zero marker in Dawson Creek. Other attractions of this small town are the Walter Wright Pioneer Village *(daily)*, with original buildings and nine flower gardens, and Dawson Creek Station Museum *(daily, summer; Tue–Sat, winter)*, housed in the old National Railroad Station, where you can watch an hour-long video about the building of the highway.

FORT ST. JOHN

After 47 miles (76km), the route runs through Fort St. John, the oldest European settlement in mainland BC; it was founded in 1794 and served as field headquarters for the US Army during construction of the highway. The Fort St. John-North Peace Museum *(daily)* features thousands of exhibits from the surrounding area, including the re-creation of a trapper's cabin. Some 11km (7 miles) north of town, you can make a left off the highway to visit W.A.C. Bennett Dam, a huge earth-filled structure, now holding back the largest body of fresh water in British Columbia.

The construction of the Alaska Highway was a monumental feat that involved not only the actual road construction, but also the building of 100 bridges, conquering a vast stretch of inhospitable country

LAIRD RIVER HOT SPRINGS

The sulfur laden pools here, at km799 (mile 496) west of Fort Nelson, have an average temperature of 42°C (107°F), and the resulting semitropical ecosystem around them even supports orchids.

WATSON LAKE

Styling itself the "Gateway to the Yukon," this town has an interpretive center *(daily)*, and also the Northern Lights Center *(daily)*, relating to the aurora borealis, but it is most famed for the "signpost forest." This was started by a homesick US Army soldier in 1942, who erected a makeshift signpost pointing the way to his home. Later, travelers added more signs, and today there are more than 42,000.

TESLIN

This place, 179km (111 miles) south of Whitehorse, was home to the Tinglit people. George Johnston (1884–1972) photographed many of them early in the 20th century, and the town museum *(daily)* displays these photographs, plus a collection of Tinglit objects.

BACKGROUND

When northwestern Canada was first conquered by settlers, its rivers provided the major routes—thousands traveled up the Yukon River in the 1890s during the Klondike gold rush, most taking the Inside Passage to Skagway before the struggle over the White Pass to reach the river. When the gold ran out, the population dropped and the Yukon almost returned to its untamed state.

Then, during World War II, Japan attacked Pearl Harbor and invaded the Aleutian Islands, threatening Alaska, and the US needed to strengthen its protection of the state. An overland route was planned, linking mainland US with Alaska across the Canadian north. The joint venture between the two countries began on March 9, 1942, and was completed on October 25 of the same year, built by 27,000 men at a rate of more than 13km (8 miles) a day. The work was hard, through mosquito-infested muskeg marshland turned into mud by the machinery. The original route was 2,452km (1,520 miles) long, but as many of the curves have since been taken out it is now 2,400km (1,488 miles).

● Although the highway is accessible all year (weather permitting), the road conditions are very variable, with loose gravel, frost heave and potholes a constant problem—drive with care.

FORT NELSON

This town, named after Admiral Lord Horatio Nelson, marks the lowest point along the highway and was originally a trapper community. Today, it has a small heritage museum *(daily)*.

A bald eagle, perched above the Chilkat River

Entertainment is in true Gold-Rush style at Diamond Tooth Gertie's

Gold fever lives on in the tourist attractions of Dawson City

RATINGS	
Good for kids	● ● ●
Historic interest	● ● ● ● ●
Photo stops	● ● ● ●
Value for money	● ● ● ●

TIP

● Dawson City airport only operates a local service, Air North, to Whitehorse and to Fairbanks, Alaska.

BASICS

✚ 374 C9

🔖 Klondike Visitors Assocation, P.O. Box 389, Dawson City, Yukon Y0B 1G0, tel 867/993-5575, 1-877/GOLD-006 (465-3006)
www.dawsoncity.org

🔖 Tourism Yukon Visitor Reception. Corner of Front and King streets, Dawson City, Yukon, tel 867/993-5566; daily 8–8, mid-May–late Sep
Parks Canada

✉ P.O. Box 390, Dawson City, Yukon, Y0B 1G0 ☎ 867/993-7237
www.parkscanada.gc.ca

IF YOU'VE TIME

For a great view of Dawson City and the surrounding mountains, take the steep, winding Dome Road for 8km (5 miles) to the top of Midnight Dome (884m/2,900ft). Go on June 21 to see how it got its name—the sun is visible at midnight on that day.

DAWSON CITY

A living historical town, once at the heart of the Klondike gold rush.
One of Canada's most unusual communities.

When gold was discovered in the Yukon in 1896, word soon got around, and Dawson City was briefly the most happening place in the world, the epicenter of this amazing phenomenon. More than 100,000 people traveled here, yet within three years the rush came to a grinding halt and Dawson City went into decline, clinging to its role as capital of Yukon Territory while its clapboard houses slowly rotted away. Whitehorse took over as capital in 1950, but Dawson never quite died, and during the following decade a movement began to preserve it as a part of Canadian heritage. Today, over 30 buildings have been saved or renovated and are operated as historic sites, mainly by Parks Canada and by the Klondike Visitors' Association, which plows the admission money back into the community. The city's small but eclectic population is swelled in summer by the visitors who come to enjoy the costumed actors re-creating those days of old.

DIAMOND TOOTH GERTIE'S

Diamond Tooth Gertie's *(daily, mid-May to mid-Sep)* is a turn-of-the-20th-century-style saloon and gambling casino. It is named after one of Dawson's most illustrious dancing girls, Gertie Lovejoy, who is said to have had a decorative diamond set into one of her front teeth. Here the atmosphere of the high-rolling gold-rush days is re-created, with costumed can-can dancers, blackjack, poker, and roulette.

MUSEUMS

Dawson City's Museum *(daily)* is housed in the neoclassical Old Territorial Administration Building on 5th Avenue and covers both the gold-rush era and Dawson in the early 20th century. The local First Nations Han Hwech'in tribe, almost forgotten in the excitement of gold-rush history, still has a thriving population and their cultural center, Tr'ondek Hwech'in Danajo Zho Cultural Center *(daily, late May–late Sep)*, depicts their hunter-gatherer lifestyle. Dawson City's two literary figures, Jack London and Robert Service, are both remembered through re-creations of the cabins *(daily, mid-May to mid-Sep)* in which they lived (on 8th Avenue). Readings of their works sometimes take place within these cabins.

Skagway, Alaska, is a busy little town on the Klondike Highway

An aerial view of the Kluane National Park shows the glaciers snaking away into the distance, creeping slowly down their valleys

KLONDIKE HIGHWAY

➕ 374 B10 ℹ️ Tourist Reception centers at Whitehorse, Dawson City and Carmacks ☎ 867/993-5575 🚌 Daily bus services between Whitehorse and Dawson City (May–Sep) ✈️ Flights from Vancouver to Whitehorse www.touryukon.com

This highway follows the trail of the thousands of prospectors who stampeded north in search of gold in the 1890s. Starting at Skagway (in Alaska, USA), where the hopefuls disembarked, the Klondike Highway—also called the Gold Rush Route—extends north to Dawson City in the Yukon. The prospectors traveled as far as Whitehorse (see pages 181–182) on foot or on horseback, then continued their journey by boat on the Yukon River. Today, this 540km (335-mile) northern section is about a six-hour drive, not counting any detours, and much of it passes through barren wilderness.

Around 6km (4 miles) from the start of the northern Klondike Highway you can take a 10km (6-mile) detour left to Takhini Hot Springs *(daily)* and relax in an outdoor pool fed by odorless mineral water at 40°C (104°F)—a great place to watch the aurora borealis in the fall and in winter.

Carmacks, 190km (118 miles) from Whitehorse, is a Tutchone First Nations village named for George Carmacks, who first discovered gold in the Klondike. Farther north, at Stewart Crossing, the Silver Trail heads east for 112km (69 miles) through the former mining communities of Mayo and Elsa to Keno City. At Glenboyle, 40km (25 miles) from Dawson City, the Klondike Highway joins the Dempster Highway (see page 175) running northeast across the Northwest Territories to Inuvik.

KLUANE NATIONAL PARK

➕ 374 B10 • P.O. Box 5495, Haines Junction, Yukon, Y0B 1L0 ☎ 867/634-7250 💲 Free; camping $10 per night www.parkscanada.gc.ca/kluane
ℹ️ Haines Junction Visitor Center, Haines Junction: daily mid-May to mid-Sep; most weekdays rest of year

Kluane National Park is the ancestral home of the Southern Tutchone First Nations people— the name is derived from a Tutchone word meaning "lake with many fish"—and is one of Canada's most environmentally diverse parks. Within it, a series of mountain ranges runs parallel with the northern Canadian/Alaskan coast, and it is these majestic mountainscapes that draw visitors here. Several giants rise to over 5,000m (16,400ft), including Canada's highest peak, Mt. Logan, at 5,959m (19,545ft).

Kluane also encompasses the world's largest non-polar ice-fields. The moist Pacific air coming directly off the water creates ideal snow-producing conditions, and there is a vast network of more than 4,000 interior glaciers. Nearly 120 species of birds nest within Kluane, and the park supports large populations of Dall sheep and bears.

There is no road access into the park's interior, and the highway that skirts the park was not easy to construct. Destruction Bay on Kluane Lake recalls the storm that almost wiped out the road-builders' camp. The road offers tantalizing views west, but to explore this area you need to set out on foot, by kayak or on horseback—or take a tour in a small plane. There are three reasonably short hiking trails (see walk on pages 294–295), but the rest involve one or more nights of wilderness camping and require good navigational skills.

NAHANNI NATIONAL PARK

➕ 374 E11 • Box 348, Fort Simpson, Northwest Territories, X0E 0N0
☎ 867/695-3151 🕐 Daily, mid-Jun to mid-Sep; Park office: daily 8–12, 1–5, mid-Jun to mid-Sep; Mon–Fri 8.30–12, 1–5, rest of year 💲 $10 per person per day
www.parkscanada.gc.ca/nahanni
www.unesco.org
www.canadianparks.com

Located in the southwest corner of the Northwest Territories, Nahanni protects sections of the Mackenzie Mountains, an unspoiled wilderness of high peaks, deep canyons, rivers, forest, hot springs, and tundra. Nahanni is one of the most remote of Canada's national parks, and in 1978 became the first place in the world to be designated a UNESCO World Heritage Site. The park is wonderful for those wanting to escape civilization, but getting there is not straightforward. There is no easy vehicular access (most visitors arrive by charter seaplane), and campers must take all supplies and equipment.

Attractions include canyons up to 1,200m (3,936 ft) deep, created by river erosion; the Ribbitkettle Hot Springs, at a constant 20°C (68°F); and Virginia Falls at 92m (302ft), twice the height of Niagara.

The South Nahanni River is the world's premier whitewater-rafting location. Only very experienced rafters are allowed to take to the rapids unescorted, and most rafters undertake the trip with a licensed outfitter. For intrepid mountaineers, there is the challenge of the sheer rocky peaks of the Cirque of the Unclimbables. **Don't miss** Charter a small plane to see the Cirque of the Unclimbables, Virginia Falls and the canyons from the air.

THE SIGHTS

The Top of the World Highway enters the Arctic at this point

TOP OF THE WORLD HIGHWAY

➕ 374 B8 🕐 Highway open mid-May to mid-Oct, weather permitting
ℹ️ Tourism Yukon Visitor Reception Center, Front and King streets, Dawson City, Yukon, tel 867/993-5566
www.touryukon.com

The 66km (41-mile) Top of the World Highway—more prosaically known as Route 9—leads from Dawson City to the Alaska border and is one of the most picturesque routes in northern Canada. Its wonderful name was inspired by its high northerly latitude, and because much of it lies above the treeline, it has breathtaking, seemingly never-ending panoramic views across mountain peaks and valleys blanketed in Yukon forest.

The route begins at the northern end of Dawson City's Front Street, with a free ferry ride *(daily 24 hours, May–Sep)* across the wide Yukon River. From here the highway climbs steadily until, just under 4.5km (3 miles) along, there's a viewpoint with a stunning vista back over Dawson City, the Yukon River and its tributaries that really highlights the settlement's remote location.

After 15km (9 miles), the highway breaks through the treeline and follows the top of the ridges, so that you really feel that you are on top of the world. After 56km (35 miles) there is a collection of strange rock formations known as Castle Rock.

The highway is surfaced with asphalt, but is not cleared of snow in winter and closes with the first major snowfall, or when the river freezes. In addition, the border crossing into the US is open only in summer.

WHITEHORSE AND THE WHITE PASS
See opposite.

Latham Island is in Yellowknife Bay on the Great Slave Lake

YELLOWKNIFE

A former gold-rush town that's now the "Diamond Capital of North America."

➕ 375 G11 ℹ️ Yellowknife Visitor Center, 4 4807–49th Street, Yellowknife, Northwest Territories, X1A 3T5, tel 867/873-4262; Mon–Fri 8.30–5.30, Sat–Sun and hols noon–4, Sep–May
www.northernfrontier.com

RATINGS			
Good for kids	●	●	●
Historic interest	●	●	● ●
Specialist shopping	●	●	●
Walkability	●	●	● ●

Yellowknife, located on the northeast shore of the Great Slave Lake, is the capital of the Northwest Territories and the jumping-off point for exploring the area's natural attractions. The intrepid traveler Samual Hearne named the settlement in 1770 after seeing the yellow- (copper-) bladed knives used by the native Dogrib Dene peoples. Prospectors discovered gold in the region in 1934, and by 1937 Yellowknife was a boom town. Although gold-mining is still active, in the 1990s Yellowknife pioneered diamond-mining in Canada—the Diavik Diamond Mines Visitor Centre demonstrates methods of mining, cutting and polishing.

The Prince of Wales Heritage Centre, on Highway 4, is the main museum for the whole of the Northwest Territories. It includes galleries with dioramas relating to the traditions and lifestyles of the First Nations from the area, European settlement, and the modern industrial and social infrastructure.

The other principal reason to come here is for the area's natural attractions, not least the midnight sun in summer and the aurora borealis in winter. There are also lots of opportunities for wildlife watching (caribou and musk-ox herds) in the surrounding wilderness and along the Mackenzie River. Outdoor pursuits include canoeing, kayaking and rafting, as well as hunting and fishing.

This stuffed 450kg (1,000lb) polar bear is on display at the Prince of Wales Heritage Center

Whitehorse and the White Pass

A fascinating gold-rush town and scenic wilderness area.

SEEING WHITEHORSE AND THE WHITE PASS

Although it's not particularly attractive, especially when compared with Dawson City or Skagway, Whitehorse is the perfect starting point for exploration of the Yukon and White Pass area. It has the only major airport in the territory, along with plenty of adventure outfitters. Whitehorse may be visited mainly as the jumping-off point for trips into the wilderness, but it has a few attractions of its own. See also tour on pages 292–293.

An old silver mine clings to the slope along the White Pass

HIGHLIGHTS

WHITEHORSE MUSEUMS

You can find out more about the gold rush at the Macbride Museum *(daily, mid-May–early Sep; Thu–Sat, rest of year)* which has a really good explanatory display about the frenzy that followed the discovery of gold in the Klondike, including a gold-rush tent housing the typical equipment used by the prospectors, and some genuine gold nuggets found in the area. There's also a series of dioramas containing stuffed animals displayed in their native surroundings.

The Old Log Church Museum *(daily)*, housed in a church built in 1900, tells the tale of the Yukon's early explorers, from whalers to missionaries. There is also an interpretive display relating to the lives

RATINGS				
Good for kids	●	●	●	
Historic interest	●	●	●	●	●
Photo stops	●	●	●	●	

The SS Klondike *was built to ply the Klondike and Yukon rivers*

SS *KLONDIKE*

✉ Docked beside 300 Main Street, Whitehorse, Yukon, Y1A 2B5

☎ 867/667-3910

Built in 1929, this was the largest paddle steamer to sail the Klondike and Yukon rivers, transporting people and goods on the seven-day journey from Whitehorse to Dawson City, and with stops at settlements along the way.

of the First Nations peoples since the arrival of Europeans. The Yukon Transportation Museum *(daily, May–Sep)* looks at Yukon's favorite methods of transportation, from dogsleds to floatplanes and riverboats, and provides information on the historic routes.

The fascinating Beringia Interpretive Center *(daily, May–Sep; Sun only, rest of year)* explores the geology of the land bridge called Beringia, that joined Russia and Alaska before the last Ice Age, together with the flora and fauna that crossed it.

THE WHITE PASS

The White Pass is a narrow and very steep ravine that runs southwest of Whitehorse to Skagway, Alaska. It is an impressively dramatic route whether traversed by car or—much more fun—by the narrow-gauge railway *(daily, mid-May to mid-Sep)* from Skagway to Lake Bennet (with a bus connection to Whitehorse), whose tracks hug the south

The Caribou Hotel (above, left) is a welcome sight for weary travelers on the White Pass. Exhibits in the Beringia Interpretive Centre (above, right) reflect life in the area in prehistoric times

✚ 374 C10 ℹ Whitehorse Visitor Reception Center, 100 Hanson Street, Whitehorse, Yukon, Y1A 3S9, tel 867/667-3084

www.touryukon.com

www.city.whitehorse.yk.ca

ℹ Skagway Convention and Visitors Bureau, 2nd Avenue and Broadway, P.O. Box 1029, Skagway, Alaska 99840, USA, tel 907/983-2854

www.skagway.org

• The Whitehorse to Skagway route involves crossing the US border. Visitors from outside North America will need to show passports, and certain nationalities will require a visa to enter Alaska (UK citizens can purchase visa waiver stamps at the border).

• The City of Whitehorse issues free three-day parking permits—ask at City Hall, Second Avenue at Steele Street (Mon–Fri 8.30–4.30).

side of the ravine, carried over seemingly rickety wooden bridges. One of the most memorable sections is Dead Horse Gulch, where the bones of over 3,000 pack animals lie. Horses, it turned out, were not tough enough to survive the harsh environment; instead, both men and dogs acted as pack animals during the gold rush.

SKAGWAY

The beautifully preserved town of Skagway, in Alaska (USA), looks very much as it did 100 years ago, when it was the port for prospectors arriving by sea for the Klondike gold fields. Several blocks of downtown are subject to a preservation order and have been designated the Klondike Goldrush National Historic Park *(daily)*, a living museum with saloons, hotels and stores—look out for for the costumed actors throughout the town. Skagway has a wonderful position, crowded by high peaks at the head of the fiord-like Lyn Canyon waterway. It is still a busy port, and on certain days of the week it can be very full. The Chilkoot Gold Rush Footpath is a popular hiking route heading north from Skagway. The climb out of town takes a full day, but in summer you can return to the town by train.

BACKGROUND

The town of Whitehorse was established during the gold rush, when, to ease their journey to the Klondike, most prospectors navigated the Yukon River, which flows north through the territory. Two of the many obstacles in their path were Miles Canyon, an impenetrable narrow funnel with sheer walls that forced them to carry their equipment for 5km (3 miles), and the fierce Whitehorse Rapids, so named because the flurry of white water resembles a horse's mane. Rudimentary towns sprang up at Canyon City and Whitehorse as prospectors rested and planned how to negotiate the obstacles.

In 1897, a tramway was built on either side of the canyon, making the journey easier, but it was superseded by the White Pass and Yukon Route Railway, which bypassed Miles Canyon. Canyon City faded away (the ramshackle remains of its timber buildings can still be seen today), while Whitehorse flourished, taking over from Dawson City as the capital of Yukon Territory in 1950.

This chapter gives information on things to do in Canada, other than sightseeing. Canada's best shops, arts venues, nightlife, activities and events are listed region by region.

What to Do

SHOPPING

Canada has some wonderful shopping, with the opportunity to buy all kinds of goods in all kinds of retail outlets: cutting-edge technology in smart downtown locations; distinctive designer fashions in chic neighborhood boutiques; superb art and crafts from First Nations and Inuit galleries; old-fashioned preserves and candies in re-created pioneer settlements; and the whole gamut of high-street stores selling just about everything you can think of.

Stores are generally well laid out, spotless and well stocked, and places to eat or grab a coffee and doughnut are never far away. In addition to the range of goods, there is a real pleasure in the retail experience that is due entirely to the exceptionally friendly and helpful service you get from the staff. It seems that they really do want you to have a nice day.

SHOPPING MALLS

The malls in Canada are huge and modern—indeed, Canada has both the largest and second-largest malls in the world at Edmonton in Alberta

The famous Wild Geese *sculpture suspended over the Eaton Centre, Toronto*

and Burnaby in British Columbia. These places are usually purpose-built, sometimes a sparkling downtown facility at its busiest during the lunch-hour and on weekends, but often on the edge of town and surrounded by massive parking lots. Many incorporate a multiplex movie theater, some have nightclubs, and all have food courts and restaurants. There might be a play area for kids, special discount offers for tourists (check at the information booth on arrival) and special events.

Some of the city malls occupy conversions of older buildings, like the splendidly upscale Queen's Quay Terminal in Toronto, or

Vancouver's characterful Lonsdale Quay, complete with a bustling market area. Eatons were the trailblazers in the world of shopping malls, and, in spite of the demise of this

department store chain, a number of downtown malls still bear their name, notably in Toronto and Montréal.

Though they can vary considerably in size, most of the malls have pretty much the same national and international chain stores, and the same fast-food chains in their food courts, which means you can set out with some confidence about finding what you are looking for. This doesn't necessarily detract from the pleasure of browsing, particularly for visitors from outside North America who are not familiar with the stores, and it certainly doesn't mean that when you've seen one, you've seen them all.

DISCOUNT MALLS

Shoppers with an eye for a bargain will want to head for one of the discount malls—and there are no shortage of these: there's even one over on Prince Edward Island. Here you'll find brand-name and designer outlets with up to 70 percent off the normal retail price, mostly for discontinued lines. One of the biggest and best known is the Dixie Mall, just outside Toronto, which has a range of low-price goods of variable quality.

DOWNTOWN SHOPPING

Main Street shopping can be tiring, particularly in the biggest, noisiest cities, but if you enjoy pounding the city streets you'll find a huge variety of stores and services, with fashion, electronics, sports goods and other specialty stores mingling with downtown malls, banks and restaurants. This kind of shopping certainly gives you a feel for the pulse of the city.

Much more interesting, though—and to be found in all of the major cities—are the little enclaves that have developed their own specialties. Most obvious are the Chinatowns, Little Italys, and other nationality-based areas, each with their own style and flavor. Some towns are entirely influenced by a particular nationality, such as Kitchener, Ontario, with a large German population (and consequently a really good *Oktoberfest*—see page 230). You will also find that in the bigger cities independent fashion designers' boutiques tend to cluster together in trendy neighborhoods; antiques dealers and fine art galleries do the same, or share one large building to create a market atmosphere; and there will always be street markets with lots of noise and character. These areas are fun to explore and can present some unique items that you won't find anywhere else. Tourist offices can point you in the right direction.

SMALL TOWN SHOPPING

Just about every province has small towns or villages that are known for their concentration of craftspeople, artists, booksellers, and individual boutiques, and these are wonderful places to visit. Invariably peaceful, low-key and friendly, you can amble in and out of stores crammed with interesting unusual items. Mennonite towns, where the lifestyle that has remained unchanged for a century, are fascinating, with residents in old-style clothing getting round by pony and trap. First Nations craft stores are also worth a visit, but not every reservation is geared toward tourists, so make inquiries locally about where you should go.

Walrus, carved in soapstone, at the Inuit Artists' Shop, Ottawa

SOUVENIRS

There are many distinctively Canadian goods that will recall your visit for many years to come, including Inuit soapstone carvings and First Nations art and crafts, that are widely available throughout the country. There are plenty of galleries that guarantee authenticity, in addition to those run by the artists and artisans themselves. Up in the Yukon there are a number of jewelry designers producing pieces from local gold and gemstones—or you can just buy a raw nugget.

Much of the clothing available is unmistakably Canadian—not just the T-shirts

and sweatshirts with destinations or maple leaves emblazoned on the front, but also real lumberjack shirts, moccasins, cowboy boots, and traditional First Nations beaded suede shirts and dresses. Sport fans will enjoy the range of team shirts and hats from the leading hockey and baseball teams.

Maple syrup is an obvious choice, available everywhere from supermarkets to the sugar shacks where it is produced. Canadian confectionary includes the Ganong brand from New Brunswick and Laura Secord chocolates.

There is nothing like the written word to bring back fond memories, and good choices here include *The Spell of the Yukon*, a collection of Robert Service's frontier ballads; *The Shipping News* by Annie Proulx, set in Newfoundland; or the Prince Edward Island classic, *Anne of Green Gables* by Lucy Maud Montgomery.

FURS

Some visitors may be surprised, even shocked, to see so many stores selling furs and clothing made from sealskin. Remember, however, that trade in these items is vital to the survival of many First Nations and Inuit communities, and that where demand has declined, these people have had to find alternatives to provide a livelihood, such as giving over their land to oil exploration or forestry, which has a devastating effect on the local ecology. None of the pelts are from rare species.

TAXES

One thing that can catch visitors out is the fact that price tags do not include tax. When you pay for goods, 7 percent will be added for GST (Goods and Service Tax; TPS in Québec) plus PST (Provincial Sales Tax; TVQ in Québec). PST varies between the provinces.

GST can be reclaimed on certain items that are to be taken

out of the country, so keep all receipts and pick up a leaflet explaining the scheme, available from duty-free stores (some of which can give an instant refund), various other retailers, or Revenue Canada's Visitor Rebate Programme (Summerside Tax Centre, Summerside, Prince Edward Island, C1N 6C6; tel: 1-800/668-4748; www.ccra-adrc.gc.ca). You must claim your refund before leaving the country, so check for the most convenient location, which may be your departure airport (allow plenty of time). PST can only be reclaimed in Manitoba and Québec; there is no PST at all in oil-rich Alberta.

New Brunswick, Nova Scotia, and Labrador/Newfoundland

Sealskin garments by Nunavut designer, Rannva

now have HST (Harmonized Sales Tax), which is a combination of GST and PST, but the rules for reclaiming tax are the same as for GST above.

OPENING HOURS

Stores are generally open from 9 or 10am to 5.30 or 6pm, with late opening on Thursday and Friday, and many are open on Sundays from noon. Times vary though, and big cities will have stores open well into the evening most days. Shopping malls also stay open late, generally closing between 7.30 and 9pm, and souvenir shops in tourist destinations will stay open as long as there's the chance of making a sale.

WHAT TO DO

NAME	Department Stores	Fashion, Leather and Haberdashery	Sports and Casual Wear	Drugstores, Eyecare, Bodycare and Fragrances	Home and Garden	Photographic and Electronics	Jewelry and Gifts	Travel Accessories	Confectionary	Books	HEAD OFFICE
Athletes World Bata			✔								416/446-2020
Banana Republic		✔			✔						888/277-8953
The Bay	✔	✔		✔	✔						416/861-9111
Bentley								✔			514/341-9333
Birks							✔				800/682-2622
Blacks						✔					800/668-3286
Body Shop				✔							800/832-7569
Canadian Tire					✔						800/387-8803
Chapters/Indigo-Coles										✔	800/561-1833
Cookies by George									✔		780/477-6853
Costco	✔			✔	✔	✔				✔	819/669-4375
Cows									✔		800/565-2697
Crabtree & Evelyn				✔							800/272-2873
Danier Leather		✔						✔			416/762-8175
Eddie Bauer			✔					✔			020 7795 6055
English Butler						✔					800/625-7935
Fabricland/Fabricville		✔									416/658-2200
Footlocker			✔								416/742-3590
Future Shop						✔					800.663-2275
Garage Clothing Co		✔									800/340-3962
Harry Rosen		✔									416/935-9020
Holt Renfrew		✔									866/465-8736
Home Hardware					✔						Independent dealers
Japan Camera						✔					800/268-7740
La Senza		✔									877/6440-0551
Laura Secord									✔		416/443-5401
Lawton's				✔							902/468-1000
Le Chateau		✔									888/577-7419
Leather Ranch		✔						✔			418/654-6364
Lenscrafters				✔							513/765-6000 (US H(
London Drugs				✔							604/272-7400
Mark's Work Wearhouse			✔								800/663-6275
McNally Robinson										✔	800/561-1833
Motherhood Maternity		✔									800/466-6223
Northern Reflections		✔									877/902-5608
Peir 1 Imports					✔		✔		✔		800/245-4595
Peoples							✔				800/211-2272
Reitmans		✔									514/384-1140
Rocky Mountain Choc Co.									✔		604/298-2462
Roots			✔								888/30-ROOTS
Running Room			✔								800/419-2906
Sears	✔	✔			✔						888/473-2772
Shoppers Drug Mart				✔							800/SHOPPERS
Suzy Shier		✔									888/260-5557
Tall Girl		✔									866/318-TALL
Unic							✔				866/341-9380

The chart below gives details of just some of the national and international chain stores that you'll find in Canada's major downtown areas and shopping malls. The US company, Sears, is a market leader in the department store category, along with Canada's own The Bay, which developed out of the historic Hudson's Bay Company of pioneer days. The latter has more lively fashion departments. Zellers and WalMart are the leading low-cost department stores.

NUMBER OF SHOPS	DESCRIPTION	SHOP WEBSITE
172	Athletics superstore for clothing and equipment	www.athletesworld.ca
62	Fashions for men and women, plus accessories, jewelry and gifts	www.bananarepublic.com
100	The historic Hudson's Bay Co is now a mid-range department store	www.hbc.com
500	Travel bags and suitcases, purses and wallets and accessories	www.onlinebags.com
38	Jewelry, timepieces, silver and gifts from Canada's foremost jewelry chain	www.birks.com
155	Quick film developing and full range of cameras, film and photo equipment	www.blackphoto.com
116	Cosmetics with a conscience and profits with principles	www.thebodyshop.ca
450+	Practical guys adore this store—tools, hardware, home and garden, sports kit	www.canadiantire.ca
234	Big stores, author readings, book signings, events and maybe coffee too	www.chapters.indigo.ca
14	Wonderful gourmet cookies in a variety of flavours and gift packs	www.cookiesbygeorge.com
61	Warehouse operation providing low prices on a big range of goods	www.costco.com
9	Famous ice cream from Prince Edward I. Locations on PEI and Halifax	www.cows.ca
42	Quality toiletries in pretty packaging, gifts, candles. In all the major malls	www.crabtree-evelyn.com
96	Leather and suede clothing for men and women. Also bags and accessories	www.danier.com
600+	Expedition wear plus fashion casuals and accessories for men and women	www.eddiebauer.com
23	Stylish gifts and home accessories including crystal, dinnerware and linens	www.englishbutler.com
170	Canada's largest retailer for fabrics, thread and sewing notions	www.fabricland.ca
69	The world's leading retailer of athletic footwear and clothing	www.footlocker.com
100+	Electronics retailer, selling TV's, computers, audio and entertainment software	www.futureshop.ca
115	Young fashions at low prices, including T-shirts, denims, skirts and pants	www.garageclothing.com
16	Men's apparel and footwear, with a long, long list of designer labels	www.harryrosen.com
11	Upscale and stylish clothes for office and home including their own label	www.holtrenfrew.com
1,000	Handiman paradise and a fun place to browse stuff impossible to take home	www.homehardware.com
100	Pioneer of 1 hour photo-processing with 10 minute process under test	www.japancamera.com
81	Stylish sensual and fun lingerie from a Quebec based company	www.lasenza.com
174	Quality chocolates, fudge, bons bons and ice cream by a famous Canadian	No website
60	Part of the Sobeys (supermarket) company with 60 stores in Atlantic Canada	www.sobeys.com
160+	Treny fashions with French flair from a Quebec based company	www.le-chateau.ca
17	Leather and suede clothing for men and women. Also bags and accessories	www.leatherranch.com
483	The place you want if you have a vacation eyeglasses problem	www.lenscrafters.com
59	Drugstore chain covering BC, Alberta and Saskatchewan	www.londondrugs.com
308	Casual and work clothes and footware. The place for a real lumberjack shirt	www.marks.com
4	Prairies bookstore chain with some stores specializing in children's books	www.mcnallyrobinson.com
15	Largest maternity wear retailer in Canada. Stylish range of easy-care clothing	http://motherhood.com
150	Ladies casual coordinates with matching pants etc in easy-care fabrics	www.northernrelections.com
65	Distinctive homeware, furnishings, gifts, candles, UNICEF cards, confectionary	No website
170	For more than 80 years this store has been selling fine jewelry across Canada	www.peoplesjewellers.com
598	Classic women's fashions including business and leisure wear	www.reitmans.com
26	Handmade chocolates at 26 outlets in BC, the Prairies, Ontario and Quebec	www.rockychoc.com
140	Outfitters of the Canadian Olympic team and the NHL. Also trendy casuals	www.roots.com
50	Alberta company specializing in running shoes and staffed by runners	www.runningroom.com
125	Traditional department store with good range of homewares and fashions	www.sears.ca
850	Premier drugstore chain in Canada. Quality service from pharmacist owners	www.shoppersdrugmart.ca
450	Trendy young fashions	www.suzyshier.com
14	Fashions for taller women or with disproportionate features	www.tallgirlshop.com
462	Suitcases, backpacks, purses, wallets and accessories such as locks and labels	http://unic.onlinebags.com

PERFORMANCE

Canada has produced many world-class performers in all branches of the arts, and the range of entertainments available is enormous. Toronto is the entertainment hub of the country, is the third-largest film and TV production center in North America (after LA and New York), and is alive with theater, orchestral concerts, comedy, and live music performances year-round. Montréal and Vancouver are close behind, with their own slant on things, and every major city has plenty going on, from classical performances to pub music. Throughout the country, arts festivals provide concentrated culture at regular intervals, and some First Nations gatherings are open to all.

THEATER
There's a thriving theater scene in Canada, including block-buster musicals and long-running plays in big city the-aters, and the classics, such as the renowned Shakespeare Theatre in Stratford, Ontario, and Shaw Festival at Niagara-

FILM
Canada's National Film Board was awarded an Oscar to mark its 50th anniversary, recogniz-ing the fine contribution it has made to the world of cinema.
Canada has a reputation for producing quality art films and animations, and its cities and

worldwide, and all the major cities have comedy clubs, notably Toronto's Second City, and the Yuk Yuks chain.

POPULAR MUSIC
Brian Adams, Avril Lavigne, Alanis Morrissette, Shania Twain, Neil Young, and Céline Dion are just a few of Canada's many musicians who are known internationally. All kinds of music can be found throughout Canada, and Toronto, Vancouver, Calgary, and Montréal feature on most world-tour schedules of the big-name singers and bands.
World-class jazz clubs are easy to find—those in Québec have a certain je ne sais quoi—and blues clubs are equally widespread.

The storm scene from Pericles, Prince of Tyre at Vancouver's 2003 Bard on the Beach season

When We Were Singing at the Belfry theater, Victoria, British Columbia

on-the-Lake. Modern plays and experimental works by local writers are frequently staged.
There are also open-air theater performances in some spectacular locations.

CLASSICAL MUSIC AND DANCE
Canada's cultural institutions include a National Ballet and National Opera Company, in addition to world-class provin-cial orchestras and soloists. There are superb concert halls in all the major cities, which attract top musicians, orches-tras and opera companies from around the world. Every major city will have a schedule of classical music concerts.

landscapes have become enormously popular among US movie and TV companies for location work: Vancouver hosted many series of the X-Files, and Toronto will have between 20 and 40 movies being shot on location on any day of the year (it's often used as a stand-in for New York).

COMEDY
Canada has produced a long, long list of comedians who have earned international fame, including Jim Carrey, Mike Myers, Dan Aykroyd, John Candy, and Martin Short.
The international Just For Laughs Festival in Montréal (see page 213) is televised

FOLK AND COUNTRY MUSIC
Singers such as Gordon Lightfood and Anne Murray introduced the world to Canadian folk music, and folk clubs are thriving throughout the country, with lots of sum-mer festivals. The Maritimes have a strong tradition of fid-dle music and Celtic song.
Country music is popular everywhere, but especially in the Prairies, where the cowboy culture is alive and well.

SMOKING
There's a general no-smoking rule in all places of public entertainment, including most open-air venues.

NIGHTLIFE

Canadians might be known as outdoors people—and they certainly do enjoy communing with nature—but they know how to party too, and the opportunities for living it up into the early hours (or even till dawn) are plentiful, at least in the cities. As everywhere, things are quieter out in the country, and in the north might be confined to gathering for a drink beneath the midnight sun or the aurora borealis, depending on the time of year.

NIGHTCLUBS

All the big cities have a choice of nightclubs. There are plenty of high-tech dance clubs, with DJs spinning the latest rhythms, big-screen music videos and perhaps more than one dance floor; some of these clubs include chill-out areas and food service. Most of them won't really get going before 11pm or midnight and will

Canada has provided the world with many of its favorite comedians

continue till between 2am and dawn.

There are also sophisticated cabaret clubs, cocktail lounges and piano bars, usually attracting a more mature crowd.

CASINOS

Gambling has only been legal in Canada since 1969, but you will find plenty of chances to indulge, with superb casinos in or near the major cities—and Niagara Falls is about to get a second huge casino complex. In addition to all the favorite table games—roulette, black-jack, craps, and so on—they usually have thousands of slot machines, fine restaurants and spectacular shows.

Unusually, some casinos are charitable or community organizations, raising funds for local causes.

There will always be an age limit—usually over 18 or 19—and admission is free (though there may be a charge to see the stage shows).

LIVE MUSIC VENUES

Canada's vibrant music scene gives rise to a huge number of venues featuring national or international bands, or showcasing local acts. You might see a soon-to-be-famous band in a fairly modest club, but even if it's just the local favorites, standards are pretty high everywhere.

Many venues specialize in a particular type of music, so it's easy to find a place to suit your taste. Others feature different styles on different nights of the week.

Some clubs levy a cover charge while other's don't; sometimes it depends what is on, or which night of the week you go. The music usually kicks off at about 9 or 10pm, and bars that are open all day will only start charging admission after a certain time.

PUBS AND BARS

Sometimes all you need is good company, and that's the time to head for one of the many pubs and neighborhood bars. If you choose well, you will get to know a lot of new people and have a great time.

Canadians are generally outgoing and interested in their visitors, so conversation comes easy. In summer you can usually find a place with tables outside to enjoy the buzzy downtown atmosphere.

Pubs vary in character, sometimes replicating an English pub, sometimes with an Irish theme and sometimes more Americanized, reminiscent of the old TV show *Cheers*.

Unlike English pubs, you will get table service for drinks as well as food (where it's available), and tips are expected.

GAY CLUBS

Canada is very gay-tolerant—actively so in some places: Toronto has huge Gay Pride and Aids Awareness events

Jill Townsend Big Band at The Cellar, Vancouver

every year, and Montréal is a renowned gay destination.

Every major city has at least one or two gay clubs (Montréal has more than 100), and they are usually brash, noisy and fun, with dancing and stage shows. Many are popular with—and welcoming to—a straight crowd too.

SMOKING

Canada is still struggling with legislation over smoking in bars. After imposing a blanket ban, many provinces had to backtrack following vociferous opposition from bar owners, who claimed they were losing custom. Rules vary from place to place, so check in advance if it's important to you.

SPORTS AND ACTIVITIES

An entire book could easily be devoted to sports and activities in Canada—especially activities. There are seemingly endless possibilities, summer and winter, in every part of the country. There is also avid support for certain spectator sports. Hockey is a national obsession, and baseball and Canadian football games attract big crowds—the atmosphere at any of these can be electric. Violence (at least off the playing surface) is not an issue, and even if you are not a sports fan, the experience of being among all the hot-dog-munching, enthusiastically vocal supporters is great fun.

HOCKEY
www.canadianhockey.ca
www.nhl.com
Don't call it ice hockey. To Canadians it's just hockey, and the other kind is called field hockey. The season runs from October to early April, when excitement reaches fever pitch as Canada's top teams vie with

Manitoba Moose on the ice

their US counterparts for the NHL (National Hockey League) championship.

The national team is among the top three in the world, and in the 2002 Winter Olympics in Salt Lake City, Canada took the gold medals in both men's and women's events.

Hockey is fast and furious (often literally), with a reputation for violence on the ice—a favorite joke goes: "I went to a boxing match last night, and a hockey game broke out"—but when the teams behave, its tremendously exciting. Wear warm clothing, including a hat and gloves—it gets very cold sitting by the ice, unless you leap up and down like the locals. (See also pages 16–17.)

BASEBALL
www.majorleaguebaseball.ca
Baseball has a strong following, particularly in Toronto—its Blue Jays have played in the American League since 1976 and won the World Series in 1992 and 1993. The city was also where the legendary Babe Ruth scored his first home run.

The season runs from April through September/October, so games are often played in bright sunshine—wear a hat, sunglasses and sunscreen, and bring binoculars if you can: some of the seats are a long way from the field. For the full experience, buy plenty of hotdogs and sodas, and join in the waves and interval keep-fit session.

CANADIAN FOOTBALL
www.cfl.ca
This is similar to American football, and therefore quite incomprehensible to most visitors from Europe, but if you're an enthusiast you can see CFL (Canadian Football League) games in Montréal, Toronto, Hamilton, Calgary, Edmonton, Saskatoon, Winnipeg, and Vancouver. The season is from late June to early November.

Important differences from American football—bigger ball, longer pitch, deeper end zone, field goalpost positioning, 12 players instead of 11, three downs instead of four—make for a faster game with more passing and less rushing at the opponents.

BASKETBALL
www.nba.com
Although the game was invented by a Canadian (see page 17), it is not that big here at a professional level, but the Toronto Raptors, only established in the mid-1990s, have made something of a mark in the NBA. The season runs from October through June.

HORSERACING
www..woodbineentertainment.com
Racetracks are located within proximity of all the major population centers, but the top one is the Woodbine track near Toronto, which hosts Canada's premier races with the richest prizes. Two-thirds of Canada's horseracing takes place in Ontario. Racetracks

Saskatchewan's Roughriders are among the teams in the CFL

usually also have casino-style slot machines, feature thoroughbred, standard-bred or harness racing (sometimes all three), and when there's no live racing, events are beamed in from the US, Hong Kong and Australia.

MOTOR RACING
www.grandprix.ca
The future of the Canadian Grand Prix is uncertain at the time of going to press, since new laws banning sponsorship by tobacco companies have robbed the sport of its financial support. How this will affect the coming season is hard to say—appeals against the Tobacco Act are pending.

During the 2003 season the following provinces had circuits with regular fixtures, including Formula events, CASCAR, motorcycle racing and demolition derbys: Québec had eight, including the Grand Prix circuit (Gilles Villeneuve, in Montréal); Ontario five; Alberta three; British Columbia two; and one each in Manitoba and Nova Scotia. The other provinces have none.

GOLF

www.golfcanada.com

Golf is hugely popular in Canada, and there are more than 2,000 courses throughout the country in all kinds of territory, from spectacular mountains to seaside links and parklands. A number were designed by famous golfers. Glen Abbey, at Oakville, Ontario, is one of the best; the Top of the World course in Dawson City, Yukon (see page 251), is the most northerly, with 24-hour daylight in mid-summer. The Canadian Open is held at a different venue each year.

For players, there's a great choice, including resort hotels that have superb golf courses on the grounds—Jasper is notable among these. Many ordinary hotels offer golf packages using nearby courses. Visitors are generally welcome, but it's advisable to make reservations for tee times, particularly in summer. Most courses have clubs and carts for rent. As everywhere, green fees vary.

The playing season very much depends on weather conditions, but summers are pretty reliable, and spring and autumn can be glorious.

WINTER SPORTS

www.ski-guide.com/canmap

Naturally, there are exceptionally good opportunities for winter sports in Canada, with plenty of competitive events to watch too. All over the country, winter snows bring the chance to do cross-country (or Nordic) and downhill skiing, snow-

boarding, snow-tubing, snow-mobiling, snowshoeing, dogsled trips, and skating on frozen lakes, ponds and rivers.

The west and the Laurentians have the best resorts, notably Whistler, where the premier downhill and extreme sports competitions take place; it is set to host the 2010 Winter Olympics. Other premier locations include Blackcomb, Banff and Lake Louise, Kicking Horse near Calgary, and Tremblant in Québec. In Ontario, head for Collingwood. Even in top resorts, ski passes tend to cost less than in Europe, and elsewhere it's even cheaper.

There are thousands of skating rinks throughout Canada, but it's much more fun out in

Snowboarding was invented in Whistler, a winter thrillseekers' destination

the open on lakes, ponds, rivers, and canals. Popular areas often have floodlighting for night-time skating, piped music and booths selling hot drinks and snacks. Rinks and some outdoor sites offer skate rental. Wear thick socks and get skates a size bigger than your shoe size.

WATER SPORTS

The popular image of Canada usually includes a canoe on a stretch of calm water, with spectacular mountain scenery in the background. It's not a false image, and anyone can place themselves into this idyllic picture. Wherever there is water, there's likely to be an outfitter providing canoes and

kayaks—and probably tuition and guided trips too.

Sea-kayaking is also popular, and is a wonderful way to explore remote areas of the Atlantic and Pacific coastlines. Best of all, you can kayak among whales off both the Atlantic and BC coasts during the season.

Inland, on the majestic rivers, you can go whitewater rafting through boiling rapids—particularly exhilarating in spring and early summer when the melt-water adds extra power to the torrent. There are plenty of companies that specialize in this and that have excellent safety records.

Divers can explore some of the clearest waters in the world off both the Atlantic and Pacific coasts, where, in addition to the wonderful marine life, there are wrecks to explore. Diving is also possible in the Great Lakes.

Swimming is good in lakes, rivers and the oceans as soon as the winter chill has gone, though really hardy souls can join one of the Polar Bear clubs on their winter dips through broken ice. There are a surprising number (i.e., more than one) of these clubs.

FISHING

There are superb fishing opportunities, summer and winter, in the rivers and lakes, but you will need a license and regulations are strictly enforced, with regular warden

patrols in even the remotest areas. Contact the tourist information office or make inquiries at an equipment store or outfitter.

Offshore fishing trips can be arranged at various points along the Atlantic and Pacific coasts. If you accidentally catch a lobster down east, throw it back immediately. Lobster fishing is a huge industry here and is strictly licensed.

In winter, ice fishing is a popular pastime, in which you venture out onto a frozen lake, saw a hole through the thick ice, drop your line through it... and wait. In some places the hole is already cut for you, and you might get a little wooden hut on the ice where you can warm yourself.

Jogging in Stanley Park, Vancouver

HUNTING

Hunting is strictly regulated in Canada. Whatever you do, do not shoot a moose—even the locals have to enter a lottery to win a license to do so, and penalties for flouting the rules are severe, including imprisonment. First Nations and Inuits are exempt from these rules.

If you want to bring your own gun into Canada, you will need to contact the Canadian embassy in your country of residence to check on the regulations and consult customs and excise officials regarding airport security.

HIKING AND WALKING

Canadians are keen hikers, and there is a huge number of

good trails of varying length all over Canada, particularly in the national and provincial parks. They are well mapped, sometimes signposted, and guided hikes with a naturalist are often available.

If you plan to set off into the wilderness, check weather conditions, make sure you are fully equipped and wearing the proper gear, and let someone know where you are going. Good maps are available from park information offices and specialist bookstores.

CLIMBING

Climbers automatically think of the Rocky Mountains and Laurentians, and those ranges certainly do have some great climbs (though they are not the only options by any means), with outfitters offering tuition, equipment and guided climbing trips. If you come in winter you can have a go at climbing a frozen waterfall too. It's sometimes hard to imagine the severity of the Canadian winter, so even experienced climbers should very carefully think about when to go.

HORSEBACK RIDING

The Prairies—known for their vast wheatfields—are also Canada's cowboy country, with great opportunities for taking to the saddle. And there are places all over the country where you can go out on horseback, either on a guided ride or on your own (as long as you can demonstrate your competence). Stables offer trail-riding by the hour, the day or multiday trip, or you can stay at a guest ranch and work on the farm, round up cattle and ride for pure pleasure.

If you just want to watch expert riders, try to get to one of the many rodeos that are regularly held on the Prairies during summer.

WILDLIFE WATCHING

The opportunity of seeing a bear or herd of caribou in the wild, or a pod of whales surfacing close to your boat, is a huge attraction in Canada, and there are plenty of companies offering organized trips. It's probably best to use these experts, since they know where to find what you are looking for and how best to maintain safety and not alarm the wildlife. Nevertheless, even a short hike in one of the national or provincial parks may offer sightings, and park offices can give advice about what is around.

You'll often see moose along the roadsides in certain areas—drive carefully. Aside from not wanting to harm the animal, it

Wild deer are protected in Québec's Réserve Faunique des Laurentides

is akin to driving into a wall in terms of damage and injury.

For birdwatchers there are countless reserves and observation points on migratory flight lines.

HEALTH AND BEAUTY

Activities are great for health and fitness, but after all the exertion there's nothing like a bit of pampering. There are lots of spas with a range of soothing options—from a single treatment to a whole day or a weekend tailored to your requirements, including nutritious meals. If you're in the Rockies, you can just go for a soak in one of the natural hot springs.

CHILDREN'S CANADA

Canada is a fun country for kids, with lots of attractions, including theme parks, waterparks, zoos and wildlife parks, open farms, and science centers full of hands-on exhibits. Even the big cities have a larger number of things specifically for children than you would find in their European counterparts, and this is equally true of more modest-size towns. In addition to the specific attractions, children will enjoy many of the same outdoor activities as their parents—enhanced, for them, by the sight of so many adults acting just like kids.

THEME PARKS AND WATERPARKS
There are plenty of amusement parks throughout the country, but Canada's Wonderland (see page 229) in Ontario is the nearest thing you'll get to a Disneyland experience; allow a full day or more to sample all the thrill rides and shows. Waterparks are abundant, and incorporate giant water slides and splash pools. These are usually open from about May to late August or September, when the weather is at its best, and some will have water that has been slightly warmed. In winter, there are some indoor amusement complexes, with everything from toddlers' ball-pools to video arcades.

NATIONAL AND PROVINCIAL PARKS
Canada has 39 national parks and hundreds of provincial parks. These are great places to let off steam and perhaps spot some wildlife you'd only see in a zoo back home—and many have special events for children. The relevant national park offices have details. Most offer canoeing or kayaking and other activities too.

MUSEUMS
Canada's museums are particularly child-friendly, and often have lively areas designed specially for kids, with interactive exhibits, interpreters to engage their interest, and fun demonstrations. Winnipeg, Ottawa and London (Ontario) have children's museums devoted entirely to the younger generation. Science museums also

have a particular appeal, and just about every provincial capital has one.

Open-air museums are good for kids, too, where they can see real people in costume, living as their forebears once did. They can explore old homes, take a wagon ride and taste traditional candy.

Schoolchildren try their hand at musket drill at Toronto's Fort York

ZOOS, WILDLIFE PARKS AND AQUARIUMS
A sure bet for entertaining the little ones is to show them some animals, and Canada has a number of excellent places, including the superb Toronto Zoo and Vancouver Aquarium. (see pages 118 and 149) There are also buffalo herds and caribou (reindeer) that can be seen in the wild.

ACTIVITIES
There's a long list of activities that children will enjoy, including panning for gold in the Yukon, horseback riding on the Prairies, whale-watching off British Columbia or the Atlantic coast, learning to ski, or just rollerblading around a city park.

SUMMER CAMPS
If your children have an independent nature (and you can bear to be separated from them), you can sign them up for a spell at summer camp (www.camppage.com/canada) where they can make new friends and have an exciting Canadian experience. There are camps for every kind of interest, from wilderness adventures to circus skills, and you can choose between fully residential or day camps, where they return to you each evening.

BEACHES
You might not think of Canada for a beach vacation, but there are some wonderful stretches of sand on both the east and west coasts. Many of the lakes have sandy beaches, too, notably on Georgian Bay and the Toronto Islands, with safe swimming. Canada's beaches are generally unspoiled, though there will probably be good facilities nearby, and they remain scenically attractive.

CONCESSIONS
There are invariably reduced admission charges for children and students (which sometimes means over 12), except in theme parks and waterparks, where only the tiniest toddlers and grandparents get a lower price.

Children are not allowed in any bars, pubs, nightclubs, or casinos.

FESTIVALS AND EVENTS

It seems that there is always something to celebrate somewhere in Canada, and there are quite literally thousands of festivals and events countrywide every year. Edmonton, Alberta, has gained the title of "Canada's Festival City," but the others aren't that far behind, and relevant tourist information offices have full details. The list of international and nationally important events is impressive, but don't overlook the little local events where you can really get to know people and gain an insight into small-town Canadian life. While many of the festivals indulge a particular interest, there is one that brings the whole country together—Canada Day, on July 1—with parades, fireworks, open-air concerts, and general partying.

invite the world to Ontario to sample their splendid beers at *Oktoberfest*.

Agricultural shows and fall fairs feature locally grown produce and culinary specialties, along with livestock and fairground attractions.

ARTS FESTIVALS

There's great enthusiasm for the arts, and the festivals that celebrate them are often world-class and internationally renowned, such as the Shaw Festival at Niagara-on-the-Lake, the Toronto Film Festival, Montréal's Just For Laughs

Over in the Maritimes and Newfoundland—and to a large extent in Québec and Ontario—traditional Celtic-style fiddle music is huge, and among the hundreds of events throughout the year the highlights are the Celtic Colours Festival in Cape Breton, Nova

WINTER FESTIVALS

When winter comes and the snow piles up to the rafters, when others might think only of staying indoors until the spring melt, Canadians hold festivals to celebrate the weather. Winter festivals are glittering affairs, with ice-sculpting competitions, winter sports, sleigh-rides, dogsled and snowmobile racing, and entertainment. The streets sparkle with lights reflecting off the ice and an aroma of warming food and drink wafts on the cold air. Christmas Lights Across Canada kicks off in the capital in December, where nearly 300,000 dazzling lights are switched on, timed to coincide with similar displays across the nation.

The winter freeze brings the glittering celebration of Québec's Neige Festival

ETHNIC FESTIVALS

In addition to Kitchener's German *Oktoberfest*, already mentioned, there are other national groups who maintain their culture through festivals. The Chinese population of Vancouver stage one of the best Chinese New Year celebrations in North America, and there's a similar event in Toronto. In Newfoundland on St. Patrick's Day, descendants of Irish immigrants do what they do best—make music and make merry—and Montréal also celebrates Paddy's Day in fine style. In August, the Scottish contingent have their turn, with highland games and bagpipe music in Fergus, Ontario, and all year there are plenty of events with a Scottish flavor in Nova Scotia (New Scotland). And in Ottawa each August, the local Greek community showcase their homeland's culture.

Comedy Festival, and Ottawa's International Writers' Festival. Every big city has a number of arts festivals, and many of the smaller places will have at least one during the year, either specializing in one aspect, or encompassing all the arts in a varied and interesting schedule of events.

MUSIC

All kinds of music are celebrated in Canada, with festivals of opera, classical and chamber music. There are also jazz, blues and rock festivals in most major cities, attracting international performers.

Folk music is extremely popular here, and there are big festivals in all the provinces.

Scotia, in October, which attracts top performers from many countries, and the Grand Masters Fiddle Championships at Nepean, Ottawa, in August, which showcases Canada's own favorite players.

FOOD AND DRINK

There is much to celebrate in the wonderful food and drink produced in Canada, and this is recognized in the various seasonal festivals.

Seafood festivals abound along the coasts in late summer. The wine regions of Ontario and British Columbia celebrate their harvest later on, in October—which is also the time when Kitchener's German-extraction population

ATLANTIC PROVINCES

The waters around the Atlantic Provinces offer excellent whale-watching

The Atlantic provinces—the Maritimes—have a character that is quite distinct from the rest of Canada, with a culture that blends the Acadian (French) heritage with that of the Irish and Scottish who settled here in large numbers. Lively cities—Halifax, Nova Scotia, is the biggest—have good shopping, nightlife and cultural entertainment, and there are captivating small towns amid spectacular scenery that is perfect for an active outdoors vacation.

There are some superb national and provincial parks that are great for hiking and wildlife spotting, including bear and moose. The region also has some of the most beautiful coastlines in the world, with opportunities for whale-watching, fishing and kayaking—and the famous Fundy tides to experience. This is also a terrific place for winter sports—winters are mild, but snowfall is among the highest in the country—and though the slopes are not as spectacular as in more mountainous areas, there are lots of scenic cross-country, dogsledding and snowmobile trails, ice-fishing, and frozen waterfall climbing.

Many visit this part of country just for the traditional Celtic music—a legacy of the Scottish and Irish immigrants. Every province has its own style, and there are countless events year-round. Provincial capitals also attract touring performers, and Halifax has its own symphony orchestra.

Shopping

FREDERICTON

BOTINICALS GIFT SHOP AND STUDIO
65 Shore Street, Fredericton, New Brunswick, E3B 1R3
Tel 506/454-7361, 877/454-7361
www.botinicalsgiftshop.com
An attractive clapboard house, next door to Bliss Carman

House, decked with window-boxes full of trailing plants, and fronted by garden foliage, is the setting for this shop. It sells unique craftwork by a number of the top artisans in the Maritimes, including superb metal floral arrangements by John L. Welling.
🕐 Tue–Fri 10–6, Sat noon–6, Sun and Mon by appointment

BOYCE FARMERS' MARKET
665 George Street, Fredericton, New Brunswick, E3A 1A3
Tel 506/451-1815
www.boycefarmersmarket.com
This Fredericton institution was founded in the early 19th century by local benefactor William Boyce, and moved to its present home in 1951. Amid a cheerful, bustling atmosphere, over 200 vendors offer local produce and specialty foods, crafts and gifts.
🕐 Sat 6am–1pm

REGENT MALL
1381 Regent Street, Fredericton, New Brunswick, E3C 1A2
Tel 506/452-1005
www.regentmall.ca

Fredericton's biggest and newest mall is bright and attractive, and home to 115 stores and services. It's anchored by Sears, Wal-Mart, Toys'R'Us, Chapters, and Sport Check, along with a good range of fashion boutiques and some interesting specialty stores.
🕐 Mon–Sat 10–9.30, Sun noon–5
🚌 116 🚗 Southern edge of town just beyond the Trans-Canada Highway/101 intersection 🍴 The food court includes New York Fries, McDonald's, KFC, Deluxe French Fries, Hardy's Subs, Mrs Vanelli, Dairy Queen, and Made in Japan

RIVER VALLEY CRAFTS AND ARTISAN GIFT SHOPS
Soldiers' Barracks, Carleton Street, Fredericton, New Brunswick
Tel 506/460-2837
Six stores and artisans' studios are grouped together on the first floor of the former

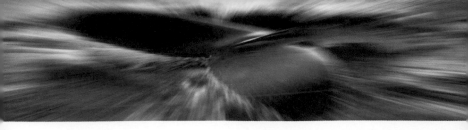

Soldiers' Barracks in the historic Garrison District. In these historic surroundings you can buy First Nations crafts, paintings, jewelry, pottery, soaps, Celtic art, and much more.
🕐 Daily, Jun–Sep

HALIFAX

HALIFAX SHOPPING CENTRE
7001 Mumford Road, Halifax,
Nova Scotia, B3L 4N7
Tel 902/453-1752
www.halifaxshoppingcentre.com
The biggest shopping mall in Halifax, anchored by Sears, Sears Outlet and Wal-Mart, with over 150 stores, including the largest Gap and Gap for Kids in the Atlantic provinces. In bright new surroundings, there's fashion, sporting goods, drugstores, homeware, and bookstores, plus banks, hair salons and fast-food outlets.
🕐 Mon–Sat 9.30–9 🚌 1–6, 9, 10, 14, 15, 18, 20, 52, 58 🚌 Ten minutes from downtown via Quinpool and Connaught

JOHN W. DOULL
1684 Barrington Street, Halifax, Nova Scotia, B3J 2A2
Tel 902/429-1652, 800/317-8613
www.doullbooks.com
Statues and sculptures among the floor-to-ceiling book shelves make for a highly entertaining visit to this downtown store (corner of Prince and Barrington). Huge stock of old books, focusing on nautical themes and books about the Atlantic provinces; also modern first editions, academic, history, and art books.
🕐 Mon–Tue 9.30–6, Wed–Fri 9.30–9, Sat 10–9 🚌 6

MONCTON

CHAMPLAIN PLACE
477 Paul Street, Dieppe, Moncton, New Brunswick, E1A 4X5
Tel 506/857-0040
The biggest shopping mall in the Atlantic provinces, attracting shoppers even from the provincial capital. It's a bright, modern place, anchored by Sears, Sobeys and Wal-mart, with a good range of specialty stores, fashions, sporting goods, electronics, and homeware. There's a multiplex

movie theater and an indoor-outdoor amusement park.
🕐 Mon–Sat 10–9, Sun and holidays noon–5 🍴 Usual food court outlets, plus Don Cherry's Grapevine and McGinnis Landing, which have more varied menus—and, of course, there's a Tim Horton's

NEWTOWN

KISSING BRIDGES GIFT SHOP
1666 Route 890, Newtown,
New Brunswick, E4G 1N4
Tel 506/433-4813
www.kissingbridges.com
It's not only Madison County that has them—Route 890 is also the "Covered Bridges Discovery Byway." There are 22 of them along this route, but only one that's converted into a shop. Covered bridge memorabilia made from pewter, pottery, stained glass, wrought iron, and wood, plus postcards, calendars and T-shirts.
🕐 Tue–Sun 9–5, May–mid-Oct (Mon and evenings by chance); by appointment mid-Oct–24 Dec 🚌 Off Trans-Canada Highway at exits 195, 233, and 239

SAINT JOHN

THE SCHOLAR'S DEN
105 Prince Edward Street, Saint John, New Brunswick, E2L 3S1
Tel 506/657-2665
www.abebooks.com/home/sden
Housed in a former drugstore, with the original 100-year-old storefront, apothecary's marble-top counter, oak shelving, and drawers. Sells not only the scholarly works indicated by the name, but also contemporary hardcover titles, paperbacks and vinyl records.
🕐 Mon–Sat 11–5, Sun 11–5, Aug–Jan

ST. JOHN'S

AVALON MALL
48 Kenmouth Road, St. John's, Newfoundland and Labrador, A1B 1W3
Tel 709/739-8088
Attractive mall on two levels, anchored by a big Empire Theatres multiplex, Wal-Mart and Sobeys supermarket. As usual, there are lots of clothing outlets, plus books, music, gifts, jewelry, and gadgets.
🕐 Mon–Sat 10–10, Sun noon–5 🚌 3, 4, 7, 14, 15 🍴 Food court has burgers,

fish and chips, Japanese, and Italian food. Restaurants include Emerald Place, Whole Health, Fog City Brewing Company

Performance

ANNAPOLIS ROYAL

KING'S
209 St. George Street, Annapolis Royal, Nova Scotia, B0S 1A0
Tel 902/532-7704, 902/532-5466
www.kingstheatre.ca

Historic building presenting 50 to 70 live shows (drama and concerts), including a summer festival and movies.
🕐 Year-round 💵 Price varies, depending on event

ANTIGONISH

BAUER
St. Francis Xavier University, Antigonish, Nova Scotia, B2G 2W5
Tel 902/863-4921
www.stfx.ca/theatre-antigonish
Nova Scotia's longest-running professional repertory theater, home to the university community theater, Theatre Antigonish and the summer Festival Antigonish season.
🕐 Year-round 💵 $9.50–23

CAPE BRETON

SAVOY
116 Commercial Street, Glace Bay, Cape Breton, Nova Scotia, B1A 3C1
Tel 902/564-6668, 902/842-1577
www.savoytheatre.com
A grand 1920s theater that was converted into a movie house, converted back again in the 1970s, and restored in the 1990s after a fire. It is now one of finest theaters in the whole of Canada.
🕐 Late Jun–mid-Oct 💵 $20–40

WHAT TO DO

CHARLOTTETOWN

EMPIRE STUDIO 8
University Avenue, West Royalty, Charlottetown, Prince Edward Island, C1E 1Z6
Tel 902/368-1922
www.empiretheatres.com
Modern multiscreen theater showing the latest mainstream releases. Located at Charlottetown Mall.
🕐 Daily 🎫 Adult $9.75, child (under 13) $5.25, or (14–17) $8

DARTMOUTH

ALDERNEY LANDING
2 Ochterloney Street, Dartmouth Waterfront Park, Dartmouth, Nova Scotia, B2Y 3Z3
Tel 902/461-8401
www.alderneylanding.com
Performing arts center with a 285-seat theater, outdoor event plaza and art gallery. Home of the Eastern Front Theatre Company, plus professional touring drama and dance companies.
🕐 Year-round 🎫 $21 (average)

FREDERICTON

EMPIRE THEATRES
1381 Regent Street, Regent Mall, Fredericton, New Brunswick, E3C 1A2
Tel 506/458-9704
www.empiretheatres.com
This 10-theater movieplex is an integral part of the Regent Mall on the south side of town; it screens the latest Hollywood releases.
🕐 Daily 🎫 Adult $9.75, child $5.25 🚌 116

OFFICERS' SQUARE
575 Queen Street, Fredericton, New Brunswick
Tel 506/460-2129
Free concerts in the historic Garrison District, including jazz, blues, folk, country and marching bands, plus theater by the Calithumpians, who perform humorous and historical productions.
🕐 Theater: Jul–Aug; concerts: late Jun–Aug 🎫 Free

THE PLAYHOUSE
686 Queen Street, Fredericton, New Brunswick E3B 5A6
Tel 506/458-8344
www.theplayhouse.nb.ca

Modern theater, next to the Legislature, with a varied schedule (all in English) of drama, comedy and all kinds of music. Home of Theatre New Brunswick, the province's leading English-language company.
🕐 Year-round 🎫 Price varies

HALIFAX

DALHOUSIE ARTS CENTRE
6100 University Avenue, Halifax, Nova Scotia, B3H 3J5
Tel 902/494-3820, 800/874-1669
www.dal.ca
The Rebecca Cohn Auditorium here hosts jazz, opera, Celtic, rock, and country music concerts; it's also home to Symphony Nova Scotia.
🕐 Year-round 🎫 Varies, depending on event 🚌 1, 3, 58

EMPIRE 17 CINEMAS AND IMAX
190 Chain Lake Drive, Bayers Lake Park, Halifax, Nova Scotia, B3S 1C5
Tel 902/876-4800
www.empireimax.com
Halifax's principal movie destination, with a multiscreen theater showing latest first-run releases; plus Atlantic Canada's only IMAX theater, which has 2D and 3D movies.
🕐 Daily 🎫 Adult $10, child $6–7.50 🚌 12, 21 🚗 West of downtown via Quinpool and St. Margaret's Bay roads

GRAFTON STREET DINNER THEATRE
1741 Grafton Street, Halifax, Nova Scotia, B3J 2W1
Tel 902/425-1961
www.graftonstdinnertheatre.com
Lighthearted musical comedies with some audience interaction. Specially written shows focus on a particular era of the

20th century, with wait staff also in character. Three-course dinner offers limited choices.
🕐 Shows 6.45–10pm 🎫 Adult $32, child (under 12) $15.65 except Sat 🚌 6

NEPTUNE
1593 Argyle Street, Halifax, Nova Scotia, B3J 2B2
Tel 902/429-7070, 800/565-7345
www.neptunetheatre.com
Dating from 1915, the theater was renovated in 1997 and is home to one of the oldest professional companies in Canada (plus a theater school). Two auditoriums feature world-class drama, music and comedy.
🕐 Year-round 🎫 Price varies, depending on show 🚌 1, 3, 10, 14

SHAKESPEARE BY THE SEA
Point Pleasant Drive, Halifax, Nova Scotia
Tel 902/422-0295
Summer season of open-air theater featuring Shakespeare favorites, an annual event since 1994, performed in beautiful Point Pleasant Park.
🕐 Jul–Aug 🎫 Donation ($8 suggested); some "pay-what-you-can" performances 🚌 9 ⊘

MONCTON

CAPITOL
811 Main Street, Moncton, New Brunswick, E1C 1G1
Tel 506/856-4377
www.capitol.nb.ca
This fine theater has been magnificently restored to its 1920s splendor, including the original stenciling and gilded boxes; it stages drama, dance, comedy, and concerts featuring all kinds of music.
🕐 Year-round. 🎫 🚌 1, 2, 3

FAMOUS PLAYERS
125 Trinity Drive, Moncton, New
Brunswick, E1G 2J7
Tel 506/854-3456
www.famousplayers.com
Eight curved wall-to-wall
screens and stadium seating,
with state-of-the-art projection
and sound.
🎬 Daily 🎟 Adult $10.25, child (under
13) $5.50 🚌 Codiac bus from down-
town

GLASGOW SQUARE
15 Riverside Parkway, New Glasgow,
Nova Scotia
Tel 902/752-4800, 888/873-0777
www.newglasgowriverfront.ca/Glasgow
Distinctive modern building,
with a full schedule of drama
and music, including some on
the outdoor stage in summer.
🎬 Year-round 🎟 Price varies, some
shows are free

PARRSBORO

SHIP'S COMPANY THEATRE
Upper Harbour, Parrsboro, Nova Scotia,
B0M 1S0
Tel 902/254-3000, 800/565-SHOW
www.shipscompany.com
Unique entertainment experience: The theater is the historic
vessel, MV *Kipawo*. Season
includes two drama productions and a concert series.
🎬 Tue–Sat, Jul–Aug 🎟 $11.75–19.75

PICTOU

**DECOSTE ENTERTAINMENT
CENTRE**
Water Street, Pictou, Nova Scotia,
B0K 1H0
Tel 902/485-8848, 800/353-5338
www.decostecentre.ca
This is a showcase for Nova
Scotia culture and contempo-
rary talent, including informal
ceilidhs, concerts, pipebands,
highland dancing and pioneer
reenactments.
🎬 Mar–Dec 🎟 $10–39

ST. JOHN'S

EMPIRE STUDIO 12
Avalon Mall, Kenmount Road, St. John's,
Newfoundland and Labrador, A1B 1W3
Tel 709/722-5775
www.empiretheatres.com
Spacious modern multiplex
showing all the latest releases,
with stadium seating.

🎬 Daily 🎟 Adult $10.25, child (under
13) $5.25 or (14–17) $8.50 🚌 3, 4, 7,
14, 15

WOLFVILLE

ATLANTIC THEATRE FESTIVAL
356 Main Street, Wolfville, Nova Scotia,
B0P 1X0
Tel 902/542-4242, 800/337-6661
http://atf.ns.ca
World-class professional performers present the classics in
a 500-seat thrust stage theater;
backstage tours and accommodations packages available.
🎬 Late Jun–end Aug 🎟 $10–37
🚌 Across from Acadia University

YARMOUTH

TH'YARC
76 Parade Street, Yarmouth, Nova Scotia,
B5A 3B4
Tel 902/742/8150
Live theater, music concerts,
and other performances are
held at this arts facility, which
also has a gallery of work by
local artists.
🎬 Mid-Mar to mid-Dec 🎟 Prices vary

Nightlife

CHARLOTTETOWN

MYRON'S CABARET
151 Kent Street, Charlottetown, Prince
Edward Island
Tel 902/892-4375
www.myrons.com
Live music nightly, including
tribute bands (Beatles, Kiss,
Pink Floyd) and Maritimes
musicians playing classic rock.
Also dance club and pub.
🎬 Daily 11am–2am 🎟 $6 after 9
Thu–Sat, otherwise free

OLDE DUBLIN PUB
131 Sydney Street, Charlottetown,
Prince Edward Island, C1A 1G5
Tel 902/892-6992
www.oldedublinpub.com
Irish theme pub upstairs from
Claddagh Room restaurant
with traditional music.
🎬 Daily. Live entertainment: Sat–Sun
nights, May–Sep 🎟 $5 Thu–Sat, $3
Sun–Wed (free before 8.30pm)

FREDERICTON

DOLAN'S
Piper's Lane, 349 King Street,
Fredericton, New Brunswick
Tel 506/454-7474

The city's only Irish-style pub,
with a Maritime Kitchen Party
Thursday, Friday and Saturday
nights, featuring best East
Coast Celtic talent. Classic rock
other nights. Full dinner menu.
🎬 Daily 🎟 $5 after 8pm Fri and Sat,
otherwise free

**TWENTY 20 CLUB/THE RIGHT
SPOT**
403 Regent Street, Fredericton, New
Brunswick
Tel 506/457-9887
Three lounges in the old
Regent Station building, one
with pool tables and another a
sports bar; '60s music.
🎬 Daily, 10pm–2am 🎟 $2.25 for spe-
cial events, otherwise free

HALIFAX

CASINO NOVA SCOTIA
1983 Upper Water Street, Halifax, Nova
Scotia, B3J 3Y5
Tel 902/425-7777, 888-6GAMES6
www.casinonovascotia.com
Waterfront casino with table
games, including baccarat,
blackjack, craps, and roulette,
over 1,000 slot machines, and
a poker room. Live entertainment in 500-seat concert hall,
plus traditional-style pub.
🎬 Daily 24 hours (table games closed
Tue–Wed 4am–noon) 🎟 Free 🚌 2, 4,
6, 12, 82

LOWER DECK PUB
Historic Properties, Upper Water Street,
Halifax, Nova Scotia, B3J 1S9
Tel 902/425-1501
A former privateers' warehouse keeps up the tradition
of rollicking, good-natured fun,
with traditional Maritimes
music every night
🎬 Daily. Music: Mon–Sat 9.30pm–
12.30am, Sun 3.30–6.30pm,
9.30pm–12.30am 🚌 2, 4, 6, 12, 82

WHAT TO DO

REFLECTIONS CABARET

5184 Sackville Street, Halifax, Nova
Scotia
Tel 902/422-2957, 877/422-2957
www.reflectionscabaret.com
The best gay dance club in
town, featuring drag shows
with pop-star impersonators,
karaoke every Tuesday, talent
nights, movies and music
videos, and live bands.
🎭 Daily 4–3.30 💵 $5–8

VELVET OLIVE

1770 Market Street, Halifax, Nova Scotia,
B3J 3X8
Tel 902/492-2233
www.velvetolive.com
Live bands, singer-songwriters,
and DJs Tuesday through
Saturday; improv comedy on
Mondays, jazz every Sunday.
Renowned for good entertain-
ment and great cocktails.
🎭 Daily, usually 11pm–2am, but some
events start earlier. Jazz: Sun 6.30–9
💵 $5 🚌 6

MONCTON

ROCKIN' RODEO

415 Elmwood Drive, Moncton, New
Brunswick, E1A 4Y2
Tel 506/384-4324
www.rockin-rodeo.com
High-energy club with a cow-
boy theme and one of the
biggest dance floors in the
Maritimes. Rock and country
videos are shown on five big
screens.
🎭 Daily 11am–2am 💵 Fri–Wed $3.75,
Thu $3; ladies free Fri–Sat 🚌 5

Sports and Activities

SPECTATOR SPORTS

HALIFAX

HALIFAX MOOSEHEADS

Halifax Metro Centre, 1800 Argyle
Street, Halifax, Nova Scotia, B3J 2V9
Tel 902/451-1221
www.halifaxmooseheads.ca
The Mooseheads hockey team
plays in the Québec League. It
may not be NHL (National
Hockey League), but games
are enthusiastically contested
and well supported.
🎭 Sep–Mar 💵 Adult $12.50–20, child
(under 12) $7.50 🚌 1, 3, 6, 10

MONCTON

MONCTON WILDCATS

Moncton Coliseum, 377 Killam Drive,
Moncton, New Brunswick, E1C 3T1
Tel 506/857-4100
www.moncton-wildcats.com

The Wildcats play visiting
teams from the Maritimes and
Québec.
🎭 Sep–Mar 💵 Adult $11, child (under
12) $8

ACTIVITIES

ALMA

FRESH AIR ADVENTURE

16 Fundy View Drive, Alma, New
Brunswick, E4H 1H6
Tel 506/887-2249, 800/545-0020
www.freshairadventure.com
Guided kayaking, from two-
hour to multiday trips, along
scenic coastline to caves and
beaches. Full days give a real
Bay of Fundy experience, on the
highest tides in the world.
🎭 Daily, mid-May–mid-Sep 💵 From
$30 for 2 hours

CAPE BRETON

CAPE BRETON HIGHLANDS NATIONAL PARK

Cheticamp Information Centre, Cape
Breton, Nova Scotia, B0C 1L0
Tel 902/224-2306

This is one of the most beautiful places in the world, with a
stunning coastline and thickly
forested mountains. There are
27 hiking trails of various
lengths—you can pick up maps
at the information pointse.
🎭 Year-round; reduced service
Oct–May 💵 Park entry permit $3.50
mid-May–mid-Oct

WESLEY'S WHALE WATCHING

The Harbour, Pleasant Bay, Cape
Breton, Nova Scotia
Tel 866/273-2593
www.cabottrail.com/whalewatching
Sightings of whales—pilot,
humpback, minke, or, more
rarely, right whales, orcas, belugas and sperm whales—are
pretty much guaranteed. Trips
are in a traditional lobster boat
or Zodiac inflatable, and
Captain Wesley is both knowledgeable and friendly.
🎭 Daily 9–6, Aug–Oct 💵 Adult
$24–36, child (6–18) $23
🚌 Northwest coast of Cape Breton, 35
minutes drive north of Chéticamp

ST. ANDREWS

RETREAT CHARTERS

155 Water Street, St. Andrews, New
Brunswick, E0G 2X0
Tel 506/529-4813, 866/541-5500
Three-hour deep-sea fishing
trip in the Bay of Fundy, with
all the gear provided. Vessel is
accessible for wheelchair
users. Reservations required.
🎭 Daily, based on weather conditions
and achieving minimum numbers
💵 Adult $49, child (under 12) $29

SAINT JOHN

JET BOAT TOURS

Box 7094, Brunswick Square, Saint
John, New Brunswick, E2L 4S5
Tel 506/634-8987, 888/634-8987
www.jetboatrides.com
Tremendous jet boat thrill ride,
departing from Market Square
up the St. John River and right
into the famous Reversing
Falls. The one-hour trip
includes 20 minutes hanging
on tight as the boat leaps
through the rapids.
🎭 Daily 1pm, 3pm, 5pm Jun–Sep
(also 7pm Jul–Aug) 💵 Adult $32, child
(under 13) $24.25 🚌 Douglas Avenue
route from City Hall, then 2-minute walk
🚌 Fallsview Park, off Douglas Avenue

SUSSEX CORNER

SUSSEX GOLF AND CURLING CLUB
148 Picadilly Road, Sussex Corner, New Brunswick, E4E 5L2
Tel 506/433-4951
Not only one of the nicest courses in New Brunswick, it's central for Fredericton, Saint John and Moncton. Challenging layout (two tough finishing holes) and reasonable prices.
🕐 Mid-May– mid-Nov, depending on weather 💲 $20–38 🚌 Trans-Canada Highway, exit 198

Health and Beauty

HALIFAX

SPIRIT
1566 Barrington Street, Level 3, Halifax, Nova Scotia, B3J 1Z6
Tel 902/431-8100
www.spiritspa.ca
In a restored historic dotwown building (above the Up Country furniture store), spa staff will soothe away the cares of the day and give you a fresh-air glow with their range of natural products. Services include Vichy Shower, sea scrub, hair and make-up, and sports massage.
🕐 Daily 💲 Treatments priced separately; massage from $70 🚌 1, 3, 6, 10

ST. JOHN'S

SPA AT THE MONASTERY
63 Patrick Street, St. John's, Newfoundland and Labrador, A1E 2S5
Tel 709/754-5800
www.monastery-spa.com
None of the rigors of monastic life, but all of the tranquility are found in this beautiful

historic building. You can get one simple treatment or an integrated schedule of ancient Oriental and Western therapies, relaxation techniques and enlightened nutrition.
🕐 Fri–Mon 10–6, Tue–Thu 10–9
💲 Treatments priced individually; massage from $40 (half-hour) or $70 (hour)

Children

BOUCTOUCHE

LE PAYS DE LA SAGOUINE
57 Acadie Street, Bouctouche, New Brunswick, E4S 2T7
Tel 506/743-1400
www.sagouine.com

In a re-created Acadian village, professional actors bring to life La Sagouine, an old woman with lots of tales to tell. It is mostly in French, but there are daily English-language tours, and the colorful musical shows and special events are always entertaining for younger children.
🕐 Daily 9.30–5.30, Jun–late Sep (10–3 in the fall) 💲 Adult $13 ($11 in fall), child (5–16) $7 ($5 in fall), family $32 ($25 in fall) 🚌 Off Route 11 at exit 32A
🍴 L'Ordre du Bon Temps restaurant serves traditional Acadian dishes and seafood (closed after end Aug)

BURLINGTON

BURLINGTON AMUSEMENT PARK
Route 234, Burlington, Prince Edward Island, C0B 1M0
Tel 902/836-3098
As well as the longest go-kart track east of Montréal, with some two-seater karts for an adult with child, this park has mini-golf, bumper cars and boats, baseball batting cages, trampolines, and a roller coaster.

🕐 Daily 10–9, Jun–early Sep 💲 Free admission, charges for rides
🍴 Restaurant serves up all the kids' favorites: burgers, hot dogs, nachos, ice cream, shakes

CAVENDISH

AVONLEA
Route 6, Cavendish, Prince Edward Island, C1E 2B7
Tel 902/963-3050
www.avonlea.ca
Anne of Green Gables was set on Prince Edward Island, and your kids can live the story and meet "Anne" at the fictional village of Avonlea, re-created in the PEI countryside. Costumed actor-guides inhabit the farm, houses and stores, and kids can attend Miss Montgomery's schoolroom. It's not just for girls—all children will enjoy the lively music shows, the games, the farm animals, and taking a wagon ride.
🕐 Daily 9–6, mid-Jun–Sep, 10–4 Sep
💲 Adult $12.95, child $9.95 🍴 The White Sands tearoom serves light meals and snacks

RAINBOW VALLEY
Route 6, Cavendish, Prince Edward Island, C0B 1M0
Tel 902/963-2221
www.rainbowvalley.pe.ca
Canada's largest privately owned amusement park, covering 16ha (40 acres). Three boating lakes, six waterslides, fairground rides, playground, and monorail. Live shows with magicians, puppets and music.
🕐 Mon–Sat 9–8, Sun 11–8, early Jun–early Sep (closes earlier in Jun)
💲 Adult $13, child (6–16) $10
🚌 On main road through Cavendish; look for giant rainbow over entrance

RIPLEY'S BELIEVE IT OR NOT!
Route 6, Cranberry Village, Cavendish, Prince Edward Island, C0A 1N0
Tel 902/963-2242
www.ripleys.com
One of about 30 Ripley's worldwide, packed with curiosities, illusions and just plain weird stuff, plus videos from the TV show.
🕐 Daily 9am–10pm, Jul–Aug; 9.30–5.30, Jun andSep 💲 Adult $7.95, child $4.95 🚌 On main road through Cavendish

CHARLOTTETOWN

FIRED UP

Leisure World Building, 95 Trans-
Canada Highway, Charlottetown, Prince
Edward Island, C1E 1E8
Tel 902/566-2270

If you want something more
creative for your kids than hurl-
ing themselves around in
amusement parks, bring them
here and let them decorate
their own mug, plate or pet
dish. Materials are provided,
help is at hand and you don't
need an appointment.

🕐 Mon–Fri noon–9, Sat noon–6
✋ Under $10 (depending on item cho-
sen to decorate) 🚌 Outskirts of
Charlottetown, off Highway 2

FREDERICTON

KINGSWOOD ENTERTAINMENT CENTRE

31 Kingswood Park, Fredericton, New
Brunswick, E3C 2L4
Tel 506/444-9500
www.kingswoodpark.com

A 72,000sq-m (80,000sq-ft)
family attraction, with indoor
playground, a big playclimber
with slides and ball-pool, laser
tag, soft-play for toddlers, and
Cosmic Zone with games of
skill. For adults there's bowling,
golf and a gymnasium.

🕐 Sun–Thu 8am–9pm, Fri–Sat
8am–midnight; hours vary seasonally
✋ Games priced individually or in
combos ranging from $5.95 to $17.95;
under-6s inflatables $1.95; playclimber
(3–11 years only) $3.95 🚌 15N
🚌 South of city, off Hanwell Road
(Route 640)

SCIENCE EAST HANDS-ON SCIENCE CENTRE

668 Brunswick Street, Fredericton, New
Brunswick, E3B 1H6
Tel 506/457-2340
www.scienceeast.nb.ca

With 100 hands-on exhibits,
kids learn the basics of science
in an exciting way. They can
step inside a giant kaleidoscope, leave their shadow on a
wall and take part in the ever
popular static-electricity display
that literally makes their hair
stand on end.

🕐 Mon–Sat 10–5, Sun 1–4, Jun–Labor
Day; Tue–Fri noon–5, Sat 10–5, Labor
Day–May; closed Jan ✋ Adult $3, child
$2, family $7

HALIFAX

MUSEUM OF NATURAL HISTORY

1747 Summer Street, Halifax, Nova
Scotia, B3H 3A6
Tel 902/424-7353. Recorded information: 902/424-6099
www.museum.gov.ns.ca/mnh

In addition to such exhibits as
a pilot whale skeleton, stuffed
moose and dinosaur fossils,
there are always live displays
that might include snakes,
amphibians, bats, spiders, and
mice, plus Gus, an 80-year-old
tortoise, and a living beehive.

🕐 Mon–Tue, Thu–Sat 9.30–5.30, Wed
9.30–8, Sun 1–5.30, Jun–Oct; Tue and
Thu–Fri 9.30–5, Wed 9.30–8, Sun 1–5,
mid-Oct–May ✋ Adult $4, child (6–17)
$2, family $8–12 🚌 8, 14, 20, 53, 59,
61, 68, 84, 86

MARYSTOWN

GOLDEN SANDS

Marystown, Newfoundland and
Labrador, A0E 2M0
Tel 709/891-2400

Miles of fine golden sand with
attractions that include freshwater swimming, a huge
waterslide, boat rentals, folk
art, minigolf, games arcade
and trackless train rides.

🕐 Daily 10am–dusk, mid-Jun to mid-
Sep (weather permitting) ✋ $4 🚌 On
Route 222, 20km (12 miles) from
Marystown

MONCTON

CRYSTAL PALACE

499 Paul Street, Dieppe, Moncton, New
Brunswick, E1A 6S5
Tel 506/859-4386
www.crystalpalace.ca

Next to the Champlain Place
shopping mall, this indoor and
outdoor amusement park is a
great reward for being good
while you shop. It includes a

roller coaster, Jumpin' Star ride,
laser-tag, Ferris wheel, bumper
boats, carousel, and karting.

🕐 Mon–Thu noon–8, Fri noon–9, Sat
10–10, Sun 10–8 (10–10 daily in summer) ✋ All-day bracelet $16.95, junior
$12.25, family $62 🚌 7, 8, 9, 10, 20, 21
🍴 McGinnis Landing has an extensive
menu

MAGIC MOUNTAIN

TCH 2, exit 450, Moncton, New
Brunswick, E1G 4R3
Tel 506/857-9283, 800/331-9283
www.magicmountain.ca

When you've experienced the
weird sensation of freewheel-
ing "uphill" in your car on
Magnetic Hill, you can explore
the rest of the complex. Magic
Mountain is Atlantic Canada's
largest waterpark, with nine
slides and a wave pool.

🕐 Daily 10–6 (till 8 in high season),
mid-Jun–early Sep ✋ $19.95 (under
1.2m/48in tall $15) 🚌 Magic Mountain
route

NEW GLASGOW

MAGIC VALLEY FUN PARK

Highway 104, New Glasgow, Nova
Scotia, B0K 2A0
Tel 902/396-4467
www.magicvalley.ca

Nova Scotia's original theme
park, established in 1971, with
huge waterslides, pedal and
bumper boats, train ride, karting, soft-play area, and live
animals. Storybook Village
takes younger children into the
world of nursery rhymes.

🕐 Daily 11–6 in summer
✋ $10.95 including all rides and attrac-
tions, $6 children's rides and soft-play
area only. Individual ride prices also
available 🚌 10km (6 miles) west of
New Glasgow off Trans-Canada
Highway at exit 20

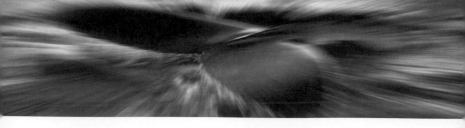

ST. JOHN'S

THE FLUVARIUM
Nagles Place, Pippy Park, St. John's, Newfoundland and Labrador, A1B 2Z2
Tel 709/754-3474
www.fluvarium.ca
A unique insight into the life of a river, with windows below the water level of a real stream showing day-to-day activities of trout, frogs and tadpoles. Feeding time is at 4pm. The second floor has interactive exibits, videos and displays.
🕐 Mon–Fri 9–5, Sat–Sun noon–5, Apr–Sep (closed some weekends Apr–Jun); Mon–Fri 9–4.30, Oct–Mar 💵 Adult $5, child (under 14) $3, family $15

NEWFOUNDLAND SCIENCE CENTRE
5 Beck's Cove, The Murray Premises, St. John's, Newfoundland and Labrador, A1C 5N5
Tel 709/754-0823
www.sciencecentre.nf.ca
Up-to-the-minute science museum in one of the oldest buildings in St. John's. Kids learn while having lots of fun—transforming into a human gyroscope, looking into the world of backyard bugs, walking like a dinosaur, or enjoying the puppet theater.
🕐 Mon–Fri 10–5, Sat 10–6, Sun noon–6 💵 Adult $6, child $4.25

SHEDIAC

SANDSPIT
Parlee Beach, 79 Ohio Road, Shediac, New Brunswick, E0A 3G0
Tel 506/532-8111
Along the best beach in the province, with its gently shelving sands and changing rooms, Sandspit has a roller coaster, karting, bumper boats, softplay, carousel, and super-slide.
🕐 Daily 10–6, mid- to end Jun; 10am–11pm, Jul–Aug; 10–9 early Sep 💵 Unlimited rides $11.30; also various coupon options 🚗 Pointe-du-Chêne, off Route 15, exit 37

UPPER CLEMENTS

UPPER CLEMENTS PARK
2931 Highway 1, Upper Clements, Nova Scotia, B0S 1A0
Tel 902/532-7557. Wildlife park 902/532-5924
www.upperclementspark.com

The Maritimes' largest amusement park. Attractions include roller coaster, log flume, fairground rides, rope swings, and paddle boats. A 12ha (30-acre) wildlife park here is home to cougars, black bears, moose, deer, and other animals.
🕐 Daily 10–7, mid-Jun–Sep. Wildlife park mid-May to mid-Oct 💵 $5.75 plus rides: premium bracelet (covers all rides) $12, small child attractions only $8 🚗 West end of Annapolis Valley, 8km (5 miles) west of Annapolis Royal

Festivals and Events

MARCH

SNO-BREAK WINTER FESTIVAL
Goose Bay, Newfoundland and Labrador
Tel 709/896-3489
www.tourismlabrador.com
A week of snowmobile races, Nordic skiing, adventure tours, parties and family fun.

JUNE/JULY

FESTIVAL 500, SHARING THE VOICES
St. John's, Newfoundland and Labrador
Tel 709/738-6013
www.festival500.com
International festival of choral singing, with choirs from all over the world.

NOVA SCOTIA INTERNATIONAL TATTOO
Halifax, Nova Scotia
Tel 902/451-1221
www.nstattoo.ca

Nightly for 10 days, the Metro Centre hosts military bands, pipe bands, dancers and military displays, featuring the cream of the world's military and civilian performers.

CANADA'S IRISH FESTIVAL
Miramichi, New Brunswick
Tel 506/778-8810
www.canadasirishfest.com
Lively festival, with a pipe and drum parade, and music from top Canadian and Irish performers.

ROLLO BAY FIDDLE FESTIVAL
Rollo Bay, Prince Edward Island
Tel 902/687-2584
Permanent festival grounds host the cream of Maritimes fiddle talent, with two concerts a day and an old-time dance each night. A friendly event.

AUGUST

HALIFAX INTERNATIONAL BUSKER FESTIVAL
Halifax, Nova Scotia
Tel 902/429-3910, 866/773-0655; http://buskers.ns.sympatico.ca
Street performers, including musicians, magicians, comedians, artists, jugglers, dancers, and mimes, do their stuff along the 1km (half-mile) waterfront site.

ATLANTIC SEAFOOD FESTIVAL
Moncton, New Brunswick
Tel 506/853-3516
Some of the best seafood in the world comes out of the waters off New Brunswick, and top international chefs come to work their magic on it.

SEPTEMBER

HARVEST JAZZ AND BLUES FESTIVAL
Fredericton, New Brunswick
Tel 506/454-2583, 888/622-5837
www.harvestjazzbllues.nb.ca
Venues and streets throughout the city are buzzing with live music, and a large marquee downtown hosts big-name jazz and blues bands.

OCTOBER

CELTIC COLOURS FESTIVAL
Sydney, Cape Breton, Nova Scotia
Tel 902/562-6700, 877/285-2321
www.celtic-colours.com
One of the best Celtic music festivals in the world, with about 300 musicians from all the Celtic nations performing in a week of concerts and ceilidhs, at more than 30 venues.

QUÉBEC

Decidedly French in a uniquely Canadian way, Québec presents the visitor with a fascinating cultural experience. French is the first language here, so you need a good grasp of it to enjoy theater productions (though there are some in English). Montréal is the biggest metropolis, and has superb shopping and entertainment with a European flavor; Québec City is known for its beautiful historic core, and also has much to offer in the way of individual stores, galleries and nightlife; and Gatineau (formerly the three adjoining towns of Hull, Gatineau and Aylmer) is only separated from Ontario and the city of Ottawa by the Ottawa River. The Québec countryside includes the wonderful Laurentians—great for hiking, climbing and winter sports—the mighty St. Lawrence River and picturesque Gaspésie. There's a distinct *joie de vivre* here that results in a huge number of festivals and special events, and ensures the success of cultural activities that are definitely outside the mainstream.

The Eaton Centre is just one of Montréal's superb modern shopping malls

Shopping

GRANBY
LA FLAMME
328 rue Principale, Granby, Québec,
J2G 2W4
Tel 450/378-8484
www.la-flamme.com
If you have underestimated the winter chill, check out this family business that specializes in warm fabric, leather and fur coats by Québec designers—Simon Chang, Marisa Minicucci, Hilary Radley, Jane Adams—and top international names.
🕐 Mon–Sat 9–5.30 (till 9 Thu–Fri)

KAHNAWAKE
5 NATIONS INDIAN ART GALLERY
Route 138 Est, P.O. Box 1435,
Kahnawake, Québec, J0L 1B0
Tel 450/638-7777
www.5nations.qc.ca
Within the Mohawk Territory of Kahnawake, this is the largest gallery of Iroquois art in Canada, housed in a beautiful wood building. Inside is a wonderful array of art and craft items, all fashioned from natural resources. It's part of a heritage village where you can visit longhouses, watch traditional dancing, and see buffalo, deer and horses.

🕐 Daily 9–5 🚇 Angrignon, then bus
🚌 CITSO Kahnawake bus 🚗 Ten minutes from Montréal, between Mercier Bridge and highways 20, 15 and 10

MONTRÉAL
ATWATER MARKET
138 avenue Atwater, Montréal, Québec
Tel 514/937-7754
www.marchespublics-mtl.com

Saved from demolition in the late 1960s, this distinctive building with a tall clock tower carries on a long tradition of supplying fresh produce from the surrounding countryside. There's also a gourmet food shop and a bakery.
🕐 Mon–Wed 8–6, Thu–Fri 8am–9pm (till 7 Thu Jan–Apr), Sat–Sun 8–5
🚇 Lionel-Groulx 🚌 36

BELLINI SHOES
1119 rue Ste-Catherine Ouest, Montréal, Québec, H3B 1H8
Tel 514/288-6144
If you are not excited by shopping for shoes, try Bellini. It has a huge range of footwear, for men and women, that bridges all tastes and budgets—you can spend $50 to $1,000 here, and all the shoes are imported from Italy.
🕐 Mon–Wed 9.30–6, Thu–Fri 9–9, Sat 9–5, Sun noon–5 🚇 Peel 🚌 15

BIDZ
3945A St-Denis, Montréal, Québec, H2W 2M4
Tel 514/286-2421
Forget the diamonds and gold, this is the place to come if it's you that's paying. There's an enormous selection of beads from all over the world, and you can have some fun string-

ing them into necklaces, bracelets and earrings. There are also some funky pieces made by artists-in-residence.
🕐 Mon–Wed 11–6, Thu–Fri 11–7, Sat–Sun noon–5 🚇 Mont-Royal 🚌 30

BOUTIQUE POM' CANELLE
4860 rue Sherbrooke Ouest, Montréal, Québec, H3Z 1H1
Tel 514/483-1787
An exclusive boutique selling designer fashions for children aged 3 to 16, much imported from top European design houses. If your young teen is brave enough to be individual, or your toddler won't drool all over the Lily Gaufrette or Pinco-Palleno creations, you can dress them up beautifully.
🕐 Mon–Fri 10–6, Sat 10–5 🚇 Vandome or Villa-Maria, then bus 24

COMPLEXE DESJARDINS
150 rue Ste-Catherine Ouest/175 boulevard René-Lévesque Ouest, Montréal, Québec, H5B 1E9
Tel 514/281-1870
www.complexedesjardins.com
Linked to the underground city, this office and shopping complex is the largest building downtown. The shopping area is around La Grande-Place, a huge space with a fountain, and has more than 100 units including fashion, gifts, services, and eateries. Events include exhibitions, charity events, cultural festivals, and even blood-donor sessions.
🕐 Mon–Wed 9–6, Thu–Fri 9.30–9, Sat 9.30–5, Sun, noon–5 🚇 Place-des-Arts 🚌 15, 150 🍴 A good selection of cafés, bistros, fast food, and quality restaurants

DUBARRY FURS
370 rue Sherbrooke Ouest, Montréal, Québec, H3A 1B2
Tel 514/844-7483
www.dubarryfurs.com
You'll find some of the best prices for quality furs here. As well as ready-made and made-to-measure designer fur coats and jackets, there is a range of hats, fur-trimmed leather, and accessories to choose from.
🕐 Mon–Fri 9–6 , Sat 9–5, Sun by appointment 🚇 Place-des-Arts or McGill 🚌 24

HEMSLEY'S
660 rue Ste-Catherine Ouest, Montréal, Québec, H3B 1B8
Tel 514/866-3706
This is Montréal's oldest jeweler, in business since 1870, with an interesting selection of unique jewelry, handmade by local craftspeople. They also have crystal, sculptures, china and clocks.
🕐 Mon–Wed 10–6, Thu–Fri 10–9, Sat 10–5, Sun noon–5 🚇 McGill 🚌 15

HENRI HENRI
189 rue Ste-Catherine Est, Montréal, Québec, H2X 1K8
Tel 514/288-0109
This hat shop may not have coined the phrase "hat trick," but they certainly did their bit when, in the 1940s and 1950s, they gave a hat to each Canadiens hockey player who scored three goals in a game. Classic headgear for men, such as Stetson, Biltmore and Borsalino, plus Donegal tweed caps from Ireland and their own-brand fur hat.
🕐 Mon–Thu 10–6, Fri 10–9, Sat 9–5 🚇 St-Laurent or Berri-UQAM 🚌 15

JEAN-TALON
7075 avenue Casgrain, Montréal, Québec
Tel 514/277-1588
www.marchespublics-mtl.com

In the heart of Little Italy, this bustling market has been a popular shopping destination for a cosmopolitan local clientele for many years, and the range of goods reflects their cultural diversity.
🕐 Mon–Wed and Sat 8–6, Thu–Fri 8am–9pm, Sun 8–5 🚇 Jean-Talon 🚌 Little Italy, south of Jean-Talon, east of St-Laurent

MAISONNEUVE MARKET
4445 rue Montréal Est, Montréal, Québec, H1V 3V3
Tel 514/937-7754
www.marchespublics-mtl.com

Opened in 1995, this lively market is on the site of the original Maisonneuve market, which was established back in 1914. As well as hosting vendors selling local produce, it is a cultural center for festivals, music, dance, theater and other activities.
🕐 Mon–Fri 8–6, Sat–Sun 8–5 🚇 Pie IX 🚌 125 🚋 Hochelaga Maisonneuve

MAISON SIMONS
977 rue Ste-Catherine Ouest, Montréal, Québec, H3B 4W3
Tel 514/282-1840
This is a great clothing store for women, some of whom travel substantial distances to stock up on outfits here. It's strong on stylishly tailored outfits, but there are clothes for all occasions. Men's clothing is equally interesting, and there are good homeware departments.
🕐 Mon–Wed 10–6, Thu–Fri 10–9, Sat 9.30–5, Sun noon–5 🚇 Peel or McGill 🚌 15

MARCHÉ BONSECOURS
350 rue St-Paul Est, Old Montréal, Québec, H2Y 1H2
Tel 514/872-7730
www.marchebonsecours.qc.ca
One subway stop from the ultramodern underground city is this magnificent old building, former home of the governors of Canada. Headquartering the Institute of Design and the Conseil des Métiers d'Art du Québec (both of which have galleries), it houses 15 boutiques selling top-quality crafts,

fashions, jewelry, furniture and gift items. Ongoing exhibitions of arts and crafts.

🕐 Mon–Sat 10–9, Sun 10–6, late Jun–early Sep; Thu–Fri 10–9, Sat–Wed 10–6, Apr–late Jun and early Sep–Dec 🚇 Champ-de-Mars 🍴 Two restaurants and a historical banquet

MONTRÉAL EATON CENTRE
705 rue St-Catherine Ouest, Montréal, Québec, H3B 4G5
Tel 514/288-3708
www.centreeaton.shopping.ca

Linked directly to the underground city and McGill subway station, this mall has about 175 units, including stores of every kind, banks and other services, and eating places There's also a movie multiplex. Spacious and chic, it's the biggest shopping destination in the city, and includes currency exchange and instant tax refunds for tourists.

🕐 Mon–Fri 10–9, Sat 9–5, Sun noon–5 🚇 McGill 🍴 A vast selection of international fast foods, coffee houses and the Restofiore restaurant.

OGILVY
1307 rue Ste-Catherine Ouest, Montréal, Québec, H3G 1P7
Tel 514/842-7711

This fine old store has a classy atmosphere and a reputation for high quality goods. Established in 1866, and in this location since 1912, it is home to about 50 smart franchises, including Guy Laroche, Aquascutum and Anne Klein. If you are there at noon you'll hear the lone bagpiper play—a store tradition that dates back to 1927.

🕐 Mon–Wed 10–6, Thu–Fri 10–9, Sat 9–5, Sun noon–5 🚇 Peel 🚌 15

OLIVIERI
5219 rue de la Côte des Neiges, Montréal, Québec, H3T 1Y1
Tel 514/739-3639

Warm, welcoming and very user-friendly, this bookstore and bistro is run with great enthusiasm by people with a passion for literature. It has a vast section devoted to Québecois, French and foreign novels, but you can also pick up a good, lightweight novel for vacation reading, and there's a kid's corner.

🕐 Mon–Sat 10–10, Sun 11–7 🚇 Côte des Neiges 🚌 165, 535 🍴 Bistro offers a selection of homemade dishes

PLACE MONTRÉAL TRUST
1500 avenue McGill College, Montréal, Québec, H3A 3J5
Tel 514/843-8000
www.placemontrealtrust.com

Linked to the underground city, midway between the two busiest subway stations, this bright and lofty mall has about 100 stores, including fashion boutiques and specialty stores, Athletes World, Indigo, and Canada's first Zara.

🕐 Mon–Wed 10–6 (till 9 Jun–Aug), Thu–Fri 10–9, Sat 9–5, Sun noon–5 🚇 McGill or Peel 🚌 15 🍴 Food court, including burgers and Oriental cuisine, plus a nice coffee shop

MONT TREMBLANT
HELLY HANSEN
Place St-Bernard, Mont Tremblant, Québec, J0T 1Z0
Tel 819/681-4990

If you wind up in Mont Tremblant in winter without the right outdoors gear, this place can fix you up for all kinds of demanding conditions. It stocks Lifa and Helly Hansen clothing, accessories and equipment, along with Merrell footwear, and helpful staff can advise about the technicalities of layering fabrics.

🕐 Daily 8.30am–10pm

PERCÉ
BOUTIQUE AU BON SECOURS
150 Ouest Route 132, Percé, Québec, G0C 2L0
Tel 418/782-2011

This artisan-owned craft shop was once a pharmacy, and is now Percé's oldest store. It carries a great selection of original craft work by the owner and others; one reason to come is for the superb sandstone bird sculptures by Québec artist, Suzanne Tétreault-Massé.

🕐 Daily 9–9, May–Oct 🚗 Corner of rue Principale and rue de l'Eglise

PIEDMONT
ANTIQUITÉS HIER POUR DEMAIN
914 boulevard des Laurentides, Piedmont, Québec, J0R 1K0
Tel 450/227-4231

An attractive white clapboard house is the home of this antiques shop, which specializes in Québec pine furniture from the 18th and 19th centuries. There's a good selection of small items, including some beautiful pieces of folk art, woodcarving and old toys.

🕐 Fri–Sun 11–5 🚗 On Route 117

QUÉBEC CITY
ARTISANS DU BAS-CANADA
30 Côte de la Fabrique, Québec City, Québec, G1R 3V7
Tel 418/692-2109, 888-339-2109
www.artisanscanada.com

For more than 50 years this family-run store has been providing a showcase for the work of around 500 Canadian artists and artisans. Everything here is guaranteed authentic, and products include Inuit and First Nations carvings, miniature lead soldiers and Mounties, ceramic cats, and clothing.

🕐 Daily 10–6

BOUTIQUE CANADEAU
1124 rue St-Jean, Québec City, Québec, G1R 1S4
Tel 418/692-4850
www.canadeau.com

On one of the main shopping streets of Old Québec City, this friendly store has a great range of Canadian-made products. In addition to Inuit soapstone sculptures from Nunavut, there are collector knives, fur and leather items, exquisite gold jewelry and brightly patterned tundra sweaters.

🕐 Daily 9–6, mid-Jun to mid-Oct; 10–6, rest of year 🚌 800, 801

LE CAPITAINE D'A BORD/PLEIN AIR D'A BORD

59 and 63 Petit-Champlain, Québec City, Québec, G1K 4H5
Tel 418/694-0624
www.capitainedabord.com

These twin stores—one with a nautical flavor, the other with landlubbers in mind—are close neighbors on the oldest street in North America. Under the same management, they stock a large range of sweaters, pants (trousers), footwear, waterproof jackets, shirts, and accessories with labels like Lacoste, Paul and Shark, and Michel Beaudouin.

🕐 Daily 9am–11pm, mid-May to mid-Oct; Thu–Fri 9–9, Sat–Wed 9–6, rest of year

CUIR LA POMME

47 rue Sous-le-Fort, Québec City, Québec, G1K 4G9
Tel 418/692-2875
www.kapomme.qc.ca

This is the outlet for the leather creations of more than a dozen Québec fashion designers. Exclusive garments are offered at extremely reasonable prices, and a multilingual staff is welcoming and helpful. If you don't see what you want, it can be tailored for you.

🕐 Daily 9am–9pm, mid-May to mid-Oct; 9.30–5.30, rest of year 🚌 1 🚇 Petit Champlain, near bottom of cable car

ÉRICO CHOCO-MUSEUM

634 rue St-Jean, Faubourg St-Jean Baptiste, Québec City, Québec, G1R 1P8
Tel 418/524-2122
www.chocomusee.com

The museum exploring the history of chocolate is interesting, of course, but it's the homemade chocolates that are the

real attraction here. The finest French and Belgian chocolate covers delectable fillings with no artificial flavors or preservatives—and they look like little works of art.

🕐 Mon–Sat 10–6, Sun 11–5.30 (closes later May–late Sep) 🚌 800, 801

5 NATIONS INDIAN ART GALLERY

20 rue Cul-de-Sac, Québec City, Québec, G1K 8L4
Tel 418/692-1009
www.5nations.qc.ca

Originally founded as an outlet for Iroquois craft, this store now represents artists from First Nations throughout North America. Sculptures in stone and wood, dreamcatchers, jewelry, masks, and many other items reflect the lives, legends and spirituality of people who lived off the land. There's another outlet on rue du Petit Champlain, and one at Kahnawake (see page 203).

🕐 Daily 9–9 (shorter hours in winter) 🚌 1

FOURRURES DU VIEUX-PORT

55 rue St-Pierre, Québec City, Québec, G1K 4A2
Tel 418/692-6686
www.quebecfur.com

A cool and classy store, with tile floor, brick walls and foliage, selling designer fur coats, jackets and hats, along with fur-trimmed leather and knitwear with labels such as Zuki, Paula Lishman, Gianfranco Ferre and Dominic Bellissimo. If the prices are just too alarming, you could always content yourself with a luxurious fur pillow or cuddlesome teddy bear.

🕐 Mon–Sat 10–5, Sun noon–4

GALERIES D'ART INUIT BROUSSEAU ET BROUSSEAU

35 rue St-Louis, Québec City, Québec, G1R 4S7
Tel 418/694-1828
www.inuitart.ca

This gallery, next to Le Château Frontenac, is dedicated to promoting the work of the finest Inuit artists from Arctic Canada, and has a superb display of museum-quality pieces with a guarantee of authenticity. The staff are very knowledgeable, and purchases can be shipped abroad.

🕐 Daily 9.30–5.30

LOUIS PERRIER JOAILLIER

48 rue Petit-Champlain, Québec City, Québec, G1K 4H4
Tel 418/692-4633
www.louisperrierjoaillier.com

In the heart of the Old City, Louis Perrier's store showcases stunning, elegant pieces of gold jewelry set with richly colored stones. Carrying on a 40-year family tradition, Louis' daughter, Brigitte, is now the designer. Pieces are not cheap, but they are hard to resist.

🕐 Sat–Wed 10–5, Thu–Fri 10–9 🚌 1

PANTOUTE

1100 rue St-Jean, Québec City, Québec, G1R 1S5
Tel 418/694-9748
www.librairiepantoute.com

The largest independent bookstore in the city, with a good section of local-interest titles—the histories of Québec and glossy picture books make good souvenirs. Most fiction is in French, but there are a few English-language novels.

🕐 Mon–Sat 10–10, Sun noon–10 🚌 800, 801 🚇 Vieux-Québec, between Côte du Palais and Ste-Agnés

PEAU SUR PEAU

66–70 boulevard Champlain, Québec City, Québec, G1K 4H7
Tel 418/692-5132

You can dress yourself up from head to toe in leather here, and then get a leather suitcase to pack it all in. It's worth coming into the store just for the smell of leather. Everything comes from Québec or from international designers who

use the best-quality skins for their original styles.
 Sat–Wed 9–6 , Thu–Fri 9–9

PLACE FLEUR DE LYS
550 boulevard Wilfrid-Hamel, Québec City, Québec, G1M 3E5
Tel 418/529-0728
This is one of the most stylish shopping malls in Canada—and that's official—it has won a number of design awards. The 250 stores are a mix of interesting boutiques and big chain stores (Sears, The Bay, Mega Sports), and it's all on one floor, with natural light to illuminate its imaginative features.
Sat–Mon 9.30–5.30, Tue–Fri 9.30–9 Fast-food outlets and restaurants

PLACE LAURIER
2700 boulevard Laurier, Ste-Foy, Québec City, Québec, G1V 2L8
Tel 418/651-7085, 800/322-1828
www.placelaurier.com

Eastern Canada's largest shopping mall, with 350 stores, anchored by Zellers, Sears and The Bay. Extended nine times since it was first built, it's a light, airy space with seemingly limitless choices for clothing, leisure, sports goods, and homewares. Tourists get free shopping bags and discount vouchers (ask at La Service).
Mon–Wed 10–5.30, Thu–Fri 10–9, Sat 9–5, Sun noon–5 (individual store hours may vary) 5km (3 miles) west near bridges on boulevard Laurier Variety of restaurants and fast food

LES PROMENADES DU VIEUX-QUÉBEC
43 rue De Buade, Québec City, Québec, G1R 4A2
Tel 418/692-6000
More of an exclusive retail

enclave than a mall in the usual sense, with just a dozen or so classy boutiques. The surroundings are equally chic, blending modern style with old wood and brass. Designer fashions for men, women and children, arts and crafts, jewelry, cosmetics, candies and Christmas items (year-round).
Daily 10–5

QUÉBEC PUBLIC MARKET
160 Quai St-André, Québec City, Québec, G1K 7C3
Tel 418/692-2517
Markets are always entertaining, but add the French element—wonderful selections of cheeses in particular—and you have something really special. This is a good place to buy maple syrup products, and the locally grown fruits and vegetables are of excellent quality.
Daily 10–6 Vieux Port area

VERRERIE LA MAILLOCHE
58 rue Sous-le-Fort, Québec City, Québec, G1K 4G8
Tel 418/694-0445
www.lamailloche.qc.ca
You can watch master glassblower Jean Vallieres and his team produce delicate works of art, then head upstairs to the showroom. Bowls and vases, bottles and paperweights, goblets and pitchers are created in glorious shades of blue, green and burgundy.
Sat–Wed 9.30–5.30, Thu–Fri 9.30–9 1

STE-ANNE-DE-BEAUPRÉ

PROMENADE STE-ANNE
10909 boulevard Ste-Anne, Ste-Anne-de-Beaupré, Québec, G0A 3C0
Tel 418/827-3555
Just for a change from the big malls and the chic boutiques, you can indulge in pure bargain-hunting at this discount strip mall. Substantial savings on designer clothes for the whole family, sportswear, leather, footwear, accessories, and homeware, including Levi's, Fila, Niko Leather, Benetton, and Liz Claiborne.
Daily 9.30–6 (till 9 Thu–Fri) 20 minutes east of Québec City, 2km (1 mile) beyond Ste-Anne-de Beaupré

Basilica on Route 138 The Mimosa restaurant serves California cuisine

ST-BERNARD-DE-LACOLLE

IGL
350 Route 15, St-Bernard de Lacolle, Québec, J01 1V0
Tel 450/246-2000
A big white building by the main highway to the US border, where you can pick up duty-free items and get GST refunds before you leave Canada. All the usual liquor, wine, perfumes, watches, jewelry, and gift items, as well as clothing and souvenirs.
Daily 24 hours South of Montréal at intersection of routes 15 and US Highway 87 Light meals

SHERBROOKE
CARREFOUR DE L'ESTRIE
3050 boulevard de Portland, Sherbrooke, Québec
Tel 819/563-1907
This is the megamall for the Eastern Townships region, with about 200 stores and 20 restaurants. It's anchored by the usual clutch of department stores—Sears, The Bay, Zellers, Maison Simons—all in bright, modern surroundings.
Mon–Wed 9.30–5.30, Thu–Fri 9.30–9, Sat 9–5, Sun noon–5pm 1, 3, 4, 6, 11 Portland Commercial District, off Highway 410 About 15 restaurants, including Chinese, Italian, Japanese, Greek, Canadian, and a pub

Performance

CHICOUTIMI
ECCE MUNDO
555 boulevard de l'Université, Chicoutimi, Québec, G7H 2B1
Tel 418/549-4101, 800/563-4101
www.eccemundo.com
Spectacular and sophisticated show featuring dance through the ages—classical to jazz and rock 'n' roll—plus acrobatics, and song (in six languages).
Tue–Sun, Jun–Aug, Adult $38, child (under 12) $18

GATINEAU
IMAX
100 Laurier Street, Gatineau, Québec, J8X 4H2
Tel 819/776-7000
www.civilization.ca/imax.html

WHAT TO DO

In the Canadian Museum of Civilization (see page 92), this big-screen theater shows large-format movies; stadium seating and surround-sound.
🕐 Tue–Thu 9–9, Fri–Sat 9am–10pm, Sun 9–6 (call for info about English screenings) 💰 Adult $9.50, child (under 13) $7 or (14–17) $8. Combined ticket with museum: adult $17, child $10 🚌 8 from downtown Ottawa

(see page 92)

GRANBY
PALACE DE GRANBY
135 Principale, bureau 20, Granby, Québec, J2G 2V1
Tel 450/375-2262, 800/387-2262
www.palace.qc.ca
Features touring theater companies, music of all kinds—rock, singer-songwriters, classical, opera and other events.
🕐 Year-round 💰 From $15

MONTRÉAL
AMC CINEMAS
Pepsi Forum, 2313 rue Ste-Catherine Ouest, Montréal, Québec, H3H 1N2
Tel 514/904-1250, 504/933-6786
www.amctheatres.com

No less than 22 of the highest-tech movie theaters, forming part of a giant entertainment complex. All the latest releases, plus some foreign-language and arthouse offerings.
🕐 Daily 💰 Adult $13 ($10 before 6pm; $8 all day Tue) 🚇 Atwater 🚌 15, 57

BELL CENTRE
1260 rue de la Gauchetière Ouest, Montréal, Québec, H3B 5E8
Tel 514/790-1245
www.centrebell.ca
The 21,000-seat home of the Montréal Canadiens (formerly the Molson Centre) doubles as a venue for mega rock

concerts, classical performances and family shows.
🕐 Specific dates year-round 💰 Price varies 🚇 Bonaventure or Lucien-L'Allier 🚌 61, 107, 150, 410, 420, 430, 535

CENTAUR
453 St-François Xavier, Montréal, Québec, H2U 2T1
Tel 514/288-3161
www.centaurtheatre.com
Historic theater, home to the city's leading English-language company, with a reputation for acclaimed ground-breaking productions.
🕐 Sep–May 💰 $36–38. Matinées and previews: $28.50 🚇 Place d'Armes

CENTRE PIERRE PELADEAU
300 boulevard Maisonneuve Est, Montréal, Québec, H2X 3X6
Tel 514/987-6919
Superb acoustics and intimate size make for enjoyable concerts, which feature music and performers from all over the world, plus dance and drama.
🕐 Year-round 💰 Price varies with event 🚇 Berri-UQAM 🚌 15

LA CHAPELLE
3700 rue Ste-Dominique., Montréal, Québec, H2X 2X7
Tel 514/843-7738
All of the drama productions here are in French, but the theater also hosts concerts, including roots, jazz, classical music and opera.
🕐 Year-round 💰 Price varies depending on event 🚇 St-Laurent, then bus 55 north to des Pins 🚌 29, 144

PLACE DES ARTS
Place des Arts, Montréal, Québec, H2X 1Y9
Tel 514/842-2112
www.pda.qc.ca

World-class venue, central to Montréal's cultural life, with five halls totalling 6,000 seats. Full schedule of classical music, ballet and opera.
🕐 Box office: Mon–Sat noon–9 💰 Price varies with event 🚇 Place des Arts 🚌 15, 80, 129 🍴 Bistro restaurant

SAIDYE BRONFMAN CENTRE FOR THE ARTS
5170 rue Côte Ste-Catherine, Montréal, Québec, H3W 1M7
Tel 514/739-2301
www.saidyebronfman.org

Internationally acclaimed venue promoting a wide range of drama, comedy and music, including English-language and Yiddish performances.
🕐 Closed Sat and major Jewish holidays 💰 Price varies with event 🚇 Côte-Ste-Catherine or Snowdon 🚌 17, 129 west

THÉÂTRE DU NOUVEAU MONDE
84 rue Ste-Catherine Ouest, Montréal, Québec, H2X 1Z6
Tel 514/878-7878
www.tnm.qc.ca
The historic Gaiety Theatre was taken over in the 1970s by this theater company, which stages drama, from Shakespeare to modern works.
🕐 All year 💰 Price varies 🚌 15 ☕ Café du Nouveau Monde serves light meals, wine, beer and coffee

NORTH HATLEY
THE PIGGERY THEATRE
215 chemin Sunard, Route 108, North Hatley, Québec
Tel 819/842-2431
This is the oldest English-speaking summer theater in the region.
🕐 Daily, Aug; Tue–Sat and alternate Sun, Jun–Jul and Sep 💰 $14–32 🚌 1

WHAT TO DO

PIERREVILLE

AU VIEUX THÉÂTRE DE PIERREVILLE
33 rue Maurault, Pierreville, Québec, J0G 1J0
Tel 450/568-0909, 877/568-0909
www.vieuxtheatre.com
This former movie theater has lots of character, and cabaret-style seating. It hosts concerts and comedy.
🕐 Shows some Saturday nights, plus summer season 💲$12–25 🚗 On route 132, 30km (19 miles) east of Sorel

QUÉBEC CITY

FAMOUS PLAYERS IN LES GALERIES DE LA CAPITALE
5401 boulevard des Galeries, Québec City, Québec, G2K 1N4
Tel 418/628-2455
www.famousplayers.com
This 12-screen multiplex in the shopping mall shows all the latest releases, sometimes in original language, sometimes in French (look for VF on the listings).
🕐 Daily 💲Adult $8.50, child $5.95) 🚗 Any going to Terminus Les Saules or Terminus Beauport

GRAND THÉÂTRE DE QUÉBEC
269 boulevard René-Lévesque Est, Québec City, Québec, G1R 2B3
Tel 418/643-8131, 877/643-8131
www.grandtheatre.qc.ca
Premier theater in the province, home to Opera de Québec and the Québec Symphony Orchestra. Two concert halls provide a full schedule of dance, drama and music.
🕐 Year-round 💲$35–80 🚌 800, 801

PETIT CHAMPLAIN
Maison de la Chanson, 68–78 rue du Petit-Champlain, Québec City, Québec, G1K 4H4
Tel 418/692-4744
Atmospheric little galleried theater, formerly a warehouse, with old stone walls. Regular performances by Francophone musicians of all kinds.
🕐 Thu–Sat night 💲Price varies

ST-FABIEN

VIEUX THÉÂTRE DE ST-FABIEN
112 Premier Rue, St-Fabien, Québec, G0L 2Z0
Tel 418/869-3202
www.libertel.org/theatre
Snug little village theater in a 1928 building, with a summer season of drama (in French) and music.
🕐 Jul–Aug, on scheduled days 💲Price varies with event 🚗 On Highway 132 just west of Rimouski in the Bas-St-Laurent 🍴 Le Petit Café serves light refreshments

SHERBROOKE

CENTRE CULTUREL DE L'UNIVERSITÉ DE SHERBROOKE
2500 boulevard de l'Université, Sherbrooke, Québec, J1K 2R1
Tel 819/820-1000
www.usherbrooke.ca
Modern campus theater with eclectic schedule—solo singers and groups, touring dance and theater companies, classical concerts, and comedy.
🕐 Year-round 💲Price varies

GRANADA
53 rue Wellington Nord, Sherbrooke, Québec, J1H 4P9
Tel 819/565-2843
Historic 1,200-seat theater that has retained its original 1929 architecture. It hosts touring theater companies, musicals, and classical and pop concerts.
🕐 Year-round 💲Price varies; dinner and show packages available 🍴 Restaurant serves French cuisine

LE VIEUX CLOCHER DE SHERBROOKE
1590 rue Galt Ouest, Sherbrooke, Québec, J1H 2B5
Tel 819/822-2102
www.vieuxclocher.com
Venue for touring performers, including rock bands, solo singers, acoustic bands, stand-up, and family entertainers.
🕐 Year-round 💲Price varies with event; from $10 🚌 3, 4, 5, 7, 8, 9

TERREBONNE

THÉÂTRE DU VIEUX-TERREBONNE
867 rue St-Pierre, Terrebonne, Québec, J6W 1E6
Tel 450/492-4777, 866/404-4777
www.theatreduvieuxterrebonne.com
This theater hosts a vibrant calendar of drama, dance, song, classical music, jazz and comedy. Most are in French, but it's worth checking for English-language productions.

🕐 Year-round 💲Price varies with event, $15–45 🚗 North of Montréal, on north bank of the Rivière des Milles-Îles (Thousand Islands River)

Nightlife

GATINEAU

CASINO DU LAC-LEAMY
1 Boulevard du Casino, Gatineau, Québec, J8Y 6W3
Tel 819/772-2100, 800/665-2274
www.casinos-quebec.com
Gaming, entertainment and conference complex with more than 60 tables, 1,800 slots, ritzy shows in the performance hall and interior gardens. Patrons must be over 18.
🕐 Daily 9am–4pm 💲Casino free; performances from $15 🚌 Outaouais bus: 21XX 🚗 East of downtown Ottawa across Ottawa River 🍴 bars and restaurants

MONTRÉAL

BOURBON COMPLEX
1474 rue Ste-Catherine Est, Montréal, Québec, H2L 2H9
Tel 514/529-6969
Montréal is a particularly gay-friendly city, with more than 100 gay establishments. This one, covering a city block, is reputedly the biggest in the world. It includes a retro disco, hotel, sauna and bathhouse.
🕐 Daily, till 3am 💲No cover charge 🍴 Bars and restaurants

CASINO DE MONTRÉAL
1 avenue du Casino, Montréal, Québec, H3C 4W7
Tel 514/392-2746, 800/665-2274
www.casinos-de-montreal.com

Spectacular waterfront building on an island in the St. Lawrence River, with five floors of gaming, entertainment and

dining. More than 115 tables and 3,000 slots, plus electronic horse racing. Glittering cabaret features world-renowned performers and dancers. Patrons must be over 18. Dress code.

🕐 Daily 24 hours 🎫 Free admission; charge for cabaret 🚇 Jean-Drapeau, Berri-UQAM, or Atwater, then bus 🚌 167 from the métro stations above 🍴 Bars and restaurants

COMEDYWORKS
1238 Bishop Street, Montréal, Québec, H3G 2E3
Tel 514/398-9661
www.comedyworks.ca.tc
In this venue, upstairs from Jimbo's pub, there's comedy every night, with definite audience participation—whether it's taking to the stage on open mike nights or just heckling the paid acts. There's regular improv comedy and headline acts on weekends.

🕐 Nightly 🎫 Mon $3, Tue–Wed $7, Thu–Sun $10 🚇 Lucien L'Allier or Guy-Concordia 🚌 15, 150

ERNIE BUTLER'S COMEDY NEST
Forum Pepsi, 2313 rue Ste-Catherine Ouest, Montréal, Québec, H3H 1N2
Tel 514/932-6378
www.comedynest.com
An international line-up of top comedians is on the bill at the Blue Cat on the 4th floor of the Pepsi Centre. Thursday nights feature the Bionic Yahoos sketch show. Wednesday is open mike night. Dinner and show packages are also available.

🕐 Wed–Sat 🎫 Thu $10, Fri–Sat $12. Dinner and show: $37 🚇 Atwater

LE FESTIN DU GOUVERNEUR
Fort Ste-Hélène, Parc Jean Drapeau, Montréal, Québec
Tel 514/879-1141, 800/713-0111
www.festin.com
Staff in period costume serve your dinner and drinks, while musicians, singers and comedians entertain in the historic surroundings of the fort on St. Helen's Island. It's a fun evening, as long as you enter into the spirit.

🕐 Year-round 🎫 Adult $39, child (under 12) $18.85 ⛴ From Old Port (summer only)

HOUSE OF JAZZ
2060 Aylmer Street, Montréal, Québec, H3A 2E3
Tel 514/842-8656
Formerly Biddle's Jazz and Ribs—until the death of Charlie Biddle in 2003—this is still one of the city's premier jazz clubs. Live music nightly from top names, local acts and jam sessions.

🕐 Mon–Sat 11.30am–1am (till 2.30am Fri–Sat), Sun 6pm–1am; live music starts around 5.30 (7 Sun–Mon) 🎫 No cover charge; mandatory coat check; drink minimum Fri–Sat 🚇 McGill 🚌 24, 125 🍴 American-style restaurant serves ribs, chicken, potato skins

BOURBON STREET WEST
1866 boulevard des Sources, Pointe-Claire, Québec H9R 5B1
Tel 514/695-6545
Street scene mural, brick walls, and polished wood, coupled with a friendly mood on the dance floor, attracts all ages. Live bands—blues (Tuesdays), R&B, soul, and rock—and comedy (Wednesdays). Drive home service available.

🕐 Music starts Tue and Sun 9.30, Wed 9, Thu 10, Fri–Sat 10.30

CAFÉ DES ARTS
1000 rue St-Jean, Québec City, Québec, Tel 418/694-1499
This is an unusual place offering unusual entertainment of a more cerebral variety—mime, poetry, jazz and *chansons*.

🕐 Shows start around 8.30 🎫 Small cover charge; depends on show

N'ICE CLUB
Hôtel de Glace, 143 route Duchesnay, Ste-Catherine-de-la-Jacques-Cartier, Québec, G0A 3M0
Tel 418/875-4522, 877/505-0423
www.icehotel-canada.com
If you're in Québec in winter, visit this cool (literally) place in a hotel made entirely of ice. The nightclub is as hot as it can be at -2°C (28°F), with dancing to a DJ on Thursday and Friday, and live music on Saturday.

🕐 Jan–early Apr (depending on weather) 🎫 $20 ❌ Sherpa Plein Air shuttle 🚌 30 minutes west of Québec City via Highway 40 and Route 367

TERRASSE D'ORSAY
65 rue de Buade, Québec City, Québec, G1R 4A2
Tel 418/694-1582
www.restaurantpubdorsay.com
Lovely old pub-restaurant, opposite City Hall, with polished wood, stained glass and snug booths, attracting a mature crowd. It has a small dance floor and DJ, and occasional live shows (also one of the best terraces in the city).

🕐 Daily 11.30am–3pm

LES YEUX BLEUS
1117 1/2 St-Jean, Québec City, Québec, G1R 1S3
Tel 418/694-9118
In the heart of the old city, this is an atmospheric bar where you are most likely to hear Québecois *chansons*, but there's a smattering of international pop on the schedule, too.

🎫 No cover charge

Sports and Activities

MONTRÉAL ALOUETTES
Percival Molson Memorial Stadium, 475 avenue des Pins, Montréal, Québec, H2W 1S4
Tel 514/871-2266
www.montrealalouettes.com
McGill University stadium, built in 1915, has been developed and expanded to a capacity of 20,000. It has hosted the Alouettes Canadian football team's home games since 1998, and the team—winners of the 2002 Grey Cup—are always worth seeing.

🕐 Late Jun–early Nov 🎫 $17.50–65 🚇 McGill 🚌 Free pre-game shuttle every 5 minutes from McGill University

MONTRÉAL CANADIENS
Bell Centre, 1260 de la Gauchetière Street West, Montréal, Québec, H3B 5E8
Tel 514/790-1245, 800/361-4595
www.canadiens.com
Superb venue, and top-quality hockey from the Canadiens attracts tumultuous support. Attending a game is quite an

experience, and when it comes to choosing who to cheer for, take your cue from those around you.
🕐 Sep–Mar 💰 From about $25
🚇 Bonaventure or Lucien-L'Allier
🚌 61, 107, 150, 410, 420, 430, 535

MONTRÉAL EXPOS
Olympic Stadium, 4549 avenue Pierre de Coubertin, Montréal, Québec, H1V 3N7
Tel 514/8GO-EXPOS
www.expos.mlb.com
One of only two Canadian baseball teams in the American Major League (the other is Toronto's Blue Jays), the Expos play to rousing support at the immense Olympic Stadium. You can't miss it—it has the world's tallest inclined tower (see page 83).
🕐 Apr–Oct 💰 $8–36 🚇 Pie-IX or Viau 🚌 97, 139, 505

(see page 83)

ACTIVITIES

BLAINVILLE
SAFARI NORDIK AVENTURE
639 boulevard Labelle, Blainville, Québec, J7C 3H8
Tel 450/971-1800, 800/361-3748
www.snowmobileincanada.com
The snowmobile was invented in Québec (see page 17), so what better place to find out why they were necessary. This outfitter rents the latest models (you also get the suit, boots, gloves, and helmet), and offers various tour packages, including fishing and hunting trips.
🕐 Daily 9–5, mid-Dec–Mar
💰 $150–175 per day (plus $1,000 refundable deposit) ❓ Transport from Montréal can be arranged

CHATHAM
RANCH ROBERT
74 chemin Fuller, Chatham, Québec, J8G 1V6
Tel 450/562-9869
There's no better way to appreciate the beautiful Québec countryside than on horseback, and here you can ride trails through woodland or across fields of wildflowers. You can get lessons here, too, and horse-drawn sleigh rides in winter.

🕐 Daily 💰 $15 per hour 🚌 In St-Philippe d'Argenteuil, south of Route 148, west of Lachute

MONTRÉAL
LACHINE RAPIDS TOUR
Clock Tower Pier, Old Port, Montréal, Québec
Tel 514/284-9607
www.jetboatingmontreal.com

The mighty St. Lawrence River flows over the Lachine Rapids just upstream from Montréal, and you can take an exhilarating ride over them on a one-hour jet-boat ride. You can also jet-boat up to the rapids and raft down them, or take a speedboat trip with high-speed twists and turns. No children under 14.
🕐 Jun–Aug 💰 Adult $55, youth (14–18) $45 🚌 14 🚇 Champ de Mars

MONT TREMBLANT
GRAY ROCKS RESORT GOLF COURSE
2322 rue Labelle, Mont Tremblant, Québec, J8E 1T8
Tel 819/425-2771, 800/567-6767
www.grayrocks.com

Two beautiful courses, in spectacular surroundings, both 18 holes and well in excess of 5,500m (6,000yd), with lush

fairways and pine woods. Voted the best family golf resort in Québec in one golf magazine, they also offer a good challenge for experienced golfers.
🕐 Spring–Oct depending on weather
💰 $23–41 🚌 5km (3 miles) north of St-Jovite on Route 327

ST-JOACHIN
CAP-TOURMENTE
Canadian Wildlife Service, 570 chemin du Cap-Tourmente, St-Joachin-de-Montmorency, Québec, G0A 3X0
Tel 418/827-3776
www.qc.ec.gc.ca/faune/faune/html
World-famous location for viewing tens of thousands of migrating snow geese in spring and fall, with 2,400ha (5,928 acres) of tidal bulrush marshland. Many other species, observation points, information center, and guide services.
🕐 Daily 8.30–5, early Jan–Oct 💰 $6. Personal guide services: $60 per hour
🚌 Highway 360 near Beaupré

Health and Beauty

ST-MARC-SUR-RICHELIEU
SPA GIVENCHY
Hostellerie Les Trois Tilleuls, 290 rue Richelieu, St-Marc-sur-Richelieu, Québec
Tel 514/856-7787
www.spagivenchy.com
Givenchy has a reputation for choosing fabulous locations, and this is no exception. Salt water pumped from far below ground feeds the swimming pool and therapeutic baths. Treatments focus on shaping, revitalizing, hydrating, and enhancing face and body.
🕐 Daily 💰 Treatments priced separately, massage $105, facials from $95; half-day packages from $361 🚌 On Route 223; to the east of Montréal (south of the river), via Highway 20

Children

CHARLESBOURG
JARDIN ZOOLOGIQUE
9300 rue de la Faune, Charlesbourg, Québec, G1G 4G4
Tel 418/622-0312
www.spsnq.qc.ca

WHAT TO DO

After a costly makeover, this long-established zoo reopened in 2003. It houses 750 animals of 300 species, plus a splendid bird collection, and kids can encounter such animals as fishing cats, tree-dwelling kangaroos and the perennial favorites—insects and reptiles.
🕐 Daily 9–5, Sep–May; 10–8, rest of year 💰 Adult $24, child $16 🚗 North of the city off Highway 73, exit 154

GRANBY

GRANBY ZOO AND AMAZOO
525 rue St-Hubert, Granby, Québec, J2G 5P3
Tel 450/372-9113; 877/472-6299
www.zoogranby.ca

There are more than 800 animals here, including the big ones children love—elephants, giraffes, bears, gorillas, alligators, camels—in addition to smaller ones such as meerkats, monkeys and tiny Przewalski's horses. Also animal rides and a waterpark
🕐 Daily 10–7, May–late Aug; Sat–Sun 10am–6pm, late Aug–mid-Oct 💰 Adult $23.45, child (2–4) $10.95, (5–12) $17.95 🚗 At intersection of routes 112 and 139 🍴 Various restaurants

MONTEBELLO

PARC OMEGA
Route 323 North, Montebello, Québec, J0V 1L0
Tel 819/423-5487
www.parc-omega.com
Here you drive through the 600ha (1,500-acre) enclosure and see wild animals, including bison, bear, deer, wild boar, moose, and wolves, in their natural habitats. And FM88.1 on the car radio gives information about the animals. Out of the car, there's a deer enclo-

sure to wander through, an otter pool and birds of prey.
🕐 Daily 9.30–6, summer; 10–5, winter 💰 Adult $10–13, child (2–5) $5 or (6–15) $7–8 🚗 2km (1.2 miles) north of Montebello on Route 323 🍴 Log-built restaurant, with terrace overlooking the lake, serves light meals

MONTRÉAL

BIOSPHÈRE
160 chemin Tour de l'Île, Île-Ste-Hélène, Montréal, Québec, H3C 4G8
Tel 514/283-5000
www.biosphere.ec.gc.ca

Invite kids to visit a museum about water and they may be less than enthusiastic, but when they see this giant transparent golf ball they can't wait to get inside. They have lots of fun with interactive displays, and there's a superb view from the top.
🕐 Daily 10am–6pm, late Jun–mid-Sep; Wed–Mon 10–6, mid-Sep–late Jun 💰 Adult $8.50, child $5 🚇 Jean-Drapeau 🍴 Light meals are served in canteen-like café; terrace is pleasant

LABYRINTHE DU HANGAR 16
Clock Tower Pier, Vieux Port, Montréal, Québec, H2L 4K3
Tel 514/499-0099
www.labyrintheduhangar16.com

A 2,430sq-m (27,000sq-ft) warehouse converted into a great maze game, where you have to discover and solve clues that lead you through the corridors, while tackling obstacles and various surprises along the way.
🕐 Sat–Sun 11.30–5.30, mid-May–mid Jun and Sep; daily 11–9, mid-Jun–Aug; Fri 6.30pm–9pm, Sat 11.30–9, Sun 11.30–5.30, Oct–early Nov 💰 Adult $11, child (4–12) $9 or (13–17) $10 🚇 Champ-de-Mars 🚌 14

MEGADÔME DE MONTRÈAL
6900 boulevard Décarie, Suite 110, Montréal, Québec
Tel 514/344-3663
www.megadome.ca
High-tech video games and laser-tag, things to climb on, ball games, and more sensitive arts and crafts activities—kids can have hours of fun at this giant complex.
🚇 Namur 🚌 17, 92, 160

MONTRÉAL BIODOME
4777 avenue Pierre-De Coubertin, Montréal, Québec, H1V 1B3
Tel 514/868-3000
www.biodome.qc.ca

Four North American ecosystems have been beautifully re-created here, and kids have fun spotting all the animals. These include snakes, capybaras and sloths in the Tropical Forest (great to visit in winter); four kinds of penguins in the Polar World; marine life in the St. Lawrence Marine Ecosystem; and beavers, porcupines and lynx in the Laurentian Forest.
🕐 Daily 9–6, Jul–Aug; 9–4, rest of year 💰 Adult $10.50, child (5–17) $5.25 🚇 Viau, then walk 🚌 132

MONTRÉAL SCIENCE CENTRE

King Edward Pier, Vieux Port, Montréal, Québec
Tel 514/496-4724, 877/496-4724
www.montrealsciencecentre.com

A superb interactive facility. Little ones have more than 20 activities in Dynamo's Lair; for older kids there are technology exhibits, including Technocity, Eureka!, and an interactive movie with three giant screens and touch-screen consoles to control the action.

⊙ Sun–Thu 10–5, Fri–Sat 10–9, late Apr–early Sep; closed Mon in winter except statutory holidays 🎫 Various options; adult $12–27, child $10–25 🚇 Place d'Armes or Champ-de-Mars 🍴 Zoomatic bistro serves light meals

PEPSI FORUM

2313 rue Ste-Catherine Ouest, Montréal, Québec, H3H 1N2
Tel 514/933-6786, 888/613-6786
www.forum-pepsi.com
Older kids who are not easily overwhelmed might meet their match in this huge complex, with more than 200 of the latest interactive games and simulators, a 30m (100ft) climbing wall, movie theaters, pool tables, bowling, and Montréal Hall of Fame.
⊙ Daily 🎫 Activities priced separately (arcade games are expensive) 🚇 Atwater 🚌 15, 57 🍴 Five restaurants featuring fusion cuisine

QUÉBEC CITY

PARC AQUARIUM DU QUÉBEC

1675 avenue des Hotels, Ste-Foy, Québec City, Québec, G1W 4S3
Tel 418/659-5264
www.spsnq.qc.ca
As a build-up to the main attraction—an acrylic tunnel walk through a 350,000-liter

(91,000-gal) tank with more than 650 marine animals—there are outdoor habitats for polar bears and seals, and a pavilion housing 3,500 fish. Dress for the cold.
⊙ Daily 10–8, Jun–Aug, 10–5 rest of year 🎫 Adult $24, child (3–5) $7, (6–12) $16 or (13–17) $19.50 🍴 Yes, there's seafood on the menu, along with burgers, salads and roast dinners

Festivals and Events

JANUARY/FEBRUARY

QUEBEC WINTER CARNIVAL

Quebec City, Québec
Tel 866/422-7628, 418/621-5555
www.carnaval.qc.ca
More than two weeks of winter fun, with parades, sporting events, dogsled and horse-drawn sleigh rides, snow sculptures, concerts and food.

MARCH

ST. PATRICK'S DAY

Montréal, Québec
Tel 514/932-0512
Parade with marching bands and floats, and lots of traditional Irish music and dancing.

APRIL

BLUE METROPOLIS INTERNATIONAL LITERARY FESTIVAL

Montréal, Québec,
Tel 514/937-BLEU
http://blue-met-bleu.com
More than 120 authors take part in on-stage interviews, an award presentation, readings, comedy and music events.

JUNE/JULY

CANADIAN GRAND PRIX

Montréal, Québec
www.grandprix.ca
The future of this event, at the Circuit Gilles-Villeneuve, is uncertain at the time of going to press (see pages 190–191).

FETES DU QUÉBEC MARITIME

Bas-St-Laurent, Gaspésie, Manicouagan, Duplessis, Îles de la Madeleine, Québec
Tel 800/657-3383, 418/722-3383
www.fetesduquebecmaritime.com
Celebrating the rich heritage of maritime Québec, with music, storytelling, tours and food.

FESTIVAL DE LANAUDIÈRE

Joliette, Québec
Tel 450/759-7636
www.lanaudiere.org
Highly acclaimed classical music event, with world-class performances in a covered amphiteater.

QUÉBEC CITY SUMMER FESTIVAL

Québec City, Québec
Tel 418/529-5200, 888/992-5200
www.infofestival.com
Long-established music event that includes experimental, rock, Celtic, and world music, plus street performers.

JUST FOR LAUGHS COMEDY FESTIVAL

Montréal, Québec
Tel 888/244-3155, 514/845-3155
www.hahaha.com

For these 10 days Montréal is the happiest city in the world, as top comedians from all over come to do their stuff. Stage shows are broadcast worldwide

LES GRANDS FEUX LOTO-QUÉBEC

Montmorency Falls Park, Québec City, Québec
Tel 418/523-3389
www.lesgrandsfeux.com
A dazzling competition for international fireworks teams, set in a natural amphitheater backed by the waterfall.

AUGUST

HOT-AIR BALLOON FESTIVAL

Gatineau, Québec
Tel 819/243-2330, 800/668-8383
www.balloongatineau.com
Around 150 hot-air balloons take to the sky, and on the ground there are fairground rides, shows and fireworks.

 WHAT TO DO

 **FESTIVALS AND EVENTS 213**

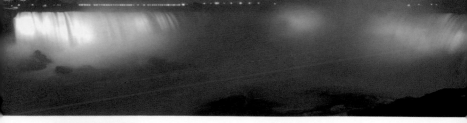

ONTARIO

The Toronto Argonauts go into action at the SkyDome

The province with two capitals—Ottawa, the national capital, and Toronto, the provincial capital—and a number of other large, vibrant cities, tops the cultural stakes in Canada. Ottawa is surprisingly low-key, and smaller than you might expect, but has some choice, high-quality theater and musical events, some good live music venues, plus high-profile festivals.

Toronto is undisputably the cultural capital of the country, with entertainment to rival New York and London in its huge number of theaters, magnificent concert halls and arenas. It's home to the national ballet and national opera, and also a number of small-scale and experimental theater companies. Toronto's Second City comedy club is world-renowned for spawning a long list of internationally famous performers, such as Mike Myers, Gilda Radner and John Candy. Nightlife is a buzzing mix of trendy dance clubs, jazz and blues clubs, gay clubs and rock music venues.

Shopping is unrivaled in Toronto, too, from the splendid malls to the chic designer boutiques, but it's also worth exploring the province for picturesque little places like Elora that have interesting craft and clothing stores.

Spectator sports include the Blue Jays baseball team at the SkyDome, plus hockey, Canadian football and basketball. Toronto also has the country's premier racetrack, the Woodbine, and the Mosport motor racing circuit. In and out of the cities, there are seemingly endless possibilities for entertaining children and for outdoor activities of all kinds, at any time of year, with watersports on lakes Ontario and Huron, winter sports at Collingwood, some superb golf courses, and hiking in wonderful parks like the Algonquin or along the Bruce Trail. Ontario is also the home of the international headquarters of the Taoist Tai Chi Society, out at Orangeville.

World-class festivals come thick and fast in Toronto and Ottawa—there are just too many to list in this guide—and elsewhere you'll find events that range from the Fergus Highland Games to fall fairs and folk festivals.

Shopping

OLDE HIDE HOUSE
49 Eastern Avenue, Acton, Ontario, L7J 2E6
Tel 519/853-1031
www.LeatherTown.com

An 1899 building houses Canada's largest leather store, and it's worth visiting just for the wonderful aroma inside. Stretching into the distance are coats, jackets, pants (trousers) and vests in many colors, plus hundreds of purses, wallets, belt, gloves, and leather furniture for home and office.
🕐 Sat–Wed 10–6, Thu–Fri 10–9 (daily 10–9 during holidays) 🚉 Off Mill Street

KARGER GALLERY
Elora Mews Unit 6a and 7, 45 Mill Street West, Elora, Ontario, N0B 1S0
Tel 519/846-2921, 877/846-1116
www.kargergallery.com
The picturesque village of Elora, with its wide river rapids, is a great place to shop, with lots of friendly boutiques and interesting specialty stores. The Karger Gallery is one of the highlights, full of high-quality works from more than 100 Canadian artists—ceramics, glass, wood, metal, paintings, and raku. Stunningly beautiful pieces sit alongside whimsical practical items, and the prices are very affordable.
🕐 Daily 11–6

CATARAQUI TOWN CENTRE
945 Gardiners Road, Kingston, Ontario, K7M 7H4
Tel 613/389-7900
www.cataraquitowncentre.ca

The largest shopping center in the area, with more than 140 stores, including Sears, The Bay, Zellers and Sport Chek. There's also a good variety of smaller stores, and a place where you can drop off children aged 1–6 years to be cared for (fee) while you shop.

🕐 Mon–Fri 9.30–9, Sat 9.30–6, Sun noon–5 🚌 West of the river, between Princess and Kidd, south of Highway 401 (exit 611) 🍴 Fast-food; Moxie's Grill, featuring European and American cuisine; Rose and Crown pub

MISSISSAUGA

SQUARE ONE
100 City Centre Drive, Mississauga, Ontario, L5B 2C9
Tel 905/279-7467
www.shopsquareone.com
It was Canada's largest shopping mall when built in 1973, and it's still Ontario's largest, with more than 350 stores and services, anchored by the big four department stores: a giant Wal-Mart, The Bay, Sears, and Zellers. Also movie multiplex and gymnasium.

🕐 Mon–Fri 10–9, Sat 9.30–6, Sun noon–6 🚌 Downtown Transit Terminal nearby 🚌 Downtown Mississauga, at highways 403 and 10 🍴 Around 40 outlets, including fast foods and licensed restaurants

NIAGARA FALLS

CANADA ONE FACTORY OUTLETS
7500 Lundy's Lane, Niagara Falls, Ontario, L2H 1G8
Tel 905/356-8989, 866/284-5781
www.canadaoneoutlets.com
Around 40 stores sell off big-name items at up to 70 percent discount—Ralph Lauren, Danier Leather, Liz Claibourne, Levi's, Tommy Hilfiger, Roots, Reebok,

and Villeroy and Bosch are just some of them.

🕐 Mon–Sat 10–9, Sun 10–6
🚌 Niagara shuttle (summer only)
🍴 Saint Cinnamon Bakery Café

NIAGARA-ON-THE-LAKE

EUROPA ANTIQUES
1523 Niagara Stone Road, Virgil, Ontario, L0S 1J0
Tel 905/468-3130
www.europa-antiques.com
You could spend hours browsing around this antiques shop, housed in an ivy-clad church building that is itself over 100 years old. Inside (and spilling out onto the lawn in summer), there's furniture (armoirs, beds, dressers, chairs) plus a whole lot of fascinating small items, such as lights and mirrors, bobbins, oil lamps, pewter and kitchenware.

🕐 Wed–Fri 10–5, Sat–Sun 11–5, Mon–Tue by appointment only (phone for winter hours) 🚌 On Highway 55, 2km (1 mile) from Niagara-on-the-Lake

FRENCH PERFUME FACTORY
393 York Road, Niagara-on-the-Lake, Ontario, L0S 1J0
Tel 905/685-6666, 800/463-0012
www.perfumefactory.ca
See antique stills, raw materials, and the laboratory at the first perfume factory and museum in North America to open to the public. Hundreds of big-name fragrances for men and women—Armani, Chanel, Givenchy, Yves Saint-Laurent—are available at less-than-duty-free prices, along with Ombra bath products and aromatherapy oils.

🕐 Daily 10–5 🚌 Off Queen Elizabeth Way, exit 38 or via Glendale Avenue from St. Catharines

OTTAWA

BOUTIQUE LE PAPILLON
136 Bank Street, Ottawa, Ontario, K1P 5N8
Tel 613/233-1003
www.boutiquelepapillon.com
Elegant, professional women in Ottawa shop at this family-run business. It's not just the fashions that set this store apart, it's the courteous, knowledgeable and honest service. Designer clothing from

around the world is selected for classic clean lines, wearability, modern textiles, and above all a contemporary sense of style.

🕐 Mon–Wed and Sat 10–5.30, Thu–Fri 10–6 🚌 1, 2, 4, 7

BYWARD MARKET
55 Byward Market Square, Ottawa, Ontario, K1N 9C3
Tel 613/241-6542
www.byward-market.com

Historic market in the oldest part of Ottawa, with a real buzzing atmosphere. Hundreds of vendors, under cover and lining the streets, sell fruit and vegetables, clothing, footwear, jewelry, crafts, ornaments and souvenirs. The whole area is a lively mix of restaurants, specialty stores and nightclubs.

🕐 Daily, hours vary 🚌 1, 2, 4, 7, 14, 16, 18 (Rideau) or 3, 4 (Dalhousie)

COLLECTED WORKS
1242 Wellington Street, Ottawa, Ontario, K1Y 3A4
Tel 613/722-1265
www.collected-works.com
This independent bookstore, in the Holland neighborhood, is owned and run by real enthusiasts—co-owner Craig Poile is a poet and playwright. You can browse at leisure, get expert advice, enjoy excellent coffee and cookies, and perhaps catch a reading or art exhibition in the back room, or a book-signing event. Strong emphasis on literary fiction, poetry and children's books, with works by Canadian, American and British writers.

🕐 Mon–Wed 7.30–5.30, Thu–Fri 7.30–9, Sat 8–5.30, Sun 11–5 🚌 2
🍴 Gourmet coffee and cookies

INUIT ARTISTS' SHOP
2081 Merivale Road, Ottawa, Ontario,
K2G 1G9
Tel 613/224-8189
www.inuitart.org

Owned and operated by the artists themselves, this is a nonprofit (which doesn't mean items are cheap) gallery with exquisite examples of Inuit art, including sculptures in caribou and whale bone and stone, prints, wall hangings, baskets, and dolls. Items can be shipped worldwide.
🕐 Mon–Sat 9–5, Sun 10–4 🚌 3, 4, 306 🚇 Byward Market area, between Sussex and King Edward

PLACE D'ORLÉANS
110 place d'Orleans Drive, Orleans, Ottawa, Ontario, K1C 2L9
Tel 613/824-9050
www.placedorleans.com
Wide sunlit aisles, a fountain and children's play areas make this a particularly pleasant mall. Anchored by Wal-Mart and The Bay, it has around 200 stores—if fatigue sets in, call at Back World and try out the orthopedic chairs.
🕐 Mon–Sat 9.30–9, Sun 11–5 🚌 95 🚇 East of Downtown, just off RR174/Highway 17 at place d'Orleans Drive and St-Joseph Boulevard 🍴 Food court, plus Beef n' Brand restaurant

RIDEAU CENTRE
50 Rideau Street, Ottawa, Ontario
K1N 9J7
Tel 613/236-6565
www.rideaucentre.net
About 200 stores share this downtown mall, with Sears as the anchor. It has a classy feel to it, though after the big out-of-town malls, it seems just a little closed-in. But it's defi-

nitely worth a visit for its many interesting specialty stores and individual fashion boutiques.
🕐 Mon–Fri 9.30–9, Sat 9.30–6, Sun 11–5 🚌 2, 7, 14, 18, 306, 316 🍴 More than a dozen food outlets, including Italian, Mexican and Chinese

R.W. KIDS
Hampton Park Plaza, Ottawa, Ontario,
K1Z 7L6
Tel 613/724-4576, 800/652-4674
www.rwkids.com
If you want to outfit your kid like a little Canadian, this is the place to come. Family-run, it stocks a range of stylish Canadian-made clothes, including tough dungarees, denim jackets and snowsuits.
🕐 Mon–Wed and Sat 9.30–5.30, Thu–Fri 9.30–8 🚌 85 Bayshore 🚇 East of Downtown, at Carling and Kirkwood–Queensway intersection 124

JOYCE SEPPALA DESIGNS
508 East Victoria Avenue, Thunder Bay, Ontario, P7C 1A7
Tel 807/624-0022
www.welcome.to/joyce_seppala_designs
English-born Joyce Seppala has introduced stunning designs to cuddly fleece fabrics, and the result is a range of wearable, easy-care garments that are stylish and fun. Imaginative patterns are inspired by Joyce's love of the Canadian northern landscapes.
🕐 Mon–Fri 9.30–5, Sat 9.30–1

TORONTO
ALGONQUIANS SWEET GRASS GALLERY
668 Queen Street West, Toronto, Ontario
Tel 416/703-1336
Owned by the Ojibway tribe, this wonderful gallery has exquisite arts and crafts, including soapstone and antler (deer and moose) sculptures, masks, porcupine-quill jewelry, moccasins, dreamcatchers and antique spearheads. There is also a range of Canadian-designed T-shirts and sweatshirts.
🕐 Mon–Fri 11–6, Sat 11–5 🚇 Osgoode, then any streetcar west 🚋 Streetcar: 501 🚇 West of Bathurst

ALL THE BEST FINE FOODS
1099 Yonge Street, Toronto, Ontario,
M4W 2L7
Tel 416/928-3330
www.allthebestfinefoods.com
The name says it all, and the window display in the century-old storefront defies you to keep on walking. Well placed for exclusive Rosedale, it has an outstanding cheese selection, fresh baked goods, gift baskets, tableware and items for stylish entertaining.
🕐 Mon–Fri 8.30–7, Sat 10–6, Sun 10–5 🚇 Summerhill 🚌 97B 🚇 Just south of Summerhill subway

BOOTMASTER INC.
609 Yonge Street, Toronto, Ontario,
M4Y 1Z5
Tel 416/927-1054
www.bootmaster.com

This store has everything for the armchair cowboy or aspiring country singer. Cowboy boots, jackets in leather or fringed and beaded suede, western shirts, belts, buckles, bolo ties, and Stetsons.
🕐 Mon–Sat 10–7 🚇 Bloor-Yonge or Wellesley 🚌 97B 🚇 Between Bloor and Wellesley

BOUNTY
Harbourfront Centre, 235 Queen's Quay West, Toronto, Ontario, M5J 2G8
Tel 416/973-4993
www.harbourfront.on.ca
A range of contemporary crafts, including ceramics, blown glass, jewelry, wood and fiber crafts. Many of the items have been made by the professional artists-in-residence at the onsite craft studios (you can watch work in progress).
🕐 Tue and Sat–Sun 11–6, Wed–Fri 11–8 🚇 Union Station 🚋 Streetcar: 509, 510

WHAT TO DO

DR. FLEA'S
8 Westmore Drive, Toronto, Ontario, M9V 3Z7
Tel 416/745-3532
www.drfleas.com
An undercover market houses more than 400 independent vendors selling all manner of goods: crafts, collectables, jewelry, clothing, baby goods, furniture, homeware, music (recordings and instruments), toys and games. The farmers' market has fresh produce, candy and bakery items.
🕒 Sat–Sun 10–5 🚇 Royal York, then bus 73 🚌 73 🚗 Highway 27 and Albion Road, 25 min from downtown

EATON CENTRE
220 Yonge Street, Toronto, Ontario, M5B 2H1
Tel 416/598-8700
www.torontoeatoncentre.com

A trailblazer in the world of shopping, this is one of the most visited places in Toronto. The architecture remains impressive, and even with a million visitors a week it rarely feels crowded (except the food court on weekday lunchtimes). There are nearly 300 stores, and since Eaton's ceased trading, Sears is the main anchor.
🕒 Mon–Fri 10–9, Sat 9.30–7, Sun noon–6 🚇 Queen or Dundas 🚌 97B
🍴 Fast food. Restaurants include Baton Rouge (see page 321), City Grill, Mr Greenjeans and the Duke of Richmond

ESKIMO ART GALLERY
12 Queen's Quay West, Toronto, Ontario, M5J 2V3
Tel 416/336-3000, 800/800-2008
www.eskimoart.com
There are touches of the Arctic about this excellent gallery of Inuit sculpture, with frosted-glass shelving, pedestals that simulate icebergs, tundra-colored carpet, and icy blue lighting. It displays Canada's largest collection of contemporary Inuit soapstone carvings, reflecting the warm emotions that exist in the cold north.
🕒 Mon–Fri 10–7, Sat–Sun 10–6 🚇 Union Station 🚋 Streetcar: 509, 510 🚌 Harbourfront

HOAX COUTURE
163 Spadina Avenue, 3rd Floor, Toronto, Ontario, M5V 2L6
Tel 416/597-8924
www.hoaxcouture.com
The name is fun, the clothes are witty, too, but are seriously stylish, and the boutique is a calm space where garments are displayed on the walls, like the artworks that they are. Jim Searle and Chris Tyrell's glamorous designs feature draping fabrics, full skirts and perfect little cocktail dresses; innovative, superbly cut designs for men wouldn't let you down at a Hollywood premiere.
🕒 Daily 🚇 Osgoode 🚋 501 west 🚌 Corner of Queen and Spadina

HOLT RENFREW
50 Bloor Street West, Toronto, Ontario, M4W 1A1
Tel 416/922-2333
www.holtrenfrew.com

This long-established, exclusive store has the oldest existing contract with Christian Dior and five generations of royal warrants. In addition to prestigious designer fashions for men and women, it has accessories, cosmetics, and fragrances. There's also an Estée Lauder spa, a nail spa and a hair salon.

🕒 Mon–Wed and Sat 10–6), Thu–Fri 10–8, Sun noon–5 🚇 Bay 🚌 6A, 6B
🚇 Downtown, west of Yonge ☕ Chic café aimed at "ladies who lunch"

HONEST ED'S
581 Bloor Street West, Toronto, Ontario, M6G 1K3
Tel 416/537-1574
A huge signboard with 22,000 flashing lights heralds a place that's world-famous for its brash, fun approach to discount retailing (a sign inside reads "don't faint at our prices, there's no place to lie down"). In business since 1948, it has 14,400sq m (160,000sq ft) of bargains including clothing, gifts, homewares, and food.
🕒 Mon–Fri 10–9, Sat 10–6, Sun 11–6 🚇 Bathurst 🚋 Streetcar: 511 🚌 Corner of Bloor and Bathurst

KALIYANA
2516 Yonge Street, Toronto, Ontario, M4P 2H7
Tel 416/480-2397
www.kaliyana.com
This is a real find–a classy store with uncluttered racks of gorgeous clothes in sleek styles and unusual colors, all in washable natural fibers. Smart enough for the office and comfortable enough for lounging around, the designs and fabrics drape well…and you won't get turned away if you're bigger than size 10 (they go up to 24).
🕒 Mon–Wed and Sat 10–6, Thu–Fri 10–7, Sun noon–5 🚇 Eglinton 🚌 97+ 🚌 Yonge and Eglinton

QUEEN'S QUAY TERMINAL
207 Queen's Quay West, Toronto, Ontario, M5J 1A7
Tel 416/203-0510
www.queens-quay-terminal.com

A very classy mall with soaring ceilings, lots of glass giving natural light (and lake views), and more than 50 outlets that have a mainly Canadian focus—Arctic Canada, Canadian Naturalist, Oh Yes! Toronto, and Proud Canadian Design. There's also designer clothing, fine art, Venetian glass and Swiss music boxes.
🕐 Daily 10–5 🚇 Union Station 🚃 Streetcar: 509, 510 🍴 Food court, overlooking the lake, includes Japanese, Chinese, seafood, deli and diner

TILLEY ENDURABLES
900 Don Mills Road, Toronto, Ontario, M3C 1V6
Tel 416/441-6141
www.tilley.com
The flagship store of a Toronto business success story (see page 35). It started with Alex Tilley's simple need for a good sailing hat, and now the hat is sold all over North America. This is one of Tilley's own stores, and sells tough, practical clothing for travelers.
🕐 Mon–Wed 9–8, Thu–Fri 9–9, Sat 9–6, Sun 11–5 🚌 25+, 403 🚃 Uptown, two traffic lights north of Eglinton

WORLD'S BIGGEST BOOKSTORE
20 Edward Street, Toronto, Ontario M5G 1C9
Tel 416/977-7009
It's not the biggest any more, but the name was accurate when it opened, and who's going to quibble when they see 27km (17 miles) of shelves and 143,000 titles in 65 departments? There's a free CD-ROM search service and a database that contains every book that is in print in the world.
🕐 Mon–Sat 9am–10pm, Sun 11–8 🚇 Dundas 🚌 97B 🚃 Downtown, off Yonge just north of the Eaton Centre

Performance

GANANOQUE

THOUSAND ISLANDS PLAYHOUSE
690 Charles Street South, Gananoque, Ontario, K7G 2T8
Tel 613/382-7020
www.1000islandsplayhouse.com

Right on the waterfront, this professional theater stages popular lightweight drama, music and comedy.
🕐 Mid-May–early Nov 💵 Adult $24.50–28.50, child $15 🚃 On bank of St. Lawrence River

HAMILTON

HAMILTON PLACE THEATRE
Ronald V. Joyce Centre for the Performing Arts, 1 Summers Lane, Hamilton, Ontario, L8P 4Y3
Tel 905/546-3100
www.hecfi.on.ca
Fine modern facility with huge stage and superior acoustics, staging drama, concerts, opera, and musicals. Adjacent Studio Theatre is more intimate.
🕐 Year-round 💵 Prices vary

THEATRE AQUARIUS
du Maurier Ltd. Centre, 190 King William Street, Hamilton, Ontario, L8R 1A8
Tel 905/522-PLAY, 800/465 PLAY
www.theatreaquarius.org
This superb modern theater complex, with four separate performing spaces, features classic drama, musicals and children's shows.
🕐 Year-round 💵 Price varies with event; usually $20–47 🚃 Downtown, between Walnut and Ferguson

KINGSTON

GRAND THEATRE
218 Princess Street, Kingston, Ontario, K7L 1B2
Tel 613/530-2050
www.grandtheatre-kingston.com
The principal performing arts venue in Kingston, with an 800-seat main theater and smaller Baby Grand Studio Theatre. Full calendar of drama, comedy and music.
🕐 Year-round 💵 Price varies

MISSISSAUGA

LIVING ARTS CENTRE
4141 Living Arts Drive, Mississauga, Ontario, L5B 4B8
Tel 905/306-6000, 888/805-8888
www.livingarts.on.ca
World-class theaters with excellent acoustics, staging drama, dance, opera, comedy, and music, including classical, jazz, blues, and folk.
🕐 Year-round 💵 Varies with individual events 🚌 6, 26 A/B, 28, 86 🚃 Downtown, near Princess Royal Drive 🍴 Lunch and pre-theater buffet

NIAGARA FALLS

OAKES GARDEN THEATRE
Niagara Parkway, Niagara Falls, Ontario, L2E 6T2
Tel 905/371-0254; 877/642-7275
www.niagaraparks.com
Constructed in 1936, this amphitheater has beautiful lawns, rock gardens, lily ponds, and borders overlooking the American Falls. The classical-style stage hosts a variety of plays and concerts.
🕐 Year-round 💵 Invariably free 🚃 5, 19, Niagara Shuttle

NIAGARA-ON-THE-LAKE

SHAW FESTIVAL THEATRE
10 Queen's Parade, Niagara-on-the-Lake, Ontario, L0S 1J0
Tel 905/468-2172, 800/511-7429
www.shawfest.com
The only theater in the world that specializes in plays by George Bernard Shaw. It is also one of the largest repertory companies in North America.
🕐 Apr–Nov 💵 $18–75

OAKVILLE

OAKVILLE CENTRE FOR THE PERFORMING ARTS
130 Navy Street, Oakville, Ontario, L6M 3A4
Tel 905/815-2021
www.oc4pa.com
Community arts center staging theater, music, comedy and family entertainment.
🕐 Year-round 💵 Average $35–40

OTTAWA

CENTREPOINTE THEATRE
Ben Franklin Place, 101 Centrepointe Drive, Nepean, Ottawa, Ontario
Tel 613/580-2700, 866/752-5231
www.centrepointetheatre.com

WHAT TO DO

Modern 967-seat theater hosting all types of performance, from international touring companies to local orchestras, dance groups and theater companies. 🕐 Year-round 🎫 Varies with event, usually $20–40 🚌 Transitway to Baseline 🚇 O-Train to Carleton, then bus 117

EDDIE MAY MYSTERIES
Marble Works, Rideau Street, Ottawa, Ontario
Tel 613/729-8832, 877/WE-SLAY-U
www.eddiemay.com
Canada's longest-running dinner theater company continues in its flagship location, a fine 1866 heritage building. As you enjoy a four-course meal, a victim succumbs, and the mystery unfolds as you play detective. Light-hearted fun.
🕐 Fri–Sat, Jan–May and Oct–Nov; Sat, Jun–Sep; Wed–Sun, Dec 🎫 $50–60 🚌 2, 7, 14, 18, 306,

GREAT CANADIAN THEATRE COMPANY
910 Gladstone Avenue, Ottawa, Ontario, K1R 6Y4
Tel 613/236-5196
www.gctc.ca
This is a long-established company staging a vibrant selection of challenging drama and comedy, and with a commitment to produce new Canadian work.
🕐 Year-round 🎫 $14–26 🚌 3, 14 🚇 West of Downtown, near intersection with Preston

KANATA 24
801 Earl Grey Drive, Kanata, Ottawa, Ontario, K2T 1E7
Tel 613/599-1200
www.amctheatres.com

AMC 24-screen megaplex with 4,764 seats, showing first-run movies. Wall-to-wall screens and stadium seating, some with retractable armrests.
🕐 Daily 🎫 Adult $13, child (under 13) $8 🚌 97 from Ottawa or 118, 161, 152 from Kanata Town Centre

NATIONAL ARTS CENTRE
53 Elgin Street, Ottawa, Ontario, K1P 5W1
Tel 613/947-7000, 866/850-ARTS
www.nac cna.ca

One of the largest and most comprehensive performing arts facilities in the world, staging theater (English and French), dance and music.
🕐 Year-round 🎫 Prices vary 🚌 1, 2, 4, 5, 6, 7, 14, 15, 16, 18 🍴 Canadian and international cuisine

ODYSSEY THEATRE
Strathcona Park, Laurier Avenue East, Ottawa, Ontario
Tel 613/232-8407
Performances in the park are in the tradition of *commedia dell'arte*, using masks, puppets and clowns.
🕐 Tue–Sun, late Jul–late Aug, 🎫 Adult $10, child (under 12) $4; pay-what-you-can on Sun 🚇 8 🚌 Downtown, intersection of Laurier and Range

OTTAWA LITTLE THEATRE
400 King Edward Street, Ottawa, Ontario, K1N 7M7
Tel 613/233-8948
www.o-l-t.com
One of Canada's oldest theaters (since 1913), producing eight plays a year. The auditorium dates from 1970—when a fire destroyed the original.
🕐 Sep–May, plus summer season 🎫 $15. Summer Theatre: musicals: $18 🚌 2, 7, 14, 18, 19 🚇 Transitway Mackenzie King Bridge (15-min walk)

STRATFORD
STRATFORD FESTIVAL OF CANADA
55 Queen Street, Stratford, Ontario, N5A 6V2
Tel 519/271-0055; 800/567-1600
www.stratfordfestival.ca
This building won accolades when it was built in 1957, and now, with a multi-million dollar remodeling, it remains a superb setting for Shakespeare and other classics.
🕐 May–Nov 🎫 From about $30

THUNDER BAY
COMMUNITY AUDITORIUM
1 Paul Shaffer Drive, Thunder Bay, Ontario, P7B 6C7
Tel 807/684-4444, 800/463-0017
www.tbca.com
Impressive 1,500-seat concert hall, home to the Thunder Bay Symphony Orchestra, with full schedule of classical concerts, musicals and rock concerts.
🕐 Year round 🎫 Price varies

MAGNUS THEATRE
Dr. S. Penny Petrone Centre for the Performing Arts, 10 South Algoma Street, Thunder Bay, Ontario, P7B 3A7
Tel 807/345-5552
www.magnus.on.ca

Northwest Ontario's professional theater company stages an interesting series of world-class drama and comedy.
Year-round $18–32 West of downtown, off Waverley Street

SILVERCITY THUNDER BAY
850 North May Street, Thunder Bay, Ontario, P7C 6A5
Tel 807/628-8445
www.famousplayers.com
Twelve big-screen, big-sound movie theaters with stadium seating.
Daily $7.95 Downtown, corner of North May and Northern

TORONTO

AIR CANADA CENTRE
40 Bay Street, Suite. 400, Toronto, Ontario, M5J 2X2
Tel 416/815-5500
www.theaircanadacentre.com
This complex includes the 5,200-seat Sears Theatre, the largest venue in the city. It stages ice shows and concerts by touring international stars.
Year round Varies Union Station Streetcar: 6A, 97B Huge food court, restaurants, pub and bar

CANADA SQUARE
2200 Yonge Street, Toronto, Ontario, M4S 2C6
Tel 416/483-9428
www.famousplayers.com
Big, curved screens, stadium seating and digital sound make for enjoyable viewing of all the latest releases.
Daily Adult $11.50, child $7.25 Eglinton 32B, 32C, 61+, 97+ Uptown, at Eglinton Avenue West

CANON
244 Victoria Street, Toronto, Ontario, M5B 1V8
Tel 416/872-1212
Formerly the Pantages, and restored in grand style, this 2,268-capacity theater specializes in long-running musicals.
Year-round $46–94 Queen or Dundas 97B One block east of Yonge, between Queen and Dundas

CANSTAGE
26 Berkeley Street, Toronto, Ontario M5A 2W3
Tel 416/368-3110; 416/367-8243
www.canstage.com

In a renovated century-old factory, this is home to Canada's largest contemporary theater company. Serious drama, classics, comedies and small-scale musicals.
Year-round $35–77 King, then eastbound streetcar to Berkeley

DOCKS DRIVE-IN THEATRE
Docks Entertainment Complex, 11 Polson Street, Toronto, Ontario, M5A 1A4
Tel 416/461-3625
www.thedocks.com
There are still a number of drive-in movie theaters in Canada, but this one has the biggest screen, showing a double bill of first-run movies.
Nightly, summer; Sat–Sun, Sep–Oct $10, $6.50 on Tue (children under 12 free) 72A East side of Inner Harbour, off Lakeshore Boulevard, then Cherry Street

ELGIN & WINTER GARDEN
189 Yonge Street, Toronto, Ontario, M5B 1M4
Tel 416/314-2871

A national historic site, this is the last "double-decker" Edwardian theater in the world—Elgin downstairs, Winter Garden above. Stages various drama, music and comedy.
Year-round $28–55 Queen or Dundas Streetcar: 97B Downtown, between Queen and Dundas

FAMOUS PEOPLE PLAYERS
110 Sudbury Street, Toronto, Ontario, M6J 3T3
Tel 416/532-1137; 1-888/453-3385
www.fpp.org
World-renowned puppeteers create a remarkably exciting show using huge, bright pup-

pets and black lighting. A meal is an integral part of the show.
Tue–Sat $46.95 Go Train: Exhibition Streetcar: 501, 504 South of Queen between Lisgar and Dovercourt Three-course meal (no choices), with dessert and coffee taken after the show

HARBOURFRONT CENTRE
See page 112–113

HUMMINGBIRD CENTRE
1 Front Street East, Toronto, Ontario, M5E 1B2
Tel 416/393-7429
www.hummingbirdcentre.com

Formerly the O'Keefe Centre. The largest venue in the city, staging opera, Broadway-style shows, ballet, and concerts by international stars.
Year-round Price varies Union Station or King Street 65A, 72A

MASSEY HALL
Shuter Street, Toronto, Ontario, M5J 2H5
Tel 416/593-4822
www.masseyhall.com

The grande dame of the city's music halls, dating back to 1894. Hosts pop, rock, and classical music.
Year-round Varies with event

🚇 Queen, then walk north
🚌 Streetcar: 97B, 501, 502 🅿 Theater District

MOLSON AMPHITHEATRE
Ontario Place, 909 Lakeshore Boulevard West, Toronto, Ontario, M6K 3L3
Tel 416/260-5600
Open-air facility with reserved seating for 9,000 and lawn space for 7,000 more. Concerts include rock, jazz, alternative, hip-hop, blues and country.
🕐 Year-round 💵 Price varies, depending on event 🚇🚌 Bathurst, then streetcar 511 🚆 GO Train: Exhibition

MYSTERIOUSLY YOURS...
2026 Yonge Street, Toronto, Ontario, M4Z 1Z9
Tel 416/486-7469, 800/668-3323
www.MysteriouslyYours.com

The audience participates in solving the crime in this highly entertaining interactive murder-mystery, which unfolds during dinner.
🕐 Thu–Sat 💵 $75–80, including dinner and taxes 🚇 Davisville or Eglinton 🚌 Streetcar: 97B, 97+ 🚉 Uptown, 4km (2.5 miles) north of Bloor on west side of Yonge 🍴 Three-course dinner, with choice of dishes, including a vegetarian option

ONTARIO PLACE CINESPHERE
955 Lakeshore Boulevard West, Toronto, Ontario, M6K 3B9
Tel 416/314-9900, 416/870-8000
www.ontarioplace.com
This distinctive golf-ball building, a landmark on the lakeshore, houses an IMAX theater with six-story screen, including large-format and 3D, plus regular feature movies.
🕐 Daily 💵 $7–10 🚇 Bathurst, then streetcar 511 south 🚌 Streetcar: 509, 511

PRINCESS OF WALES
300 King Street West, Toronto, M5V 1J2
Tel 416/593-4142, 800/724-6420
www.mirvish.com

Built in the 1990s for the Mirvish Productions empire, this superb 2,000-seat theater has a huge stage suitable for the most spectacular productions, such as *The Lion King*.
🕐 Year-round 💵 $26–116 🚇 St. Andrew 🚌 Streetcar: King Street

ROYAL ALEXANDRA
260 King Street West, Toronto, M5V 1H9
Tel 416/593-4142, 800/724-6420
www.mirvish.com
Restored *beaux-arts* theater with 1,495 capacity. It's the oldest continuously operating theater in North America, staging mostly musicals.
🕐 Year-round 💵 $26–94 🚇 St. Andrew 🚌 Streetcar: King Street 🅿 Between Simcoe and Duncan

ROY THOMSON HALL
60 Simcoe Street, Toronto, Ontario, M5J 2H5
Tel 416/872-4255
www.roythomson.com

Superb modern hall, home to Toronto's Symphony Orchestra and Mendelssohn Choir.

Presents top international (mostly classical) performers.
🕐 Year-round 💵 Varies with event
🚇 St. Andrew 🚌 Streetcar: 504

ST. LAWRENCE CENTRE FOR THE ARTS
27 Front Street East, Toronto, Ontario, M5E 1B4
Tel 416/366-7723, 800/708-6754
www.stlc.com
This arts center with two small theaters is a nonprofit venue featuring drama, comedies, classical concerts and recitals.
🕐 Year-round 💵 $26–77 🚇 Union Station 🚉 Downtown, east of Yonge

SKYDOME
1 Blue Jays Way, Toronto, Ontario, M5V 1J3
Tel 416/341-3000
www.skydome.com

In addition to sporting events, SkyDome hosts concerts by megastars, opera, circus, ice shows, and such events as the Chinese New Year Festival and Canadian Aboriginal Festival.
🕐 Year-round; check local listings for schedule 💵 Price varies depending on event 🚇🚌 Union Station or St. Andrew 🚌 Streetcar: 510 🍴 Buffet restaurant and fast food

TORONTO CENTRE FOR THE ARTS
5040 Yonge Street, Toronto, Ontario, M2N 6R8
Tel 416/733-9388
www.tocentre.com
A beautiful modern building containing three halls—the mainstage theater, a studio theater and a recital hall—for drama, musicals and concerts.
🕐 Year-round 💵 Varies with event
🚇 North York or Sheppard
🚌 Streetcar: 97B, 97C 🚉 North York, north of Sheppard

TORONTO TRUCK THEATRE
94 Belmont Street, Toronto, Ontario,
M5R1P8
Tel 416/922-0084
www.mousetraptheatre.com
Agatha Christie's *The Mousetrap* has been showing here for almost 30 years.
🕐 Year-round 💰 $26 🚇 Rosedale
🚌 6, 97B

Nightlife

HAMILTON
JAZZ CELLAR MARTINI LOUNGE
69 Main Street East, Hamilton, Ontario
Tel 905/522-3155
www.jazzcellarmartinilounge.ca
Hamilton's ultimate cool live jazz and blues venue, where you can soak up the music and sample some of the 400 martinis on offer.
🕐 Wed–Sun 🍴 Food available

KINGSTON
TIME TO LAUGH
237 Ontario Street, Kingston, Ontario,
K7L 2Z4
Tel 613/542-5233
North America's top touring comedians are on stage here. Amateur night first Wednesday of each month; improv third Wednesday.
🕐 Thu–Sat 💰 Thu–Fri $9.95, Sat $12.95 🚇 Downtown, in Howard Johnson Hotel on the waterfront between Princess and Brock

TOUCAN AND KIRKPATRICK'S
76 Princess Street, Kingston, Ontario,
K7L 1A5
Tel 613/544-1966
www.thetoucan.ca
The Toucan and Kirkpatrick's (upstairs) are both Irish pubs. It's the Toucan that has music—traditional folk to hot new bands, with soul, blues, funk, and Motown on Mondays.
🕐 Daily; music Mon, Fri or Sat 💰 Mon free, other nights $2 🚌 1 🚇 Downtown, between Wellington and King Street East

NIAGARA FALLS
CASINO NIAGARA
5705 Falls Avenue, P.O. Box 300, Niagara Falls, Ontario, L2E 6T3
Tel 888/946-3255
www.casinoniagara.com
World-class gaming, with more than 2,700 slots and 135 gaming tables, including roulette, blackjack, poker, baccarat, and pai-gow. Restaurants, lounges and shopping.
🕐 Daily, 24 hours 💰 Admission free 🚌 Niagara Shuttle 🚇 Close to Rainbow Bridge

NIAGARA FALLSVIEW CASINO RESORT
Corner of Buchanan Avenue and Murray Street, Niagara Falls, Ontario
Tel 416/326-0163 (Ontario Casino Corporation) for information
When it opens in April 2004, Niagara's new casino will have 230,000sq m (2.5 million sq ft) of gaming space and other facilities, including 3,000 slots and 150 tables, on a site overlooking the falls. Patrons must be over 19.

OTTAWA
BARRYMORES MUSIC HALL
323 Bank Street, Ottawa, Ontario,
K2P 1X9
Tel 613/233-0307
www.barrymores.on.ca
One of Ottawa's top live rock music venues since 1978, with some big names featured in its history. Original and tribute bands, theme nights. Sundays are Retro 80s nights with DJ and no cover charge.
🕐 Thu–Sun 💰 $6–15 🚌 1, 2, 4, 7

D'ARCY MCGEE'S
44 Sparks Street, Ottawa, Ontario
Tel 613/230-4433
In its prime downtown location, this is a lovely pub with handcarved wood, and etched and stained glass that was handcrafted in Ireland and shipped over. Traditional Celtic and East Coast music from first-rate live bands.
🕐 Daily; live music Wed–Sat 💰 No cover charge 🚌 2, 5, 6, 7

DUKE OF SOMERSET
352 Somerset Street West, Ottawa, Ontario, K2P 0J9
Tel 613/233-7762
www.dukeofsomerset.com
Buzzing historic Somerset Village pub complex featuring regular live music from local rock bands, karaoke, international sport on satellite TV, and traditional pub league games.
🕐 Daily 💰 No cover charge (except charity events) 🚌 1, 2, 4, 7, 316 🚇 Corner of Bank

EI8HTEEN
18 York Street, Ottawa, Ontario,
K1N 5T5
Tel 613/244-1188
www.restaurant18.com

An ultra-chic nightspot, which attracts a casually sophisticated crowd. Cutting-edge cuisine, well-stocked wine bar, and regular jazz or DJ.
🕐 Daily 💰 No cover charge 🚌 3, 4, 306. Transitway: 95, 97 Mackenzie King or Laurier 🚇 Byward Market

THE INSTITUTION
145 Besserer Street, Nepean, Ontario
Tel 613/564-7000
www.theinstitution.cc
High-energy improv comedy. Thursdays and Fridays feature Laff Lines—like *Whose Line is it, Anyway?* On Saturdays the audience chooses a theme, and the cast play it out for maximum laughs.
🕐 Thu–Sat 💰 $12 ($10 Thu)

IRISH VILLAGE
67 Clarence Street, Ottawa, Ontario,
K1N 5P5
Tel 613/562-0674
www.irishvillage.ca
Four Irish pubs cluster together in this corner of Byward Market, with live music at Mother McGintey's and the Heart and Crown. It's mostly traditional Irish, but McGintey's also has rock on Sundays and jazz on Mondays.
🕐 Daily 💰 Rarely a cover charge 🚌 3, 4

WHAT TO DO

OLE BISTRO LATINO

352 Somerset Street West, Ottawa, Ontario, K2P 0J9
Tel 613/569-6397
The owner of this brightly decorated venue is in a salsa band and entertainment majors in Latin and Afro-Cuban music. Be prepared to dance—even if you don't know how.
🕐 Daily 💷 No cover charge 🚌 1, 7, 14, 316 🚉 Downtown, east of Bank Street

VINEYARDS WINE BAR BISTRO

54 York Street, Ottawa, Ontario, K1N 5T1
Tel 613/241-4270
www.ottawakiosk.com/vineyards
Atmospheric cellar wine bar, with snug booths and well-stocked bar of fine wines, single malts and imported beer. Jazz from top local artists.
🕐 Daily 💷 No cover charge 🚌 3, 4, 306. Transitway: 95, 97 to Mackenzie King or Laurier 🚉 Byward Market

YUK YUK'S COMEDY CABARET

88 Albert Street, Ottawa, Ontario, K1P 5E9
Tel 613/236-5233
www.yukyuks.com
This comedy-club's Ottawa location seats 200 for touring professional stand-up comedians. Amateur night Wednesday.
🕐 Wed–Sat 💷 Wed $6, Thu $12, Fri–Sat $16. Dinner and show $40–46 🚌 16, 18, 316

ZAPHOD BEEBLEBROX

27 York Street, Ottawa, Ontario, K1N 5S7
Tel 613/562-1010
Not for nothing was this place voted Ottawa's best live music and dance venue. Jewel, Alanis Morrissette and Fun Loving Criminals are among countless international stars who have played to the eclectic crowd. DJs on other nights.
🕐 Daily 💷 Cover charge varies 🚌 3, 4, 306. Transitway: 95, 97 to Mackenzie King or Laurier 🚉 Byward Market

RAMA

CASINO RAMA

RR #6, P.O. Box 178, Rama, Ontario, L0K 1T0
Tel 705/329-3325, 800/832-7529
www.casino-rama.com

More than 2,200 slots and 120 gaming tables, nine restaurants, an all-suite hotel, and a 5,000-seat venue hosting big-name concerts (Joe Cocker, David Cassidy, Cyndi Lauper) and shows. Patrons must be over 19.
🕐 Daily, 24 hours 💷 Admission free; Concerts and shows: $15–35 🚌 Call 705/329-5228 for special bus services 🚉 90 min north of Toronto, off Highway 11

TORONTO

BABAL·Ú

136 Yorkville Avenue, Lower Level, Toronto, Ontario, M5R 1C4
Tel 416/515-0587
www.babluu.com
Soft seating and pools of light on the hardwood dance floor create a party atmosphere at this tapas bar. DJ spins modern and classic salsa, mambo, Afro-Cuban, and Brazilian sounds. Free salsa lessons 9–10pm.
🕐 Wed–Sun (free salsa tuition 9–10pm) 💷 Cover $8–10 🚇 Bay or Bloor-Yonge 🚋 Streetcar: 6, A, B 🚉 Bloor-Yorkville; north of Bloor between Yonge Street and Avenue Road

C'EST WHAT?

67 Front Street East (music room around the corner at 19 Church), Toronto, Ontario, M5E 1B5
Tel 416/867-9499
www.cestwhat.com

A young (early 20s) crowd come to this brewpub show-bar to relax on the comfy couches and enjoy an eclectic mix of quality indie pop, jazz, folk, and blues. Good food and 29 draft beers.
🕐 Daily (no music on Mon) 💷 $5–8 🚇 King 🚋 Streetcar: 504 (King) 🚉 Downtown, corner of Church

FLY

8 Gloucester Street, Toronto, Ontario, M4Y 1L5
Tel 416/925-6222
Currently the hottest gay club in Toronto, popular with straight clubbers, too, for its top-rated DJs, superior sound and light systems, and party atmosphere. Three floors include dance floor, chill-out area, bars, and bistro.
🕐 Sat 10pm–7am 💷 $10–20 🚇 Wellesley 🚌 97B 🚉 Downtown at Gloucester and Yonge, two blocks north of Wellesley

THE GUVERNMENT

132 Queen's Quay East, Toronto, Ontario, M5A 3Y5
Tel 416/869-0045
www.theguvernment.com

Incorporating the huge and classy Kool Haus venue, this multi-faceted club complex (formerly The Warehouse) hosts Canadian and international big-name performers and DJs in seven separate rooms. Dress code and age limits may apply.
🕐 Fri–Sat (also Thu in summer, but only the Skybar is open) 💷 $10–15 cover charge 🚇 Union Station 🚋 Streetcar: 75 🚉 Corner of Lower Jarvis Street

HEALEY'S

178 Bathurst Street, Toronto, Ontario, M5V 2R4
Tel 416/703-5882
www.jeffhealeys.com
One of the best live music clubs in Toronto, co-owned by great vocalist-guitarist Jeff Healey. The man himself performs (with guests) Thursday nights, and with The Jazz Wizards on Saturday afternoons (free).

More top performers other nights; open jam Tuesdays.
🕐 Tue–Sat 💵 $5–25 depending on act 🚇 Osgoode, then 501 west 🚋 Streetcar: 511, 501 🚗 Just off Queen Street West

HORSESHOE
368 Queen Street West, Toronto, Ontario, M5V 2A2
Tel 416/598-4226
Among the hottest live music venues in the city, with an eclectic schedule of top-quality alternative rock, pop and contemporary country music, including many rising (and risen) stars. In the back room of a traditional-style pub, it has a great sound system and room for about 350 people.
🕐 Daily noon–2am 💵 $5–10 🚇 Queen then streetcar west to Spadina, or Spadina then streetcar south to Queen

LAUGH RESORT
370 King Street West, Toronto, Ontario, M5V 1J9
Tel 416/364-5233
www.toronto.com/infosite/312463
Top international comedians bring down the house here: Adam Sandler, Chris Rock, David Spade, Ray Romano and Ellen Degeneres have all been on the bill. Food available.
🕐 Tue–Sat 💵 $7–15 🚇 St. Andrew 🚋 Streetcar: 504 🚗 Within Peter, John, University and Spadina quadrant

MONTRÉAL BISTRO AND JAZZ CLUB
65 Sherbourne Street, Toronto, Ontario, M5A 2P9
Tel 416/363-0179
www.montrealbistro.com
Jazz and blues mecca; an atmospheric venue featuring some of the best musicians on the circuit—Oscar Peterson, Doc Cheatham and George Shearing have played here.
🕐 Mon–Sat 💵 King, then streetcar east 🚋 Streetcar to Sherbourne 🚗 Corner of Adelaide

SECOND CITY
56 Blue Jays Way, Toronto, Ontario, M5V 2G3
Tel 416/343-0011
The company that inspired the long-running US hit TV show,

Saturday Night Live presents revues, improv, character performers, comedic debate, and short plays. Past company members include Mike Myers, John Candy and Gilda Radner.
🕐 Daily 💵 $8–25 (improv show free after main performance) 🚇 St. Andrew 🚋 Streetcar: 504 (King), 510 (Spadina) 🚗 Just south of King Street West

YUK YUK'S COMEDY CABARET
224 Richmond Street West, Toronto, Ontario
Tel 416/967-6425
www.yukyuks.com

Founded here in Toronto in the 1960s, this comedy club chain has fostered much Canadian talent, and hosted the likes of David Letterman, Jerry Seinfeld and Robin Williams from the US. Amateur nights (Mon), college comedy (Tue).
🕐 Daily 💵 $10–17 🚇 Osgoode 🚋 Streetcar: 501 🚗 Downtown, between Duncan and Simcoe

Sports and Activities

SPECTATOR SPORTS

BOWMANVILLE
MOSPORT INTERNATIONAL RACEWAY
3233 Concession Road #10, RR #5, Bowmanville, Ontario, L1C 3K6
Tel 905/983-9141
www.mosport.com
A principal venue for Canadian motor racing, with a 4km (2.5-mile), 10-turn road course, a 0.8km (half-mile) oval, a 1km (half-mile) kart track, and Driver Development Centre. Formula Ford, CASCAR and Superbike events.

🕐 Jun–Sep 💵 Usually $10–50; weekend rates available 🚗 100km (62 miles) east of Toronto off Highway 401 (exit 531) then east on RR #20

CAMPBELLVILLE
MOHAWK RACETRACK
9430 Guelph Line, Campbellville, Ontario, L0P 1B0
Tel 416/675-RACE, -888/675-RACE
www.woodbineentertainment.com
Beautiful woodland setting, with exciting major league harness (trotting) racing over a 1.5km (just under a mile) oval track, featuring many of North America's champion horses.
🕐 Spring and fall 💵 Free 🚗 Off Highway 401, west of Toronto

OTTAWA
OTTAWA LYNX
Ottawa Lynx Stadium, JetForm Park, 300 Coventry Road, Ottawa, Ontario, K1K 4P5
Tel 613/747-9947, 800/663-0985
www.ottawalynx.com

Ottawa's baseball team, the Lynx, plays visiting teams from the AAA league at the 10,000-seat open stadium on the edge of the city. Enthusiastic fans are as entertaining as the game.
🕐 Apr–Sep 💵 Adult $7.50–9.50, child (under 15) $6.50–8.50 🚗 103 Lynx Shuttle, 3, 18, 111 🚗 South edge of city off Queensway (exit 117) at Vanier Parkway and Coventry Road

OTTAWA REBEL
Corel Centre, 100 Palladium Drive, Kanata, Ontario, K2V 1A5
Tel 613/599-0183
Lacrosse is officially Canada's national sport, and it's fast, furious and physical. In addition to the game, the crowd is entertained with music and a dance team.

🎫 Late Dec–Apr 🎟 Adult $22–25, child (under 17) $14–17 🚇 1, 7 🚌 West of city off Highway 417

OTTAWA RENEGADES
Frank Clair Stadium, 1015 Bank Street, Ottawa, Ontario, K1S 3W7
Tel 613/231-5608, 888/881-7298 ext 224
www.ottawarenegades.net
A fairly new team for the city (though it has a long history in Canadian Football with other teams), the Renegades came into being in 2001, and play their home games at a 31,000-seat open-air stadium with some canopied seating.
🎫 Season: late Jun–early Nov 🎟 $25–60 🚌 1, 2, 4, 7

OTTAWA SENATORS
Corel Centre, 1000 Palladium Drive, Kanata, Ontario, K2V 1A5
Tel 613/599-0250, 800/444-SENS
www.ottawasenators.com
The Senators play about 40 home games at the Corel Centre, against visiting National Hockey League teams, and the excitement runs high.
🎫 Season: Sep–May or Jun 🎟 Ticket price varies 🚌 401, 402, 403, 404, 405, 406 🚌 West of city off Highway 417 (Queensway) to arena-specific interchange

RIDEAU CARLETON RACEWAY
4837 Albion Road, Gloucester, Ottawa, Ontario, K1X 1A3
Tel 613/822-2211
www.rcr.net
One of Canada's fastest 1km (slightly more than a half-mile) harness racing tracks, with prime seating in the grandstands. Also simulcast racing from tracks across North America and Australia, and 1,250 slot machines.
🎫 Live racing: Thu–Sun 6.30pm; late Mar–Dec 26; Mon, Jul; Simulcast racing and slots: daily 9am–3am 🚌 Track's own shuttle service (tel: 613/822-8980) 🚌 Southeast of downtown beyond airport

TORONTO

TORONTO ARGONAUTS
SkyDome, 1 Blue Jays Way, Toronto, Ontario, M5V 1J1
Tel 905/607-5328
www.argonauts.on.ca

Founded in 1873, this team, whose home is the SkyDome, holds the Canadian Football League record for the most—14—championship victories.
🎫 Season Jun–Nov 🚇 🚇 Union Station 🚃 Streetcar: 510

TORONTO BLUE JAYS
SkyDome, 1 Blue Jays Way, Suite 3200, Toronto, Ontario, M5V 1J1
Tel 416/341-1234, 888/OK-GO-JAY
www.bluejays.ca
Major league baseball team, twice winners of the World Series, based at the SkyDome. Great action on the field and a buzzing atmosphere.
🎫 Apr–Sep 🎟 $7–44 🚇 Union Station 🚃 Streetcar: 510

TORONTO LYNX
100 East Mall, Suite 11, Toronto, Ontario, M8Z 5X2
Tel 416/251-4625
www.lynxsoccer.com

Soccer is not big here, but the Lynx play in the North American A-League and get good results. Home games are played to enthusiastic support at the Centennial Stadium.
🎫 Apr–Aug 🎟 $15 🚇 Royal York, then bus 48 🚌 48 🚌 West of city, between Eglinton and Rathburn

TORONTO MAPLE LEAFS
Air Canada Centre, 40 Bay Street, Suite 400, Toronto, Ontario, M5J 2X2
Tel 416/815-5700
www.mapleleafs.com
Toronto's National Hockey League team whips up the excitement at the Air Canada Centre, playing against major North American teams.
🎫 Season: Oct–early Apr 🎟 From $24 🚇 Union Station 🚃 Streetcar: 6, 6A, 97B

TORONTO RAPTORS
Air Canada Centre, 40 Bay Street, Suite 400, Toronto, Ontario, M5J 2X2
Tel 416/872-5000
www.nba.com/raptors
Without a basketball team for 50 years, Toronto got the Raptors up and running in 1995, and they've made their mark in the NBA, frequently reaching the playoffs. The fan base is growing, and there's strong support at home games at the Air Canada Centre.
🎫 Oct–Jun 🎟 🚇 Union Station 🚃 Streetcar: 6, 6A, 97B

WOODBINE RACETRACK
555 Rexdale Boulevard, Toronto, Ontario, M9W 5L2
Tel 416/675-1101
www.woodbineentertainment.com

Canada's most famous racetrack, home to the major classic races, with thoroughbred and standard-bred racing (sometimes on same day), and some big-money races. It features both dirt and turf tracks, and also hosts harness (trotting) racing.
🎫 Year-round 🎟 Free 🚇 Islington then 37A bus, or Kipling then 191 Highway 27 Rocket Bus 🚌 Northwest of Toronto, off Highway 27

Activities

COLLINGWOOD

BLUE MOUNTAIN RESORT
RR #3, Collingwood, Ontario, L9Y 3Z2
Tel 705/445-0231
www.bluemountain.ca
This is Ontario's premier winter resort, located on its highest mountain, with downhill and cross-country skiing, snow-boarding, tubing, and tuition. Also hiking, mountain-biking, water sports, etc in summer.
🕐 Year-round 🎿 Rentals: skis $30, snowboard $38; Lift tickets: $47 per day 🚗 11km (7 miles) west of Collingwood off Highway 26

LAFONTAINE

GEORGIAN TRIANGLE CHARTERS
Albert's Cove Marina, Lafontaine.
Mailing address: 20 Forest Dale Drive, Barrie, Ontario L4N 6M7
Tel 705/791-4176
www.georgiantrianglecharters.com

Freshwater salmon and trout fishing in the pristine waters of beautiful Georgian Bay. Tackle is provided, and the vessel has an underwater camera so you can watch the fish bite.
🕐 Dawn–dusk May–Oct 🎣 Up to 4 people $100 per hour (minimum 3 hours) 🚗 Northeast end of Nottawasaga Bay off County Road #6 and 17th concession

NIAGARA FALLS

BRUCE TRAIL
Ball's Falls Conservation Area, Niagara Falls, Ontario
Tel 905/529-6821
www.brucetrail.org
Canada's oldest and longest footpath stretches 800km (496 miles) from Tobermory in northern Ontario to Niagara. This 8km (5-mile) loop will

take about three hours to complete. Take a copy of the Bruce Trail Reference Map (No. 23)
🕐 Year-round 🎟 Free 🚗 Turn off Queen Elizabeth Way at exit 57, go south on Victoria Avenue, through Vineland, to Niagara Road 75

WHIRLPOOL GOLF COURSE
3351 Niagara Parkway, Niagara Falls, Ontario, L2E 6T2
Tel 905/356-1140, 866/465-3642
www.whirlpoolgolf.com
This has been one of Canada's top public courses since 1951, an 18-hole par 72 championship course with the backdrop of the Niagara River whirlpool and gorge. Full rental service and clubhouse.
🕐 Whenever weather permits 🏌 Green fees: $64–74 ($80–90 with cart). Club rental: $30 🚗 Short drive north of Rainbow Bridge on Niagara Parkway

NIAGARA-ON-THE-LAKE

WHIRLPOOL JET BOAT
61 Melville Street, Niagara-on-the-Lake, Ontario, L0S 1J0
Tel 905/468-4800, 999/438-4444
www.whirlpooljet.com

This thrilling ride takes you over the Devil's Hole Rapids. You get waterproof clothing (and life jacket), but you'll probably need change of clothes afterward.
🕐 May–Oct 🎟 Adult $54, child (6–14) $44 🚗 Niagara Parks shuttle (daily Jun–Oct, Sat–Sun May) 🚗 Corner of Delater (off King Street) and Melville

OTTAWA

GREAT CANADIAN BUNGEE
22 Aldridge Way, Nepean, Ottawa, Ontario, K2G 4H8
Tel 819/459-3714, 877/828-8170
www.bungee.ca

North America's highest bungee jump, 61m (200ft) above a lagoon, with head or body dip into the water. Ripride is a terrifying 308m (1,015ft) cable slide over the lagoon, at speeds up to 85kph (53mph).
🕐 Sat–Sun 11–6, May–Oct; Mon–Fri 3–6, Jul–mid-Sep 🎟 Bungee $86.95; Ripride $29.90 🚗 Morrison's Quarry, on Route 105 north of Ottawa

RENT-A-BIKE
Fairmont Chateau Laurier Hotel, 1 Rideau Street, Ottawa, Ontario, K1N 8S7
Tel 613/241-4140
www.cyberus.ca/~rentabike
Ottawa is great for cycling, with cycle paths and weekend road closures. This company has a large selection of bicycles and in-line skates for rent.
🕐 Daily 9–6 Apr–Oct and late Aug–Oct; 9–7.30, Jul–late Aug 🚲 From $8 per hour; $23 per day

TORONTO

DON VALLEY GOLF COURSE
4200 Yonge Street, Toronto, Ontario, M2P 1N9
Tel 416/392-2465
Howard Watson designed this 18-hole course, taking advantage of the rolling landscape. It's a challenging par 71, with signature par 5 at the 12th hole. Pro shop, club rental, power carts.
🕐 Year-round, weather permitting 🏌 $45–49 (9 holes $23–26) 🚇 York Mills 🚗 97 🚗 At intersection of Yonge Street and William Carson Crescent

HARBOURFRONT CANOE AND KAYAK CENTRE
283A Queen's Quay West, Toronto, Ontario, M5V 1A2
Tel 416/203-2277, 800/960-8886
www.paddletoronto.com

You can take to the water right in the city and explore the secluded beaches, bird sanctuaries and picnic areas of the Toronto Islands. Go it alone or join a group.

🕐 Daily 10am–dusk, Apr–Sep
💲 $15–30 per hour; $40–60 per day (plus damage deposit) 🚇 Union Station, then Queen's Quay West streetcar 🚋 Streetcar: 509, 510

HELICOPTER COMPANY INC.
Toronto City Centre Airport, Toronto, Ontario, M5V 1A1
Tel 416/203-3280
www.helitours.ca

If you think the view from the top of the CN Tower is impressive, wait until you've seen it from a helicopter! Flights of six to ten minutes whisk you over the city and offer spectacular photo-opportunities. Other exciting packages are available.

🕐 Daily; reservations required
💲 From $90 per passenger 🚇 Union Station, then streetcar 🚋 Streetcar: 509 to Bathurst, then airport ferry

Health and Beauty

OTTAWA
HOLTZ
45 Rideau Street, Ottawa, Ontario, K1N 5W8
Tel 613/241-7770
www.holtzspa.ca
Years of soothing away the cares of political titans and business brains is good recommendation for the treatments here. Try the one where you get a cocooning body masque, lie on a warm flotation bed, then relax with candlelight and soothing music.

🕐 Mon–Fri 9–8, Sat 9–6, Sun 11–5,
💆 Treatments priced individually or as packages. Half-hour massage $40 🚌 2, 7, 14, 18, 306, 316

TORONTO
CLEAR
300 York Mills, Toronto, Ontario, M2L 2Y5
Tel 416/386-0300
www.cleardayspa.com
Chic, modernist spa. Highly trained professionals pamper the Toronto elite here, and the Waterfall Room's wet-body treatments are a highlight.

🕐 Mon 11–6, Tue 10–6, Wed 9–7, Thu–Fri 9–8, Sat 9–6. Closed Sun
💆 Treatments priced individually: manicure $22, 1-hour massage $90
🚇 Northwest corner of Bayview and York Mills Road

ICI PARIS
370 Danforth Avenue, Toronto, Ontario, Tel 416/461-1774
www.iciparis.ca
An oasis of calm in dynamic Riverdale, focusing on holistic treatments and natural skin care.

🕐 Mon–Fri 9–8, Sat 9–6, Sun 10–3
💆 Treatments priced separately; facials from $65, massage from $15
🚇 Chester 🚋 Streetcar: 504, 505

Children

BRAMPTON
WILD WATER KINGDOM
7855 Finch Avenue West, Brampton, Ontario, L6T 3Y7
Tel 905/794-0565, 866/794-9453
www.wildwaterkingdom.com
A terrific waterpark, with a wave pool, 15 water slides of varying fright levels, rides and a safe play area for tinies. The Double Tipping Bucket tips 3,000 liters (800 gal) of water over you.

🕐 Daily 10–6 (till 8 high season), mid-Jun–early Sep 💲 $24.50, child (under 10) $18.50 or under 3 free 🅿 $6
🚇 Yorkdale or York Mills, then GO Bus; 22 from Mississauga; 11 from Brampton
🚗 Off Highway 427

CAMBRIDGE
AFRICAN LION SAFARI
Safari Road, #RR1, Cambridge, Ontario, N1R 5S2
Tel 519/623-2620, 800/461-WILD
www.lionsafari.com

Established for more than 30 years, this huge park houses 1,000-plus exotic animals (big cats, elephants, giraffe, monkeys) that roam freely in large game reserves. You can drive through or take the safari bus, and there's a lake cruise and scenic railroad. Don't miss the elephant swim. There's also the Jungle Playground and wet play area.

🕐 Daily, late Apr–mid-Oct 💲 Adult $19.95–22.95, child (3–12) $13.95–16.95 🚗 One hour southwest of Toronto, off Highway 401 at exit 299 (westbound) or exit 268A (eastbound)

LONDON
CHILDREN'S MUSEUM
21 Wharncliffe Road South, London, Ontario, N6J 4G5
Tel 519/434-5726
www.londonchildrensmuseum.ca

Canada's first children's museum, and still one of the best. Kids can dig for dinosaur bones, hunt "underground" for cave dwellers, experience an Arctic adventure, explore life 100 years ago, and dress up like an astronaut. Outdoor playground with maze. Day camps for 5–10s in summer. Saturday workshops all year.

🕐 Mon–Thu and Sat–Sun 10–5, Fri 10–8, Jun–Aug and holidays 💲 $5 (under 2s free) 🚌 12 🚗 Between Queens Avenue/Riverside Drive and Horton Street

MISSISSAUGA
PLAYDIUM
99 Rathburn Road, Mississauga, Ontario, L5B 4C1
Tel 905/273-9000
www.playdium.com
More than 5ha (11.5 acres) of indoor and outdoor activities.

Indoor complex has 200 virtual and interactive games, plus a Ridefilm motion simulator with wrap-around screen. Outside (weather permitting), there are baseball batting cages, a 1.6km (1-mile) go-kart track, golf greens, volleyball and basketball courts, and a climbing tower.

🕐 Mon–Thu noon–midnight, Fri noon–2am, Sat 10am–2am, Sun 10am–midnight 🎟 $10–25 🚌 9, 10, 61 🚗 Center of Mississauga, just north of Square One Shopping Mall

MARINELAND
7657 Portage Road, Niagara Falls, Ontario, L2E 6X8
Tel 905/356-9565
www.marinelandcanada.com

Kids can touch beluga whales and orcas and help feed them, then watch their show, which includes sea lions and walruses. There are also thrill rides (included in the entrance fee), many designed with younger children in mind. The world's largest aquarium complex, covering 8ha (20 acres), is under construction.

🕐 Daily 10–5, mid-May–Jun and Sep–mid-Oct; 9–6 Jul–Aug; rides open until dusk 🎟 $33.95, children (5–9) $28.95 🚌 Niagara Parks shuttle (summer only) 🚗 1.6km (1 mile) from Horseshoe Falls 🍴 Two cafeterias serving pizza, burgers, hotdogs, etc. Also snack wagons

ABORIGINAL EXPERIENCES
12 Stirling Avenue, Victoria Island, Ottawa, Ontario, K1Y 1P8
Tel 613/564-9494, 877/811-3233
www.aboriginalexperiences.com
Experiencing Canadian and American aboriginal culture is fascinating for both children and adults. Here, on an island that has been a place of celebration for 1,000 years, you can enjoy songs, drumming and dancing, and hear ancient legends. There are tepees, totem poles and canoes.

🕐 Daily 11–6, mid-Jun–Sep 🎟 Adult $14, child $11. Taste of Native Spirit: adult $19, child $13 🚌 1, 2, 4, 7 🍴 Traditional aboriginal food prepared by award-winning First Nations chef

CANADA SCIENCE AND TECHNOLOGY MUSEUM
1867 St. Laurent Boulevard, Ottawa, Ontario, K1G 5A3
Tel 613/991-3044
www.sciencetech.technomuses.ca

This national museum is a fantastic place for children to learn not only about science in general, but also about specific Canadian achievements. The Space exhibit has plenty of interactive exhibits, multimedia presentations and a simulator ride. Special holiday activities include how DJ equipment works, robotics demonstrations, astronomy, and crafts.

🕐 Daily 9–5 May–Aug; Tue–Sun 9–5, Sep–Apr 🎟 Adult $6, child (4–14) $3 🚌 85, 86 🚗 10 minutes southeast of downtown off Highway 417 at St. Laurent South exit 🍴 Light meals and snacks

CANADIAN MUSEUM OF NATURE
Victoria Memorial Building, 240 McLeod Street, Ottawa, Ontario
Tel 613/566-4700, 800/263-4433
www.nature.ca
Children are captivated by natural history museums, and this one is particularly good, with items they can pick up and examine in the Exploration Station, superb dioramas of mammals in their natural habitats, giant dinosaur skeletons, a Creepy Critters Gallery, and the occasional eye-popper (like a jar of parasites from a whale's stomach) for good measure.

🕐 Fri–Wed 9.30–5, Thu 9.30–8, May–mid-Oct; Tue–Wed and Fri–Sun 10–5, Thu 10–8, late-Oct–Apr 🎟 Adult $8, child (3–12) $3.50; free Thu 5–8, Sat 10–noon 🚌 5, 6, 14 🚗 Corner of Metcalfe and McLeod; Metcalfe Street exit from Highway 417 🍴 Drinks and snacks; also a place to eat packed lunches

RCMP MUSICAL RIDE CENTRE
1 Sandridge Road, Ottawa, Ontario, K1G 3J2
Tel 613/998-8199
www.rcmp-grc.gc.ca
See the legendary Mounties putting their horses through their paces in the choreographed Music Ride (check in summer because the team travels a lot). You can tour the stables, meet the horses, visit the riding school and farrier station, and see the gleaming tack and ceremonial carriages.

🕐 Daily 9–4, May–Oct; Mon–Fri 10–2, Nov–Apr 🎟 Free 🚌 7 🚗 Just beyond Rockcliffe Park, at St. Laurent Boulevard

VALLEYVIEW LITTLE ANIMAL FARM
4750 Fallowfield Road, Nepean, Ottawa, Ontario, K2J 4S4
Tel 613/591-1126
www.vvlittleanimalfarm.com
You can't beat ordinary farm animals for amusing little kids, especially when the babies arrive in the spring. There's a train ride through the fields, country walks, a play area, old farm equipment, puppet shows, and special events.

🕐 Tue–Sun 10–3, 4 or 5, Mar–Oct 🎟 $4.25 🚗 West on Highway 12 🍴 Sunflower Café serves light meals

CENTREVILLE
Centre Island, Toronto, Ontario, M5J 2G2
Tel 416/203-0405
www.centreisland.ca
This 240ha (600-acre) park,

WHAT TO DO

themed around a century-old Ontario village, has more than 30 rides and attractions that include an antique carousel, Ferris wheel, log flume, boats, bumper cars, train rides, and pony rides. It appeals most to children under 10.

🕐 Daily 10.30am–dusk, mid-May–early Sep; Sat–Sun rest of May and Sep (subject to change) 💵 Admission free. All-day pass for rides: adult $23, child $16.50 🚌 From foot of Bay Street and Queen's Quay 🍴 Fast food

FANTASY FAIR
500 Rexdale Boulevard, Toronto, Ontario, M9W 6K5
Tel 416/674-5437
www.fantasyfair.ca
Ontario's largest indoor play complex, with nine full-size rides, including an antique carousel, bumper boats, Ferris wheel, and balloon ride. The enormous play area has tubes, slides and mazes for little ones, plus a video arcade.

🕐 Mon–Fri 11–8, Sat–Sun noon–6 💵 Day pass: adult $11.95, child $10.95–13.95 🚌 Islington, then 37A bus or Kipling, then 191 Highway 27 Rocket Bus 🅿 Upper level of Woodbine Centre, corner of Rexdale and Queens Plate Drive (Highway 27)

ONTARIO PLACE
See page 111

ONTARIO SCIENCE CENTRE
770 Don Mills Road, Toronto, Ontario, M3C 1T3
Tel 416/696-3127
www.ontariosciencecentre.ca

The Science Centre has more than 800 high-tech interactive exhibits in 13 multithemed exhibition halls, and there are demonstrations from experts

who know how to work the crowd. The children's enthusiasm is audible and infectious. There's also the Shoppers' Drug Mart Omnimax Theater.

🕐 Daily 10–5 (subject to change) 💵 Adult $13, child (5–12) $7 or (13–17) $9; combined ticket with Omnimax: adult $18, child (5–12) $10 or (13–17) $12 🚇 Eglinton, then bus 34 east; Pape, then bus 25 north 🅿 East of downtown off Don Valley Parkway 🍴 Bistro and fast food court 🛗

RIVERDALE FARM
201 Winchester Street, Toronto, Ontario, Tel 416/392-6794
Little ones will love this turn-of-the-20th-century farmstead in the heart of the city, where they can see horses, donkeys, sheep, chickens, cows, goats, and pigs. There are regular demonstrations, including cow and goat milking, buttermaking, sheep-shearing, spinning, storytelling, and sing-alongs.

🕐 Daily 9–6, spring and summer; 9–4 fall and winter 💵 Free 🚇 Castle Frank, then bus 65+ south 🚋 Streetcar: 506 🚌 Cabbagetown, off Parliament Street

TORONTO ZOO
See page 118

VAUGHAN
CANADA'S WONDERLAND
9580 Jane Street, Vaughan, Ontario, L6A 1S6
Tel 905/832-7000, ext 8000
www.canadas-wonderland.com

Canada's premier theme park with over 200 attractions, including North America's greatest variety of roller coasters. For toddlers there's a cartoon-themed area; bigger kids and adults can scream the day away as they're hurtled

around on ever more scary rides. There's a full schedule of entertainment, and a 3D ocean-motion movie.

🕐 Daily from 10am, late May–early Sep; Sat–Sun May and Sep–mid-Oct; closing time varies with season: 6, 8, 10 or 10.30pm 💵 Adult $47, child (under 7) $23.49. Grounds only: $24.99; 🅿 $7.50 per day 🚌 Wonderland Express GO bus from Toronto's Yorkdale, or York Mills subway station 🚌 North of Toronto, off Highway 400, beyond the 401 🍴 Many food outlets:

Festivals and Events

JANUARY
NIAGARA ICEWINE CELEBRATIONS
Niagara Falls, Ontario
Tel 905/688-0212
www.grapeandwine.com
Celebrating internationally renowned ice wine (see page 300), with wines from more than 30 of Ontario's wineries.

WINTERLUDE
Ottawa, Ontario
www.canadascapital.gc.ca/winterlude
The capital celebrates winter with street parties, a stew cook-off, ice-carving and snow-sculpture, Inuit cultural events, the Canadian Ski Marathon, snowshoe racing, and other entertainment.

FEBRUARY
WINTERCITY
Toronto, Ontario
Tel 416/395-0490
www.toronto.ca/special_events
Indoor and outdoor events bring the city to life in the depths of winter, with music, skating shows, street theater, acrobatics, and comedy.

MARCH
CANADA BLOOMS: THE TORONTO FLOWER AND GARDEN SHOW
Toronto, Ontario
www.canadablooms.com
Some 2.4ha (6 acres) of gardens and 150-plus stands promoting horticulture. Fun events, such as a celebrity flower-arranging competition.

APRIL

WORLD STAGE INTERNATIONAL THEATRE FESTIVAL
Toronto, Ontario
Tel 416/973-4000
www.harbourfront.on.ca
Theater from around the world at the Harbourfront Centre, with nearly 20 main-stage productions, workshops, music, and readings.

SHAW FESTIVAL
Niagara-on-the-Lake, Ontario
Tel 800/511-7429, 905/468-2172
www.shawfest.com
The works of George Bernard Shaw are performed during this festival, which lasts until November.

SHAKESPEARE FESTIVAL
Stratford, Ontario
Tel 800/567-1600
www.stratfordfestival.ca
World-class theater on four stages from the largest classical repertory company in North America. About 16 plays (not all Shakespeare) and fringe events until November.

MAY

MILK INTERNATIONAL CHILDREN'S FESTIVAL OF THE ARTS
Toronto, Ontario
Tel 416/973-4000
www.harbourfront.on.ca
One of the best children's festivals in North America, with theater, music and puppet shows.

JUNE

CANADA DANCE FESTIVAL (CDF)
Ottawa, Ontario
Tel 613/947-7000 ext 576
www.canadadance.ca
Showcases the work of contemporary Canadian choreographers.

JULY

CISCO SYSTEMS BLUESFEST
Ottawa, Ontario
Tel 613/247-1188
http://ottawa-bluesfest.ca
The biggest outdoor festival of its kind, with international performers. Main stage on the grounds of City Hall. Also includes Cajun, jazz, zydeco, and world music.

KINGSTON BUSKERS RENDEZVOUS
Kingston, Ontario
www.kingstonbuskers.com
Street performers from around the world, including magicians, musicians, acrobats, and actors.

AUGUST

FERGUS SCOTTISH FESTIVAL AND HIGHLAND GAMES
Fergus, Ontario
Tel 519/787-0099
www.fergusscottishfestival.com
One of North America's oldest and biggest highland games, with pipe bands, Celtic music and traditional sports.

FESTIVAL OF THE ISLANDS
Gananoque, Ontario
Tel 613/382-3250
www.gananoque.com/festival
Boat races, battle reenactments, dances, and barbecues celebrate the Loyalist heritage.

CANADIAN NATIONAL EXHIBITION
Toronto, Ontario
Tel 416/263-3800
www.theex.com
One of the biggest exhibitions in North America, with a permanent home on the lakefront. "The Ex" has hundreds of exhibitors and attractions.

CANADIAN GRAND MASTERS FIDDLE CHAMPIONSHIP
Nepean, Ottawa, Ontario
Tel 613/727-6650
http://cgmfiddle.cyberus.ca/contest.htm
The cream of Canada's top fiddle players compete for the national crown.

SEPTEMBER

TORONTO INTERNATIONAL FILM FESTIVAL
Toronto, Ontario
Tel 416/968-FILM (from mid-July),
www.e.bell.ca/filmfest
The movie industry comes to Toronto to showcase hundreds of movies, and the place is heaving with celebrities.

NIAGARA GRAPE AND WINE FESTIVAL
St. Catharines, Ontario
Tel 905/688-0212
www.grapeandwine.com

Celebrating the bounty of Niagara's wineries, with tastings, tours and entertainment.

OCTOBER

OKTOBERFEST
Kitchener, Ontario
Tel 519/570-4267
www.oktoberfest.ca
With its German heritage, this is the obvious place to enjoy traditional *Oktoberfest* celebrations.

CANADIAN INTERNATIONAL MARATHON
Toronto, Ontario
Tel 416/972-1062
www.runtoronto.com
A serious event for the runners (qualifying speed; no walkers), but there's ancillary entertainment for spectators.

NOVEMBER

CANADIAN ABORIGINAL FESTIVAL
Toronto, Ontario
Tel 519/751-0040
www.canab.com
This three-day event at the SkyDome is a celebration of First Nations culture, including a pow wow, music awards, lacrosse, and the arts.

DECEMBER

CHRISTMAS LIGHTS ACROSS CANADA
Ottawa, Ontario
Tel 800/465-1867 or 613/239-5000,
www.canadascapital.gc.ca/winter/xmaslights
A parade along Confederation Boulevard, where more than 70 sites are illuminated, to Parliament Hill. The governor general switches on nearly 300,000 colorful lights, timed to coincide with similar displays across the nation.

DESIGNS IN ICE
Toronto, Ontario
416/395-0490,
www.toronto.ca/special_events
Top Ontario artists carve some really cool (literally) creations in a three-day exhibition and competition in Nathan Phillips Square. Also multimedia shows and family ice-skating parties.

THE PRAIRIES

Wagon races, a highlight of the Calgary Stampede, recall the desperate quest to stake out the best parcels of land when the Prairies were settled

There is so much more to the Prairies than the vast plains of wheat and the oilfields that everyone has heard of. Its cities are modern and vibrant, with a huge range of cultural activities and festivals, including classical music, touring international performers and, of course, the Calgary Stampede. Shopping is almost reason enough to come here—Alberta not only has the world largest mall, but, because it's oil-rich, levies no Provincial Sales Tax. The range of goods is excellent.

Cowboy culture is strong here (there are vast cattle ranches besides all that wheat), resulting in plenty of horseback activities, a penchant for country music and Stetsons, and, of course, the continuing popularity of rodeos. Anglers flock here for the superb river fishing, and the national and provincial parks have some great hikes. In winter, there's plenty of snow for cross-country skiing, snowshoeing, dogsledding, and snowmobiling, and to the west the foothills of the Rockies provide for downhill sports (see the British Columbia and the Rockies section for Alberta's mountain resorts).

its exciting range of retailers, restaurants, nightlife and street entertainers. The range of goods is enormous, from clothing to food and crafts.
🕐 Mon–Wed and Sat 10–6, Thu–Fri 10–8, Sun noon–5 (some retailers keep longer hours) 🚌 31, 419, 433
🅿 Prince's Island Park, at 2nd Avenue and 2nd Street Southwest 🍴 A dozen food-court eateries and 10 international restaurants

WEST EDMONTON MALL
8882 170 Street, Edmonton, Alberta, T5T 4M2
Tel 780/444-5200
www.westedmall.com

The world's biggest shopping mall, with more than 800 stores, but it doesn't stop there. World-class leisure attractions include Deep Sea Adventure (with real submarine trips), a 2ha (5-acre) indoor waterpark, a huge amusement park with thrill rides, the Dolphin Lagoon, and an ice rink. Also lots of entertainment venues, sports facilities, and special events.
🕐 Mon–Fri 10–9, Sat 10–6, Sun

Shopping

ALBERTA BOOT
614 10th Avenue Southwest, Calgary, Alberta, T2R 1M3
Tel 403/263-4605
www.albertaboot.com
Alberta's only western boot maker, producing over 10,000 pairs a year from cow and bull hide, as well as various kinds of snake, alligator, lizard, kangaroo, and even ostrich skin. There are always 12,000 pairs in stock, and you can also get jeans, hats, shirts, and belts.
🕐 Mon–Fri 9–9, Sat 9–6, Sun 11–4,

Jul–end of the Calgary Stampede; Mon–Sat 9–6, rest of year 🚇 C-train: 7th Avenue 🅿 Downtown at 10th Avenue Southwest and 5th Street Southwest

EAU CLAIRE FESTIVAL MARKET
200 Barclay Parade Southwest, Calgary, Alberta, T2P 4R5
Tel 403/264-6450
www.eauclairemarket.com
Established in 1993, this 21,600sq-m (240,000sq-ft) shopping and entertainment complex soon became central to the Calgary experience, with

noon–6 🚆 1, 2, 100, 112 and many other routes 🚌 West, off Highway 16; between 87 and 90 avenues 🍴 More than 100 eating options, notably Bourbon Street, with several restaurants

MEACHAM

HAND WAVE GALLERY
409 3rd Avenue North, Meacham, Saskatchewan, S0K 2V0
Tel 306/376-2221
www.handwave.ca
The tiny village of Meacham is home to a large number of artists and craftspeople, and this interesting little gallery sells high-quality individual pieces. It showcases the work of about 75 Saskatchewan artists, including fine art, ceramics, quilting, woodcarving, and metalwork.
🕐 Thu–Mon 11–6, Jun–Sep; 1–6, Oct–Dec and Apr–May; by appointment Jan–Mar 🚌 52km (32 miles) east of Saskatoon on Highway 5, then 5km (3 miles) south on Highway 2

REGINA

BOOK AND BRIER PATCH
4065 Albert Street, Regina, Saskatchewan, S4S 3R6
Tel 306/586-5814
Three generations of a local family have run this large independent bookstore, which covers 900sq m (10,000sq ft) and contains 30,000-plus titles, including mass-market paperbacks and children's books. The magazine section is huge, and there are also cassettes and CDs.
🕐 Mon–Fri 9–9, Sat 9–6 🚌 11, 13 🚌 South Regina ☕ Cappuccino bar (Mon–Sat 8.30am–10pm)

SASKATOON

THE ANTIQUE MALL
Saskatoon Emporium, 126 20th Street West, Saskatoon, Saskatchewan, S7M 0W7
Tel 306/653-5595
The largest antiques mall in western Canada houses about 40 dealers. It's in a historic former department store from 1911, with 1930s art-deco features, and the variety of goods is incredible.
🕐 Tue–Sat 10–5, Sun noon–5 🚌 Riverdale route 🚌 Between Avenue BN and Idylwyld Drive South

WINNIPEG

BAYAT GALLERY
163 Stafford Street, Winnipeg, Manitoba, R3M 2W9
Tel 204/475-5873
www.inuitgallery.com
This is one of the largest and finest galleries for the work of Inuit artists from Canada's Arctic regions. Beautiful sculptures, carvings and prints are set against a stark white background. The wildlife wood sculptures by Ed Brown are a highlight.
🕐 Mon–Sat 10–5.30, Sun by appointment 🚌 Downtown, at Stafford and Grosvenor

THE FORKS MARKET
201 One Forks Market Road, Winnipeg, Manitoba, R3C 4L9
Tel 204/942-6302
www.theforks.com

This is Winnipeg's best shopping experience, an old market building that's part of a complex at the confluence of the Red and Assiniboine rivers. There's a huge array of specialty foods, and the second floor has local arts and crafts, including aboriginal works.
🕐 Mon–Sat 9.30–9, Sun 9.30–6.30, summer; Sat–Thu 9.30–6.30, Fri 9.30–9, rest of year 🚌 99 (10am–3.30pm), 38 (after 3.30pm) 🚌 Downtown, east of Main Street and Union Station 🍴 Fast-food outlets, including Caribbean, Sri Lankan and Ukrainian food, plus more formal restaurants

Performance

CALGARY

COLISEUM
100 – 16061 MacLeod Trail Southeast, Calgary, Alberta, T2Y 3S5
Tel 403/974-0472
Ten-screen, out-of-town multiplex showing latest movies.
🕐 Daily 🎬 Adult $12.95, child (under 13) $6.95 🚇 LRT: 201 to Anderson 🚌 81 🚌 Beside South Calgary Shopping Centre, MacLeod Trail Southeast and 162nd Street ☕ Concessions include Pizza Hut, New York Fries and Taco Bell

EPCOR CENTRE FOR THE PERFORMING ARTS
205 8th Avenue Southeast, Calgary, Alberta, T2G 0K9
Tel 403/294-7455
www.theartscentre.org
A 2,000-seat concert hall and four theaters of various sizes are home to five arts companies, with a diverse schedule of dance, music, theater, cabaret, and comedy.

🕐 Year-round 🎬 Price varies with event 🚇 LRT: C-Train to Centre Street, City Hall or Olympic Plaza 🚌 Downtown, overlooking Olympic Plaza ☕ Coffee bar with snacks

IMAX THEATRE EAU CLAIRE MARKET
132 – 200 Barclay Parade Southwest, Calgary, Alberta, T2P 4R5
Tel 403/974-4629
www.imax.com/calgary
Huge screen six stories high, showing IMAX movies and adapted blockbusters such as the *Star Wars* epics.
🕐 Daily 🎬 Adult $9.90, child $6.90 🚌 31, 419, 433 🚇 LRT: 201, 202 🚌 Downtown, at 2nd Avenue and 2nd Street

SOUTHERN ALBERTA JUBILEE AUDITORIUM
1415 14th Avenue Northwest, Calgary, Alberta, T2N 1M4
Tel 403/297-8000
www.jubileeauditorium.com/southern

WHAT TO DO

This superb building, at South Alberta Institute of Technology, is home to the Calgary Opera and Alberta Ballet, and also hosts touring companies. ⊙ Year-round 💵 Price varies with event 🚋 C-train: SAIT/ACAD/Jubilee

DRUMHELLER

CANADIAN BADLANDS PASSION PLAY

Box 457, Drumheller, Alberta, T0J 0Y0
Tel 403/823-2001
www.canadianpassionplay.com

In a natural rocky amphitheater (uncannily resembling ancient Judea), a permanent set has been built with seating for 2,300. A huge cast puts on a three-hour passion play here every summer. Site open for viewing at other times. ⊙ Two weekends (Fri–Sun), mid-Jul 💵 Adult $25, child (12 and under) $12.50 🅿 Just west of Drumheller on South Dinosaur Trail, off Highway 9 🍴 Stands for light snacks and drinks

EDMONTON

CITADEL THEATRE

9828 – 101A Avenue, Edmonton, Alberta, T5J 3C6
Tel 780/425-1820, 888/425-1820
www.citadeltheatre.com
One of Canada's foremost arts facilities, housing five theaters and a theater school. Full calendar of drama, comedy, musicals, and children's shows. ⊙ Year-round 💵 Price varies 🚋 LRT: Churchill 🚌 52, 100, 112, 308 🅿 Arts District 🍴 Formal Oriental restaurant

FRANCIS WINSPEAR CENTRE FOR MUSIC

4 Sir Winston Churchill Square, Edmonton, Alberta, T5J 4B2
Tel 780/428-1414, 800/563-5081
www.esowinspear.com

World-class concert hall, home of the Edmonton Symphony, featuring classical, country, folk, and jazz and dance in a dramatic, modern setting. ⊙ Year-round 💵 Price varies with event 🚌 52, 112 🚋 LRT: Churchill 🅿 Arts District

NORTHERN ALBERTA JUBILEE AUDITORIUM

11455 – 87 Avenue Northwest, Edmonton, Alberta, T6G 2T2
Tel 780/427-2760
www.jubileeauditorium.com/northern
Fan-shaped auditorium with 2,750 capacity on a 5ha (13-acre) site. Entertainments here include Broadway-style musicals, comedy and concerts featuring all kinds of music. ⊙ Year-round 💵 Price varies with event 🚌 4, 6, 30, 50, 51 🚋 LRT: University 🅿 University of Alberta

SILVERCITY WEST EDMONTON MALL

#3030, 8882 – 170 Street, Edmonton, Alberta, T5T 4M2
Tel 780/444-2400
www.famousplayers.com
There's a huge choice of movie theaters in Edmonton, and this 13-screen multiplex is one of three in West Edmonton Mall. It has wide, curved screens, surround-sound and stadium seating. ⊙ Daily 💵 Adult $13.95, child $8 🚌 1, 2, 100, 112, and many others

REGINA

GLOBE THEATRE

1801 Scarth Street, Regina, Saskatchewan, S4P 2G9
Tel 306/525-6400
www.globetheatrelive.com
A 400-seat theater-in-the-round, staging six main-stage productions and four "Sandbox Series," including excellent contemporary Canadian works and international drama. ⊙ Year-round 💵 Main stage: $25, Sandbox Series: $16.50 🚌 Cornwall Centre service 🅿 Downtown, in Old City Hall Mall, corner of 11th Avenue

REGINA LITTLE THEATRE

1077 Angus Street, Regina, Saskatchewan, S4T 1Y4
Tel 306/352-5535
www.reginalittletheatre.com

The oldest continually producing English-language theater group in western Canada. ⊙ Oct–Jun 💵 $15–16 🚌 5 🅿 North of downtown, just beyond 4th Avenue

SASKATCHEWAN CENTRE OF THE ARTS

200 Lakeshore Drive, Regina, Saskatchewan, S4P 3V7
Tel 306/525-9999, 800/667-8497
www.centreofthearts.sk.ca
Home of Opera Saskatchewan, producing world-class performances in a grand theater with superb acoustics. Also hosts the Regina Symphony and touring companies. ⊙ Year-round 💵 Price varies with event 🚌 1 (you must tell the driver you want the center and he/she will detour there) 🅿 Downtown

ROSTHERN

STATION ARTS CENTRE

Railway Avenue, Rosthern, Saskatchewan, S0K 3R0
Tel 306/232-5332
www.stationarts.com
A converted train station houses this highly regarded arts facility, with various concerts and summer theater. ⊙ Year-round 💵 Price varies with event 🅿 At entrance to Rosthern from Highway 11 🍴 Tearoom serves light meals

SASKATOON

PERSEPHONE THEATRE

2802 Rusholme Road, Saskatoon, Saskatchewan, S7L 0H2
Tel 306/384-7727 (24-hour information line)
www.persephonetheatre.org
The city's premier professional company, staging six productions a year, including classics, contemporary drama, comedy, and musicals. ⊙ Tue–Sun, Sep–Apr 💵 Varies with event, $14–30 🅿 Near Confederation Mall, 10-minute drive from downtown

WINNIPEG

BURTON CUMMINGS THEATRE

364 Smith Street, Winnipeg, Manitoba, R3B 2H2
Tel 204/956-5656 (tickets available only from Ticketmaster, tel 204/780-3333)
A national historic theater, formerly the Walker, now named after the Winnipeg rock star

who has pledged financial aid. Concerts, drama and musicals.
🎭 Year-round 💵 Price varies with events 🚌 Downtown, near Notre Dame and Ellice

CANWEST GLOBAL PERFORMING ARTS CENTRE
The Forks, Winnipeg, Manitoba, R3C 4X1
Tel 204/942-8898, 877/871-6897
www.mtyp.ca
Splendid modern theater building that also houses the Manitoba Theatre for Young People (see page 238).
🎭 Oct–May or Jun 💵 $10–12 🚌 Free shuttle bus on circular route downtown

CENTENNIAL CONCERT HALL
555 Main Street, Winnipeg, Manitoba, R3B 1C3
Tel 204/956-2792
www.wso.mb.ca
Home of Winnipeg's Symphony Orchestra, this is a first-class modern facility offering a full calendar of classical concerts.
🎭 Year-round 💵 Price varies depending on event 🚌 21, 22, 24, 28, 67

MANITOBA THEATRE CENTRE
174 Market Avenue, Winnipeg, Manitoba
Tel 204/942-6537, 877/446-4500
www.mtc.mb.ca
Canada's oldest English-language theater, producing 10 world-class plays a year, plus other shows. Venue for the Fringe Theatre Festival in July.
🎭 Oct–May 💵 $20–75 🚌 21, 22, 24, 28, 31, 33, 67 🚌 Exchange District

PANTAGES PLAYHOUSE THEATRE
180 Market Avenue, Winnipeg, Manitoba, R3B 0P7
Tel 204/989-2889
www.pantagesplayhouse.com
Lavish theater, built in 1913–14. It now hosts varied entertainments, including professional and amateur theater and all types of music.
🎭 Year-round 💵 Price varies 🚌 1, 2, 3, 4 🚌 Exchange District

RAINBOW STAGE, KILDONAN PARK
2021 Main Street, Winnipeg, Manitoba, Tel 204/780-7328
www.rainbowstage.net

A covered, comfortable outdoor amphitheater with a popular summer season of musical productions.
🎭 Tue–Sun, late Jul–late Aug, 💵 Adult $12–36 (plus agency fee) 🚌 🚌 11, 75, 77 to the main entrance to Kildonan Park 🚗 15km (9 miles) northeast of downtown's Main/Portage intersection

SHAKESPEARE IN THE RUINS
I. J. Dremen Building and Parkade, 246 Portage Avenue, Winnipeg, Manitoba
Tel 204/957-1753
www.shakespeareintheruins.com
After 10 years at the ruins of St. Norbert's monastery, the company now stages imaginative Shakespeare productions on a vast downtown rooftop. Folding chairs are provided, and the audience moves with the actors as plays progress.
🎭 Tue–Sun, mid-May–early Jul 💵 $10–22 🚌 🚌 11 🚌 Downtown, at Garry Street intersection

WEST END CULTURAL CENTRE
586 Ellice Avenue, Winnipeg, Manitoba, R3B 1Z8
Tel 204/783-6918
www.wecc.ca

Arty paintings cover this converted church, now a dynamic hall featuring music and

performance of all kinds, including internationally known names.
🎭 Year-round 💵 Price varies with events 🚌 14, 31 (Ellice) and 29 (Sherbrooke) 🚗 At Sherbrooke 🍴 Snacks, plus a bar

WINNIPEG JEWISH THEATRE
Asper Jewish Community Campus, 123 Doncaster Boulevard, Winnipeg, Manitoba, R3N 2B2
Tel 204/477-7478
www.jhcwc.mb.ca
Canada's only professional Jewish theater company, promoting an understanding of Jewish culture through top-quality productions of established and new plays.
🎭 Oct–May 💵 Price varies

Nightlife

BACK ALLEY NIGHTCLUB
4630 MacLeod Trail South West, Calgary, Alberta, T2G 5E8
Tel 403/287-2500
The name might conjure up dubious images, but don't be deterred—this is a big, fun, friendly place where you can listen to a good variety of live rock and alternative music.
🎭 Wed–Sat 7pm–2am 💵 Wed and Sat $4, Thu $3, Fri free 🚌 81 🚊 LRT: 201

KING EDWARD HOTEL
438 9th Avenue Southeast, Calgary, Alberta, T2G 0R9
Tel 403/262-1680
The "King Eddie," Calgary's number one venue for blues, has just the right atmosphere. It hosts touring big-name musicians and the cream of the local acts. Jam sessions on Saturday afternoons.
🎭 Mon–Sat 11am–2am 🚌 Downtown, Eau Claire area

WOODY'S TAPHOUSE
225 – 4307 130 Avenue Southeast, Calgary, Alberta, T3K 4Y7
Tel 403/257-1666
One of three Woody's in Calgary, and all of them provide an energetic mix of live rock bands, karaoke, special event, and pub sports leagues.
🎭 Daily 11am–2am

WHAT TO DO

EDMONTON

YARDBIRD SUITE
11 Tommy Banks Way, Edmonton, Alberta, T6E 2M2
Tel 780/432-0428
www.yardbirdsuite.com
Named after a Charlie Parker tune, this club is run by the local nonprofit Jazz Society for a discerning bunch of regulars, and delivers quality jazz from big-name performers.
🕐 Fri–Sat 8–1, mid-Sep–Jun. Jam session Tue 🎵 Varies 🚌 52 🚉 Corner of 102 Street and 86 Avenue

HILL SPRING

GREAT CANADIAN BARN DANCE
Box 163, Hill Spring, Alberta, T0K 1E0
Tel 403/626-3407, 866/626-3407
www.greatcanadianbarndance.com

It may not be sophisticated, but it's great fun: roast beef dinner, horse-drawn hayride, then old-style barn dance with live music (and tuition).
🕐 Fri–Sat, late Jun–Aug; Sat, mid-May–late Jun and Sep–mid-Oct 🎵 Adult $22.50, child (under 9) $6.50 or (9–17) $16 🚉 Northeast of Hill Spring off the 505 on Wynder Road

SASKATOON

CRAWDADDY'S LOUISIANA BAR AND GRILL
244 1st Avenue North, Saskatoon, Saskatchewan, S7K 1X1
Tel 306/978-2729
www.goforthegumbo.com
All the atmosphere of a New Orleans bar, with jazz, swing, zydeco, blues and Cajun.
🕐 Music Thu–Sat

WATROUS

DANCELAND
RR#1, Manitou Beach, Watrous, Saskatchewan, S0K 4T0
Tel 306/946-2743, 800/267-5037

Traditional dance hall, dating from 1928 and famous for its dance floor, built on a cushion of horsehair. It hosts old-style dances, country rock 'n' roll, bluegrass shows, and dance competitions.
🕐 Dances: Fri–Sat nights. Gospel shows: Sun (call for details of other events; open daily for tours) 🎵 $12.50 🚌 Free shuttle service from town on dance nights 🚉 North of Watrous, off Highway 2

WINNIPEG

TIMES CHANGE HIGH AND LONESOME
234 Main Street, Winnipeg, Manitoba, Tel 204/957-0982
Best venue in the city for live roots, blues, bluegrass, country, and soul, showcasing local and touring bands, with jam sessions Sunday nights.
🕐 Thu–Sun 8pm–2am; also Mon–Wed 4pm–2am, but no live music 🚉 Downtown, corner of St. Mary Avenue

Sports and Activities

SPECTATOR SPORTS

CALGARY

CALGARY FLAMES
Pengrowth Saddledome, 555 Saddledome Rise Southeast, Calgary, Alberta, T2P 3B9
Tel 403/777-2177
www.calgaryflames.com
One of the premier franchises in the National Hockey League (NHL), the Flames attract passionate support. The splendid stadium was used in the XV Winter Olympics.
🕐 Season: Oct–Apr 🎵 $21.50–155 🚉 LRT: 201 Victoria Park/Stampede 🚉 Next to Stampede Ground

CALGARY STAMPEDERS
McMahon Stadium, 1817 Crowchild Trail Northwest, Calgary, Alberta, T2M 4R6
Tel 403/289-0258
www.stampeders.com
One of the top Canadian football teams in the west, with a loyal and enthusiastic set of fans. Games are played in the 36,000-seat stadium that hosted the opening and

closing ceremonies of the XV Winter Olympics.
🕐 Season: late Jun–early Nov 🎵 $27-55 🚉 University of Calgary

STAMPEDE PARK
2300 Stampede Trail Southeast, Calgary, Alberta, T2G 2W1
Tel 403/261-0214
Thoroughbred and harness racing bring excitement to Stampede Park for seven months of the year, including the Nat Christie Memorial Stake, western Canada's richest race; at other times there's simulcast betting.
🕐 Thoroughbred racing: Apr–Jun. Harness racing: late Jul–late Oct. Simulcast: Wed and Fri–Sun, year-round 🎵 Free 🅿 $5 🚉 LRT: 201 Victoria Park/Stampede

EDMONTON

EDMONTON ESKIMOS
Commonwealth Stadium, 11000 Stadium Road, Edmonton, Alberta, T5J 2J7
Tel 780/448-ESKS
www.esks.com
Eskimos home games are played in the 60,000-capacity stadium built to host the 1978 Commonwealth Games. It's the only one in Canada with natural turf—one of North America's best playing surfaces.
🕐 Season: late Jun–early Nov 🎵 Adult $25–43, child $14–23 🚉 2, 120, 127 🚉 LRT: Stadium 🚉 4km (1.5 miles) northeast, near 112 Avenue and 86 Street intersection

EDMONTON OILERS
Skyreach Centre, Northlands Park, Edmonton, Alberta, T5J 2N5
Tel 780/414-4625, 866/414-4625
www.edmontonoilers.com
Massive renovations in 1999 gave the hockey stadium a new look, and excellent sightlines make it a good place to watch the rapid-action games.
🕐 Season: Oct–Apr 🎵 $28–150 🚉 5, 8, 10, 127, 141, 142, 143 🚉 LRT: Coliseum 🚉 Downtown, near 74th Street and Wayne Gretzky Drive

EDMONTON TRAPPERS
Telus Field, 10233 96th Avenue, Edmonton, Alberta, T5K 0A5
Tel 780/414-4450
www.trappersbaseball.com

The Trappers baseball team, in the Pacific League, play home games at the 9,200-capacity Telus Field, one of the Minor League's best baseball parks.
🎫 Season: Apr–Sep 💰 Adult $8–11, child (3–14) $5–8 🚌 52 🚆 LRT: Government Centre 🚉 Rossdale

REGINA
SASKATCHEWAN ROUGHRIDERS
Taylor Field, 2940 10th Avenue, Regina, Saskatchewan, S4P 3B8
Tel 306/566-4280, 888/474-3377
www.saskriders.com26

Canadian Football League players, and two-time winners of the Grey Cup (but not for a while), the Riders hosted the 2003 championships.
🎫 Season: late Jun–Oct or early Nov 💰 $9–38 🚌 Services from 11 city locations on game days; call 306/777-7433 for information 🚉 Just west of downtown, between Saskatchewan Drive and Dewdney Avenue

SASKATOON
RODEO
Various locations; contact the Canadian Cowboys' Association, RR4, Site 412, Box 287, Saskatoon, Saskatchewan, S7K 3J7
Tel 306/931-2700
www.canadiancowboys.sk.ca

Spectacular showmanship, truly courageous feats of daring, and unique sounds and smells make the rodeo a fantastic Prairies experience. Events all over the province every weekend, with the Finals Rodeo in Edmonton (see page 238) in November.
🎫 Season: Mar–Oct

WINNIPEG
ASSINIBOIA DOWNS
3975 Portage Avenue West, Winnipeg, Manitoba, R3K 2E9
Tel 204/885-3330
www.assiniboiadowns.com
Hosts 75 days of thoroughbred racing a year, including the Manitoba Derby. Sundays and holidays are festive, with family entertainment. Rest of the year features simulcast wagering from major tracks in Canada, the US and Australia.
🎫 Live racing: May–Sep. Gaming lounge: daily 9am–2am 💰 Free 🚌 "A" Trip from Main and William; "B" Trip from Portage and Ronald 🚉 Southwest of downtown, at the Perimeter Highway

MANITOBA MOOSE
Winnipeg Arena, 1430 Maroons Road, Winnipeg, Manitoba, R3G 0L5
Tel 204/987-7825. Tickets: 204/780-7328
www.moosehockey.com

Top National Hockey League affiliate of the Vancouver Canucks, known for high-caliber hockey and great entertainment, the Moose, now play in the American Hockey League. They'll be moving to the new MTS Centre downtown in November 2004.
🎫 Season: Oct–Apr 💰 $12–33 🚉 Polo Park area, between Empress and St. James streets

WINNIPEG BLUE BOMBERS
Canad Inns Stadium, 1465 Maroons Road, Winnipeg, Manitoba, R3G 0L5
Tel 204/784-2583
www.bluebombers.com
The Blue Bombers Canadian football team has an enthusiastic set of fans, and it's fun to join them in cheering on the players at the Canad Inns Stadium, an open venue seating nearly 34,000.
🎫 Season: late Jun–early Nov 💰 $12–55 🚌 11, 12, 20, 24, 26, 66, 67, 77, 78, 79, 97 🚉 Just east of the airport, across from Winnipeg Arena

ACTIVITIES

BEZANSON
ADAM RANCH
Box 332, Bezanson, Alberta, T0H 0G0
Tel 780/814-5618, 866/232-6283
www.adamranch.net
Saddle up cowboy-style for guided rides over vast, pristine grasslands where the buffalo really do roam, along with cattle, bear, moose, and coyotes. Ranch activities include roping and calf-"rassling." You sleep in a modernized bunkhouse.
🎫 Year-round 💰 Various packages, from $486 for inclusive weekend; free pickup from Grande Prairie airport 🚉 Peace Country, southeast of Grande Prairie

COLEMAN
ALBERTA FLY FISHING ADVENTURES
Box 1094, Coleman, Alberta, T0K 0M0
Tel 403/563-3258, 877/363-3258
www.albertaflyfishing.ab.ca

Three great trout rivers meet here, and there are 20 more less than an hour away. You can get walk-and-wade, float trips and heli-fishing with local

WHAT TO DO

experts, customized to anglers' abilities. Equipment and travel are included in the price.
🕐 Year-round 💲 Prices depend on requirements 🚗 On Highway 3 at Crowsnest Pass in southwest Alberta

HORIZONS UNLIMITED
Churchill River Canoe Outfitters, La Ronge, Missinipe, Saskatchewan, S0J 1L0
Tel 877/511-2726
www.churchillrivercanoe.com
This company is run by experienced canoeists offering tuition, guided trips, equipment rental and shuttle service (sometimes by floatplane).
🕐 Mid-May–late Sep 💲 Canoe rental from $27.50 per day 🚗 80km (50 miles) north of La Ronge at Otter Lake

Health and Beauty

MANITOU SPRINGS
Box 610, Manitou Beach, Watrous, Saskatchewan, S0K 4T0
Tel 306/946-2233
www.manitousprings.ca
This is one of only three places in the world where the water is so mineral-rich it keeps you afloat, and it has legendary therapeutic properties. Canada's largest indoor mineral spa has a huge pool filled with it, plus various treatments.
🕐 Daily 9am–10pm 💲 Day pass: adult $11.68, child (7–12) $4.21 or (13–17) $5.61. Treatments priced separately 🚗 North of town on Route 365

Children

BUTTERFIELD ACRES
254077 Rocky Ridge Road, Calgary, Alberta, T3R 1A6
Tel 403/547-3595
www.butterfieldacres.com
This is a hands-on farm, where children can pet the animals, collect eggs, try milking, and take a hayride or a pony ride. Nursery Rhyme Park is being developed, featuring appropriate animals. There are also summer day camps and special events.

🕐 Daily 10–4, Jul–Aug; Mon–Fri 10–2, Sat–Sun 10–4, Apr–Jun and Sep; winter special events by advance ticket purchase only 💲 Adult $7, child (toddlers–18) $5.25 🚗 Northwest of Calgary, 3km (2 miles) north of the Crowchild Trail (Highway 1A) 🍴 Hot and cold drinks and snacks

CALAWAY PARK
254033 Range Road 33, Calgary, Alberta, T3Z 2E9
Tel 403/240-3822
www.calawaypark.com
Western Canada's largest outdoor amusement park, offering 27 rides—for thrill-seekers and small children. Live entertainment, soft-play area, mini-golf, and haunted mansion.
🕐 Daily 10–8, late Jun–Aug; Fri 5–10, Sat–Sun 10–8, mid-May to mid-Jun; Sat–Sun 11–6, Sep–mid-Oct 💲 Adult $21, child (3–6) $15 🚗 10km (6 miles) west of Calgary on Trans-Canada Highway (Highway 1) at Springbank Road 🍴 Fast food and snacks

CALGARY ZOO, BOTANICAL GARDEN AND PREHISTORIC PARK
1300 Zoo Road Northeast, Calgary, Alberta, T2E 7V6
Tel 403/232-9300, 800/588-9993
www.calgaryzoo.ab.ca

One of the finest zoos on the continent, known for the breeding of endangered species. The Destination Africa exhibit includes tropical rain forest with lowland gorillas and indoor hippo viewing pool. The 6.5ha (16-acre) Prehistoric Park recreates the Canada of the dinosaurs, and the Botanical Garden has a butterfly garden.
🕐 Daily 9–5 💲 Adult $13, child (3–17) $6.50 🚊 LRT: C-train 🚗 At Memorial Drive/Deerfoot Trail interchange

🍴 Five food outlets; Safari Lodge offers a hot buffet breakfas

THE ODYSSIUM
11211 – 142 Street, Edmonton, Alberta, T5M 4A1
Tel 780/452-9100
www.odyssium.com
Six fascinating galleries include the natural world at the Green's House; the Gallery of the Gross, with everything weird about the human body; crime solving in Mystery Avenue; and extraterrestrial stuff in the Space Place. DiscoveryLand is specifically for two- to eight-year-olds, and there's the Star Theatre, observatory and an IMAX theater.
🕐 Sun–Thu 10–5, Fri–Sat 10–9. IMAX theater, from 11am 💲 Adult $9.95, child (3–12) $6.95 or (13–17) $7.95 🚌 5, 115, 125, 127, 128, 135, 150, 203, 305 🚊 LRT: Westmount 🚗 Coronation Park, at 111 Avenue and 142 Street 🍴 Light meals, snacks and beverages

WEST EDMONTON MALL
8882 – 170 Street, Edmonton, Alberta, T5T 4M2
Tel 800/661-8890, 780/444-5200
www.westedmall.com

The world-class attractions within this vast shopping mall include Deep Sea Adventure, Galaxyland Amusement Park, Dolphin Lagoon and Sea Life Caverns, World Waterpark, Ice Palace, and Professor Wem's Adventure Golf.
🕐 Daily from 11am; closing times vary depending on day and season 💲 Adult $9.95, child (3–10) $5 🚌 1, 2, 100, 112 and many other routes 🍴 Huge choice of fast food, snacks and restaurants within the mall

WHAT TO DO

KENOSEE LAKE

KENOSEE SUPERSLIDE
Highway 9, Kenosee Lake,
Saskatchewan
Tel 306/577-2343
www.kenoseesuperslides.com
Waterslides range from gentle
slopes to the terrifying Freefall
that drops you eight stories in
less than three seconds, and
Bonzai Slides that bounce you
to the bottom (you can rent
tubes to cushion the effect).
Also pools and a play area.
🕐 Mon–Fri 10–5, Sat–Sun 10–6,
mid-end Jun; Mon–Fri 10–6,
Sat–Sun 10–7, Jul–Aug 🎟 Adult $16.50,
child (4–6) $9; half-price last 2hrs of the
day 🚌 At entrance to Moose Mountain
Provincial Park and Kenosee Lake
Village 🍴 Cruisers Family Diner

REGINA

MAXWELL'S AMUSEMENTS
Victoria Avenue East, Regina,
Saskatchewan, S4P 3B1
Tel 306/789-6200
www.maxwellsamusements.com
The main attractions are the
three go-kart tracks, suitable
for anyone over the age of
four, and the waterpark, with
eight slides and the River Ride.
Also baseball batting cages
and basketball courts.
🕐 Daily 11–10, Jun–Aug; reduced
hours early Apr–May and Sep–early
Oct, depending on weather 🎟 Price
varies 🚌 North Service Road
🥤 Snacks stands and western-style bar

WINNIPEG

FORT WHYTE CENTRE
1961 McCreary Road, Winnipeg,
Manitoba
Tel 204/989-8355
www.fortwhyte.org
One of Canada's foremost outdoor recreation facilities, with
more than 160ha (400 acres)
of woods, lakes and grassland.
There's a large herd of bison, a
prairie dog town and an aquarium. In summer there's a
tepee encampment, boating
and fishing, and in winter
there's a toboggan slide, skating on the lake and ice fishing.
🕐 Mon–Fri 9–5, Sat–Sun 10–5
(extended hours Jun–Oct) 🎟 Adult $5,
child (3 and over) $3 🚌 Southwest of
downtown 🍴 Light lunches and specialty coffees; also bison meat for sale

**MANITOBA CHILDREN'S
MUSEUM**
Kinsmen Building, 45 Forks Market
Road, Winnipeg, Manitoba, R3C 4T6
Tel 204/924-4000
www.childrensmuseum.com

This terrific museum, seemingly devoted entirely to fun
and make-believe, is where
learning flourishes. Kids can
dig, build, and play with water,
dress in costumes, play at driving a real locomotive, make
their own TV show, and record
a video that might get aired on
a local TV kids' show.
🕐 Sun–Thu 9.30–4.30, Fri–Sat 9.30–8
🎟 Adult $5.50, child (2–17) $6 🚌 34,
45

**MANITOBA THEATRE FOR YOUNG
PEOPLE**
CanWest Global Performing Arts
Centre, Forks Market Road, The Forks,
Winnipeg, Manitoba, R3C 4X1
Tel 204/942-8898, 877/871-6897
www.mtyp.ca
This professional theater com-
pany with a national profile
specializes in performances for
young people, including tradi-
tional tales and innovative
theater for teens.
🕐 Fri 7pm, Sat–Sun 1pm and 4pm,
Oct–May/Jun 🎟 $10–12 🚌 Free
shuttle

Festivals and
Events

MARCH

ROYAL MANITOBA WINTER FAIR
Brandon, Manitoba
Tel 204/726-3590, 877/729-0001,
www.brandonfairs.com
Six-day agricultural show,
including horse shows and
rural and commercial exhibits.

JULY

CALGARY STAMPEDE
Calgary, Alberta
Tel 403/261-0101, 800/661-1260
www.calgary-stampede.com

Recalling pioneer days, this is a
huge event that takes over the
whole city, starting with the big
parade on opening day. After
that, it's 10 days of big-name
concerts, a first-rate rodeo and
cultural events.

**TASTE OF MANITOBA FOOD
FESTIVAL**
Winnipeg, Manitoba
Tel 204/783-9955
www.dinemanitoba.com
Around 30 of Manitoba's top
restaurants congregate in
Memorial Park to serve up
their signature dishes, accompanied by live entertainment
and other attractions.

AUGUST

FOLKORAMA
Winnipeg, Manitoba
Tel 204/982-6210
www.folklorama.ca
Canada's largest and longest-
running multicultural festival.
Two weeks of events, showcasing more than 40 ethnic
cultures.

NOVEMBER

**CANADIAN FINALS RODEO AND
FARMFAIR INTERNATIONAL**
Northlands Park, Edmonton, Alberta
Tel 780/471-7210, 888/800-7255
www.canadianfinalsrodeo.ca
The city fills up with cowboys
and livestock for this event.
The rodeo, at the Skyreach
Centre, stars Canada's tough-
est professionals; Farmfair, at
Northlands Park, is a huge
agricultural show.

WHAT TO DO

BRITISH COLUMBIA AND THE ROCKIES

Vancouver's Pacific Centre is a bright and inviting downtown shopping mall

This is a spectacular region of massive mountains, wild coastline and offshore islands teeming with marine- and bird-life, and verdant landscapes where vineyards and fruit orchards thrive. You can ski in the morning and swim in the ocean in the afternoon; you can soak in a naturally heated spring-water pool while the snow falls on you; you can kayak among whales and dolphins; or you can just enjoy a round of golf, a hike or a horseback ride across meadows, with a backdrop of majestic snow-capped mountains. Winter sports facilities are first-class, and world-famous Whistler hosts international competitions, including the upcoming 2010 Winter Olympics. Naturally, there are challenging climbs, too, and guided hikes over glaciers. Divers can explore crystal-clear waters rated by the late Jacques Cousteau as second only to the Red Sea.

Beautiful Victoria is the capital of British Columbia, but Vancouver is bigger, a lively and immensely attractive waterfront city with every kind of entertainment. There might also be US movie-makers in town—the area is popular for location work, and casts and crews relax in the city's trendy nightspots. There's great shopping in Vancouver, too, including arts and crafts, innovative designer boutiques and the second-largest mall in the world (at Burnaby). Up in the mountains, Banff has the best shopping.

Shopping

ARMSTRONG

ARMSTRONG FARMERS' MARKET
IPE Fairgrounds, Pleasant Valley Road, Armstrong, British Columbia
Tel 250/546-1986
In an area that's full of farms, orchards and wineries, there's no shortage of fruit stands and food shops, but this market offers a great variety and a great experience. It's the oldest of its kind in the region.
🕐 Sat 8–noon, Apr–Oct

BANFF

THE FUDGERY
215 Banff Avenue, Banff, Alberta
Tel 403/762-3003
www.thefudgery.com
It's just impossible to walk past this store—the tempting aroma of cooking chocolate and the sweet smell of fudge in the making grab you by the taste buds and haul you inside. The Fudgery has been in business here since 1976, and you can watch the candies being made by hand.
🕐 Daily 9am–11pm

JASPER

TOTEM SKI SHOP
408 Connaught Drive, Jasper, Alberta, T0E 1E0
Tel 780/852-3078
www.totemskishop.com
If your outdoor wear proves inadequate for rugged national park activities, pay this store a visit. They have mountain wear, sweatshirts and handknit Cowichan sweaters, and there's a good selection of footwear (including hiking boots) and souvenirs.
🕐 Daily 9.30am–10pm, summer; Sun–Fri 8–6 , Sat 8–8, winter 🚌 Ski Bus (winter only) 🚏 On main street, by Astoria Hotel

KELOWNA

SUMMERHILL ESTATE WINERY
4870 Chute Lake Road, Kelowna, British Columbia, V1W 4M3
Tel 250/764-8000; 800/667-3538
www.summerhill.bc.ca
There are a number of wineries in the Thompson Okanagan area, but this one is particularly interesting, with good visitor facilities. Wine here is aged in a four-story-high pyramid to enhance the flavor. You can tour the facility—and a reconstructed native earth house—sample the wine, and maybe stay to watch the sunset over dinner.
🕐 Daily 9–6 🚗 20-min drive from Kelowna 🍴 Sunset Verandah (see page 330)

RICHMOND

RIVERGEMS
220–12240 Second Avenue, Richmond, British Columbia, V7E 3L8
Tel 604/241-4367
www.rivergems.com
This is more than just a jewelry store, though it does have some gorgeous pieces made from richly colored Alberta ammolite and some shark-tooth necklaces. But how many other jewelers could sell you a dinosaur egg? The most stunning displays, though, are the minerals that glitter or glow in the light.
🕐 Daily 10–6; by appointment after hours 🚌 401 🚏 Across from Steveson Landing and docks

WHAT TO DO

SIDNEY

TANNERS—A BOOKSTORE AND MORE

2436 Beacon Avenue, Sidney, British Columbia, V8L 1X6

Tel 250/656-2345

Sidney is known for its bookstores, most specializing in rare and secondhand books. This one has a more universal appeal, with classics, the latest paperbacks, Canadian literature, and local interest books. Also international newspapers and 3,000 magazines.

Daily 8–9 70, 75 Downtown, corner of Beacon and 4th

VANCOUVER

BLACKBERRY BOOKS

1663 Duranleau Street, Granville Island, Vancouver, British Columbia, V6L 3B2

Tel 604/685-6188, 604/685-4113

www.bbooks.ca

Carefully selected piped music adds to the welcoming atmosphere in this bookstore, run by the enthusiastic Stewart family in the same location for more than 20 years. In addition to the latest fiction, it has a good selection of works by Canadian writers and local interest titles.

Daily 9–6 4, 7, 8 Granville Island Ferry or Aquabus

CRAFTHOUSE

1386 Cartwright Street, Granville Island, Vancouver, British Columbia, V6H 3R8

Tel 604/687-7270

www.cabc.net

Run by the Crafts Association of British Columbia, this gallery is a nonprofit organization showcasing the work of more than 150 of its members. The imaginative layout and careful spotlighting highlight pieces that include ceramics, glass, metal, wood, fabrics, and furniture (shipping arranged), at prices from $5 to $2,500.

Daily 10.30–5.30; closed Mon in Jan 4, 7, 8 Granville Island Ferry, Aquabus Near ferry terminal

ESSENTIAL BOUTIQUE

375 Water Street, Vancouver, British Columbia, V6B 5C6

Tel 604/689-8544

www.essentialboutique.com

Creative, distinctive and wearable garments are produced by a team that includes First Nations fashion designers—and some reflect First Nations traditions. Luxury fabrics are decorated with appliqué, embroidery and inserts.

Mon–Sat 10–6, Sun noon–5 50 Skytrain: Waterfront The Landing, Gastown

IMAGES FOR A CANADIAN HERITAGE

164 Water Street, Vancouver, British Columbia, V6B 1B2

Tel 604/685-7046, 877/212-8900

www.imagesforcanada.com

This is one of Canada's finest galleries with works by Canadians, including First Nations and Inuit artists and artisans. Pieces from BC artists include Kevin Peters soapstone sculptures, Ken Curley bronzes, Shannon Ravenhall abstract paintings, and Lynne Rae Mercer wildlife scenes on slate. Also bird decoys, glass and limited edition prints.

Daily 10–6 (extended hours in summer) 50 Skytrain: Waterfront Gastown, southeast corner of Cambie Street intersection

INTRA-VENUS

1072 Mainland Street, Yaletown, Vancouver, British Columbia, V6B 2T4

Tel 604/685-9696

www.intra-venus.com

This little store has brought together two often incompatible concepts in footwear—fashion and comfort. Admittedly, a lot of the shoes are like sneakers, but there's a good range of colors and styles, and your feet will love you for dropping by. There's also casual clothing and accessories sourced worldwide.

Mon–Thu and Sat 11–6, Fri 11–7, Sun 1–5 15, 17 Skytrain: Granville Between Helmcken and Nelson

INUIT GALLERY OF VANCOUVER

206 Cambie Street, Gastown, Vancouver, British Columbia, V6B 2M9

Tel 604/688-7323, 888/615-8399

www.inuit.com

A spacious gallery, with huge wooden pillars and a hardwood floor, where individual works by Inuits of the eastern Canadian Arctic and Northwest Coast First Nations artists are displayed. Plain white plinths show soapstone animal sculptures to their best advantage, and there are also prints and drawings, traditional masks, jewelry, gift items, and boxes.

Mon–Sat 10–6, Sun 11–5 17, 50 Skytrain: Waterfront Corner of Cambie and Water streets

LEONE

757 West Hastings Street, Sinclair Centre, Vancouver, British Columbia, V6C 1A1

Tel 604/683-1133

www.leone.ca

It's like stepping into the glamorous world of celebrity shopping at this fashion store. It has been constructed to look just like an Italian street lined with exclusive designer boutiques—Versace, Dolce and Gabbana, Armani, and Hugo Boss are just some of the labels. There's valet parking, and A-list customers can arrange private after-hours shopping.

Mon–Fri 9.30–6, Sat 9.30–5.30, Sun noon–5 10, 44 Skytrain: Waterfront Downtown, near Cruise Ship and Seabus Terminal

LONSDALE QUAY

Lonsdale Avenue, North Vancouver, British Columbia, V7M 3KY
Tel 604/985-6261
www.lonsdalequay.com

In a spectacular location over-looking the harbor, this mall has more than 90 stores and services, plus a traditional market with more than 60 vendors selling local produce and fish. Upstairs there are specialty boutiques and a playroom, and there's daily entertainment.
🕐 Sat–Thu 9.30–6.30, Fri 9.30–8 or 9 depending on season 🚌 246 ⛴ Sea Bus from downtown (15 min)
🍴 British-style pub and hip lounge bar-restaurant ☕ European-style coffee house and café

METROTOWN

604–4720 Kingsway, Burnaby, Vancouver, British Columbia, V5K 1A1
Tel 604/438-4700
www.metrotown.info

British Columbia's biggest shopping and entertainment complex, and the second-largest shopping mall in the world. It can be daunting, but there are handy maps on each level. There are around 500 stores, including Sears, The Bay, Zellers, and two super-markets, plus 22 movie theaters and the Metropolis Entertainment Centre.
🕐 Mon–Fri 10–9, Sat 9.30–6, Sun 11–6
🚌 19, 49, 130 🚇 Skytrain: Metrotown
🍴 90 places to eat, including fast food and snacks, coffee houses, restaurants and hotel dining rooms

PACIFIC CENTRE

700 West Georgia Street, Vancouver, British Columbia, V7Y 1A1
Tel 604/688-7236
www.pacificcentre.com

Occupying three blocks between West Georgia and Dunsmuir, this sparkling three-story mall has upward of 200 stores, including Holt Renfrew, and all the major chain stores and services. It also links with The Bay, Sears and the Vancouver Centre.
🕐 Mon–Wed and Sat 9.30–7, Thu–Fri 9.30–9, Sun 9.30–6 🚌 4, 6, 7, 8, 10, 15, 17 🚇 Skytrain: Granville 🚇 Downtown, between Georgia, Dunsmuir, Howe and Seymour 🍴 Fast-food ☕ Specialty coffee shops; Sierra Café and Grill

PUBLIC MARKET

Johnston Street, Granville Island, Vancouver, British Columbia, V6H 3R8
Tel 604/666-6655
www.granvilleisland.com

At the heart of Granville Island, this market is a sensory delight, with colorful displays of fresh produce, an all-pervading aroma of ethnic foods, roasting coffee, fragrant flowers and candy; and the sound of happy shoppers and street entertainers. There are 50 permanent vendors, plus visiting farmers, craftworkers and food producers.
🕐 Daily 9–6 (seasonal variations)
🚌 4, 7, 8 ⛴ Granville Island Ferry, Aquabus 🚇 Near Ferry terminal at Duranleau 🍴 Food options include seafood and Mexican ☕ Coffee house

SALMAGUNDI

321 West Cordova Street, Gastown, Vancouver, British Columbia, V6B 1E5
Tel 604/681-4648
In an area that is just bursting with antiques shops and other funky little stores, you should seek out this one. It special-izes, it says, in "interesting things," and this encompasses a wide range of antiques, col-lectibles, and quirky novelty items. It's great fun to go through the drawers down in the basement just to see what's there.
🕐 Daily 10.30–5.30 🚌 6 🚇 Skytrain: Waterfront

THE SOURCE

929 Main Street, Vancouver, British Columbia, V6A 2V8
Tel 604/684-9914
www.sourceenterprises.bc.ca
This vast emporium is stuffed with mostly small objects. There's a strong slant toward British pub items, including about 300 original pub signs, darts and dartboards, door-knobs and knockers, telescopes and other nautical items, and swords. A great place to find curios for your basement bar.
🕐 Mon–Sat 9–5 🚌 3, 8, 19, 22
🚇 Skytrain: Main Street-Science World
🚇 Between Union and East Georgia

SPIRIT OF THE NORTH

1026 Alberni Street, Vancouver, British Columbia, V6E 1A3
Tel 604/683-2416
You don't have to wait until you get to the airport to buy

your duty-free items—Canada's largest tax- and duty-free store, with more than 2,500sq m (28,000sq ft) on two floors, is right downtown. It has the full range of fragrances, tobacco, liquor, jewelry and watches, and electronic items.
🕐 Daily 10–9, summer; 10–7, winter 🚌 240, 250, 251, 252, 257 🚇 Skytrain: Burrard, then bus 135 🚉 Downtown, between Burrard and Thurlow

VERNON
OKANAGAN OPAL
7879 Highway 97, Vernon, British Columbia, V1T 6M2
Tel 250/542-1103
www.opalscanada.com

The only opal mine in Canada has is own jewelry design studio and store. Stones in many different shades—some more richly colored than you might expect—are set into gold-, silver- and rhodium-plated earrings, pendants and rings, or you can buy loose stones. You can also arrange a trip to the mine site (Fri–Sun in summer) to dig for your own opals.
🕐 Year-round (phone first in winter) 🚉 6.4km (4 miles) north of Vernon; take Pleasant Valley exit and follow signs

VICTORIA
ROYAL BC MUSEUM SHOP
675 Belleville Street, Victoria, British Columbia, V8W 9W2
Tel 250/356-0505
www.royalmuseumshop.com
You don't have to pay admission to the museum to visit this superb store, which stocks First Nations artwork sourced from Northwest Coast tribes. Items include carved silver and gold jewelry, masks, ceremo-

nial sticks, crests, dolls, totem poles, clothing, books and kids' stuff.
🕐 Daily 9–5 🚌 30, 31 🚉 Downtown, corner of Belleville and Douglas

WHISTLER
BRICK SHIRT HOUSE
C-4227 Village Stroll, Whistler, British Columbia, V0N 1B4
Tel 604/932-5320
The name is eye-catching, and so is the clothing—perfect for the outdoor life. The great Whistler branded sweaters, T-shirts and hats make practical souvenirs of your visit.
🕐 Daily 8am–11pm

Performance

BANFF
THE BANFF CENTRE
107 Tunnel Mountain Drive, Banff, Alberta, T1L 1H5
Tel 403/762-6301
www.banffcentre.ca

An arts, culture and conference venue in a spectacular mountain location. It has an interesting calendar of music, dance and comedy.
🕐 Year-round 💵 Price varies with event 🚉 On slope of Tunnell Mountain, four blocks east from Banff Avenue

CHEMAINUS
CHEMAINUS THEATRE
9737 Chemainus Road, Chemainus, Vancouver Island, British Columbia, V0R 1K0
Tel 250/246-9820
This is a beautiful theater building, offering a good variety of new and classic drama and musicals, such as *The Mousetrap, Godspell, Arms and the Man*.

🕐 Year-round 💵 $24–32. Dinner and theater: $42–52 🍴 Playbill Dining Room (licensed) with hot and cold buffet

VANCOUVER
BARD ON THE BEACH
Theatre Tent, Vanier Park, Vancouver, British Columbia
Tel 604/739 0559, 877/739-0559
www.bardonthebeach.org

An annual professional Shakespeare festival presenting three classical productions and various special events.
🕐 Tue–Sun, mid-Jun–late Sep 💵 $14–27 🚢 Granville Island Ferry 🚌 2, 22

CAPITOL 6 VANCOUVER
820 Granville Street, Vancouver, British Columbia, V6Z 1K3
Tel 604/669-6000
Only six screens, and conventional seating, but its 1,000-seat Theatre One is the largest in the city, so it's great for opening nights. Upstairs theaters are small.
🕐 Daily 💵 Adult $10.75, child (under 13) $6.50 🚇 Skytrain: Granville

CN IMAX
Canada Place, 201–999 Canada Place, Vancouver, British Columbia, V6C 3C1
Tel 604/682-4629

www.imax.com/vancouver
Nest to Canada Place, jutting out into the bay, this theater offers the usual IMAX huge-screen experience.
🕐 Mon–Fri 5.30–9, Sat–Sun and holidays 11.30–9 💵 Adult $11–14, child (under 13) $9–12 🚇 Skytrain: Waterfront

FIREHALL ARTS CENTRE
280 East Cordova Street, Vancouver, British Columbia, V6A 1L3
Tel 604/689-0926
www.firehallartscentre.ca

Housed in the atmospheric old fire station, this is one of the busiest venues in the city, staging around 300 events a year: dance, theater and music.
🕐 Year-round 💵 Prices vary 🚌 3, 4, 7, 8 🚇 Skytrain: Waterfront 🚍 Eastside, corner of Gore Avenue 🍴 Gallery lounge serves snacks

GENERAL MOTORS PLACE
800 Griffiths Way, Vancouver, British Columbia, V6B 6G1
Tel 604/899-7889
When it's not staging hockey or basketball, this 20,000-seat state-of-the-art arena hosts nearly 200 events a year, including big-name concerts.
🕐 Year-round 💵 $20–100 🚌 15, 17, 19 🚇 Skytrain: Stadium 🍴 More than 20 fast-food concessions and three formal restaurants; Brew House Grill has dinner-and-view tables

GRANVILLE ISLAND STAGE
1585 Johnston Street, Granville Island, Vancouver, British Columbia, V6H 3R9
Tel 604/687-1644
www.artsclub.com
The Arts Club Theatre Company stages popular plays, new works and musicals—here and at the Stanley Theatre.

🕐 Year-round 💵 $17.50–55 🚌 4, 7, 10, 17 ⛴ Granville Island Ferry or Aquabus

ORPHEUM
Smithe Street, Vancouver, British Columbia
Tel 604/665-3050
www.city.vancouver.bc.ca/theatres/orpheum/orpheum.html

Lavish 1927 building, now a national historic site, home to the Vancouver Symphony and BC Entertainment Hall of Fame. It has a full schedule of classical, pop, choral, and chamber recitals.
🕐 Year-round 💵 $20–100 🚌 4, 6, 7, 10 🚇 Granville 🚍 Downtown, at Seymour

QUEEN ELIZABETH THEATRE COMPLEX
600 Hamilton Street, Vancouver, British Columbia, V6B 2R3
Tel 604/665-3050
Incorporating the Queen Elizabeth Theatre and the Vancouver Playhouse, this complex hosts a full and varied calendar of world-class dance, opera, musicals, and rock concerts.
🕐 Year-round 💵 $20–100 🚌 17 🚇 Stadium 🚍 Downtown, between Georgia and Dunsmuir

STANLEY THEATRE
2750 Granville Street, Vancouver, British Columbia, V6H 3J3
Tel 604/687-1644
www.artsclub.com
The Arts Club Theatre Company stages popular plays, new works and musicals—here and at the Granville Island Stage (see left).
🕐 Tue–Sat 💵 $17.50–55 🚌 8, 98B 🚇 Granville at 12th

THEATRE UNDER THE STARS
Stanley Park, Vancouver, British Columbia
Tel 604/687-0174
www.tuts.bc.ca
Nonprofit company staging popular musicals at the Malkin Bowl in Stanley Park. Two shows alternate nightly.
🕐 Mid-Jul–late Aug 💵 $29–34 🚇 🚍 Stanley Park loop

VANCOUVER EAST CULTURAL CENTRE
1895 Venables Street, Vancouver, British Columbia, V5L 2H6
Tel 604/251-1363
www.vecc.bc.ca
Widely regarded as a cultural treasure, this converted 1909 church hosts an exciting schedule of theater, music and dance, including Canadian and world premieres.
🕐 Year-round 💵 Price varies, average $28 🚌 20 🚇 Skytrain: Broadway, then bus 20 🚍 Downtown Eastside, Corner of Venables and Victoria

VICTORIA

BELFRY
1291 Gladstone Avenue, Victoria, British Columbia, V0T 1G5
Tel 250/385-6815
www.belfry.bc.ca

An old church has been converted into this beautiful theater, renowned for new drama, comedy and musicals. It hosts nine shows a year, as well as jazz and pop concerts.
🕐 Aug–mid-May 💵 $16–29 🚌 22 🚍 Corner of Fernwood Road

LANGHAM COURT
805 Langham Court, Victoria, British Columbia, V8V 4J3
Tel 250/384-2142
www.langhamcourttheatre.bc.ca

Old carriage house and barn (c1880), converted in 1940 into this intimate theater. It stages classic and new drama, and comedies.
🕐 Year-round 💷 $15 🚌 2, 16, 76 🚇 South of Rockland Avenue

MCPHERSON
3 Centennial Square, Victoria, British Columbia, V8W 1E5
Tel 250/386-6121, 888/717-6121
www.rmts.bc.ca
Formerly The Pantages, this 1914 theater is central to the city's entertainment scene, and hosts a variety of local and touring shows.
🕐 Year-round 💷 Depends on event, average $30 🚌 Corner of Pandora and Government, behind City Hall 🍴 Snack concessions and bar

NATIONAL GEOGRAPHIC IMAX
Royal BC Museum, 675 Belleville Street, Victoria, British Columbia, V8W 1A1
Tel 250/356-7226, 888/447-7977
www.imaxvictoria.com

The screen is 6-stories high and 21m (70ft) wide, so even though it's only 2-D, you still get a powerful and involving movie experience.
🕐 Daily 9–8 💷 Adult $9.75, child (under 5) $3.50 or (5–18) $6.50 🚌 30, 31 🚇 Corner of Belleville and Douglas

PORT
125 Front Street, Victoria, British Columbia
Tel 250/754-8550
Distinctive modern building in superb waterfront location. Top local and touring artists provide a broad range of entertainment.
🕐 Year-round 💷 From $5 to more than $60, depending on show 🚌 Next to Coast Bastion Inn

ROYAL
805 Broughton Street, Victoria, British Columbia, V8W 1E5
Tel 250/386-6121, 888/717-6121
www.rmts.bc.ca
Home to Pacific Opera Victoria and the Victoria Symphony, this splendid 1913 building, with a 1,445 audience capacity, hosts varied events.
🕐 Year-round 💷 $23–60 🚌 16, 76 🚇 At Blanchard intersection

WESTBANK
BARD IN THE VINEYARD
Mission Hill Winery, 1730 Mission Hill Road, Westbank, Okanaga Valley, British Columbia, V4T 2E4
Tel 250/768-7611
www.missionhillwinery.com
www.bardinthevineyard.org
Concerts, plays, readings, and summer Shakespeare events are staged in a grassy amphitheater, with a beautiful lake as a backdrop.
🕐 Shakespeare: Tue–Sun, Aug. Call for details of other events 💷 Shakespeare: $30, or $79 including dinner; price varies for other events 🚇 🚌 Just over the floating bridge from Kelowna 🍴 Three-course dinners on the terrace

WHISTLER
RAINBOW THEATRE
4010 Whistler Way, Whistler, British Columbia, V0N 1B4
Tel 604/932-2422
Single movie theater showing kids' matinees and two evening performances of first-run blockbusters. Also venue for Whistler Film Festival.
🕐 Daily 💷 Adult $10 ($5 on Tue). Matinees: adult $6.50, child $2–5

Nightlife

JASPER
ATHA-B CLUB
Athabasca Hotel, 510 Patricia Street, Jasper, Alberta, T0E 1E0
Tel 780/852-3386
www.athabascahotel.com
This is a buzzing nightclub in a landmark hotel that dates from 1929. It's a fun, noisy place with dancing every night, and live music most nights, including some internationally known touring bands
🕐 Daily 4pm–2am 🚌 Near ViaRail station and bus depots

PETE'S ON PATRICIA
614 Patricia Street, Jasper, Alberta, T0E 1E0
Tel 780/852-6262
One of the liveliest and most modern places in Jasper, with occasional live blues and alternative music, but mostly a DJ and high-energy dancing. Mainly young crowd.
🕐 Daily noon–2am 💷

VANCOUVER
BACKSTAGE LOUNGE
1585 Johnston Street, Vancouver, British Columbia, V6H 3R9
Tel 604/687-1354
www.artsclub.com
Run by the Arts Club Theatre Company, behind the Granville Island Stage (see page 243), this is one of the city's foremost live music venues showcasing the best local bands.
🕐 Daily, from noon 💷 Cover charge varies 🍴 Pub food; 11 brews on tap

THE CELLAR
3611 West Broadway, Vancouver, British Columbia, V6R 2B8
Tel 604/738-1959
www.cellarjazz.com

Opened in 2000 to fill a gap in the Vancouver jazz scene, the Cellar quickly became *the* place to see the best local and touring jazz performers. Snug room; cabaret-style seating.
💷 Minimum food/drinks order: Thu $10, Fri–Sun $15

DUFFERIN
900 Seymour Street, Vancouver, British Columbia, V6B 3L9
Tel 604/683-4251
www.bars.dufferinhotel.com
Three venues in one—pub, karaoke lounge and Backdoor Tavern—catering to the gay

WHAT TO DO

community for nearly 30 years. Male strippers, go-go boys, drag shows, comedy nights, DJ music and billiards.
🕐 Mon–Sat noon–2am, Sun noon–midnight 🚌 4, 7, 8 🚇 Skytrain: Granville 🚇 Downtown, opposite Orpheum Theatre

ODYSSEY
1251 Howe Street, Vancouver, British Columbia, V6Z 1R3
Tel 604/689-5256
www.theodysseynightclub.com
In the heart of the city's gay village, this gay nightclub attracts straight clientele, too. Each night is different: the latest tracks, drag shows, and naked male dancers.. Age limit: 19.
🕐 Mon–Sat 9pm–2am, Sun 9–midnight 🍷 Mon–Fri $3, Sat–Sun $5 🚇 Skytrain: Bay 🚇 Between Drake and Davie, parallel with Granville Street

PLAZA
881 Granville Street, Vancouver, British Columbia, V6V 1K7
Tel 604/646-0064
www.plazaclub.net
Classy club with huge dance floor, comfortable booth seats, mezzanine overlook and the best nightclub washrooms in town. Dance to Top 40, R&B, Latin, alternative, hip-hop, and latest club hits. Dress code Friday and Saturday.
🕐 Wed–Thu from 9pm, Fri–Sat from 8 🍷 $3–10 🚇 Skytrain: Granville 🚇 Between Robson and Smithe

PURPLE ONION
15 Water Street, Gastown, Vancouver, British Columbia, V6A 1A1
Tel 604/602-9442
www.purpleonion.com
This is where the celebs come to groove when they are in town. Two-room venue features live music (sometimes international stars on stage) and DJs playing Top 40, R&B, and dance hits.
🕐 Daily 🚌 50 🚇 Skytrain: Waterfront 🚇 At Carrall, one block east of the Steam Clock

RICHARDS ON RICHARDS
1036 Richards Street, Vancouver, British Columbia
Tel 604/688-1099
www.richardsonrichards.com

Affectionately known as Dicks on Dicks, this is a cool venue for international touring bands, including progressive country, indie rock, world music, singer-songwriters, and hip-hop.
🕐 Daily 🍷 $10 Fri–Sat 🚇 Skytrain: Granville 🚇 Downtown, between Nelson and Helmcken

VANCOUVER THEATRE SPORTS LEAGUE
New Revue Theatre, 1601 Johnston Street, Granville Island, Vancouver, British Columbia
Tel 604/738-7013
www.vtsl.com
Highly entertaining improv comedy company that uses various themes to showcase its considerable talent, including competitive improv.
🕐 Wed–Sat 🚌 50 ⛴ Aquabus or Granville Island Ferry

Sports and Activities

SURREY

FRASER DOWNS RACE TRACK
17755 60th Avenue, Surrey, British Columbia, V3S 1V3
Tel 604/576-9141
www.fraserdowns.com
A good long season of harness-racing events, plus simulcast from Hong Kong.
🕐 Live racing: Sep–Apr. Simulcast: year-round 🍷 Free 🅿 $2 for live racing, otherwise free 🚌 320 from Surrey Central station 🚇 Skytrain: Surrey Central, then bus 🚇 Cloverdale, east of Pacific Highway

VANCOUVER

BC LIONS
BC Place Stadium, 777 Pacific Boulevard, Vancouver, British Columbia, V6B 4Y8
Tel 604/589-7627
www.bclions.com
The BC Lions Canadian football team plays at the superb BC Place Stadium, which has a capacity for more than 60,000 and the biggest air-supported dome in the world.
🕐 Season: late Jun–early Nov 🍷 $20–60 🚌 15, 17 🚇 Skytrain: Stadium

VANCOUVER CANUCKS
General Motors Place, 800 Griffiths Way, Vancouver, British Columbia, V6B 6G1
Tel 604/899-7550. Tickets: 604/280-4400
www.canucks.com
The Canucks hockey team play home games at the superb General Motors Place, also one of the most active entertainment venues in North America.
🕐 Sep–Mar 🚇 Skytrain: Stadium

ACTIVITIES

CANMORE

M AND W GUIDES
Box 8020, Canmore, Alberta, T1W 2T8
Tel 403/678-2642
www.mwguides.com
Licensed mountain guides provide personalized adventures in spectacular locations, for beginners and experts. Half-day to multiday excursions include tuition, mountain and frozen waterfall climbs, glacier crossing, and skiing.
🕐 Year-round 🍷 Price depends on requirements

SILVER TIP RESORT
1000 Silver Tip Trail, Canmore, Alberta, T1W 2V1
Tel 403/678-1600, 877/877-5444
www.silvertipresort.com
A spectacular, world-class 6,552m (7,200yd) golf course on the mountainside, with a 182m (600ft) elevation change and a 360-degree view.
🕐 Daily, late May–early Oct 🍷 $79–150 ($55 for 9 holes in evening) ❓ Power cart rule 🚇 Off Trans-Canada Highway (Canmore exit), 23km (14 miles) east of Banff National Park

GRAND CACHE

U BAR TRAIL RIDES
Box 929, Grande Cache, Alberta, T0E 0Y0
Tel 780/827-4884
www.ubartrailrides.com
Take overnight pack trips or spend just a few hours in the saddle. Beginners get instruction, then set off with a guide through meadows and mountains for wonderful views. Reservation required.
🕐 Day rides begin 9am, last ride 7pm 🍷 1 hour $20, 2 hours $35, 3.5 hours

WHAT TO DO

$55, 5 hours $85 🚗 Northern edge of Willmore Wilderness Park on the Big Horn Highway (40), 2.5 hours drive north of Jasper via Trans-Canada 16

JASPER

JASPER RAFT TOURS
Box 398, Jasper National Park, Jasper, Alberta, TOE 1E0
Tel 780/852-2665; 1-888-55FLOAT
www.JasperRaftTours.com
A great trip for families, following the fur-traders' route down the Athabasca River in big inflatables. The two- to three-hour round trip has some small rapids and calm stretches where you can enjoy the natural beauty.
🕐 Tours depart Jasper 9am, 12.30pm and 7pm Jul–Aug; 12.30pm, mid-May–Jun and Sep 💵 Adult $47, child (6–16) £15, under 6 free
❓ Transportation from Jasper provided Meet at the totem pole beside the train station, at 607 Connaught Drive

NANAIMO

OCEAN EXPLORERS DIVING
5450 Westdale Road, Nanaimo, British Columbia, V9S 5T9
Tel 250/753-2055, 800/233-4145
Renowned diver and broadcaster Jacques Cousteau rated the crystal-clear waters off British Columbia as second only to the Red Sea for world-class diving. This outfitter offers diving charters that take you to explore artificial reefs and wrecks, and the package can include tuition and supplies.
🕐 Year-round 💵 Two-diver charters $90–100, snorkeling $50 🚢 BC Ferries: Horseshoe Bay, Vancouver, to Nanaimo
❓ Free pick-up/drop-off to ferry terminal and airport 🚗 Near Departure Bay ferry terminal

TELEGRAPH COVE

STUBBS ISLAND WHALE-WATCHING
Box 2, Telegraph Cove, British Columbia, V0N 3J0
Tel 250/928-3185, 250/928-3117, 800/665-3066
www.stubbs-island.com
This was the first whale-watching company established in British Columbia, and its experienced captains take you to some of the best whale-watching waters in the world

in vessels with cabin heating, restrooms, and hydro-phones to hear the whales. Extended tours also available.
🕐 Late May–mid-Oct (call for specific dates and times), arrive 45 minutes prior to departure time 💵 Adult $59–68, child (under 13) $59 🚌 Island Coach Lines: Victoria–Port Hardy 🚗 At the north end of Vancouver Island, 11km (7 miles) from Highway 19 via Beaver Cove Road

WHISTLER

ADULT SKI SCHOOL
Activity and Information Centre, Box 621, Whistler, British Columbia, V0N 1B0
Tel 604/664-5624, 800/944-7853
www.mywhistler.com

Whistler is one of the premier winter sports resorts in the whole of North America (some say its the absolute best), and you can get some of the best tuition in skiing and snowboarding in the world here. The courses range from half-day to three-day packages, and there is something to suit all ages and levels of competence.
🕐 Daily, throughout winter season 💵 Adult from $70 (half-day), child from $91 (full day)

Health and Beauty

CLINTON

ECHO VALLEY RANCH AND SPA
Clinton, Jesmond, British Columbia
Tel 250/459-2386, 800/253-8831
www.evranch.com
A little bit of Thailand has been set down amid beautiful BC landscape, with a traditional Thai Baan building and Thai spa treatments, including massage, *Ruesri-dat-ton* stretching exercises and rejuvenation
🕐 Year-round; minimum three-night stay in summer, two nights in winter
💵 Three nights all-inclusive from $720
🚗 About 30km (81 miles) northwest of Kamloops, off Highway 97 at Clinton

108 MILE RANCH

CANADIAN WELLNESS CENTRE
The Hills Health Ranch, 108 Mile Ranch, British Columbia
Tel 250/791-5225
www.spabc.com
A world-class spa on a vast western ranch. The Canadian Wellness Centre here has the largest staff of any spa in the country, and offers the full treatment, from health analysis and advice to a full range of treatments and diet regimes.
🕐 Packages range from 2-night weekend to 30-night Weight Loss Special 💵 From $350 to more than $4,000 (based on 2 sharing a double room)
🚌 Greyhound Bus to 100 Mile House, then taxi 🚆 BC Rail to 100 Mile House, then taxi 🚗 Off Route 9, 12km (7.7 miles) north of 100 Mile House

VANCOUVER

LA RAFFINAGE SPIRIT SPA
521 West Georgia Street, Vancouver, British Columbia, V6B 1Z5
Tel 604/681-9933
www.laraffinage.com
Body, mind and spirit are soothed and nurtured in this relaxing haven in the heart of the city. Besides massage and facials, you can explore tarot, yoga, reiki, numerology and meditation.
🕐 Mon–Wed 10–7, Thu–Fri 10–8, Sat 9–6 💵 Treatments priced individually or as packages; massage/facials from about $70 🚇 15, 17 🚗 Downtown, between Richards and Seymour

WHAT TO DO

Children

ALDERGROVE

GREATER VANCOUVER ZOO

5048 264th Street, Aldergrove, British
Columbia, V4W 1N7
Tel 604/856-6825
www.greatervancouverzoo.com
The only place in the world
where you can see an albino
black bear (Albus), just one of
more than 700 animals that
live at this 48ha (120-acre)
park. There's a zoo train, with
commentary, and a tour bus
that goes inside the North
American Wilds exhibit.
🕐 Daily 9.30–7, Apr–Sep; 9.30–4, rest
of year 🎟 Adult $13, child $10 🚗 Off
Trans-Canada Highway between
Vancouver and Abbotsford, south of exit
73 🍴 Fast food

BRIDAL FALLS

DINOTOWN

53480 Bridal Falls Road, Rosedale,
British Columbia, V0X 1X0
Tel 604/794-7410
www.dinotown.com
This theme park in the Fraser
Valley is one for young children. The 5ha (12-acre) park
has cute dinosaur characters,
gentle rides and a wet play
area. There's a parade through
a prehistoric town and a live
stage show in the clubhouse.
🕐 Daily 10–7, Jul–Aug; daily 10–5
mid-Jun–end Jun; Sat–Sun 10–5,
May–Jun and Sep 🎟 $13 (children
under 3 free) 🍴 Dinersaurus serves
burgers, chicken strips and hot dogs

BRITANNIA BEACH

BC MUSEUM OF MINING

Highway 99, Britannia Beach, British
Columbia
Tel 604/896-2233, 800/896-4044
www.bcmuseumofmining.org
A filming location for dozens of
movies and TV shows, this
national historic site preserves
the copper mining heritage of
BC. The highlight is climbing
aboard the train in hard hats for
a trip 364m (1,200ft) underground, where old mining
methods are demonstrated.
🕐 Daily 9–4.30, early May–mid-Oct;
Mon–Fri 9–4.30, mid-Oct–Nov and
Feb–early May 🎟 Adult $12.95, child (6
and over) $10.95 🚗 52km (32 miles)
north of Vancouver on Sea-to-Sky route

BURNABY

PLAYDIUM

Unit E5, 4700 Kingsway, Burnaby,
British Columbia, V5H 4M1
Tel 604/433-7529
www.playdium.com
Teenagers love this 3,600sq-m
(40,000sq-ft) entertainment
complex, with more than 200
high-tech attractions, including
table and interactive console
games. They can drive a virtual
Indy Car, fly a virtual glider or
hurtle down a virtual ski slope.
🕐 Sun–Thu 10am–midnight, Fri–Sat
10am–2am 🎟 $10–25 🚌 19, 49, 130
🚆 Skytrain: Metrotown

SURREY

SEA MONSTER MAZE

4623 168th Street, Surrey, British
Columbia, V4P 0L2
Tel 604/576-1449
www.thecornmaze.com
This 3ha (7-acre) maze, laid
out by a Guinness world
record holder, can take up to
two hours. You get a booklet
with puzzles and a quiz trail,
and a family flag to wave as
you cross the victory bridge.
Also farm tours, hayrides and
a farm market
🕐 Sun–Thu 11–6, Fri–Sat 11–10, mid-
Jul–Oct 🎟 Adult $7, child $5.50
🚗 3km (2 miles) south of 168th Street
and 32nd Avenue intersection

VANCOUVER

ALCAN CHILDREN'S MARITIME DISCOVERY CENTRE

Vancouver Maritime Museum, 1905
Ogden Avenue, Vancouver, British
Columbia, V6J 1A3
Tel 604/257-8300
www.vmm.bc.ca
There's plenty of opportunity
for make-believe as well as
educational fun here, taking
the controls in a replica tug-
boat wheelhouse, working a
remote-controlled deep-sea
robot or visiting Pirate's Cove.
There are also real boats to
visit in the harbor.
🕐 Daily 10–5 🚌 Aquabus 🚗 Vanier
Park

H. R. MACMILLAN SPACE CENTRE

1100 Chestnut Street, Vancouver, British
Columbia, V6J 3J9
Tel 604/738-7827
www.hrmacmillanspacecentre.com

This spectacular attraction
offers exciting space-related
activities. Best is the realistic
virtual voyage, with a pre-
mission briefing then a ride in
a spacecraft simulator. You can
morph yourself into an alien,
dock with the International
Space Station, touch a moon
rock, and visit the multimedia
show and planetarium.
🕐 Tue–Sun 10–5 (also Mon during
holidays) 🎟 Adult $12.75, child (5–10)
$8.75 or (11–18) $9.75 🚌 Aquabus

LYNN CANYON ECOLOGY CENTRE

Lynn Canyon Park, North Vancouver,
British Columbia
Tel 604/981-3103
www.dnv.org/ecology/
The center interprets the park's
temperate rain forest, and children particularly enjoy the
Exploratorium—make sure they
find the banana slugs, up to
26cm (10in) long. Outside,
they can clamber across the
suspension bridge over the
creek and explore forests and
waterfalls.
🕐 Daily 10–5 (noon–4 on winter
weekends and holidays) 🎟 Park: free;
Ecology Centre: donation 🚌 210, 228,
229, 998 🚢 Sea Bus from Lonsdale
Quay, then bus 🚗 North Vancouver off
Trans-Canada Highway, via Lynn Valley
Road and Peters Road 🍴 Snack concession stand Apr–Oct

SCIENCE WORLD AND OMNIMAX THEATRE

1455 Québec Street, Vancouver, British
Columbia, V6A 3Z7
Tel 604/443-7440; 604/443-7443
www.scienceworld.bc.ca

There are masses of interactive
exhibits in this huge geodesic
dome. Centre Stage offers
entertaining demonstrations

WHAT TO DO

and kids are sometimes called on to participate. The Science Theatre has electronic and live shows. KidSpace Gallery has lots of bright exhibits that teach through play, and there's an Omnimax theater.

⊕ Mon–Fri 10–5, Sat, Sun and holidays 10–6 🕲 Adult $12.75, child (4–18) $8.50 🚇 Skytrain: Main Street/Science World ⛴ Aquabus or False Creek Ferry

VANCOUVER AQUARIUM
See page 149

VANCOUVER AQUARIUM SLEEPOVER
845 Avison Way, Stanley Park, Vancouver, British Columbia, V6B 3X8
Tel 604/659-3504
www.vanaqua.org/visit_us/sleepovers
After the aquarium closes, you can stay on to enjoy various activities, then sleep in front of the huge whale tank. After breakfast there's a tour of the Marine Mammal Deck and Amazon Free Flight Gallery. Under-16s must be accompanied by an adult.

⊕ Specific dates; call for information 🕲 $83 🚌 Stanley Park Express Bus and Stanley Park Shuttle; 23, 35, 135 🍴 Light evening meal and breakfast included in the price

VICTORIA
VICTORIA BUG ZOO
631 Courtney street, Victoria, British Columbia, V8W 1B8
Tel 250/384-BUGS
www.bugzoo.bc.ca
See some of the most incredible live insects and creepy-crawlies, including huge grasshoppers, colorful beetles, giant stick insects, and tarantulas—you can hold some, and there are even bugs for sale.

🕲 Daily 9–9, Jun–Labor Day weekend; Mon–Sat 9.30–5.30, Sun 11–5.30, rest of year 🕲 Adult $6, child (3–16) $4 🚌 Between Government and Douglas, a block north of Empress hotel

WHISTLER
ADVENTURE ZONE
Whistler, British Columbia
Tel 604/938-2769, 877/991-9988
www.mywhistler.com
In summer this place has lots of exciting activities, including sliding down the mountainside

on the Westcoaster Luge, climbing the 8m (25ft) wall, flying through the air on the All-Canadian Trapeze, and bouncing up and down on the trampoline. Also guided horseback tours on the mountain.

🕲 Daily 8.30–5, depending on weather 🕲 Activities $4–10 each, horseback tour $50

Festivals and Events

JANUARY/FEBRUARY
CHINESE NEW YEAR CELEBRATIONS
Vancouver, British Columbia
Tel 604/662-320
www.vancouverchinesegarden.com
The third-largest Chinese community in North America celebrates Chinese New Year in style, with lion dances at numerous city locations and various other events, centered on the Dr. Sun Yat-Sen Classical Chinese Garden.

MARCH
VANCOUVER INTERNATIONAL DANCE FESTIVAL
Vancouver, British Columbia
Tel 604/662-7441
http://vidf.ca
Local, national and international dancers gather for nearly three weeks, with shows, films and workshops.

APRIL
BRANT WILDLIFE FESTIVAL
Qualicum Beach, British Columbia
Tel 205/752-9171
www.brantfestival.bc.ca
Celebrates the return of over 20,000 Brent geese en route from Mexico to Alaska, with birdwatching, wildlife art, carving competition, lectures, and guided walks.

WORLD SKI AND SNOWBOARD FESTIVAL
Whistler, British Columbia
Tel 604/938-3399
www.wssf.com
Action-packed 10 days of events featuring Olympic champions and extreme sports legends, plus live music and other entertainment.

MAY/JUNE
VANCOUVER INTERNATIONAL MARATHON
Vancouver, British Columbia
Tel 604/872-2928
www.adidasvanmarathon.ca
The whole city seems to be on the move, with the marathon, the half-marathon, wheelchair half-marathon, a kids' MaraFun; lots of accompanying events.

VANCOUVER INTERNATIONAL CHILDREN'S FESTIVAL
Vancouver, British Columbia
Tel 604/708-5655,
www.vancouverchildrensfestival.com
Entertainment, the arts and lots of hands-on activities designed specifically for children, in candy-striped tents beside English Bay.

JUNE/JULY
INTERNATIONAL JAZZ FESTIVAL
Vancouver, British Columbia
Tel 604/872-5200,
www.jazzvancouver.com
A great line-up of world-class performers delight jazz fans for 10 days. This is one of the best events of its kind in the world.

ICA FOLKFEST
Victoria, British Columbia
www.icafolkfest.com
Nine-day multicultural festival of world music, dance, theater, visual, and culinary arts.

SEPTEMBER
VANCOUVER FRINGE FESTIVAL
Vancouver, British Columbia
Tel 604/257-0366
www.vancouverfringe.com
Theater for everyone is the purpose of this popular festival showcasing thought-provoking, hilarious, mysterious, or just plain unusual shows.

NOVEMBER/DECEMBER
NORTH AMERICAN NATIVE ARTS AND CRAFTS FESTIVAL
Vancouver, British Columbia
Tel 604/253-1020,
www.geocities.com/Kakilani2000/nativeartsfestival
The Vancouver Aboriginal Friendship Centre hosts this event, featuring traditional performances, food, and arts and crafts.

248 **BRITISH COLUMBIA AND THE ROCKIES**

THE NORTH

A team of well-trained huskies from the Blue Kennels provides dogsled trips for winter visitors

It's a different world up here, with small settlements perched on the edge of a vast wilderness. Needless to say, it's not a shopping and entertainment mecca by any means, but in true Gold-Rush style, there are treasures to be discovered, including designer clothing and jewelry. There are also cultural jewels in the Yukon Arts Centre in Whitehorse and Aurora Village.

Visitors come to the region for the pioneer experience, to explore one of the world's great wilderness areas and to see its wildlife in natural surroundings. There are quite a number of outfitters—mostly based in Whitehorse, Yellowknife, Dawson City, and Iqalut—organizing day trips and longer expeditions in summer and winter, including hiking and climbing, canoeing, flightseeing, snowmobiling and dogsledding. And you can play golf at midnight at the height of summer.

Though many of the activities are far too gruelling for children, there is plenty to attract families with small children too, including gold-panning, easy walks, dogsled trips and, of course, the prospect of seeing a polar bear in the wild.

Shopping

CARCROSS

CARIBOU CROSSING TRADING POST
Carcross, Yukon, Y0B 1B0
Tel 867/821-4055
www.cariboucrossing.ca
Within a museum of Yukon natural history, this store specializes in Yukon-made gifts and products, including hand-carved antler and horn, and fur products. Some of the items on sale are made for this outlet by local artisans, and there's an artist-in-residence.

Mid-May to mid-Sep, call for hours 3km (2 miles) north of Carcross off the Klondike Highway Restaurant (reservation required) Coffee house and ice cream parlor

DAWSON CITY

BONANZA MARKET
2nd Avenue and Princess Street, Bag 5020, Dawson City, Yukon, Y0B 1G0
Tel 867/993-6567
More of a food store than a traditional-style market, really, but it's a good place to meet the locals, and if you're looking for provisions for a picnic, it's well worth a visit. It's the only place in town that has fresh fruit and vegetables, and there's a good European/Canadian deli counter that's strong on German delicacies. Mon–Sat 9–7

RIVERS OF GOLD
952 2nd Avenue, Box 805, Dawson City, Yukon, Y0B 1G0
Tel 867/993-6909 (winter: 250/494-0131)
It doesn't seem right to leave Dawson City without a gold nugget, and if you don't want to spend time panning in the river, you can cheat and buy one here. The Lee family also create individual pieces of jewelry, and sell jade sculptures, mineral specimens, and the family's book, *Rivers of Gold: A Yukon True Story*. Daily 9–9, mid-May–Sep

IQALUIT

RANNVA DESIGN
Apex Beach, Old Hudson Bay Building 3606, Iqaluit, Nunavut, X0A 0H0
Tel 867/979-0333
www.rannva.com
You might find Rannva's sealskin garments elsewhere in Canada (they're even exported to Italy), but there's a real thrill in buying direct from the designer in such a far-flung

Performance

PALACE GRAND THEATRE
King Street, Dawson City, Yukon, Y0B 1G0
Tel 867/993-6217
Lavish theater dating to 1899, now superbly restored. It's home to the Gaslight Follies, a professional musical comedy with a gold-rush theme.
🕐 Mid-May–Sep 🎫 Adult $15–17, child $7.50

WHITEHORSE

FRANTIC FOLLIES
Westmark Whitehorse Hotel, 201 Wood Street, Whitehorse, Yukon, Y1A 2E4
Tel 867/393-9700
www.franticfollies.com

The vaudeville tradition of the gold-rush era brought to life. Don't expect cerebral entertainment—just old-fashioned singing, dancing and skits.
🕐 Late May–mid-Sep 🎫 Adult $19, child (under 12) $9.50

YUKON ARTS CENTRE
300 College Drive, Yukon College Campus, Whitehorse, Yukon, Y1A 5X9
Tel 867/667-8574; 867/667-8575 (and press 2)
www.yukonartscentre.org

corner of the world—and in the old Hudson's Bay Company trading post at that. Fur has long been a traditional trade up here, and Rannva uses it to create beautiful, exclusive and original designs.
🕐 Sat 2–6, Sun 2–4, or by appointment during the week

WHITEHORSE

FOLKNITS
2151 2nd Avenue, Whitehorse, Yukon, Y1A 1C6
Tel 867/668-7771
www.folknits.yukon.net

Life-size battling moose on the roof are just a hint of something a little unusual. Fiber artist Wendy Chambers' store specializes in qiviut (the down of the musk ox), one of the rarest natural fibers in the world, plus garments made from handspun dog hair, arctic fox fur, mountain goat wool, and regular yarns. Also knitting kits and classes.
🕐 Mon–Fri 10–5.30, Sat 10–5

GOLDSMITHS
106 Main Street, Whitehorse, Yukon, Y1A 2A7
Tel 867/667-7340
www.yukoninfo.com/goldsmith
David Ashley and Cheryl Rivest

create and sell beautiful original pieces of jewelry and metal art, which are all designed and made on the premises. You can also get gold nuggets (with a certificate of authenticity) and Canadian Polar Bear Diamonds that originate in the Arctic. Commissions accepted.
🕐 Tue–Sat 10.30–5, or by appointment

MAC'S FIREWEED BOOKS
203 Main Street, Whitehorse, Yukon, Y1A 2B2
Tel 867/668-6104, 800/661-0508
www.yukonbooks.com
This is one of the best-known bookstores in the Yukon, and you can't miss the big blue storefront on Main Street. Inside, you will find a modern layout with a great selection of books about the Yukon, including evocative tales of pioneer days, sumptuous picture books to remind you of your visit, travel planners and maps, plus all the usual bestsellers, magazines and newspapers.
🕐 Daily, summer: 8am–midnight, winter 8am–9pm

UNIQUE TAILORS
4101 4th Avenue, Whitehorse, Yukon, Y1A 1H6
Tel 867/633-6088
www.uniquetailors-yukon.com
There's a crucial need to keep warm up here, and this store has a good selection of very distinctive parkas and anoraks, fur hats and gloves that will keep the winter chill at bay. It also has some First Nations clothing, such as beaded leather dresses and shirts, moccasins and mukluks, as well as beaded necklaces, earrings, and dreamcatchers.

WHAT TO DO

Foremost arts facility in the north, with a 424-seat theater featuring innovative drama, modern dance, classical recitals, country, roots, singer-songwriters, and cabaret.
🕐 Year-round 💵 $10–20

YUKON CINEMA CENTRE
304 Wood Street, Whitehorse, Yukon Y1A 2E6
Tel 867/668-6644
www.cinema.yk.ca
Modern movie house with two theaters, each seating just over 200, showing selected latest releases and kids' movies.
🕐 Daily 💵 Adult $8.50 (matinees and Tue $5), child $5–7

YELLOWKNIFE
CAPITOL THEATRE
4920 – 52 Street, Yellowknife, Northern Territories, X1A 3S9
Tel 867/873-2302
www.movies.yk.com
Three comfortable, modern theaters with superb acoustics and sight lines.
🕐 Daily 💵 Adult $13 (matinees $8), child (under 14) $8

Nightlife

DAWSON CITY
DIAMOND TOOTH GERTIES GAMBLING HALL
Queen Street, Dawson City, Yukon, Y0B 1G0
Tel 867/993-5525

Canada's oldest casino, in a 1901 building named after a famous dance-hall queen. Blackjack, roulette, *sic bo*, slots and cancan shows raise money for the community and local conservation projects. Age limit applies.
🕐 Daily 7–2 💵 $6

Sports and Activities

ACTIVITIES

DAWSON CITY
KODIAK WILDERNESS TOURS
Box 248, Dawson City, Yukon, Y0B 1G0
Tel 867/993-6333
www.kodiaktours.ca
You can build your own trip with this company, run by local guides who'll take you out on quads, by riverboat or canoe, and in winter by snowmobile, to explore the wild north.
🕐 Year-round 💵 Depends on the package you want

TOP OF THE WORLD GOLF COURSE
Dawson City, Yukon
Tel 867/993-5888
www.topoftheworldgolf.com
Canada's most northerly course with grass greens has nine challenging holes amid rugged scenery. Hazards may include old mining equipment and moose. Driving range, pro shop, cart and club rentals.
🕐 Depends on weather; no tee-time reservations required; 24-hour daylight in high summer

WHITEHORSE
KANOE PEOPLE
P.O. Box 5152, Whitehorse, Yukon, Y1A 4S3
Tel 867/668-4899
www.kanoepeople.com
Experts here make sure you get just what you need for a canoe trip: suitable craft, dry bags, coolers, cooking equipment, and bear repellent spray. Then they get it, and you, to your starting point.
🕐 Daily 9–6 mid-May to mid-Sep; call for information about winter tours 💵 From $25 a day, plus optional insurance ❓ Transportation can be provided to put-in or pick-up point 🚐 First Avenue and Strickland Street, on the Yukon River

MEADOW LAKES GOLF COURSE
Whitehorse, Yukon
Tel 867/668-4653
Public nine-hole, par 36 course of 1,756–2,548m (1,930–2,800yds), designed for target

golfers, with lots of hazards, but suitable for beginners too. Wonderful views, practice areas, pro shop and rentals.
🕐 Year-round, weather and light permitting 🚐 South of Whitehorse on Alaska Highway

YUKON CONSERVATION SOCIETY
302 Hawkins Street, Whitehorse, Yukon, Y1A 1X6
Tel 867/668-5678
www.yukonconservation.org
A variety of hikes with YCS trail guides, including easy two-hour walks to the Yukon Fish Ladder or Canyon City, day-long hikes up Grey Mountain or through forests to visit remote lakes.
🕐 Tue–Sat, starting 10am, 2 or 3pm, Jul–Aug; phone for details. Office: Mon–Fri 10–2 💵 Free 🚐 Most hikes meet at YCS office in Whitehorse; Canyon City Hike meets at Miles Canyon suspension bridge

YUKON ESCAPES
4158 4th Avenue, Whitehorse, Yukon
Tel 867/668-6005
www.yukonescapes.com
Ice fishing is just one of many tours organized by this company. You get a snowmobile driving lesson, then head out with your guide on a scenic route before cutting a hole in a frozen lake and fishing through the ice.
🕐 Year-round for various tours; this one depends on weather 💵 $200 includes lunch and beverages, but not fishing license; $1,000 damage deposit ❓ Door-to-door service offered from your accommodations

YELLOWKNIFE
AURORA VILLAGE
Box 1827, Aurora Village, Yellowknife, Northern Territories, X1A 2P4
Tel 867/669-0006
www.auroravillage.com
A winter experience, based at an authentic tepee village, offering a taste of First Nations life. Various packages include dogsledding, snowmobiling, ice fishing, snowshoeing, wildlife flight tours, and aurora borealis viewing. Winter clothing for rent.
🕐 Late Nov–mid-Apr 💵 Packages start at $78 🚐 Pick-up from Yellowknife included

Children

GOLDBOTTOM MINE TOURS
Hunker Creek Road, Dawson City,
Yukon, Y0B 1G0
Tel 867/993-5023
www.goldbottom.com
Finding a glittering fragment of
gold among the gravel evokes
the excitement of the Gold
Rush. You get a tour with
guides who tell lots of fascinating stories before they let you
loose on the creek. You keep
what you pan, and you might
even see bear or moose. Wear
sturdy footwear.
🕐 Daily 11–7, Jun until freeze-up
💰 Panning: $2 per hour ($5 for guaranteed gold). Tour and panning: $15
($25 including bus from Dawson City)
🚌 Shuttle from Dawson City 🚗 East
of Dawson City, 15km (9 miles) south
of intersection of Klondike Highway
North and Hunker Creek Road

BERINGIA
Km 1,473 Alaska Highway, Whitehorse,
Yukon, Y1A 2C6
Tel 867/667-8855
www.beringia.com

This unique interpretive center
about animals that roamed
Beringia 40,000 years ago is
full of models, skeletons and
dioramas of strange-looking
creatures—the 4m-high (13ft)
woolly mammoth, the 3m-long
(10ft) giant sloth, scimitar cat,
yesterday's camel, American
lion, giant beaver and many
more. There are also displays
about early First Nations, and
a movie theater.
🕐 Daily 8.30–7, Jun–Aug; 9–6, mid-
May–Jun and Sep; Sun 1–5 or by
appointment rest of year 💰 Adult $6,

child (6 and over) $4 🚗 Next to
Whitehorse International Airport
🍴 Light refreshments and drinks

BLUE KENNELS
Box 31523, Whitehorse, Yukon, Y1A 6K8
Tel 867/633-2219
www.bluekennels.de

A dogsled trip is one of the
ultimate Canadian experi-
ences, and not just a winter
activity. In summer, to keep the
dogs fit and in training, they
pull buggies instead. You can
help put the huskies into their
harnesses, and after the trip
there's a barbecue.
🕐 Call for details 💰 $25 ($35 including barbecue) 🚗 50km (31 miles) west
of Whitehorse at km1,530 (mile 956)
on Alaska Highway

YUKON CONSERVATION SOCIETY
302 Hawkins Street, Whitehorse, Yukon,
Y1A 1X6
Tel 867/668-5678
www.yukonconservation.org
Two-hour hikes are specially
designed for families, so that
parents and children can share
the natural wonders of the
north in the expert company of
YCS trail guides. Tuesday hikes
are for four- to six-year-olds,
while Thursdays are aimed at
seven- to ten-year-olds.
🕐 Tue and Thu 1–3pm, Jul–Aug.
Office: Mon–Fri 10–2 💰 Free

YUKON WILDLIFE PRESERVE
Box 31429, Whitehorse, Yukon, Y1A 6K8
Tel 867/668-3225
Caribou, moose, Dall sheep,
musk oxen and other animals
roam relatively freely in their
natural habitat, which is as
close as you'll get to a real
wildlife experience. Sadly, the
preserve is struggling for finan-

cial support and faces an
uncertain future.
🕐 Daily, mid-May to mid-Sep 🚗 At
km8 (mile 5) on Takhini Hot Springs
Road, 25 minutes north of Whitehorse

Festivals and Events

**YUKON QUEST INTERNATIONAL
SLED DOG RACE**
Whitehorse, Yukon
Tel 867/668-4711,
www.yukonquest.com

A 1,637km (1,023-mile) race
between Whitehorse and
Fairbanks (Alaska), alternating
in direction each year.
Between 20 and 40 teams
complete, and Whitehorse,
Braeburn, Carmacks, Pelly
Crossing, and Dawson City are
good viewing places.

**YUKON INTERNATIONAL
STORYTELLING FESTIVAL**
Whitehorse, Yukon
Tel 867/633-7550
www.yukonstory.com
The third-largest festival of its
kind in the world, gathering
together storytellers from
many countries.

KITIKMEOT NORTHERN GAMES
Kitikmeot Region, Nunavut
Tel 867/979-6551 (Nunavut Tourism)
www.nunavuttourism.com
You can witness the intense
competition as entrants from
across the region compete in
traditional and modern games
over three days. The event also
includes a northern feast.
Locations change each year.

WHAT TO DO

The eight driving tours and 12 walks in this chapter explore Canada's National Parks, scenic areas and major cities. Their locations are marked on the map on page 254. In each area, the walk starts from a point on a driving tour (except those within cities), and are marked by a red star on the tour map. Walks follow well-trodden, waymarked paths, or most interesting parts of a city.

Out and About

The map below shows the starting points of the driving and walking tours featured in this section of the book. Each driving tour also has a route map on the relevant page.

Beaufort Sea

DK

IS

USA

Dawson

Arctic Circle

Davis Strait

Labrador Sea

20 19
Whitehorse

Yellowknife

Nain

Goose Bay

Fort Smith

Churchill

Hudson Bay

Chisasibi

St John's

2

Hazelton

Peace River

Lynn Lake

Prince Rupert

Prince George

Edmonton

13 12

QUÉBEC CITY

5
7

6

3

1

14 15 **CALGARY**

Prince Albert

4

18 17
VANCOUVER

Medicine Hat

16

WINNIPEG

Thunder Bay

MONTRÉAL

Saint John

Halifax

8

OTTAWA

9

TORONTO

USA

Windsor

10 11

Walks and drives lead to spectacular viewpoints, such as this one at Peyto Lake, Banff National Park

OUT AND ABOUT

BEAUTIFUL BONNE BAY DRIVE, NEWFOUNDLAND

Stretching deep inland from the Gulf of St. Lawrence, Bonne Bay is surrounded by the Long Range Mountains and Tablelands of Gros Morne National Park. Because of the bay's rich and diverse variety of organisms, Newfoundland's Memorial University has operated a marine biology research laboratory at Norris Point since 1970. The bay penetrates inland and divides into two sections; choose between driving the north side or the south, or do both.

THE DRIVE

Distance: north side 39km (24 miles); south side 52km (32 miles)

Allow: A half-day for each drive

Start: Wiltondale

End: North side drive at Lobster Cove Head Lighthouse, Rocky Harbour; south side drive at Trout River Pond

How to get there: Turn off the Trans-Canada Highway onto Route 422 at Deer Lake, for west coast of Newfoundland

NORTH SIDE DRIVE

From Wiltondale, take Route 430 north in the direction of Gros Morne National Park. The highway climbs steeply and, after 13km (8 miles), there is a view of Bonne Bay below.

The waters of Bonne Bay glow with the colors of sunset

❶ The mountains drop straight into this fiord, which is over 200m (700ft) deep. It has two main arms—the east, which is beside you, and the south—connected by a narrow strait of water known as a "tickle" hereabouts.

Drive 14km (9 miles) to reach an excellent place on the left to stop and admire the bay.

❷ From here, on a clear day, Gros Morne Mountain is visible to your right.

Continue for 5km (3 miles) and you will see a parking area for hikers wishing to scale Gros Morne. This is a tough climb that takes about eight hours. After another 2km (1.2 miles) you will reach the visitor center.

❸ In addition to background information on the park, the center *(daily, May–Oct; other times by appointment)* has several interesting videos explaining the park's outstanding geology.

From here, there's a detour to Norris Point (8km/5 miles), with a spectacular viewpoint on the right 2km (1.2 miles) after taking the turning. You can see the Tablelands across the water. After crossing a narrow isthmus, you will arrive at the water's edge.

❹ The Bonne Bay Marine Station here offers displays and interpretive programs in the summer months. There are also boat tours and a water taxi service to Woody Point.

Return to Route 430. Drive 4km (2.5 miles) from the visitor center to Rocky Harbour. Take a left turn off Route 430 and drive 1km (0.5 mile) to Salmon Point (you may see whales, if you're lucky). A further 1km (0.5 mile) takes you to Lobster Cove Head Lighthouse. Park and walk (five minutes) to the lighthouse.

❺ The lighthouse has been a beacon to shipping since 1897. The old lightkeeper's house *(Jun–Sep)* has displays on the lives of the people who have lived on this coast for the last 4,000 years.

WHEN TO GO

Late summer is best for weather, but there's more chance of spotting whales earlier in the year. December brings the caribou down from the Tablelands, and they are often seen, along with moose, on the roadsides.

WHERE TO EAT

Fisherman's Landing Restaurant, Rocky Harbour, tel: 709/458-2060.

WHERE TO STAY

Wildflowers Bed-and-Breakfast, Main Street North, Rocky Harbour, tel: 709/458-3000.

The watery landscape along the South Side Drive

OUT AND ABOUT

Woody Point Cemetery, a more scenic last resting place would be hard to find

SOUTH SIDE DRIVE

From Wiltondale, take Route 431 and follow signs for Woody Point and Trout River. After 10km (6 miles) you will cross the Lomond River and enter the Gros Morne National Park. After another 3km (2 miles), turn right and continue for 4km (2.5 miles) to Lomond.

❶ This former logging community is a great place to stop for a picnic, or even a quick dip (although the water is too cold to stay in for long).

Return to Route 431. You will climb steeply up the "Struggle" for 7km (4 miles) to the top.

❷ From this viewpoint there is an impressive view of the Tablelands over the top of the Peak of Teneriffe. Their orange-rust color is in marked contrast with the deep green elsewhere.

Continue on Route 431 for 5km (3 miles), enjoying views of

Glenburnie and the other small communities. Beyond Glenburnie, the road follows the eastern shore, with views of the surrounding hills and Woody Point up front.

❸ In early summer, whales are sometimes seen here chasing schools of capelin, herring and mackerel.

Drive 9km (5 miles) beyond Glenburnie, taking the detour off Route 431 into Woody Point.

❹ The community of Woody Point was once the hub of the fishing and lumbering industries around Bonne Bay; it's fine old homes recall the wealth of those days.

Return to Route 431, drive 1km (0.5 mile) from Woody Point to the Discovery Centre.

❺ Displays at the Discovery Centre *(daily, May–Oct)* explain the interesting geological phenomena of the Gros Morne National Park, which was declared a World Heritage Site in 1987.

Continue for another 6km (4 miles) beyond the Discovery Centre and you come to the Tablelands Walk.

❻ On the drive here from the Discovery Centre, notice the difference between the ocher-colored Tablelands and Winterhouse Brook Canyon to your left, and the green valley ahead and to your right. The road marks the division between these two geological formations.

As you continue, there are views ahead of the Gulf of St. Lawrence

Glenburnie, within the national park, has some fine buildings (above). Fishing has been a vital part of Newfoundland's heritage for centuries. Fishing boats (right) on the Trout River

Lobster Cove Head Lighthouse (below), with its array of flags (right), is the distinctive destination of the North Side Drive

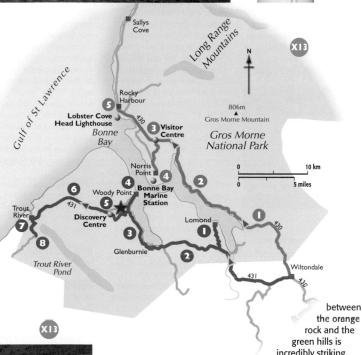

X13

between the orange rock and the green hills is incredibly striking. There are boat tours on Trout River Pond *(mid-Jun to mid-Sep)*.

as the road descends to Trout River, which lies 12km (7 miles) from Tablelands.

❼ Trout River has an active fishing industry. Notice the black volcanic rock all around.

Some 2km (1.2 miles) along on the road to the campground, is Viewpoint Trout River Pond.

❽ Here you get a magnificent view of this long narrow fiord set between the Tablelands and the Gregory Plateau Hills. Again, the contrast in color

WHEN TO GO
Bright, sunny days highlight the colors; avoid winter if you want to visit the Discovery Centre—it's closed November through April.

WHERE TO EAT
Tabletop Eatery, Discovery Centre, Woody Point, tel: 709/453-2452.

WHERE TO STAY
Crocker Cabins, 57–61 Duke Street, Trout River, tel: 709/451-3236.

A WALK ON THE EARTH'S MANTLE

This unique walk on flat-topped and almost barren ocher-colored rock, never usually seen at the earth's surface, is in Newfoundland's Gros Morne Tablelands. Composed of peridotite from the earth's mantle, the Tablelands record a time when the continents of Eurasia and North America collided. Formed far below the ocean floor, they were transported hundreds of kilometers to their present position some 450 million years ago. Gros Morne National Park (see page 61) was placed on UNESCO's World Heritage List because of the importance of its geological features.

THE WALK

Distance: 4km (2.5 miles)

Allow: 1–2 hours

Start and end: in the parking area on Highway 431, 5km (3 miles) from the Discovery Centre in Woody Point (direction Trout River)

Ascent: about 60m (200ft)

How to get there: Gros Morne is in the west of Newfoundland. Turn off the Trans-Canada Highway onto Route 422 at Deer Lake, then Route 431 from Wiltondale

After reading explanatory panels about the geology of the area, begin your walk. You will soon pass a second trail—part of a 500m (540yd) loop, which can be made by those not wishing to walk the whole trail (take this loop on your return). Much of the trail, except the last section, follows an old gravel roadbed, so it's reasonably flat and easy.

The path is marked by stones, and you should not wander off it—with little vegetation, it is hard to judge distances (and heights) in the Tablelands. What looks like a short, flat and easy hike can actually be a long, hard struggle over jumbled boulders.

The ocher-colored rock here is virtually devoid of vegetation—almost desert-like. Peridotite weathers from a dark green to the rusty brown you see around you as oxygen reacts with the iron in the rock. The twisted and gnarled larch trees and alders growing here are small but they are hundreds of years old.

Continue about 1km (0.5 mile).

To your right and high above you, a deep, steep-walled basin can be made out in the mountainside. Known as a cirque, it's a remnant of retreating glaciers and is best viewed from the largish bridge over the stream flowing from it. Along the trail you will cross many streams by boardwalk bridges. At dusk or in foggy weather, take particular care—it's easy to miss your footing.

Soon afterward, to the left there's a splendid view of the verdant South Arm of Bonne Bay below. After about 1.5km (1 mile), the path leaves the old roadway and bears right, marked by man-made stone ridges. After 2km (1.2 miles), you will reach the bottom of Winterhouse Canyon, from which the Winterhouse Brook issues.

This is a lovely place to sit on the rocks and have a picnic. Note the rocks in the stream bed, with surfaces resembling snake skin. This is peridotite which has reacted to the passage of water by breaking up into a series of tiny cracks. You can walk farther into the canyon but there is no trail and the going is rough.

Return by the same route. Just before reaching the parking area, which you can see ahead, you can follow the alternative loop trail mentioned at the start.

This loop enables you to appreciate some of the plants that have managed to adapt and grow in this very harsh environment. The pitcher plant consumes insects to make up for the nutrient-poor soil; the yellow lady's slipper grows beside streams where it can benefit from the calcium leaching out of the rock. You will also see Arctic plants, which are at the southern limit of their growing range here.

WHEN TO GO

During the national park's Summer Interpretation Program (late Jun–early Sep), when wardens lead guided tours.

PUBLIC RESTROOMS

None.

WHERE TO EAT

Tabletop Eatery, Discovery Centre, Woody Point, tel: 709/453-2452.

WHERE TO STAY

Victorian Manor Heritage Properties, Main Road, Woody Point, tel: 709/453-2485.

The Tableland rocks (below) have great geological importance, and wild flowers (top left) add color. The footbridge (right) takes walkers across a river in the Tablelands

OUT AND ABOUT

DRIVE THE CABOT TRAIL

The Cabot Trail, in the northern part of Cape Breton Island in Nova Scotia, is named after an Italian explorer who is said to have landed at its northern tip in 1497. Hugging the coast, the road winds up and down, with fine views of ocean, craggy mountains, rocky inlets and dense forests. Along the way, look for moose, bald eagles, whales and a multitude of seabirds.

Distance: 292km (181 miles)

Allow: 2 days

Start and end: Baddeck

How to get there: From the Canso Causeway, take Trans-Canada 105 east to Baddeck.

Warning: Cape Breton, especially the Atlantic coast, is well known for its fogs. Switchbacks and almost dizzying changes of altitude can make the drive hazardous; it is not for the faint of heart.

Drive west from Baddeck (see page 59) on Trans-Canada Highway 105 toward Canso Causeway, along the shore of Bras d'Or Lake. After 8km (5 miles), at Nyanza, turn right on the Cabot Trail. Drive 52km (32 miles) and the Margaree River and harbor come into view.

❶ You follow the Margaree River through mostly agricultural country, and you'll cross the river, driving north on the undulating Gulf Coast. After crossing the river, all the village names are French and you'll definitely see the tricolor Acadian flag along the way.

After driving another 24km (15 miles), you'll come to Chéticamp.

❷ Chéticamp is a sprawling fishing village, along the coast opposite the island that protects the harbor. At 15067 Main Street, close to the Roman Catholic church of St-Pierre, is the Coopérative Artisanale Acadienne *(daily, mid-May to mid-Oct; Tue–Thu pm, rest of year)*. The community is famous for its handmade hooked rugs and mats, and the co-op offers a good selection. There's also a restaurant and a small museum, where visitors can watch demonstrations of this craft *(daily mid-May to mid-Oct)*.

Drive on 8km (5 miles) to enter Cape Breton Highlands National Park. This is one of the most spectacular parts of the drive, but the road is very steep and winding in some places, with frequent switchbacks.

❸ If you drive the trail between May and October, stop at the Information Centre at the park entrance to buy a permit *(adult $5, child ages 6–16 $2.50, family $12.50)*. Take time here to view the interesting exhibitions and videos, and browse around the excellent bookstore *(daily mid-May to mid-Oct)*.

At regular intervals on the route you'll find turnouts (pull-offs, or lay-bys) where you can stop and admire the views of the Gulf of St. Lawrence or take one of the walks that lead off the highway. The drive climbs 455m (1,493ft) up French Mountain, followed by 355m (1,165ft) up Mackenzie Mountain—the switchback descent from here is particularly dramatic, with views along the coast to Pleasant Bay. Drive 14km (9 miles) beyond Pleasant Bay to the Lone Shieling (parking on right).

❹ The short but rewarding 15- to 20-minute walk to the Lone Shieling, a stone cottage, is through maple forest beside a stream. The tiny cottage itself is a replica of a Scottish sheep crofter's hut common to the Highlands and islands of Scotland. It is a tribute to the many Scots who settled in this area after the terrible Highland Clearances in Scotland in the 18th and 19th centuries.

There are fine views as you enter the valley of the North Aspy River and as you descend to the village of Cape North on Aspy Bay. The next section of the Cabot Trail is far less scenic, being inland, but there is a very good chance that you'll see moose, especially in early morning or evening. After 34km (21 miles), there's a detour to Neil's Harbour.

❺ The 2km (1.2-mile) detour into Neil's Harbour takes you to this attractive fishing village and its sandy bay. Park by the lighthouse.

Return to the Cabot Trail and drive 6km (4 miles) to Black Brook Cove (park and walk to the beach).

❻ This scenic spot has pink granite rocks stretching into the sea, contrasting with the lush green forest that clads the hillsides inland. If you have time, walk along the coast. Strung along the next 20km (12 miles) or so of the Cabot Trail around North Bay and Ingonish Harbour, is a series of communities that together form a resort area popular for fishing, swimming, boating, golf, and whale-watching.

Continue your drive beyond Middle Head for 7km (4 miles) to Cape Smokey, which rises 366m (1,200ft) out of the sea.

❼ The trail climbs steeply up Cape Smokey. From the lookout at the summit, the view is one of the most dramatic along the whole of the drive. The descent, a series of vertiginous switchbacks, returns to sea-level and continues south along the Gaelic Coast. Offshore are the Bird Islands, a sanctuary where vast numbers of seabirds nest in summer.

Remain on the Cabot Trail and follow the winding shoreline of St. Ann's Bay to South Gut St. Ann's, or take the scenic alternative on Route 312 along a narrow spit of land, then cross St. Ann's Bay by a two-minute ferry ride *(cars $3)* across the narrow outlet to join Trans-Canada Highway 105 and the Cabot Trail. After joining Trans-Canada Highway 105, turn right and continue for 19km (12 miles) for the return to Baddeck.

OUT AND ABOUT

WHEN TO GO
It's good in all seasons if you avoid the foggy days, but summer is best for whale-spotting.

WHERE TO EAT
Rusty Anchor, Pleasant Bay, Cape Breton, tel: 902/224 1313.

Whales break the waters around Cape Breton, and bald eagles swoop down for fish (below left). The glorious coastline (right and bottom) is one of the most spectacular in the world

WHERE TO STAY
Inverary Resort, 368 Shore Road, Baddeck, tel: 902/295-3500; Bellefontaine Bed-and-Breakfast, 606 Belle Marche Road, Cheticamp, tel: 902/224-1224.

OUT AND ABOUT

MIDDLE HEAD ON THE CABOT TRAIL

Middle Head, in Cape Breton, Nova Scotia, is a long, narrow protrusion into the Atlantic Ocean. It separates North Bay from Ingonish Harbour and offers fabulous views of the rocky coast and mountains. In 1890, Henry Corson, a friend of inventor Alexander Graham Bell, built a house here after discovering this area while staying with Bell in Baddeck (see page 59). His home became part of the national park in 1938 and, in 1951, it was replaced by Keltic Lodge, a fine hotel that's run by the provincial government of Nova Scotia.

THE WALK

Distance: 4km (2.5 miles)

Allow: about 2 hours

Start and end: Parking area signed "Trail No. 25 Middle Head" just beyond Keltic Lodge.

How to get there: From the Canso Causeway, take Trans-Canada 105 through Baddeck, then turn left onto the Cabot Trail at South Gut St. Ann's or reach it via the Englishtown ferry. Drive north toward Ingonish Beach (88km/55 miles from Baddeck). Follow signs for Keltic Lodge, pass the lodge and park in designated area.

Warning: The cliffs at the tip are extremely steep and mists can descend quickly. Take care with children.

At the beginning of the trail, note the old gate posts—this was once a carriage road linking a country estate with summer fishing shacks, and the gates kept the cows from wandering along the trail. The path goes up and down, with viewpoints of Cape Smokey across Ingonish Harbour on the right. After 1km (0.5 mile) you come to Trail Junction, an alternative route that you can take on your return. After a steep descent with views ahead of the tip of the peninsula, you will reach the narrowest section of the headland. There are superb views in both directions—to Ingonish Island in North Bay to the left, and across Ingonish Harbour to the right.

Until fairly recently, there were fishermen's shacks here, along with nets, traps and drying racks. These have all been gone since the 1980s, as have the cod that were fished.

The path continues up and down, with several lookouts and benches where you can pause to rest and enjoy the surroundings. The forest of mainly beech trees gives way to dense fir on the approach to the tip of the peninsula.

In addition to the trees, other plants here include creeping juniper, black crowberry and stunted white spruce. In the winter, the wild Atlantic winds batter this peninsula, and the salt-laden fog and rain flow over the cliffs, permeating the thin soil. Plants really need to cling on to survive.

After about 1.5km (1 mile) you come to Trail Junction No. 2, which you can follow on the return. Several paths lead from here to the cliffs at the end of Middle Head, which drop abruptly to the sea.

A plaque marks the official end of the trail. The cliffs are very impressive, with great Atlantic breakers crashing in far below. This is a very wild place and can be dangerous, as mists can descend very fast.

Return to the trail you passed earlier. A very short walk leads to a lookout at the tip of the peninsula, this time on the North Bay side.

This is where seabirds nest in spring (see When to Go,

The rocky Atlantic coast of Cape Breton provides magnificent vistas along the walk

OUT AND ABOUT

Keltic Lodge has a wonderful view (above) of the wooded coastline that stretches toward Ingonish

below). You will see great cormorants, black guillemots, common terns and great black-backed gulls. Explanatory panels are positioned to help you identify each species. Occasionally, pods of whales, dolphins and seals can be seen breaking the waves offshore. In addition, the national park is home to moose, black bear, coyote, fox, and bald eagles.

Retrace your steps to the narrow section and climb the steep slope to the trail junction. About 500m (540yd) along, is an alternative route, which is slightly longer.

This route offers great views of North Bay and barren Ingonish Island, which is topped by a lighthouse. The island is another nesting area for birds, and in 1976 it was the site of an important archeological find. Basalt chippings were found, which were the residue of centuries of spear- and arrow-point production by the Mi'kmaq. These finds have been dated as early as 9000BC, and were used to spear fish and shellfish.

Return to the parking area.

WHEN TO GO
The trail is closed in springtime, when seabirds are nesting on the cliffs. At other times, try to choose a day when the notorious Atlantic fog is unlikely to roll in off the ocean. In the fall, the foliage colors are beautiful, and this, combined with the Celtic Colours Festival, makes October a good time to be here. The information center at Ingonish is only open mid-May to mid-October.

PUBLIC RESTROOMS
At Keltic Lodge.

WHERE TO EAT
Atlantic Restaurant or Purple Thistle Room, Keltic Lodge, Middle Head Peninsula, Ingonish Beach, tel: 902/285-2880.

WHERE TO STAY
Keltic Lodge, Middle Head Peninsula, Ingonish Beach, tel: 902/285-2880. Castle Rock Country Inn, 39339 Cabot Trail, Ingonish Ferry, tel: 902/285-2700.

SOME PARK REGULATIONS
Consult on-site publications and important safety messages, and, in order to protect the environment and ensure your own safety, keep the following national park rules in mind:

It is illegal to disturb or collect any natural, cultural or historic objects, including rocks, driftwood, plants or animals.
Feeding, touching, enticing, or hunting any wildlife is unlawful, and these activities place not only the animals at risk, but you as well.
Store all food in the trunk of your car (where it won't attract the attention of animals) and do not drop litter—it harms wildlife, spoils the view and is subject to a $2,000 fine.
Gathering twigs, branches, bark, and dead wood for firewood is prohibited.
Stay on established trails to avoid trampling vegetation.
Pets are welcome (except on swimming beaches), but must be kept on a leash at all times and droppings must be picked up, even in remote areas.

Cormorants are among the seabirds found on this coast

OUT AND ABOUT

THE RESPLENDENT GASPÉ PENINSULA

This drive offers some of the most dramatic landscapes in all of Québec, including the extraordinary cliffs of Forillon National Park, and culminates in the scenic wonder of Percé. The native peoples, the Mi'kmaq, called it *gespeq*, meaning "end of land."

THE DRIVE

Distance: 237km (147 miles)

Allow: 2 days if possible

Start: Just before Grande-Vallée on the north shore.

End: Grande-Rivière on the south shore on Highway 132.

How to get there: The start point is on Highway 132.

Just before Route 132 descends into Grande-Vallée, there is a turnout (pull-off, or lay-by) with a fine view of the town nestled around its bay. Route 132 winds up and down, sometimes at water level, sometimes high above it. Drive 64km (40 miles) to Rivière-au-Renard.

❶ Rivière-au-Renard is the most important fishing community of Gaspésie. There are commercial wharves, fish-processing plants and an impressive fishing fleet. Today, shellfish dominates the market.

Continue 6km (4 miles). You will pass an information office for Forillon National Park on the right. If you intend to spend time in the park you must purchase a daily permit *(May–Oct)*. About 10km (6 miles) from Rivière-au-Renard is L'Anse-au-Griffon.

❷ This small fishing community's name may come from a ship, the *Griffon,* or it may refer to the gray color of the seabed—*gris fonds.* As you drive through, notice the large yellow clapboard house on the right. The Manoir LeBouthillier was built in the 1850s by John LeBouthillier, a wealthy cod merchant and exporter from Jersey, in the Channel Islands. This was a secondary home, where he stayed on business trips, and is open to the public *(daily, Jun–mid-Oct).*

Some 11km (7 miles) farther on is Cap-des-Rosiers.

❸ Stop at the lighthouse, Canada's tallest, for views of Cap Bon Ami and Cap Gaspé.

It stands in a park with picnic tables and other amenities.

After leaving Cap-des-Rosiers, you enter Forillon National Park.

❹ This wonderful park is like a huge tilted block rising from the sea. Shaped by erosion, it has a rugged coastline of sheer limestone. It is worth detouring to the Interpretive Centre, 2km (1.2 miles) along the Cap Bon Ami road.

Continue on Route 132 across the peninsula. The mountains are part of the Appalachian chain, which starts far to the south in Alabama, USA. The final 50km (31 miles) of the International Appalachian Trail cross the park to end at Cap Gaspé.

❺ About 8km (5 miles) farther on, you will get a sudden view of the Baie de Gaspé and beyond, toward Percé. If it is clear, you may be able to distinguish the famous rock.

Continue 11km (7 miles) to Penouille Peninsula and the Information Centre.

❻ This sandy protrusion into the bay boasts the best beach in the area. You can walk or bicycle (no cars allowed) along the 4km (2-mile) trail or take the small train *(modest fee).*

Route 132 leaves Forillon National Park and detours around the Baie de Gaspé crossing the Dartmouth River at its mouth by a long bridge. After driving 20km (12 miles) from Penouille (or 42km/26 miles from Cap-des-Rosiers) you will reach Gaspé.

❼ Gaspé, the administrative and commercial hub of the peninsula, has a fine site on a hillside sloping down to the York River where it joins the Dartmouth River as it widens out to become the Baie de Gaspé. The town is dominated

by a former religious building, which today houses the hospital.

Leave Gaspé by the bridge over the York River and then turn left, keeping on Route 132. (Be careful not to take the straighter and faster Route 198.) After 48km (30 miles), at Pointe-St-Pierre, take rue du Quai, on the left opposite the white episcopal church, for a short distance to the water's edge for a view of the famous rock at Percé. Slowly, Rocher Percé disappears from view and you begin your entry to Percé by a steep, winding, undulating route over about 6km (4 miles). Percé is 29km (18 miles) from Pointe-St-Pierre.

❽ Renowned for its beauty, Percé is the scenic culmination of the Gaspé Peninsula. Most famous of all is the great pierced rock that gave the town its name. Rocher Percé is a huge limestone block 438m (1,437ft) long and 88m (289ft) high, which was formed by layers of sediment deposited on the seabed about 375 million years ago. Until 1848, it had two arches. Then one of them collapsed, leaving just one hole and a separate block known as the Obelisk. You can park in the town and walk out (at low tide) to the rock. There are fine views from all of Percé's headlands, but the best is the one from the top of the craggy red peak that dominates the town. You can hike to the top of Mont-Ste-Anne (see pages 266–267). Don't miss the boat tour to Bonaventure Island (see page 97). Information is available from the tourist office on the main street.

Drive 9km (5.5 miles) from Percé to L'Anse-à-Beaufils.

❾ This small community has a general store, built in 1928, which still has its original wainscoting (paneling) and a

OUT AND ABOUT

collection of the tools that were used in an earlier age *(mid-June to mid-Sep)*.

Continue 7km (4 miles) to reach Cap d'Espoir, the last place with a view of Percé. The coast begins to swing west. Some 16km (10 miles) farther on is Grande-Rivière, where the drive ends.

WHEN TO GO

Boats only cross to Bonaventure Island from June to mid-October; Percé is splendid year-round, but can get overcrowded in high season.

Homes on the Rivière-au-Renard (below). A waterfall (right) in the Forillon National Park

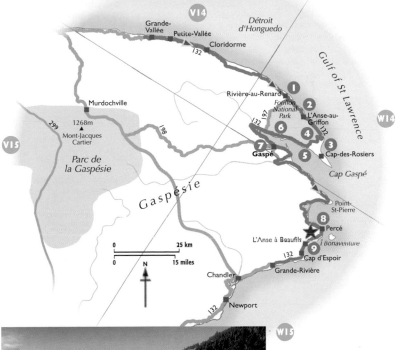

WHERE TO EAT

Restaurant de la Vallée, 44 St-François-Xavier O, Grande-Vallée, tel: 418/393-2880. Adams Restaurant, 20 rue Adams, Gaspé, tel: 418/368-4949.

WHERE TO STAY

Motel Atlantique, Cap des-Rosiers, Gaspé, tel: 418/892-5533; Motel Adams, 20 rue Adams, Gaspé, tel: 418/368-2244.

Jagged rocks jut out from the coastline of Forillon National Park

PANORAMA FROM MONT-STE-ANNE

The summit of Québec's Mont-Ste-Anne, visible from afar in the Gulf of St. Lawrence, offers magnificent panoramas of the town of Percé, the surrounding area (including Bonaventure Island), and, if conditions are clear, the coast of New Brunswick and Île d'Anticosti. The reddish conglomerate rock dramatically distinguishes it from the limestone of Rocher Percé.

THE WALK

Distance: 5km (3 miles)

Allow: at least 2.5 hours

Start and End: Church of St-Michel-de-Percé, on rue de l'Église.

Ascent: 320m (1,100ft)

How to get there: Take Highway 132 along the north coast of Gaspésie, then follow directions to Percé as detailed in the drive on pages 264–265.

There's some parking next to the church; otherwise town parking areas are not far away. Walk behind the church and follow the rough gravel road signed "Chemin du Mont-Ste-Anne." Walk about 500m (540yd) until you reach a trail intersection; take the left fork. The trail continues to climb steeply. In another 500m (540yd), you come to the Belvédère One viewpoint.

From here there's a splendid view over the town, its famous rock and the stone church from where you set off.

Instead of continuing on the main trail, take the Sentier des Belvédères by the viewpoint on your right. This woodland trail is more pleasant than the main trail, and takes in two more viewpoints.

From Belvédère Two, you can see Bonaventure Island, the famous bird sanctuary (see page 97). From Belvédère Three, the view is much the same as from Belvédère One except that you are higher. The town of Percé below was an important fishing center for many years. The Mi'kmaq came here for the cod, and a French fishing station was established in 1673. It was, however, after the British conquest that development really began. In 1781, Charles Robin came from Jersey and established the Robins

Mont-Ste-Anne's Belvedere One has a spectacular view over the town and Gulf of St. Lawrence

Company to market cod. By 1850, the company owned about 30 buildings, many of which still stand, and by the end of the century, Percé was Canada's cod capital. In 1912 the railway arrived, followed by the road in 1920. These brought tourists, today the lifeblood of Percé since there are practically no cod left.

The Sentier des Belvédères rejoins the main trail, which climbs very steeply. You will get a view of the mountain peak ahead. The trail climbs the north side of the peak; the south side falls away very abruptly. At this point, you seem to be almost directly on top of the *rocher*. Another 1km (0.5 mile) along, you'll see the intersection of the Sentier de la Falaise trail, but continue up the main trail—you can descend by this alternate trail from the summit. The main trail is very obvious, because it is used by vehicles and thus wider

St. Anne's statue atop Mont-Ste-Anne draws pilgrims in summer

and rutted. Some 500m (540yd) along, having climbed 320m (1,050ft), you reach the summit.

The statue of St. Anne here is the focus of pilgrimages in summer, especially on July 26, St. Anne's day. The mountain was a holy place for the native peoples, who talked of "the god on the mountain." The French dedicated the summit to St. Anne, the patron saint of

fishermen, because its height made it a landmark for shipping in the gulf. The view embraces the whole bay, Bonaventure Island and, to your right, the coast of New Brunswick. The land that you can see in front and to the left is the Île d'Anticosti (see page 91).

Take the Sentier de la Falaise trail for the first part of the descent. It is only very slightly longer, and less steep than the road. About 500m (540yd) down, you come to lookouts Belvédères Four and Five, which offer the best views of Percé. You can avoid Belvédère Four and return directly to the main trail if you wish to save a few minutes.

The peninsulas visible below are, right to left: Cap Blanc, Cap Canon, Mont Joli (with a cross), Cap Barré, Les Trois Soeurs (Three Sisters), and the Pic de l'Aurore.

Rejoin the main trail and be prepared for a steep descent. Don't try to do it too quickly and don't look directly down if you suffer from vertigo! On your right, you will pass the beginning and end points of the Sentier des Belvédères and other trails. On the main trail, signs indicate that the descent will be 10 percent over the next section. On reaching the intersection with the Chemin de la Grotte, turn right to return to the church.

WHEN TO GO
Unless you want to join them, avoid the summer pilgrimage days, notably July 26, when the route is crowded with followers.

PUBLIC RESTROOMS
There are wilderness latrines at the summit.

WHERE TO EAT
Café le Croque-Lune, 1623 Route 132 Ouest, Percé, tel: 418/7782-5353. You can purchase food for a picnic at the Boulangerie Le Fournand on Percé's main street (194 Route 132 Ouest).

WHERE TO STAY
Hotel-Motel Manoir de Percé, 212 Route 132 Ouest, Percé, tel: 418/782-2022.

QUÉBEC CITY RAMPARTS

Not only is Québec the oldest city in Canada, it is also North America's only walled city. Strolling around these impressive fortifications is a unique way to appreciate its spendid site, its captivating architecture and its natural beauty.

THE WALK

Distance: 5km (3 miles)

Allow: about 2 hours

Start and end: Place d'Armes in front of the tourist office (Infotouriste) on rue Ste-Anne.

How to get there: Place d'Armes is in the heart of Québec City near the Château Frontenac hotel.

From Infotouriste *(daily)* in Place d'Armes, walk to your right toward the UNESCO monument. Behind it, there is a monument commemorating Samuel de Champlain, founder of Québec in 1608. You are now on the Terrasse Dufferin (see page 90). Walk along it to your right past the top of the cable car (funicular) to the Lower Town, and past the covered pavilions. To your left, beyond the Château Frontenac, is the Jardin du Gouverneurs, with its monument to both Wolfe and Montcalm. Cross the end of the toboggan slide to rue des Carrières and take the Escalier de la Terrasse up 65 steps to rue St-Denis (there's a big sign for Parc des Champs de Bataille) to reach the slopes of the Citadelle.

Climb about another 50 steps for a really splendid view. High above the river and town, this is a great place to sit and picnic, especially on hot summer evenings. You can look down into the outer moat of this formidable defense fortress whose construction began in 1820 on the orders of the Duke of Wellington.

Follow the star-shape of the Citadelle, to your right, to the main entrance, which you will see below you. Cross the entrance road—Côte de la Citadelle—using the pedestrian bridge. Bear right to follow the city walls.

You might prefer to walk just inside the walls rather than on top of them—although this is possible, the walls are

The Château Frontenac Hotel overlooks Terrasse Dufferin

regularly pierced by gun emplacements (there are no guns in them), and you have to jump a metre or more over them. There are views ahead (outside the walls) of the Québec Parliament building and the Cross of Sacrifice, a memorial to Canadians who lost their lives in World War I. It was inaugurated in 1924.

You then come to Porte St-Louis (St-Louis Gate), which is one of the three picturesque gates that were built into the walls between 1878 and 1881. You can cross rue St-Louis on top of the wall or you can descend to the street to visit the Fortifications of Québec Initiation Centre *(summer months only)*. Return to the walls and continue your walk along the top.

To your left is the Québec Parliament and the site where the Ice Palace is constructed every February for the Québec winter Carnaval. To your right is the Québec Esplanade, once a military parade ground but now a children's playground.

Next you come to Porte Kent (Kent Gate), which you can use as a bridge to cross rue Dauphine.

This gate is named after the Duke of Kent, father of Queen Victoria, who lived nearby when he was Governor General of Canada 1792–94.

The wall and path descend to Porte St-Jean (St. Jean Gate), crossing rue St-Jean as it exits the Upper Town and becomes Place d'Youville, to your left.

Note the restored Théâtre Capitole. The first silent movies were shown here as well as the first "talkies" in the early 1930s.

You can descend into Parc de l'Artillerie (Artillery Park) after crossing the Porte St-Jean.

This section of the Upper Town just inside the walls contains a series of buildings originally used for military purposes and later for the manufacture of armaments. Until World War II, this was the Canadian Arsenal in Québec. To your right, a brick former armaments building today houses an interpretive center *(summer months)*.

Cross rue Richelieu. Parc de l'Artillerie continues with the Dauphine Redoubt *(summer months)*, to your right.

Built in 1712–48, it was part of the defense system that Governor Frontenac put in place in case the city was attacked from the west. It was later used by British troops and then became a munitions factory in 1882.

Follow the walls and descend the steps. Cross Côte-du-Palais. The buildings of the Hôtel-Dieu loom large ahead to the right. Continue to follow the walls—you are now on rue des Remparts, which leads around the northeast corner of the walls, offering fine views over the city below. To

OUT AND ABOUT

your right is the Augustinian monastery.

The Augustinian nuns founded the Hôtel-Dieu in 1637, making it the oldest hospital in North America. It's been on this site since 1644.

Rue des Remparts swings to the right beyond rue Hébert, and there are views of the Château Frontenac ahead. Walk into Parc de Montmorency (Montmorency Park) from rue des Remparts.

Montmorency Park was the site of the Canadian Parliament in 1850–66, when the capital alternated between Toronto and Québec. Parliament met in the old Bishop's Palace, and the Québec Conference of 1864 which led to confederation was held there. The palace burned down, and by the time it was rebuilt Parliament had moved

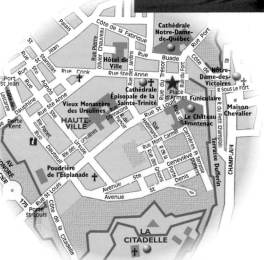

Horse-drawn carriages are a fitting form of transport, along rue St-Louis, one of the lovely old streets in historic Québec City

to Ottawa. It burned down again in 1883.

From the park, take the pedestrian bridge across Côte de la Montagne and climb the 83 steps back to Place d'Armes. A walk into the Haute-Ville (Upper Town) is also possible from here (see map on page 356).

WHEN TO GO
The walk is possible year-round, except in heavy snow; it's superb on a mild summer evening.

PUBLIC RESTROOMS
In tourist office on Place d'Armes.

WHERE TO EAT
Restaurant Gambrinus, 15 rue du Fort, tel: 418/692-5144.

WHERE TO STAY
Le Château de Pierre, 17 avenue Ste-Genevieve, tel: 418/694-0429.

Interesting rooflines around Place d'Armes feature dormer windows, shown here atop a restaurant

OUT AND ABOUT

MONTRÉAL'S OLD CITY AND PORT

Walking around the old quarter of Montréal evokes the days when the tiny French mission struggled for survival, but also provides evidence of the city's phenomenal growth in the 19th century. Highlights include the magnificent Basilique Notre-Dame, the 19th-century buildings of rue Ste-Hélène, and some wonderful viewpoints of the city old and new.

THE WALK

Distance: 3.5km (2 miles)
Allow: 2.5 hours (not including visits)
Start and end: Place d'Armes
How to get there: Take the métro to Place d'Armes station, which is actually two blocks north of the starting point on Place d'Armes.

Start the tour by visiting Basilique Notre-Dame and the Sulpician Seminary, both located on the south side of Place d'Armes.

When it was built in 1829, the Basilique Notre-Dame was the largest church on the North American continent. The interior is gorgeous (see pages 76–77). To the left is the Sulpician Seminary. The rustic building behind the wall is the oldest in the city, built by the Sulpician priests, and is a fine example of fieldstone construction, notable for its dormer windows and clock dating from 1701.

Walk across Place d'Armes to the Bank of Montréal at 119 St-Jacques.

The bank's head office occupies an imposing neo-classical structure built in 1848 by John Wells, inspired by the Pantheon in Rome.

Leave the bank and turn right. Cross St-Jacques to see the Old Royal Bank.

This massive Florentine palace, built in 1928 by York and Sawyer, was the first building in Montréal to rise higher than the towers of Notre-Dame. Go up the stairs into the huge banking hall to see the splendid coffered ceiling. Side rooms have vaulted ceilings decorated with gold leaf.

Turn left after leaving the bank and go left on rue Dollard. Cross Notre-Dame, turn right, then turn left along picturesque rue Ste-Hélène, with its gas lamps and fine stone buildings. Turn left on Lemoyne, then right on St-Pierre, and walk into Place d'Youville to visit the Centre d'Histoire de Montréal at No. 335 and the Youville Stables at No. 298.

Built in 1903, the red-brick building housing the Centre d'Histoire de Montréal was once the Central Fire Station. Now it charts the history of the city with a series of interesting displays. The squat but substantial 1828 Youville Stables were constructed as potash warehouses. Walk through the *porte cochère* into the lovely central courtyard.

Continue along Place d'Youville to Pointe-à-Callière

On May 17, 1642, Montréal was established here, where once the St. Pierre River joined the St. Lawrence River. Construction of the port facilities has pushed the St. Lawrence some distance away and the St. Pierre River has been underneath Place d'Youville since the 19th century. Today, Pointe-à-Callière is dominated by the huge concrete building housing the Musée d'Archéologie et d'Histoire de Montréal (see page 82).

Cross rue de la Commune. Turn right and walk to the entrance to the Vieux Port (where you can cross the railroad). Turn left, and then left again at the Promenade du Vieux-Port to come to the Esplanade du Vieux-Port.

This pleasant park offers a wide variety of attractions, as well as fine views of the city and the river. On the King Edward Pier is the Montréal Science Centre (see page 83).

Continue to Quai Jacques Cartier for more views. Turn left, leave the Vieux Port, and cross rue de la Commune into Place Jacques Cartier.

Lined with outdoor cafés and full of street performers, flower vendors and artists, this street is lively all summer long, especially in the evenings.

Walk along rue St-Paul to your right to visit Marché Bonsecours and then the Chapelle Notre-Dame-de-Bon-Secours.

The impressive stone façade and Renaissance-style dome of the former Bonsecours Market building, built in 1845 by William Footner, today houses an interesting collection of boutiques, craft stores and restaurants. The "sailors' church" of Notre-Dame-de-Bon-Secours (see page 75) has long had a special place in the hearts of Montréalers. Before the expansion of the port necessitated the reclaiming of land behind the church, the statue of the Virgin was a landmark from far downstream. It is worth taking a look inside and visiting the church's museum.

Cross St-Paul and walk up rue Bonsecours on your left. Turn left on rue Notre-Dame, and on your left, at No. 280, is Château Ramezay.

Today, Château Ramezay houses a fascinating museum devoted to the city's history. At the rear of the building, the Jardin du Gouverneurs is cultivated with the types of flowers, fruit and vegetables that would have been grown here during the French regime. Across the street from the garden is the monumental Second Empire Hôtel-de-Ville, Montréal's City Hall. Originally built in 1870, it was rebuilt after a fire in 1922. Above the main entrance is the balcony

OUT AND ABOUT

from which French President Charles de Gaulle made his famous "Vive le Québec libre" speech in 1967.

Walk back to Place d'Armes along rue St-Paul—the oldest street in Montréal, which dates to 1672—and through Cours Le Royer, where old stone warehouses, constructed in 1861–74 are now condominium apartments. This completes the tour.

WHEN TO GO

This is a year-round walk, but it's especially splendid early on a summer evening or on a crisp day in the fall.

Montréal's Place Jacques Cartier is a vibrant area, full of street entertainers and artists. Nearby, horse drawn carriages wait to take visitors around the old city

PUBLIC RESTROOMS

Centre de Commerce Mondial, Bonsecours Market, City Hall.

WHERE TO EAT

Boris Bistro, 465 rue McGill, tel: 514/848-9575. Le Bourlingueur, 363 rue St-François-Xavier, tel: 514/845-3646. Bonaparte, 443 rue St-François-Xavier, tel: 514/844-4368.

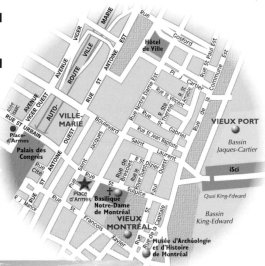

WHERE TO STAY

Auberge du Vieux-Port, 97 rue de la Commune Est, tel: 514/876-0081. Auberge Bonsecours, 353 rue St-Paul Est, tel: 514/396-2662. Hotel du Fort, 1390 rue du Fort, tel: 514/938-8333.

Montréal's Vieux-Port (left) now contains some very modern craft. This statue of Maisonneuve (below left) stands in place d'Armes, at the spot where he killed an Iroquois chief. Marché Bonsecours (below) is a great place to shop

THE HEART OF TORONTO

This walk in Canada's most important city includes a glimpse of the vibrant financial area, the underground system of passageways lined with stores and food outlets, a number of unusual art works, and a look at what Toronto has done with its magnificent waterfront.

THE WALK

Distance: 4.8km (3 miles)
Allow: 2–2.5 hours (not including visits)
Start and end: Nathan Phillips Square in front of Toronto City Hall.
How to get there: Nathan Phillips Square is on Queen Street West; subway: Queen or Osgoode.

Nathan Phillips Square is an attractive focal point for the distinctive 1965 City Hall. In front of the curved, twin buildings, there's an open area and water feature where office workers sun themselves in summer, and where people come to skate in winter.

From here, cross Bay Street to your left. On the corner with Queen Street you see Old City Hall.

Built in 1889–99 by Edward James Lennox at a cost of $2.5 million, it served as both a courthouse and municipal offices. Today, it houses the criminal court.

Walk behind Old City Hall, cross James Street and enter the Eaton Centre.

Designed by Eberhard Zeidler in 1977, the impressive atrium, with its arched glass and steel roof, is over 262m (860ft) long. It features a flock of sculpted Canada geese in full flight by Michael Snow, as well as more than 285 stores, restaurants and other services.

Walk through and out on the other side onto Yonge Street.

"The longest street in Canada" was built by Governor Simcoe in 1795 as a military road connecting Toronto to Lake Simcoe to the north.

Continue south on Yonge Street for four blocks, then turn right on King Street.

This is the financial heart of Canada. To your right is Scotia Plaza, owned by the Bank of Nova Scotia. Across the street, step inside Commerce Court, owned by the Canadian Imperial Bank of Commerce, which was created in 1929–30 by architects York and Sawyer. In the early 1970s, the tower was added next door, to your right.

You walk through a sort of metal kaleidoscope that joins the two together. Turn left in the newer building and walk outside into the courtyard. Turn right and walk out onto Bay Street. Then turn left and cross Wellington Street. Across the street, the two triangular gold-sheathed towers house the Royal Bank of Canada. At 181 Bay Street, enter BCE Place.

This complex boasts the most elegant galleria in the city. Designed by Skidmore, Owings, and Merrill in 1993, the long, elegant atrium is five floors high and incorporates two older buildings, plus two unusually shaped office towers.

Return to Bay Street and turn left, cross Front Street and look to your right for a great view of the CN Tower. Here, Bay Street goes under the railroad tracks. Cross the street to the west sidewalk (pavement) leading through a tunnel. Just before you emerge from the tunnel, on your right is the Air Canada Centre, home to the Toronto Maple Leafs (see page 220). Walk alongside the stadium and then under the Gardiner Expressway. This is a horrible section of the route and you may wonder where it's all leading, but the waterfront is really worth the effort. Cross Harbour Street and Queen's Quay, and then walk between

Yonge Street, the longest in the world, cuts through the heart of Toronto's downtown shopping areas

the Westin Harbour Castle Hotel and Harbour Square to come to the waterfront.

Across the water, you can see the Toronto Islands. Ferries to the islands leave from the dock to your left.

Turn right at the water's edge and follow the path in front of the condominiums and around the York Street slip. Ahead to your right is Queen's Quay Terminal.

Classy stores occupy the light and airy ground level of Queen's Quay Terminal (see page 113). At the far end there are waterfront restaurants and cafés.

Cross Queen's Quay and walk away from the lake on York Street. Go under the expressway and railroad tracks again. You can take the Teamway, a covered sidewalk on the west side of York Street, leaving it to go outside at Front Street. Cross the street and walk past the Fairmont Royal York Hotel. Walk one more block and then turn right at Wellington Street. The black glass buildings on both sides of the street are part of the Toronto Dominion Centre. Go into the Maritime Life Tower on your right to visit the TD Gallery of Inuit Art.

The TD Gallery contains a superb collection of Inuit art that should not be missed (daily).

Walk back outside again, cross Wellington Street, and enter the middle of the buildings of the TD Centre across the street to see Joe Fafard's *Cows*.

In the courtyard, officially called Pasture, *Cows* is the work of Saskatchewan sculptor, Joe Fafard.

Cross King Street and enter First Canadian Place. Take the escalator down to experience a bit of Toronto's underground city on the PATH Walkway, a subterranean shopping complex that connects the major buildings of Toronto's business district. From First Canadian Place, you can follow the signs to City Hall. You will pass below the

Stone carving at the Toronto Dominion Gallery of Inuit Art

Richmond Adelaide Centre and the Sheraton Centre. You will then find yourself in the parking area of Nathan Phillips Square. Take the steps up and you are back where you started.

WHEN TO GO
You can do this walk anytime, but spring, early summer and fall are the best. High summer gets very hot and humid, which also exacerbates the effect of traffic pollution. Winters, of course, can be very cold.

PUBLIC RESTROOMS
City Hall, Eaton Centre, Queen's Quay Terminal, and most major buildings visited on the route.

WHERE TO EAT
Acqua, 10 Front Street, tel: 416/368-7171. Pier 4 Storehouse Restaurant, 245 Queen's Quay West, tel. 416/203-1440. Baton Rouge, 216 Yonge Street, tel: 416/593-9667 (see page 321).

WHERE TO STAY
Toronto Colony Hotel, 89 Chestnut Street, tel: 416/977-0707.

A brightly decorated bagel stand in Toronto's Eaton Centre

OUT AND ABOUT

NIAGARA PARKWAY

This scenic drive encompasses the impressively powerful Niagara Falls, one of the world's great tourist attractions, as well as tranquil river scenes, beautiful gardens and the picturesque community of Niagara-on-the-Lake.

THE DRIVE

Distance: 53km (33 miles)

Allow: a half-day

Start: Old Fort Erie

End: Niagara-on-the-Lake

How to get there: Old Fort Erie is on Route 1, 32km (20 miles) south of Niagara Falls and 2km (1 mile) from the Peace Bridge, a major entry point from the US (from Buffalo, New York state).

The Niagara Parkway officially begins at Mather Arch on the left side of Route 1.

① Mather Arch was constructed in 1933 as a gateway for visitors entering Canada from the US over the Peace Bridge. Surrounded by beautiful flower beds in summer, the bridge connects Fort Erie in Ontario with Buffalo in New York across Niagara River. It was opened in 1927 by the then Prince of Wales, and is one of four international bridges across the river.

There are many rest stops and picnic areas along the parkway. About 16km (10 miles) into the drive, you will see Navy Island.

② This small island was where rebel leader William Lyon Mackenzie sought refuge after the failure of his revolt in Upper Canada in 1837.

Another 2km (1.2 miles) along, in Chippawa, the parkway follows a one-way system to cross the Welland River over King's Bridge, then passes the Dufferin Islands, a series of small island parks with paths and bridges. Immediately after these islands is the International Niagara Control Works.

③ At night, the control dam channels up to 50 percent of the water for 90m (300ft) below the city of Niagara Falls to Sir Adam Beck Generating Station near Queenston or to the Robert Moses Generating Station on the American side.

Immediately beyond the control works, the river is impressive moving at nearly 100kph (60mph) through great rapids. After 28km (17 miles) from the start of the drive, you come to Horseshoe Falls. Park across from the Table Rock complex *(parking $10)* and go for a stroll to view this amazing sight.

④ The Horseshoe (or Canadian) Falls (see pages 122–125) are nearly 800m (2,600ft) wide and 50m (160ft) high. From inside the Table Rock building, you can descend 38m (150ft) by elevator and walk to two observation decks behind the Falls *(daily)*. Protective rain gear is provided. A little farther along, the American Falls can be seen on the US side of the river, and you reach the starting point for the *Maid of the Mist* boat trip.

Another 2km (1.2 miles) along the parkway is Rainbow Bridge.

⑤ The steel-arched Rainbow (or Honeymoon) Bridge is the fifth to be built at this location. Completed in 1941, it replaced a bridge destroyed in an ice jam in 1938. On the Canadian side, there is a carillon tower with 55 bells, the largest of which weighs 10 tons.

The parkway passes underneath the Whirlpool Rapids Bridge, 2km (1.2 miles) along, then it's another 1km (0.5 mile) to the Whirlpool, Spanish Aero Car, and White Water Walk (see page 127), and a Buddhist temple.

⑥ The river makes an abrupt turn northeast, and the force of the water creates a powerful whirlpool. A cable car is suspended high above it, offering impressive views *(daily)*. The Whirlpool can be seen from the riverbank here, but there is a better view from the other side if you continue driving another 2km (1.2 miles). Near the cable car, an elevator takes you down to the White Water Walk at the bottom of the gorge, a board-walk alongside the rapids *(daily)*. It is almost impossible to see these rapids from above. Across the street from the White Water Walk is a large Buddhist temple, known as the Ten Thousand Buddhas Sarira Stupa—an amazing sight.

Drive almost 3km (2 miles) from here to Niagara Glen.

⑦ Here you can hike down the gorge, carved out by the river between 7,000 and 8,000 years ago. For the descent of over 60m (200ft), allow about

The Spanish Aero Car crosses directly above the Whirlpool

OUT AND ABOUT

A leafy walk in the Niagara Parks Botanical Gardens

15 minutes to descend and 30 minutes to climb back up.

Continue on the parkway for 1km (0.5 mile) to reach the Botanical Gardens and Butterfly Conservatory *(daily)*. In another 2km (1.2 miles), you'll pass two important power plants.

❽ Below, the Sir Adam Beck Generating Station is one of Ontario Hydro's largest facilities. Across the river, the Robert Moses Generating Station serves an industrial part of New York state.

One kilometer (0.5 mile) farther, the Queenston-Lewiston Bridge crosses the river. The parkway steeply descends the escarpment and bypasses the small village of Queenston at its foot then continues through an area of large, beautiful estates, orchards and vineyards as it approaches Niagara-on-the-Lake.

❾ Niagara-on-the-Lake was settled by Loyalists after the American Revolution, and was the first capital of Upper Canada. The Americans burned it to the ground during the War of 1812, but it was rebuilt soon afterward. The town is well known for the Shaw Festival (see page 230) and is also the jewel at the heart of the burgeoning Niagara wine industry (see page 300).

WHEN TO GO
Though Niagara Falls is always busy, you don't have to drive far to get away from the crowds. Spring is lovely, fall offers local wine festivals and, in winter, the falls freeze—an incredible sight.

WHERE TO EAT
Anchorage Bar and Grill, 186 Ricardo Street, Niagara-on-the-Lake, tel: 905/468-2141.

WHERE TO STAY
Holiday Inn, 1485 Garrison Road, Fort Erie, tel: 905/871-8333. Century Farmhouse B&B, 758 Niagara Stone Road, Niagara-on-the-Lake, tel: 905/682-6820 or 888/473-7335.

The Maid of the Mist *heads right into the spray of the falls*

OUT AND ABOUT

NIAGARA WALK

This walk follows part of the scenic Niagara River Recreation Trail, begun in 1986. In its entirety, the paved pedestrian path stretches some 58km (35 miles) along the Niagara River from Niagara-on-the-Lake to Fort Erie.

THE WALK

Distance: Just over 5km (3 miles)

Allow: 1.5 hours

Start and end: Rainbow Bridge, Niagara Falls

How to get there: From Queen Elizabeth Way, take Highway 420 into Niagara Falls and exit on River Road. From US, just cross the Rainbow Bridge.

Warning: The spray given off by the falls is likely to drench you if the wind carries it. You may need a raincoat and hat.

From Rainbow Bridge walk toward the falls.

The steel-arched Rainbow Bridge, or Honeymoon Bridge, is the fifth to be built here, its predecessor destroyed in an ice jam in 1938. You can walk under the bridge if you don't mind the roar of traffic.

At the end of the bridge to the right, there is a carillon tower with 55 bells. Concerts are given from time to time. The cloud of spray issuing from the falls dominates the view ahead. Cross Clifton Hill Street and follow the footpath away from the road close to the river and you come to the *Maid of the Mist*.

You can buy a ticket here and take the *Maid of the Mist* boat trip, which rates among the most exciting in the world (see page 122–123).

About 500m (540yd) ahead you'll see Goat Island, separating the American Falls from the Horseshoe Falls.

The American Falls, on the US side of the river, are 300m (1,000ft) wide and more than 50m (164ft) high, but count for only 10 percent of the river's flow.

Soon after this point, you will start to feel the spray from Horseshoe Falls, about 0.8km (0.5 mile) along.

At Table Rock, you can approach the very edge, where the water plunges over the cliff—a compelling sight. It is both spectacular and powerful, nearly 800m (2,600ft) wide and 50m (160ft) high, and carries 90 percent of the river's flow. The force of water continually causes large sections of rock to erode and break off (see chart on page 124), but water diversion to the power plants and generating stations has spread the flow more evenly over the falls, thus reducing the rate of erosion.

Continue walking upstream for about another 0.8km (0.5 mile).

Huge boiling rapids upstream are an impressive precursor to the falls, with water flowing at nearly 100kph (60mph). The rusty old boat caught in the midst has been there since 1918. It was a dumping scow that broke loose from its towing tug some way upstream and finally ran aground here. It took 29 hours to rescue the men on board—a breeches buoy connected to a line was shot out to them from the roof of the Electrical Development Corporation building, which you can see directly ahead.

Turn around at the Electrical Development Corporation and return to Rainbow Bridge.

WHEN TO GO
It's never quiet here, but arrive early or come in the evening, when the falls are floodlit, to avoid the crowds and longest lines for the *Maid of the Mist*.

PUBLIC RESTROOMS
At Table Rock.

WHERE TO EAT
Hard Times, 5759 Victoria Avenue, Niagara Falls, tel: 905/374-3650. Victoria Park, Niagara Falls, tel: 905/356-2217 (see page 318).

WHERE TO STAY
Lion's Head Bed-and-Breakfast, 5239 River Road, Niagara Falls, tel: 905/374-1681.

OUT AND ABOUT

From whatever angle you view the falls—from the edge of the precipice, from the water or from a helicopter sightseeing tour—it never fails to impress. The incredible spray is bound to make you wet at some point, but waterproofs are provided on the Maid of the Mist

PRINCE ALBERT PARK DRIVE

Prince Albert National Park, the largest protected wilderness in Saskatchewan, covers 3,875sq km (1,534sq miles) of rare environment, a mixture of boreal evergreen forest plains and fescue grassland, which at one time covered much of the prairies but has been all but usurped by crops since the arrival of Europeans. Water makes up over 10 percent of the area with over 1,500 lakes and streams. There are few roads in the park and many of its highlights are a couple of kilometers' walk from vehicular access. However, this scenic route explores Prince Albert's forest ecosystem and the underlying effect of glaciation on the landscape.

THE DRIVE

Distance: 135km (84 miles)

Allow: 3 hours

Start: Prince Albert town

End: Grey Owl parking area in Prince Albert National Park.

How to get there: The starting point at Prince Albert town is located 144km (90 miles) north of Saskatoon, along Route 11.

After 10km (6 miles) you'll cross the marshy Spruce River valley. The Spruce Highlands Walk (see pages 280–281) starts just over the bridge. Continue through Prince Albert Burn, 62km (38 miles) along the route.

❸ This is an area seemingly devastated by fire, but in fact, most forest areas rely to a certain extent on fire for their continuation. Some species of plants germinate only after a fire, so in many areas controlled burning takes place.

As you come to the outskirts of Waskesiu Lake, 66km (41 miles) from Prince Albert, you'll see the banks of the lake on your left before the settlement appears.

❹ The town has a pleasant setting amid dense forest with several small beaches. Log cabins and clapboard cottages, set in ample gardens, are available for rent. The oldest buildings—the Community Hall, Golf Clubhouse and Nature Centre—were built during the Depression of the 1930s by single unemployed men, who earned $5 per month plus food and housing.

When you reach Waskesiu Lake, turn left at the crossroads and drive past Kipasiwin Camping. The road leads around the lake, traveling west, and crosses the Waskesiu River. You'll also pass the marina, 6km (4 miles) farther along, before the road ends in a gravel parking area some 32km (20 miles) from Waskesiu Lake.

❺ From here you can walk or go by kayak into the heart of the park's wilderness. The best of the trails (21km/13 miles one way) is Grey Owl Trail, leading to the last resting place of writer-naturalist Grey Owl, born Archibald Stansfeld Belaney in England, who lived here during the 1930s (see page 281).

Return to your car and drive back the way you came.

Windsurfers enjoy the huge expanse of Waskesiu Lake (left), a resort that derives its name from the Cree word for "red deer"

Head north out of Prince Albert on Route 2. After 37km (23 miles), turn left on Route 263, signposted "Prince Albert National Park Scenic Route." The small settlement of Christopher Lake, just over 1km (0.5 mile) along, has a filling station and general store. Later, you'll pass the decaying wooden shacks and warehouses of a long abandoned settlement. The southern boundary of the national park *(entrance fee)* comes into view after 18km (11 miles).

❶ In the park, the first natural attraction is Sandy Lake on the left, where summer visitors can fish or go boating, and there is a turnout (pull-off, or lay-by) with a great view.

The road leads on through thick, mainly evergreen, forest.

❷ It is common to see deer or elk grazing on the wide shoulder (verge) of the road.

The cabin where Grey Owl lived and wrote in the 1930s

Controlled burning of the forest is essential to its long-term survival

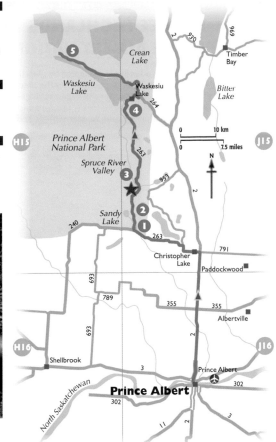

Crean Lake

Timber Bay

Waskesiu Lake

Waskesiu Lake

Bitter Lake

H15

Prince Albert National Park

0   10 km

0   7.5 miles

N

J15

Spruce River Valley

Sandy Lake

Christopher Lake

791

Paddockwood

789

355   355

Albertville

H16

693

Shellbrook

3

North Saskatchewan

J16

Prince Albert

302

Prince Albert

302

11   2   3

SPRUCE HIGHLANDS TRAIL IN PRINCE ALBERT NATIONAL PARK

Prince Albert National Park is a landscape sculpted by glacial action. The Spruce Highlands are composed of glacial moraine—rocks deposited after the glaciers advanced and retreated over several stages of the last Ice Age. Several separate ridges of moraine have created an undulating landscape now overlaid with totally unspoiled forest, a mixture of evergreen and deciduous trees that is home to deer, wolves and the occasional bear.

THE WALK

Distance: 8.5km (5 miles)

Allow: 5 hours

Start and end: Spruce Highlands Trail parking area on Route 263

How to get there: From Prince Albert town (see page 278), take Route 2 north to the Route 263 intersection. Turn left here for the Spruce Highlands Trail parking area.

Warning: Read the advice leaflets regarding animal encounters offered by the park office before you depart. Take drinking water and snacks with you.

From the parking area follow the path next to the information plaque on the south side. Early in the walk there is a sharp rise in elevation with a seat at the top. If it's too soon to take a rest, make a right turn here.

The path levels out and leads left past a large erratic – a boulder left behind when the

Parks Canada has placed information boards at suitable points in the park

glaciers melted at the end of the last Ice Age. This area was under as much as 1,600m (5,200ft) of glacial ice, which formed some of the major lakes, carved the river valleys and shaped the drumlins, eskers, ridges, and moraines that are much in evidence throughout the park.

After 700m (765yd) you'll reach a wooden lookout tower, from where you can view much of the southern part of park.

Notice the effect of erosion on the valley by the Spruce River. The southwestern section of the Prince Albert National Park is home to a sizable herd of plains bison.

From the tower. the path leads down and up across another moraine valley to reach the start of the walk loop 300m (330yd) away. Take the left path.

You'll find that the walk is easier on the return section; the steeper undulations are on the outward section.

The path leads on through thick, mainly deciduous, forest, sometimes cutting across the

Glorious sunsets bring a golden glow to the park

OUT AND ABOUT

Clearly defined paths make following the Spruce Highlands Trail easy

slope of the hills, which can be hard on the ankles. After 1km (0.5 mile) the path widens into a bright valley, then climbs to its highest point: 1,500m (4,920ft).

From here there are far-reaching views southwest.

Eventually, 3.4km (2.1 miles) from the loop start, you'll reach an intersection in the trail where it's possible to take a left to Anglin Lake. To continue on the circular Spruce River Highlands route, keep to the right. From the intersection, the route begins to swing back toward your starting point. You'll enter an area of mainly evergreen forest 1.3km (0.75 mile) beyond, where the climbs and drops are not as steep as they were on the outward path. Just before you reach the start of the loop and head back past the lookout tower for the parking area, glance over to the left.

You will see another typical geological feature of a glacial landscape. The small lake set deep in a bowl below you is known as a kettle, created when a block of ice was left behind as the main glacier retreated. The ice became covered in layers of earth but later melted, causing the earth to drop into the now empty space and fill with water.

WHEN TO GO

The park is open year-round, but the information center is closed from early September to mid-May, and hotels and restaurants are closed from October to May.

PUBLIC RESTROOMS

No facilities along the walk; the nearest are in Waskesiu Lake.

WHERE TO EAT

The nearest place for refreshments is in Waskesiu Lake, 27km (17 miles) distant. Beach House, 911 Lake View Drive, Waskesiu Lake, tel: 306/663-5288. Park Centre Café, 929 Waskesiu Drive, Waskesiu Lake, tel: 306/663-5233.

WHERE TO STAY

Again, Waskesiu Lake is the nearest: Hawood Inn, Waskesiu Lake, tel: 306/663-5911. Elk Ridge Resort, Waskesiu Lake, tel: 306/663-4653.

PARK WILDLIFE

Prince Albert National Park is one of the few areas in the world where timber wolves live free and undisturbed. It is also the only Canadian park with a herd of free-roaming bison. Six bison (out of 50 that were released nearby in 1969) found their way into this protected area and have now increased in number to around 220. Other wildlife includes lynx, woodland caribou, elk, moose, and black bear. There are around 200 species of birds, the list including eagles, osprey, loons, and hawks. The park also has Canada's largest breeding colony of white pelicans—numbering more than 15,000—on and around Lavallée Lake, but access is restricted.

GREY OWL

Credited with being the first ecologist, Grey Owl was born Archibald Stansfield Belaney in Hasings, England, in 1888. He was drawn to life in the wilderness and emigrated to Canada in 1906, living as a trapper and marrying an Ojibway woman. In 1925 he met his second wife, a Mohawk, and became a conservationist and writer, taking the name Grey Owl. He wrote three best-selling novels about life at his small cabin (pictured on page 279) at Ajawan Lake at the heart of the Prince Albert National Park, and 1930s films about his life and his pet beavers made him a household name. Grey Owl died in 1938 and is buried near his cabin, now a popular summer hike for devotees, in spite of being a 40km (24-mile) round trip from the nearest parking area. A 1999 movie about Grey Owl was directed by Richard Attenborough and starred Pierce Brosnan in the title role.

OUT AND ABOUT

ICEFIELDS PARKWAY DRIVE

This drive from Lake Louise to Jasper leads through some of the most majestic scenery in the Canadian Rockies, from Crowfoot Glacier in the south to the Athabasca Glacier in the north. It also puts you within easy walking distance of some of the area's most glorious natural sites, including Peyto Lake view, Mistaya Canyon, Sunwapta Falls, and Athabasca Falls, and leads to the Columbia Icefields Centre from where you can take an excursion onto a glacier.

THE DRIVE

Distance: 227km (143 miles)
Allow: One day, two if you want to undertake longer walks and the Athabasca Glacier trip
Start: Lake Louise village
End: Jasper
How to get there: Lake Louise is a two-hour drive north of Calgary on Route 1.

Stock up on snacks and water at the small shopping mall in Lake Louise village, then take Route 1 north. Take the right exit for Route 93 (Icefields Parkway). About 2km (1.2 miles) along, you'll enter the park. If you don't have a valid park pass, buy one here *(adult $5 per day, child 6–16 $2.50 per day)*. You'll pass tiny Hector Lake some 16km (10 miles) beyond the ticket office, but the first important landmark comes when you've driven 34km (21 miles) from Lake Louise.

❶ Crowfoot Glacier, off to the left, is so named because the several fingers of ice hanging over the rock face resemble a bird's foot, though gradual melting is altering its shape.

After 6km (4 miles) look for the left turn to Peyto Lake view.

❷ From the parking area it is an easy 750m (820yd) walk to one of the most impressive panoramas in the Rockies, with turquoise Peyto Lake nestling at the base of the surrounding peaks.

Drive 26km (16 miles) to the parking area for Mistaya Canyon.

❸ Leave your car to take the 10-minute walk down a well-worn path to explore the water-eroded landscape.

Some 5km (3 miles) farther north you'll cross the wide boulder-strewn path of the North Saskatchewan River.

❹ Here you'll find refreshments, lodging and fuel—the last till Jasper, 130km (81 miles) north.

Beyond the crossing, the highway follows the route of the North Saskatchewan River.

❺ You'll see a series of jagged peaks on either side. Look particularly for Cirrus Mountain on the right (parking area on the left side of the road) before you reach a huge curve, called Big Bend, that leads on up to a still higher plain. A parking area at the top of the bend is a great photo spot for the view back down the valley. Once on the plain, the 2.5km (1.5-mile) steep walk along Parker Ridge—120km (74 miles) from Lake Louise—on the left leads to excellent views of the Saskatchewan Glacier.

Past Parker Ridge you'll cross the boundary of Banff National Park and enter Jasper National Park. Only 10km (6 miles) farther on are the Columbia Icefields.

❻ Here you can travel out onto Athabasca Glacier on a Snocoach from Columbia Icefields Centre (see page 158).

At North Columbia Icefield the mountains recede a little as the highway follows the wider flood plain of the Sunwapta River.

❼ The two main attractions on this section of the drive are both waterfalls. At the first, Sunwapta Falls, the river plunges 60m (197ft) down through a narrow gorge.

Continue northward for another 16km (10 miles) to reach the Athabasca Falls.

❽ At this waterfall, the drop is deeper and the gorge even narrower, allowing for more dramatic photos.

From here it is 30km (19 miles) to Jasper (see page 160).

(see page 160)

From here it is 30km (19 miles) to Jasper

WHEN TO GO

The road is open all year, weather permitting, but many of the accommodations and restaurants are open only April through October. Most footpaths are closed in winter.

WHERE TO EAT

Baker Creek Bistro, Highway 1A, Bow Valley Parkway, Lake Louise, tel: 403/522-3761. There are also places to eat at the North Saskatchewan River crossing.

WHERE TO STAY

Fairmont Château Lake Louise Hotel, 111 Lake Louise Drive, Lake Louise, tel: 403/522-3511. Other accommodations can be found en route at the North Saskatchewan River crossing.

A snowy trail (opposite) in Banff National Park. The Athabasca Waterfall (below) and Cirrus Mountain viewpoint (bottom)

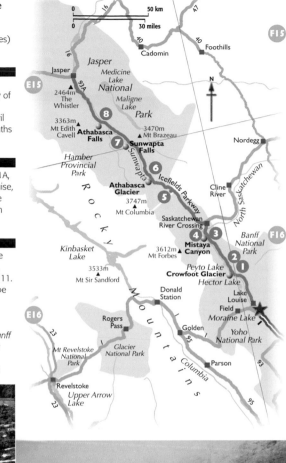

OUT AND ABOUT

LAKE AGNES WALK

Follow in the footsteps of the genteel Victorian and Edwardian visitors to the Tea House at Lake Agnes high above Lake Louise, along a route that offers some excellent mountain panoramas. There are only two teahouses still operating in the Rockies, and the route to this one is the most popular walk in Banff National Park.

THE WALK

Distance:	3.8km (2 miles)
Allow:	6 hours (one way)
Start:	Lake Louise parking area
End:	Lake Agnes Tea House

How to get there: Lake Louise is a two-hour drive north of Calgary on Route 1.

Warning: The path has some steep sections. The upper part of the walk follows the same route as the horse trek route from Lake Louise to the Tea House, so be careful around the horses and watch where you tread—horse droppings are not only unpleasant, but are also slippery underfoot.

From the Lake Louise parking area, make your way to the lakeshore promenade for exceptional water-level views of the landscape and the Château Lake Louise Hotel. Keep the water on your left and walk along the lakefront until the path splits. Take the right-hand fork, which climbs immediately from the water's edge. The climb is quite steep, with few places to rest, so take your time. After 1.2km (0.75 mile) a magnificent lake view presents itself on the left.

From above the waterline, the unreal-looking blue tone of the lake is even more apparent. The coloration is caused by the minerals in the water absorbing some parts of the spectrum of light shining on them, and reflecting others. The viewpoint is a perfect place to take a photograph, especially when there are kayakers on the water.

The route takes a tight dogleg here, but the ascent continues to be just as steep. The path eventually reaches a plateau after 2km (1 mile).

Here you can pause for a while and admire Mirror Lake, a small body of water backed by a wall of rock and surrounded by mature shady trees. From here there are two possible routes onward to Lake Agnes.

The Bridal Veil Waterfall (above) is passed on the way up to Lake Agnes, and is most impressive during the spring melt

Take the path to the right from the lake where it sweeps around to the east.

You have views across acres of woodland carpeting Bow Valley and stretching to the mountains on the lake's far flank. Notice the green strips on the mountain sides—in winter, these become the Lake Louise ski runs.

The path then swings left, west of the Little Beehive rock formation, before the final ascent to Lake Agnes. Climb the steps to the right of the rock wall.

This steep flight of steps often turns into a waterfall with overflow from the lake. At the top of the steps, the pretty setting of Lake Agnes presents itself immediately, with a curtain of peaks on all sides and the Big Beehive rock formation to your left. The lake is generally thought to have been named after Lady Agnes Macdonald, wife of the first prime minister of Canada, who hiked up here in 1886. The redoubtable lady is also known

for taking a trip on a Canadian Pacific steam locomotive—riding on the cowcatcher at the front.

Take time for some refreshment at the historic Tea House before the return journey. It was constructed in 1901 by the Canadian Pacific Railway and was one of several in the park—this is the highest at 2,134m (6,999ft)—to provide refreshment for parties of upper-class hikers. King Edward VIII, then the Prince of Wales, made his way up from the hotel to the Tea House during an official visit to Canada.

At this point you can return to the parking area by retracing your steps.

OPTIONAL EXTENDED WALK

If you prefer, you can extend the walk into a circular route of 12km (8 miles) in total.

Leave the Lake Agnes Tea House, keeping the lake on your left (walk away from the path you took on your arrival at this point). After 1km (0.5 mile) you will see the left turning to the top of the Big Beehive. The route is a short but hard climb of 125m (135yd) to the summit for extensive views across Mirror Lake, but the footpath is not maintained and is unclear in parts.

Return to the main path and continue walking away from Lake Agnes (turn left at the junction of the two footpaths). This is a steep descent into the valley bottom. After 900m (0.4 mile) this path intersects the Highline Trail. Turn right here, then after 1km (0.5 mile), fork left and after 700m (760yd) you'll meet the Plain of Six Glaciers Trail.

As you approach the intersection, you have panoramic views up to the left to the Victoria Glacier above the Plain of Six Glaciers (the Plain of Six Glaciers is where the second teahouse is located, on the right 2km/1.2

OUT AND ABOUT

miles along the trail).

Turn left where the Highland Trail meets the Plains of Six Glaciers Trail and walk just over 1km (0.5 mile) down the valley to the head of Lake Louise.

Your final 2km (1.2 miles) is a flat walk by the lakeshore toward Fairmont Château Lake Louise Hotel, with views of the reflections of the surrounding peaks on the surface of the azure water.

WHEN TO GO

You might want to take a lead from the Tea House, which opens when the snow melts and closes after the first snow falls (generally open May–Oct). This is one of the most popular hikes

in the country, so you might want to avoid the height of the summer and weekends. Set out as early as you can. Wildflowers up in the mountains will be in bloom around late July/early August; the larch trees are beautiful in the fall.

PUBLIC RESTROOMS

Fairmont Château Lake Louise Hotel and Lake Agnes Tea House.

WHERE TO EAT

Lake Agnes Tea House, Lake Agnes (there are also picnic tables up at the Tea House, if you want to carry your own supplies— these can be bought from the Château Deli, Fairmont Château Lake Louise Hotel). Mount

Fairview Dining Room, Deer Lodge, tel: 403/522-3747.

WHERE TO STAY

Paradise Lodge and Bungalows, Lake Louise, tel: 403/522-3595. Fairmont Château Lake Louise Hotel, 111 Lake Louise Drive, Lake Louise, tel: 403/522-3511. Post Hotel, 200 Pipestone Road, Lake Louise, tel: 403/265-4900.

THINGS TO DO

As an alternative to the walk, you can go up to Lake Agnes on horseback. Treks are organized by the Fairmont Château Lake Louise Hotel twice a day (weather permitting), with a duration of about three hours.

The climb up to Lake Agnes is well rewarded with views such as this, over Lake Louise and the mountains

AROUND STANLEY PARK'S SEAWALL

This walk around Vancouver's famous Stanley Park starts off with plenty of city views and park attractions, with the western section providing wonderful panoramas out to sea, invigorating fresh air, and peace and quiet.

The city skyline is a backdrop to the Royal Vancouver Yacht Club

THE WALK

Distance: 10.5km (6.5 miles)

Allow: 5 hours

Start and end: Parking area at the intersection of Denman Street and West Georgia Avenue.

How to get there: Bus 5 stops at the intersection one block west of the start point, while routes 35 and 135 will take you to the information center in the park (see directions below); or its a 500m (550yd) walk west of Canada Place.

Warning: There are clearly marked lanes for walkers and joggers, and for cyclists and in-line skaters. For safety reasons, stay in the appropriate lane.

From the parking area, walk in the direction of the waterfront. Go left at the walkway, skirting between the ornamental gardens. This is the path you'll stay on all the way around the seawall. The path sweeps around to the right and the first way point along your walk is the boathouse of the Vancouver Rowing Club, 200m (220yd) from the park entrance. The tourist information kiosk is 500m (550yd) from the park entrance, where you can pick up a map. Go past the yacht club boathouse on the left and continue for 1.2km (0.75 mile).

You pass the entrance of Deadman's Island, now a naval shore base named HMCS *Discovery*.

After another 300m (330yd), you'll see the totem garden on the left and pass the Nine O'Clock Gun, fired every evening across the harbor.

Here you can get some excellent photographs of the Vancouver skyline with Canada Place (see page 146) directly across the water.

From Hallelujah Point, just beyond the gun, the path heads north around Brockton Point before turning to the west.

There are views at this point of the North Shore with its dramatic curtain of mountains behind.

Continue 400m (440yd) to the small bronze statue, *Girl in a Wetsuit*.

This life-size statue (1970), just offshore, is a homage to Copenhagen's *Little Mermaid*, and is the work of Budapest-born sculptor Elek Imredy.

OUT AND ABOUT

Another 100m (110yd) brings you to the bright oriental prow of the SS *Empress of China*, which sits in an ornamental shrub looking out over the narrowing waters. Continue past the children's play area before heading northwest.

You'll see the high Lion's Gate Bridge that spans the outlet as the open sea looms ever closer.

After you pass under the bridge, it's another 50m (55yd) to Prospect Point.

This is the northernmost point in the park, and from here your views will be to the west across the Pacific Ocean.

The Nine O'Clock Gun (above) is along Stanley Park's seawall

Girl in a Wetsuit *mimics Copenhagen's* Little Mermaid

From Prospect Point it's 1km (0.5 mile) to Siwash Rock, with views across English Bay, and then almost another 1km (0.5 mile) to Third Beach.

Whatever the time of year, you'll find bathers or beachcombers here.

Just beyond Third Beach is Ferguson Point, the most westerly place in Stanley Park. Some 8km (5 miles) from the start of the walk, you come to Second Beach.

Here you'll find the large artificial Stanley Park Swimming Pool.

The path leaves the waterfront here and continues through some ornamental lawns. You come to an intersection, where you go left (follow signs for Lost Lagoon) under Stanley Park Road. You'll see a golf course on your right. Turn right at the far side of the golf course and walk past the Ted and Mary Greig Rhododendron Gardens on the right. Lost Lagoon will come into view on the left.

Lost Lagoon was given its name when the building of the Stanley Park Causeway cut it off from Coal Harbour.

Follow the path around the lake to reach the pass under the main road. At the intersection, go right, and after 200m (220yd) you'll be back at the starting point.

WHEN TO GO
Year-round, any fine day will be a great time to join health-conscious Vancouverites in their perambulations round the park.

PUBLIC RESTROOMS
Behind the information office.

WHERE TO EAT
Teahouse Restaurant, Ferguson Point, Stanley Park, tel: 604/669-3281. In addition, there are cafés at the totem poles, Lumbermen's Arch and Third Beach, and restaurants at Prospect Point and Stanley Park Pavilion.

WHERE TO STAY
London Guard Motel, 2227 Kingsway, tel: 604/430-4646.

The group of totem poles at Brockton Point attracts much attention

ACROSS VANCOUVER ISLAND

This long day trip links such highlights of south Vancouver Island as the First Nations totems at Duncan, the beautiful murals at Chemainus and the natural splendor of Cathedral Grove. You'll leave the relative bustle of Victoria in the morning and by late afternoon arrive at the solitude of the Pacific Rim National Park to watch the sun set over the vast Pacific Ocean.

THE DRIVE

Distance: 316km (196 miles)
Allow: 6 hours (not including visits)
Start: Victoria
End: Tofino (Pacific Rim National Park)

From the Empress Hotel on Victoria's waterfront at Inner Harbour, travel via Route 1, or Island Highway. Take Douglas Street, which becomes Route 1 and head through the northern suburbs. The road leads up and over Malahat Pass, at 352m (1,155ft) one of the highest points in southern Vancouver Island. Visibility may be limited by low cloud and fog. Some 60km (37 miles) from Victoria is Duncan (see page 152).

❶ Known as the City of Totems (there are more than 80 of them in town and along the highway), Duncan is home to the Cowichan people, who are renowned for their carving skills. You can see carving in progress at the Quw'utsun Cultural and Conference Centre, and explore other aspects of their cultural background.

Some 11km (7 miles) north of the Lake Cowichan intersection, turn right on Westholme to Chemainus. This approach is much more picturesque than carrying on along the main road and taking the shorter link road farther north. When you reach the next junction (a T-junction), turn left into Chemainus (see page 152). You'll see an old steam engine opposite you at the junction.

❷ Chemainus is famed for its murals and attractive shops. It is also known as "The Little Town That Did" because of its dramatic recovery from what seemed to be a terminal decline back in the early 1980s. The depression followed the closure of the town's traditional industries, but the idea of it becoming an artists'

Many walls in Chemainus are covered with remarkable murals

enclave—to breathe new life into the community—was championed. Many people said it couldn't be done, but after they were proved wrong, the plucky little town earned its cheery sobriquet.

Head back to Route 1 and continue your drive north. When you've reached 110km (68 miles) from Victoria, you can visit Nanaimo (see page 164). Route 1 runs through the town, but if you'd rather carry on, take Route 19—a four-lane bypass—and reconnect with Route 1 north of town.

❸ Nanaimo is a lively town with an active fishing fleet and an interesting First Nations heritage. There's a pleasant seafront walk around the harbor and to the estuary of the Millstone River, where salmon come to spawn.

Travel north of Nanaimo for 38km (24 miles) to reach a sign at the intersection of Route 4 pointing the way to Port Alberni and the Pacific Rim National Park (also signposted to Tofino and Ucluelet). Turn left here and begin the westward drive. About 15km (9 miles) from the turning, Cameron Lake comes into view, followed after another 6km (4 miles) by Cathedral Grove and Port Alberni.

❹ The road skirts Cameron Lake, traveling through thick pine forest, then the majestic old growth forest of Cathedral Grove (see page152). Port

Alberni is the leading town of the region, from where you can take boat trips down the Alberni Inlet to Barkley Sound in the Pacific Rim.

To reach Tofino and Ucluelet, make a right at the waterfront, following Route 4 the whole way.

❺ This final section of the trip really takes you into untamed landscape. After Sproat Lake there is no fuel for 85km (53 miles), so check your tank.

Around 46km (29 miles) from Port Alberni, the road rises 175m (574ft) at Sutton Pass through a series of dramatic switchbacks along the boulder-strewn Taylor River valley up onto the Clayoquot Plateau. You'll climb again at the other side of the plateau, before passing Lake Kennedy, on your right, on your final descent to the coast, eventually reaching a T-junction that signposts Ucluelet south and Tofino north. Take the right turn to Tofino. You travel through the mainland section of Pacific Rim National Park (see pages 166–167) before reaching Tofino.

WHEN TO GO

Some of the attractions, including guided tours of the Duncan totems, may operate only between May and September. However, storm-watching is a popular winter pastime on the coastline near Tofino.

WHERE TO EAT

Wharfside Eatery and Decks, 1208 Wharf Street, Victoria, tel: 250/360-1808. Loft Restaurant, 346 Campbell Street, Tofino, tel: 250/725-4241.

WHERE TO STAY

The Vineyard B&B, 4740 Beaverdale Road, Victoria, tel: 250/727-6449. Best Western Tin Wis Resort, 1119 Pacific Rim Highway, Tofino, tel: 250/725-4445 or 800/661-9995.

OUT AND ABOUT

Huge hardwood trees in Cathedral Grove (below). The Empress Hotel (right), Victoria

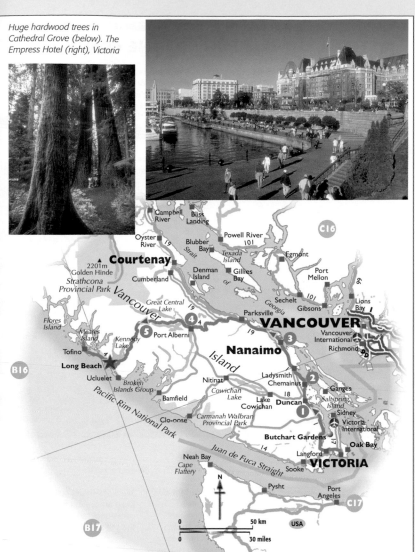

Campbell River
Bliss Landing
Powell River
101
C16
Oyster River
19
Blubber Bay
Texada Island
Egmont
Port Mellon
Courtenay
2201m Golden Hinde
Strathcona Provincial Park
Cumberland
Denman Island
Gillies Bay
Sechelt
101
Gibsons
99
Lions Bay
Vancouver
Great Central Lake
19
4
Parksville
VANCOUVER
Flores Island
Meares Island
Kennedy Lake
5
Port Alberni
4
Island
Nanaimo
3
Vancouver International
Richmond
99
Tofino
4
Long Beach
Ladysmith
Chemainus
2
Ganges
Ucluelet
Broken Islands Group
Nitinat
Cowichan Lake
18
Lake Cowichan
Duncan
1
Saltspring Island
Sidney
Bamfield
Pacific Rim National Park
Clo-oose
Carmanah Walbran Provincial Park
Carmanah Walbran
Butchart Gardens
Victoria International
Neah Bay
Cape Flattery
Juan de Fuca Straight
14
Langford
Oak Bay
VICTORIA
N
Sooke
Pysht
Port Angeles
C17
B16
B17
0   50 km
0   30 miles
USA

Duncan, famous for totems, also has this colorful carved whale

Port Alberni's busy, business-like harbor is where 20 percent of BC salmon are landed. It's also a hub for the forestry industry

A STROLL ON THE EDGE OF THE CONTINENT

Long Beach in Pacific Rim National Park Reserve is noted for its big waves, famed throughout the surfing world. Long, smooth strands backed by temperate rainforest make this the perfect place for strolling, while just offshore you may spot migrating whales or frolicking sea lions.
Rather than taking in all 21km (13 miles) of Long Beach, this walk introduces you to the delights of its northernmost section of Long Beach, nearest to the region's main town, Tofino.

THE WALK

Distance: 7.2km (4 miles) round-trip

Allow: 4 hours

Start and end: Long Beach north parking area

How to get there: From Victoria, take Route 1 north and after 38km (23.7 miles)—north of Nanaimo—turn left on Route 4, a total distance of 316km (196 miles).

Between mid-March and mid-October you'll need to display a Park Use Permit in your car, available from the Park Information Centre on Highway 4 at Long Beach. From the Long Beach north parking area, head straight out onto the sand.

This part of Long Beach is the most popular with surfers, and you'll normally find a small group out on the water here in almost all weather conditions.

When you reach the waterline, turn left, walking along the shore with the ocean on your right.

Driftwood piled up on Long Beach is in stark contrast with the lush, living rain forest stretching away in the distance

Whatever the state of the tide, Long Beach presents a wonderful vista—high tide leaves only the soft golden grains visible, but low tide widens the strand considerably and provides lots of firm sand underfoot. As you stroll you'll

Boardwalks make the going easy and also protect the delicate vegetation from trampling feet in the Long Beach hinterland

see a small islet just offshore. Keep an eye out for the occasional sea lion basking in the sea spray.

Continue walking along the waterline. You'll see a rocky headland ahead (if the tide is coming in and is close to the rocks, don't walk on the water-side of the headland as the waves can be powerful, take the footpath that runs along the landward side).

The north flank of the rocky outcrop has a bronze plaque

commemorating the visit of Her Royal Highness Princess Anne when she officially opened the park in 1971. The top of the outcrop is a great vantage point out to the open ocean, and to the left and right along Long Beach.

If you take the shore-side route you'll pass the path to Green Point Campground on your left, leading inland through thick shoreline vegetation. Beyond the outcrop is another long sandy bay. Walk along until you reach a stream of water cutting across your path (look also for a parking area at the top of the beach). Make your way to the vegetation line to reach the start of the 1.5km (1-mile) loop known as Combers Beach interpretive walk.

This boardwalk route leads through various levels of coastal vegetation, starting with the intercoastal tideland spruce forest at sea-level, before moving inland and climbing as the land level rises. Here you'll find mixed woodland and cedar-hemlock forest, containing some rare Sitka spruces, which are one of the world's tallest tree species. This is old growth forest with some gargantuan examples, along with a forest floor of ferns and dead fallen trees.

When you've completed the boardwalk, retrace your steps to the Long Beach parking area.

WHEN TO GO

Any time of year is good here, with whales offshore from March to October, beautiful sunsets in summer, and mild weather interspersed with spectacular storms in winter. The most important thing you should do is consult tide tables—you will get most out of the walk if you come at low tide, when there's more beach, more firm sand to walk on and more tidepools to explore. Tides change every six hours, so there are two low tides a day. High tide is best for kayaking or storm-watching, but for the latter stay off the beach—for safety and for better views,

find a high vantage point away from the crashing waves. Park facilities are open only mid-March through mid-October.

PUBLIC RESTROOMS

North beach parking area.

WHERE TO EAT

Pointe Restaurant, Wickaninnish Inn, 500 Osprey Lane, Tofino, tel: 250/725-3100.

WHERE TO STAY

A Snug Harbour Inn, 460 Marine Drive, Ucluelet, tel: 250/726-2686. Wickaninnish Inn, 500 Osprey Lane, Tofino, tel: 250/725-3100.

SOME ADVICE

To protect the environment and ensure your safety, heed the following advice:

It is illegal to remove shells, stones, driftwood, or any creatures—alive or dead.

Explore rockpools gently, and respect the life in them.

Watch where you tread on the rocks—they are covered with life, which is simply dormant until the sea returns.

Beware of rogue waves and fast incoming tides.

WILDLIFE

Marine mammals abound in this protected environment, including whales offshore from March to October, and curious seals and sea lions that peer at you from the surfline or bask on the rocks. There's a bird sanctuary close by, and you'll see bald eagles, herons, oystercatchers and other species, including migrating shore birds. Inland, there are bears—some local outfitters run tours to view them safely.

High tide is the best time for kayakers to take to the waters off Long Beach, and is also best for storm-watching in winter

THE GOLDEN CIRCLE DRIVE

This spectacular drive, following in the footsteps of the Gold Rush prospectors, traverses some of the most pristine landscapes in North America, and takes you to two countries as you cross the Canadian border into Alaska. Majestic peaks in Kluane National Park, the Bald Eagle preserve near Haines City, the fierce incline of the White Pass, and the world's smallest desert are just some of the natural highlights.

THE DRIVE

Distance: 483km (299 miles)
Allow: 2 days (not including time for hiking on park trails)
Start and end: Whitehorse
How to get there: The best way to reach Whitehorse is by air—regular flights from Vancouver (4hrs) and Edmonton (about 3hrs). Overland, from Vancouver take routes 97, 16, then 37, or 97 then the Alaska Highway; from Edmonton take Route 43 then the Alaska Highway.
Warning: Distances between settlements are large. Keep an eye on your fuel gauge at all times and plan ahead for overnight stops. You'll be crossing into the US, so have necessary documentation for the vehicle and all passengers, plus US$6 per person for the visa waiver green card. If you need a visa to enter the US, obtain it from the US embassy in your home country before leaving.

From Whitehorse, travel via 4th Avenue and Two Mile Hill to Route 1, the famed Alaska Highway (see pages 176–177), which takes you in a northwest direction toward Haines Junction.

❶ This is pretty unremarkable countryside by Yukon standards, but as you get within 1.5km (1 mile) or so of Haines Junction, the mighty peaks of Kluane National Park (see page 179) come into view directly ahead.

At Haines Junction, 161km (100 miles) along the route, take the Haines Highway south toward Haines City; in 27km (17 miles) you'll see a turning right to Kathleen Lake, popular for hiking and camping, but continue to the 44km (27-mile) point.

❷ You can stop here to take the 800m-long (875yd) Rock Glacier Trail, leading through a glacial landscape.

Sweep on past Dezadeash Lake at 51km (31.5 miles), to Klukshu.

❸ At this traditional First Nations fall camp, 500m (550yd) left off the highway, you can see fish being smoked during the salmon run (late Oct–early Nov), and shop at the craft store (Jun–Sep). The camp is deserted early November through May.

Some 90km (56 miles) from Haines Junction you'll cross from the Yukon into British Columbia. The views here are dominated by the St. Elias Mountains to the right, and the road leads gradually up to the Chilkat Pass.

❹ The Chilkat Pass is the highest point on this highway, at 1,065m (3,493ft), and was one of the main conduits for prospectors in the 1898 Gold Rush. Beyond, there are wonderful sweeping views south into Alaska.

You'll cross into Alaska, USA, after traveling 179km (111 miles).

❺ The customs post is open 7am–11pm, Alaska Time (one hour ahead of the time on the Canadian side).

Once the formalities are over, head on to the Chilkat Bald Eagle Preserve, 33km (20 miles) farther.

❻ Thousands of bald eagles gather on the Chilkat Valley flats, especially in late fall when salmon spawn. Don't park at the roadside—only use designated parking spaces.

From the preserve it's only 35km (22 miles) to diminutive Haines City, a good place for an overnight stop. Take the one-hour ferry ride from here to Skagway, an old Gold Rush town, and follow the Klondike Highway north, climbing the steep ascent to White Pass, completed 1978.

❼ Over 90,000 prospectors traveled on foot through this and the parallel Chilkoot Pass in the late 1890s. There are dramatic views of the footpath, White Pass and Yukon narrow-gauge rail tracks climbing through the narrow ravine.

White Pass summit is 23km (14 miles) from Skagway, just before the Canadian border. It's another 12km (7 miles) to the customs post (daily 24 hours in summer). At 50km (31 miles), Tushti Lake comes into view and the road follows its banks for a few miles until you cross from BC back into the Yukon. North of Carcross, at 106km (66 miles), is a surprising landscape.

❽ The Carcross Desert is the world's smallest, at just over 2km (1 mile) long.

Some 117km (73 miles) from Skagway is Emerald Lake, known for its brilliant blue-green hues. Klondike Highway meets the Alaska Highway 40km (25 miles) on, from where it's only 15km (9 miles) back to Whitehorse, although you should take the turn to the right 11km (7 miles) from the intersection to view Miles Canyon before heading back into town.

WHEN TO GO

Extra-long summer days make this an ideal time to travel in the north. The best time to see bald eagles is during the salmon spawn (mid-Oct to mid-Nov), but most hotels and restaurants will close October through April.

WHERE TO EAT

Antonio's Vineyard, 202 Strickland Street, Whitehorse, tel: 867/668-6266. Raven Hotel, Haines Junction, tel: 867/634-2500.

WHERE TO STAY

Best Western Gold Rush Inn, 411 Main Street, Whitehorse, tel: 867/668-4500.

OUT AND ABOUT

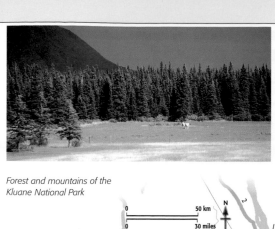

Forest and mountains of the
Kluane National Park

Fraser Station, by the railroad
track at White Pass

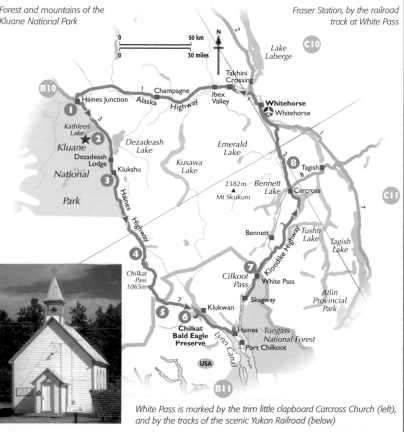

*White Pass is marked by the trim little clapboard Carcross Church (left),
and by the tracks of the scenic Yukon Railroad (below)*

KING'S THRONE TRAIL IN KLUANE NATIONAL PARK

One of the most spectacular of the shorter trails in Kluane National Park, the King's Throne Trail climbs steeply from the shores of Kathleen Lake to a wonderful mountain cirque, offering panoramic views north across the Dezadeash Valley and the Kluane mountain range. Then, if you feel fit enough, climb above the cirque onto the King's Throne, with majestic vistas to the west across the glacial mountainscapes that make Kluane famous.

THE WALK

Distance: 10km (6 miles)

Allow: 6 hours

Start and end: Kathleen Lake parking area

How to get there: From Whitehorse (see Golden Circle Drive, pages 292–293), take the Alaska Highway. Total distance is 165km (101 miles) and the journey takes about 2 hours.

Make your way to the trailhead to the left side of the parking area as you look at the lake. The route is wide here and well worn, but watch out for the huge tree roots crisscrossing it. After 750m (820yd) the footpath skirts the lake on your right. Continue 350m (380yd) along the trail to where the route splits, and follow the King's Throne Trail signs that lead left.

The Cottonwood Trail, which leads on beside the lakeshore, is one of the longest trails in the park at 83km (52 miles).

The King's Throne route begins to climb through the mature woodland away from the lake. When you reach a second split in the trail, take the left route and continue climbing.

The path soon becomes a series of tight switchbacks and narrows to a single file. Then it breaks through the treeline, offering the first panoramic view north—a breathtaking vista, with Kathleen Lake in the

OUT AND ABOUT

foreground, a carpet of forest along the valley and the high peaks of the park to the left. It's also worth looking up at the route ahead, which is almost vertical at this point with a tightly twisting trail.

Keep on climbing until you arrive at the lip of the cirque, a rock bowl gouged out of the mountain peak by glacial action.

After the climb, you will want to take time to sit and admire the full spectacle of the Yukon countryside spread out far below. Then explore the rock-strewn surface of the cirque, with its relatively smooth sides.

From the cirque it's possible to hike along the ridge to the King's Throne summit.

There are stunning views to the west over some of the most typical Kluane landscape, the remote Kennedey-Hubbard-Alverstone peaks seemingly set in the icefields.

This part of the trail is not marked as clearly as on the lower section, so extra care is needed. Return to your car by retracing the route.

WHEN TO GO
With its very steep sections and poorer markings in the higher reaches, this walk definitely calls for a bright, clear day when the ground is dry and free of ice.

PUBLIC RESTROOMS
Kathleen Lake parking area.

WHERE TO EAT
Kluane Park Inn, Haines Junction, tel: 867/634-2261.

WHERE TO STAY
The Cabin Bed-and-Breakfast, Haines Junction, tel: 867-634-2626. Alcan Motor Inn, Junction of Alaska and Haines Highways, tel: 867/634-2371.

Hikers along the King's Throne Trail (right), and the panorama of the Dezadeash Valley in Kluane National Park (below)

There are a great many companies and organizations that offer tours in Canada of every type and employing every mode of transportation imaginable. The following list includes a selection of the more specialized, as well as a few major operators for general tours.

Snow streaks the Tablelands (above left); kayaker (above) off Long Beach; Lake Minnewanka (above right)

ADVENTURE

ALBERTA CANOE HOLIDAYS
17240 113 Street, Edmonton, Alberta, T5X 5Y4 , tel: 780/970-3015
www.albertacanoeholidays.com
Guided canoe and camping adventure holidays on western Canadian rivers and lakes.

BEAR MOUNTAINEERING
Box 4222, Smithers, British Columbia, V0J 2N0, tel: 250/847-2854
www.bearmountaineering.bc.ca
Mountain adventure tours in northwestern British Columbia and Yukon.

CANADIAN TRAILS ADVENTURE TOURS
Suite 153, 162-2025 Corydon Avenue, Winnipeg, Manitoba, R3P 0N5, tel: 800/668-BIKE (2453)
www.canadiantrails.com
All-inclusive group bicycle tours for all ranges of ability.

CLIPPER CRUISES
11969 Westline Industrial Drive, St. Louis, Missouri, USA, 63146-9840, tel: 314/655-6700, 800/990-0354)
www.clippercruises.com
Exciting small-ship cruises on the West Coast, Great Lakes, Québec, and the Maritimes.

GLOBE-TROTTER AVENTURE CANADA
4764 Papineau, Montréal, Québec, H2H 1V5, tel: 514/849-8768, 888/598-7688
www.adventurecanada.com
Outdoor adventure and eco-tourism packages in Québec.

THE GREAT CANADIAN TRAVEL COMPANY
158 Fort Street, Winnipeg, Manitoba R3C 1C9, tel: 204/949-0188,800/661-3830)
www.greatcanadiantravel.com

Tours of Nunavut, Northwest Territories and Yukon, including an Arctic odyssey.

GROS MORNE ADVENTURES
Box 275, Norris Point, Newfoundland, A0K 3V0, tel: 709/458-2722, 800/685-4624
www.grosmorneadventures.com
Adventure tours in Gros Morne National Park, the Viking Trail of Newfoundland/Labrador.

HIDDEN TRAILS
202-380 West 1st Avenue, Vancouver, British Columbia, V5Y 3T7, tel: 604/323-1141, 888/9-TRAILS (872457)
www.hiddentrails.com
Horseback vacations in Alberta, British Columbia and Québec.

ROCKY MOUNTAINEER
100-1150 Station Street, Vancouver, British Columbia, V6A 2X7, tel: 604/606-7245, 800/665-7245
www.rockymountaineer.com
Spectacular train trips in the Canadian Rocky Mountains.

ROUTES TO LEARNING CANADA
4 Cataraqui Street, Kingston, Ontario, K7K 1Z7, tel: 613/530-2222
www.routestolearning.ca
Educational travel.

TIMBERWOLF ADVENTURES
16-161 Broadway Boulevard, Sherwood Park, Alberta, T8H 2A8, tel: 780/467-9697, 888/467-9697
www.timberwolftours.com
Adventure excursions in the Canadian Rockies, northern British Columbia and Yukon.

MAJOR TOUR OPERATORS

ATLANTIC TOURS
1660 Hollis Street, Suite 211, Halifax, Nova Scotia, B3J 1V7, tel: 902/423-6242, 800/565-7173

www.atlantictours.com
Package tours of the Maritimes, Newfoundland and Labrador.

BREWSTER VACATIONS
Box 1140, 100 Gopher Street, Banff, Alberta, T1L 1J3, tel: 403/762-6700, 1-877/791-5500
www.brewster.ca
The largest tour operator in the Canadian Rockies; also packages in the Martimes, Ontario, Montréal and Yellowknife.

CARDINAL TRAVEL TOURS
732 – 41st Avenue NE, Calgary, Alberta, T2E 3P9, tel: 403/531-3945, 800/661-6161
www.cardinaltraveltours.com
Group tours through western Canada, the north and the Atlantic provinces.

COLLETTE VACATIONS
162 Middle Street, Pawtucket, Rhode Island, USA, 02860, tel: 401/728-3805, 800/340-5158
www.collettevacations.com
Wide variety of escorted tours by bus and train in Ontario, the Maritimes and the Rockies.

INDEPENDENT VACATIONS

CANADA À LA CARTE
1402 3rd Avenue, Suite 717, Seattle, Washington, USA, 98116-2118, tel: 206/622-9155, 877/977-6500)
www.canadaalacarte.com/Holidays
Custom-designed independent vacations to suit individual interests and budgets.

GENERAL WEBSITES

www.canada-adventures-guide.com
Information on a wide variety of wilderness trips and adventures.
www.listingsca.com/Travel/Tours_and_ Cruises provides information on a wide variety of packages.

OUT AND ABOUT

This chapter lists places to eat and places to stay alphabetically by town within Canada's regions. In each town places to eat precede places to stay although some of the establishments offer both food and accommodation.

Eating and Staying

CANADIAN CUISINE

Canadian cuisine is a somewhat nebulous concept, given that it's such a young country with so many outside influences. Some say it doesn't exist at all, and in some restaurants it simply means they are using the best Canadian products. Nevertheless, there are certainly a few traditional dishes that you won't find anywhere else in the world, and top chefs in all the major cities are producing inventive and exciting dishes that can truly be regarded as Canadian.

Dining with a view (above left), at Cadero's Restaurant, Vancouver. Super shredded beef nacho skillet (above center), a Manitoba specialty. Wonderful seafood is available in all coastal areas (above right)

Fusion remains a buzz word on the restaurant scene, notably in the Pacific Rim cuisine of the West Coast, incorporating Canadian and Oriental influences. Elsewhere, the longer established French and British cuisines are mixed with Native Canadian, and further embellished with the ethnic culinary skills of more recent arrivals. This has created such exotic dishes as seared sea scallops on a potato pancake with lemongrass lobster sauce, or venison wellington stuffed with enoki mushrooms. The original Canadian cuisine is, of course, that of the First Nations, and there are opportunities to sample this, for instance at one of the many tribal pow-wows that take place during the year. Tourist offices will have details.

The choice of restaurants in Canada has increased enormously in recent years as the immigrant population has brought about a gastronomic revolution. Cities such as Toronto, Montréal and Vancouver are now compared to New York for quality and diversity. The abundance of fresh produce, wild game, locally reared beef, and freshly caught fish and shellfish, along with award-winning Canadian beers and wines, makes dining throughout Canada a delectably memorable experience. In the major cities you'll find Greek, Italian, Polish, Ukrainian, Chinese, Vietnamese, Korean, and Thai restaurants, to name just a few. Not surprisingly, American chain restaurants have a strong presence. While meat and fish play a central role in many regional dishes, vegetarians and vegans can today find enough choice in most of the country, especially in the larger cities. Away from the cities choice of cuisine is more limited, but home-style cooking with local ingredients is often excellent and the service is friendly.

REGIONAL SPECIALTIES
The Atlantic provinces have their Acadian French, English and Scottish traditions, and proudly serve a tantalizing variety of seafood, from robust chowders to dainty deep-sea scallops. Freshly caught Atlantic cod, lobster, shrimp, and mussels are equally traditional fare. Steakhouses are popular, serving top-quality beef cooked to order, and many restaurants offer bison and caribou, adding their uniquely Canadian tastes and textures to many dishes. The rich ethnic flavors are reflected in dessert choices such as shoofly pie, chocolate mousse and strawberry cheesecake. Newfoundland's unusual cuisine includes brewis, a hard bread soaked and boiled with salt cod, which is eaten with fried salt-pork squares called scrunchions. Cod tongues and cheeks, and seal-flipper pie are other traditional dishes.

In Québec, restaurants offer a gastronomic pageant of fine French-style cooking. Laurentian pea soup, made of yellow split peas, is a Québecois specialty, as are fiddleheads (also a favorite in the Maritimes), the young shoots of the ostrich fern. The musical name refers to the similarity of the tightly curled fronds to the scroll of a violin head; they taste like a blend of broccoli, asparagus and globe artichoke. *Tarte au sucre* (sugar pie) is the favorite dessert choice here. Visitors to Montréal should sample the smoked meats, served piled high-rise style between two slices of rye bread. Most restaurants have an English-language menu, but you may have to ask for it. If you wish to save on the cost of a bottle of wine, it's common practice to bring your own in many of Québec's restaurants, and they will happily open your bottle and provide glasses.

EATING AND STAYING

Ontario, especially Toronto, is where fusion cooking excels. Here, chefs create masterpieces using a palette of fine ingredients mixed with the inspiration of the world's cuisines in dishes such as maple-glazed duck or tea-smoked sea bass. Toronto's multiethnic population is reflected in the abundance of restaurants, from Japanese *robata* bars to Mexican cantinas. Locally produced Canadian cheddar originated in Ingersoll, Ontario, where raw milk is used to make this tasty cheese. Corn, pumpkin, beans, and peaches are locally grown and provide inspiration for such delights as pumpkin mousse. Traditional shoofly pie is a molasses dessert that satisfies anyone with a sweet tooth. Ottawa, like Toronto, offers a wide variety of choices.

In the Prairies the abundance of grain and game feature on menus in the form of sourdough bread, bannocks (a griddle-baked flatbread made of oats or barley), Manitoba wild rice, barbecued ribs, Prairie-grazed beef, caribou, wild boar, and bison. Traditional Native American fare, including turkey, cornbread, and Saskatoon pie, made of berries similar to blueberries, is popular.

In the Rockies and British Columbia, Pacific and Arctic fish, Alaskan king crab and Fanny Bay oysters, plus wild game, appear on menus. Vancouver is recognized as having some of the best restaurant chefs in the country, who import the latest trends from Seattle, across the border. This city also has one of North America's largest Chinatowns, with some exceptionally good, authentic Chinese restaurants. However, it is the Ukrainian *pierogi* (filled dumpling) that is practically a national dish here.

The sparsely populated north is rather limited compared to other regions, but the quality, quantity and freshness of such wonderful homemade fare as home-smoked salmon, moose sausages, breads, and jams guarantee wholesome, tasty meals.

MEALS

Breakfast and brunch: A typical Canadian breakfast includes fresh fruit, yogurt, cereal, bacon and eggs, sausages, home-smoked kippers, pancakes or waffles with maple syrup, hash browns, bannocks, forach (oatmeal, cream and sugar), toast, bagels, homemade preserves, and muffins. Continental breakfasts of croissant, bread, butter, and jam are a lighter option, while brunch is a feast of breakfast and lunch dishes. Usually available weekends only, and generally a buffet, brunch may come with complimentary cocktails or wine, and can cost as little as $10 in some places.
Lunch: Set menus are excellent value in the larger cities, where you can eat for between $6 and $15.
Dinner: Dinner for two in a restaurant (excluding drinks) averages out to between $25 and $150. At top restaurants, the decor is often exquisite, but equally enjoyable are the little family-run restaurants that proudly show off local heritage. The views from your table can

An authentic taste of Canada's pioneering days— salmon cooked whole over a wood fire

offer such exotic sights as the aurora borealis in the north or Niagara Falls in Ontario, and you don't have to pay a lot for the pleasure.

WHERE TO EAT

Cafés and bistros: Cafés in all the cities offer an informal atmosphere with simple but good food at reasonable prices. Bistros are less formal than restaurants and the food is often of a very high standard.
Bars, brewpubs and pubs: Many bars in the cities have a happy hour, where you can enjoy free snacks along with your half-price drinks. Brewpubs offer a great selection of beers and standard pub food such as fish and chips, nachos and burgers. Pubs are informal, offering simple, inexpensive burgers, pasta and the like.
Restaurants: Some restaurants offer table d'hôte—a set menu with a set price, which is less expensive than choosing from the à la carte menu, although choices are limited.

WHAT TO DRINK

Coffee: In most diners and restaurants you pay for your first cup of coffee and the waiter or waitress refills it as many times as you like. Coffee is either regular (caffeinated) or decaf, black or with half-and-half (half milk, half cream) or cream—Canadians don't understand the term "white coffee." Sidewalk cafés like the Toronto-based Second Cup offer a large selection of excellent Italian coffees, and the US chain Starbucks has also moved in, although Tim Horton's is the one you'll see most.
Tea: Tea shops offer a selection of teas, including herbal, served with your choice of milk or lemon. If you want your tea brewed in the correct way—boiling water poured directly onto the tea or tea bag—you will have to spell it

out carefully, otherwise you are likely to get a cup of hot water and a tea bag in the saucer.
Beer: Canadian beers, like American brews, are light and fizzy, and are always served ice cold. Canadians are fond of their native Molson and Labatts beers, and Moosehead, brewed in New Brunswick, and Great Western Beer from Saskatchewan are also popular. Foreign beers, including Heineken made under license in Canada, are widely available. Real-ale devotees should not despair. Canada has an increasing number of microbreweries producing a variety of British-style real ales, along with lagers, pilsners and bock. Brewpubs offer beers brewed on the premises (tours are sometimes available). If you are in a group, it's cheaper to purchase a pitcher of beer to share.
Wine: Wine drinking has gained popularity in the past decade as the health benefits have hit the news. Most restaurants offer a fine selection of imported wines, but do try Canada's own. Since the 1980s, Canadian wines, both red and white, under a VQA (Vintner's Quality Assurance) have gained international acclaim. Ontario's Niagara Peninsula produces wines similar to those of Burgundy and the Loire Valley. British Columbia's Okanagan region and Vancouver's coastal islands produce some very

good Chardonnay, Merlot and Pinot Noir, as well as German varieties such as Riesling and Gewürztraminer. In addition, BC has become the largest producer of ice wine, a pricey dessert wine made from grapes picked and crushed while still frozen. There are also some vineyards in Québec and the Maritimes.
Spirits: A wide selection of spirits is available. Canadian Club is known all over the world, and has been based in Walkerville, Ontario, for about 150 years ago. VO rye whiskey is another domestic favorite. Cocktails using gin, rum, vodka, kahlua, and other spirits usually run from $4 up to $10, depending on the establishment.
Non-alcoholic drinks: Sodas, milkshakes, floats (soda and ice cream), and juice smoothies are a tasty, healthy alternative. Note that in Canada, cider is a non-alcoholic apple drink.

PRICES

In the listings that follow, these abbreviations are used within price information:
L – lunch (2-courses for two, without drinks)
D – dinner (3-courses for two, without drinks)
W – wine (least expensive bottle)
Remember that throughout Canada, the tax (see page 342) and tip (see page 345) are not included in the restaurant check.

MENU READER

apple butter: thick, dark brown apple preserve
Arctic char: a fish from the salmon family
assiette anglaise: cold meats
bangbelly: pork rice bun
biscuit: savory scone
brewis: hard bread boiled with salt cod
butter tarts: tarts made with butter, brown sugar, corn syrup, and raisins
capelin: tiny fish similar to smelts
chokeberry: small deep-purple berry also called aronia
chowder: thick seafood soup usually made with milk or cream
cipate chicken: meat and vegetable casserole with biscuit topping
cookie: biscuit
cranberry: a red North American berry rich in vitamin C
crème brûlée: creamy baked custard with caramelized sugar
cretons: spicy pork pâté
decaf: decaffeinated coffee
dim sum: Chinese breakfast and lunch buffet of hors d'oeuvres
dulse edible: dried deep-purple seaweed from the Bay of Fundy
escargot: snails in garlic butter
fat archie: Cape Breton molasses cookie
fiddleheads: young green shoots of the ostrich fern
finnan haddie: smoked haddock
foie gras: liver of specially fattened goose or duck
fricot: a hearty chicken soup
grunt: stewed fruit and dumplings
hash browns/home fries: pan-fried diced potatoes

ice wine: white wine made from pressed frozen grapes
Lunenburg sausage: Nova Scotia's hot spicy sausage
maple taffy: hot maple syrup chilled on snow and wrapped onto a stick
molasses thick: dark syrup produced from refining sugar or sorghum
Nanaimo bars: chocolate bars, originating in Nanaimo, Vancouver Island
partridgeberry: red berries used in preserves and pies
pemmican: dried meat preserved in cranberries and fat; a staple for mountaineers
pierogi: Ukrainian dumplings filled with cheese, potato, meat, or vegetables
Posole stew: hominy and meat stew
poutine: french fries, curd cheese and gravy
poutine rappé: potato dumpling with salt-pork filling
rapie pie: meat pie topped with potato
Saskatoon pie: berry pie popular in Saskatchewan
scone: small, round, sweet cake
scrapple: fried pork
scrunchions: fried salt-pork squares
shoofly pie: molasses or brown-sugar pie
snow crab: crab of polar waters with enormously long legs
Solomon Grundy: marinated herring
sourdough: bread made from fermented dough
sugar pie/tarte au sucre: open tart with a caramel-flavor or molasses filling
tourtière: meat and potato pie
toutons: pork bread
trempette: bread, cream and maple syrup

EATING AND STAYING

MAJOR RESTAURANT CHAINS

A useful selection of national and international restaurant chains available in Canada.

RESTAURANT CHAINS

A&W	Quality burgers and fries, and deservedly top-selling root beer in the world.	www.aw.ca
Arby's	Roast beef piled high in sandwiches and buns; also turkey and chicken, appetizers and desserts. 150 locations across Canada.	www.arbysrestaurant.com
Boston Pizza	Family restaurants with ribs, chicken, steak, and shrimp dishes, as well as the pizza and pasta. 113 locations in Canada.	www.bostonpizza.com
Chicken Delight	Canadian-owned company with 37 restaurants serving crispy-coated chicken, pizzas, wings, ribs, crinkle-cut fries. Eat in, take out, or drive-through.	www.chickendelight.com
Cultures	Toronto-based company, with 42 locations across Canada. Contemporary interior design; wide variety of soups, salads, sandwiches, baked goods, and yogurt.	tel:416/368-1440
Dairy Queen	The name is synonymous with soft ice cream, but you can also get burgers, chicken sandwiches, hot dogs, and fries.	www.dairyqueen.com
Dunkin Donuts	The biggest coffee and baked goods chain in the world, with quality coffee, plus a big range of doughnuts and bagels.	www.dunkindonuts.com
Golden Griddle	Comfort food (roasts, steaks, fish and chips, pasta, etc.) and table service. More than 60 locations in Canada, with one-third open 24 hours.	www.goldengriddlecorp.com
Greco Pizza Donair	New Brunswick company, specializing in pizzas, oven subs and donairs (doner kebabs). 55 locations in eastern Canada as far west as Ontario.	www.greco.ca
Hard Rock Café	Fajitas, steaks and grilled chicken, plus rock music and memorabilia (but only five branches in Canada so far).	www.hardrock.com
Harveys	Cheap fast food in formica surroundings; good for hot breakfasts.	www.harveys.ca
Hooters	Chicken wings, hotdogs, steaks, burgers, and sandwiches, but guys like it for the waitresses! Ten locations in Canada.	www.hooters.com
Humpty's	Calgary-based chain offering a huge menu, including meatloaf, fried chicken, burgers, liver and onions, omelets, and crisp salads. Great breakfasts.	www.humptys.com
Lone Star	Great Tex-Mex with cowboy theme; they make their own tortillas fresh on site. Just eight locations so far in Ontario and the Maritimes.	www.lonestarcafe.com
Made in Japan— A Teriyaki Experience	A secret recipe for teriyaki sauce and dishes prepared from fresh ingredients right before your eyes is the attraction here. Food court operation.	www.donatogroup.com
Manchu Wok	Freshly cooked Chinese food in about 100 locations in Canada; build-your-own or buffet-style options, plus two new drive-through outlets in Greater Toronto.	www.manchuwok.com
Mike's	Full-service Italian restaurants that are an eastern Canada favorite. They grow their own tomatoes, make pasta fresh each day and cure their own pepperoni.	www.mikes.ca
Mr Mike's West Coast Grill	Full-service casual restaurants with a West Coast feel, specializing in beef and promising "affordable indulgence" 22 outlets in Canada.	www.mrmikes.ca
Mrs Vanelli's	Food-court restaurants serving fresh Italian food, including pizza, panzerotti, pasta, and salads.	www.donatogroup.com
New York Fries	Superior fries are hand-cut, skin on, and cooked to order using a unique three-stage process. Just fries and soft drinks.	www.newyorkfries.com
Old Spaghetti Factory	Classic fresh pasta dishes, soups and salads in pleasant surroundings.	www.osf.com
Pizza Pizza	You'll find this popular pizza chain all over Ontario (and a few in Québec). Not just pizzas, but also stuffed burgers, chicken wings and nuggets, oven-toasted sandwiches, hotdogs, fries and salads.	www.pizzapizza.com
Ponderosa Steakhouse	Inexpensive, basic steakhouse, with cafeteria style for appetizers and ordering main course (which is then brought to your table). Six locations in Atlantic provinces. No-tipping policy.	www.ponderosasteakhouses.com
Red Lobster	Good fresh lobster, crab, shrimp, and other seafood, plus a couple of chicken dishes.	www.redlobster.com
Saint Cinnamon	Freshly baked cinnamon rolls and other pastries.	www.saintcinnamon.com
Smitty's	Family restaurants offering all-day breakfasts, burgers, pasta, stir-fries, wraps, soups, and salads.	www.smittys.ca
Swiss Chalet	Established in Toronto in 1954. Its specialty is chicken cooked in a slow-roasting rotisserie oven, with fresh-cut fries and crisp salads, plus stir-fries and burgers.	www.swisschalet.com
Taco Bell	Mexican fast food, including tacos, burritos, gorditas, and chalupas, all with beef, chicken, or steak-based fillings.	www.tacobell.com
Taco Time	Crisp and soft tacos, tortillas and burritos, with lots of tasty fillings, available at 110 Canadian locations.	www.tacotime.com
TGI Friday's	Steaks and ribs, chicken, shrimp, fajitas, cajun chicken, and burgers, usually served by hyperactive wait staff.	www.tgifridays.com
Tim Horton's	A Canadian institution for good coffee and fresh doughnuts. Any average-size town will have about 30 of them.	www.timhortons.com
Wendy's	Burgers –the best of this bunch, with freshly made patties, nothing frozen. 235 Canadian locations	www.wendys.com

STAYING IN CANADA

Canadians in general have a reputation for being polite and friendly, and this is nowhere more apparent than in the hospitality industry. You may occasionally meet an indifferent motel receptionist or a tetchy waiter, but it's extremely unusual, and for the most part you are made to feel very welcome wherever you go—and this is true across the board, from swanky downtown hotels to budget motels.

L'Hôtel Tadoussac (above left), on the Saguenay Fjord. Wood cabins (above center) provide delightful accommodations. The Carcross Hotel (top right) is on the scenic White Pass up in the Yukon

Canada has every type of accommodations: luxury hotels and vacation resorts equal to any in the world; chic boutique-style "designer" hotels in the cities; and beautiful historic properties serving as intimate bed-and-breakfasts. There are international-style, mid-range chain hotels in all the main towns and cities, and roadside motels are dotted along all the principal highways. To all of these, you can add the places that offer something particular, like the ranches where you can experience the cowboy's life, the fishing lodges that give access to Canada's premier fishing lakes and rivers, hotels with a championship golf course on the grounds, and winter resorts that have snowmobile parking and a handy ski-lift. Every kind of location is there, whether you want to be in the hub of the downtown action, or get so far away from it all that you have to fly in on a floatplane.

RESERVATIONS AND LATE ARRIVALS
Usually you can travel at will in Canada and find somewhere to stay without too much difficulty. In most cases, the supply fits the demand, and all towns, cities and vacation hotspots are well served with hotels, motels and restaurants. However, popular locations do fill up quickly in high season, so you'd be well advised to make a reservation well in advance. This is also true if your requirements are specific, or if there's a festival or convention coinciding with your visit. If you are heading north to the more remote areas, take a look at a map, make sure you understand the scale and get to grips with the enormous distances that can exist between settlements. These trips will need careful planning and you should make sure you have a

room waiting for you at the end of each day. Should you be running late on your journey, it's a wise precaution to call the hotel and let them know your expected arrival time so that you don't lose the room. If you do show up in town without a reservation, the tourist office may be able to help.

CATEGORIES OF ACCOMMODATIONS
Hotels in large cities range from high-priced luxury establishments to inexpensive dingy downtown joints, with fewer in the mid-priced range. Luxury hotels charge between $150 and $500 for a double room, with $250 getting you a deluxe room with amenities such as refrigerator, microwave, high-speed Internet access, CD, and VCR. For a mid-priced hotel, around $90 for a double, head for one of the chains such as Best Western or Holiday Inn, where you'll get a room that's comfortable and clean, but without the fine linen and extras. The lower end of the scale, at about $25 to $45 for a double, gets you a room that is central, often above a bar, and clean but run down.

Motels are usually found on the highways outside of towns and may be called motor hotels, lodges or inns. Prices mostly range from $45 to $80 for a double, with many offering free beds for children sharing a room with parents. Weekly rates can reduce the overall price, so don't forget to ask if you're interested. Motels vary in what they have to offer, but all will provide a comfortable bed, private bathroom, TV, and phone. Food is not usually available on the premises other than from a vending machine, so ask where the nearest restaurant is before you settle in. Some motels have a few self-catering rooms with small kitchenettes, which add little if anything to the price. Parking is free.

Cottages and cabins with one or more bedrooms, bathroom and kitchens are available in many areas, and can be rented for a single night or longer. They are often in scenic areas, and may have a veranda and barbecue, with onsite facilities such as laundry rooms and playgrounds. Prices can start at little more than you'd pay for a motel room. Holiday home rentals, in regular houses and apartments, are usually available only by the week, and are considerably more expensive.

Bed-and-breakfasts, or **gîtes du passant**, offer pleasantly furnished, comfortable rooms with a double bed and breakfast for around $50, more in some places. In some cities and towns hosts provide transportation to and from the airport, which can be very useful. Ask ahead if they offer a full hot breakfast or only a continental breakfast so that you are sure what you will be getting for your money. Tourist offices are very helpful in finding available bed-and-breakfasts for you and can often show you pictures to help you decide. Location is important, as some are well outside of the town or city.

Hostels affiliated with Hostelling International (HI) are graded as basic, simple, standard, and superior. These normally have single-sex dormitories and range in price from around $10 to $25 for members, many offering membership on the spot or a surcharge for non-members that can double the price. Most hostels will accept credit card bookings, some for up to six months in advance. There are HI offices around the world where you can obtain the Hostelling North America handbook. In Canada, contact Hostelling International, Room 400, 205 Catherine Street, Ottawa, Ontario, K2P 1C3 (tel: 613/237-7884 or 1-800/444-6111). City university residences are also available during the summer vacation period.

Campgrounds, usually open from May to October, run on a first-come, first-served basis, but some are beginning to offer advance reservations. July and August are the high season, when campgrounds in or near resorts fill up early in the day. Municipal campgrounds are inexpensive, normally about $5 per tent and $10 per RV, but are very basic. Private grounds often have more facilities, including stores, laundries, restaurants, swimming pools, tennis courts, and other amenities. Some have fully winterized tepees for rent, and provide winter sports such as dogsledding and showshoeing. Prices vary. National and provincial parks offer camping between May and September, but if you wish to camp outside of this period, it is often permitted and an "honesty box" is provided for collecting your fees. Backcountry camping is not for most people, but if you want to rough it in the wild, check that fires are permitted before starting one and use fire pits if provided. If you are in bear country, make sure you know all the necessary safety precautions, especially regarding the storage of food (racoons will also raid tents for food at night).

Resorts are usually open year round and range from luxurious hotel accommodations to cozy log cabins in the mountains and tepees alongside lakes, with prices between $100 and $500 depending on the location and facilities. Mountain resorts have spectacular views and offer winter sports such as skiiing, skating, bobsledding, and snowshoeing. Lakeside resorts are pleasant and relaxing, with boating, waterskiing and swimming in summer, skating and cross-country skiing in winter. Many resorts have superb restaurants, some have pools, health and fitness suites, weekly entertainment, and kids clubs, and some have their own golf course.

The Hampton Court is one of Toronto's modern hotels

Farms, ranches and fishing lodges offer a real Canadian experience. On farms and ranches you can often give a hand with the chores and will certainly have the opportunity to explore (or perhaps help round up the cattle) on horseback. You can expect great home-cooked food, lots of fresh air and as much exercise as you like. Fishing lodges cater to the real angling enthusiast, and are often located right on the edge of a scenic lake or riverbank.

RATINGS

Standards in Canada are generally high, and there are a couple of organizations that back this up with a ratings system. The AAA (commonly called Triple A), the US motoring organization, inspects and rates many hotels and restaurants across Canada using its one-to five-diamond categories. Information is published, in conjunction with the CAA (Canadian Automobile Association), in three regional guidebooks. Not all Canadian accommodations are covered, and they tend to major on the big guys—chain hotels and more luxurious places—though not to the total exclusion of more individual establishments. The other outfit is called Canada Select (www.canadaselect.com), which inspects and rates participating hotels and B&Bs with a one-to five-star system. Properties within this scheme show a distinctive "maple leaf with a roof" symbol. Canada Select also has a scheme for campgrounds, called Camping Select, but this is currently limited to the Atlantic provinces.

PRICES

The prices given in the listings in the following pages are for two people sharing a double room, per night. The quoted prices may or may not include breakfast and taxes, so check when making your reservations. Prices were correct at the time of printing, but may change during the lifetime of this book.

MAJOR HOTEL CHAINS

Company name	Company statement and regional coverage	Number of hotels	Website and contact number
Best Western	The world's biggest hotel chain, with 167 locations in Canada. Mid-range accommodations, some in interesting old buildings. Reward card.	167	800/WESTERN www.bestwestern.com
Choice	Nine brands, including Comfort, Clarion, Econo Lodge, Quality Inn, and Sleep Inn, provide good budget accommodations. Econo Lodge has rooms designed specially for seniors. Kids stay free. Air miles.	200	800/4-CHOICE www3.choicehotels.com
Crowne Plaza	Part of the Holiday Inn family, providing upscale, good-value accommodations aimed primarily at the business community.	8	www.crowneplaza.com
Days Inn	Five brands of budget hotels, most offering complimentary continental breakfast and newspaper.	72	800/DAYSINN www.daysinn.com
Delta	Canadian company with 37 luxury hotels and resorts countrywide. Big rooms, big beds, plush furnishings, and lots of amenities. Delta Privilege Club.	57	800/268-1133 www.deltahotels.com
Fairmont	North America's largest luxury hotel chain, most occupying historic landmark buildings. President's Club recognition program.	21	800/257-7544 www.fairmont.com
Four Points	A Sheraton brand with 15 Canadian locations, offering mid-scale, modern, full-service hotels that compete vigorously for the business market.	15	888/625-5144 www.starwood.com/fourpoints
Hilton	Not the biggest chain (though 500 hotels worldwide is not shabby), but one which has a reputation for quality and style. 18 prime locations in Canada.	18	800/HILTONS www.hilton.com
Holiday Inn	One of the best-known chains in the world, with modern, full-service hotels that have large rooms and a range of leisure facilities. Express brand provides good-value limited service options; Select is aimed at business people. Priority Club.	92	800/HOLIDAY www.sixcontinents hotels.com
Howard Johnson	A familiar name in North America for many decades, with a reputation for honest, good-value accommodations. Children stay free in parents' room.	49	800/446-4656 www.hojo.com
Hyatt	Luxury accommodations, with three brands: Regency forms the core, Grand serves culturally rich destinations and Park has a more intimate style.	3	800/532-1496 www.hyatt.com
Marriott	Upscale hotels with lots of leisure amenities; Courtyard brand has moderately priced business hotels; Residence and TownePlace Suites cater to long-stay guests; Fairfield Inns are quality motor lodges.	31	866/211-4607 www.marriott.com
Radisson	US company, with a strong presence in Canada. Quality hotels in strategic locations, run by upbeat management. Radisson Gold Rewards.	20	800/333-3333 www.radisson.com
Ramada	Part of Marriott family, with a range of mid-price hotels, boutique hotels and quality inns. Locations throughout Canada. Various reward schemes, including Air Miles.	61	888/835-0078 www.ramada.ca
Renaissance	Part of the Marriott company, Renaissance hotels, resorts and suites provide high-end boutique-style accommodations.	4	800/HOTELS-1 www.renaissancehotels.com
Sheraton	Long-established US chain, with 17 prime locations in Canada. Upscale modern accommodations with deluxe guest rooms and full range of services.	17	888/625-5144 www.starwood.com/sheraton
Super 8	One of the largest, fastest-growing motel chains in North America, with locations right across Canada. Properties inspected four times a year to maintain standards.	95	800/800-8000 www.super8.com
Travelodge/ Thriftlodge	About 90 Travelodge locations across Canada. Good-value rooms for short-stay visitors, some designed with kids in mind. Thriftlodge is its no-frills sister.	89	800/578-7878 www.travelodge.com
Wandlyn Inns	Nearly 20 full-service mid-range hotels in the Maritimes and Québec, most with indoor pool and hot tub. Kids Eat Free and Kids Stay Free, subject to availability.	20	800/561-0000 www.wandlyninns.com
Westin	Luxury hotels with distinctive architecture in superb settings, known for innovative features. 10 locations in Canada, including many cities and Whistler ski resort.	10	877/678-9330 www.starwood.com/westin

EATING

If you like seafood, you will think you have died and gone to heaven. Every province in the Maritimes has a strong fishing tradition, and the Atlantic Ocean's bounty, fresh from the sea, features heavily on many restaurant menus. Shediac, New Brunswick, is the lobster capital of the world, hauling in millions every year for shipping worldwide or for canning, but along every coast fishermen are landing fish and shellfish destined for local restaurants. Even the most modest diner might serve you the best you have ever tasted, and community lobster suppers, open to all, offer incredibly low-priced feasts.

Acadian cuisine includes a number of dishes that you won't find anywhere else, such as chicken *fricot*, a delicious and hearty soup, and *poutine rappé*, a potato dumpling filled with salt pork—quite rare now outside the home, but worth trying if you see it. Other specialties include beer from the Alexander Keith brewery and Cow's ice cream from PEI.

There are restaurants of every kind here. The bigger towns and cities will have fine dining and many kinds of cuisine from around the world. Out in the country, they'll probably be more homey. And there are plenty of American-style chains and diners, too.

STAYING

The provincial capitals make a good choice for a base. Halifax is big and brash, while the other capitals are more laid-back, with tree-lined streets in place of highrise blocks. Moncton, New Brunswick, is another good base—not especially pretty in itself, but with plenty of amenities, and an easy drive to the rest of the province, Prince Edward Island and Nova Scotia.

Outside of the cities, there are some enchanting bed-and-breakfasts, many in historic homes, cottage rentals and quality motels—some of which have wonderful coast or countryside views. There are also good campgrounds, including some within the national and provincial parks.

ALMA

⊘ CAPTAIN'S INN

8602 Main Street, Alma, New Brunswick, E4H 1N5
Tel 506/887-2017
A picturesque clapboard building with picket fence and orchard, just across from the little harbor (and those Fundy tides), and close to the Fundy National Park. Comfortable bedrooms are in a cheerful country style, with pale blue walls, pretty matching fabrics and pine furniture. All have private bathroom and TV;

some have ocean views. Snug parlor with fireplace, sunroom, and pleasant breakfast room where you can enjoy hot breakfasts, with homemade preserves and fresh fruit.
⊙ Year-round, but may close for a period in winter
🛏 $80, breakfast included
🚪 10 (all non-smoking)
⊗
🅿
🚌 In the village

ANNAPOLIS ROYAL

⊘ QUEEN ANNE INN

494 Upper St. George Street, Annapolis Royal, Nova Scotia, B0S 1A0
Tel 902/532-7850
www.queenanneinn.ns.ca
No expense was spared when this Victorian home was originally built, with a grand staircase, gleaming woodwork and elegant rooms, all set in spacious grounds with mature trees. Greg and Val Pyle are the welcoming hosts, and have given each of the large bedrooms an individual style, with Victorian furniture, luxury fabrics and distinctive design schemes. Each has a private bathroom. Breakfast is served at one large table.
⊙ Closed Nov–mid-Apr
🛏 $95–135, breakfast included
🚪 10 (all no-smoking)
⊗
🅿

BIG POND

⊕ RITA'S

Big Pond, Cape Breton, Nova Scotia, B1J 2E2
Tel 902/828-2667
www.ritamacneil.com
Singer-songwriter Rita MacNeil, a Canadian legend (her 18th album was released in 2002), bought this former schoolhouse, in the place where she grew up, as her family home.

When fans dropped by they were welcomed in, and her hospitality became so popular that Rita decided to open up as a tearoom. A comfortable, attractive place to enjoy home-baked goodies and a fresh pot of tea, and afterward you can take a look at Rita's awards and photographs, and visit the gift shop.
⊙ Daily 9–7, Jun–mid-Oct
🍴 L $22
⊗
🅿
🚌 40km (25 miles) west of Sydney on Highway 4

CHARLOTTETOWN

⊕ GAHAN HOUSE

126 Sydney Street, Charlottetown, Prince Edward Island, C1A 1G4
Tel 902/626-2337
www.peimenu.com/brewing
Traditional-style brewpub with polished dark wood and brick interior, in a historic building on the city's liveliest street. Six excellent ales are brewed on the premises, and brewery tours are available for groups of four or more (phone in advance). Above-average pub food includes soups and sandwiches, stir-fries, pizza, pasta, steaks, and seafood; most famous is the "Brown Bag Fish and Chips," fresh haddock coated in batter made with the brewery's own ale.
⊙ Mon–Thu 11am–midnight, Fri–Sat 11am–1am, Sun 11am–9pm
🍴 L $35, D $45, W $21
⊗ Section

P On site evenings and weekends, otherwise on street
National Historic District

☺INNS ON GREAT GEORGE
58 Great George Street, Charlottetown, Prince Edward Island, C1A 4K3
Tel 902/892-0606; 800/361-1118
www.innsongreatgeorge.com

In the heart of Charlottetown's National Historic District, this renowned inn consists of 12 properties that have been beautifully restored to provide luxury accommodations in 19th-century style. And

because they are separate buildings, there's a more intimate feel than in many hotels of similar size. The best rooms have an open fireplace and Jacuzzi, and all are elegantly furnished with antiques. The Pavilion building includes the breakfast room and a fitness room.
Year-round
$109–325, breakfast included
48 (all non-smoking)
P Street or nearby lots (charge)
Downtown, in the National Historic District

DINGWALL

☺MARKLAND COASTAL RESORT
Cabot Trail, Dingwall, Cape Breton, Nova Scotia, B0C 1G0
Tel 902/383-2246, 800/872-6084
www.marklandresort.com

About as far north as you can get on Cape Breton Island. You can't get here without being overwhelmed by the scenery, and this resort is no let-down. It consists of wooden cabins, surrounded by mountains, forests and unspoiled beaches. The natural warmth of the wooden floors, ceilings and walls sets the scene in the well-furnished but uncluttered cabins. The restaurant features fresh-caught seafood and organic local produce. There is

also a concert hall on site with weekly entertainment.
Year-round
$99–319
25
Outdoor
P
Northern tip of Cape Breton Island on the Cabot Trail

FREDERICTON

ⓘBREWBAKERS
546 King Street, Fredericton, New Brunswick, E3B 1E6
Tel 506/459-0067

Crispy pizzas from the wood-fired oven, pasta, fresh seafood, interesting salads, and entrées such as maple ginger salmon, Thai grilled chicken, and osso bucco are on the extensive menu. The open kitchen adds to the lively atmosphere. Warren of rooms with booths and tables, plus a stylish bar and patio seating on an upper deck. Fascinating array of antiques and curios.
Mon–Wed 11.30–10, Thu–Fri 11.30am–midnight, Sat 4–midnight, Sun 4–10
L $30, D $55, W $20
Section
P Nearby (charge)
Downtown

ⓘEL BURRITO LOCO
304 King Street, Fredericton, New Brunswick E3B 1E3
Tel 506/459-5626
www.elburritoloco-vallarta.com

The Mexican owner ensures authentic Mexican food. Guacamole made to order, fresh salsa made to a family recipe, interesting fillings for burritos, tortillas, tacos, tamales, and enchiladas. Platters include a taste of everything, and there are various combos—make sure you are very hungry. Wash it all down with Mexican beer.

Friendly, informal atmosphere enhanced by mismatched furniture, and bright Mexican

tablecloths, and the whole place is hung with a papel picado, with family photographs and Mexican posters adorning the walls.
Hours vary daily
L $12–16, D $45, W $17.99
P Nearby (charge)
Downtown

☺LORD BEAVERBROOK
659 Queen Street, Fredericton, New Brunswick, E3B 5A6
Tel 506/455-3371, 866/444-1946
www.lordbeaverbrookhotel.com

Behind a distinguished façade is an elegant and comfortable hotel, a city landmark since 1947. It couldn't have a better location, neighboring the art gallery, Playhouse and Legislature, and backing onto the wide St. John River. Governor's Room is the formal restaurant, the airy Terrace Restaurant overlooks the river and there's a smart bar lounge. Rooms are spacious, with cable TV and dark furniture.

The Oasis leisure club features a good-size swimming pool, whirlpool, sauna, and pool tables.
Year-round
$150
168 (150 non-smoking)
Indoor
P
11
Downtown

HALIFAX

ⓘSALTY'S ON THE WATERFRONT
1869 Upper Water Street, Halifax, Nova Scotia, B3J 1S9
Tel 902/423-6818
www.saltys.ca

Waterfront restaurant with a nautical theme, but get a window table and you won't care about the decor—the view across the harbor is stunning. Seafood fresh out of the water is the specialty, notably lobster, mussels, Atlantic salmon,

EATING AND STAYING

⑪ RYAN DUFFY'S STEAK AND SEAFOOD

5640 Spring Garden Road, Halifax, Nova Scotia, B3J 3M7
Tel 902/421-1116
www.rcr.ca

One of Canada's top 100 restaurants every year since 1987. Steak is a serious business here. You choose your cut of corn-fed American beef at the table, then it's taken away and cooked to your liking (they have no less than five different kinds of "rare"). Also has a good range of Atlantic seafood. Comfortable, stylish seating with velvet upholstery, subdued lighting and antiques.

🕐 Mon–Wed 11.30–11, Thu–Sat 11.30am–midnight, Sun 5–10
🍴 L $30, D $70, W $23
Ⓢ Section
🚌 1, 10, 80; free bus (called Fred) in summer
📍 Downtown, near Citadel Hill

and deep-sea scallops. Try the haddock baked with banana and almonds, or the rich seafood chowder. Kids' menu has a short selection of under-10s favorites, including peanut butter and honey sandwiches. Lunch and dinner are also available in the bar downstairs.

🕐 Daily 11.30–10 (varies seasonally)
🍴 L $30, D $50, W $25
Ⓢ
📍 Next door (charge)
🚌 2, 4, 6, 12, 32
⚓ End of Historic Properties pier

⊖ HALLIBURTON HOUSE INN

5184 Morris Street, Halifax, Nova Scotia, B3J 1B3
Tel 902/420-0658
www.halliburton.ns.ca

Historic property in the old part of town, elegantly

furnished with antiques. Rooms and suites all have private bathrooms (some with whirlpools), goose-down comforters (duvets), and cable TV. Four small adjoining dining rooms provide an intimate atmosphere in which to enjoy innovative cuisine featuring Atlantic seafood, bison and caribou. Pretty garden courtyard for cocktails and light meals on fine days; in winter, guests can relax by an open fire in the library.

🕐 Year-round
🛏 $110–210, continental breakfast included
🛌 29
Ⓢ
📍
🚌 7, 9

L'ANSE AU CLAIR

⊖ NORTHERN LIGHT INN

58 Main Street, P.O. Box 92, L'Anse au Clair, Newfoundland and Labrador, A0K 3K0
Tel 709/931-2332, 800/563-3188
http://nli.labradorstraits.net

Close to the border with Québec and one of the ferry services to Newfoundland, this is a good place to begin a trip to Labrador. It has some housekeeping cottages and RV sites with power hook-ups in addition to its hotel rooms and suites, all of which have cable TV and telephones. The Basque Dining Room is listed as one of the top 500 restaurants in Canada.

🕐 Year-round
🛏 $65–120
🛌 54
Ⓢ
📍
⚓ On Labrador Strait

LUNENBURG

⊖ LINCOLN HOUSE

130 Lincoln Street P.O. Box 322, Lunenburg, Nova Scotia, B0J 2C0
Tel 902/634-7179, 877/634-7179
www.lincolnhouse.ca

With its turret, dormer windows and wrought-iron fence, this historic B&B is right at home in the Lunenburg UNESCO World Heritage Site. Inside, the decor is pure Victorian, with hardwood floors, ornate fireplaces, stained glass, antique furniture and quality linens, plus handmade soap in the bathrooms. There's a sitting room and solarium

overlooking the harbor, and a shop selling exotic paper goods and rubber art stamps.

🕐 Mid-May to mid-Oct
🛏 $85–120, breakfast and afternoon tea included
🛌 4 (all non-smoking)
📍

MOBILE

⑪ CAPTAIN'S TABLE

Mobile, Newfoundland and Labrador, A0A 3A0
Tel 709/334-2278
www.captainstable.nf.ca

This restaurant is named after Newfoundland's greatest hero, Captain William Jackman, great-grandfather of the current owner-chef. The dining room has an open fireplace and is hung with Anne Meredith Barry prints. Delicious fresh seafood, including a hearty chowder, oven-baked Atlantic cod and other traditional Newfoundland dishes. Also excellent non-fish dishes and children's menu. For dessert, try the wonderful bumbleberry pie or apple dumpling.

🕐 Daily 11.30–9, mid-Apr to mid-Oct
🍴 L $28, D $44, W $12.50
Ⓢ
📍
🚌 Halleran's or Lawlor's Irish Loop service from St. John's
⚓ On south coast, a 35-minute drive from St. John's along Route 10

MONCTON

⑪ MAVERICK'S STEAK AND LOBSTERHOUSE

40 Weldon Street, Moncton, New Brunswick, E1C 5V8
Tel 506/855-3346

Don't expect a full Texan cowpoke theme or country-and-western music—this is an upscale restaurant with plush furnishings and just a few understated paintings featuring cattle. The charbroiled steaks here are succulent—juicy and full of flavor—and vegetables are perfectly cooked. Hors

d'oeuvres include lobster-stuffed mushrooms, coconut shrimp and seafood chowder; desserts such as cheesecake, pecan pie and chocolate mousse come in generous portions.

🕐 Mon–Fri 11.30–2, 5–10, Sun 4–9
🍴 L $60, D $80, W $20
🚭 Section
🅿 Nearby (charge)
🚌 1, 2, 3, 4, 7, 8, 9, 10, 16, 23
🚇 Downtown

⊖CHATEAU MONCTON

100 Main Street, Moncton, New Brunswick, E1C 1B9
Tel 506/870-4444, 800/576-4040
www.chateau-moncton.nb.ca

This motel is a cut above the average, in a distinctive five-story building right beside the Petitcodiac River. Le Galion bar has a superb river view and an open-air deck, perfect for

viewing the tidal bore that surges upstream at high tide. The interior is European-style elegance, with coordinated fabrics and friendly uniformed staff. Bedrooms and suites (some with whirlpool bathtub) have extended cable TV, high-speed Internet access and free local calls.

🕐 Year-round
🛏 $119–139, continental breakfast included
ⓘ 106 (70 percent non-smoking)
♿ 🛎
🅿
🚌 1, 2, 3, 4, 7, 8, 9, 10, 16, 23
🚇 Downtown, near train station

NORTH RUSTICO

⊖NORTH RUSTICO MOTEL AND COTTAGES

RR 2, Hunter River, North Rustico, Prince Edward Island, C0A 1N0
Tel 902/963-2253, 800/285-8966
www.isn.net/~cottages

Overlooking lovely North Rustico Harbour, and handy for the attractions of Cavendish and the national park, this is a friendly family-run establishment. There's a range of wooden cottages with porches, and a small motel block. The snug cottages, all warm pine inside, are equipped with full-size refrigerator, microwave and a gas barbecue outside. In the morning, guests congregate in the enclosed sundeck at the house for the complementary breakfast buffet. There is a swimming pool, playground and laundry room on site.

🕐 May–Oct
🛏 $80–160, breakfast included
ⓘ 38
🏊 Outdoor
🅿
🚌 Route 6, 8km (5 miles) east of Cavendish

ST. JOHN'S

⊕CABOT CLUB

The Fairmont Newfoundland, Cavendish Square, St. John's, Newfoundland and Labrador, A1C 5W8
Tel 709/726-4980

A superb, upscale restaurant, its refined atmosphere enhanced by classical music, would be enough for anyone, but here you can add a spectacular view of Signal Hill and the harbor (and passing icebergs in winter) through picture windows. Traditional Newfoundland cuisine,

expertly prepared, includes fresh local seafood and sumptuous desserts. Dress code is casual-dressy. Reservations recommended.

🕐 Mon–Sat 6–10pm

⊖THE MURRAY PREMISES HOTEL

5 Becks Cove, St. John's, Newfoundland and Labrador, A1C 6H1
Tel 709/738-7773, 866/738-7773
www.murraypremiseshotel.com

Overlooking the harbor, this former salt-cod warehouse dating from 1846 is now a luxurious boutique hotel with handmade furniture, top-quality furnishings and up-to-the-minute facilities that include whirlpool baths, cable TV, Internet connections, and voice mail. Dotted around are fascinating reminders of its past, and the old beams, exposed brickwork and quirkily slanting roofs all add to the atmosphere. The seafood restaurant and Italian restaurant here are each under separate ownership.

🕐 Year-round
🛏 $199–249
ⓘ 28 (all non-smoking)
♿
🅿

🍴 D $40–50, W $15
🚭 Section
🅿
🚌 3, 5, 15
🚇 Downtown

SUMMERSIDE

⊕STARLITE DINER AND DAIRY BAR

810 Water Street, Summerside, Prince Edward Island, C1N 4J8
Tel 902/436-7752
www.starlitediner.pe.ca

A total 1950s experience, with a neon-lit frontage, jukeboxes in the booths (bring plenty of quarters), waitresses in 1950s fashions and old gas pumps and Coca Cola memorabilia inside. Good down-home cooking features burgers, hot dogs, fried clams, barbecued chicken, and "the biggest breakfast in town." Desserts major on ice-cream sundaes, and beverages include sodas, milk shakes, floats, and cherry Coke.

🕐 Daily 7am–10pm
🍴 L $16, D $25
🚭
🅿
🚌 East of town at Read's Corner, intersection of Highways 1A and 11

EATING AND STAYING

Maple syrup for sale at a Québec City store

EATING

As you would expect, there's a strong French influence in the food of this staunchly Gallic province. The combination of traditional French recipes with top-quality local ingredients produces some stunning dishes. Seafood comes direct from the Gulf of St. Lawrence on the day it is caught, and meat dishes might include caribou from the northern tundra and other local game. Among the dessert choices, try the *tarte au sucre* (sugar pie).

Montérégie, to the south of Montréal, is known as the Garden of Québec, an area of plains and low hills that are perfect for its apple orchards, vineyards and maple groves. Québec also has some fine local beers and cheeses. Lac Brome, in the Eastern Townships, is famous for its duck, featured in a gastronomic fall festival.

Around March, when the sap starts to rise, head for a *cabane à sucre* (sugar shack) to try maple taffy—hot syrup is poured onto clean snow, and as it starts to harden, you wrap it round a little stick and pop it into your mouth.

There are all kinds of eateries here, particularly in cosmopolitan Montréal, ranging from charming historic *auberge* properties to bar food and sophisticated restaurants.

STAYING

Montréal is the place to stay if you are looking for a big-city buzz and all that goes with it—fantastic shopping, quality entertainment and nightlife, and the brash atmosphere of a busy metropolis. Québec City is quieter, but full of character, with a gorgeous historic heart.

Beyond the major towns and cities, there are some splendid resort hotels, *hôtelleries champétre*, with superb views, gourmet cuisine and a range of activities. In the Laurentians, Mont Tremblant is a chic resort, well placed for hiking and winter sports in magnificent surroundings. Meanwhile, along the coast, there are enchanting settlements with terrific sea views.

AYER'S CLIFF

❶ AUBERGE RIPPLECOVE INN

700 Ripplecove Road, Ayer's Cliff, Québec, J0B 1C0
Tel 819/838-4296, 800/668-4296
www.ripplecove.com
A beautiful building on a peninsula overlooking Lake Massawippi. Refined international cuisine is served in a superb dining room, with upholstered chairs and formal table settings set amid the glow of a warm-toned decor. The varied lunch menu

might include snow-crab cake, Wiener schnitzel and stir-fried Szechuan shrimp, while at dinner there's a four-course table d'hôte menu, a Canadian menu and a Québec menu. The wine list is huge.
🕙 Year-round for lunch and dinner
💷 L $44, D $108 (4 courses), W $20
🚭 Section
🅿
🚌 On Route 141, 8km (5 miles) south of Highway 55 intersection 21

BAIE-ST-PAUL

⊖ AUBERGE LA MAISON OTIS

23 rue St. Jean Baptiste, Baie-St-Paul, Québec G3Z 1M2
Tel 418/435-2255, 800/267-2254
www.quebecweb.com/maisonotis
A traditional Québec-style hotel, extended to provide a health and beauty suite, an indoor swimming pool, a renowned restaurant, and a café. Attractive bedrooms come in various sizes (some in the original building are a bit compact) and have beautiful furniture, including French colonial-style beds, plus fireplaces and a decor of pastel shades and pretty fabrics. Outside, there are lovely gardens and a stylish terrace.
🕙 Year-round
💷 $155–223, breakfast and dinner included
🛏 30
🏊 Indoor
🅿

BEAUPORT

❶ MANOIR MONTMORENCY

2490 avenue Royale, Parc de la Chute-Montmorency, Beauport, Québec, G1C 1S1
Tel 418/663-3330
www.sepaq.com/chutemontmorency
Don't be deterred by the fee to enter the park—it will be refunded on production of your restaurant receipt. Bay windows in the dining room give spectacular views of the Montmorency Falls and river, but even this won't distract you from the excellent Québec cuisine, blending traditional French recipes with such local ingredients as cranberries and game.
🕙 Daily 10–10
💷 L $26, D $60, W $29.95
🚭 Section
🅿
🚌 Metrobus 800, then bus 50

CHATHAM

⊖ LA 5EME SAISON

265 chemin du Lac Louisa, Chatham, Québec, J8G 2C9
Tel 450/533-1130
www.la5emesaison.com
A unique camping experience is offered here in authentic tepees that have comfortable beds, a raised floor and a woodburning stove—you even get breakfast delivered. Set amid pinewoods, sites have private bathrooms, picnic table, hammock, and firewood, and are close to the lake for swimming and canoeing; also nature trails, badminton courts and horseshoe pits.

Tepees are fully winterized and amazingly snug; dog-sledding, snowshoeing and ice-fishing can be arranged. Credit cards not accepted.

🕐 Year-round
💲 $100–300
🛏 3 tepees
🅿
🚗 Off Route 327 near Brownsburg

GASPÉ

🍴 CAFÉ DES ARTISTES

249 boulevard de Gaspé, Gaspé, Québec, G4X 1A5
Tel 418/368-2255

Just over 1km (half a mile) from the Musée de la Gaspésie, this charming café doubles as a gallery for the work of local artists, notably the owners. You can watch artists at work in the atelier, too. There's a warm atmosphere, with natural wood tones, in this lovingly restored home. The simple table d'hôte menu includes homemade ice creams and home-roasted coffee.

🕐 Daily 11am–10pm, Jun–mid-Sep
🍴 L $20, D $30–40
🚭

MONT TREMBLANT

🍴 LA TABLE ENCHANTÉE

1842 Route 117 North, Mont Tremblant, Québec, J8E 2Y2
Tel 819/425-7113
www.mt-tremblant.com/table

Attractive gardens and hanging baskets out front, and hanging houseplants and natural wood inside give a nice country feel to this little restaurant in the heart of the Laurentians. The accomplished cook specializes in game and traditional cuisine. Hors d'oeuvres include fiddlehead greens au gratin, wild mushrooms, brown-bean soup, and roast-pork jelly. Main courses feature game pie, medallions of caribou, sauté of chicken with maple sauce, or Atlantic salmon. There's a moderate, well-

chosen wine list to accompany the food.

🕐 Tue–Sat 5–10
🍴 D $50, W $22.50
🚭
🅿
🚗 On Route 117, 1km (half-mile) north of intersection wth Montée Ryan

🏨 FAIRMONT TREMBLANT

3045 chemin Principale, Mont Tremblant, Québec, J0T 1Z0
Tel 819/681-7000
www.fairmont.com

Superb Year-round resort set beneath the highest peaks in the Laurentians. Popular with winter sports enthusiasts, but there's lots to do all year, much of it right in the hotel, including swimming pools, a health and fitness suite, and a kids' club. Regular rooms and suites have fairly standard hotel furnishings, cable TV, coffeemaker, hairdryer, and minibar. Fairmont Gold guests get special treatment, with their own lounge, concierge and check-in. Many rooms have wonderful mountain views and windows open to let in the clean air.

🕐 Year-round
💲 $127–429
🛏 316
🏊 🐾 🔥 Indoor and outdoor, heated
🅿
🚗 In resort village

MONTRÉAL

🍴 AUBERGE LE ST-GABRIEL

426 rue St-Gabriel, Montréal, Québec, H2Y 2Z9
Tel 514/878-3561
www.auberge1754.com

Formal, but family-friendly, this is the oldest (1754) *auberge* in North America, with a historic dining room and two lovely terraces. Food is an inventive mixture of traditional French and Québec, with hors d'oeuvres such as apple caribou terrine and Florentine Atlantic salmon; main courses

include cranberry-stuffed turkey with mandarin devil sauce and fried chestnuts, and piglet filet mignon with wild mushrooms. The wine list has a good international selection. Sunday brunch (with a clown for the kids) is popular.

🕐 Daily 6–10pm; also open for lunch daily 11–2.30, Apr–Nov
🍴 L $37, D $60, W $25
🚭
🚌 14, 53
🚗 Old Montréal, between rue Notre-Dame and St-Paul

🍴 BEN'S MONTREAL-DELI

990 boulevard de Maisonneuve Ouest, Montréal, Québec, H3A 1M5
Tel 514/844-1000

Locked into the 1950s, with its formica and chrome interior, soda-fountain counter and diner-style seating, this deli goes back even further—to 1908, when the Kravitz family started the business. It's big on smoked-meat sandwiches and platters, but also has other basics like burgers and pasta. Strawberry cheesecake is a popular dessert. Everything is decidedly no-frills here, but that doesn't detract from the appeal; the walls are adorned with photographs of celebrity patrons of many years ago.

🕐 Sun–Wed 7.30am–2am, Thu 7.30am–3am, Fri–Sat 7.30am–4am
🍴 L $12–30, D $12–30
🚭
🅿 (Charge)
🚇 Peel or McGill
🚌 15, 420
🚗 Downtown, corner of Metcalfe

🍴 BISTRO 2000

2000 rue St-Denis, Montréal, Québec, H2X 3K7
Tel 514/843-2000
www.bar-resto.com/bistro2000

In the heart of the Latin Quarter, this lively, Paris-style bistro is something of an international meeting place, particularly at festival time, when a table out front under the awning is a prime people-watching place. There's also a quieter patio at the back. The cool, pale blue interior is set off by green plants, and the menu includes such bistro favorites as escargots, French onion soup, mussels, poached salmon, and bison burgers.

🕐 Daily 11.30am–midnight
🍴 L $25, D $45, W $20
🚭

P Street (free) or parking area at rear (charge)
Sherbrooke or Berri-UQAM
24, 125
Latin Quarter, near intersection with Sherbrooke

CAFÉ DES BEAUX-ARTS
Museum des Beaux-Arts, 1384 rue Sherbrooke Ouest, Montréal, Québec, H3G 1J5
Tel 514/843-3233
www.mmfa.qc.ca
A great place to take a break from the artworks, rest your feet and refuel for the afternoon. This is an elegant bistro with dark wood, honey-toned walls, white table linen, and a chic bar area. The menu has such offerings as duck confit, deer steak with mush-rooms, walnuts, cranberries and red wine sauce, and warm mesclun salad with sautéed beef filet and pine nuts. Save some room for the heavenly crème brûlée.
Thu–Tue 11–5, Wed 11–8; lunch served 11.30–2.30
L $40, D $50, W $24
S
P Nearby (charge)
Guy-Concordia
24
Downtown, at Sherbrooke and Bishop

CASA CUBA
4218 rue de la Roche, Montréal, Québec, H2J 3H9
Tel 514/526-2822
www.bar-resto.com/casacuba
Exuberant Latin American atmosphere created by Cuban music, vast murals and memorabilia on the bright blue walls, and—not least—friendly Cuban staff. The menu includes plenty of shrimp and chicken dishes seasoned with Caribbean herbs, spices and sauces, and some pastas and fajitas. There is also a long list of cocktails for an added dash of tropical atmosphere.
Tue–Sun 6–10pm
D $45, W $16.50
S
P Nearby
Sherbrooke
24
Corner of Rachel

GIBBY'S
298 Place d'Youville, Montréal, Québec, H2Y 2B6
Tel 514/282-1837
www.gibbys.ca

L'EXPRESS
3927 rue St-Denis, Montréal, Québec, H2W 2M4
Tel 514/845-5333
A lively bistro with the special atmosphere that comes from lots of regulars having a good time. In a long, narrow room, with a checkerboard floor, zinc bar and pub-style furniture, classic, unpretentious bistro fare includes pâté, caviar, bouillabaisse, steak tartare, fresh seafood, and steak-frites. The wine list is exclusively French, and cocktails are also available. Reservations are essential, though you might get in without one if you turn up at 2am; when you call, ask for directions—it's not easy to spot from the outside.
Daily 8am–3am
L $25–40, D $40–60, W $19
S
P Street (charge)
Sherbrooke
30, 144
Latin Quarter/Mont-Royal, between Duluth and Roy

If you like oysters, this is the place to go. It's equally renowned for succulent steaks and seafood (more than a dozen kinds, including salmon smoked on the premises), plus homemade bread, pastries and chocolates. A fine old archway leads into the courtyard where Gibby's occupies a converted 17th-century stable, with old beams and stone walls. There's a snug lounge with fireplace where you can await your table, plus courtyard seating for bar patrons in summer.
Daily 5–11 or 11.30pm (opens 4.30pm Sat)
D $120, W $28
S Section
P Valet (free)
Square Victoria
61, 75
Old Montréal, just east of McGill

LE COMMENSAL
1204 avenue McGill College, Montréal, Québec, H3B 4J8
Tel 514/871-1480
One of a popular chain of vegetarian restaurants offering a vast buffet that includes some clearly indicated vegan

options. You help yourself and then pay by the weight of the food on your plate, so it's difficult to anticipate the cost, particularly when everything looks so tempting. There are about a dozen desserts, too, again with vegan possibilities.
Daily 11.30–10
L $20–30, D $30–40
S
P
McGill
15
Corner of rue Ste-Catherine

LE PIMENT ROUGE
1170 rue Peel, Montréal, Québec, H3B 4P2
Tel 514/866-7816
Widely regarded as serving the best Szechuan cuisine in the city, this is a chic restaurant in a historic building. Pastel hues and huge windows, plus a tower of 3,000 wine bottles (priced up to $3,000) in the

middle, set the scene for elegant dining. The carefully prepared and presented dishes include Szechuan shrimp and beef with mango strips and Kahlua sauce, General Tao's chicken, crispy duck, and orange beef. You'll be mixing with local tycoons, politicians and celebrities, and dressy casual attire is the norm.
Mon–Fri 11.30–11 (midnight Fri), Sat noon–midnight, Sun noon–11. Closed major holidays
L $40, D $60, W $33
S
P Nearby (charge)
Peel
15, 107, 150
Downtown, between Ste-Catherine and René Lévesque

MARCHÉ MÖVENPICK
1 place Ville-Marie, Montréal, Québec, H3B 2C3
Tel 514/861-8181, 800/695-5771
www.movenpickcanada.com
If you're shopping in the Ville Souterraine, this is a fun place

EATING AND STAYING

to take a break. First you get a "passport" that includes a map showing the huge number of restaurants and food stores on site: pasta, pizza, grills, sushi, seafood, deli, bakery, and lots more. Then you move among them, picking and choosing as you go, and getting a stamp on your card from each outlet you use. You pay at the end at a single cashier. It's a great way to please everyone.

🕐 Daily 7am–2am
🍽 L $25, D $35, W $30
🚭
🅿 Nearby (charge, but free after 5pm and Sat–Sun)
Ⓜ McGill or Bonaventure
🚌 150, 410, 420, 535, 935

⑪ NUANCES

Casino du Montréal, 1 avenue du Casino, Montréal, Québec, H3C 4W7
Tel 514/392-2708, 800/665-2274
www.casino-de-montreal.com

On the fifth floor of the casino, Nuances is one of the top-rated restaurants in North America, presenting gourmet French cuisine in formal surroundings: rich mahogany, white linen and fine tableware. The large windows offer panoramic view over the St. Lawrence River and the city. The combinations of tastes and textures is nothing short of artistic: asparagus and lobster chartreuse appetizer, loin of lamb cooked in clay with gnocchi, parmesan-breaded eggplant (aubergine), and bell-pepper ratatouille, or lobster and scallops with vegetables and pesto linguini. Dress code calls for business-style attire; no diners under 18.

🕐 Mon–Fri 5.30–11pm, Sat–Sun 5.30–11.30pm
🍽 D $120, W $54
🚭
🅿 On site (free) and valet (charge)
Ⓜ Jean-Drapeau then free shuttle bus
🚌 Casino bus 167
🚗 Autoroute Bonaventure exit 2, then cross Port de la Concorde

⑪ SOTO

3527 boulevard St-Laurent, Montréal, Québec, H2X 2T6
Tel 514/842-1150
www.restaurantsoto.com

Cool and classy, with pale green walls, modern art and architectural features, this is one of three Soto restaurants in Québec. You can choose from 80 varieties of sushi, sashimi, tempura, and yakitori—and no less than 20 brands of sake—all beautifully prepared by Japanese chefs. In addition to the dining room with conventional seating, there's a private dining room where you sit Japanese style on the floor.

🕐 Sun–Wed 5.30–10, Thu 5.30–11, Fri–Sat 5.30–11.30
🍽 D $60
🚭
🅿 Nearby (charge)
Ⓜ St-Laurent
🚌 55
🚗 Just south of rue Prince Arthur

⑪ WEINSTEIN AND GAVINO'S PASTA BAR

1434 rue Crescent, Montréal, Québec, H3G 2B6
Tel 514/288-2231

There's always a buzzing atmosphere in this trendy Italian place on Montréal's nightclub strip. The interior has warm tones, and there's an open gallery upstairs, plus a terrace for warm weather. Long list of fresh, homemade antipasti, soups, salads, pastas,

and pizzas, along with main courses that include chicken, steak, lamb, and fish dishes, and—a curious departure from the Italian—*pad Thai*. Floor-to-ceiling shelves are stacked with bottles from Italian, French and New World wineries.

🕐 Sun–Wed 11–11, Thu–Sat 11–midnight
🍽 L $40, D $50, W $28
🚭
🅿 Street (charge)
Ⓜ Guy-Concordia
🚌 15
🚗 Between Maisonneuve and Ste-Catherine

⑪ WITLOOF

3619 rue St-Denis, Montréal, Québec, H2X 3L6
Tel 514/281-0100

In the midst of so many French eateries, this Belgian bistro offers something similar but markedly different. It has a chic, uncluttered interior, convivial cosmopolitan atmosphere and pleasant, professional service. The Belgian (largely Flemish) dishes include the usual steaming bowls of mussels, steak tartare, fish stew, and *frites* with mayonnaise, and the menu has been expanded to include dishes with a South of France influence. Belgian beers are also available. Incidentally, *witloof* is Flemish for endive (chicory).

🕐 Mon–Wed 11–3, 5–10, Thu–Fri 11–3, 5–midnight, Sat 5–midnight, Sun 5–10
🍽 L $25–45, D $30–55, W $25
🚭
🅿 Street (charge)
Ⓜ Sherbrooke
🚌 Mont Royal, north of Sherbrooke

🛏 AU GÎTE OLYMPIQUE

2752 boulevard Pie IX, Montréal, Québec, H1V 2E9
Tel 514/254-5423, 888/254-5423
www.gomontrealgo.com

A warm welcome is assured at this B&B, not just from the owner, but from pet shnauzer Sasha (she doesn't lick). Rooms are individually decorated with pastel shades—one has a classical arch and columns framing the headboard; another has a

bright Mexican theme. In addition to the ground-level lounge, there's a snug basement sitting room with rattan furniture and a second TV. Breakfast is taken at one large table in the dining room or, in summer, on garden terraces. It's all very restful, in spite of its location on a busy road.

🕐 Year-round
🛏 $95–125, breakfast included
🛈 5 (all non-smoking)
🚭
Ⓜ Pie IX

AUBERGE DE LA FONTAINE
1301 rue Rachel Est, Montréal, Québec, H2J 2K1
Tel 514/597-0166, 800/597-0597
www.aubergedelafontaine.com
B&B in a peaceful location on Mont Royal, overlooking pretty Parc Lafontaine. Beautiful rooms and suites are decorated in bold tones, sometimes paired with brick walls, and furniture and fabrics are modern; some rooms have whirlpool tub, balcony or view over the park. Continental breakfast buffet includes bread, pastries, cheese and cold meats, yogurt and fresh fruit. Guests have free access

to kitchen noon to midnight for beverages and snacks, or to use the stove or microwave.
- Year-round
- $129–243, breakfast included
- 21
-
- Limited; street parking (free)
- Mont Royal
- 14

AUBERGE DU VIEUX-PORT
97 rue de la Commune Est, Montréal, Québec, H2Y 1J1
Tel 514/876-0081, 888/660-7678
www.aubergeduvieuxport.com
An 1882 building houses this fine hotel, with stone walls, wooden beams and gleaming hardwood floors. Bedrooms have huge brass or wooden beds, private bathroom, cable TV, stereo system, and voice mail—there's even an umbrella. Windows stretch almost from

floor to ceiling and have views over the St. Lawrence River or historic rue St-Paul. The roof terrace also has wonderful views, and gourmet dinners are served here when the city puts on fireworks displays.
- Year-round
- $165–290
- 27 (all non-smoking)
-
- Valet (charge)
- Champ-de-Mars
- 55
- Vieux Montréal

CHÂTEAU VERSAILLES
1659 rue Sherbrooke Ouest, Montréal, Québec, H3H 1E3
Tel 514/933-8111, 888/933-8111
www.versailleshotels.com
A complete renovation has added imaginative touches to the historic architectural features in this luxury hotel, with bold shades offset by ornate white plaster moldings and huge old fireplaces. The richly toned walls are hung

with Matisse reproductions and the wooden furniture has been custom made. Bathrobes and Fruits et Passion bathroom packs are provided, and rooms all have cable TV, Nintendo, minibar, hairdryer, coffee-maker, and modem point. Stylish bar and restaurant, plus a comfortable lounge.
- Year-round
- $165–315
- 65
-
- On site and valet (charge for both)
- Guy-Concordia
- 15, 57, 165
- Downtown, corner rue St-Mathieu

FAIRMONT QUEEN ELIZABETH
900 boulevard René Lévesque Ouest, Montréal, Québec, H3B 4A5
Tel 514/861-3511
www.fairmont.com
The choice of royalty and celebrities ever since it opened

in 1958. John Lennon's famous bed-in, during which he wrote and recorded "Give Peace a Chance," was held here in Suite 1742 in 1969. Rooms are decorated in warm tones, with contemporary furniture, cable TV, Play Station, and a video check-out facility. Premier rooms and suites have best views. The Beaver Club restaurant is renowned for gastronomic dining, and there's an extensive modern health club. Immediate access to underground city.
- Year-round
- $135–279
- 1,050
- Indoor
- On site and valet (charge)
- Bonaventure
- 150, 410, 420, 535, 935
- Downtown, above train station

LE GERMAINE
2050 rue Mansfield, Montréal, Québec, H3A 1Y9
Tel 514/849-2050, 877/333-2050
www.hotelboutique.com
The high-gloss, black and glass doorway framed in shiny bronze clearly indicates you are entering a hotel that's supremely cool and classy. The

theme is stylish loft living, with natural lighting enhancing the earth tones, leather chairs, dark wood, glass, and mirrors. Furniture is sleek and modern, beds have cuddly down comforters (duvets) and high-quality linen; other little luxuries include fresh fruit, bottled water, bathrobe, large-screen TV (with cable and VCR), minibar, and CD-clock-radio. Efficient room service and excellent breakfast buffet.
- Year-round
- $210–450, breakfast included
- 101 (16 non-smoking)
-
- On site and valet (charge)
- Peel
- 24

⊙MANOIR HARVARD

4805 avenue Harvard, Notre-Dame de Grâce, Montréal, Québec, H3X 3P1

Tel 514/488-3570, 888/373-3570

www.manoirharvard.com

Proudly displaying its Grand Prix du Tourisme awards, this picturesque B&B in a Victorian mansion offers five large rooms that are stylishly designed with plain, pale walls, dark antique furniture and hardwood floors. All have a private bathroom, and some overlook the beautiful garden, which guests are welcome to enjoy. Breakfasts, served at one big table, are a real feast— Belgian waffles, French toast with maple syrup, quiches, pancakes, and eggs, as well as croissants, muffins, cereals, and fruit.

⊙ Year-round

🖐 $175, breakfast included

🛏 5 (all non-smoking)

💲

🅿

🚇 Villa Maria

🚌 West of downtown

⊙PIERRE DU CALVET

405 rue Bonsecours, Montréal, Québec, H2Y 3C3

Tel 514/282-1725

www.pierreducalvet.ca

You won't find a more historic place to stay in Montréal. Built in 1725, the hotel is named after an influential free-thinker (they'll tell you his story if you ask). Built in typical French colonial style, it contains a pleasing array of antiques, family heirlooms and portraits. Bedrooms have some huge old beds, including four-posters, and such modern conveniences as modem points. Breakfast is served in the Greenhouse, a Victorian conservatory with plants, a fountain and exotic birds.

⊙ Year-round

🖐 $225–300

🛏 9

💲

🅿 Charge

🚇 Champ-de-Mars

🚌 Vieux Montréal

⊙RÉSIDENCES UNIVERSITAIRES DE L'UQAM

303 boulevard René Lévesque Est, Montréal, Québec, H2X 3Y3

Tel 514/987-6669

www.residences-uqam.qc.ca

Budget accommodations on campus, close to the lively Latin Quarter. The studio rooms, with one double bed, private bathroom and kitchen/dining area, are most compact; there are also two-bedroom units (one double, one single) with full kitchen and bathroom, and some with eight bedrooms that are good for groups. Bed linen and towels are provided, and there's a café and laundry room on the premises. Guests have the use of the university sports facility.

⊙ Mid-May to mid-Aug

🖐 $47.50–55

🛏 332

🅿 Indoor parking nearby (charge)

🚇 Berri-UQAM

🚌 14, 15, 150

🚌 East of downtown

⊙RUBY FOO'S

7655 boulevard Decarie, Montréal, Québec, H4P 2H2

Tel 514/731-7701, 800/361-5419

www.hotelrubyfoos.com

If you don't want to drive into the city, this motel is a perfect alternative, just off the Trans-Canada Highway. Rooms and two-bedroom suites are modern, with light-wood furniture, and some have kitchenettes. All rooms have cable TV, coffeemaker and high-speed Internet access. Restaurants include Italian, continental, seafood, and a sushi bar.

⊙ Year-round

🖐 $155–240

🛏 198

💲 🧖 🏊 Outdoor heated

🅿

🚌 Near intersection of highways 40 (exit 66) and 15 (exit 69)

PERCÉ

⊕LA NORMANDIE DINING ROOM

Hotel La Normandie, 221 Route 132 Ouest, Percé, Québec, G0C 2L0

Tel 418/782-2112

www.normandieperce.com

White walls and bright red roof stand out on the seashore, and the hotel restaurant, with a smart interior of rattan chairs and crisp white table linen, looks out over Percé Rock and Bonaventure Island. It is known for some of the best food in the area, and the extensive four-course table d'hôte menu includes artistic arrangements such as roasted stuffed quail, lobster feuillete au Champagne, and guinea hen with almond, garlic and sherry sauce.

⊙ Daily 7.30–10am, 6–9pm Jun–Sep

🖐 D $50–80, W $28

💲

🅿

🚌 Orléans Express, Gaspé route

🚌 Downtown, on waterfront

⊙LE MIRAGE

288 Route 132 Ouest, Percé, Québec, G0C 2L0

Tel 418/782-5151, 800/463-9011

www.hotellemirage.com

Every single room in this friendly, family-run hotel has a spectacular view of the famous Percé Rock and Bonaventure Island, and they have nice big windows to make the most of it. Some rooms have glossy

hardwood floors, while others are carpeted, and all have quality fabrics that coordinate with the stylish design; extended cable TV and hairdryers are provided. The dining room has picture windows, and the extensive grounds include a tennis court and pool. Boat trips and whale watching can be arranged.

⊙ Mid-May to mid-Oct

🖐 $65–185

🛏 67 (50 non-smoking)

💲 🏊 Outdoor, heated

🅿

🚌 60

🚌 West of Percé on Route 132

QUÉBEC CITY

⊕AU PETIT COIN BRETON

1029 rue St-Jean, Québec City, Québec, G1R 1R9

Tel 418/694-0758

One of three locations in the city (the others are on boulevard Laurier and Grande Allée) serving around 80 varieties of crêpes. These range from the gourmet brunch variety (weekends only) to delicious desserts, with a huge variety of main-course fillings, including ham, cheese,

EATING AND STAYING

mushrooms, peppers, asparagus, and many other choices. There is also a large range of salads. Staff in costume evoke an atmosphere of old Brittany, and table linen is printed with a Brittany map.

🕐 Mon–Thu 11–2, 5–9, Fri 11–2, 5–10, Sat 10–10, Sun 9–9
💷 L $20–40, D $20–40
Ⓢ
🚇 Vieux Québec

⑪ AUX ANCIENS CANADIENS

34 rue St-Louis, CP 175, Succursale Haute-Ville, Québec City, Québec, G1R 4P3
Tel 418/692-1627
www.auxancienscanadiens.qc.ca
Come here for Canadian cuisine at its finest, served in the oldest building in Québec City (1675). The five dining rooms here retain their historic features and atmosphere, and the menu features such local dishes as boar and pig's knuckles ragout with meat-

balls, meat pie with pheasant, buffalo casserole, caribou cooked with creamy blueberry wine sauce, and other interesting meat and fish dishes. Maple syrup features strongly in the desserts, and other sweet temptations include apple cheesecake with creamy caramel sauce.

🕐 Daily noon–9
💷 L $44, D $70, W $29
Ⓢ
🅿 Nearby (charge)
🚌 7, 11
🚇 Corner of rue Desjardins

⑪ GUIDO LE GOURMET

73 rue St-Anne, Québec City, Québec, G1R 3X4
Tel 418/692-3856
A classy, understated frontage introduces this elegant restaurant and its exquisite French cuisine. You'll probably want to dress up to feel comfortable in these surroundings. There are

creative dishes such as bison with a lobster tail and trio of foie gras; other creations might feature quail, veal, and salmon. Sumptuous desserts include soufflés and the classic crème brûlée. The wine list is extensive.

🕐 Mon–Fri 11.30–2, 5.30–10, Sat–Sun 5.30–10
💷 L $24–34, D $55–65, W $24
Ⓢ
🅿 Valet (charge)
🚇 Vieux Québec, between rue des Jardins and rue Pierre-Olivier-Chauveau

⊖ L'HÔTEL DU CAPITOLE

972 rue St-Jean, Québec City, Québec, G1R 1R5
Tel 418/694-4040
www.lecapitole.com
Part of the complex that includes the Théâtre Capitole and an Italian restaurant, this four-story hotel has modern rooms that may not be huge, but are decidedly mellow and stylish. There are interesting ornaments and pictures—and the showbiz theme is fun; stage-struck guests will appreciate the star on the bedroom door. Some rooms feature a whirlpool bath, and all have soft feather comforters (duvets), plus cable TV, CD player, honor bar and hairdryer.

🕐 Year-round
💷 $119–285
🛏 40
Ⓢ
🅿 On site and valet (charge)
🚇 Place d'Youville, near Vieux Québec

⊖ AUBERGE ST-ANTOINE

10 rue St-Antoine, Québec City, Québec, G1K 4C9
Tel 418/692-2211
www.saint-antoine.com
Massive restoration of a derelict warehouse, completed in May 2003, has created a hotel of enormous character, and the owners must have had great fun designing the bedrooms: Whether it's brick walls, huge beams and traditional-style furnishings, or clean lines, plain pastel walls and ultra-modern pieces all have plenty of flair and just a touch of whimsy. The 007 Suite

has both in abundance. Some rooms have a rooftop terrace or balcony. Public areas include a snug lounge with a fireplace and a wrought-iron staircase.

🕐 Year-round
💷 $179–549
🛏 95 (89 non-smoking)
Ⓢ
🅿 Valet
🚇 Lower Town, near Vieux Port

⊖ LE CHÂTEAU FRONTENAC

1 rue des Carrières, Québec City, Québec, G1R 4P5
Tel 418/692-3861, 800/257-7544
www.fairmont.com
This landmark hotel is the city's most prestigious place to stay, with a commanding presence above it. The rooms are restful, in warm autumnal shades, and classic dark wood furniture, and have individual climate control. There's a superb leisure suite with large pool, kid's wading pool, whirlpool, steam rooms, exercise room, and spa. The variety of eating options ranges from formal restaurant to bistro and afternoon teas.

🕐 Year-round

🛏 $179–389
🛎 618
🔲 🔳 🛋 Indoor
🅿 On site (access via rue St-Louis) and valet (charge)
🗺 Vieux Québec

⊖LE PRIORI

15 Sault-au-Matelot, Québec City, Québec, G1K 3Y7
Tel 418/692-3992

In an 18th-century building in the Vieux Port, this hotel has a stylish modern interior featuring exposed brick walls, hardwood floors and designer furniture. Some bedrooms have an old-fashioned bathtub right in the room, and all have bathrooms with massaging showers. Loft-style suites have feature fireplaces, kitchens and double whirlpool baths. Coffee machines, TV, modem points, and down comforters (duvets) are provided. There's a fine restaurant and a terrace.

🕐 Year-round
🛏 $99–159, continental breakfast included
🛎 26
🔲
🅿 Parking area across the street (charge)
🍽 1
🗺 Lower Town, between Côte de la Montagne and rue St-Antoine

⊖L'HÔTEL DU VIEUX QUÉBEC

1190 rue St-Jean, Québec City, Québec, G1R 1S6
Tel 418/692-1850, 800/361-7787
www.hvq.com

This is a privately owned hotel standing in a prime location within the walls of North America's only fortified city. There's a very friendly atmosphere throughout, and the owners offer free guided walks in July and August.

A rather eccentric arrangement of staircases leads to no-frills rooms that reflect the age of the building, some with exposed stone walls and

sloping ceilings, and all with private bathroom, cable TV and mini-refrigerator. Local calls are free. A lively bistro-restaurant spills onto the sidewalk in summer. Minimum two-night stay required.

🕐 Year-round
🛏 $99–255; high-season rate includes Continental breakfast
🛎 41 (23 non-smoking)
🔲
🅿 Nearby (charge)
🗺 Vieux Québec

ST-FAUSTIN-LAC-CARRÉ

🍴LA CABANE À SUCRE MILLETTE INC.

1357 rue St-Faustin, St-Faustin-Lac-Carré, Québec, J0T 1J3
Tel 819/688-2101, 877/688-2101
www.tremblant-sugar-shack.com

Sugar shacks are great to visit when the sap is flowing (Mar–Apr), and you can view the delicious maple syrup being produced, but here you can tour the boiling room and maple grove year-round. More to the point, you can sample real down-home Canadian cooking in a traditional log building: Laurentian pea soup, smoked maple syrup ham, baked beans (not the canned variety), and sausages in maple syrup. Desserts include scrumptious sugar pie, pancakes with maple syrup, and maple taffy on snow. Reservation essential.

🕐 Tue–Sun 11–8, Mar–Apr; rest of year meals only available when it's also open for a group reservation
🛏 $14–33 (all courses, maple taffy and tea or coffee included)
🔲 Section
🅿
🗺 15 minutes' drive south of Tremblant on Highway 117

TADOUSSAC

🍴RESTAURANT LE BÂTEAU

246 rue des Forgerons, CP 127, Tadoussac, Québec, G0T 2A0
Tel 418/235-4427
www.lebateau.com

A big model sailboat on the signboard heralds your arrival at this informal restaurant, which has a wonderful view over the water, both from the picture windows of the dining room and the spacious deck outside. Lunch and dinner are both served buffet style, with tasty Québecois dishes that include delicious homemade soups, beef and vegetables,

seafood, and traditional pies for dessert—apple and other seasonal fruits, raisin, *tarte au sucre*, etc. The menu isn't what you'd call extensive, but it's wholesome, plentiful and immensely enjoyable.

🕐 Daily 11–2.30, 5–9.30, May–Oct
🛏 L $22, D $34, W $18
🔲 Section
🅿
🗺 Downtown

WAKEFIELD

⊖WAKEFIELD MILL

60 Mill Road, Wakefield, Québec, J0X 3G0
Tel 819/459-1838, 888/567-1838
www.wakefieldmill.com

An 1838 watermill straddling a picturesque waterfall on La Peche River now houses this lovely inn, in the heart of the hills and forests of Gatineau Park. Exposed brick walls, hardwood floors and mellow tones are set off by soft calico sofas and historical pictures. Some rooms include a Jacuzzi and a fireplace, and many have wonderful views of the falls; all have old-Canadian furnishings and satellite TV. There are also some luxury suites, housed in a converted grain silo.

🕐 Year-round
🛏 $90–136, breakfast included
🛎 26
🔲
🔳
🅿
🗺 Half-hour drive north of Ottawa off Highway 5, and along Highway 105

EATING AND STAYING

EATING

Toronto is reputed to have no fewer than 7,000 restaurants, and though these include all the fast-food joints and neighborhood diners, you are still spoilt for choice in really excellent and interesting places to eat. This cosmopolitan city not only encompasses just about every culture in its cuisine, it also prides itself on being Canada's trendsetter. So whatever the latest fad might be, you'll find it here—or discover that Torontonians are already moving on to the next big thing.

Ontario has a thriving wine industry, based in the Niagara region, and is also known for its microbreweries, which produce full-bodied beers. In addition, it is the home of Canadian Club whiskey—lighter than Scotch, smoother than bourbon—which has been distilled and bottled in Walkerville for about 150 years.

STAYING

This is one of the most popular provinces for visitors from Europe, and those who aren't staying with emigrant relatives will find the full range of accommodations options, from the finest downtown and resort hotels to the most charming and secluded country inns.

Toronto is an obvious hub, sometimes dubbed the New York of Canada, and has plenty of budget and mid-price options as well as luxury hotels. A good alternative to staying in the city is to choose one of the satellite towns that have good rail connections on the GO-train routes.

Although it's the national capital, Ottawa is much smaller and far less frantic than Toronto—and many consider that it is all the better for it. Choose a top hotel here and you're likely to be rubbing shoulders with government types and visiting dignitaries.

Niagara is another place people flock to, and it's full of honeymoon hotels with heart-shaped whirlpool baths right in the room. Discerning visitors choose to stay instead at the nearby stately little town of Niagara-on-the-Lake.

ALGONQUIN

⊖PARKWAY CORRIDOR CAMPGROUNDS

Algonquin Provincial Park, Box 219, Whitney, Ontario, K0J 2M0
Tel 705/633-5572, 888/668-7275
www.ontarioparks.com

There is camping within the park, but access is only on foot or by canoe. Less intrepid campers have a choice of eight organized campgrounds in the Parkway Corridor (Highway 60), and you don't even have to have your own equipment—the one at Mew Lake has some yurts (semipermanent structures, fully equipped and furnished) for rent. Many of the campgrounds have lakeside beaches; there are some electrical hookups, and there is boating plus hiking and cycling trails.

🕐 May–Thanksgiving weekend
🍽 $20 28 (maximum 6 people) per site; yurt rental $60
ℹ️ More than 1,200 sites (pitches), 446 with electricity; 8 yurts for rent
🅿
🚌 Just over 200km (124 miles) north of Toronto, south of TCH 17

GANANOQUE

⊕GANANOQUE INN

550 Stone Street South, Gananoque, Ontario, K7G 2A8
Tel 613/382-2165
www.gananoqueinn.com

Historic pub on the St. Lawrence River with a sophisticated formal dining room serving Continental cuisine. For lunch, try grilled breast of chicken on guacamole and spinach salad, or PEI mussels flambéed in Pernod; the dinner specialty is prime rib of beef au jus, slow roasted and served with Yorkshire pudding. There are other imaginative concoctions based on Atlantic salmon, chicken, steaks, and seafood. The informal pub, with its patio deck, has pasta, burgers and

daily specials. Thousand Islands tour boats dock nearby.

🕐 Daily 7–10, 11.30–2, 5.30–10, May–Nov; Fri–Sun 5.30–10, Apr and Dec
🍽 L $21, D $42, W $25
🚭
🅿
🚌 Downtown, on waterfront

HAMILTON

⊖VISITORS INN

649 Main Street West, Hamilton, Ontario, L8S 1A2
Tel 905/529-6979, 800/387-4620
www.visitorsinn.com

Accommodations here are way above average for an inn, including an oasis-style indoor pool complex with Jacuzzi, sauna and fitness room.

Rooms are very stylish, and have satellite or cable TV, phones, refrigerators, and minibars, and there are some efficiency units and luxury suites with their own Jacuzzi. The dining room is open all day, and beverages are available at the poolside. Free local calls and newspaper.

🕐 Year-round
🍽 $99–115
ℹ️ 60 (47 non-smoking)
🚭 🐾 Indoor
🅿
🚌 Corner of Highway 403 and Main Street West

KINGSTON

⊕CHEZ PIGGY

68-R Princess Street, Kingston, Ontario, K7L 1A5
Tel 613/549-7673

It has been said that Chez Piggy serves the kind of food you might have in a private home in Turkey, or Vietnam, or Italy, and the place oozes the same kind of warmth and friendliness. The staff is bright and lively, the building is a beautifully restored 1812 stable with garden and patio, and the company will include Kingston's academics, artists

and business folk, who know a good thing when they taste it. Pick up a copy of the *Chez Piggy Cookbook*, a Canadian bestseller, so you can re-create the experience back home.

🕐 Mon–Sat 11.30am–midnight, Sun 11am–midnight
🍽 L $16, D $30, W $25
🚭
🅿 Nearby (charge)
🚌 Downtown, at Princess and King (68-R means at the rear)

🏠BELVEDERE
141 King Street East, Kingston, Ontario, K7L 2Z9
Tel 613/548-1565, 800/559-0584
www.hotelbelvedere.com
Built in the 1880s, this mansion has suffered mixed fortunes but has now been restored to its original

opulence and converted into a hotel, and many interesting architectural motifs have been preserved. It's furnished with fine antiques, including early Canadian and Victorian pieces. Rooms and suites have restful tones set off by lush foliage plants, and old fireplaces are a feature. Some of the bathrooms are fitted with a whirlpool bath.

🕐 Year-round
🛏 $110–195, light breakfast included
🛎 22 (10 non-smoking)
🚭
🅿
🚌 3
🚌 Downtown, on the waterfront. Near City Hall and University

🏠PILLAR AND POST INN
48 John Street, Niagara-on-the-Lake, Ontario, L0S 1J0
Tel 905/468-2123, 888/669-5566
www.vintageinns.com
One of Canada's loveliest country inns, dating from 1890, with a long list of guest services and amenities, including 24-hour concierge, valet, babysitting, business facilities, ticket reservations,

and free shuttle. Individually designed bedrooms combine floral fabrics with dark greens and reds, and each has a Victorian fireplace, large-screen TV, Play Station and Nintendo, and bathrobes. Meals are created by award-winning chefs, and there's a full spa and a conference venue.

🕐 Year-round
🛏 $150–305
🛎 123
🚭 🚷 🏊 Indoor and outdoor
🅿
🚌 Middle of town

NIAGARA FALLS
🍽VICTORIA PARK
6345 Niagara Parkway, Niagara Falls, Ontario, L2E 6T2
Tel 905/356-2217
Within a beautiful floral park, next to an illuminated stage (with kids' shows on summer weekends), this family restaurant has spectacular views of the Horseshoe and American falls, particularly from the large balcony. The menu has a wide selection, including some Canadian cuisine, all prepared from fresh local ingredients—a children's menu is also available.

🕐 Daily 11.30–9, 10 or 11, May–mid-Oct (closes 3pm weekdays in early May)
🍽 L $27, D $60, W $30
🚭

🅿 Nearby (charge)
🚗 4, 20
🚌 In Queen Victoria Park

🏠SHERATON FALLSVIEW
6755 Fallsview Boulevard, Niagara Falls, Ontario, L2G 3W7
Tel 905/374-1077, 800/267-8439
www.fallsview.com
The best location in town, directly overlooking both the Horseshoe and American falls. Modern high-rise hotel with standard and superior rooms and suites; the nicest ones are furnished with reproduction pieces—and, of course, you'll

want to ask for one with a falls view. There's an indoor pool, Jacuzzi and fitness suite, and the dining room (with that view again) offers North American, Asian and European cuisines; there's also an Italian bistro where kids eat free, a pub and room service.

🕐 Year-round
🛏 From $239
🛎 402 (354 non-smoking)
🚭 🚷 🏊 Indoor
🅿
🚌 6; Niagara Parks Shuttle (in summer)

NIAGARA-ON-THE-LAKE
🍽TERROIR LA CACHETTE
1339 Lakeshore Road, Niagara-on-the-Lake, Ontario, L0S 1J0
Tel 905/468-1222
www.lacachette.com
Delicious tastes of Provence are brought to fruition using top-quality Niagara produce in a chic restaurant within the Strewn Winery (the wine list is

EATING AND STAYING

exclusively Ontario). Fish soup, Provençal tart with braised onions and roasted pepper, and Atlantic salmon are among lunch offerings, while the dinner menu includes duck confit, fennel-seed-crusted Atlantic salmon, and beef tenderloin with Cabernet-basil reductions and sun-dried tomato compound butter. There's informal dining in the wine bar and a patio.

🕐 Daily
🍽 L $40, D $80, W $24
🚫
🅿
🚌 About 6km (4 miles) west of town

NOBEL

◉WINNETOU RESORT
RR#1, Nobel, Ontario, P0G 1G0
Tel 705/342-9967, 800/567-4550
www.holidayjunction.com/winnetou
Snug housekeeping cottages set on the rocky shore of Georgian Bay, with a fine sandy beach on site. Available for single nights and weekends, as well as longer stays. In addition to wonderful views, the rustic-style timber cottages have full bathroom and kitchen, and outside you get your own barbecue and lawn furniture. There's a health suite within the complex, as well as all kinds of boats, windsurfers, fishing, and such activities as beach volleyball and horseshoe-tossing.

🕐 May–Oct
🍽 $113–208
🛏 10 units
🍷
🅿
🚌 14km (9 miles) north of Parry Sound on Highway 69, then 10km (6 miles) west on Highway 559

OTTAWA

◉JOHNNY FARINA
216 Elgin Street, Ottawa, Ontario, K2P 1L7
Tel 613/565-5155
www.johnnyfarina.com
Part of the old Elgin movie theater, with incredibly high ceiling, brick walls, ceramic floor tiles, a feature staircase up to the gallery level, and typical Italian atmosphere. Open kitchen area provides greater entertainment than the unobtrusive piped music or the discreet muted-sound TV. The owner's mother makes most of the sumptuous desserts and the biscotti, while

the chefs concentrate on imaginative fresh pasta dishes and crispy wood-oven pizzas.

🕐 Mon–Wed 11.30–10 or 10.30, Thu–Sat 11.30–11 or 11.30, Sun 4–10 or 10.30
🍽 L $25, D $30, W $25
🚫
🅿 Street
🚌 5, 14

◉MERLOT
Marriott Hotel, 100 Kent Street, Ottawa, Ontario, K1P 5R7
Tel 613/783-4212
Revolving restaurant on 29th-floor of the Marriott Hotel, giving superb views of the city and the Ottawa River—a complete circuit takes about two hours, so come for a leisurely lunch. All seats are near the windows, so everyone enjoys the view. This is the hotel's formal eating option, and it has a good, varied menu. The Sunday lunch buffet is particularly popular.

🕐 Daily 6–10, also Sun 10.30am–2 or 3pm
🚫
🅿
🚌 1, 2, 4
🚇 Downtown

◉YANGTZE
700 Somerset Street West, Ottawa, Ontario, K1R 6P6
Tel 613/236-0555
Stands out in a long street full of restaurants, not only for the first-rate Chinese food, but also for the illuminated dome high above the entrance. The large room has a token dragon at one end, huge chandeliers and big tables accommodating local Chinese families and other devotees. Try the crispy baskets with various fillings and the excellent won ton soup. Service is a little on the reserved side, but the place is buzzing with cheerful diners.

🕐 Mon–Fri 11am–12.30am, Sat 10am–1am, Sun 10am–12.30am
🍽 L $25, D $40, W $17.95
🚫
🅿 Street
🚌 2, 85, 316
🚇 Near Cambridge intersection

◉ALBERT HOUSE
478 Albert Street, Ottawa, Ontario, K1R 5B5
Tel 613/236-4479, 1-800/267-1982
www.albertinn.com
Queen Anne-style inn, built in 1875 by Canada's first chief

architect, close to all downtown attractions. Bedrooms are individually designed, with old-style furniture and wallpapers, coordinated fabrics, shams and soft lighting. All have private

bathrooms, some with whirlpool baths; some only have a shower. Also TV, desk, and dataport telephone. The famous breakfasts include freshly baked muffins and croissants, as well as traditional hot dishes and some unusual items.

🕐 Year-round
🍽 $88–158, breakfast and beverages included
🛏 17 (13 non-smoking)
🚫
🅿 Charge
🚌 16, 18, 316; Transitway 95, 97
🚇 Downtown

◉ARC, THE HOTEL
140 Slater Street, Ottawa, Ontario, K1P 5H6
Tel 613/238-2888, 800/699-2516
www.arcthehotel.com
Ottawa's only designer boutique hotel, just four blocks from the parliament buildings and close to shopping streets and National Arts Centre. The lobby, with pale limestone floor and black paneling, is pure minimalist chic. The bedrooms are also stylishly elegant, with muted natural shades and soft gray Egyptian cotton bed linen, and have welcoming touches of mohair throws, terry-cloth bathrobes, fresh orchids, and Granny Smith apples; baths are so deep that you can wallow up to your chin, and Bulgari toiletries add to the pleasure.

🍽 $135–425
🛏 110 (non-smoking rooms available)
🚫 🍷
🅿
🚌 1, 2, 4, 7, 16, 18, 316
🚇 Between Metcalfe and O'Connor

EATING AND STAYING

SAULT STE MARIE

❶ A THYMELY MANNER

531 Albert Street East, Sault Ste Marie, Ontario, P6A 2K3

Tel 705/759-3262

Located in a conversion of an old home, this is widely regarded as the best restaurant in the area. Only the finest natural ingredients are used to produce the creative menu of steak, pasta and fish dishes. A delightfully snug and intimate atmosphere adds to the dining pleasure.

🕐 Tue–Sat 5.30–11; closed public holidays and 2 weeks in Jul

🍴 D $50, W $25

🚭

🅿

🚌 Between Spring and Brock

❖ ALGOMA WATER TOWER INN

360 Great Northern Road, Sault Ste Marie, Ontario, P6A 5N3

Tel 705/949-8111

www.watertowerinn.com

Independent motor inn with exceptional facilities. Some rooms have woodburning stove, some have whirlpool baths, and all are decorated with coordinating fabrics and stylish pine furniture. Leisure facilities include a feature swimming pool, with kids' wading pool, whirlpool, sauna, and fitness room; the outdoor section consists of a landscaped courtyard with waterfall and rivers. Food is fast and friendly rather than haute cuisine, with Tex-Mex in the Lone Star restaurant.

🕐 Year-round

🍴 $129–165

🛏 180

🏊 🚹 Indoor and outdoor

🅿

🚌 North edge of town at intersection of the Great Northern Road (Highway 178) and Second Line (Highway 550)

SUDBURY

❶ CULPEPPER'S EATERY

1835 Regent Street South, Sudbury, Ontario, P3E 3Z7

Tel 705/522-2422

www.sud-biz.com/culpeppersrestaurant

A bright and cheerful atrium overlooks the dining area of this popular restaurant. It has an enormous menu of Italian, Greek and North American food: soups, sandwiches, burgers, and wings are joined by pastas, salads, stir-fries, fajitas, chicken, steaks, ribs,

and seafood. You would have to be a very choosy person not to find something on this menu to please. There's also a children's menu, a salad bar, and brunch and lunch buffets.

🕐 Mon–Thu 11–11, Fri–Sat 11–midnight, Sun 10–10, holidays 4–11

🍴 L $16, D $35, W $22

🚭

🅿

🚍 501

🚌 South End, corner of Paris

❖ PARKER HOUSE INN

259 Elm Street, Sudbury, Ontario, P3C 1V5

Tel 705/674-2442, 888/250-4453

www.bbcanada.com/sudburyparkerhouse

Kathryn and Michael Cull's renowned hospitality and good cooking bring visitors

back to their elegant home, convenient to downtown, Science North and the Big Nickel. All the bedrooms have queen-size pillow-top beds (some four-posters), private bathrooms, and facilities that include TV, VCR and modem point. There are also three suites, a snug living room and a sunroom, plus a secluded garden patio. Jazz club every Sunday night.

🕐 Year-round

🍴 $75–140

🛏 7 (all non-smoking)

🚭

🅿

🚌 Downtown

THUNDER BAY

❶ PORT ARTHUR BRASSERIE AND BREWPUB

901 Red River Road, Thunder Bay, Ontario, P7B 1K3

Tel 807/767-4415

www.pabrewpub.com

The vision in 1987 was to provide a neighborhood meeting place and supply it with great beer and food. That is certainly what the Port Arthur does. Extensive Chinese

menu, as well as the popular pub dishes of beef, chicken or shrimp sizzlers, *pierogies* (Polish filled dumplings), burgers, pastas, pizzas, chicken, steaks, and sandwiches. Desserts include Elvis banana pudding. There are children's and 55+ menus, and don't forget the beers— there are seven to choose from (some seasonal), all brewed on the premises.

🕐 Mon–Sat 11am–1am, Sun 9am–midnight

🍴 L $30, D $55, W $16.50

🚭

🅿

🚍 3

🚌 Downtown, corner of Red River and Dunant

❖ PRINCE ARTHUR

17 North Cumberland Street, Thunder Bay, Ontario, P7A 4K8

Tel 807/345-5411, 1-800/267-2675

www.princearthur.on.ca

This hotel has the best view in the city, overlooking the lake and marina, and it's right in the heart of the action, just a block from the casino. Rooms are in plain, modern style, with light-wood furniture, big beds, satellite TV, and no distinguishing features to speak of; executive suites have more of the same in their roomy lounge area. There's a large indoor pool, plus sauna and whirlpool, and the Landing restaurant overlooks the waterfront scene.

🕐 Year-round

🍴 $95

🛏 123

🏊 🚹 Indoor

🅿

🚌 Downtown, on the waterfront

❖ WHITE FOX INN

1345 Mountain Road, Thunder Bay, Ontario, P7J 4C2

Tel 807/577-3699, 800/603-3699

www.whitefox.com

Elegant mansion on a 6ha (15-acre) wooded estate. Spacious rooms have a pleasing combination of plain, pastel shades and interesting furniture, including handcarved Indonesian hardwood pieces; some have whirlpool baths right in the bedroom. Thick terry-cloth bathrobes are provided, and, as well as the usual TV/VCR, each room has a mini-stereo and telephone with modem point. Renowned

EATING AND STAYING

restaurant harmonizes New World and European cuisines.

🕐 Year round
🍴 $110–299
🍷 9
🚭
🈲
🅿
🚆 2km (1.2 miles) southeast of the city, just off Highway 61

TORONTO

🍴 BATON ROUGE

Toronto Eaton Centre, 216 Yonge Street, Toronto, Ontario, M5B 1N5
Tel 416/593-9667
www.batonrouge-restaurant.com

Cool and classy bar-restaurant, with dark polished wood, red leather upholstery and huge pots of foliage. There are tables and booths, some overlooking the busy street. The ribs are legendary, and there's fresh seafood, tender chicken and other southern American dishes cooked over hickory and aromatic hardwoods. Popular with business people, shoppers, families, and pre-theater crowd. Uniformed staff are efficient and friendly. Nothing to do with Louisiana—this company originated in Montréal and the name means "Red Stick."

🕐 Mon–Thu 11–11, Fri 11am–midnight, Sat 11.30am–midnight, Sun noon–10
🍴 L $45, D $70, W $28
🚭
🅿 Nearby (charge)
🚇 Dundas or Queen
🚌 97B

🍴 BISTRO 990

990 Bay Street, Toronto, Ontario, M5S 3A8
Tel 416/921-9990

A bright, striped awning, a Citroen 2CV parked outside, intimate dining spaces with vaulted ceilings and Picasso-style drawings, fresh flowers, French doors… it's a little corner of Paris in downtown Toronto. The menu is bursting with French bistro classics, from the garlic-crusted shrimp to the filet mignon and the delectable raspberry mille-feuille. And you are likely to be rubbing shoulders with celebs if Hollywood happens to be in town (which it often is).

🕐 Lunch Mon–Fri, dinner Mon–Sat
🍴 L $50, D $90, W $15
🚭

🅿 Next door or north on Church (charge for both, Church is cheaper)
🚇 Wellesley
🚌 6A, 6B
🚆 Downtown, just north of Wellesley

🍴 BOUJADI

999 Eglinton Avenue West, Toronto, Ontario, M6C 2C7
Tel 416/440-0258
www.boujadi.com

The sand-colored frontage, and the North African objects and music set the scene for first-rate Moroccan cuisine in this family-run restaurant. It's very intimate (some call it cramped), and there's often a wait for tables, but the food is definitely worth it. Authentic dishes are perfectly cooked and delicately balanced with exactly the right amount of spicing: traditional *tagines*, *harira*, *pastilla*, homemade *merguez* beef sausages, and moist and tasty couscous. Limited selection of desserts.

🕐 Wed–Sun 5–10
🍴 D $60, W $22
🚭
🅿 Nearby (charge)
🚇 Eglinton West
🚌 7, 7A, 32
🚆 Near Eglinton and Bathurst, one block east of Allen Road

🍴 CAPTAIN JOHN'S HARBOUR BOAT

1 Queen's Quay West, Toronto, Ontario, M5J 2H1
Tel 416/363-6062
www.toronto.com/captainjohns

Run by well-known local philanthropist John Letnik, this restaurant is on a ship, with its prow pointing straight up the longest street in the world (Yonge). Decorated wardroom style, with plush red velvet upholstery, gold drapes, crisp white tablecloths, and gleaming dark wood set off by brass portholes and other nautical accoutrements. The menu is mostly seafood—the Alaskan king crab feast is highly recommended—with a few meat dishes, including a tender stroganoff and Swiss steak. There's a bar up on deck, with lakeshore views.

🕐 Mon–Sat 11–11, Sun 10.30am–11pm
🍴 L $50, D $60, W $22
🚭
🅿 Nearby (charge)
🚇 Union Station
🚌 6, 97B

🚆 Downtown, on lake at foot of Yonge Street, next to Island Ferry Terminal

🍴 INSOMNIA

563 Bloor Street West, Toronto, Ontario, M5S 1Y6
Tel 416/588-3907
www.insomniacafe.com

More than just snacks and surfing, Insomnia is a friendly, chic place as popular for food as for web access. Eclectic international menu ranging from gourmet sandwiches to interesting vegetarian options and meat dishes: grilled shrimp with horseradish, chili and sesame honey dip; Asian barbecued ribs; baked goat's cheese with artichoke, tomato, fresh basil and garlic. Huge liquor selection. Five private cubicles have PCs with 53cm (21in) monitors ($9 per hour); also 79cm (31in) screen for multiple-player games.

🕐 Mon–Thu 11am–3am, Fri 11am–5am, Sat 10am–5am, Sun 10am–3am
🍴 L $40, D $60, W $29
🚭
🅿 Nearby (charge)
🚇 Bathurst
🚌 Streetcar 511
🚆 Downtown, near corner of Bloor and Bathurst

🍴 MONTANA

145 John Street, Toronto, Ontario, M5V 2E4
Tel 416/595-5949
www.montanaonline.ca

Huge, brash, lively restaurant, with some of the most cheerful and energetic wait staff you'll see anywhere. The food inclines in various directions, with Italian (wood-oven pizzas, pastas) and Oriental (satay) elements, but in its heart it is steadfastly North American: The baby back ribs are highly recommended, and there are also steaks, salmon, chicken, burgers, and the like. Upstairs there's a sports bar with pool table and the Mustang Room with DJ Thursday to Saturday. No children.

🕐 Sun–Wed 11.30am–midnight, Thu 11.30am–1am, Fri–Sat 11.30am–2am
🍴 L $30, D $50, W $25
🚭 Section
🅿 Nearby
🚇 Osgoode
🚌 Streetcar 501
🚆 Entertainment district, southeast corner of John and Richmond

⓫ MOONBEAN COFFEE COMPANY

30 St Andrew Street, Toronto, Ontario, M5T 1K6

Tel 416/595-0327

This coffeehouse developed from a retail store selling coffee beans and speciality teas, and is a great place to relax amid the bustle of Kensington Market. The snug café has a wide range of

gourmet coffees, smoothies, juices and sodas, along with light snacks, including bagels with toppings, samosas, cakes, and pastries. The walls are given over to works (for sale) by Toronto artists, forming a constantly changing exhibition. And there's outdoor seating for people-watching on the market.

🕑 Daily 7am–9pm

🍴 $15

🚫

🅿 Parking garage next door (charge)

🚇 St. Patrick, then streetcar 505

🚌 Streetcar 505 on Dundas, 510 on Spadina

⓫ PONY

488 College Street, Toronto, Ontario, M6G 1A4

Tel 416/923-7665

www.ponyrestaurant.com

Interesting combinations, expertly prepared by Marc Zegers, in a charming three-room restaurant. Maple-glazed duck with vanilla poached pear, and pecan Thai rice and hoisin wilted bok choy are good examples. There are

some excellent choices for vegetarians, and you can get hors d'oeuvres in main course size for an extra $5. The latter include classic bouillabaisse, grilled calamari with chipotle aioli, and warm goat's cheese fondue. The interior makes use of warm tones, antiques and soft lighting, and there's a leafy deck for alfresco dining.

🕑 Mon–Sat 5–11

🍴 D $55, W $24

🚫

🅿 Nearby (charge)

🚇 Queen's Park, then streetcar 506 west

🚌 Streetcars 506, 511

🚆 Downtown, intersection of College and Bathurst

⓫ REAL THAILAND

350 Bloor Street West, Toronto, Ontario, M5S 1W9

Tel 416/924-7444

www.realthailand.ca

Superbly fragrant Thai food is expertly cooked here, and served in the uncluttered restaurant or on the patio outside. About 20 appetizers include a lot of shrimp dishes, the ever-popular satays and interesting soups; then comes a seemingly endless list of main courses and just three desserts. The quality of the food, the impeccable service and the warm atmosphere are all good reasons to eat here.

🕑 Daily 11.30am–midnight

🍴 L $16, D $30, W $25

🚫 Except patio

🅿 Next door (charge)

🚇 Spadina

🚌 127, 510

🚆 Spadina and Bloor

⓫ SHOPSY'S DELI AND RESTAURANT

33 Yonge Street, Toronto, Ontario, M5E 1G4

Tel 416/365-3333

On the up since it was founded in 1921, Shopsy's attracts an eclectic clientele of locals, visitors, politicians, and celebrities. Busy and noisy, it has a modern interior design and a vast menu, featuring such entrées as corned beef and cabbage, chicken parmigiana, New York steak, chili, chicken pot pie, and cabbage rolls. There is a huge range of sandwiches, subs, wraps and pitas, platters, soups, salads, all-day breakfasts, and famous hot

dogs. Also on King Street and at 1535 Yonge Street.

🕑 Mon–Wed 7am–11pm, Thu–Fri 7am–midnight, Sat 8am–midnight, Sun 8am–9pm

🍴 L $25, D $35, W $20

🚫

🅿 On site after 6pm, or below restaurant

🚇 Union Station or King

🚌 97B

🚆 Downtown

⓫ 360 THE RESTAURANT AT THE CN TOWER

CN Tower, 301 Front Street West, Toronto, Ontario, M5V 2T6

Tel 416/362-5411

www.cntower.ca

A tourist trap? Definitely not. The world's highest revolving restaurant has won some of the highest awards for its food and wine (from the world's highest wine cellar). An appetizer of crisp salad, homemade soup or Canadian smoked salmon might be followed by Ontario rainbow

trout, Atlantic salmon, Canadian prime rib of beef, or vegetarian options; save room for a slice of the Québec maple syrup cheesecake. All diners enjoy the spectacular views, and the complete circuit takes 72 minutes.

🕑 Sun–Thu 11–2, 4.30–1, Fri–Sat 11–2, 4.30–10.30; Sun brunch 10.30–2

🍴 L $75, D $120, W $27

🚫

🅿 Nearby (charge)

🚇 Union Station, then via SkyWalk

⓫ TIGER LILY'S NOODLE HOUSE

257 Queen Street West, Toronto, Ontario, M5V 1Z4

Tel 416/977-5499

This is a hugely popular stop for lunch, buzzing with a mix of TV types from the nearby City TV, trendies and families. You can create your own Chinese and Thai soups, choosing the type of broth, the

EATING AND STAYING

type of noodles (there are six), and whatever meat, vegetables or wontons you want them to throw in. It really makes a meal in itself, but there's more on the menu, including dim sum, spring rolls, *pad Thai*, satays and salads.

🕐 Daily, year-round
🍽 L $20, D $20–30, W $23
Ⓢ
🅿 Street (metered)
Ⓜ Osgoode
🚋 Streetcar 501
🚇 Downtown, west of University Avenue

⊖ABERDEEN GUESTHOUSE

52 Aberdeen Avenue, Toronto, Ontario, M4X 1A2
Tel 416/922-8697
www.aberdeenguesthouse.com
This B&B is in historic Cabbagetown, a quiet residential area of leafy streets and Victorian homes. It has tasteful bedrooms with fireplaces, TV and traditional-style furnishings, and two roomy bathrooms are shared between the three bedrooms; bathrobes are provided.

Continental breakfast is served weekdays; hot breakfasts on Saturday and Sunday. There's a secluded garden and patio. No children under 16 or pets.

🕐 Year-round
🍽 $100–140, breakfast included
🛏 3 (all non-smoking)
Ⓢ
🅿 Street (free)
Ⓜ College
🚋 Streetcar 506
🚇 Downtown, Cabbagetown

⊖AINSLEY HOUSE

19 Elm Avenue, Toronto, Ontario, M4W 1M9
Tel 416/972-0533; 1-888/423-3337
Gracious B&B in leafy Rosedale, Toronto's smartest residential area. The spacious rooms have gleaming hardwood floors with rugs, nice old furniture and design schemes that

❶TRUFFLES

Four Season's Hotel, 21 Avenue Road, Toronto, Ontario, M5R 2G1
Tel 416/964-0411
www.fourseasons.com
Experts agree that Truffles serves the best food in Toronto—maybe the best in the country—and it has a long list of accolades. Contemporary French cuisine is presented in extremely classy surroundings. Roasted yellowtail snapper with saffron minestrone *nage*, chicken-liver parfait with lemon ravioli, and prime beef tenderloin with two sauces are just a few of the mouthwatering concoctions. The signature dish features spaghettini with Perigord "black gold" truffles. Dress code is casual but dressy; jackets not required.

🕐 Mon–Sat 6–10.30, Sun 5.30–10.30
🍽 D $130, W $30
Ⓢ
🅿
Ⓜ Museum (then walk north) or Bay (then walk west)
🚇 Downtown, north of Bloor

promote a serene atmosphere. Breakfast includes freshly baked breads and muffins, fresh fruit, and bacon and eggs.

🕐 Year-round
🍽 $49.50, breakfast included
🛏 3 (all non-smoking)
Ⓢ
🅿
Ⓜ Rosedale, then bus 82 to South Drive
🚌 75

⊖AMBASSADOR INN

280 Jarvis Street, Toronto, Ontario, M5B 2C5
Tel 416/260-2608
www.ambassadorinntoronto.com
A fine redbrick home dating to 1899, and yet just 10 minutes' walk from the Eaton Centre

and two blocks from the subway. It's been lovingly restored to retain an air of less hurried times, and original features include exposed brick walls, a cathedral ceiling, fireplaces, bay windows, and stained glass. All the bedrooms have private bathrooms (most with Jacuzzis) and some are incredibly spacious. There's no B&B sign outside because they prefer guests to reserve; you'll get directions when you call.

🕐 Year-round
🍽 $149–319, breakfast included
🛏 20 (all non-smoking)
Ⓢ
🅿 Nearby (free)
Ⓜ College
🚋 Streetcar 506 (Carlton)
🚇 Downtown, corner of Jarvis and Gerrard, two blocks east of Yonge

⊖CAMBRIDGE SUITES HOTEL

15 Richmond Street East, Toronto, Ontario, M5C 1N2
Tel 416/368-1990, 800/463-1990
www.cambridgesuiteshotel.com
This is a real haven of tranquility in the midst of the bustling financial and entertainment district—a cool and classy modern hotel that offers two-room suites. These have a bedroom that can be closed off from the spacious living room, and amenities that include microwave, refrigerator and coffeemaker. Cityscape and Penthouse suites on the top floors have great views and extra luxuries such as high-speed Internet access, CD, VCR, safe, and turndown service.

🕐 Year-round
🍽 $175–360, continental breakfast included
🛏 229
Ⓢ 🍴
🅿 Charge
Ⓜ Queen
🚌 97B
🚇 Corner of Yonge and Richmond

⊖FAIRMONT ROYAL YORK

100 Front Street West, Toronto, Ontario, M5J 1E3
Tel 416/368-2511, 800/441-1414
www.fairmont.com
A Toronto landmark since 1929 and long-time choice of visiting royalty and celebrities. The 28-story hotel retains its original hand-painted ceilings, travertine pillars and glittering chandeliers. Guest rooms are

exceptionally elegant, but even more opulent are the suites and the exclusive Fairmont Gold section, where the level of pampering reaches monumental heights. There

are five restaurants, a sky-lit swimming pool, a spa, and a fitness facility. The hotel is directly connected to underground shops and the subway.
🕐 Year-round
💷 $169–309
ℹ️ 1,365 (1,089 non-smoking)
🚭 🍴 🏊 Indoor
🅿️
🚇 Union Station
🚋 Downtown, opposite Union Station

🏨 GVB TORONTO
460 King Street West, Toronto, Ontario, M5V 1L7
Tel 416/703-8540, 888/844-7875
www.globalbackpackers.com
Bright and lively hostel in a central location, near CN Tower, and housed in a former Spadina Hotel that was once a celebrity haunt for the likes of Jack Nicholson and Canadian band, The Tragically Hip. Accommodations are in spacious dormitories with

linens supplied free. Self-serve kitchen, laundry, secure storage for luggage and Internet access. Public areas with bright native-art murals include a games room with pool table, bar and outdoor deck with barbecue parties in summer.
🕐 Year-round

💷 $56 (double occupancy); $22 per person in dormitory
ℹ️ 200 beds
🚭
🍴
🅿️ Nearby (charge)
🚇 St. Andrews
🚋 Streetcars 509, 510 west from Union Station
🚋 Downtown, King and Spadina

🏨 JARVIS HOUSE
344 Jarvis Street, Toronto, Ontario, M4Y 2G6
Tel 416/975-3838
www.jarvishouse.com
Restored Victorian house, now a delightful B&B, within walking distance of theaters, museums, shopping districts, and other attractions. Three room sizes all have coordinated design schemes and private bathroom, and honeymoon rooms have a Jacuzzi. There's a breakfast room where you can start the day with ham or bacon and eggs, pancakes, French toast, home-baked muffins, and cereals. Complementary beverages and fresh fruit are available all day.
🕐 Year-round
💷 $85–169, breakfast included
ℹ️ 11 (all non-smoking)
🚭
🅿️
🚇 Yonge or College
🚋 Streetcar 506 from College subway
🚋 Downtown, Jarvis and Carlton

🏨 NEILL-WYCIK COLLEGE HOTEL
96 Gerrard Street East, Toronto, Ontario, M5B 1G7
Tel 416/977-2320, 800/268-4358
www.neill-wycik.com
Relaxed and friendly students' residence with compact rooms, close to downtown and 10 minutes' walk from the bus station. Occupies 16 floors of a 22-story building; each floor has four apartments, consisting of four or five bedrooms, two bathrooms and

a kitchen/lounge area. Linen is supplied, but no crockery or kitchen utensils. A renovated on-site café with outdoor patio is where breakfast is served 7–11am. There's a sauna, rooftop sundeck and 24-hour concierge.
🕐 Early May–late Aug
💷 $66, continental breakfast included (upgrade to hot breakfast $1)
ℹ️ 300
🚭
🅿️ Limited on site; also nearby (charge)
🚇 Dundas or College
🚋 Gerrard East and Church

🏨 RENAISSANCE TORONTO HOTEL AT SKYDOME
1 Blue Jays Way, Toronto, Ontario, M5V 1J4
Tel 416/341-7100, 800/237-1512
Next door to the CN Tower, this is the first hotel ever to be an

integral part of a sports complex—the 11-story building curves around one side of the SkyDome. Inside it's sheer luxury, and 70 rooms have picture windows overlooking the stadium. If you get one of these rooms, be aware that TV cameras often pan across here during games—one couple famously got caught on camera engaged in an entirely different sport.
🕐 Year-round
💷 $179–249
ℹ️ 384 (248 non-smoking)
🚭 🍴 🏊 Indoor
🅿️
🚇 Union Station
🚋 Streetcar 510

🏨 VICTORIA
56 Yonge Street, Toronto, Ontario, M5E 1G5
Tel 416/363-1666, 800/363-8228
www.hotelvictoria-toronto.com
In an ideal location, this European-style boutique hotel is close to all the action of downtown Toronto, at the heart of the theater and financial districts. Its classy

lobby leads straight onto Yonge Street. The bedrooms all have identical Regency stripe wallpaper and coordinated fabrics, with private bathroom, cable TV and voice mail. Deluxe rooms also have mini-refrigerator and coffeemaker. Guests can use the health club at the nearby Plaza Club.

⏰ Year-round
🛏 $129–169, continental breakfast included
ℹ 56 (48 non-smoking)
♿
🅿 Nearby (charge)
🛌 King
📶 97B

⏰WESTIN HARBOUR CASTLE
1 Harbour Square, Toronto, Ontario, M5J 1A6
Tel: 416/869-1600
This huge, glittering, classy hotel has a wonderful lakeshore setting. Rooms have extended cable TV, video games, dual phone lines, voice mail and honor bars. In addition to a revolving rooftop restaurant, there's the trendy Toula, offering Italian cuisine along with more great views across the harbor.

⏰ Year-round
🛏 $149–389
ℹ 981
♿ 🛁 🏊 Indoor
🅿
🚇 Union Station

⏰WINDSOR ARMS
18 St. Thomas Street, Toronto, Ontario, M5S 3E7
Tel 416/971-9666
A five-story luxury hotel in a peaceful residential area, with tasteful furnishings. All rooms and suites have whirlpool, cable TV, CD player, and honor bar.

⏰ Year-round
🛏 $425–2,000
ℹ 28
♿ 🛁 🏊 Indoor
🅿
📶 Downtown, at junction with Bloor

Succulent Alberta beef is renowned throughout Canada

THE PRAIRIES

EATING
The breadbasket of Canada produces much more than wheat, and Alberta beef is renowned for being supremely juicy and succulent. There's superb river and lake fish on menus here, too, as well as bison, duck, pork, and game.

Outside of the cities, agriculture reigns supreme, supplying first-class produce to the region's restaurants. There's also nature's bounty in the form of wild rice and berries, such as the saskatoon berry, highbush cranberries, chokecherries, and buffalo berries.

Though the area is famed for its cowboy culture, there is a degree of sophistication in the main cities, and you can certainly find more choices than the chuckwagon and Tex-Mex favorites and barbecues that abound. There are international influences from the various immigrant communities, too, including Ukrainian (try their sausages).

STAYING
As everywhere else in Canada there is a full range of accommodations available, with first-rate city hotels, splendid out-of-town, all-inclusive resorts, motels and roadside inns.

If you're an outdoors type you can get the full Prairies experience on a guest ranch, where you get to help out with the chores around the ranch, then saddle up to round up cattle, maybe try out your rodeo skills, or just follow trails with magnificent views. Days usually wind up with a highly social barbecue.

There are also luxurious

fishing lodges catering to anglers, either right on the water or close by the region's wonderful rivers and lakes. In the far north, there are places that specialize in exploring the tundra and its wildlife.

BATTLEFORD
⏰HARVELLE HOUSE
P.O. Box 538, Battleford, Saskatchewan, S0M 0E0
Tel 306/937-6105
www3.sk.sympatico.ca/harvelle
Nestled in the Eagle Hills south of Battleford, this lovely Victorian-style B&B is just minutes from Fort Battleford and a half-hour from the provincial park. Set in farmland, with a little brook, it offers spacious rooms with antique-style queen-size beds, a hearty country breakfast and a host of things to do. There are plenty of hiking, skiing and horseback-riding trails (you can even bring your own horse), as well as fishing and wildlife-watching—not to mention simply relaxing and enjoying the views.

⏰ Year-round
🛏 $55, breakfast included (horses accommodated, $5 a night)
ℹ 2
♿
🅿
📶 14km (9 miles) south of Battleford on Highway 658

CALGARY
🍴BUZZARDS COWBOY CUISINE
140 10th Avenue Southwest, Calgary, Alberta, T2R 0A3
Tel 403/264-6959
www.cowboycuisine.com
If you like western movies, if you ever played at cowboys as

⊖HILLCREST HOUSE

600 Hillcrest Avenue SW, Calgary,
Alberta, T2S 0M9
Tel 403/228-6164
www.hillcresthouse.com

In her 1914 home Janis King has created a warm, friendly B&B. The house retains its old wood beams, fireplaces, hardwood floors, and tiffany-style fixtures. Each bedroom has a gleaming, modern private bathroom. Bedrooms are light and airy, with individual design schemes, plain walls and pretty cotton bedspreads and drapes, plus TV and VCR and a phone jack for free internet access. Lavish breakfasts are served, and it's only a couple of minutes' walk from trendy 4th Street and its restaurants.

🕐 Year-round
🛏 $79.50–119.50, breakfast included
🛈 4 (all non-smoking)
🚭
🅿
🚌 13
🗺 Downtown, in Mount Royal area

a child, or even if you simply enjoy steak and ribs, this place is great. It's full of cowboy memorabilia (including the chuckwagon from the Demi Moore movie, *The Scarlet Letter*), and the interior takes you back 100 years. There are even taped cowboy poetry readings in the lavatory. It's not all steak and ribs (though these are prominent); there are also chicken and fish dishes, soups and salads—you can even try prairie oysters as an hors d'oeuvre.

🕐 Daily 11am–1am
🛏 L $30, D $65, W $23
🚭
🅿 Street (metered; free after 6)
🚊 C-train
🗺 Downtown, near 10th Avenue/ 1st Street intersection

⊕LA DOLCE VITA

916 1st Avenue Northeast, Calgary,
Alberta, T2E 0C5
Tel 403/263-3445

This Little Italy restaurant has a distinctive white exterior with wrought-iron balconies, and a chic formal interior of white tablecloths, upholstered chairs with wooden arms, and

Italian paintings. Traditional recipes using fresh pasta, seafood and veal combine with imaginative presentation, and the soft ambient music and attentive service make this a great place for a romantic dinner. There's a more casual dining room upstairs that's perfect for a family outing.

🕐 Mon–Fri 11.30–2, 5.30–10.30, Sat 2.30–11; closed Sun
🛏 L $50, D $90, W $30
🚭
🅿 Street, and at rear (both free)
🚌 9
🗺 Little Italy, between 8th and 9th

DAUPHIN

⊖CANWAY INN AND SUITES

1601 Main Street, Dauphin, Manitoba,
R7N 2V4
Tel 204/638-5102, 888/325-3335
www.canwayinn.com

This is a modern, low-rise hotel, conveniently located for visiting Riding Mountain National Park. The modern bedrooms are fairly plain and functional, but there are deluxe rooms and suites that offer more spacious accommodations, in-room two-person Jacuzzis and other extras. The indoor pool complex, for guests only, includes a hot tub and sauna, and there's a bright, modern restaurant open throughout the day (room service is also available).

🕐 Year-round
🛏 $68–78
🛈 67 (12 non-smoking)
🚭 ⊠ Indoor
🅿 With winter plug-ins
🗺 2.4km (1.5 miles) south of Dauphin on highways 5A and 10A

DRUMHELLER

⊖HEARTWOOD MANOR

320 North Railway Avenue East,
Drumheller, Alberta, T0J 0Y4
Tel 403/823-6495, 888/823-6495
www.innsatheartwood.com

Good place to stay in the Badlands. This is a 1920s heritage building of clapboard, turrets, dormers, and many classic old-fashioned touches. Each of the rooms in the inn is quite individual: spacious suites with whirlpool baths, rooms with sloping ceilings and dormer windows, rooms with fireplaces, separate Honeymoon Cottage. All have their own design scheme, with antique-style pine furniture and tasteful fabrics, along with superb modern bathrooms. A range of professional spa treatments is also available.

🕐 Year-round
🛏 $110–250
🛈 10 (all non-smoking)
🚭
🅿 With winter plug-ins
🗺 Downtown, just east of Highway 9

EDMONTON

⊕THE CREPERIE

111, 10220 103rd Street, Edmonton,
Alberta, T5J 0Y8
Tel 780/420-6656
www.thecreperie.com

Small, snug dining rooms below street level, wine racks lining the walls and intimate candlelight make this a romantic spot. The French cuisine is delectable. The house dish is, of course, stuffed crepes, including vegetarian options, and the more unusual combinations feature chicken, shrimp and fruit cocktail in a light curry cream sauce. There are other delights on the menu such as mussels Marseillaise, baked salmon, filet mignon and chicken à la Fiorentina, plus scrumptious desserts such as chocolate fondue.

🕐 Mon–Fri 11.30–10, Sat 5–11, Sun 11.30–9
🛏 L $30, D $55, W $22.50
🚭
🅿 Charge
🚊 LRT to Bay
🚌 1, 2, 8, 52, 112, 308
🗺 Downtown in the Boardwalk, just north of 102nd Avenue

⊖FANTASYLAND AT WEST EDMONTON MALL

17700 87th Avenue, Edmonton, Alberta,
T5T 4V4
Tel 780/444-3000, 800/737-3783
www.fantasylandhotel.com

If you want the complete West Edmonton Mall experience, you should reserve one of

Fantasyland's 11 luxury theme rooms: African jungle, ancient Rome, Polynesia, igloo...you can even sleep in the back of a pick-up truck or in a Wild West

stagecoach. It's great fun for anyone with a modicum of imagination, and off-season specials make it very affordable. There are regular rooms, too, in case of sensory overload from the mall itself, and these are spacious and modern, using toning shades in their design and dark wood furniture.
🕐 Year-round
🛏 $175–305
ℹ 355 (158 non-smoking)
🚭 🍽
🅿 On site (free), valet (charge)
🚌 1, 2, 100, 112 (and many other routes)
🚍 Southwest end of the mall

⊖UNION BANK INN
10053 Jasper Avenue, Edmonton, Alberta, T5J 1S5
Tel 780/423-3600, 888/423-3601
www.unionbankinn.com
Built in 1911 for the Union Bank, this fine old building has been extended and converted into a chic, classy boutique hotel. Designer rooms and suites are individually styled, with restful pastel tones, distinctive fabrics, antique or modern furniture, and goose-down comforters (duvets). Some bathrooms have jet tubs. Lovely soft fleece bathrobes are provided, and free cheese and wine are delivered to guest rooms every evening. The stylish Madison Grill is renowned for its excellent regional Canadian cuisine.
🕐 Year-round
🛏 $145–269
ℹ 34
🚭 🍽
🅿 At rear, free 3pm–9am
🚊 LRT to Central
🚌 3, 5, 100, 120, 135
🚍 Downtown, corner of 101st Street

REGINA
①BUSHWAKKER BREWING CO. LTD.
2206 Dewdney Avenue, Regina, Saskatchewan, S4R 1H3
Tel 306/359-7276
www.bushwakker.com
Created from an old warehouse, this renowned brewpub retains many original features, including its restored pressed-tin ceiling. Historical pictures and contemporary artworks adorn the walls, and you can see the brewhouse

through large windows. The excellent beers are accompanied by memorable pub food, including fish and chips, burgers and nachos. There's also a great variety of Scotch whiskeys, and a range of Bushwakker merchandise.
🕐 Sun–Thu 11am–1am, Fri–Sat 11am–2am
🛏 L $12, D $32, W $17
🅂 Section
🅿
🚍 Old warehouse district, at Dewdney and Cornwall

①MEDITERRANEAN BISTRO
2589 Quance Street East, Regina, Saskatchewan, S4V 2Y7
Tel 306/757-1666
www.mbistro.ca
Handy for through travelers and Regina visitors, this smart modern bistro just off the Trans-Canada Highway is big and boisterous. It has a lengthy menu of bistro favorites, including coq au vin, linguini carbonara, shrimp seafood ravioli, and medallions of beef. The fish specials are invariably excellent. Hors d'oeuvres have some light exotic touches in the use of chili, wasabi, coconut curry, and soy sauce yet also include the standards: mussels, prosciutto and escargots.
🕐 Daily 11–3, 5–11
🛏 L $30, D $50, W $20
🅂

🅿
🚍 East of Regina, on Trans-Canada Highway (Highway 1), just southeast of Fleet Street intersection

⊖FIELDSTONE INN
Box 26038, Craven, Regina, Saskatchewan S4R 8R7
Tel 306/731-2377
www.sasktourism.com/fieldstone
Hundred-year-old stone house on a 200ha (500-acre) farm in the beautiful Qu'Appelle River Valley, which is teeming with wildlife. You can get just bed-and-breakfast or a complete farm-stay experience, with horseback riding, farm chores, nature hikes, and cooking and craft courses. The house is furnished with antiques and retains a historic atmosphere. Guests have use of the library (with books, TV, VCR, and telescope), plus bicycles and canoes. Breakfast is served on verandah on warm days, with wonderful views. Pick up can be arranged (extra charge).
🕐 May–Oct
🛏 $95
ℹ 3
🅿
🚍 Near Craven, 35km (22 miles) north of Regina off Highways 11 or 6

SASKATOON
①CRAWDADDY'S LOUISIANA BAR AND GRILL
244 1st Avenue North, Saskatoon, Saskatchewan S7K 1X1
Tel 306/978-2729
www.goforthegumbo.com
Bourbon Street has been re-created in this former paint warehouse bringing 1900s New Orleans to Saskatoon, with wrought iron, hardwood floors and brick walls. There's a boisterous atmosphere to accompany Creole and Cajun cuisine (and music). Crawfish, of course, is on the menu, together with jambalayas, gumbos, catfish, and alligator— all prepared to authentic recipes. There are also more conventional choices, and hot sauces are on the tables, not in the food.
🕐 Mon 11–9.30, Tue–Thu 11–10, Fri–Sat 11–midnight, Sun and public holidays 4–9.30
🛏 L $25, D $32, W $16
🅂
🅿 Parking area adjacent (charge)
🚌 2
🚍 Downtown between 23rd and 24th streets

SASKATOON STATION PLACE

221 Idylwyld Drive North, Saskatoon, SK, S7L 6V6
Tel 306/244-7777
www.stn-biz.com/saskatoonrestaurant

You can't miss this place—it has two Pullman railcars parked outside. You can choose between dining in these fine old railroad relics or in the historic station building itself. Inside, the station is decorated in Victorian style with authentic antiques and railroad memorabilia. The 8.5m (28ft) mahogany and stained-glass bar is a work of art. Tender ribs and succulent steaks are cooked to various recipes and are sometimes paired with chicken, shrimp or lobster tail. There are also a variety of Greek dishes, pastas, salads, and chicken dishes.

Mon–Sat 10.30am–midnight, Sun 10–10
L $35, D $50, W $22
P
1, 7
At intersection with 23rd Street

PARK TOWN

924 Spadina Crescent East, Saskatoon, Saskatchewan, S7K 3H5
Tel 306/244-5564, 800/667-3999
www.parktownhotel.com

This is a distinctive and superbly renovated hotel with lovely river and parkland views. All rooms are fitted out with oak furniture and have huge windows to take full advantage of the views—the suites on the top two floors have a complete wall of glass. Other extras include coffeemakers, hairdryers, voice mail, and TV. The Jacuzzi rooms have a two-person tub right in the bedroom, and the Presidential Suite is on two floors with a spiral staircase to a loft bedroom (it has a Jacuzzi and a shower with six shower heads). Yuk Yuk's Comedy Club stages a weekly show at the hotel, and there's a pub and lounge in addition to the formal restaurant.

Year-round
$65–93
173
Indoor
P
6A, 7, 11, 19
Downtown, corner of 25th Street by University Bridge

SPECIAL

TAVERN IN THE PARK

55 Pavilion Crescent, Assiniboine Park, Winnipeg, Manitoba, R3P 2N6
Tel 204/896-7275

With its tall tower and mock-Tudor architecture, this is a landmark building surrounded by lovely parkland. The restaurant is in an atrium, with a glass roof, huge indoor plants and formal table settings; there is also outdoor seating on the garden terrace in summer. The food is equally memorable, with gourmet European dishes bringing out the intense flavors of the fresh fish, meat and poultry. Vegetarian options are also available.

Tue–Sat 11.30–2.30, 5–10, Sun 10–2, 5–9
L $30, D $100, W $25
P
67
In Assiniboine Park Pavilion

WINNIPEG

AMICI

326 Broadway, Winnipeg, Manitoba, R3C 0S5
Tel 204/943-4997
www.amiciwpg.com

Very classy upstairs Italian restaurant attracting a lot of business and special-occasion diners. In low-lit modern surroundings, comfortable upholstered chairs are pulled up to tables that are simply laid with white tablecloths. It is the food that creates the color, with Tuscan specialties on a daily-changing menu. Favorite dishes are always retained and might include roast quail, breast of duck or linguini with salmon. Exotic items include ostrich, wild boar and bison.

Mon–Fri 11.30–2, 5–11, Sat 5–11
L $50, D $80, W $20
P
29
At Hargrave Street

BANNER

164 Harrow Street, Winnipeg, Manitoba, R3M 2Z2
Tel 204/256-8721

In historic Crescentwood, a short drive or bus ride from downtown, this is a beautiful Victorian B&B on a shady lot with mature trees and lawns. Inside, it's decorated and furnished in traditional style, with dark wood furniture and beams contrasting with the plain, light walls. Rooms are large and snug, and the one called Secret Harbor has a delightful private sunroom hidden away behind a corner door. Wayfarer's Rest is larger, and has its own sitting area, dressing room and private bathroom.

Year-round
$60–70, breakfast included
2
P
Crescentwood, to the south of the downtown area

PLACE LOUIS RIEL ALL-SUITE HOTEL

190 Smith Street, Winnipeg, Manitoba, R3C 1J8
Tel 204/947-6961, 800/665-0569
www.placelouisriel.com

This is undoubtedly the best place to stay in Winnipeg, the only all-suite hotel in the city, with wonderful original artworks by Native Canadians adorning the walls. Suites include studios and one- and two-bedroom units, and those

up on the Premier (23rd) floor are extra luxurious and have far-reaching views. All rooms have a fully equipped kitchen, cable TV, video games, voice mail, and Internet access. In addition to the restaurant, there's a convenience store and an ATM within the hotel. The well-trained staff are extremely friendly—and so is the hotel's cat.

Year-round
$78–240
290
P Charge
Downtown, between York and St. Mary

Vancouver has a number of superb Chinese restaurants

EATING

Vancouver has a number of restaurants that showcase Pacific Rim cuisine, which looks to the Orient for flavors that combine with the top-quality local produce in new and interesting ways. Many other cuisines are also featured in the city's eclectic collection of eateries, including some of the best Chinese restaurants in the country and several excellent brewpubs. And, not least, the Pacific and Arctic seafood on offer is superb, and could hardly be fresher if you caught it yourself.

Rural BC includes the Okanagan region, which is known for its fruit orchards and is where the province's best wines are produced.

STAYING

Vancouver is the West's biggest city and deservedly popular with visitors—it's consistently at the top of polls of the best place in the world to live and has excellent tourism facilities. Many Vancouver accommodations take advantage of the views out across the water, and though it has the appearance of a modern city, there are some lovely historic properties offering bed-and-breakfast.

Another place with huge pulling power is Whistler, North America's premier ski resort, which is popular year round for superb accommodations surrounded by spectacular mountain scenery. Banff and Jasper are also beautifully sited in the mountains, and offer winter sports and outdoors activities.

BANFF

ⓘMAPLE LEAF GRILLE AND SPIRITS
137 Banff Avenue, Banff, Alberta, T1L 1C8
Tel 403/760-7680
www.banffmapleleaf.com
The two floors of this restaurant and bar-lounge are separated by a grand staircase, and natural wood creates a rustic elegance. Real Canadian cuisine is the focus of the menu, with game (bison, venison, duck), lobster from the tank, fresh fish from the Pacific, Atlantic and Arctic oceans, and prime Alberta beef. There are 300 wines to choose from, including ice wine, and the main-floor lounge has a great selection of beers and spirits (particularly Scotch), making it popular with the après-ski crowd.
🕐 Daily 11–11
🍴 L $35, D $45, W $28
Ⓢ Section
Ⓟ Street and nearby parking areas (all free)
🚌 Banff Shuttle
🚉 Near Caribou Street intersection

ⓑBREWSTER'S MOUNTAIN LODGE
208 Caribou Street, Banff, Alberta, T1L 1C1
Tel 403/762-2900, 888/762-2900
www.brewsteradventures.com
Generations of the enterprising Brewster family—pioneers, cowboys, outdoor adventure operators—have run this hotel in the Rockies. In the style of traditional grand mountain lodges, it has various rooms and suites, with log furniture, rich decor, comforters (duvets), satellite TV, and full granite and tile bathrooms, some with jetted bathtubs. Some rooms have a private balcony. Public areas have log furniture and a western theme, and there is a sauna and whirlpool. Themed packages are available.
🕐 Year-round
🛏 $159–279
🛌 73
Ⓢ
Ⓟ Underground heated
🚉 Downtown

CHASE

ⓠQUAAOUT LODGE
Little Shuswap Lake Road, Chase, British Columbia, V0E 1M0
Tel 250/679-3090
www.quaaout.bcresorts.com

ⓒCASTLE MOUNTAIN CHALETS
Box 1655, Banff, Alberta, T1L 1B5
Tel 403/762-3868
www.decorehotels.com
Midway between Banff and Lake Louise, this isolated spot offers a true taste of the wilderness without the inconvenience. One- and two-bedroom log cabins have cathedral ceilings, Jacuzzis, fully equipped kitchens with dishwasher and microwave, open stone fireplaces and satellite TV/VCR. The 2 ha (4-acre) site is at the base of Castle Mountain, with excellent skiing, hiking and fishing opportunities, and includes an old-fashioned style grocery store, laundry, steam room and library.
🕐 Year-round
🛏 $195–330
🛌 21 chalets
🍴
Ⓟ
🚉 Castle Junction, on Bow Valley Parkway (Highway 1A), short distance off the Trans-Canada Highway.

Owned and run by the Little Shuswap tribe, this lakeside resort combines modern accommodations with native culture. The lobby is in the style of a traditional winter home, with pictographs and carvings; the dining room, supported by log beams, offers international cuisine and native delicacies. The modern rooms have private bathrooms, some with whirlpool, plus TV and refrigerator. There are also tepee accommodations. Guests can swim, waterski and go boating on the lake, or follow hiking trails through the surrounding woodland.
🕐 Year-round
🛏 $140–175
🛌 72
Ⓢ 🍴 Ⓟ
🚉 2.5km (1.5 miles) from Trans-Canada Highway, east of Kamloops, exit Squilax Bridge

DAWSON CREEK

ⓘALASKA CAFÉ AND DINING ROOM
10213 10th Street, Dawson Creek, British Columbia, V1G 3T5
Tel 250/782-7998
www.alaskahotel.com

EATING AND STAYING

Just 55 paces from Mile Zero of the Alaska Highway—that is, 2,400km (1,500 miles) south of Alaska—this restaurant is in a historic hostelry, the landmark Alaska Hotel. A member of the World Famous Restaurants group, it has an extensive menu of European and Canadian cuisine, so there are bison burgers, steaks, Alaskan king crab, and clam chowder alongside crêpes, quiche, pasta, schnitzels, and spanakopita with tzatziki. Desserts include European tortes and homemade pies.

🕐 Daily 11–10
🍴 L $30, D $50, W $19
🚭
🅿
📠 1

JASPER

🍴 PAPA GEORGE'S

Astoria Hotel, 404 Connaught Drive, Jasper, Alberta, T0E 1E0
Tel 780/852-3351, 800/661-7343
www.astoriahotel.com

On the main floor of a family-run heritage hotel, this is a snug, casual restaurant with a pub-style interior featuring a big stone fireplace. If you're just looking for a hearty

sandwich for lunch, this is absolutely the best place, but there's also a varied menu (including a children's menu) of well-cooked dishes that include homemade burgers, pasta, duck à l'orange, fresh fish, and Alberta steaks. The freshly baked bread and pastries are particularly good.

🕐 Daily 7–3, 5–10
🍴 L $25, D $50, W $18
🚭
🅿 Street (free)

🏨 JASPER PARK LODGE

Lodge Road, Jasper, Alberta, T0E 1E0
Tel 780/852-3301, 800/257-7544
www.fairmont.com

Set out like a village of picturesque cedar chalets and

log cabins, this hotel is sympathetic to the spectacular mountains and lake scenery. Cabins with between one and eight bedrooms are available, all with cable TV, telephone, hairdryer, and iron and board. The sitting rooms have wood-burning stoves. Summer activities include golf, boating, horseback riding, and fishing, and there's a resident guide for scenic hikes. In winter, there's skating on the lake, horse-drawn sleigh rides and various winter sports.

🕐 Year-round
🛏 $119–543
🛈 446
🅴 🦽 ≋ Heated outdoor
🅿 On site (with winter plug-ins) and valet
🚗 4.8km (3 miles) northeast of Jasper via Highway 16

KELOWNA

🍴 SUNSET VERANDAH

Summerhill Pyramid Winery, 4870 Chute Lake Road, Kelowna, British Columbia, V1W 4M3
Tel 250/764-8000, 800/667-3538
www.summerhill.bc.ca

If you're on the Okanagan Wine Route, you should stop for lunch—or better still dinner at sunset—at this winery restaurant, with big picture windows overlooking Okanagan Lake. The wide

selection of creative dishes incorporate seafood and organic meats with interesting accompaniments. Main courses might include pine-nut and cilantro-crusted halibut, vine-smoked curried pork tenderloin or Pacific sablefish, or you can get a simple soup, sandwich, burger or pasta dish.

🕐 Daily 11–10
🍴 L $45, D $75, W $20
🚭
🅿
📠 1
🚗 12km (7 miles) from Kelowna on Lakeshore Road

SECHELT

🏨 PEACESCAPES WATERFRONT RETREAT

Site 9 RR#3, 6321 Marmot Road, Sechelt, British Columbia, V0N 3A4
Tel 604/740-0734
www.waterfront-retreat.bc.ca

A supremely tranquil spot and a nature-lover's paradise, this elegant B&B is right on the water's edge, where you'll see abundant wildlife and spectacular sunsets. There are

just two suites (reserve the Honeymoon Suite and you'll get your own waterfront patio) and both have separate entrances. To maintain the peace, under-12s and pets are not accommodated—or you can just rent the whole place.

🕐 Year-round
🛏 $150–185, breakfast included
🛈 2 (both non-smoking)
🅿
🚗 North of Sechelt, on Porpoise Bay

VANCOUVER

🍴 STEAMWORKS BREWPUB

375 Water Street, Vancouver, British Columbia, V6B 5C6
Tel 604/689-2739
www.steamworks.com

The same steam that runs the famous Gastown clock heats the mash tun for Steamtown's wonderful beers—about 15 in total, with seven or eight on tap at any one time. In this 100-year-old building, the quality of the food also attracts some high-profile diners. The pub menu, including seafood, burgers and wood-oven pizzas,

is augmented on lunch and dinner menus by entrées such as wood-oven roasted chicken, steaks marinaded in beer, pasta, and more seafood. There's also a great brunch, with cocktails.

🕐 Mon–Fri 11.30–2.30, 5–10, Sat–Sun 11.30–3. Pub: daily 2.30–10

🍷 L $30, D $70, W $23

🚭

🅿 Charge

🚊 Skytrain and West Coast Express to Waterfront

🚌 50

🚍 Edge of Gastown, intersection with Cordova Street

🎌 SUN SUI WAH SEAFOOD

3888 Main Street, Vancouver, British Columbia, V5V 3N9
Tel 604/872-8822
www.sunsuiwah.com

For more than 30 years this has been one of the favorite restaurants of Vancouver's large and discerning Chinese community. Occupying an ultramodern building, it offers superb Cantonese cuisine, including its signature dish of roast squab, a succulent, crispy-skinned treat that's served whole. Aside from that the emphasis is on seafood— the huge tank has many kinds of live fish and shellfish waiting to be selected. The dim sum is excellent and the atmosphere is buzzing.

🕐 Mon–Fri 10.30–3, 5–10.30, Sat–Sun 10–3, 5–10.30

🍷 L $80, D $120, W $24

🚭

🅿 Underground

🚊 Skytrain to Main Street

🚌 3

🚍 Downtown, at 23rd Avenue

🎌 ZEV'S

1906 Haro Street, Vancouver, British Columbia, V6G 1H7
Tel 604/408-4783
www.zevs.ca

Hip and sophisticated, this restaurant has a casual New

SPECIAL

🎌 BLUE WATER CAFÉ AND RAW BAR

1095 Hamilton Street, Vancouver, British Columbia, V6B 5T4
Tel 604/688-8078
www.bluewatercafe.net

In the heart of hip Yaletown, this equally hip seafood and sushi restaurant has been getting rave reviews since it opened in 2000. The converted warehouse, with brick walls, exposed heating pipes and a warm glow from subdued lighting, attracts movers, shakers and celebrities to dine on the wonderful fresh wild seafood or one of the excellent meat dishes. Two- or three-tier seafood towers (expensive), piled high with succulent shellfish, are great for sharing. Delectable desserts feature either chocolate or fruit.

🕐 Daily 11.30–3, 5–midnight

🍷 L $50, D $120, W $27.50

🚭 Except patio

🅿 Valet Thu–Sat (charge)

🚌 1

🚍 Yaletown, at Hamilton and Helmcken

York-style flair and a chic designer interior of plum-toned mohair upholstery, leopard-skin patterned carpet, dark wood, and low lighting.

The cuisine is an ingenious blend of French, Italian and Asian influences, including roasted wild mushrooms, crispy sushi salmon roll, baked sea bass, and seared Ahi tuna with Oriental vegetables and soba noodle salad. The desserts are divine—try the wet chocolate decadence. In summer you can dine on the heated patio, surrounded by lush vegetation.

🕐 Tue–Sun 5.30–11 (Sun brunch 10–2 in summer)

🍷 Brunch $25, D $90, W $28

🚭 Except patio

🅿 Street and valet (charge)

🚊 Skytrain to Burrard

🚌 5

🚍 Below Buchan Hotel, one block west of Denman at Gilford and one block south of Robson

🏨 BARCLAY HOUSE IN THE WEST END

1351 Barclay Street, Vancouver, British Columbia, V6E 1H6
Tel 604/605-1351, 800/971-1351
www.barclayhouse.com

A peaceful oasis amid the skyscrapers of trendy West End, this B&B is in a restored Victorian home, complete with porch and garden. It has high ceilings and antique furniture, and uses restful natural tones, while the pictures, ornaments and pianos give it a comforting visiting-grandma feel. Each room has a private bathroom, some with clawfoot bathtubs, and TV/VCR and CD players are provided (with an extensive video and CD library). The first-floor Garden Suite enjoys even greater privacy, with its own entrance and sitting room.

🕐 Year-round

🏨 $125–225, breakfast included

🛏 5

🅿

🚊 Skytrain to Burrard

🚍 Downtown between Broughton and Jervis

🏨 BEAUTIFUL BED AND BREAKFAST

428 West 40th Avenue, Vancouver, British Columbia, V5Y 2R4
Tel 604/327-1102
www.beautifulbandb.bc.ca

In a quiet residential area with convenient bus links to all the downtown attractions, this B&B is in a fine colonial home with antique furniture. There are always vases of fresh flowers, and the plain, white walls are set off by the dark wood furniture. Guests can enjoy some splendid views of the North Shore mountains, Vancouver Island and Mt. Baker, particularly from the balcony of the Honeymoon Suite (which also has double sinks and an extra-large bathtub in its private bathroom). Breakfast is served in the formal dining room.

EATING AND STAYING

🕐 Year-round
🍴 $125–225, breakfast included
🛏 3 (all non-smoking)
🅿
🚌 15, 41, airport shuttle
🚗 First block east of Cambie, in residential area

🏨 GRANVILLE ISLAND
1253 Johnston Street, Vancouver, British Columbia, V6H 3R9
Tel 604/683-7373
www.granvilleislandhotel.com
On the waterfront on vibrant Granville Island, this hotel has wonderful views across the water to the city and mountains—particularly if your budget runs to the Penthouse Suite on the top floor.

Individually designed rooms feature pastel shades paired with dark wood furniture, with big windows to make the most of the views. In addition to the Dockside Restaurant with its famous open kitchen, there's a pub serving beer brewed on the premises and a beautiful patio overlooking the water.
🕐 Year-round
🍴 $160–230
🛏 85 (70 non-smoking)
🔆 🍷
🅿 Charge
🚌 15, 17, 488. 492
🚗 Northeast tip of Granville Island

🏨 GROUSE INN
1633 Capilano Road North, Vancouver, British Columbia, V7P 3B3
Tel 604/988-7101
www.grouseinn.com

Great if you're driving and prefer a location out of the city that is handy for North Shore and the mountains. Variously

sized accommodations (standard up to two-bedroom suites with full kitchen) are arranged around a landscaped courtyard; rooms are rather plain and functional, but have amenities such as TV/VCR, coffeemaker, hairdryer, iron and board, and mini-refrigerator. On site there's a restaurant serving breakfast and lunch, a 12m (40ft) heated swimming pool and a children's playground.
🕐 Year-round
🍴 $69–138, continental breakfast included
🛏 80
🔆 🌊 Heated outdoor
🅿
🚌 240, 246
🚢 Seabus to Lonsdale Quay, then bus 239 to Marine Drive
🚗 North Vancouver, off Trans-Canada Highway (Highway 1), exit 14

🏨 HOSTELLING INTERNATIONAL
1025 Granville Street, Vancouver, British Columbia, V6Z 1L4
Tel 604/685-5335, 888/203-8333
www.hihostels.ca
On bustling Granville Street, within easy walking distance of the main shopping and entertainment areas. This is an above-average hostel, having some private rooms with TV and en-suite bathroom as well as the four-bed dormitories. There's a lively bar on the premises, where visitors get to know each other in the evening and daily activities are organized—hikes, bicycle tours, city tours, pub nights.
🕐 Year-round
🍴 $48
🛏 230 beds
🔆
🚊 Skytrain to Granville
🚌 Free shuttle from train station

🏨 "O CANADA" HOUSE
1114 Barclay Street, Vancouver, British Columbia, V6E 1H1
Tel 604/688-0555, 877/688-1114
www.ocanadahouse.com
The name is not just patriotic fervor—the words to the national anthem were actually written here in 1909 by Ewing Buchan, who built this fine home in 1897. Victorian charm is retained in the B&B's architectural detail and antique furniture. Spacious bedrooms and suites all include a sitting area, TV, VCR, refrigerator, telephone, and en-suite bathroom. Three-course breakfasts served at separate tables in elegant dining room. Evening sherry is provided in front parlor; also guest pantry stocked with snacks and beverages, available 24 hours.
🕐 Year-round
🍴 $135–255, breakfast included
🛏 6 (all non-smoking)
🅿
🚊 Skytrain to Burrard
🚗 Downtown, west of Thurlow

🏨 SUTTON PLACE
845 Burrard Street, Vancouver, British Columbia, V6Z 2K6
Tel 604/682-5511, 800/961-7555
www.suttonplace.com
The luxurious rooms and suites in this 21-story downtown hotel have a sleek, modern design and such amenities as plush bathrobes, in-room entertainment (including Internet TV), dual-line telephone, and individual climate control. There's a formal restaurant, a bistro and afternoon teas in La Promenade, with live music daily. Extensive health and fitness facility, including body treatments and personal trainers. Complementary downtown limousine service. Cell phones for rent.
🕐 Year-round
🍴 $179–450
🛏 397
🔆 🍷 🌊 Indoor
🅿 Underground; valet service
🚊 Skytrain to Burrard
🚌 98, 98b

🏨 WEDGEWOOD
845 Hornby Street, Vancouver, British Columbia, V6Z 1V1
Tel 604/689-7777, 800/663-0666
www.wedgewoodhotel.com
A uniformed doorman stands beneath a traditional-style

canopy to usher you into the city's foremost intimate luxury hotel. Bedrooms are individually designed with antique pieces, fresh flowers

and houseplants, coordinating tones, and original works of art. French windows open onto balconies for views over Robson Square gardens, the city or the mountains, away in the distance. The penthouse suites have their own garden terraces. The Bacchus restaurant is highly regarded, and the bar and piano lounge are popular places to gather for cocktails.

🕐 Year-round
💰 $300–800
ⓘ 83 (75 non-smoking)
🚭 🍽
Ⓟ On site (free) and valet (charge)
🚇 Skytrain to Burrard
🚌 8, 98, 98b
📍 Downtown, between Smithe and Robson

VICTORIA
🕚 THE BLETHERING PLACE
2250 Oak Bay Avenue, Victoria, British Columbia, V8R 1G5
Tel 250/598-1413
www.thebletheringplace.com

In an old Tudor-style building, with bow windows and bright flowers, this oak-paneled tearoom is the setting for a wonderful menu of teatime treats: dainty little sandwiches, scones with cream and jam, cakes and English trifle. In addition to the classic pot of orange pekoe, there are more unusual teas and good Columbian coffee. Breakfasts and traditional lunches (roast beef and Yorkshire pudding, Welsh rarebit, and the like) are also served, and there's entertainment on Saturday nights. Regular Residents' Choice award-winner.

🕐 Daily 8am–9pm
💰 L $25, D $35, W $20
🚭
Ⓟ
🚌 2, 8
📍 Oak Bay Village, corner of Monterey

🕚 MARINA
1327 Beach Drive, Victoria, BC, V8S 2N4
Tel 250/598-8555
www.marinarestaurant.com
Perched on the water's edge, with all-round windows looking out over the marina, Haro Strait, the San Juan Islands, and Mt. Baker. A Pacific Northwest slant is given to dishes that focus on fresh local and exotic seafood, but that also include such entrées as fig-crusted lamb with raisin mint couscous, pasta and steaks. There's also a sushi bar, bar meals and a gargantuan Sunday brunch buffet (hot and cold breakfast items, deli food, seafood, roast meat, and desserts) with cocktails.

🕐 Mon–Thu 11.30–2.30, 5–10, Fri–Sat 11.30–2.30, 5–11, Sun 10 2.30, 5–10
💰 L $30, D $50, W $21
🚭
Ⓟ
🚌 2, 8
📍 6km (4 miles) east of Victoria via Oak Bay Avenue

🅰 ABIGAIL'S
906 McClure Street, Victoria, British Columbia, V8V 3E7
Tel 250/388-5363, 800/561-6565
www.abigailshotel.com
Tudor-style B&B with English gardens, just three blocks from the inner harbor and downtown. The bedrooms have antiques, including some

four-poster beds, and coordinated interior designs; the ones on the top floor have dormer windows and most have a wood-burning fireplace. All have private bathrooms, some with Jacuzzis. Fresh coffee is served in the library for early risers; gourmet breakfast includes homemade bread, scones and muffins, kippers (smoked on the premises), quality meats and omelettes.

🕐 Year-round
💰 $122–389, breakfast included
ⓘ 23 (all non-smoking)
Ⓟ At rear (free)
🚌 Bus from ferry port
📍 East of downtown, between Quadra and Vancouver

WHISTLER
🕚 VAL D'ISERE
8-4314 Main Street, Bear Lodge, Town Plaza, Whistler, British Columbia, V0N 1B0
Tel 604/932-4666
www.valdisere-restaurant.com
Very French, with a zinc bar, checkerboard floor, oak furniture, tapestries and a fireplace, this restaurant harks back to 1920s Paris, and the summer patio also has a distinctly Continental feel. The

food marries regional French cuisine (Alsace, Burgundy) with such fresh Canadian ingredients as Prince Edward Island mussels, Fanny Bay oysters and Pacific salmon in creative dishes that are wonderful to look at and unbelievably tasty. The excellent wine list features fine French vintages and North American varieties, including some bottles from British Columbia vineyards.

🕐 Daily 11.30–10, early Jan–mid-Nov; 5.30–10, rest of year
💰 L $70, D $100, W $25
🚭
Ⓟ
📍 Next to Sheraton Hotel

⊘DURLACHER HOF ALPINE INN

7055 Nesters Road, Whistler, British
Columbia, V0N 1B7
Tel 604/932-1924
www.durlacherhof.com

It may be somewhat surprising
to find an authentic-looking
alpine chalet, complete with a
flower-decked wooden
balcony, up here, but this
lovely little mountain hideaway
was built and is run by an
authentic alpine (Austrian)
family. Rooms and suites have
tasteful fabrics, goose-down
comforters (duvets) and handcarved pine furniture; Alpine
Rooms on the top floor have
vaulted, pine-clad ceilings. All
have private bathrooms, some
with whirlpool, and to
maintain the peace, they lack
TVs and telephones. Lavish
breakfasts are served here,
including *Kaiserschmarren*
(sweet pancakes), and dinner
is also available on some
evenings.

⊙ Year-round
💷 $130–295
🚹 8 (all non-smoking)
🅿 Oudoor
🅿
🚌 North on Highway 99

⊘WESTIN RESORT AND SPA

4090 Whistler Way, Whistler,
British Columbia V0N 1B4
Tel 604/905-5000, 888/634-5577
www.westinwhistler.net

This splendid hotel offers the
ultimate Whistler experience—
with luxury accommodations,
breathtaking mountain views,
superb gourmet cuisine, and a
fantastic range of leisure
amenities. The suites—there
are no ordinary rooms—have
chic modern furnishings
combined with the occasional
rustic touch in the use of
natural wood and gas
fireplaces. The spa facility is
among the finest in Canada,
and other services include ski
and golf valets to take care of
your every sporting
requirement. There are several
eating options, and there's a
kid's club to keep your
offspring happily occupied.

⊙ Year-round
💷 $469–2,559 plus "resort fee"
🚹 419
🚭
🚬 🎿 🏊 Heated indoor/outdoor
🅿 Charge, also valet service
🚌 Highway 99

EATING AND STAYING (vertical, left margin)

THE NORTH

EATING

Not surprisingly, choices can
be somewhat limited in an
area that is largely wilderness
dotted with tiny settlements.
Don't rely on all towns marked
on the map to have a place to
eat—some have no more than
a filling station, a store and
maybe a motel. However,
Whitehorse, Dawson City and
Yellowknife have a number of
good restaurants, including
hotel dining rooms, where the
menu might include Arctic
char, Alaskan king crab,
caribou baked in a bordelaise
sauce, or sushi.

Laid-back eating places
serving simply cooked steaks
and ribs, fresh fish and game
are what you'll find most often.
In summer, residents and
visitors enjoy barbecues and
eating in the open air. Bars and
pubs serving simple food are
popular for meeting the locals
and sampling the local beers.
Coffee is served everywhere,
but you won't find many
specialist cafés or teashops.
Vegetarians will find that some,
but not all, restaurants cater to
their requirements.

STAYING

The north has luxury and mid-
priced hotels, hostels, motels,
B&Bs, and campgrounds, but
in some areas they're
decidedly thin on the ground.
Whitehorse has the most
choice of hotels, while other
places, including Dawson City,
have a more limited selection.
Wherever you choose to base
yourself, they all fill up fast in
summer. Reservations are
advisable for July and August,
and Select Reservations (18
Tagish Road, Whitehorse,
Yukon, 877/735-3281
www.selectrez.com/
wats_oth.htm) provides
information on places to stay
across the Yukon and northern
BC. If you arrive without a
reservation, the visitor center
may be able to help.

If you intend to drive the
Alaska Highway, it's a comfort
to know that food, fuel and
lodgings are available at 40km
(25-mile) to 80km (50-mile)
intervals, but it's still advisable
to reserve places to stay. There
are also government-run
campgrounds along this route.

DAWSON CITY

⊘KLONDIKE KATE'S

Box 417, Dawson City, Yukon, Y0B 1G0
Tel 867/993-6527
www.klondikekates.ca

This original gold-rush
building, dating to 1904, is
named after the notorious
"Queen of the Klondike." It's a
distinctive landmark on its
corner lot, and you can dine
inside or on the covered (and
heated) patio. Canadian and

ethnic food is on the menu,
and the $4.99 breakfast special
is renowned.

⊙ Daily 6.30am–11pm, mid-May to
mid-Sep
💷 L $25, D $35, W $26.21
🚭
🅿 Street (free)
🚌 At Third and King streets

⊘BOMBAY PEGGY'S

Box 411, 2nd Avenue, Dawson City,
Yukon, Y0B 1G0
Tel 867/993-6969
www.bombaypeggys.com

Built in 1900, this hotel has a
mixed history, but it's the era
when it was a brothel that lives
on, albeit only in the name.
Luxuriously restored, it retains
a touch of decadence with
hardwood floors, plush

furnishings, deep claw-foot
bathtubs, and richly shaded
walls. The Lipstick Room has
red walls and black velvet
bedding; the exotic Purple
Room has Oriental fabrics and
a 2m-high (7ft) carved
headboard. The pub offers an

appetizer menu, a range of malt whiskeys and cocktails.

🕐 Year-round
💷 $77–189
🛏 9 (all non-smoking)
🚭
🅿
🚗 One street back from the river front at 2nd and Princess Street

⊖WESTMARK INN

P.O. Box 420, Dawson City,
Yukon, Y0B 1G0
Tel 867/993-5542, 800/283-6622
www.westmarkhotels.com
Cheerful complex built around a central lawned courtyard, where locally renowned Klondike barbecues are held. Two levels, some with outside corridors, feature modern rooms and suites with private bathroom, TV, honor bar, hairdryer and iron; some have a kitchen. There's a dining room open throughout the day, and a coin laundry and gift shop on site. Local phone calls are free.

🕐 May–Sep
💷 $152
🛏 131
🅿
🚗 Downtown at 5th and Harper streets

HAINES JUNCTION

⊖THE RAVEN

Box 5470, Haines Junction, Yukon,
Y0B 1L0
Tel 867/634-2500
www.yukonweb.com/tourism/raven
Stupendous views of the St. Elias Mountains and a gourmet restaurant top the list of attractions at this delightful

little hotel in a picturesque Alaska Highway village close to the Kluane National Park and Tatshenshini-Alsek Provincial Park. Rooms all have private bathroom, TV and telephone and modern hardwood furniture. The renowned restaurant features European cuisine. There's also a large sundeck and a small RV park.

🕐 May–Sep
💷 $125, continental breakfast included
🛏 12
🚭
🅿
🚗 Short drive out of town

INUVIK

⊖ARCTIC CHALET

25 Carn Street, Inuvik, Northwest Territories, X0E 0T0
Tel 867/777-3535
www.arcticchalet.com
In a beautiful location between two lakes and the Mackenzie River, this B&B offers a wonderful northern experience. Rooms and cabins all feature the golden glow of natural wood, and all have satellite TV and phone; most have private bathroom and private entrance. The owners have a team of gorgeous white huskies, which enjoy being taken for walks, and in winter you can take a dogsledding trip. In summer there's fishing and canoeing on site. Guests who fly in to the resort have the use of a vehicle for getting around town.

🕐 Year-round
💷 $110–130, breakfast included
🛏 9 (all non-smoking)
🅿
🚗 Edge of Inuvik, off Airport Road

IQALUIT

⊖FROBISHER INN

P.O. Box 4209, Iqaluit,
Nunavut X0A 0H0
Tel 867/979-2222, 877/422-9422
www.frobisherinn.com
There are plenty of opportunities for roughing it in Nunavut, but you don't have to. This modern hotel, with spectacular views over Koojesse Inlet, is where visiting dignitaries from around the world choose to stay, most likely in the corner suites, which have fireplaces and Jacuzzis. The standard rooms, which have plain walls in pastel shades, feature quality furnishings, full bathroom, coffee, hairdryer and TV; deluxe rooms feature Inuit artworks, larger-screen TV and VCR. The hotel also has a formal dining room, café and gourmet coffee bar.

🕐 Year-round
💷 $205–255
🛏 95; no smoking floors
🏊 Indoor
🚗 Downtown

WATSON LAKE

⊖WATSON LAKE HOTEL

Alaska Highway, Watson Lake,
Yukon, Y0A 1C0
Tel 867/536-7712
www.watsonlakehotels.com
This hotel was built to service the personnel involved in the Alaska Highway project, and occupies a rustic log building dating from 1942; you can trace the history in the old photographs on the walls of the lobby and lounge. Renovations have kept it up to date, and rooms are spacious and modern, with cable TV and private bathroom; family suites have a full kitchen. There's a stylish dining room, an informal coffee shop and the Red Feather Saloon.

🕐 Year-round
💷 $100
🛏 48
🅿

WHITEHORSE

⊕TALISMAN

2112 2nd Avenue, Whitehorse,
Yukon, Y1A 1B9
Tel 867/667-2736
www.yuk-biz.com/talismancafe
With works by First Nations artist Ivan Sawrenko on one wall (including the original of the restaurant logo), this is indeed a great little café. It's geared toward families and vegetarians, and offers a good selection of international dishes that come in generous portions, including excellent home baking and a wide choice of breakfast dishes. Try one of the bannocks (shrimp, caribou, eggs and ham) or ask about the catch of the day. A take-out service is also available.

🕐 Mon–Wed 9–7, Thu–Sat 9–9, Sun 10–3
💷 L $25, D $25
🚭
🅿
🚗 Downtown, next to Toronto Dominion Bank

⊖HAWKINS HOUSE

303 Hawkins Street, Whitehorse,
Yukon, Y1A 1X5
Tel 867/668-7638
www.hawkinshouse.yk.ca
High ceilings, hardwood floors, and stained glass bring Victorian style to this two-story 1994 B&B. The rooms, all with private bathroom, are imaginatively and artistically

themed, each with videos, books, and objects relevant to the theme. Breakfasts may be themed too, and include homemade moose sausages,

breads and jams, and home-smoked salmon. The interesting and accomplished hosts can provide local information, and there is complementary laundry service.
🕐 Year-round
💲 $104–163, breakfast included
🚭 4 (all non-smoking)
🅿 With winter plug-ins
🚌 Downtown

⊖HIGH COUNTRY INN
4051 4th Avenue, Whitehorse, Yukon, Y1A 1H1
Tel 867/667-4471, 800/554-4471
www.highcountryinn.yk.ca
You can't miss this inn—it has a 15m-high (50ft) Mountie guarding its door. Inside, apart from the 1938 Harley-Davidson in the lobby, you'll find four floors of rooms ranging from standard doubles to sumptuous suites with two-person Jacuzzis. Rooms with kitchenette are also available.

All have private bathroom, cable TV, two telephone lines and a modem outlet, and tea/coffee. The large, sunny restaurant has a mainly steaks-and-ribs menu, and the Yukon Mining Company Deck is a popular meeting place.
🕐 Year-round
💲 $109–229
🚭 84

🎦
🅿 With winter plug-ins
🚌 East of Main Street

YELLOWKNIFE
❶L'ATITUDES
Yellowknife Inn, Central Square Mall, 5010 49th Street, Yellowknife, Northwest Territories, X1A 2N4
Tel 867/873-2601
www.yellowknifeinn.com
This is a modern eatery, with no-frills interior, that serves up a good range of food throughout the day, from the continental or big hot breakfasts to a dinner of

fresh Arctic char with lemon garlic butter, a ginger beef stir-fry, or caribou baked in a bordelaise sauce. The all-day menu features pasta, sandwiches, subs, stir-fries, and fajitas. There's a limited selection of European wines.
🕐 Daily 7am–9pm
💲 L $25, D $45, W $30
🚭
🅿 Mall parking (free)
🚌 1, 2 (also 3 on Sat and during summer school vacation)
🚌 Downtown, off Main Street beside shopping mall

❶THE PROSPECTOR
3506 Wiley Road, P.O. Box 400, Yellowknife, Northwest Territories X1A 2N3
Tel 867/920-7639
This is a welcoming bar and grill, with wood paneling, foliage plants and—best of all—big windows with stunning views. It's also something of a tourist attraction for its array of mining and aviation memorabilia, and maps of the area are built right into the table tops. When the weather is fine, get a table outside on the deck, directly on the water's edge. The food is good, too, with a menu of juicy steaks and other grills.
🕐 Mon–Fri 11–2, 5–10, Sat 9am–11pm, Sun 10–3

💲 L $25, D $45, W $31
🚭
🅿
🚌 1, 2 (also 3 on Sat and during summer school vacation)
🚌 Back Bay Waterfront

⊖BACK BAY BOAT BED AND BREAKFAST
3530 Ingraham Drive, Yellowknife, Northwest Territories, X1A 2E9
Tel 867/873-4080
www.backbayboat.com
This delightful B&B is in a mixture of traditional and contemporary styles, with input from local artist Ann Peters. One of the bedrooms and the bright dining room have wonderful lake views, and there's a billiard room and a good collection of local-interest books and videos. Guests also have access to a kitchenette with complimentary beverages. The European-style breakfast includes fruit, cheese, cold cuts, cereal, yogurt, and delicious home-baked sourdough rye bread.
🕐 Year-round
💲 $80, breakfast included
🚭 3 (all non-smoking)
🅿
🚌 2 (also 3 on Sat and during summer school vacation)
🚌 East of downtown, on peninsula between Back Bay and Great Slave Lake

⊖CHATEAU NOVA
4401 50th Avenue, Yellowknife, Northwest Territories, X1A 2N2
Tel 867/873-9700, 877/839-1236
www.chateaunova.com
One of Yellowknife's newest hotels, opened late 2000, provides big-city standards, with large, elegant rooms and suites. All have private bathroom, bathrobes, tea- and coffee-making facilities and hairdryer, plus high-speed Internet connection, TV, and telephone with voice mail. Reminders of less comfortable times take the form of archive pictures throughout the hotel. Think of those early explorers while you relax in the hot tub. The restaurant has an eclectic menu, including sushi, fresh fish and caribou steaks.
🕐 Year-round
💲 $161–200
🚭 59
♿ 🎦
🅿 With winter plug-ins
🚌 Downtown

Planning

Canada is an enormous country, the second largest in the world, encompassing many different climatic zones with tremendous variations from summer to winter. The country's cold winters and heavy snowfall produce some spectacular skiing, and the warmth of summer gives rise to a myriad of outdoor festivals and activities. Although any time of year has its attractions depending on your interests, the vast majority of visitors seek the pleasures of Canada between mid-May and mid-October. Outside these months, facilities may be much reduced, unless you are going to a ski area or a major city. It is thus advisable to check in advance that hotels and sights will be open if you plan to travel outside the peak season.

WHAT TO EXPECT— REGIONAL VARIATIONS

East Coast

The East Coast has lovely warm summers, but rain and fog are always a possibility, especially on or near the coast. The Atlantic shores can also be very

Wasaga Beach on Georgian Bay

WEATHER WEBSITE

The federal government agency, Environment Canada, has an excellent website (http://weatheroffice.ec.gc.ca), which gives a good idea of what to expect in any given part of the country in any particular month.

windy, particularly in Newfoundland. The fall colors in this area are spectacular. Winters are relatively mild, but there is snow too—in New Brunswick it often figures among the highest in the country—and ice floes (or massive icebergs in the case of Newfoundland and Labrador) can be seen drifting not far offshore.

Canadian Shield—Ontario and Québec

Because of their size, there is considerable variation within these two huge central provinces. Québec, covering an area greater than Texas, stretches from the temperate south to the Arctic and the weather varies accordingly.

The southern parts of both Ontario and Québec are extremely hot and humid in mid-summer. From the end of June through August the temperature can easily remain in the 30s Celsius (90s Fahrenheit) for days on end. This can be extremely uncomfortable in the big cities as there is high humidity. As a result, central Canadians

PLANNING

VANCOUVER

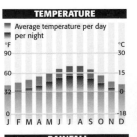

WINNIPEG

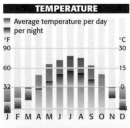

TORONTO

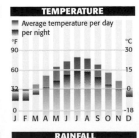

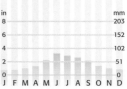

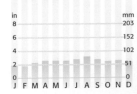

use air conditioning in summer and humidification in winter—in some homes, the same machine does both jobs.

In the winter you can expect the other extreme, with cold temperatures and lots of snow. Central Canadians continue life as normal whatever the season and adjust to the extremes. Visitors must do the same.

The Niagara Peninsula, the country's top fruit-growing and wine-producing region, has relatively milder winters. Snow does occasionally fall, and in particularly cold winters Niagara Falls looks spectacular when it freezes.

Between winter and summer, there is a short, crisp spring. Later, the mild fall produces brilliant foliage, and, not surprisingly, this is a popular time to visit.

Prairies

The landlocked Prairies have bitterly cold and drawn-out winters, but beautiful warm summers. They don't suffer from the humidity of the Canadian Shield country (Ontario and Québec) and they don't suffer from bugs either. Thunder storms occur in summer: They can be seen coming from a long way off, so you can usually avoid getting soaked. Night skies in mid-summer are unbelievable, with more stars than can possibly be counted.

Rocky Mountains

Famous for their rocky profiles and snow-capped peaks, the

QUÉBEC

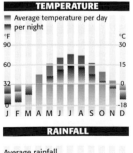

TEMPERATURE

Average temperature per day
per night

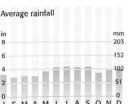

RAINFALL

Average rainfall

Canadian Rockies experience heavy snowfall in the winter. Roads are icy and dangerous at this time. The season draws skiers, snowboarders and enthusiasts for dangerous sports such as climbing frozen waterfalls.

Like all mountain areas, the weather can change dramatically in a few hours in any month of the year. Rainstorms can appear from nowhere and turn to snow at high altitudes, even in July. In May the lakes are often still frozen over, so most visitors prefer to enjoy the great mountain parks (Banff, Jasper) from June through August.

West Coast

The weather of the west coast, especially Vancouver Island, is tempered by the Pacific Ocean. It's not too hot in summer and the winters are mild with little or no snow, but both seasons can be wet.

Away from the coast the climate is much hotter and drier. Inland, the Okanagan is a major fruit-growing and wine-making region, though rainfall is so low that irrigation is required to grow the crops.

The North

In the north of the country summers are short and warm with 24 hours of daylight. Winters are long, dark and Siberia-like, with incredibly low temperatures. Plan any trip here carefully, getting as much information as possible from the tourist offices or local outfitters.

TIME ZONES

Though Canada spans six of the world's 24 time zones, there's only a four-hour difference between the east and west coasts because Newfoundland and a part of Labrador have their own special zone—half an hour ahead of Atlantic Standard Time which, itself, is 4 hours ahead of UTC (formerly known as GMT). AST is observed in the rest of Labrador and the other Maritime provinces.

Most of Québec (except a section of the North Shore) and Ontario (except the extreme west) observe Eastern Standard Time (UTC +5). Manitoba and Saskatchewan observe Central Standard Time (UTC +6). Alberta and a section of south eastern British Columbia observe

Mountain Standard Time (UTC +7). The rest of British Columbia and the Yukon observe Pacific Standard Time (UTC +8). The Northwest Territories observes the two time zones to the south—Central and Mountain—while Nunavut observes Eastern Standard.

Daylight Saving Time is effective in all provinces and territories except Saskatchewan from the first Sunday in April, when the clocks are advanced by one hour, until the last Sunday in October. Saskatchewan keeps the same time all year (see Time Zones map on page 7).

Snowboarding Canada-style

TIME ZONES		
City	Time difference	Time at 12 noon EST (Ottawa)
Amsterdam	+6	6pm
Berlin	+6	6pm
Brussels	+6	6pm
Buenos Aires	+2	2pm
Calgary	-2	10am
Chicago	-1	11am
Dublin	+5	5pm
Halifax	+1	1pm
Johannesburg	+7	7pm
London	+5	5pm
Los Angeles	-3	9am
Madrid	+6	6pm
Miami	0	12 noon
New York	0	12 noon
Paris	+6	6pm
Perth, Australia	+15	3am
Rome	+6	6pm
San Francisco	-3	9am
Sydney	+17	5am
Tokyo	+14	2am
Vancouver	-3	9am

PLANNING

Pack for seasonal weather

light in the north is surprisingly bright and daylight lasts for 24 hours in summer.

On northern trips sunscreen is important in summer; dress relatively lightly but cover against lengthy exposure to the sun. Insects are a problem in the early part of the season (April and May). Long-sleeve shirts, slacks and a hat with mosquito netting are recommended for any prolonged outdoor activity, such as camping or canoeing.

WHAT TO PACK
Long hot summer days, fierce rainstorms, tornadoes, beautiful evenings, bright, cold winters— packing can be a problem.

East Coast
Rainwear and sweaters for evenings are a good idea on the East Coast even in mid-summer. The wind can be fierce on the Atlantic coast, so pack a light windbreaker if spending time outside.

West Coast
Make sure you are equipped with rainwear if you plan to hike or do other outdoor activities. An umbrella is handy in Vancouver. In the winter months you will only need warm clothing if you go to a ski resort.

The North
Sunglasses are important as the

Winter Wear
For winter visits to Canada, except for the west coast (see above), pack warm clothing: a parka or coat, a woolen hat (preferably with earflaps), gloves, long underwear, and also waterproof boots. All the above can be purchased in the country if necessary, though you could freeze between the airport and the nearest clothing store. In the north in January especially, cover up in thermal Arctic gear from head to foot.

DOCUMENTATION AND CUSTOMS

ENTRY REQUIREMENTS
Entry requirements differ depending on your nationality, and are also subject to change without notice. Check prior to a visit and follow news events that may affect your situation.

US Visitors
American citizens must show proof of citizenship when entering Canada. At the present

time a passport is not essential, though it is the best and easiest means to prove your citizenship. Otherwise any documentation with photo ID can be used, such as your certificate of naturalization, if you were not born in the US; a birth or baptismal certificate with photo ID; a social security card; or a voter's card. No visa is necessary. If you are a permanent US

resident but not a citizen, you must carry your Alien Registration Card (green card).

Visitors from the European Union and Australia
Citizens of Australia and of European countries that are part of the European Union do not require a visa to enter Canada, but they must carry a valid passport.

CANADIAN EMBASSIES AND CONSULATES ABROAD		
Country	**Address**	**Website**
Australia	Commonwealth Avenue, Canberra, ACT 2600 Tel (02) 6270 4000	www.dfait-maeci.gc.ca/australia
France	35–37 avenue Montaigne, Paris, 75008 Tel 01 44 43 29 00	www.dfait.maecigc.ca/~paris
Germany	Friedrichstrasse 95, 10117 Berlin; tel (030) 20 31 20.	www.dfait-maeci.gc.ca/~bonn
Ireland	65 St. Stephen's Green, Dublin 2; tel 01 417 4100.	www.canadaeuropa.gc.ca/ireland
Italy	Via G. B. de Rossi 27, 00161 Rome; tel (06) 44 59 81	www.dfait-maeci.gc.ca/ canadaeuropa/italy
New Zealand	P.O. Box 12049, Thorndon, Wellington Tel (04) 473 9577	www.dfair-maeci.gc.ca/newzealand
Spain	Calle Nunez de Balboa 35, 28001 Madrid; tel (034) 91 423 3250	www.canada-es.org
South Africa	1103 Arcadia Street, Hatfield, Pretoria 0028 Tel (012) 422 3000	www.consulfrance-jhb.org
UK	Macdonald House, 1 Grosvenor Square, London, W1X 0AB Tel (020) 7258 6600	www.dfait-maeci.gc.ca/london
USA (Los Angeles)	550 South Hope Street, 9th Floor, Los Angeles, CA90071-2627. Tel 213/346-2700	www.losangeles.gc.ca

PLANNING

Visitors From Other Parts of the World

Entry visas are required for citizens of more than 130 countries. As political and economic changes take place around the world, the list of countries changes frequently, depending on what's going on at the time. You can check the situation for any particular country by getting in touch with the local Canadian embassy, or by visiting the website of the Canadian government's Citizenship and Immigration (http://cicnet.ci.gc.ca).

If you do require a visa, you will need to apply for it at the Canadian embassy in your home country. The visa must be issued before you leave home—and you'll need to plan this well in advance because the process is not always speedy.

Young People and Seniors

Any person under 19, alone or in a group, is required to show a letter from their parent or guardian giving them permission to visit Canada; the letter must state the individual's name and the duration of the trip. In addition they must carry proof of identity. Students should also have their ID handy for claiming reductions on travel fares and admission charges.

Throughout Canada, seniors need to prove their age to benefit from any reduced fares or admission charges.

CUSTOMS

Firearms

Strict regulations apply to bringing firearms into Canada. If you are going on a hunting trip, make sure you check restrictions and have the necessary documentation before you arrive at the border. If you are flying in, consult airport security for advice.

Mountain goat in the Yukon

Organic Imports

There are strict regulations concerning the importation of plants, flowers and other vegetation. It is not advisable to bring anything of this sort into Canada. Details of the regulations are available from: Revenue Canada, Customs and Excise. Tel 800/461-9999 (within Canada), 204/983-3500 or 506/636-5064 (from outside Canada), or consult their website: www.ccra-adrc.gc.ca

Pets

Pets can accompany you to Canada, but they must have been vaccinated against rabies within the preceding 12 months, and you must carry the vaccination certificate with you.

VEHICLE DOCUMENTATION

If you drive a vehicle into Canada, you must carry its registration papers and proof of insurance coverage, in addition to a valid driver's license. Be aware that your vehicle is likely to be searched for illegal substances at the border, and be prepared to show your documentation to police officers if you are pulled over while driving within Canada.

INSURANCE

To enter Canada you are not obliged to have any personal form of insurance other than for your vehicle. It is advisable, however, to arrange some kind of health coverage. Canada's health system is available free to Canadians, but is not similarly available to foreigners. Bills for quite simple procedures can be more than you would pay at home, and sometimes there is even an out-of-province premium to pay.

Your own insurance company is probably the best source of advice on what is best for you. Insurance on your personal property, especially if you will be carrying valuables with you, is also important.

Most residential insurance policies provide some kind of coverage, even when you are journeying in a foreign country—check with your insurer before leaving home. If anything does get lost or stolen, it is usually necessary to have a police report in order to make a claim.

PRACTICALITIES

ELECTRICAL ADAPTERS

Throughout Canada, the voltage is 110 volts A.C., the same as in the US. European appliances require an adapter and a plug with two flat prongs (occasionally three prongs).

Modern electric razors and hairdryers are often designed to work on both 220 volts and 110 volts, but you still need the appropriate adapter. You can buy these at most airports and travel stores in Canada, though it is advisable to purchase one before you leave home.

LAUNDRY SERVICES

Dry cleaning and laundry services are widely available in Canadian cities. Your hotel can make arrangements for you or provide some addresses; tourist offices can also supply this information.

Be warned that laundry services are not necessarily cheap. If you wish to do your own laundry and find a hotel washbasin inadequate, don't expect to find laundromats on every downtown corner—instead seek out a student area, where they are more plentiful.

MEASUREMENT

Canada uses the metric system of weights and measures, with fuel sold in litres, and food in grams and kilograms. However, clothing sizes and food amounts may still be given in the imperial (American) system.

PUBLIC WASHROOMS

Canadian cities are not usually equipped with public washrooms (toilets) accessed from the outdoors, as is often the case in Europe. The main reason for this is the problem of servicing them in winter and making sure they don't freeze up.

One of the best places to find washrooms is the local tourist office, where they will be clean. Train and bus stations also provide washrooms though they are not always spotlessly clean. Other good places include the lobbies of major hotels, department stores, museums and other tourist attractions, restaurants (but only if you are eating there) and filling stations. Public washrooms are usually free of charge and of a high standard.

CONVERSION CHART		
From	**To**	**Multiply by**
Inches	Centimeters	2.54
Centimeters	Inches	0.3937
Feet	Meters	0.3048
Meters	Feet	3.2810
Yards	Meters	0.9144
Meters	Yards	1.0940
Miles	Kilometers	1.6090
Kilometers	Miles	0.6214
Acres	Hectares	0.4047
Hectares	Acres	2.4710
Gallons	Liters	4.5460
Liters	Gallons	0.2200
Ounces	Grams	28.35
Grams	Ounces	0.0353
Pounds	Grams	453.6
Grams	Pounds	0.0022
Pounds	Kilograms	0.4536
Kilograms	Pounds	2.205
Tons	Tonnes	1.0160
Tonnes	Tons	0.9842

SMOKING AND ALCOHOL

Smoking is increasingly frowned upon in Canada, and is forbidden in office buildings, in most indoor public places, and on buses and subway systems. Some provinces are experimenting with a no-smoking policy for restaurants and bars. In other provinces it is generally the law that public places (including hotels, restaurants, bars and cafés) have at least a section set aside for non-smokers.

Cigarettes are sold in supermarkets and other grocery stores, newspaper and magazine stores, and bars.

The legal age to purchase and drink alcoholic beverages is 19 in all provinces except Alberta, Manitoba and Québec, where the age is 18. Laws regarding the sale of beer, wine and other alcoholic beverages vary from province to province.

In most provinces hard liquor can be purchased only at government stores, or at special stores in Ontario. An exception is Québec, where wine and beer are sold in food stores.

Once purchased, alcohol must be carried out of sight in the trunk (boot) of your car, and must not be consumed in public (including a picnic).

TAXES

A 7 percent Goods and Services Tax (GST) is added to everything

CLOTHING SIZES			
See www.bsi-global.com for BS EN 13402-3; final European standard expected 2004.			
Australia	**UK**	**CAN/US**	
90	36	36	SUITS
96	38	38	
102	40	40	
108	42	42	
114	44	44	
120	46	46	
7	6	8	SHOES
8	7	8.5	
9	8	9.5	
10	9	10.5	
11	10	11.5	
12	11	12	
37	14.5	14.5	SHIRTS
38	15	15	
39/40	15.5	15.5	
41	16	16	
42	16.5	16.5	
43	17	17	
8	8	6	DRESSES
10	10	8	
12	12	10	
14	14	12	
16	16	14	
18	18	16	
20	20	18	
6	4.5	6	SHOES
6.5	5	6.5	
7	5.5	7	
7.5	6	7.5	
8	6.5	8	
8.5	7	8.5	
9	7.5	9	

you buy in Canada except food from a supermarket or grocery store. It is also applicable on all hotel and restaurant checks (bills), on tickets for all types of transportation and on admission charges to tourist sights.

In addition, most provinces add their own Provincial Sales Tax (PST), so you may find yourself paying a surcharge of anything between 7 percent in Alberta (GST only—there is no PST) to 19 percent in Newfoundland, where the rate of PST is 12 percent. The Atlantic provinces operate a Harmonized Sales Tax (HST), which combines GST and PST into one system. These are not hidden taxes: They are added to

PLANNING

the check (bill) and itemized on the sales slip.

In certain cases, the GST is refundable to visitors for hotel checks (bills) and for goods being taken out of the country. Certain conditions apply (type of product, minimum purchase value), so obtain the refund slip at the time of purchase (all major hotels and tourist offices have a supply of them). The PST is also refundable in certain provinces—Québec, for example. For more information on refunds, contact: Revenue Canada Visitor Rebate Program Summerside Tax Centre, Canada Customs and Revenue Agency, 275 Pope Road, Suite 104, Summerside, Prince Edward Island, C1N 6C6, tel 800/668-4748 (in Canada) or 902/432-5608 (from abroad); www.ccra-adrc.gc.ca/visitors.

VISITING WITH KIDS

If you take children to Canada, they must have their own documentation, such as a birth certificate and passport. If you are a parent traveling without the child's other parent, or if you are not the legal guardian, you must carry a letter of permission from the other parent, parents or legal guardian. Divorced parents are required to carry legal documents establishing their status. These restrictions have recently been imposed because of the number of divorced parents absconding to Canada with their children, against the wishes of the other parent.

When renting a car, request a child's car seat at the time of making the reservation. When flying, check the carry-on allowance, especially in the case of buggies; some airlines require that they are checked as baggage. You should ask for children's meals in advance too.

Most hotels in Canada allow children under a certain age to stay free in their parents' room. The age limit for this varies from establishment to establishment, and some places treat children as extra adults and charge accordingly. Check carefully when reserving.

Most restaurants, especially those in popular tourist areas, will offer a children's menu and have high chairs or booster seats, but this is worth checking in advance. Certain museums

Helpful signposting in Ontario

(for example, the National Gallery of Canada) offer children's activity rooms in addition to child-related exhibits.

CULTURE AND ETIQUETTE

Although Canadians may appear just like Americans to some Europeans, many of them do not appreciate being told so. It's probably a topic to avoid. If you push the cultural similarities too far expect to receive a lecture on how Canada developed and just how different it is. Having said that, Canadians are increasingly informal and there is very little that shocks them.

Dress Code

Visitors can dress casually in jeans, T-shirts and sneakers and feel at home in most parts of the country, especially during the daytime. Outside the major cities, in some of the popular resorts for example, you may find that Canadians tend to dress a little more formally in the evening.

Toronto, Montréal and Vancouver are important business places, with well-dressed office workers, and you may therefore prefer to dress up a little, especially for shopping trips and when visiting museums. All three cities have world-class restaurants, and while they may not impose a dress code you are unlikely to get the best service or a good table if you are dressed too casually.

Visiting Churches

As everywhere else in the world, you should be appropriately dressed when visiting a church or other place of religious worship. The Basilique Notre-Dame de Montréal will not admit people in very short shorts or in tank tops with "spaghetti" straps, and visitors must wear shoes.

First Nations

It is important to respect the traditional lifestyle of Canada's native peoples. It is an insult, for example, to call the northern peoples Eskimos—a derogatory word meaning "eaters of raw meat." Likewise, the word Indians should be used only in the context of the people of the Indian subcontinent. Canada's native peoples, or First Nations, are generally referred to by their tribal affiliation, such as the Cree of northern Québec, the Ojibwa of northern Ontario, and the Assiniboine of the Prairies.

French Canada

In Québec and parts of New Brunswick be prepared to acknowledge that French is the first and sometimes the only language of the resident population. Learning a few words can only enhance your visit (see page 354). If you do have a problem expressing yourself, a friendly smile and a polite apology for not knowing the language will go a long way to assuring help and good service.

Tipping

For etiquette regarding tipping, see page 345.

Places of Religious Worship

Major hotels in the cities usually have a list of places of worship close to them. If not, the local tourist office can provide a list. There will normally be a Roman Catholic church, an Anglican church (Episcopal), a United church (Methodists and Presbyterians), and sometimes a Baptist church. In addition, all the major cities have synagogues and most have a mosque, and a Buddhist and Hindu temple.

PLANNING

MONEY

CURRENCY

Canada's currency is the Canadian dollar, which consists of 100 cents. Canadian currency has almost the same denominations as US money, with the exception of the $1 and $2 bills, which no longer exist. Single Canadian dollars are in the form of a gold-colored coin bearing an image of a loon (a bird found in Canada) and, as a result, the coin has been nicknamed the "loonie". Two-dollar coins have gold centers and silver rims (and are familiarly called "twonies").

EXCHANGING MONEY

Exchange facilities are found in large hotels, airports and train stations, but rates are often poor and commission fees high. Most banks offer exchange facilities, but may charge a fee. Outside major cities and resort areas, there are few places devoted solely to currency exchange. American dollars are widely accepted in Canada, but be aware of the official exchange rate.

EXCHANGE RATES

The Bank of Canada gives the official exchange rate for foreign currencies in Canada (www.bank--banque-canada.ca/en/exchform.htm). At the time of going to print, the rates were as follows:

$1 Can	$ 0.76 US
$1 Can	$1.10 Australian
$1 Can	£0.46 UK
$1 Can	€0.65

Exchange rates vary over time, so check the current rate before leaving on a trip.

TRAVELER'S CHECKS

The best way to carry money is in the form of traveler's checks (cheques). You can purchase American Express or Visa checks from your own bank before you leave home. Have the traveler's checks made out in Canadian dollars and they can then be used as cash in most stores, restaurants and filling stations

across the country. There is no limit to the amount of Canadian or foreign currency that can be exchanged in or brought into or out of the country.

AUTOMATED BANKING MACHINES

The simplest means of obtaining money is by using your bank card at an automated banking or telling machine (ABM or ATM). In this way, you avoid worrying about currency exchange rates and service charges since your own bank does the exchange. But be aware that there will be a charge. Bank cards are generally connected to either the MasterCard (Cirrus) or Visa (Plus) system. You may have to check a couple of machines before you find one that accepts your card.

CREDIT AND DEBIT CARDS

A credit card is a convenient means to pay for things when visiting Canada. It is also safer than carrying a lot of cash. Most hotels, restaurants and stores

Like all banks, the Royal Bank of Canada has user-friendly ATM's across the country

TIPPING

Just as in the United States, tipping is widespread across Canada and people who work in service industries often rely on tips to make ends meet. Nonetheless, tipping remains an acknowledgment of good service and if the service you have received is not satisfactory, don't leave a tip. Service charges are not automatically added to restaurant checks (bills), except in a few rare cases.

It is customary to tip as follows:

● About 15 percent of the check (bill), before taxes, for waiters and waitresses.
● About 15 percent for taxi drivers and hairdressers.
● At your hotel, you should give the bellman (porter) $1 per bag, the valet $2, and room service staff 10 percent of the check before taxes have been calculated.
● If you take a guided city tour, it is customary to offer the tour guide a small token of your

ABM/ATM TIPS

● To be able to use your bank card at an ABM/ATM in Canada, it must be programmed with a personal identification number, or PIN. Without this you will not be able to access either your bank or credit card account.
● Before leaving home, you should check the restrictions on the amount of money you can withdraw at any one time or on any one day.

appreciation. In general, if you are satisfied with the service, $1 per person is adequate.

TAXES

See page 342.

accept the major cards. However, you will probably need cash in local grocery stores, newsstands and other small establishments.

Before leaving home, you should check with your bank as to whether your debit card will be accepted out of your home country.

10 EVERYDAY ITEMS AND HOW MUCH THEY COST

Takeaway sandwich	$4–5
Bottle of water	$1
Cup of tea or coffee	$1.50
Bottle of beer	$2.50
Glass of wine	$5–6
Daily newspaper	75 cents
Roll of camera film	$5–6
20 cigarettes	$6
An ice cream	$2.50
A liter of fuel (petrol)	79 cents

BANKS

Name	Telephone	Website
Bank of Montréal	416/867-5050	www.bankofmontreal.com
Royal Bank of Canada	800/769-2511	www.royalbank.com
Scotiabank	416/866-6161	www.scotiabank.com/
Toronto Dominion	866/567-8888	www.td.com

HEALTH

BEFORE YOU GO

Vaccinations

No vaccinations are required before entering Canada for visitors from Europe, the US, Australia or New Zealand. You should check current requirements if you are arriving from the Far or Middle East, Africa, or South or Central America, and especially if you are coming from a known infected area. For details contact the Canadian embassy in your country or visit the Canadian government's Citizenship and Immigration website, http://cicnet.ci.gc.ca.

Prescription Drugs

You should carry a full supply of any prescription drug that you have to take. Over-the-counter drugs are readily available in

pharmacies (see below), but no Canadian pharmacy will accept or refill an out-of-province prescription. If you run out of or lose your supply, you will have to visit a Canadian doctor and get a new prescription recognized locally. There will be a cost for this service.

HEALTH HAZARDS

For most visitors there are no significant health hazards involved in a trip to Canada. The few problems that could occur are associated with the outdoors. For example, "beaver fever" comes from a parasite (*Giardi lamblia*) that thrives in small streams or shallow lakes in summer. You are well advised to boil all drinking water when camping. Beaver fever normally lasts only a day or so, but seek medical aid if it persists.

In southern Ontario and Québec poison ivy can be prevalent in woodland. It causes inflammation and rashes, and can be very uncomfortable, but will normally disappear after about 10 days. Rag-weed can cause similar irritations. Creams are available in pharmacies to help alleviate any discomfort.

Less serious but still irritating are the hordes of biting insects that are common in central Canada and the north any time after April, but especially in May and June. Insect repellents work with only limited effectiveness on some people. You should wear long-sleeve, light-toned clothing when outdoors—especially after 5pm on a hot day.

PHARMACIES

There is no shortage of pharmacies (chemists) in

PLANNING

Canadian cities, some staying open 24 hours. Ask at your hotel reception or call the police in an emergency for addresses.

City pharmacies are generally large stores selling a variety of cosmetics and other beauty products in addition to prescription and over-the-counter drugs. The pharmacist is a good source of advice if you are not sure what to buy for a particular condition, such as the effects of poison ivy (see page 345), or if you are suffering from an unknown malady.

In case of emergency, it is wise to make a note of the generic name of any prescription medications that you take before you leave home—they may be sold under a different trade name in Canada. See also the section on prescription drugs (page 345).

DOCTORS AND DENTISTS

If you require medical or dental help in Canada, ask at your hotel reception. Most hotels keep a list of doctors, dentists and medical centers handy, which can save you considerable time. Otherwise, try the local visitor center or the Yellow Pages telephone book; emergency services, such as an ambulance, are usually listed inside the front cover. When you pay for any medical services, keep the receipts and other paperwork for future insurance claims.

HOSPITALS

In an emergency, call 911 (see page 348); an ambulance will take you to the nearest or most suitable local hospital. There will be a charge for the service, so keep your receipts.

HEALTH INSURANCE

See page 341.

Visitors coming to Canada via long-haul flights may be concerned about the effect on their health. The most widely publicized fear is Deep Vein Thrombosis, or DVT. Misleadingly labeled "economy class syndrome", DVT is the clotting of the blood in a vein deep below the skin, particularly in the legs. The clot can move around the bloodstream and may be fatal.

Flying increases the likelihood of DVT because passengers are often seated in a cramped position for long periods of time and may become dehydrated. Those most at risk include the elderly, pregnant women and those using the contraceptive pill, smokers, and the overweight. If you are at increased risk of DVT, see your doctor before departing.

To minimize the risk of DVT:
● Drink water (not alcohol)
● Don't stay immobile for hours at a time—stretch and exercise your legs periodically
● Wear elastic flight socks, which support veins and reduce the chances of a clot forming
● A small dose of aspirin may be recommended; this thins the blood slightly

EXERCISES

1 ANKLE ROTATIONS **2 CALF STRETCHES** **3 KNEE LIFTS**

Lift feet off the floor. Draw a circle with the toes, moving one foot clockwise and the other counterclockwise

Start with heel on the floor and point foot upward as high as you can. Then lift heels high, keeping balls of feet on the floor

Lift leg with knee bent while contracting your thigh muscle. Then straighten leg, pressing foot flat to the floor

Other health hazards are airborne diseases and bugs spread by the plane's air-conditioning system. If you have a serious medical condition, seek advice from a doctor before leaving home.

Shoppers Drug Mart is a nationwide pharmacy chain

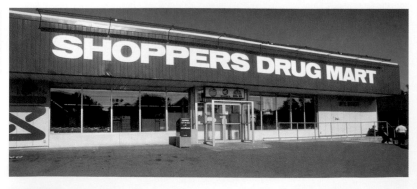

COMMUNICATIONS

TELEPHONES
Public phones are widely available. They accept coins, telephone credit cards and pre-paid phone cards. US telephone credit cards are also readily accepted.

Pre-paid phone cards are sold in most convenience stores, visitor centers and some hotels, and are available in various amounts starting at $10. They are probably the most convenient means to make a long-distance call from a public phone.

MAKING CALLS
To call within Canada, press 1 followed by the provincial or city code (see panel) unless you are making a local call, where, in most places, you just press the telephone number. In the major cities you must use the provincial or city code even for local calls.

It is easy to make calls directly to the US. Again, press 1 followed by the state or city code and telephone number.

To make calls to Europe or elsewhere outside North America, you must know the country code. Most phone books list country codes (see panel), along with instructions for making an overseas call. If you have any problems placing a call or you don't know or cannot find the country code, press 0 and ask for the overseas operator.

To call Canada from overseas, use the country code 1, the same as for the US (see panel).

COUNTRY CODES FROM CANADA

Australia	011 61
Belgium	011 32
France	011 33
Germany	011 49
Greece	011 30
Ireland	011 353
Italy	011 39
Netherlands	011 31
New Zealand	011 64
Spain	011 34
Sweden	011 46
UK	011 44
US	1

CELL PHONES
Check with your server to find out whether your cell phone will work in Canada—some do, some don't and you may need to organize a "roaming agreement" prior to your trip. Making calls this way can be expensive.

POSTAL SERVICES
Canada is not noted for speedy mail delivery. In addition, the cost of postage stamps tends to rise frequently.

There is one mail delivery per day, Monday to Friday. For more information on the mail service, contact Canada Post, www.canadapost.ca.

Alternatively, Priority Post is a fast and somewhat expensive service that promises "next day delivery" within Canada. It is available 24 hours a day, seven days a week.

Stamps
Post offices are generally open Monday to Friday 8.30 to 5.30. Certain small convenience stores are licensed to sell stamps, and postal outlets are often found inside larger stores and train stations—look for the "Canada Post" sign. Such outlets may open on Saturday mornings and keep longer hours on weekdays than regular post offices. Stamps may also be available at hotel reception desks.

EMAIL AND INTERNET ACCESS
Almost every Canadian is online, so emails are an efficient form of communication. Many hotels offer Internet access, though this comes at a price. You are

PROVINCIAL TELEPHONE CODES

Alberta	South	403
	North	780
British Columbia	Vancouver	604
	rest of BC	250
Manitoba		204
New Brunswick		506
Newfoundland and Labrador		709
Northwest Territories		867
Nunavut		867
Nova Scotia		902
Ontario	Toronto	416 and 647
	region	905 and 289
Central and North		705
Southwest		519
Ottawa region		613
Northwest		807
Prince Edward Island		902
Québec	Montréal	514
	region	450
Central and North		819
East		418
Saskatchewan		306
Yukon		867

probably better off seeking out the nearest Internet café. Visitor centers have the addresses of local Internet cafés, or there may be Internet access at the nearest large bookstore or a university campus. Internet cafés are also listed in the Yellow Pages telephone book.

POSTAGE RATES
At the time of going to print, a regular letter cost:

Within Canada	from 48 cents
To the US	from 65 cents
Overseas	from $1.25

PLANNING

FINDING HELP

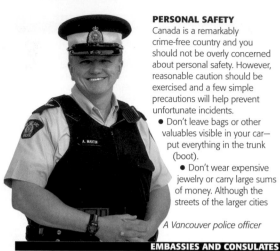

A Vancouver police officer

PERSONAL SAFETY

Canada is a remarkably crime-free country and you should not be overly concerned about personal safety. However, reasonable caution should be exercised and a few simple precautions will help prevent unfortunate incidents.

● Don't leave bags or other valuables visible in your car—put everything in the trunk (boot).

● Don't wear expensive jewelry or carry large sums of money. Although the streets of the larger cities are much safer than those in the US, there is always a danger of pickpockets.

● Consider carrying your passport and credit cards in a pouch or belt, and walk along only well-lit streets at night. If you do have anything stolen, report it immediately to the police and/or your hotel.

EMERGENCIES

To contact the police, the fire department, or ambulance service in most parts of Canada, dial **911**. Where the 911 service is not in effect (Vancouver Island, Prince Edward Island, Nova Scotia, Yukon, Northwest

EMBASSIES AND CONSULATES

Australian High Commission
7th Floor, Suite 710, 50 O'Connor Street, Ottawa, Ontario, K1P 6L2
Tel 613/236-0841
www.ahc-ottawa.org

In addition to its embassy, Australia maintains consulates in the following cities:

Australian Consulate General Toronto
Suite 314, 175 Bloor Street East, Toronto, Ontario, M4W 3R8
Tel 416/323-1155, 416/323-3910

Australian Consulate Vancouver
Suite 1225, 888 Dunsmuir Street, Vancouver, British Columbia, V6C 3K4
Tel 604/684-1177

French Embassy Canada
42 Sussex Drive, Ottawa, Ontario, K1M 2C9
Tel 613/789-1795
www.ambafrance-ca.org/english

There are French consulates in Moncton, Halifax, Québec, Montréal, Toronto and Vancouver.

Embassy of the Federal Republic of Germany, Canada
1 Waverley Street, Ottawa, Ontario, K2P 0T8
Tel 613/232-1101
www.germanembassyottawa.org

There are German consulates in Montréal, Toronto and Vancouver.

Italian Embassy Canada
275 Slater Street, 21st Floor, Ottawa, Ontario, K1P 5H9

Tel 613/232-2401
www.italyincanada.com

There are Italian consulates in Montréal, Toronto, Edmonton and Vancouver.

Spanish Embassy Canada
74 Stanley Avenue, Ottawa, Ontario, K1M 1P4
Tel 613/747-2252, 613/747-7293
www.DocuWeb.ca/EmbassiesOttawa/Spain

There are Spanish consulates in Toronto and Montréal.

US Embassy Ottawa
490 Sussex Drive, Ottawa, Ontario, K1N 1G8
Tel 613/238-5335
www.usembassycanada.gov

In addition to its embassy, the US maintains consulates in the following cities:

US Consulate Halifax
Suite 904, Purdy's Wharf Tower II, 1969 Upper Water Street, Halifax, Nova Scotia, B3J 3R7
Tel 902/429-2485

US Consulate Montréal
1155 rue St-Alexandre, Montréal, Québec, H2Z 1Z2
P.O. Box 65, Postal Station Desjardins, Montréal, Québec, H5B 1G1
Tel 514/398-9695

US Consulate Québec City
2 place Terrasse-Dufferin, C.P. 939, Québec City, Québec, G1R 4T9
Tel 418/692-2095

US Consulate Toronto
360 University Avenue, Toronto, Ontario, M5G 1S4
Tel 416/595-1700

US Consulate Winnipeg
860-201 Portage Avenue, Winnipeg, Manitoba, R3B 3K6
Tel 204/940-1800

US Consulate Calgary
615 Macleod Trail S.E., Room 1000, Calgary, Alberta, T2G 4T8
Tel 403/266-8962

US Consulate Vancouver
1095 West Pender Street, Vancouver, British Columbia, V6E 2M6
Tel 604/685-4311

UK/British High Commission
80 Elgin Street, Ottawa, Ontario, K1P 5K7
Tel 613/237-1303
www.britainincanada.org

In addition to its embassy, the United Kingdom maintains consulates in the following cities:

British Consulate General Montréal
Suite 4200, 1000 rue de la Gauchetière Ouest, Montréal, Québec, H3B 4W5
Tel 514/866-5863

British Consulate General Toronto
777 Bay Street, Suite 280, College Park, Toronto, Ontario, M5G 2G2
Tel 416/593-1290

British Consulate General Vancouver
1111 Melville Street, Suite 800, Vancouver, British Columbia, V6E 3V6
Tel 604/683-4421

PLANNING

Territories and Nunavut), press **0** for the operator instead and say that it is an emergency. This is much the best way to report a crime or other emergency situation and saves you searching for a police station or hospital.

POLICE
The Royal Canadian Mounted Police is Canada's federal police force. The "Mounties" also act as the regular police in all provinces except Ontario and Québec, which have their own provincial forces. On duty, RCMP officers look just like those of any other police force and drive cars. (Horses are no longer used, and the red jackets, stetson hats and boots with spurs are worn only on ceremonial occasions). All major cities have their own police forces in addition to the RCMP and/or provincial force.

LOST PROPERTY
The police are the best people to contact if you mislay something valuable. Don't use the emergency 911 number in such cases, but instead check the phone book or ask your hotel reception for the local number. If you make an insurance claim for any losses, you must obtain a police report (see Insurance, page 341).

Lost Passports
In the case of a lost or stolen passport, you will have to contact your local embassy or consulate. Generally, these are in Ottawa, Montréal, Toronto and Vancouver, and occasionally elsewhere (see panel, page 348).

MEDIA

NEWSPAPERS AND MAGAZINES

Nationals
There are two so-called "national" newspapers in Canada, *The Globe and Mail* and *The National Post*. Both are sold at newsstands and convenience stores across the country, though because they are published in Toronto some Canadians do not consider them truly "national."

Macleans Magazine is a monthly news magazine published in Toronto, and contains good listings of what is happening throughout Canada; you can usually find it at newsstands across the country.

For lifestyle issues in the major cities, try either *Toronto Life* magazine, famous for its restaurant listings, or *Vancouver* magazine, which is a similar publication. Montréal does not have a comparable magazine.

Local Newspapers
The major Canadian cities have their own newspapers, with circulations that can be greater than that of the nationals. Toronto newspapers include the *Toronto Star* and the *Toronto Sun*.

In Montréal the major daily in English is the *Montréal Gazette*. There are several newspapers in French, the most popular being *La Presse* and the tabloid *Le Journal de Montréal*.

The two major newspapers in Vancouver are the *Vancouver Province* and the *Vancouver*

Halifax coin-op newsstand

Sun. Ottawa has two major dailies, the *Ottawa Citizen* and the *Ottawa Sun*. In Québec City, the major newspaper is *Le Soleil*. All the above have Internet versions.

Other important publications include the *Calgary Herald*, the *Edmonton Journal* and the *Winnipeg Free Press*. There is also a variety of ethnic publications in the major cities.

The following website provides access to a wide range of Canadian newspapers as soon as they are published. www.broadcast-live.com/newspapers/canadian.html

Foreign Press
American newspapers are sold at newsstands in the major cities, notably the *New York Times*, the *Financial Post*, the *Wall Street Journal* and *USA Today*. They are less common elsewhere.

Certain other foreign newspapers are avaiable in specialized stores in the major cities (tourist offices can supply the names of these outlets), including *The Times* of the UK, the French paper, *Le Monde*, and *Der Spiegel* from Germany.

TELEVISION AND RADIO
Television goes into every home across Canada, even in the extreme north, which benefits from satellite service. The major broadcaster of English and French television and radio across Canada is the publicly funded Canadian Broadcasting Corporation, or CBC (www.cbc.ca). CBC television has commercials, though there are no advertisements on the radio stations.

On the cable network, the CBC has a 24-hour news channel, "CBC Newsworld," which boadcasts in both official languages. Other national broadcasters include CTV and Global.

CABLE CHANNELS
Where cable service is available, there is a wide choice of channels. Popular Canadian cable channels include the Weather Network; Bravo!, an arts channel; TSN, the Sports Network; MuchMusic, Canada's rock music channel; the Discovery Channel (Canadian science); the Canadian History Channel; and the Life Network, a Canadian lifestyles channel.

Many American cable networks are also accessible, including the major television networks CBS, ABC, NBC, and PBS.

OPENING TIMES AND PUBLIC HOLIDAYS

BANKS

Banking hours are usually Monday through Friday 10 to 4, though this can vary with the branch (some open at 9am, others close at 3pm). In addition, some branches have extended hours (until 5pm or 6pm) on certain days, usually Thursday or Friday. All banks are closed on public holidays. As far as changing money is concerned, currency exchange offices have longer operating hours than banks and often lower service charges. Hours tend to be Monday to Friday 9am to 5pm, and Saturday 9am to 12 noon.

DOCTORS AND PHARMACIES

Every Canadian town or city has a pharmacy that is open 24 hours, and in major urban areas pharmacies are often open until 11pm. Tourist offices or police stations can supply their addresses and also the locations of medical clinics and their hours. Major urban areas have clinics operating seven days a week, but not necessarily all night.

MUSEUMS AND GALLERIES

Opening hours of museums and the principal art galleries can vary widely. Museums usually open Tuesday to Sunday 10am to 5pm; art galleries often open at 11am. Many museums are closed on Mondays, especially off-season. Most major museums have one evening a week when they are open late (until about 9pm) and they are usually free after 5.30pm on that evening. Small museums in out-of-the-way places may close for lunch.

OFFICES

Canadian offices have increasingly gone over to flexible working hours, with employees arriving and leaving over a staggered period. In general, though, someone should always be available Monday to Friday between 9am and 5pm (or 4pm in government offices).

STORES

In general, stores open Monday to Friday 9am to 6pm, with later hours (usually 9pm) on Thursday and Friday evenings. In some cities, the downtown stores open Monday to Friday at 10am. Normal Saturday hours are 9am to 5pm, and, where open, Sunday hours are usually 12 noon to 5pm.

Shopping malls tend to have longer hours than the downtown stores; they often close between 7.30pm and 9pm. In certain tourist areas (for example Old Montréal and Québec), stores selling souvenirs and other tourist-related items will remain open late into the night if there's any chance of customers dropping by.

SUPERMARKETS

Supermarkets in the suburban areas of the large towns and cities often have longer hours than regular stores, though they can suffer from a shortage of check-out personnel at certain times of the day. These supermarkets tend to stay open until 10pm or 11pm every night.

RESTAURANTS

Restaurants that offer breakfast will naturally be open early—6am or even before that. Otherwise they generally open for lunch from around 12noon to 3pm, close for the afternoon, and then open again at around 6pm or 7pm for the evening. All of the big cities will have numerous late-night establishments, catering to the after-theater and nightclub crowd.

Fast food restaurants and coffee shops stay open all day, as do restaurants in shopping malls and the downtown areas of some towns and cities.

Outside the major urban areas, restaurants are unlikely to be open after about 9pm.

PUBLIC HOLIDAYS	
Seven national holidays are celebrated across the country:	
(Government offices and banks are closed, some stores are open)	
New Year's Day	January 1
Good Friday	Easter
Victoria Day	3rd Monday of May
Canada Day	July 1
Labour Day	1st Monday of September
Thanksgiving	2nd Monday of October
Christmas Day	December 25

Other holidays celebrated in different parts of the country:	
(Government offices and banks are closed, some stores are open)	
Easter Monday	After Good Friday
Remembrance Day	November 11 (not celebrated in Québec)
Boxing Day	December 26

Holidays in particular provinces or regions:		
Family Day	3rd Monday of February	Alberta
St. Patrick's Day	March 17	Newfoundland and Labrador
Nunavut Day	April 1	Nunavut
St. George's Day	April 23	Newfoundland and Labrador
St-Jean-Baptiste Day	June 24	Québec
Discovery Day	June 24	Newfoundland and Labrador
Orangeman's Day	July 12	Newfoundland and Labrador
Heritage Day	1st Monday of August	Alberta
British Columbia Day	1st Monday of August	British Columbia
New Brunswick Day	1st Monday of August	New Brunswick
Civic holiday	1st Monday of August	Ontario, Manitoba, Saskatchewan, Northwest Territories, Nunavut
Natal Day	1st Monday of August (varies in Halifax— usually July or August)	Nova Scotia
Natal Day	Usually 1st Monday of August (by proclamation)	Prince Edward Island
Regatta Day/ civic holiday	August (fixed by council orders)	Newfoundland and Labrador
Discovery Day	3rd Monday of August	Yukon

PLANNING

TOURIST OFFICES

PROVINCIAL TOURIST OFFICES

The best place to start collecting information on Canada or on a particular region is at the provincial tourist departments. Each Canadian province or territory operates a tourist office, which you can contact for free information (see panel below). They will send you a map of the province or territory, a list of accommodations, a list of things to do, and a host of other information. Contact them by mail, phone or email. Normally you cannot visit in person but they all operate websites. Some are really helpful and user-friendly, but others are more commercial and have less to interest visitors.

LOCAL AND CITY TOURIST OFFICES

It's worthwhile stopping at the local tourist office in the towns and cities you visit. They can help you find accommodations, supply you with free maps, and direct you to sights, tourist attractions and restaurants.

Gas stations sell useful maps. However, they will not be as good as the maps that you can get free at the tourist office.

Montréal

Montréal's tourist office, Centre Infotouriste, is at 1001 Dorchester Square in the heart of downtown. It's open daily 9 to 6, with extended hours in the summer months. Maps, a visitor guide and a variety of free information are available for the whole of Québec, as well as the city. Bus tours start from here.
Tel 514/873-2015
www.tourism-montreal.org

Vancouver

Vancouver's TouristInfo Centre is at 200 Burrard Street in the Waterfront Centre. Free maps, a visitor guide and information on local attractions are available, and city bus tours start here. Open daily with extended hours in the summer months.
Tel 604/683-2000
www.tourism-vancouver.org

Toronto

Toronto does not have a good central tourist office, but you can visit Tourism Toronto at 207 Queens Quay West on the waterfront. This is not a proper tourist office, though the staff will give you a free visitor guide and map if you ask, and there are a few brochures you can pick up

Halifax tourist information flag

here. The office is open only business hours.
Tel 416/203-2500
www.torontotourism.com

Ottawa

The National Capital Commission runs an information center opposite the Parliament Buildings at 90 Wellington Street. Free maps, a visitor guide and other information are available. The center is open daily and there is a selection of videos.

PROVINCIAL TOURIST OFFICES

Alberta
Travel Alberta
P.O. Box 2500, Edmonton, Alberta, T5J 4L6
Tel 800/661-8888
www.travelalberta.com

British Columbia
Tourism British Columbia
Parliament Buildings, Victoria, British Columbia, V8V 1XA
Tel 800/663-6000
www.hellobc.com

Manitoba
Travel Manitoba
7th Floor, 155 Carlton Street, Winnipeg, Manitoba, R3C 3H8
Tel 800/665-0040
www.travelmanitoba.com

New Brunswick
Tourism New Brunswick
P.O. Box 12345, Campbellton

New Brunswick, E3N 3T6
Tel 800/561-0123
www.tourismnbcanada.com

Newfoundland and Labrador
Newfoundland and Labrador Department of Tourism, Recreation and Culture
P.O. Box 8700, St. John's, Newfoundland, A1B 4J6
Tel 800/563-6353
www.gov.nf.ca/tourism

Northwest Territories
Northwest Territories Tourism
P.O. Box 610, Yellowknife, Northwest Territories, X1A 2N5
Tel 800/661-0788
www.explorenwt.com

Nova Scotia
Nova Scotia Tourism
P.O. Box 456, 1800 Argyle Street, Halifax, Nova Scotia,

B3J 2R5
Tel 800/565-0000;
www.novascotia.com

Nunavut
Nunavut Tourism
P.O. Box 1450, Iqaluit, Nunavut, X0A 0H0
Tel 867/979-6551,
866/686-2888
www.nunavuttourism.com

Ontario
Ontario Tourism
10th Floor, Hearst Block, 900 Bay Street, Toronto, Ontario, M7A 2E1
Tel 800/668-2746
www.ontariotravel.net

Prince Edward Island
Prince Edward Island Department of Tourism, Parks and Recreation
P.O. Box 940, Charlottetown, Prince Edward Island,

C1A 7M5
Tel 800/463-4734
www.peiplay.com

Québec
Tourisme Québec
P.O. Box 979, Montréal, Québec, H3C 2W3
Tel 800/363-7777
www.bonjourquebec.com

Saskatchewan
Tourism Saskatchewan
1922 Park Street, Regina, Saskatchewan, S4P 3V7
Tel 800/667-7191
www.sasktourism.com

Yukon
Tourism Yukon
P.O. Box 2703, Whitehorse, Yukon, Y1A 2C6
Tel 867/667-5340
www.touryukon.com

PLANNING

Tel 800/465-1867 or 613/239-5000
www.capcan.ca

Québec City
Québec's tourist office, Centre Infotouriste, is at 12 rue Ste.-Anne, across place d'Armes from the Chateau Frontenac Hotel. Free maps, a visitor guide and information on all attractions in the province are available. The office is open daily 9 to 5 with extended hours in the summer.
Tel 418/649-2608
www.quebecregion.com

Halifax
The International Visitor Centre in Halifax is at 1595 Barrington Street. Here you can pick up a free map of the city and the province, a visitor guide to the city and to each region of Nova Scotia, and a whole range of other tourist information. The center is open daily.
Tel 902/490-5946
www.halifaxinfo.com

Information on other Canadian cities is available from the relevant provincial tourist office (see page 351).

Tourism staff can help you choose places to stay and visit

BOOKS AND MOVIES

BOOKS

Canada has a number of writers of international acclaim. In recent years three have won the Booker prize—Yan Martel (*The Life of Pi*; 2002), Margaret Atwood (*The Blind Assassin*; 2000) and Michael Ondaatje (*The English Patient*; 1992), though none of these books is set in Canada.

Considered the grand old man of Canadian literature, Robertson Davies set many of his books in his native Ontario. The Deptford Trilogy is among his best-known works: *Fifth Business* (1970), *The Manticore* (1972) and *World of Wonders* (1975). Among others, he also wrote the Cornish Trilogy: *The Rebel Angels* (1981), *What's Bred in the Bone* (1985) and *The Lyre of Orpheus* (1988).

Two other Ontario classics are Stephen Leacock's *Sunshine Sketches of a Little Town* (1912) and Ralph Connor's *The Man from Glengarry* (1901).

Farley Mowat's eloquent adventure stories are mainly set in northern Canada: *People of the Deer* (1952), *Lost in the Barrens* (1956), *Never Cry Wolf* (1963) and *The Snow Walker* (1975). He wrote a fascinating but somewhat controversial book on Newfoundland, *A Whale for the Killing* (1972).

Two splendid historical novels are set in Québec City during the French Regime: William Kirby's *The Golden Dog* (1877), and Willa Cathar's *Shadows on the Rock* (1931).

Distinctive bookstore and IMAX theater complex in Toronto

To understand linguistic tensions, read Hugh Maclennan's *Two Solitudes* (1945), or Gabrielle Roy's *The Tin Flute*—a translation of *Bonheur d'Occasion* (1945).

Two very different views of Montréal life include the works of playwright Michel Tremblay, *Albertine in Five Times* (1986) and *Les Belles Soeurs* (1992); and Mordecai Richler's stories of Jewish Montréal, *St. Urbain's Horseman* (1984).

A Prairie classic is W. O. Mitchell's *Who has Seen the Wind* (1947), while a unique take on the First Peoples of British Columbia is artist Emily Carr's *Klee Wyck* (1941).

The nature books of Archie Belaney (a.k.a. Grey Owl) include *Pilgrims of the Wild* (1934), *The Adventures of Sajo and her Beaver People* (1935) and *Tales of an Empty Cabin* (1936). His life was made into a movie—see opposite.

Pierre Berton has written many popular, readable history books. His volumes on the construction of the Canadian Pacific Railway, *The National Dream* (1970) and *The Last Spike* (1971), are required reading before taking the train across Canada. He also wrote two books on the War of 1812: *The Invasion of Canada* (1980) and *Flames across the Border* (1982).

Before visiting Prince Edward Island, read Lucy Maud Montgomery's wonderful *Anne of Green Gables* (1908). Of the several film versions, the best was a series produced by the CBC in the 1980s.

The books of Thomas Raddall bring Nova Scotia to life, notably *The Governor's Lady* (1960). American writer E. Annie Proulx's *The Shipping News* (1993) won a Pulitzer prize; this tale of outpost life in Newfoundland was made into a movie starring Kevin Spacey (2001).

PLANNING

MOVIES

***I Confess* (Alfred Hitchcock, 1953)**
Montgomery Clift plays a priest framed for murder in Québec.

***Kamouraska* (Claude Jutra, 1973)**
French writer Anne Hébert set this classic love story in the village of Kamouraska in the Lower St. Lawrence.

***The Apprenticeship of Duddy Kravitz* (Ted Kotcheff, 1974)**
Mordecai Richler's best-selling novel, set in Montréal, features a young schemer (played by Richard Dreyfuss) growing up in a poor Jewish neighborhood.

***Maria Chapdelaine* (Gilles Carle, 1985)**
Louis Hémon's haunting story of a young girl and the three men who loved her stars Carole Laure.

***Jesus of Montréal* (Denys Arcand, 1989)**
Lothaire Bluteau stars in this dramatic story set in Montréal.

***Black Robe* (Bruce Beresford, 1991)**
Beresford's splendid historical movie traces the life of a young Jesuit priest in the 17th century in the area that is now Ontario. It stars Lothaire Bluteau.

***Grey Owl* (Richard Attenborough, 1999)**
This dramatic movie relates the life of Englishman, Archie Belaney, who took an Amerindian name, Grey Owl, and ethnic identity. Pierce Brosnan portrays the alter ego.

USEFUL WEBSITES

GENERAL INFORMATION ABOUT CANADA
http://canada.gc.ca
http://canadainternational.gc.ca
These government of Canada websites provide information and services about culture, immigration, tourism and more.
www.travelcanada.ca
This is the dedicated travel website of the Canadian Tourism Commission.
www.canadianculture.com
A useful one-stop national lifestyle guide.

Customs
www.ccra-adrc.gc.ca
Find out what you can and cannot import or take out of Canada. Or contact:
Revenue Canada
Customs and Excise, Ottawa, Ontario, K1A 0L5

Culture and History
www.pch.gc.ca (Canadian Heritage)
http://culturecanada.gc.ca
Canadian government websites for visitors seeking Canadian culture and heritage.
www.histori.ca
The bilingual educational website of the magazine *Historica* promotes the teaching of Canadian history and heritage.

Currency
www.bank-banque-canada.ca/en/exchform.htm
To see how many Canadian dollars you can buy, check the Bank of Canada's website.

Festivals
www.festivalseeker.com
A one-stop website for details on the multitude of festivals and other events that are held across Canada, especially during the summer months.

Food and Wine
www.agr.gc.ca/food/profiles/wine
The Agriculture Canada website has much useful information.

Parks Canada
www.parkscanada.gc.ca
There are more than 40 national parks in Canada and numerous national historic sites. For further information, contact:
Parks Canada
25 Eddy Street, Gatineau, Québec, K1A 0M5
Tel 888/773-8888

Post
www.canadapost.ca
Information on postage rates within Canada, or else ask at a local post office.

Rail
www.viarail.ca
For details on passenger train travel. Or contact:
VIA Rail (see pages 50–52)
Tel 888/VIA-RAIL

Sport
www.pch.gc.ca/progs/sc
Information on Canadian sports at the government's Sport Canada website.

Visas
http://cicnet.ci.gc.ca
The Canadian Government Citizenship and Immigration Service website gives details of

Log in at an internet café

the requirements for entry into Canada.

Visitors with Disabilities
www.ccdonline.ca
Council of Canadians with Disabilities
926–294 Portage Avenue, Winnipeg, Manitoba
Tel 204/947-0303
www.canparaplegic.org
Canadian Paraplegic Association
Tel 888/654-5444
Both of the above organizations offer advice to mobility-challenged visitors.

Weather
http://weatheroffice.ec.gc.ca
Environment Canada's website is a good stop for planning for the weather.

PLANNING

LANGUAGES OF CANADA

Canada has two official languages—English and French. The reasons for this are historical. French settlement in the St. Lawrence Valley started in the early 17th century. No English-speaking settlers arrived until after the British conquest of 1760. At the time of Canadian Confederation in 1867, the English- and French-speaking populations were more or less equal in size. Today, less than a quarter of Canadians speak French as their mother tongue (6.7 million out of 31 million).

The country has large communities of peoples of other nationalities and languages, but none has official recognition.

FRENCH-SPEAKING COMMUNITIES

French Canadians are in every province, but their greatest concentration is in the province of Québec, where they comprise more than 85 percent of the population. These are the people known as the Québécois.

French-speaking people form more than a third of the population of New Brunswick, and are also prominent in Nova Scotia and Prince Edward Island—these are the Acadiens. Ontario has a sizable French-speaking population in Toronto and in the eastern part of the province, who are known as Franco-Ontariens.

Manitoba's distinct French-speaking community is in St.-Boniface and are known as Franco-Manitobins. There are also small French-speaking communities in Saskatchewan, Alberta and British Columbia.

THE FRENCH LANGUAGE

If you speak the French of France, you will find the language Québec has a strong and highly recognizable accent—as close to the language of the mother country as the Texas accent is to the English of the UK.

The French spoken by the Acadiens is different again. For instance, *oui* sounds like "why," and *non* is pronounced "nah." If you have a good ear, you can detect the difference and a somewhat softer accent. It resembles the French of old France more than the dynamic language of French Montréal.

Differences of vocabulary that can cause unfortunate misunderstandings include words used for meals. In Québec, you eat *déjeuner* first thing in the morning, *dîner* at lunchtime, and *souper* in the evening. In France, breakfast is *petit-déjeuner,* the lunchtime meal is *déjeuner*, and *dîner* is the evening meal. You need to know the origin of your French-speaking hosts if you are invited for *dîner* or you may arrive for the wrong meal.

OTHER LANGUAGES

The official Canadian census of 2001 recorded a population of just over 31 million, of whom more than 17.4 million spoke English as their mother tongue and 6.7 million spoke French. The third-largest language group was Chinese, with over 850,000 people, followed by Italian and German, with just under half a million each.

Polish, Spanish, Portuguese, Punjabi, and Arabic were the mother tongue of about 200,000 people each. Dutch, Filipino, Greek and Vietnamese are each spoken by about 100,000 individuals. Of First Nations languages, Cree has the most speakers, with 73,000. Inuktitut (Eskimo) is spoken by about 29,000 people.

USEFUL FRENCH WORDS AND PHRASES	
French	**English**
bonjour / bonsoir / bon nuit	good day / good evening / good night
au revoir	goodbye
oui / non	yes / no
merci / bienvenue	thank you / you're welcome
s'il vous plaît	please
Comment ça va?	How are you?
Très bien, merci	Very well, thank you
Ça va?	How's it going? (more colloquial)
douanes / frontière	customs / international border
autoroute / chemins / rue	highway / road / street
arrêt	stop (road sign)
aéroport	airport
métro / autobus / taxi	subway / bus / taxi
gare / train / billets	station / train / tickets
entrée / sortie	entrance / exit
droit / gauche	right / left
tout droit	straight ahead
nord / sud / est / ouest	north / south / east / west
matin / après-midi	morning / afternoon
soir / nuit	evening / night
Où est le restaurant / hôtel?	Where's the restaurant / hotel?
le menu / table d'hôte	the menu / table d'hote (fixed-price meal)
L'addition / la facture, s'il vous plaît	The check (bill), please
Combien?	How much?
déjeuner / dîner / souper / le thé	breakfast / lunch / dinner / tea
banque / toilettes	bank / washrooms / toilets
cinéma / théâtre / concert	cinema / theater / concert
librarie / bibliothèque	bookstore / library
cathédrale / église	cathedral / church
musée / galerie d'art	museum / art gallery
centre d'achat / boutique de souvenirs	shopping mall / souvenir store
édifice / place	building / city square
hôtel de ville / palais de justice	city hall / courthouse
fontaine / chute(s)	fountain / waterfall
rivière / fleuve	river / major river
ruisseau / lac	stream / lake
montagne / colline / vallée / falaise	mountain / hill / valley / cliff
baie / champ / île	bay / field / island
ville / cité / village	town / city / village
maison / pont / jardin	house / bridge / garden
salle / porte / fenêtre	room / door / window
moulin / belvédère	mill / viewpoint

PLANNING

Maps

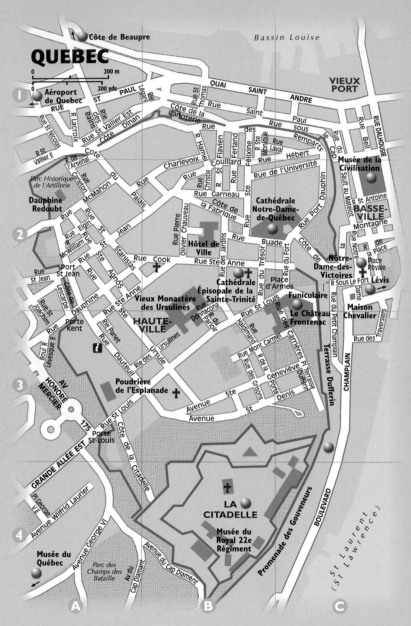

QUEBEC

0 — 200 m
0 — 200 yds

Côte de Beaupre

Aéroport de Quebec

Bassin Louise

VIEUX PORT

QUAI SAINT ANDRE

Musée de la Civilisation

BASSE-VILLE

Parc Historique de l'Artillerie

Dauphine Redoubt

Cathédrale Notre-Dame-de-Québec

Nôtre-Dame-des-Victoires

Lévis

Hôtel de Ville

Maison Chevalier

Cathédrale Épisopale de la Sainte-Trinité

Funiculaire

Vieux Monastère des Ursulines

Le Château Frontenac

HAUTE-VILLE

Poudrière de l'Esplanade

Porte Kent

Terrasse Dufferin

Porte St-Louis

LA CITADELLE

Musée du Royal 22e Régiment

Musée du Québec

Parc des Champs des Bataille

Promenade des Gouverneurs

BOULEVARD

(St Laurent / St Lawrence)

OTTAWA

MONTREAL

Biodôme de Montréal,
Parc Olympique,
Jardin Botanique
de Montréal

Le Parc du
Mont Royal

Musée d'Art
Contemporain,
Place des Arts

Musée McCord
d'Histoire Canadienne

Musée des
Beaux Arts
de Montréal

Les Aisles de la
Monde (Centre Eaton)

Cathédrale Épiscopale
de Christ-Church

Cathédrale
Marie-Reine-
du Monde

GARE CENTRAL

1000 de la
Gauchetière

Place
due
Canada

Carré
Dorchester

Place
Ville-Marie

Square-
Victoria

Place-
des-Arts

McGill

Phillips
Sq

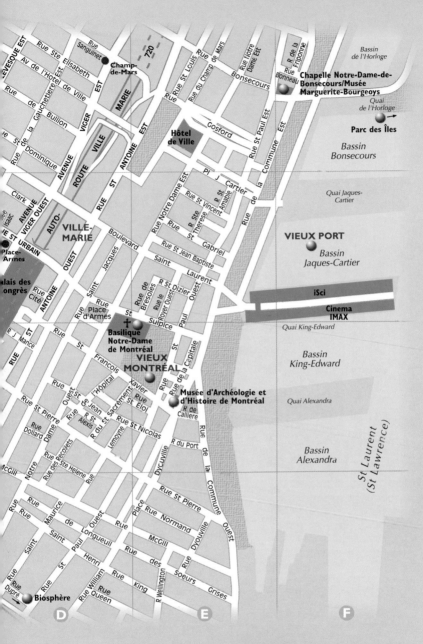

Street	Grid	Street	Grid	Street	Grid	Street	Grid
Marais, Rue du	C1	Pl Mount Royal	E3	Ste Elisabeth, Rue	D1	St Paul Ouest, Rue	D4
Marché, Pl du	C1	President Kennedy,		St Edward, Rue	B2	St Pierre, Rue	D3
Mayor, Rue	B2	Avenue du	A2	St Éloi, Rue	D3	St Sulpice, Rue	D2
McGill College, Avenue	A3	Queen, Rue	D4	Ste Helene, Rue	D3	St Urbain, Rue	B1
McGill, Rue	C3	Recollets, Rue des	D4	Ste Therese, Rue	E2	St Vincent, Rue	E2
Metcalfe, Rue	A4	René Lévesque Quest,		St Francois Xavier, Rue	D3	Sanguinet, Rue	D1
Montigny Ouest, Rue de	B1	Boulevard	B4	St Gabriel, Rue	E2	Sherbrooke Ouest, Rue	A2
Normand, Rue	E4	Royer Ouest, Rue le	E2	Saint Henri, Rue	D4	Soeurs Grises, Rue des	E4
Notre Dame Est, Rue	E2	Sacrément, Rue de	D3	Saint Jacques, Rue	D2	Stanley, Rue	A4
Notre Dame Ouest, Rue	D4	St Alexandre, Rue	C3	St Jean Baptiste, Rue	E2	Union, Avenue	A2
Ontario Ouest, Rue	B1	St Alexis, Rue	D3	St Jean, Rue	D3	Université, Rue	B3
Palace, Rle	A3	St Amable, Rue	E2	Saint Laurent, Boulevard	B1	Victoria, Rue	A3
Parc, Avenue du	A1	St Antoine Est, Rue	D2	St Louis, Rue	E1	Viger Ouest, Avenue	C3
Peel, Rue	A4	St Antoine Ouest, Rue	D3	Saint Maurice, Rue	D4	Ville-Marie, Place	B3
Philips Square	B3	St Dizier, Rue	E2	St Nicolas, Rue	D3	Wellington, Rue	E4
Phillips, Place	B3	St Dominique, Rue	D1	St Paul Est, Rue	E1	William, Rue	D4

TORONTO

Barton
Avenue — Casa Loma
Black Creek Pioneer Village,
McMichael Canadian Collection
Scollard — Street
BAY

400 m
400 yds

Prince — Arthur — Avenue
St.
George
YORKVILLE
Yorkville
Cumberland
AVENUE ROAD
Bellair St.
BAY ST

Lennox — Street
Howland — Ave
BP
Nichol Ln
Devonshire
BLOOR — STREET — WEST
Royal Ontario Museum
Gardiner Museum of Ceramic Art
Sultan St
Charles Street West
Saint Mary

Herrick St
BATHURST — STREET
Sussex Ave
SPADINA
Glen Morris St
George St
Huron St
Museum
Queen's Park
Saint Joseph
Elmsley Pl
Irwin Ave
Phipr St

HARBORD — STREET
Lippincott
Croft
Borden
Brunswick
Major
Robert
Mews
Classic Ave
HOSKIN — AVE
Tower Rd
Hart House Cir
Queen's Park
QUEENS PARK CRES E
Saint
Wellesley Street W

Markham St
Ulster St
Bancroft Ave
University of Toronto
Galbraith Rd
Kings Rd
College Rd
Taddle Creek
QUEENS PARK CRES W
Parliament Buildings
Grosvenor
Surrey Pl
Breada
BAY STREET

Willcocks Street
Russell St
Queens Park
COLLEGE — STREET
COLLEGE
Elizabeth
Laplante Ave
STR

College
Palmerston Blvd
Oxford
Bellevue
Augusta — Street
Glasgow St
Cecil
Huron
Ross St
Henry
Street
Orde St
McCaul
Murray St
Gerrard Street
Walton
Barnaby Pl

Nassau — Street
Leonard Ave
CHINATOWN
Baldwin — Street
Elm
Edward

Palmerston
DUNDAS ST W
Kensington Market
Wales Ave
Kensington Ave
Darcy — Street
St Patrick
UNIVERSITY — AVENUE
Centre Ave
Chestnut St
BAY STREET
Ea
Ce

Robinson St
Ways Ln
Denison Avenue
Augusta Avenue
DUNDAS — STREET
Willison Sq
SPADINA AVE
Larch
Grange Ave
Art Gallery of Ontario
The Grange
Grange Park
Grange Rd
Saint Patrick Street
Simcoe Street
Armoury
Toronto City Hall
Albe
Nathan Phillips Square

Alexandra Park
Carr
Riverson Ave
Cameron St
Vanauley Street
Sullivan
Phoebe
Soho
Stephanie
John
Osgoode

Wolseley Street
Ace Ln
QUEEN — STREET — WEST
Bulwer St
Duncan
Sheppard St
York St
Tempe

RICHMOND — STREET
Camden St
Peter
Nelson — St
St Andrew

Tecumseth
Portugal Sq
BATHURST — STREET
Brant
Portland
Maud
ADELAIDE — STREET — WEST
Charlotte St
Oxley St
Pearl — Street

KING — STREET — WEST
Morrison St
Brant Pl
Clarence Sq
Mercer St
John
Millstone Lane

Niagara — Street
Stewart St
Draper St
Wellington — Street — West
Windsor
Simcoe
Hockey of Fa

Piper Street

FRONT — STREET — WEST
Station St
York
Union
UNION STATION

Fort York 2
Housey Street
Blue Jays
SkyDome
CN Tower
Bremner
Rees St
Lower Simcoe
Blvd
GARDINER EXPRESS

Ontario Place
GARDINER EXPRESSWAY
Spadina Ave
Lower
Robertson
Queens Quay West

LAKESHORE BLVD W
Queens Quay West
Nautical Centre
York Quay Centre
Power Plant
Queens Quay Terminal

Stadium Road
HARBOURFRONT
Harbourfront Centre
Toronto — Harbou

A — B — C

1 · 2 · 3 · 4 · 5

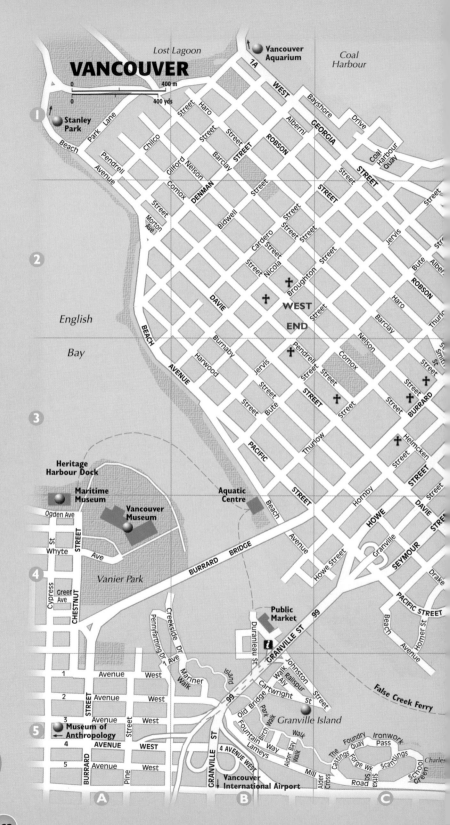

VANCOUVER

Lost Lagoon

Coal Harbour

Vancouver Aquarium

Stanley Park

0   400 m
0   400 yds

English

Bay

Park Lane

Beach

Pendrell

Avenue

Chilco

Haro

Street

Street

Barclay

Clifford Nelson

Comox

Morton Ave

Bidwell

DENMAN

Street

Cardero Street

Street

Nicola

WEST

1A

ROBSON

STREET

Alberni

GEORGIA

Bayshore

Drive

Coal Harbour Quay

STREET

Street

Street

Jervis

Street

Broughton

Street

Haro

Bute Alber

Barclay

Jervis Nelson

Nelson

Thurlow

ROBSON

WEST

END

Smith St

DAVIE

AVENUE

BEACH

Burnaby

Harwood

Street

Jervis

Street

Bute

Pendrell Street

Comox

Street

STREET

Street

Street

Street

BURRARD

Street

PACIFIC

Thurlow

Street

Helmcken

STREET

Street

Street

Heritage Harbour Dock

Maritime Museum

Ogden Ave

Whyte

STREET

Ave

Vancouver Museum

Vanier Park

Aquatic Centre

Beach

Avenue

PACIFIC

STREET

Hornby

Granville

HOWE

Howe Street

DAVIE

STRE

SEYMOUR

Drake

PACIFIC STREET

Beach

Homer st

Avenue

Cypress

Greer Ave

St

CHESTNUT

BURRARD

STREET

Creekside Dr

Pennyfarthing Dr

1 Ave

Mariner Walk

Island

BURRARD BRIDGE

Duranleau st

Public Market

GRANVILLE ST

99

Johnston

Railspur

Walk

Street

Aly

99

Cartwright

St

Old Bridge

Park

Walk

False Creek Ferry

1   Avenue   West

2   Avenue   West

STREET

3   Avenue   West

Museum of Anthropology

4   AVENUE   WEST

BURRARD

5   Avenue   West

Pine

GRANVILLE ST

4 AVENUE WEST

Vancouver International Airport

Granville Island

Fountain Way

Lameys

Church Alder Bay

Walk

Mill

The Castings

Cross

Alder

Road

Foundry Quay

Forge Wk

Ironwork Pass

Scantlings

Sds Sitka

School Green

Charles

A

B

C

362

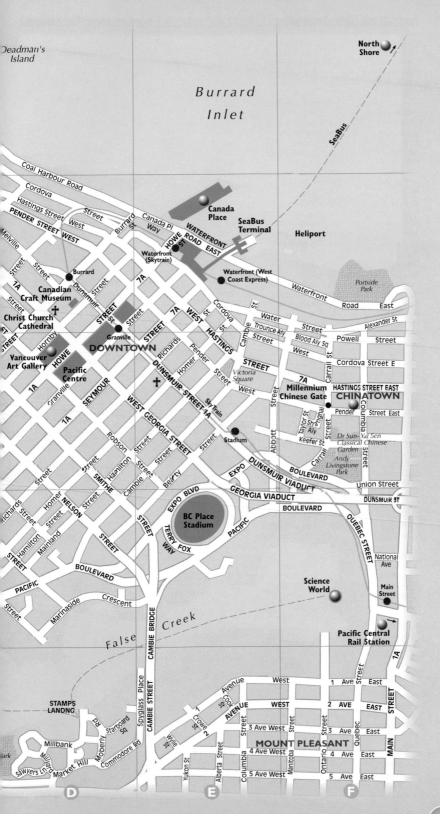

Deadman's
Island

*Burrard
Inlet*

SeaBus

North
Shore

Coal Harbour Road

Cordova

Hastings Street   West   Street

PENDER STREET WEST   Burrard   Canada Pl   Way   HOWE ROAD EAST   WATERFRONT

Melville   Street

Street   St   Canada Place

Street   Street   SeaBus
Terminal

Heliport

1A   Dunsmuir   7A   Waterfront
(Skytrain)

Burrard   Canadian
Craft Museum

Waterfront (West
Coast Express)   Waterfront   Road   East   Portside
Park

Christ Church
Cathedral   Hornby

STREET   St   Cordova   Water   Street   Alexander St

Street   7A   WEST   Street   Trounce Aly   Street   Powell   Street

Vancouver
Art Gallery   HOWE   Granville   DOWNTOWN   HASTINGS   Cambie   Blood Aly Sq   Cordova Street E

Richards   Pender   STREET   West   Carrall St

Pacific
Centre   SEYMOUR   DUNSMUIR STREET 1A   Homer   Street   Victoria
Square   Street   7A   Cordova Street E   HASTINGS STREET EAST

Granville   1A   Street   SkyTrain   West   Millennium
Chinese Gate   CHINATOWN

WEST GEORGIA STREET   Robson   Street   Street   Pender   Columbia   Street East

Street   Street   Street   Street   Stadium   Taylor St   Shanghai
Aly   Carrall   Dr Sun- Yat Sen
Classical Chinese
Garden

SMITHE   Hamilton   Cambie   Beatty   Abbott   Keefer St   Street   Andy
Livingstone
Park

Richards   Homer   NELSON   Street   DUNSMUIR VIADUCT   BOULEVARD   Carrall   Union Street

Street   EXPO   GEORGIA VIADUCT   DUNSMUIR ST

Hamilton   Mainland   NELSON   STREET   EXPO BLVD   BC Place
Stadium   BOULEVARD   QUEBEC STREET

STREET   TERRY FOX   WAY   PACIFIC   National
Ave

BOULEVARD   Crescent   Science
World   Main
Street

PACIFIC   Marinaside   CAMBIE BRIDGE   False   Creek   Pacific Central
Rail Station   1A

STAMPS
LANDNG   Spyglass Place   Willie St   Avenue   West   1 Ave   East   STREET   MAIN

Rd   Starboard
Sq   CAMBIE STREET   Crowe St   COR St   WEST   2 AVE   EAST

Millbank   Moberly   Commodore Rd   Yukon St   3 Ave West   AVENUE   Columbia   Manitoba   Ontario   Quebec   3 Ave East

SaWyers Ln   Market Hill   Millard   Alberta Street   4 Ave West   MOUNT PLEASANT   4 Ave East

Park   Rd   5 Ave West   5 Ave East

D   E   F

363

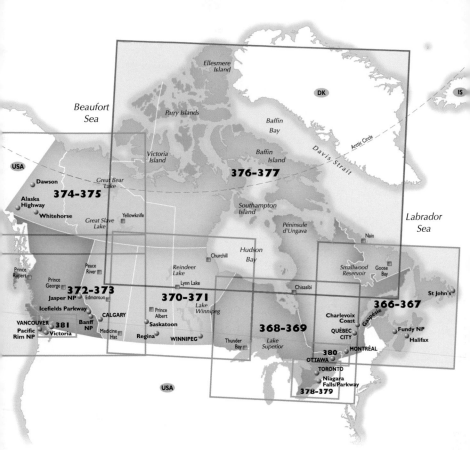

Beaufort
Sea

Ellesmere
Island

DK

IS

Parry Islands

Baffin
Bay

Victoria
Island

Baffin
Island

376-377

Davis Strait

Arctic Circle

USA

Dawson

Great Bear
Lake

374-375

Alaska
Highway

Whitehorse

Great Slave
Lake

Yellowknife

Southampton
Island

Labrador
Sea

Péninsule
d'Ungava

Nain

Prince
Rupert

Prince
George

Peace
River

372-373

Jasper NP

Edmonton

Icefields Parkway

Reindeer
Lake

Lynn Lake

Churchill

Hudson
Bay

Chisasibi

Smallwood
Reservoir

Goose
Bay

366-367

St John's

370-371

Lake
Winnipeg

CALGARY

Prince
Albert

Saskatoon

Charlevoix
Coast

Gaspésie

VANCOUVER

381

Banff
NP

Medicine
Hat

Regina

WINNIPEG

368-369

Lake
Superior

QUÉBEC
CITY

Fundy NP

Pacific
Rim NP

Victoria

Thunder
Bay

380

MONTRÉAL

Halifax

OTTAWA

TORONTO

USA

Niagara
Falls/Parkway

378-379

Toll Motorway (Turnpike)

Motorway

National road

Other road

International boundary

Administrative region boundary

■ **City / Town**

National park

● **Featured place of interest**

✈ **Airport**

1531
▲
Mt Zeil **Height in metres**

--- **Ferry route**

= **Mountain pass**

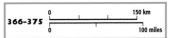

366-375

0   150 km
0   100 miles

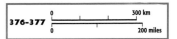

376-377

0   300 km
0   200 miles

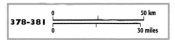

378-381

0   50 km
0   30 miles

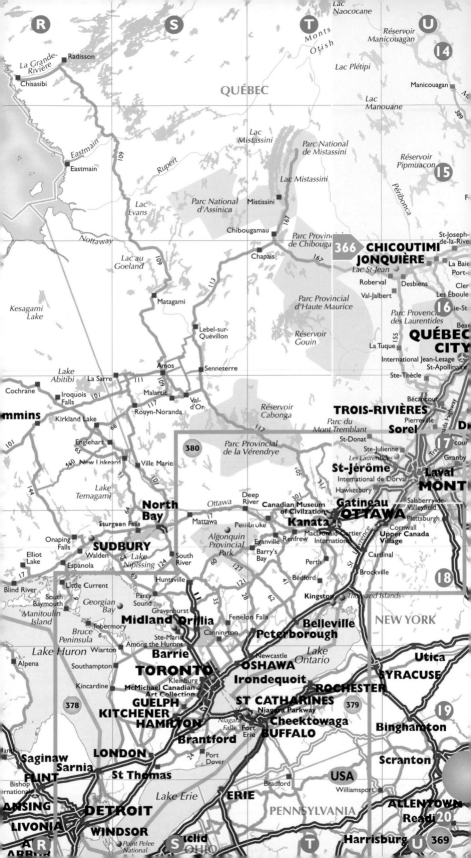

L

M

N

12

NUNAVUT

Arviat
(Eskimo Point)

*Nueltin
Lake*

Hudson Bay

13

*Cape
Churchill*

Churchill

*Southern
Indian
Lake*

Fort Severn

14

South Indian Lake

Churchill

Gillam

*Winisk River
Provincial Park*

Leaf Rapids

Nelson

280

Winisk

39

Thompson

MANITOBA

*Gods
Lake*

Snow Lake

Severn

*Big Trout
Lake*

15

*Cross
Lake*

*Moose
Lakes*

*Island
Lake*

*Opasquia
Provincial Park*

North
Caribou
Lake

*Cedar
Lake*

*Sandy
Lake*

*Lake
Winnipeg*

368

*Lake
innipegosis*

ONTARIO

16

Albany

*Lake
St Joseph*

20

*Woodland
Caribou
Provincial
Park*

Red Lake

Armstrong

Dauphin

Ste Rose du Lac

*Lac
Seul*

*Riding Mountain
National Park*

68

*Nopiming
Provincial
Park*

*Lake
Nipigon*

19

7

17

Gimli

11

*Lake
Manitoba*

9

Sioux Lookout

542

17

Neepawa

12

Lac du
Bonnet

Stonewall

Selkirk

*Whiteshell
Provincial
Park*

Vermillion
Bay

72

innedosa

Portage
la Prairie

Beausejour

Dryden

599

Ignace

Carberry

44

WINNIPEG

uris

Niverville

Winnipeg
International

17

Kenora

Brandon

13

502

17

issevain

Carman

Steinbach

622

Atikokan

THUNDER BAY

23

Morden

14

Morris

*Lake of the
Woods*

*Rainy
Lake*

18

Cartwright

Altona

12

Fort
Frances

*Quetico
Provincial
Park*

**NORTH
DAKOTA**

L

Red

MINNESOTA

M

11

N

371

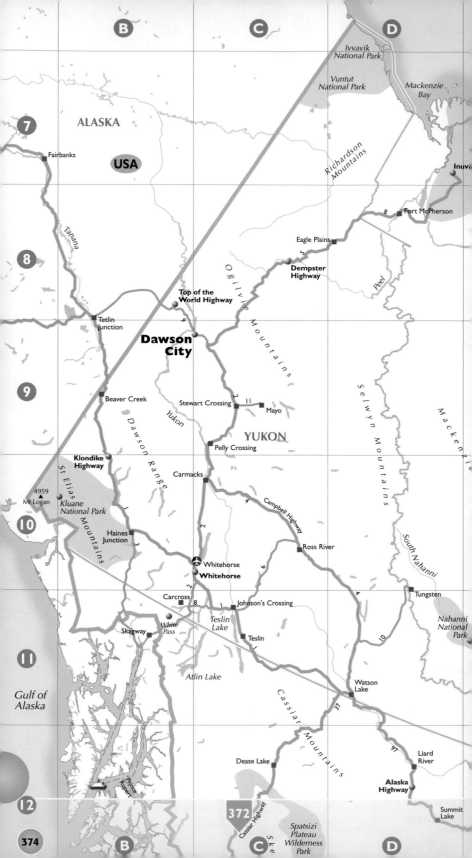

Beaufort
Sea

Banks
Island

Sachs
Harbour

Tuktoyaktuk

Cape
Parry

Amundsen
Gulf

Victoria
Island

Holman

Tukluk Nogait
National Park

Paulatuk

8

Fort
Good Hope

Coronation Gulf

Kugluktuk
(Coppermine)

Franklin
Mountains

NUNAVUT

9

Mackenzie

Great Bear
Lake

Port
Radium

Contwoyto
Lake

NORTHWEST TERRITORIES

untains

10

Wrigley

Rae-Edzo

Yellowknife

11

Fort
Simpson

Yellowknife

Liard

Fort
Providence

Great Slave
Lake

Hay
River

Fort
Resolution

Enterprise

373

Fort
Nelson

12

Fort
Smith

Wood Buffalo
National Park

Caribou

P Q R S T U V

2

3

GREENLAND

DK

4

5

Baffin Bay

6

Kangiqlugaapik
(Clyde River)

Davis Strait

7

Baffin Island

Auyuittuq National Park

8

Nettilling Lake

Pangnirtung

Cumberland Sound

Prince Charles Island

Foxe Basin

Amadjuak Lake

9

Apex

Frobisher Bay

Labrador Sea

Kingait
(Cape Dorset)

Kimmirut

10

Hudson Strait

Cape Chidley
1729
▲ Mt Caubvick

...rait

Quaqtaq

11

Ivujivik

Mansel Island

Péninsule d'Ungava

Ungava Bay

366 NEWFOUNDLAND

Cartwrigh

Labrador

North West River

Kuujjuaq

12

Smallwood Reservoir

Happy Valle
To... Goose Bay

Inukjuak

Caniapiscau

Lake Melvi

QUÉBEC

Schefferville

Lac Caniapiscau

500 *Churchill*

13

Lac Bienville

Labrador City

Kuujjuarapik

Polar Bear

Réservoir

Rivi...
To...
Sept-...

Île

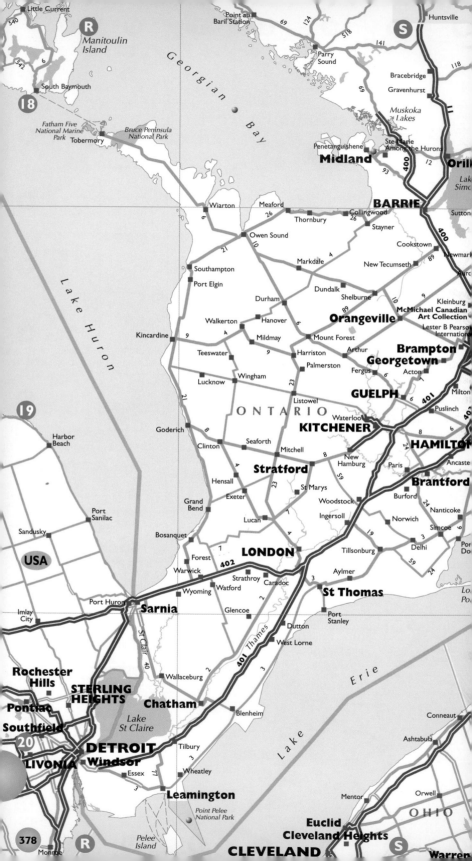

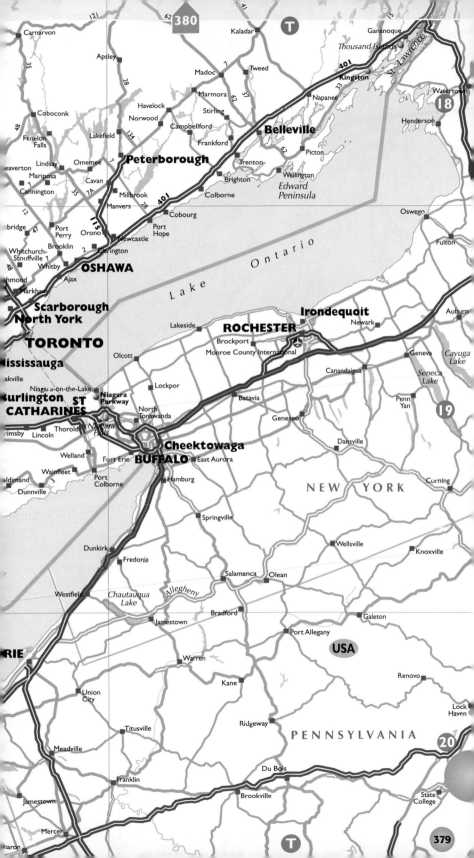

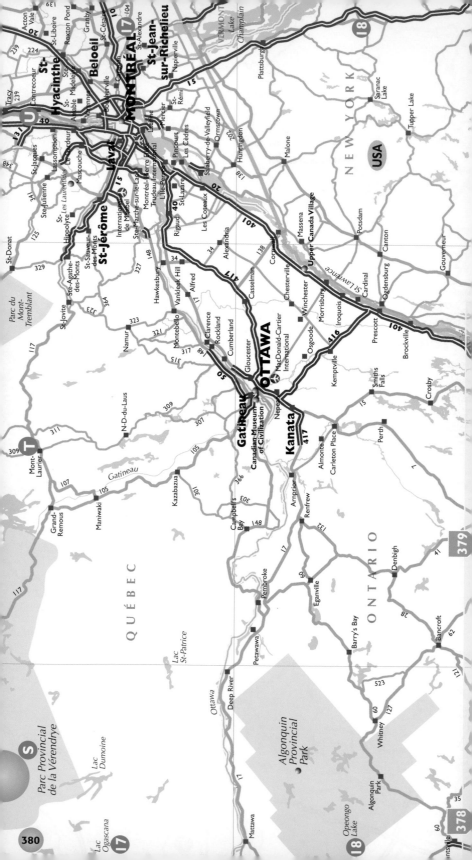

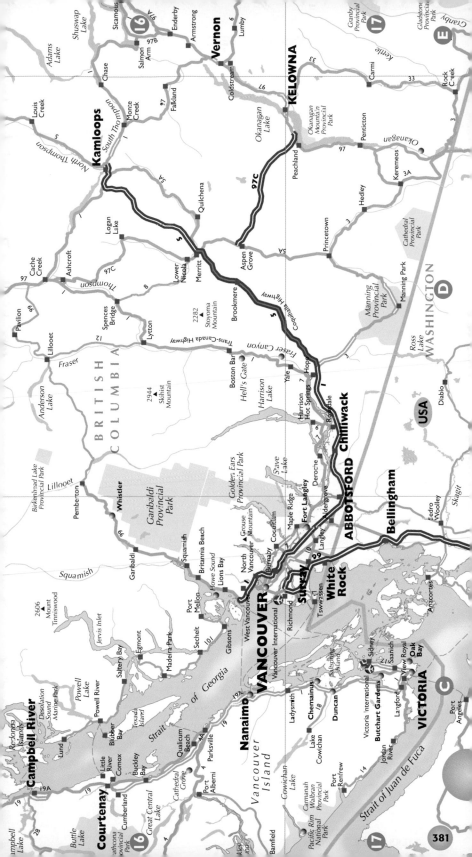

CANADA ATLAS INDEX

Shaunavon	370 H17	Strathroy	378 S19	Wausau, USA	368 P19
Shediac	367 W15	Sturgeon Falls	369 S18	Wawa	368 Q17
Shelburne,		Sudbury	369 R18	Welland	379 S19
Nova Scotia	367 X17	Summerside	367 W15	Wellington,	
Shelburne, Ontario	378 S19	Summit Lake	372 D12	Ontario	379 T18
Shellbrooke	370 H16	Sundre	373 F16	Wellington, Prince	
Sherbrooke	366 U17	Surray	381 C17	Edward Island	367 W15
Sicamous	381 E16	Sussex	367 W16	Wellsville, USA	379 T19
Sidney	381 C17	Sutton	378 S19	Wenatchee, USA	372 D18
Simcoe	378 S19	Swan Hills	373 F15	West Lorne	378 S20
Sioux Lookout	371 N17	Swan River	370 K16	West Vancouver	381 C16
Sirit River	373 E14	Swift Current	370 H17	Westaskiwin	373 F16
Skagway, USA	374 B11	Sydney	367 X15	Westfield	379 S19
Skidegate	372 B14	Sylvan Lake	373 F16	Westlock	373 F15
Slave Lake	373 F14	Syracuse, USA	369 T19	Weyburn	370 J17
Smithers	372 C14			Wheatley	378 S20
Smiths Falls	380 T18	**T**		Whistler	381 C16
Smokey Lake	373 G15			Whitby	379 S19
Snow Lake	371 K15	Tacoma, USA	372 C17	Whitchurch-	
Sorel	366 U17	Tadoussac	366 U16	Stouffville	379 S19
Souris, Manitoba	371 K17	Taloyoak	376 L8	White Rock	381 C17
Souris, Prince		Teeswater	378 S19	Whitecourt	373 F15
Edward Island	367 X15	Terrace	372 C14	Whitehorse	374 D10
South Baymouth	378 R18	Terrace Bay	368 P17	Whitney	380 S18
South Indian Lake	371 K14	Teslin	374 C11	Wiarton	378 S19
South River,		Tetlin Junction,		Wilkie	370 H16
Newfoundland	367 Z13	USA	374 B8	Williams Lake	372 D15
South River, Ontario	369 S18	The Pas	370 K15	Williamsport, USA	369 T20
Southampton	378 S19	Thessalon	368 R18	Winchester	380 T18
Southend	370 J14	Thompson	371 L14	Windsor, Nova	
Southfield, USA	378 R20	Thornbury	378 S19	Scotia	367 X16
Spences Bridge	381 D16	Thorold	379 S19	Windsor, Ontario	378 R20
Spokane, USA	373 E18	Three Hills	373 F16	Wingham	378 S19
Springdale	367 X13	Thunder Bay	368 P18	Winnipeg	371 L17
Springfield	367 W16	Tilbury, USA	378 R20	Wonowon	373 E13
Springhill	367 X16	Tillsonburg	378 S19	Woodstock,	
Springville, USA	379 T19	Timmins	369 R17	New Brunswick	366 V16
Squamish	381 C16	Tisdale	370 J16	Woodstock,	
State College, USA	379 T20	Titusville, USA	379 T20	Ontario	378 S19
Stayner	378 S19	Tobermory	378 R18	Wrigley	375 E10
Steinbach	371 L17	Tofino	372 B16	Wynyard	370 J16
Stephenville		Torbay	367 Z13	Wyoming, Ontario	378 S19
Crossing	367 X14	Toronto	379 S19	Wyoming,	
Sterling Heights,		Tracy	380 U17	Michigan, USA	368 Q20
USA	378 R20	Traverse City, USA	368 Q19		
Stettler	373 G16	Trenton	379 T18	**Y**	
Stevens Point, USA	368 P19	Trois-Rivières	366 U17		
Stewart Crossing	374 C9	Truro	367 X16	Yakima, USA	372 D18
Stirling	379 T18	Tswwassen	381 C17	Yale	381 D17
Stirling	373 F17	Tuktoyaktuk	375 E7	Yarmouth	367 W17
Stonewall	371 L17	Tumbler Ridge	373 E14	Yellowknife	375 G11
Stoney Plain	373 F15	Tungsten	374 D11	Yorkton	370 K17
Stony Rapids	370 J13	Tupper Lake, USA	380 U18		
Stratford	378 S19	La Tuque	366 U16		
Strathmore	373 F16	Tweed	379 T18		

U			
Union City, USA	379 S20		
Unity	370 H16		
Upper Canada			
Village	380 T18		
Uranium City	370 H13		
Ursuqtuq (Gjoa			
Haven)	376 L9		
Utica, USA	369 U19		
Uxbridge	379 S19		
V			
Val-d'Or	369 S17		
Val-Jalbert	366 U16		
Vallée-Jonction	366 U17		
Valleyview	373 F14		
Vancouver	381 C16		
Vanderhoof	372 D14		
Vankleek Hill	380 T17		
Varennes	380 U17		
Vegreville	373 G15		
Vermillion Bay	371 M17		
Vermillon	373 G15		
Vernon	381 E16		
Victoria	381 C17		
Victoriaville	366 U17		
View Royal	381 C17		
Viking	373 G16		
Ville-Marie	369 S17		
Virden	370 K17		
Virginia, USA	368 N18		
Vulcan	373 F17		
W			
Wabana	367 Z13		
Wainfleet	379 S19		
Wainwright	373 G16		
Walden	369 R18		
Walkerton	378 S19		
Wallaceburg	378 R20		
Warman	370 H16		
Warren, Ohio, USA	378 S20		
Warren,			
Pennsylvania,			
USA	379 T20		
Warwick	378 S19		
Waterloo	378 S19		
Watertown, USA	379 T18		
Watford	378 S19		
Watrous	370 J16		
Watson Lake	374 D11		
Waukesha, USA	368 P20		

ACKNOWLEDGMENTS

Abbreviations for the credits are as follows:
AA = AA World Travel Library, t (top), b (bottom), c (center), l (left), r (right), h/g (background)

UNDERSTANDING CANADA

4 AA/C Coe; 5l AA/J F Pin; 5c AA/P Timmermans; 5r AA/C Coe; 6l AA/C Sawyer; 6c Courtesy of Newfoundland & Labrador Tourism/Michael Hockney; 6r Photo Courtesy of Tourism Calgary/www.tourismcalgary.com; 7 AA/P Timmermans; 8cl AA/C Coe; 8tr AA/N Sumner; 8ctr AA/M Dent; 8ccr AA/N Sumner; 8cbr AA/N Sumner; 8br AA/J F Pin; 9tl AA/C Sawyer; 9ctl AA/P Bennett; 9ccl AA/N Sumner; 9bl AA/P Bennett; 9br Courtesy of Newfoundland & Labrador Tourism/Barrett & MacKay; 10tl AA/N Sumner; 10tr AA/N Sumner; 10ctr AA/N Sumner; 10ccr AA/C Sawyer; 10cbr Calgary Stampede; 10cbl AA/C Coe; 10bl AA/P Bennett; 10br AA/C Coe.

LIVING CANADA

11 AA/J F Pin; 12tl AA/C Sawyer; 12tr AA/C Sawyer; 12cr AA/P Bennett; 12br AA/N Sumner; 12/3 b/g AA/C Sawyer; 12/3c © Tourisme Montréal/Festival International de Jazz de Montréal, Caroline Hayeur; 13tl AA/N Sumner; 13tr AA/P Bennett; 13br IFC Films/The Kobal Collection/Giraud, Sophie; 14tl Digital-vision; 14tr AA/J F Pin; 14tcr AA/C Sawyer; 14bl © Tourisme Montréal/Les Grands Ballet Canadiens, Andrew Oxenham; 14cl © Tourisme Montréal/Festival International de Jazz de Montréal 2001, Jean-François LeBlanc; 14/5 b/g Digitalvision; 15tl AA/J Davison; 15tc Getty Images; 15tr AA/J F Pin; 15cr Rex Features; 16tl Calgary Stampede; 16tcl AA/J F Pin; 16tr Tourism Saskatoon; 16cr Getty Images; 16c Sebastian Larose; 16/7 b/g Calgary Stampede; 17tl Calgary Stampede; 17tr AA/J F Pin; 17cl Productions de l'Oeil; 17cc Musée J. A. Bombardier, www.bombardiermuseum.com; 17cr AA/J Davison; 18tl AA/J F Pin; 18tr Rex Features; 18cl AA/J F Pin; 18bl AA/N Sumner; 18/9 b/g © Tourisme Montréal/ Stéphan Poulin; 19tl AA/J F Pin; 19tc AA/N Sumner; 19tr AA/N Sumner; 19tcr AA/J F Pin; 19cl AA/P Bennett; 19br AA/P Bennett; 20tl Reproduction authorized by the Library of Parliament/Reproduction autorisée par la Bibliotèque du Parlement, Stephen Fenn; 20tr Rex Features; 20c J F Pin; 20 b/g AA/M Dent.

THE STORY OF CANADA

21 AA/J Davison; 22cc AA/C Coe; 22cr AA/J F Pin; 22bl AA/ P Bennett; 22bc AA; 22cbr AA/C Sawyer; 22/3 b/g AA/P Bennett; 22/3 AA/P Bennett; 23cbl AA/M Dent; 23cc Mary Evans Picture Library; 23cr AA/P Bennett; 23bl AA/J F Pin; 23bcr Newfoundland & Labrador Tourism; 23br AA/ N Sumner; 24cc AA/J F Pin; 24cr AA/J F Pin; 24bl AA/J F Pin; 24bc AA; 24/5 b/g AA/N Sumner; 24/5 AA/P Bennett; 25cbl AA/P Bennett; 25cl AA/J F Pin; 25cc AA; 25cr Hulton Getty; 25bl AA/ J F Pin; 25br AA/ N Sumner; 26tl City of Toronto Culture Division Historic Fort York; 26cc AA/C Coe; 26cr AA/P Bennett; 26bl AA/C Coe; 26/7 AA/ N Sumner; 26/7 b/g AA/J F Pin; 27cl Mary Evans Picture Library; 27cc AA; 27cr AA/J F Pin; 27cbc Hulton Getty; 27bc Fredericton Tourism; 27br AA; 28cc AA; 28cr AA/C Coe; 28bl AA/J F Pin; 28/9 Hulton Getty; 28/9 b/g AA; 29cl Illustrated London News; 29cc AA/C Coe; 29cbl AA/P Bennett; 29bl AA/P Bennett; 29br AA/J Beazley; 30cl Hulton Getty; 30cr AA/J F Pin; 30bl AA/N Sumner; 30/1 Hulton Getty; 30/1 b/g AA/P Aithie; 31cl Hulton Getty; 31cr Hulton Getty; 31cbr Mary Evans Picture Library; 31bl AA/P Aithie; 31br AA/C Coe; 32cr Hulton Gerry; 32bl The St Lawrence Seaway Management Corporation; 32ct Musée J. A. Bombardier, www.bombardiermuseum.com; 32cb Hulton Getty; 32/3 Hulton Getty; 32/3 b/g AA/J Davsion; 33cl Hulton Getty; 33ccl Tourism Thunder Bay; 33ccr Musée J. A. Bombardier, www.bombardiermuseum.com; 33cr Hulton Getty; 33bc AA/N Sumner; 33br AA/J Davison; 34cc AA/P Bennett; 34bl AA/J F Pin; 34bcr AA/J F Pin; 34/5 b/g AA/J F Pin;

34/5 AA/J F Pin; 34cr Rex Features; 35l Rex Features; 35cr Rex Features; 35br Rex Features/Ponopresse; 36cr AA/C Coe; 36bl AA/ N Sumner; 36bc AA/ N Sumner; 36b Rex Features; 36b inset Rex Features; 36 b/g AA/ P Timmermans.

ON THE MOVE

37 AA/C Coe; 38/9 Digitalvision; 38 Aéroports de Montréal; 40/1 Digitalvision; 40 Quebec City Jean Lesage Airport; 41 AA/P Bennett; 42t Digitalvision; 42c Edmonton International Airport; 42b Aéroports de Montréal; 43t AA/B Smith; 43c AA/N Sumner; 43b AA/N Sumner; 44/5 AA/B Smith; 46c STM; 46/7 AA/B Smith; 47c AA/P Bennett; 47b AA/P Bennett; 48/9 AA/M Jourdan; 48 AA/P Bennett; 49ct AA/P Bennett; 49cb AA/J Beazley; 49b AA/P Bennett; 50/1 Digitalvision; 50c VIA Rail; 52t Digitalvision; 52ct VIA Rail; 52cb AA/P Bennett; 52b VIA Rail; 53t Digitalvision; 53c AA/J F Pin; 54/5 Digitalvision; 54ct AA/P Bennett; 54cb AA/C Coe; 54cbc AA/P Bennett; 54cbr AA/P Bennett; 54btr AA/C Coe; 54bl AA/P Bennett; 54bc AA/N Sumner; 54br AA/J F Pin; 55b AA/C Sawyer; 56t AA/S McBride.

THE SIGHTS

57 AA/J F Pin; 59l AA/N Sumner; 59c AA/N Sumner; 59r AA/N Sumner; 60l AA/J F Pin; 60r AA/N Sumner; 61tl Beaverbrook Art Gallery, Fredericton; 61tr AA/J F Pin; 61b AA/N Sumner; 62t AA/C Coe; 62b AA/N Sumner; 63t AA/N Sumner; 63b AA/N Sumner; 64t AA/N Sumner; 64c AA/N Sumner; 64b AA/N Sumner; 64/5 AA/N Sumner; 65t AA/N Sumner; 65b; AA/N Sumner; 66l AA/N Sumner; 66c Courtesy of Newfoundland & Labrador Tourism; 66r AA/N Sumner; 67t AA/N Sumner; 67c AA/N Sumner; 67b AA/N Sumner; 68t AA/N Sumner; 68b AA/N Sumner; 68/9 John Sylvester; 69t AA/N Sumner; 69c John Sylvester; 69b AA/N Sumner; 70t AA/J F Pin; 70b AA/J F Pin; 70/1 AA/J F Pin; 71l AA/J F Pin; 71r AA/J F Pin; 72tl AA/N Sumner; 72tr AA/N Sumner; 72b AA/N Sumner; 74tl AA/J F Pin; 74tr AA/J F Pin; 74b AA/J F Pin; 75l AA/N Sumner; 75r AA/J F Pin; 76/7 AA/J F Pin; 77 © Tourisme Montréal , Canadian Tourist Commission/Pierre St Jacques, 78l AA/J F Pin; 78r AA/J F Pin; 79tl © Tourisme Montréal/ Copilia; 79tr AA/J F Pin; 79b © Tourisme Montréal/Parc Jean-Drapeau; 80 © Tourisme Montréal/Stéphan Poulin; 80/1 © Tourisme Montréal/Stéphan Poulin; 81t © Tourisme Montréal/Stéphan Poulin; 81b AA/J F Pin; 82t Roderick Chen, Pointe-a-Callière, Montréal Museum of Archaeology and History; 82c AA/J F Pin; 82b Roderick Chen, Pointe-a-Callière, Montréal Museum of Archaeology and History; 83l AA/J F Pin; 83c AA/J F Pin; 83r © Tourisme Montréal/ Pierre Girard; 84t Le 1000 de La Gauchetière; 84b AA/J F Pin; 85 Le 1000 de La Gauchetière; 86l AA/N Sumner; 86r AA/J F Pin; 87l AA/N Sumner; 87r AA/J F Pin; 88t AA/N Sumner; 88c AA/J F Pin; 88b AA/N Sumner; 89t AA/N Sumner; 89b AA/J F Pin; 90t AA/N Sumner; 90b AA/N Sumner; 91tl AA/N Sumner; 91r AA/N Sumner; 91b AA/N Sumner; 92t © Canadian Museum of Civilization, photographer Stephen Alsford, 1994, Image no. S94-11986; 92b AA/J F Pin; 93l AA/N Sumner; 93r AA/N Sumner; 94t AA/J F Pin; 94c AA/N Sumner; 94b AA/N Sumner; 94/5 AA/N Sumner; 95t AA/N Sumner; 95c AA/J F Pin; 95b AA/N Sumner; 96t AA/ J F Pin; 96b AA/J F Pin; 96/7 AA/J F Pin; 97 AA/J F Pin; 98t AA/N Sumner; 98c AA/N Sumner; 98b AA/N Sumner; 99t AA/N Sumner; 99c AA/N Sumner; 100t AA/N Sumner; 100b Courtesy of Newfoundland & Labrador Tourism/Barrett & MacKay; 102l Canada Aviation Museum; 102r Science & Technology Museum; 103l AA/N Sumner; 103r AA/N Sumner; 104t AA/J F Pin; 104b National Gallery of Canada; 105t National Gallery of Canada; 106t AA/N Sumner; 106b AA/N

Sumner; 107l AA/J F Pin; 107r AA/J Beazley; 108t AA/N Sumner; 108c AA/N Sumner; 109t AA/N Sumner; 109c AA/N Sumner; 109b AA/N Sumner; 110l AA/J Davison; 110r AA/J Davison; 111l Ontario Place; 111r Ontario Place; 112t AA/N Sumner; 112bl AA/N Sumner; 112br AA/N Sumner; 113t Harbourfront Centre, 235 Queens Quay West, Toronto, Ontario, www.harbourfront.on.ca; 113b AA/N Sumner; 114t AA/J Davison; 114b AA/J Davison; 114/5 AA/J Davison; 115t AA/J Beazley; 115b AA/J Davison; 116l AA/J Davison; 116r AA/J F Pin; 117l AA/J Davison; 117r Tourism Toronto; 118t AA/N Sumner; 118b AA/N Sumner; 119l AA/N Sumner; 119r McMichael Canadian Art Collection; 120t AA/N Sumner; 120l AA/N Sumner; 121t AA/N Sumner; 121r AA/N Sumner; 122t AA/N Sumner; 122bl AA/N Sumner; 122bc AA/N Sumner; 122br AA/N Sumner; 123 AA/N Sumner; 124 AA/N Sumner; 124/5 AA/N Sumner; 125ct AA/N Sumner; 125cb AA/N Sumner; 125b AA/N Sumner; 126 Marineland, Niagara Falls; 26cl AA/N Sumner; 126cc Marineland, Niagara Falls; 126cr AA/N Sumner; 126b AA/N Sumner; 127t AA/N Sumner; 127c AA/N Sumner; 127b AA/J Davison; 128tl AA/N Sumner; 128tr Tourism Thunder Bay; 128b AA/N Sumner; 129tl Tourism Thunder Bay; 129r Courtesy of Upper Canada Village; 131t AA/P Bennett; 131c AA/P Bennett; 131b AA/C Sawyer; 132t AA/P Bennett; 132b AA/P Bennett; 132/3 Tourism Calgary/www.tourismcalgary.com; 133t AA/C Sawyer; 133b Tourism Calgary/www.tourismcalgary.com; 134t AA/C Sawyer; 134cl AA/P Bennett; 134cc AA/P Bennett; 134cr AA/P Bennett; 134b Tourism Calgary/www.tourismcalgary.com; 135t Tourism Calgary/ www.tourismcalgary.com; 135b Tourism Calgary/ www.tourismcalgary.com; 136t AA/C Sawyer; 136b Calgary Stampede; 137l AA/P Bennett; 137r Historic Sites Service. Alberta Community Development/Remington Carriage Museum; 138t AA/P Bennett; 139l AA/P Bennett; 138r AA/P Bennett; 140t Courtesy of the Royal Saskatchewan Museum; 140b AA/P Bennett; 141t Tourism Saskatoon, Irene Sosulski; 141c AA/P Bennett; 141b AA/P Bennett; 142t AA/P Bennett; 142c AA/P Bennett; 142b AA/P Bennett; 142/3 AA/P Bennett; 143t AA/P Bennett; 143b AA/P Bennett; 144t AA/P Bennett; 144b AA/P Bennett; 146l AA/P Bennett; 146c AA/P Bennett; 146r AA/C Sawyer; 147t AA/C Coe; 147b AA/P Bennett; 148l AA/P Bennett; 148c AA/P Bennett; 148r AA/P Bennett; 149t Vancouver Aquarium; 149b Vancouver Aquarium; 150c AA/P Bennett; 150/1 AA/C Sawyer; 150b AA/P Bennett; 151t AA/P Bennett; 151b AA/P Bennett; 152l AA/P Bennett; 152c AA/P Bennett; 152r AA/P Bennett; 153l AA/C Coe; 153r Robert Harding Picture Library; 154t AA/P Bennett; 154b AA/C Sawyer; 154/5 AA/C Sawyer; 155t AA/C Coe; 155b AA/P Timmermans; 156l AA/P Bennett; 156tr AA/P Bennett; 156cl AA/P Bennett; 156b AA/P Bennett; 157t AA/P Bennett; 157b AA/C Sawyer; 158t AA/P Bennett; 158l AA/P Bennett; 158c AA/P Bennett; 158r AA/C Sawyer; 158b AA/C Sawyer; 159t AA/P Bennett; 159c AA/P Bennett; 159b AA/P Bennett; 160 AA/C Sawyer; 160/1 AA/C Sawyer; 161t AA/C Sawyer; 161b AA/C Coe; 162t AA/C Coe; 162b AA/C Coe; 163t AA/P Bennett; 163b AA/C Sawyer; 164tl AA/P Bennett; 164tr AA/P Bennett; 164b AA/P Bennett; 165tl AA/C Sawyer; 165tr AA/C Coe; 165b AA/C Coe; 166t AA/P Bennett; 166cl AA/P Bennett; 166cc AA/P Bennett; 166cr AA/P Bennett; 166b AA/P Bennett; 167t AA/P Bennett; 167c AA/P Bennett; 167b AA/C Bennett; 168 AA/P Bennett; 169t AA/P Bennett; 169bl AA/P Bennett; 169bc AA/C Sawyer; 169br AA/P Bennett; 170t AA/P Bennett; 170cl AA/P Bennett; 170cr AA/P Bennett; 170b AA/C Sawyer; 171t AA/P Bennett; 171b AA/C Sawyer; 172tl AA/P Bennett; 172tr AA/P Bennett; 172b AA/P Bennett; 173t AA/P Timmermans; 173b AA/P Bennett; 175t Robert Harding Picture Library; 175r Robert Harding Picture Library; 176t AA/C Coe; 176cl AA/P Bennett; 176cc AA/P Bennett; 176cr AA/P Bennett; 176tb AA/C Coe; 177t AA/C Coe; 177b AA/P Bennett; 178t Pictures Colour Library; 178b AA/C Coe; 179l Robert Harding Picture Library; 179r AA/C Coe; 180tl Robert Harding Picture Library; 180tr Winston Fraser; 180b Winston Fraser; 181t AA/P Bennett; 181cc AA/C Coe; 181b AA/P Bennett; 182l AA/C Coe; 182r Yukon Beringia Interpretive Centre.

183 Ontario Tourist Board; 184t AA/N Sumner; 184c AA/N Sumner; 185t AA/N Sumner; 185cl Inuit Art Quarterley; 185cr Rannva Designs; 188t Banff Centre, Donald Lee; 188cl Bard on the Beach/David Blue; 188t Belfry Theatre, Victoria/Tim Matheson; 189t The Guvernment Club; 189cl Yuk Yuk's Club, Toronto; 189cr The Cellar/Cory Weeds; 190t Toronto Argonauts Football Club; 190cl Manitoba Moose Hockey Club; 190cr Saskatoon Roughriders Football Club/P Dunn; 191t Toronto Argonauts Football Club; 191c Gray Rocks; 192t Toronto Argonauts Football Club; 192cl AA/P Timmermans; 192cr AA/J F Pin; 193t Toronto Argonauts Football Club; 193c AA/J Davison; 194t Courtesy of Newfoundland & Labrador Tourism; 194c Claude Hout; 195t Courtesy of Newfoundland & Labrador Tourism/Barrett & MacKay; 195c Courtesy of Newfoundland & Labrador Tourism/Barrett & MacKay; 195b Regent Mall Shopping Centre, NB; 196t Courtesy of Newfoundland & Labrador Tourism/Barrett & MacKay; 196c Kings Theatre; 197t Courtesy of Newfoundland & Labrador Tourism/Barrett & MacKay; 197cl Fredericton Playhouse Inc.; 197cr Grafton Street Dinner Theatre; 198t Courtesy of Newfoundland & Labrador Tourism/Barrett & MacKay; 198c AA/T Souter; 199t Courtesy of Newfoundland & Labrador Tourism/Barrett & MacKay; 199ct Moncton Wildcats; 199cr AA/N Sumner; 200t Courtesy of Newfoundland & Labrador Tourism/Barrett & MacKay; 200c Le Pays de la Sagouine; 200bl Spa At the Monastery, St John's; 201t Courtesy of Newfoundland & Labrador Tourism/ Barrett & MacKay; 201c Nova Scotia Museum of Natural History, Halifax; 202t Courtesy of Newfoundland & Labrador Tourism/Barrett & MacKay; 202b Magic Valley Family Fun Park; 202b Nova Scotia International Tattoo; 203t Choco-Musée Énrico, Quebec City; 203cl © Tourisme Montréal/Daniel Choinière; 203cr CGMPM; 204t Choco-Musée Énrico, Quebec City; 204b CGMPM; 204cr CGMPM; 205t Choco-Musée Énrico, Quebec City; 205c © Tourism Montréal/ Daniel Choinière; 206t Choco-Musée Énrico, Quebec City; 205b Artisans Bas-Canada; 206c Choco-Musée Énrico, Quebec City; 207t Choco-Musée Énrico, Quebec City; 207b Place Laurier; 208t Choco-Musée Énrico, Quebec City; 208cl AMC Entertainment Inc.; 208cr Saidye Bronfman Centre for the Arts; 208b © Tourisme Montréal/Stéphan Poulin; 209t Choco-Musée Énrico; Quebec City; 209b AA/J F Pin; 210t Choco-Musée Énrico, Quebec City; 211t Choco-Musée Énrico, Quebec City; 211c Tourism Montréal/© Les Descentes sur Le St-Laurent; 211b Gray Rocks; 212t Choco-Musée Énrico, Quebec City; 212cl AA/N Sumner; 212cr © Biosphere-Environment Canada; 212br © Biodôme, Michel Tremblay; 212bc Labyrinthe du Hanger 16; 213t Choco-Musée Énrico, Quebec City; 213cl © Christian Deserochers; 213cr Tourism Montréal/©Just for Laughs Festival, Gilles Menon; 214t AA/N Sumner; 214cl Toronto Argonauts Football Club; 214cr Olde Hide House, Acton; 215t AA/N Sumner; 215cl Cataraqui Town Centre; 215cr AA/N Sumner; 216t AA/N Sumner; 216c Inuit Art Quarterley; 216br Bootmaster Inc.; 217t AA/N Sumner; 217bc Holt Renfrew; 217cl AA/N Sumner; 217br AA/N Sumner; 218t AA/N Sumner; 218c Thousand Island Playhouse; 219t AA/N Sumner; 219cl Centrepoint Theatre, Ottawa; 219ct AMC Entertainment Inc.; 219cc National Arts Centre, Wilfrie Hösl; 219b Magnus Theatre, Thunder Bay/Deak Peltier; 220t AA/N Sumner; 220cb AA/N Sumner; 220cr Hummingbird Centre for the Performing Arts; 220b Massey Hall; 221cl Mysteriously Yours...; 221t AA/N Sumner; 221ct Mirvish Productions/Ron Steinberg; 221cr AA/N Sumner; 221b AA/N Sumner; 222t AA/N Sumner; 222c Restaurant 18/Ilesh Parmer B.I.D.; 223t AA/N Sumner; 223b C'est What?; 223cr The Guvernment Club; 224t AA/N Sumner; 224c Yuk Yuk's, Toronto; 224br Ontario Place; 225t AA/N Sumner; 225bc Toronto Lynx; 225br Woodbine Racetrack; 225ct Toronto Argonauts Football Club; 226t AA/N Sumner; 226cl Georgian Triangle Charters; 226b AA/N Sumner; 226ctr Great Canadian Bugee Jump; 227t AA/N Sumner; 227cl The Helicopter Inc.; 227cr London Childrens

Museum; **228t** AA/N Sumner; **228cl** Marineland, Niagara Falls; **228cc** The Canada Science & Technology Museum; **229t** AA/N Sumner; **229bl** AA/J Beazley; **229bc** Paramount Canada Wonderland; **230t** AA/N Sumner; **231t** AA/P Bennett; **231cl** Calgary Stampede; **231cr** AA/P Bennett; **231b** AA/P Bennett; **232t** AA/P Bennett; **232c** The Forks North Portage Partnership Centrecourt; **232cr** Epcor Centre for the Performing Arts; **233t** AA/P Bennett; **233cl** Canadian Badlands Passion Play; **234t** AA/P Bennett; **234c** Rainbow Stage Winnipeg/Amanda Marsland, Nicholas Matthew as Joseph and Kevin Aichele as Pharaoh; **234b** West End Cultural Centre/Brock Hamilton; **235t** AA/P Bennett; **235c** Great Canadian Barn Dance; **236t** AA/P Bennett; **236cl** Saskatoon Roughriders Football Cub/P Dunn; **236ctl** Edmonton Trappers; **236br** Alberta Fly Fishing Adventures; **236cb** Manitoba Moose Hockey Club; **237t** AA/P Bennett; **237cb** AA/P Bennett; **237br** AA/C Coe; **238ct** Manitoba Children's Museum; **238t** AA/P Bennett; **238cr** Calgary Stampede; **239t** AA/P Bennett; **239c** Pacific Centre, Vancouver; **240t** AA/P Bennett; **240b** Crafthouse; **240c** AA/C Coe; **241t** AA/P Bennett; **241c** Pacific Centre, Vancouver; **241bl** AA/P Bennett; **241tl** Londsdale Quay; **241bc** AA/P Bennett; **242t** AA/P Bennett; **242cl** Okanagan Opal Inc.; **242cc** Banff Centre, Donald Lee; **242ct** AA/P Bennett; **242cr** Bard on the Beach/David Blue; **243t** AA/P Bennett; **243cl** Firehall Arts Centre, An Enemy of the People. Adaption By Donna Spencer. Picture Front, Marie Clements; **243ct** AA/P Timmermans; **243br** Belfry Theatre; **244t** AA/P Bennett; **244bl** National Geographic Imax Theatre; **244br** The Celler/Cory Weeds; **245t** AA/P Bennett; **246t** AA/P Bennett; **246ct** Stubbs Island Whale Watching; **246b** AA/P Bennett; **247t** AA/P Bennett; **247b** AA/M Dent; **248t** AA/P Bennett; **249t** Blue Kennels & Dog Sled Trips; **249c** Blue Kennels & Dog Sled Trips; **250t** Blue Kennels & Dog Sled Trips; **250ctl** Rannva Design; **250ctc** AA/P Bennett; **250cl** Folknits; **250cr** Frantic Follies; **250br** Blue Kennels & Dog Sled Trips; **251bl** Yukon Arts Centre; **251bl** Pat Reece-www.yukoninfo.com; **252t** Blue Kennels & Dog Sled Trips; **252bl** Yukon Beringia Interpretive Centre; **252c** Blue Kennels & Dog Sled Trips; **252cr** Yukon Quest/Carsten Thies.

OUT & ABOUT

253 AA/P Bennett; **254** AA/P Bennett; **255c** AA/N Sumner; **255b** AA/N Sumner; **256t** AA/N Sumner; **256bl** AA/N Sumner; **256br** AA/N Sumner, **257br** AA/N Sumner; **257tl** AA/N Sumner; **257tr** AA/N Sumner; **258cl** AA/N Sumner; **258b** AA/N Sumner; **259** AA/N Sumner; **261tl** AA; **261tr** AA/J F Pin; **261c** Photodisc; **261b** AA/N Sumner; **262** Kim Thomas; **263b** AA/N Sumner; **263t** Corbis UK/ Wolfgang Kaehler; **265tl** Corbis/Nathan Benn; **265tr** AA/J F Pin; **265b** AA/J F Pin; **266/7** Marie LeBlanc; **267t** Marie LeBlanc; **268** AA/N Sumner; **279t** AA/N Sumner; **269b** AA/J F Pin; **271t** © Tourisme Montréal/Stéphan Poulin; **271c** Old Port of Montréal Corporation © Benoit Chalifour; **271bl** AA/J F Pin; **271br** © Tourisme Montréal/Stéphan Poulin; **272** AA/N Sumner; **273t** AA/J Davison; **273b** AA/J Davison; **274** AA/N Sumner; **275t** AA/N Sumner; **275b** AA/J F Pin; **276/7** AA/N Sumner; **277t** AA/N Sumner; **277b** AA/N Sumner; **278** Prince Albert National Park; **279** Prince Albert National Park; **278/9** Darin Longhorst/ Longhorst Photography; **280** AA/P Bennett; **280/1** AA/P Bennett; **281** AA/P Bennett; **282** AA/P Bennett; **283t** AA/P Bennett; **283b** AA/P Bennett; **284** AA/P Bennett; **285** AA/P Bennett; **286** AA/P Bennett; **286/7** AA/P Bennett; **287c** AA/P Bennett; **287b** AA/P Bennett; **288** AA/P Bennett; **289tl** AA/P Timmermans; **289tr** AA/C Sawyer; **289bl** AA/C Sawyer; **289br** AA/C Sawyer; **290/1** AA/C Coe; **290b** Parks Canada/Hikers Log Bridge rainforest & trail by A. Corneluer; **291bl** Parks Canada/July 1997; **291br** Parks Canada/Walkers on Long Beach by W. McIntyre, 1975; **293tl** AA/C Coe; **293tr** AA/C Coe; **293c** AA/C Coe; **293b** AA/C Coe; **294/5** Parks Canada; **295** Parks Canada; **296l** AA/N Sumner; **296c** Parks Canada/Llarson Paddling Hand Island by B Brittain, 2002; **296r** AA/P Bennett.

EATING & STAYING

297 AA/N Sumner; **298cl** AA/C Sawyer; **298cc** AA/P Bennett; **298cr** AA/J F Pin; **299tr** AA/C Coe; **302cl** AA/ N Sumner; **302cc** AA/C Sawyer; **302cr** AA/C Coe; **303cr** J Beazley; **305cc** Penny Phenix, **305cr** Rita's Tea Room; **306cl** Inn's on Great George; **306bc** Penny Phenix; **306cr** Lord Beaverbrook Hotel; **307cl** Salty's on the Waterfront; **307tr** Lincoln House Bed & Breakfast; **308tl** Maverick's Steakhouse; **308cl** Château Moncton; **308bc** The Fairmont Newfoundland; **309tl** AA/J F Pin; **309cc** Ripplecove Inn; **310** Fairmont Tremblant; **310tl** La 5eme Saison; **311cc** Le Piment Rouge; **312c** Wienstein and Gavino's Pasta Bar Factory; **312br** Au Gite Olympique; **313bl** Auberge de Vieux-Port; **313c** Château Versailles Hotel; **313cr** Hotel Le Germaine; **314cr** Hotel-Motel Le Mirage; **315cl** Aux Anciens Canadiens; **315cc** Guido le Gourmet; **315cr** Auberge St-Antoine; **315br** L'Hôtel du Capitole; **316bl** L'Hôtel de Vieux Québec; **316tr** Restaurant Le Bateau; **316cr** Wakefield Mill; **317tc** Whiskey Rapids Algonquin Parkway; **317cr** Visitors Inn; **318tl** Chez Piggy Restaurant; **318cl** Hotel Belvedere; **318cc** Pillar and Post Inn; **318cr** Sheraton Fallsview; **318br** Terroir La Cachette; **319tr** Albert House Inn; **320cc** Parker House Inn; **322tl** Moonbeam Coffee Company; **322bl** Pony Restaurant; **322cr** 360 The Restaurant at the CN Tower; **323cl** Aberdeen Guesthouse & B&B; **323bc** Ambassador Inn; **324tl** The Fairmont Royal York; **324bl** GVB Toronto; **324bc** Neill-Wycik College Hotel; **324cr** Renaissance Toronto Hotel at Skydome; **325tl** Hotel Victoria; **325tr** AA/P Bennett; **326bc** The Inns and Spa at Heartwood; **327tl** Fantasyland Hotel; **327cc** Bushwakker Brewpub; **328cr** Place Louis Riel All-Suite Hotel; **329tl** AA/P Timmermans; **330cl** Papa George's Restaurant; **330cc** Sunset Verandah; **330tr** Peacescapes Waterfront Retreat; **330cl** Sun Sui Wah Seafood Restaurant; **330br** Steamworks Brewing Co.; **331bc** Zev's; **332tl** Beautiful Bed and Breakfast; **332cl** Granville Island Hotel; **332tc** Grouse Inn; **333tl** The Wedgewood Hotel; **333bl** The Blethering Place Tea Room Restaurant; **333bc** Abigail's Hotel; **333cr** Val d'Isere Restaurant; **334cr** Klondike Kate's Cabins and Restaurant; **334br** Bombay Peggy's; **335cl** Raven Hotel & Gourmet Dining; **336tl** Hawkins House Bed & Breakfast; **336bl** High Country Inn; **336cc** L'Attitudes

PLANNING

337 AA/C Sawyer; **338** AA/N Sumner; **339** AA/P Bennett; **340** AA/C Sawyer; **341b** AA/C Coe; **343** AA/J Davison; **344** AA/N Sumner; **346** AA/N Sumner; **348** AA/C Coe; **349** AA/N Sumner; **351** AA/N Sumner; **352t** AA/P Bennett; **352b** N Sumner; **353** AA/N Sumner.

MAPS

355 AA/P Timmermans

CONTRIBUTORS' ACKNOWLEDGMENTS

The contributors to this guide would like to extend special thanks to the following for their assistance (along with all the Canadian provincial and city tourist organisations) for their help in the preparation of this book:

Gillian Marx (Tourism Newfoundland); Provincial Airways Limited (Newfoundland); Sue Rendell (Gros Morne Adventures); Randy Brooks (Tourism Nova Scotia); Valerie Kidney (Tourism New Brunswick); Patrice Poisson and Nathalie Beauchamp (Tourisme Québec); Gilles O. Bengle (Tourisme Montréal); Ann and Pat (Church of Toronto); The Westin Grand (Vancouver) A Snug Harbour Inn (Ucleulet); Sheila Dodd (City of Whitehorse); Kate Rogers (Travel Alberta); Kevin Johnston (Air Canada); and Nim Singh (Canadian Tourism Commission).

Project editor
Allen Stidwill

Interior Design
David Austin, Glyn Barlow, Alan Gooch, Kate Harling,
Bob Johnson, Nick Otway, Carole Philp, Keith Russell

Additional Design Work
Peter Davies, Jo Tapper

Picture research
Liz Allen, Chris Butler

Internal repro work
Michael Moody, Ian Little, Susan Crowhurst

Production
Lyn Kirby, Caroline Nyman

Mapping
Maps produced by the Cartography Department of AA Publishing

Main contributors
Terry Arsenault, Susi Bailey, Lindsay Bennett, Jenni Davis, Fiona Malins,
Penny Phenix, Paul Waters

Copy editors
Josephine Perry, Coleen Degnan-Veness

Published by AA Publishing, a trading name of Automobile Association Developments Limited,
whose registered office is Millstream, Maidenhead Road, Windsor, Berkshire SL4 5GD. Registered
number 1878835.

A CIP catalogue record for this book is available from the British Library.

ISBN 0 7495 4003 6

Binding style with plastic section dividers by permission of AA Publishing.

Colour separation by Keenes
Printed and bound by Leo, China

Find out more about AA Publishing and the wide range of travel publications and services the AA
provides by visiting our website at www.theAA.com

A01515
Mapping in this title produced from Canada data © Tele Atlas N.V. 2003
Relief map images supplied by Mountain High Maps ® Copyright © 1993 Digital Wisdom, Inc.
Weather chart statistics supplied by Weatherbase © Copyright 2003 Canty and Associates, LLC.
TCS assistance with distance/time charts gratefully acknowledged

We believe the contents of this book are correct at the time of printing.
However, some details, particularly prices, opening times and telephone numbers do change.
We do not accept responsibility for any consequences arising from the use of this book.
This does not affect your statutory rights. We would be grateful if readers would advise us of
any inaccuracies they may encounter, or any suggestions they might like to make to improve
the book. There is a form provided at the back of the book for this purpose, or you can
email us at Keyguides@theaa.com

COVER PICTURE CREDITS

Front Cover and spine: AA/P Bennett
Back Cover, top to bottom: AA/N Sumner; Ontario Tourist Board; AA/J F Pin; AA/N Sumner

Dear Key Guide Reader

●

Thank you for buying Key Guide Canada.
Your comments and opinions are very important to us, so please help us to
improve our travel guides by taking a few minutes to complete this
questionnaire.

You do not need a stamp (unless posted outside the UK). If you do not want to
cut this page from your guide, then photocopy it or write your answers on a plain
sheet of paper.

Send to: **Key Guide Editor, AA World Travel Guides**
FREEPOST SCE 4598, Basingstoke RG21 4GY

ABOUT THIS GUIDE Where did you buy it?_____

_____

When? _ _ month/ _ _ year

Why did you choose AA Key Guide Canada?
❏ Price
❏ AA Publication
❏ Used this series before; title_____
❏ Cover
❏ Other_____

_____

Please rate how helpful the following features of the guide
are to you: very helpful (**VH**), helpful (**H**) or little help (**LH**)

Size	**VH**	**H**	**LH**
Layout	**VH**	**H**	**LH**
Photos	**VH**	**H**	**LH**
Excursions	**VH**	**H**	**LH**
Entertainment	**VH**	**H**	**LH**
Hotels	**VH**	**H**	**LH**
Maps	**VH**	**H**	**LH**
Practical info	**VH**	**H**	**LH**
Restaurants	**VH**	**H**	**LH**
Shopping	**VH**	**H**	**LH**
Walks	**VH**	**H**	**LH**
Sights	**VH**	**H**	**LH**
Transport info	**VH**	**H**	**LH**

continued on next page

What was your favourite sight, attraction or feature listed in the guide?
Page ______________________________

Please give your reason ______________________________

____

Which features in the guide could be changed or improved, or any other comment you would like to make:

____

____

ABOUT YOU

Name (*Mr/Mrs/Ms*) ______________________________

Address ______________________________

____

______________________________ Postcode ______________

Daytime tel nos ______________________________

Which age group are you in?

Under 25 ❑ 25–34 ❑ 35–44 ❑ 45–54 ❑ 55+ ❑

How many trips do you make a year?

Less than one ❑ One ❑ Two ❑ Three or more ❑

Are you an AA member? Yes ❑ No ❑

ABOUT YOUR TRIP

When did you book? _ _ month/_ _ year

When did you travel? _ _ month/_ _ year

Were you travelling for business or leisure? ______________

How many nights did you stay? ______________

How did you travel?

Individual ❑ Couple ❑ Family ❑ Group ❑

Did you buy any other travel guides for your trip? ______________

If yes, which ones? ______________________________

____

____

Thank you for taking the time to complete this questionnaire. Please send it to us as soon as possible, and remember, you do not need a stamp (*unless posted outside the UK*).

The AA and the Automobile Association Limited, their subsidiaries and any other companies or bodies in which either has an interest ('the AA Group') may use information about you to provide you with details of other products and services, by telephone or in writing. The AA Group as a matter of policy does not release its lists to third parties.

If you do not wish to receive further information please tick the box ❑